W9-ASY-848

FOCUS
ON COLLEGE SUCCESS

Fourth Edition

Constance Staley

University of Colorado, Colorado Springs

CENGAGE
Learning®

Australia • Brazil • Japan • Korea • Mexico • Singapore • Spain • United Kingdom • United States

CENGAGE
Learning®

FOCUS on College Success, Fourth Edition
Constance Staley

Senior Product Manager: Shani Fisher

Senior Content Developer: Marita Sermolins

Content Developer: Damaris Curran Herlihy

Content Coordinator: Rebecca Donahue

Senior Media Developer: Amy Gibbons

Senior Content Project Manager: Jessica Rasile

Production Manager: Elena Montillo

Senior Art Director: Pam Galbreath

Rights Acquisition Specialist:
Shalice Shah-Caldwell

Manufacturing Planner: Sandee Milewski

Production Service/Compositor:
MPS Limited

Cover and Text Designer: Lisa Delgado

Cover Images: Larry Harwood Photography

For product information and technology assistance, contact us at
Cengage Learning Customer & Sales Support, 1-800-354-9706
For permission to use material from this text or product,
submit all requests online at **www.cengage.com/permissions**.
Further permissions questions can be emailed to
permissionrequest@cengage.com.

Library of Congress Control Number: 2013952159

Student Edition:

ISBN-13: 978-1-285-43007-2

ISBN-10: 1-285-43007-7

Annotated Instructor's Edition:

ISBN-13: 978-1-285-43737-8

ISBN-10: 1-285-43737-3

Cengage Learning
20 Channel Center Street
Boston, MA 02210
USA

Cengage Learning is a leading provider of customized learning solutions with office locations around the globe, including Singapore, the United Kingdom, Australia, Mexico, Brazil and Japan. Locate your local office at **international.cengage.com/region**

Cengage Learning products are represented in Canada by Nelson Education, Ltd.

For your course and learning solutions, visit **www.cengage.com.**

Purchase any of our products at your local college store or at our preferred online store **www.cengagebrain.com.**

Instructors: Please visit **login.cengage.com** and log in to access instructor-specific resources.

Printed in the United States of America
1 2 3 4 5 6 7 18 17 16 15 14

FOCUS

ON COLLEGE SUCCESS

Constance Staley

Thirty-how-many-years? she thought. What a long time to work at one job in one place. But she had learned so much over that time, especially about students and about teaching, about learning and about knowing.

When she first began, the campus consisted of a few buildings and a dirt parking lot. Now it was a thriving community with thousands of students and buildings going up everywhere. *Of course, you can enhance your career by moving from one school to another,* she thought to herself, but you can also learn a lot by sticking with a good thing over a long period of time. So that's what she'd done. There had been brief excursions, working in private industry and teaching students in the former Soviet Union as a Fulbright Scholar. But for the most part, Constance Staley had spent her entire career as a professor on one campus, University of Colorado, Colorado Springs. As the campus had "grown up," so had she as a teacher.

Over her years as a professor, she'd worked with thousands of students. She concentrated on being the kind of teacher who listened and cared, who sent encouraging e-mails to students when they needed them, or congratulatory ones when they made brilliant contributions in class, or sometimes "reality check" e-mails when they needed an academic pep talk because they weren't doing so well. She loved the give and take, convincing students that this class wasn't about how much she knew. It was about how much they could learn.

About halfway through her career, Connie decided to focus on first-year students by directing the Freshman Seminar Program on her campus. She saw that many students eased into college as if they were finally in their element. But then there were students like Ethan Cole in this book, who lost his focus and considered dropping out of college, and Sylvia Sanchez, who wasn't sure college would be worth it or whether her first-year seminar class could really teach her anything new. And there were students like Katie Alexander, a kinesthetic learner who found it hard to engage in material that wasn't naturally interesting to her, or Anthony Lopez, who partied too much and studied too little.

But it was challenges like the ones presented by these students—and all the others in this book—that motivated Constance Staley to write *FOCUS on College Success*. She knew that getting a college degree was their key to a better life, a more fulfilling career, and most importantly, achieving their potential. She knew it was her job to help them through the rough patches and find the motivation within themselves to accomplish something they'd always be proud of. The Roman poet Manlius said it well centuries ago: "The end depends on the beginning."

Since her early days of teaching, Constance Staley has seen substantial change. Today's students are busy, impatient multi-taskers who want *efficient* learning. Many aren't fully invested in college and the effort it requires, yet they want a degree that leads to a high-paying career. They want to learn what they see as valuable, *their* way, with *results*. Overwhelmingly, they work at jobs in order to finance college, crowd their days with too many obligations, and don't slow down long enough to hone their metacognitive skills. They see a college education as a *product*, rather than a *process*. And on top of these formidable challenges, today's students often come to college with emotional issues that add another layer of complexity for instructors. Simply put, many require considerable support: academically, psychologically, and emotionally.

Her goal was to build much of what she has learned into a single tool: a book that would almost teach itself, freeing instructors to do what they need to do with their students, collectively and individually. According to over 100 reviewers, some of the strengths of *FOCUS on College Success* are its ability to build rapport with students, engage them, unlock intrinsic motivation, demonstrate that learning is taking place, and help them learn how to focus. The visual display on the following pages will walk you through *FOCUS on College Success,* feature by feature.

It's been said that teaching is the ultimate act of optimism. When a Sylvia Sanchez, an Ethan Cole, or a Serena Jackson is engaged and succeeds, we know why we do what we do as instructors. And we continually challenge ourselves to do it better.

FOCUS is for all the first-year students who sit in your classrooms, and for you in your own personal and professional journey as their teacher.

Connie has seen the credibility of first year seminars challenged by results-oriented administrators, skeptical faculty, and students who assume they "already know this stuff." Yet she has witnessed their power to effect change in thousands of students, firsthand, because she has developed engaging teaching strategies that work.

"I really like the assessment in the text as well as the up-to-date scenarios and stories throughout each chapter. The pictures, visuals, and overall feel of the book is relevant, applicable, and speaks to my students. I often hear my students discussing the activities they complete in the text–even when it's not a required assignment."
—Christy Cheney, Valencia College

What makes FOCUS } Unique?

Not only is *FOCUS* customizable for your specific campus, but three different *FOCUS* books are available for the types and levels of student-readers at your institution. If you teach at a four-year public or private institution, the fourth edition of this book—*FOCUS on College Success*—is most likely right for your students. You will see examples referring to fraternities and sororities, roommates, and a broad array of campus activities. Second, *FOCUS on Community College Success* has been written with highly varied community college students in mind—non-residential; traditional to non-traditional; honors to developmental; and certificate, degree-earning, or transfer-bound. Third, *FOCUS on College and Career Success* is written for student-readers at career and technical schools, who are often (but not always) non-traditional students who know why they're in college and what they want. The good news is, however, there are no hard and fast rules about which *FOCUS* book is the right choice. If your course invests heavily in career readiness, you may choose *FOCUS on College and Career Success* even though your students attend a four-year institution. Although the old saying goes, you can't be all things to all people, the three different *FOCUS* books attempt to do just that. They are written very intentionally with specific types of readers in mind and provide you as an instructor with a range of choices.

Why Does *FOCUS on College Success* Stand Out?

More than other college success textbooks, *FOCUS on College Success* knows what today's traditional students need. The fourth edition contains cutting-edge research and genuine wisdom collected by well-known author Constance Staley, an active educator who still teaches full-time and has worked with literally thousands of students over nearly 40 years. Today's students say "Don't lecture me," "Just tell me what I need to know," and "How will this help me be successful in a world of uncertainties?" *FOCUS* offers your students what they need, want, and value.

Here's What Real Students Have to Say....

> ➤ **FOCUS has the right content.** "*FOCUS on College Success* covers every subject a college student needs to know about. It is so much better than a book that only teaches you how to study. It covers everything critical to success." Ethan, political science major

> • "*FOCUS* gives real life examples, and it's just the right length." Alex, political science major, pre-law minor

> ➤ **FOCUS speaks to today's students.** "*FOCUS* helps students who are struggling to focus and not get distracted by things like media. About a month ago I realized how much time I was spending on YouTube and Facebook. It's obvious the author is more savvy about social media than most professors." David, psychology major

> ➤ **FOCUS is readable and relatable.** "This textbook is really interactive and doesn't have the boring feel of information overload as you read through." Shannon, biology/pre-physical therapy major

> • "*FOCUS* relates to my everyday life." Mallory, elementary education major

> • "This textbook has helped me be completely content with my chosen major because now I know it is my passion." Glory, nursing major

> ➤ **FOCUS actually changes outlooks and behaviors.** "*FOCUS* definitely helped me with my college journey. From time management to studying, I will now be more successful." Nathan, sociology major

> • "I like this book because it keeps me interested while I'm reading. Other textbooks are just dull. After reading this book, I have changed as a student. I find myself more attentive, less distracted, and more eager to learn than I was prior." Noah, electrical engineering major

> • "*FOCUS* helped me tremendously in my academic life because it showed me that I have so many resources available to me that I should be utilizing more often. Great book!" Jonathan, pre-engineering major

How does FOCUS address the issue of } Engagement?

Q: Many first-year students today are NOT AVID READERS and are in a college success course that they often don't feel they need to take. How does *FOCUS* help GET STUDENTS MORE ENGAGED?

A: Today's students could be called "Generation Why." Why is this course important? Why should I learn how to study when I've already been doing it for years? Why? Why? Why? They are pragmatic and have competing distractions. First-year students need a college success textbook that not only tells them what to do, but also why doing these things is important. Recognizing "the truth" and having known it previously are two different things, as are "knowing" and "doing." For real learning to take place, students must find personal meaning in what they read, and *FOCUS* is all about students. These features are intended to bring readers into the course:

> "My favorite part of the book are the challenge cases. They cover so many issues and every student can relate to at least a portion of every case study.
> **—Shane Y. Williamson, Lindenwood University**

FOCUS Challenge Cases

Readers have the opportunity to read and react to a real student facing a challenge in each case and revisit it at the end of the chapter to see if and how their perceptions have changed. These cases provide an applied, real-life, kinesthetic approach to learning, and allow students a "safe" way to discuss problems they may be facing themselves.

> *TEACHING TIP:* Try using the Challenge Case students' handwritten notes in the margins to show students how to engage with a text and apply course material to themselves.

Voice

FOCUS offers a conversational tone that is accessible, non-condescending, and treats readers as adults. The tone is one of an older, wiser coach or mentor who gives readers not only "straight talk," but also encourages them to give academics their best effort. It builds rapport with student readers, and works to convince them of key concepts rather than simply telling them.

Activities and Self-Assessments

"What's in it for me?" is a relevant question student readers ask, and by the end of *FOCUS*, they will know a great deal about themselves. *FOCUS* provides dozens of classroom ready exercises, so you'll no longer have to locate or create them on your own. And since students are most interested in themselves, the variety of self-assessments that appear in *FOCUS* keeps them engaged in the chapter material.

> *Connie Staley's 'voice' comes through so clearly! Having been to many of her workshops, I can hear her saying these words as she directs this exercise!*
> **—Sally Firmin, Baylor University**

Q: Because they lack focus, many first-year students become discouraged, find college to be less exciting than they expected, or recognize that they are not well prepared for the sustained investment college requires over time. How does *FOCUS* help address this PROBLEM OF MOTIVATION?

A: Many students today go to college because their parents want them to, because their friends are going, or because it's the expected "next step." They don't realize how much their own motivation to propel themselves toward a degree is at the heart of their success. In addition to helping students develop realistic expectations of what it takes to learn, throughout *FOCUS* they are reminded that they are central to the learning process and that they must be fully invested.

Academic Intrinsic Motivation Scale (AIMS)

To trigger students' intrinsic motivation these features appear in every chapter:

 Curiosity: piques students' curiosity about chapter content

 Control: helps students control outcomes in their toughest class (or a chosen learning community "target" class)

 Career Outlook: offers strategies for applying college skills to the workplace

 Challenge: quizzes for students available on the Instructor's Website.

Emotional Intelligence (EI) Coverage

FOCUS uses research on emotional intelligence and intrinsic motivation to get at underlying issues that influence college success. Because they lack focus, many first-year students become discouraged, are caught unaware when and if academic problems arise, or begin to doubt their own abilities. Retaining first-year students is a serious concern on many campuses, and many students give up due to EI factors like discouragement, disillusionment, or a lack of problem-solving skills.

Readiness Checks and Reality Checks

FOCUS asks students at the beginning of every chapter to assess their level of motivation, interest, knowledge, readiness to begin, and intentions to complete reading via Readiness Checks. Students connect to the material before them and narrow the gap between initial expectations of what's required to work through the chapters and the reality of what it actually took via the end of chapter Reality Checks. These checks help students develop a more personalized, realistic approach to learning.

Based on the students I've had the pleasure of working with in the past, they would approach this as a game . . .wanting to "win" by knowing it all at the conclusion of the lesson. This section also helps students to actually prepare for the chapter BEFORE the teacher goes over it (imagine that!).
—Phebe Simmons, Blinn College

How does FOCUS address the issue of } Multitasking?

Q: Today's first-year students face many potentially derailing distractions. How does *FOCUS* help STUDENTS AVOID EXCESSIVE DISTRACTIONS?

A: Between balancing course loads, busy work schedules, family life, and social activities, first-year students have a lot going on. And that doesn't even take into account the distractions that technology brings to the table. With e-mail, text messages, and Facebook and other social networking sites, it's harder than ever for students to focus. The following content and features have been developed in this text to help students become better *uni-taskers* instead of distracted *multitaskers*.

Time Management Tools

According to research, it can take anywhere from seconds to *hours* to reboot after you've interrupted yourself to bounce out to something else.[1] It's too easy for students to lose valuable study time; they need real-world strategies that they can try out right away. Are your students having trouble staying focused on their important tasks? Have them set a kitchen timer for forty minutes and get to work. When they hear the "ding," they'll get a real feeling of accomplishment and a bit of relief from stress.[2] *FOCUS* offers dozens of strategies just like this one that students can try out for themselves, many of which are based on the most current research and actual career advice for professionals. Through exercises and self-assessments, students can find strategies that work for them.

Stress Management Strategies

Research also says that your stress level can skyrocket when you fragment your attention in dozens of directions at the same time.[3] Practical strategies for managing stress in order to stay focused can be found throughout the text and interactive online activities suggested in instructor's annotations show students how a lack of focus generates stress. Students can learn how to manage stress in their daily lives as it applies to making decisions, listening in the classroom, taking tests, and succeeding in the workplace.

Strategies That Transfer to Careers

Multitasking is not just an issue in college. When students enter the workforce, they'll need to deal with even more tasks on their to-do list, and they may feel overwhelmed by even more distractions. Many of the success strategies needed for the workplace are the same strategies needed for academic success, and today's employers are concerned that college graduates are not equipped with sufficient skills or the right skills for their careers. The *FOCUS* **Career Outlook** feature highlights these skills and suggests to students that they begin to practice these skills now. New content on working in groups and teams teaches students that today's employers are looking for "soft skills"—the ability to work collaboratively, build productive relationships, and manage conflict, for example—and that cultivating soft skills is hard!

> "A text is helpful when it is clear, concise, engaging, relevant— Focus on College Success is all that and more. We are introduced to students and have an opportunity to 'get to know them' through the text. The annotations in the instructor's edition are lifesavers. Text activities are meaningful, and not just busy work. Videos are informational and entertaining. Focus is the ultimate FYE course package."
>
> **—Peg Adams, Northern Kentucky University**

How does FOCUS address the issue of } Retention?

Q: Many colleges and universities seem to be STRUGGLING WITH RETENTION and are trying to understand why many students don't return after their first year. How does *FOCUS* help with this?

A: Helping instructors flag potential risk factors for individual students is key to guiding students through misperceptions (for example, finding the optimal amount of study time) and problematic situations (making use of computer labs on campus when the entire family shares one computer at home). This type of "early alert" system can make all the difference when it comes to retention.

Entrance and Exit Interviews

The fourth edition of FOCUS features the revised and redesigned *Entrance and Exit Interviews*. These tools allow students to record their expectations about college, their strengths, and their challenges both at the beginning of the course *and* at the end. When used together, the interviews can show students just how much progress they have made, which is key to unlocking motivation. Students will gain a better understanding of what they learned in this course and what it takes to succeed in college and life.

How can you, as an instructor, best use FOCUS Entrance and Exit Interviews to make a difference for your students? There are several ways! For example:

1. Have students print or tear out their interview sheets and bring them to your office. Students' responses can serve as the basis for a one-on-one discussion.

2. Have students summarize their own responses and write a journal or blog entry about their learning.

3. Have your peer mentors use the instruments as the basis for a face-to-face meeting with each student in your class.

4. Have your students complete the online versions of the interviews available through Aplia for *FOCUS on College Success*.

Entrance Interviews can help you accomplish several things. First, you will see "Red Flags" immediately! Often "early alert" programs on campus take place at mid-term. This may be too late for students who have already given up or opted out. The Entrance Interview also helps you learn more about individual students, identify their level of motivation, and provides you with a snapshot of the class as a whole.

Refer to the Instructor's Resource Manual for additional strategies for successfully using the Entrance and Exit Interviews in your course.

© Larry Harwood Photography. Property of Cengage Learning

} Credibility?

Q: CREDIBILITY seems to be an issue with first-year seminar courses; students and administrators sometimes question the value of the college success course. How does *FOCUS* help address the credibility issue?

A: *FOCUS* demonstrates to students that recognizing good advice and implementing it are two different things, and that real learning in a first-year seminar course requires actual behavioral change. Woven through *FOCUS* is a learning system that makes a distinction between insight and action. While students may know (or think they know) how to use particular academic tools, knowing and doing are two different things. *FOCUS* emphasizes doing. In a sense, the "final exam" in a college success course is students' first-semester GPA!

> The author uses respected research among several disciplines more broadly and more effectively than other current books on this subject matter.
>
> —**Marty Marty, Missouri State University**

Research-Based

Instructors can appreciate that the text is built on a solid foundation of current research and that the advice to students is relevant. The extensive research base (invisible to students) assures faculty that *FOCUS* is grounded in the scholarship of teaching and learning. Although *FOCUS* is written for students and therefore highly interactive and relevant to students' lives, beneath the surface runs a solid foundation of broad cross-disciplinary research and highly current national reports on students, learning, and academic success.

Challenge → Reaction → Insight → Action (CRIA) Learning System

The CRIA method of learning used in *FOCUS* includes these four steps:

? challenge	1. a challenge is presented
❝ reaction	2. initial reactions, perceptions, and misperceptions are uncovered
✳ insight	3. content/resources/new knowledge is presented, leading to new insights
! action	4. final thoughts and discoveries lead to action/change

TEACHING TIP: Use the Challenge → Reaction and Insight → Action questions as journal prompts, classroom discussion topics, or group project assignments. Making use of this system will show students their existing level of understanding and what remains to be learned.

In *FOCUS*, readers are prompted to identify what they already know about particular topics before they read about them with the Readiness Checks and the recurring Challenge → Reaction questions. After they read, they are asked to apply the information to themselves as learners through the Insight → Action questions. As students cycle through this learning chain reaction, they realize that real learning is taking place.

How does FOCUS address the issue of Varied Learning Styles?

Q: Today's INCOMING STUDENTS HAVE VARIED LEARNING STYLES. How does *FOCUS* ensure that students identify their learning style and gain the skills necessary to improve their learning throughout their college career?

A: *FOCUS* informs students about their own learning styles right away so that they can streamline their efforts and translate between the teaching "language" spoken by their instructors and learning "language" they themselves prefer. *FOCUS* encourages students to realize that learning is a process, and helps them customize their learning, just as they customize products in their lives—everything from tablet color schemes and cell phone covers to specialty coffee drinks!

Revised for the third edition and kept for the fourth, the VARK It! activities are even more relatable to the chapter content than ever. The VARK It! feature has been moved to the beginning of chapters so that students can practice using the strategies *as* they read. Rather than appearing to be "busywork" by being placed at the end or middle of chapters, they are applied immediately to the reading process itself in each chapter. If students are multimodal, they will be encouraged to select activities from several modalities. And as a first-year seminar course should be, the book has been "VARKed," by including:

iStockphoto.com/Marcela Barsse; Johanna Goodyear/Dreamstime.com;
© iStockphoto.com/Nadezda Firsova; © iStockphoto.com/Pascal Genest

Visual memorable, unusual photographs with powerful, famous quotations as captions, and bold colors to add appeal

Aural content-rich chapter summary podcasts with a humorous twist to capture student interest

Read/Write research-based, comprehensive chapters on timely topics written for today's students

Kinesthetic real-life students as the FOCUS Challenge Case students and *FOCUS* TV Episodes to reinforce chapter points

Success Types Learning Style Type Indicator (a brief MBTI-based instrument)

In Chapter 3, students can take the MBTI-based SuccessTypes Learning Style Type Indicator, to see how their psychological type affects their preferred way of learning. "Your Type is Showing," a feature throughout the text, provides students with opportunities to read MBTI research related to the chapter's content.

How does FOCUS *help me* } Teach the Course?

Q: Most instructors have multiple course preps per semester, and though they want to make the college success course as engaging and interactive as possible, they just don't have time to write CLASSROOM ACTIVITIES or research ways to invigorate LECTURES AND DISCUSSIONS in the classroom. How does *FOCUS* help?

A: *FOCUS* is designed as a learning system with built-in motivational tools, activities, and potential journal/discussion prompts. *FOCUS* was created as a single, multifaceted teaching tool: a book that would encourage instructors to stress high expectations, while also providing a high level of support. Teaching a first-year seminar is challenging, and instructors need support, too. Constance Staley knows firsthand the range of challenges instructors face and what would give them what they need—conveniently and comprehensively—to do the best job they can.

Annotated Instructor's Edition

The Annotated Instructor's Edition of *FOCUS* helps instructors at any stage of their teaching careers succeed and provides the guidance needed with any new text. Annotations are categorized into five groups for easy recognition, allowing instructors to pay attention to annotations they are most interested in:

> **Teachable Moments** note places where instructors can pause to capitalize on chapter content by making particular points that enrich the learning environment.

> **Sensitive Situations** point out places where an in-class discussion could generate potential discomfort and help keep instructors from being caught off guard by these triggers, providing suggestions for how to handle these teaching challenges.

> **Activity Options** offer further active learning strategies to use in class and provide a variety of quick yet powerful classroom activities.

> **Teaching with Technology** annotations give advice for both current users of and novices to classroom technology about how to seamlessly weave technology that students are so familiar with into the academic setting of the classroom.

> **Diversity Discussion** annotations give you ways to incorporate the topic of diversity throughout the entire textbook.

We chose this text because it effectively covers many of the theories we wanted to cover … and because it is relevant and engaging. I like that the text treats the student respectfully. I appreciate the ideas for group activities in the margins and use them frequently. The topics are very relevant and address problems that the students themselves don't realize they have. When we talk about time management, for example, I hear a lot of, 'Wow, I did not realize how planning ahead could make such a difference.' I believe students are enjoying the text.

— *Sherry Ash, San Jacinto College-Central*

Preface **xiii**

Instructor's Manual and Test Bank

The Instructor's Manual serves as a quick guide to every chapter, providing all the frequently asked questions about how to teach the course, from what the main focus of every chapter should be to yet more activity options. It is organized by questions most frequently asked by both new and seasoned instructors; for example, How should I launch this chapter? What important features does this chapter include? What additional exercises might enrich students' learning? This time-saving resource also includes a Test Bank.

Cognero Online Testing Program

FOCUS on College Success, fourth edition, provides a flexible online testing system that allows you to author, edit, and manage the author-created Test Bank content. You can create multiple test versions instantly and deliver them through your Learning Management System from your classroom or wherever you may be with no special installs or downloads.

Managing Your Time, Energy, and Money

Menu Options:
- Lecture/ Discussion
- Chapter Exercises
- Audio Chapter Summary
- Focus TV
- Other

DEREK JOHNSON

© 2015 Cengage Learning

Aplia

Aplia for *FOCUS on College Success* helps students thrive in the classroom and beyond. Engaging, interactive assignments ensure that students meet learning objectives, while automatic grading offers immediate and constructive feedback. Randomized problems in Aplia allow for multiple attempts and help students develop the critical thinking skills that they need to earn better grades, discover their potential, and chart a course for the future. Aplia for *FOCUS on College Success* also includes digital versions of the chapter exercises from the book; an eBook with search, highlighting and notetaking capabilities; and additional resources that support the book, which may be accessed via the Course Materials section.

Instructor Website with *FOCUS*Points

Created to help instructors teach their course, the Instructor Website features multiple instructor resources, including the Instructor's Manual and *FOCUS*-Points. *FOCUS*Points is an interactive Teaching Tool that allows you to select from varied, multimedia options in class—all located in one spot. You (and your students) decide where to focus during class and then point and click. Using this interactive tool with invisible links inserted, you can lecture, do activities in the text, show *FOCUS* TV episodes, listen to Chapter iAudio summaries, add YouTube videos or other Internet content, or your own materials—easily and conveniently—all with this one, flexible teaching tool. No other first-year seminar textbook includes this powerful, innovative, convenient teaching aid.

50 Ways to Leave Your Lectern

How do we leave our lecterns? How can teachers engage students? This supplement offers you a proven way to stimulate thinking, discussion, and group interaction. Each exercise is organized according to Goals, Group Size, Time Required, Materials, Physical Setting, Process, and Possible Variations. This invaluable, creative resource provides dozens of ideas for kinesthetic classroom activities.

Assessment Tools

If you're looking for additional ways to assess your students, Cengage Learning has additional resources for you to consider. For more in-depth information on any of these items, talk with your Cengage Learning sales representative.

> **College Success Factors Index:** The College Success Factors Index (CSFI) is an online survey that students complete to assess their strengths and weaknesses in areas that have been proven to affect student outcomes for success in higher education. Accessed online, the CSFI is a perfect assessment tool for demonstrating the difference your college success course makes in your students' academic success. At the start of your course, the CSFI helps assess incoming students and allows you to tailor your course topics to meet their needs. As a post-test, it provides an opportunity for you and your students to measure their progress.

> **CL Assessment and Portfolio Builder:** This personal development tool engages students in self-assessment, critical-thinking, and goal-setting activities to prepare them for college and the workplace. The access code for this item also provides students with access to the Career Resource Center.

> **Noel-Levitz College Student Inventory:** *The Retention Management System™ College Student Inventory* (CSI from Noel-Levitz) is an early-alert, early-intervention program that identifies students with tendencies that contribute to dropping out of school. Cengage Learning offers you three assessment options that evaluate students on nineteen different scales: Form A (194 items), Form B (100 items), or an online etoken (that provides access to either Form A, B, or C; 74 items).

> ***The Myers-Briggs Type Indicator® (MBTI®) Instrument1:*** MBTI is the most widely used personality inventory in history—and it is also available for packaging with *FOCUS on College Success*. The standard Form M self-scorable instrument contains ninety-three items that determine preferences on four scales: Extraversion-Introversion, Sensing-Intuition, Thinking-Feeling, and Judging-Perceiving.

College Success Planner

Package *FOCUS on College Success* with this twelve month, week-at-a-glance academic planner. The College Success Planner assists students in making the best use of their time both on and off campus, and includes additional reading about key learning strategies and life skills for success in college. Ask your Cengage Learning sales representative for more details.

Cengage Learning's TeamUP Faculty Program Consultants

For more than a decade, our consultants have helped faculty reach and engage first-year students by offering peer-to-peer consulting on curriculum and assessment, faculty training, and workshops. Our consultants are higher-education professionals who provide full-time support to help educators establish and maintain effective student success programs. They are available to help you to establish or improve your student success program and provide training on the implementation of our textbooks and technology. To connect with your TeamUP Consultant, call 1-800-528-8323 or visit www.cengage.com/teamup.

Updated for the fourth edition

This edition has an increased emphasis on the topics of resilience, teamwork, and professionalism.

New research. The research on today's students—their characteristics, learning styles, strengths, and challenges—is continually evolving. New studies appear in online and print journals daily. This edition of *FOCUS* contains updated research in every chapter to keep abreast of the prolific material available on the scholarship of teaching and learning. Specific areas of new research that are crucial to success include the specific effects of being distracted by technology interruptions, (like the time it takes to "reboot" after interrupting a task), and the role a college degree has on living a happier, healthier life.

This edition has **more coverage on creativity** in organizations and affording college; **new material on social media** and job searching; and a **renewed focus on succeeding in online classes** and writing effective online messages.

New FOCUS Challenge Case design allows students to immediately connect each student's story visually to the real world of social media.

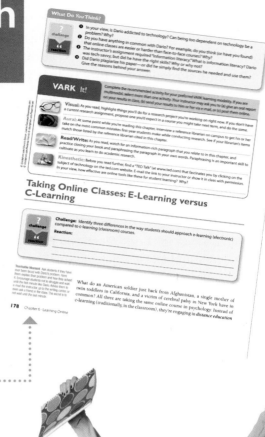

New Readiness Check design and content allows students to immediately connect the material in the chapter to their own lives.

The **updated quote and photo design** plugs into student engagement by offering photos of real students who are in college, stimulating students' interest and appealing to visual learners.

Throughout the instructor edition, Diversity Discussion, Teachable Moments, Sensitive Situation, Teaching with Technology, and Activity Option annotations provide useful instructor ideas. The Emotional Intelligence (EI) Research annotation has been removed, based on reviewers' input.

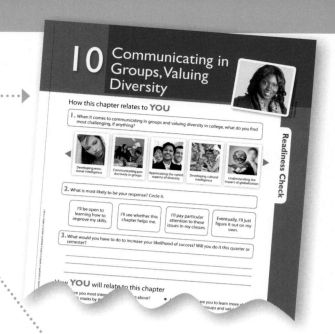

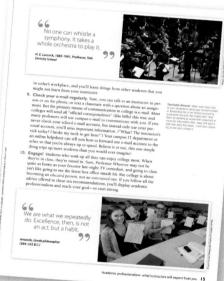

CHAPTER HIGHLIGHTS

> **NEW Chapter 1**—Starting Strong, Building Resilience—covers resilience, providing students with the tools to commit to long-term goals, despite obstacles that will undoubtedly arise along the way. It also covers academic professionalism—what instructors will expect of students and what students should expect of themselves. The FOCUS Challenge Case highlights Carson Reed, a first-year student caught unaware by critical academic challenges that make him consider dropping out of college.

> **NEW FOCUS Challenge Case in Chapter 10**—Communicating in Groups, Valuing Diversity—highlights Serena Jackson, a first-year student left to do all the work herself for a group project, setting the scene for a focus on teamwork in this chapter.

> Key content has been shifted and updated as follows:

- **Chapter 2** (previously Chapter 1), "Setting Goals, Achieving Dreams," includes new sections discussing positivity and happiness; tools to help students focus in a multitasking world; and self-motivation, explaining new ways to think about motivation.

- **Chapter 3** (previously Chapter 2), "Learning Styles and Studying," now combines the topics of Learning Styles and Study Skills so students will understand how learning preferences can lead to optimal ways to study, allowing students to learn more productively and efficiently.

- **Chapter 8,** "Reading, Writing, and Presenting," now allows students to make connections between three important skills, with a major emphasis on reading, considered to be an undesirable "chore" by some of today's students.

- **Chapter 9** (previously Chapters 7 and 9), "Developing Memory, Taking Tests," combines the topics of memory skills and test taking, giving students an opportunity to put memory strategies immediately into practice when studying for quizzes and exams.

Chapter Level Revisions

NEW Chapter 1: Starting Strong, Building Resilience

This new chapter covers resilience, providing students with the tools to commit to long-term goals. It also covers academic professionalism—what instructors will expect of students and what students should expect of themselves. The FOCUS Challenge Case highlights Carson Reed, a first-year student whose resilience is tested when he learns mid-term that his academic performance turns up sub-par across the board.

Chapter 2: Setting Goals, Achieving Dreams (previously Chapter 1)

Chapter Content

> **NEW** Chapter 2 includes new sections discussing positivity and happiness; tools to help students focus in a multitasking world; and self-motivation, explaining how and why people are motivated in new ways that students most likely have not considered.

> The topic "Who Are You? And What Do You Want?" has an increased emphasis on students' critical need to zoom in on academic work and focus (**NEW** "Zoom In and Focus"), while simultaneously taking advantage of college as a time to zoom out, wander, and discover their passions (**NEW** "Zoom Out and Wander").

> The introductory portion of "Positivity Pays Off" (previously "Give Yourself an Attitude Adjustment") has an increased emphasis on the different opinions on the subject of attitude.

> **NEW** "Self-Motivation Works Best" discusses the factors that affect how and why people are motivated.

Features

> **NEW** Box 2.2 "How to Read a Case Study" and Exercise 2.5 "Write Your Own Case Study" help students connect to and make the most of this popular chapter opening feature in *FOCUS*.

> **NEW** Exercise 2.1 "Wise Wanderings" (previously in Chapter 12) prompts students to build a "wandering map" and get creative about the thought process that should underlie choosing a career.

> **NEW** Figure 2.1 highlights multitasking.

Chapter 3: Learning Styles and Studying (previously Chapter 2)

Chapter Content

> Chapter 3 now combines the topics of Learning Styles and Study Skills so students will understand how their learning preferences connect with ways to study, allowing them to learn more productively and efficiently.

> **NEW** "Apply Your Learning Style to Your Study Style"

> The following topics or features have moved to this chapter from Chapter 8 in the previous edition:

- **NEW** "Metacognition: Take Charge of How You Study" (previously "Meta what? Metacognition, Reading, and Studying").
- **NEW** "Becoming an Intentional Learner: Make a Master Study Plan."
- **NEW** "Sprinting to the Finish Line: How to Study When the Heat Is On."

Features

> **NEW** Box 3.1 "Learning Disability? Five Ways to Help Yourself."

> **NEW** Exercise 3.4 "Study Habit Self-Assessment" (previously Exercise 8.4).

> **NEW** Exercise 3.5 "'Disciplined' Studying" (previously Exercise 8.5).

Chapter 4: Managing Your Time, Energy, and Money (previously Chapter 3)

Chapter Content

> "Time Management Isn't Enough" now includes updated information on cell phones as a time waster, as well as a **NEW** topic "Monitor How Your Life Works."

> "To Do or Not to Do? There *Is* No Question" has been updated with the most important to-do list techniques used by top executives.

Features

> Exercise 4.4 "So Much to Do—So Little Time" now includes additional instructions to aid the student.

Chapter 5: Thinking Critically and Creatively (previously Chapter 4)

Features

> **NEW** The pyramid in Figure 5.2 "Critical Thinking Is Focused" now appears next to each heading that describes the four-part model of critical thinking.

> **NEW** Exercise 5.5 "Generating Creative Captions" highlights a cartoon and how it relates to creativity.

Chapter 6: Learning Online (previously Chapter 5)

Chapter Content

> **NEW** "Taking Online Classes: E-Learning versus C-Learning" highlights the advantages of online classes and provides concrete strategies students can use to increase their chances for success.

> **NEW** "Writing Effective Online Messages" highlights rules that must be followed when communicating online.

Features

> **NEW** Exercise 6.1 "A Day in the Life of an Online Student" features the common challenges online students face and gives the reader an opportunity to think of solutions for solving these challenges.

> **NEW** "The Internet: The Good, the Bad, and the Ugly" now includes a Challenge/Reaction.

> **NEW** Box 6.1 "Are Bullets, Bits, and Bytes Enough?" shows students how information highlighted online doesn't always give the full story; it's necessary to dig deeper.

> **NEW** Exercise 6.4 "Channel Chooser" asks students to think about which form of communication to choose in different situations.

> **NEW** Box 6.2 "There's an App for That" describes the top apps for college students.

> "Now What Do You Think?" has been updated.

> **NEW** "Your Type is Showing"

Chapter 7: Engaging, Listening, and Note-taking in Class (previously Chapter 6)

Features

> **NEW** Box 7.2 "BYOD: Taking Notes Using e-Tools" includes valuable information the latest and greatest in study tool technology, including Evernote.

Chapter 8: Reading, Writing, and Presenting

Chapter Content

> Chapter 8 now allows you to make connections between three important skills, with a particular emphasis on reading.

> **NEW** "Write Right!" explores how to build necessary writing skills.

> The following topics come from previous Chapter 5:
>   • **NEW** "Writing as a Process."
>   • **NEW** "In a Manner of Speaking."

Features

> **NEW** The Career Outlook is now "Start a New Habit," describing the three parts to the "habit loop."

> **NEW** "Your Type is Showing" is from the previous edition's Chapter 5.

> **NEW** Exercise 8.4 "What's in an 'A'?" (previously Exercise 5.4).

> **NEW** Box 8.1 "Ten Ways to Oust Speaking Anxiety" (previously Box 5.3).

> **NEW** Figure 8.2 "Storyboarding a PowerPoint" shows students how helpful it is to create a storyboard, a map, or a flowchart of your slides on paper before moving to the screen.

> **NEW** "PowerPoint or PowerPointless? Five Ways to Make Your Presentations Stand Out" (previously Box 5.4).

Chapter 9: Developing Memory, Taking Tests

Chapter Content

> Chapter 9 combines the topics of memory skills and test taking, giving you an opportunity to put the memory strategies you learn immediately into practice when studying for quizzes and exams.

> The following topics come from previous Chapter 7:
> - **NEW** "Memory: The *Long* and *Short* of It."
> - **NEW** "The Three R's of Remembering: Record, Retain, Retrieve."
> - **NEW** "Your Long-Term Memory: Retain and Retrieve" (previously "Retain and Retrieve: Your Long-Term Memory").
> - **NEW** "Twenty Ways to Master Your Memory."

> **NEW** "*Reduce* Math Anxiety and *Increase* Your Test Scores" comes from the previous edition's "Curiosity: Reduce Math Anxiety and Increase Your Test Scores" in Chapter 9, with five new suggestions to keep in mind.

> **NEW** "Taking Objective Tests" (including "True-False: Truly a 50–50 Chance of Getting It Right?" and "Multiple *Choice* or Multiple *Guess*? Taking the Guesswork Out") provides strategies to improve objective test-taking skills.

> **NEW** "Deepen Your Learning" discusses the difference between effective and ineffective learners.

Features

> **NEW** The FOCUS Challenge Case highlights Darnell Williams.

> The following topics come from the previous Chapter 7:
> - **NEW** Exercise 9.1 "Subjective Memory Test" (previously Exercise 7.1).
> - **NEW** Exercise 9.2 "Test Your Memory" (previously Exercise 7.2).

- NEW "Curiosity: Act On Your Memory!"
  - NEW Figure 9.2 "Twenty Ways to Master Your Memory" (previously Figure 7.2) has been significantly updated.
- NEW "Control: Your Toughest Class" is previously from Chapter 8.
- NEW The Cast on Careers in the "Career Outlook: Command Crucial Conversations" now focuses on Serena.

Chapter 10: Communicating in Groups, Valuing Diversity

Chapter Content

- NEW "Communicating in Groups: Soft Skills Are Hard!" defines the importance of emotional intelligence and teamwork.

Features

- NEW The FOCUS Challenge Case highlights Serena Jackson, a first-year student left to do all the work herself for a group project, setting the scene for a focus on working in groups in the chapter.
- NEW Exercise 10.2 "What Are Your Views on Groupwork?" help students determine how groups should work.
- NEW Box 10.1 "How Well Do You 'Play with Others'?" discusses people skills as a necessity in the workplace.
- NEW "Your Type Is Showing" discusses how your psychological type plays into group communication.
- NEW Exercise 10.4 "Winning Is Sweet!" demonstrates conflict management.
- Statistics have been updated in Box 10.2 "Service Learning: Learning By Serving."

Chapter 11: Working Toward Wellness

Features

- NEW "Curiosity: Get the Happiness Advantage" explores why happiness seems to be on the decline. This feature replaces "Curiosity: A Sustainable Life-Style? 'It Isn't Easy Being Green'" from the previous edition.

Chapter 12: Choosing a College Major and Career

Chapter Content

- NEW "Brand Yourself" explores how personal branding is the key to job searches and career success today.

- > **NEW** "Interview at Your Best" discusses the in's and out's of creating the best impression during interviews.
- > **NEW** "Build Your Professionalism Skills: Ten Things Employers Hope You Will Learn in College" caps off this chapter by identifying what employers want in today's new hires.

Features

- > **NEW** Box 12.1 "Did I Really Post That?" describes the importance of personal information posted publicly online.

Brief Contents

Contents

1 Starting Strong, Building Resilience · 1

2 Setting Goals, Achieving Dreams · 29

3 Learning Styles and Studying   63

4 Managing Your Time, Energy, and Money   101

5 Thinking Critically and Creatively 139

6 Learning Online 175

7 Engaging, Listening, and Note-Taking in Class   211

8 Reading, Writing, and Presenting   249

11 Working Toward Wellness   359

12 Choosing a College Major and Career   395

Acknowledgments

It's been said that "Achievement is a *we* thing, not a *me* thing, always the product of many heads and hands." There are so many people to thank that this acknowledgements section could be as long as a chapter of *FOCUS*! However, here I'll at least mention those who have contributed the most, including all the students over the last 30-plus years who have taught me more than I've ever taught them.

Family   Let me start at the center of my life. My deepest thanks go to Steve, my Sean Connery look-alike husband (How do I put up with it?), who almost forgot what I looked like over the last few years. As I *FOCUS*ed away in my attic office day after day and night after night, he brought me too many cups of coffee to count. I cherish his devotion. My daughters Shannon and Stephanie helped bring some much-needed balance to my life, and aside from being the most adorable children on the planet, my grandtwins Aidan and Ailie have been a living learning laboratory for me. As growing children mastering one new thing after another, they truly have taught me about of the pure joy of learning. And to my beautiful almost 90-something Mom, who lovingly alternated between urging me to "slow down and relax" and "hurry up and finish," thanks for all your motherly love.

Reviewers   The list of reviewers who have contributed their insights and expertise to *FOCUS on College Success* is long. I'd particularly like to thank the following reviewers, who helped to shape the fourth edition with their feedback. My heartfelt thanks to all of them: Beverly Brucks, Illinois Central College; Stefanie Mitchell, San Jacinto College, Central Campus; Darla Rocha, San Jacinto College-North Campus; Miranda Ashman, Utah Valley University; Ingrid Thompson-Sellers, Georgia Perimeter College; Roxanne Hose, Georgia Perimeter College; Shane Williamson, Lindenwood University; Tamra Ortgies-Young, Georgia Perimeter College; Wendy McNeeley, Howard Payne University; Sherry Ash, San Jacinto College-Central; Charles (Chip) Frederick, Indiana University-Bloomington; Christy Cheney, Valencia College.

Thank you also to the students who shared their feedback for this edition: CaSandra Allen; Nicole Bergeron; Courtney Coulter; Spencer Davis; Ashley Fite; Katrina Hanna; Paul Hatfield; Evan Howell; Samuel B. Jones III; Meagan Klomfas; Joe Leslie; Chelsey Lower; Maggie McCormack; Zachery A. McCormick; and Tim McCoy; Hillary Presler; Brittany Price; Trashun L. Pringle; Rachel Rhinehart; Kayla Russell; Mai Sawada; Abdool Shakur; Emily Six; Jennifer Skovgaard; Paige Spence; Erin Steinman; Danielle Van Mater; Victoria Williams; Devan Young; Victoria Williams.

I'd also like to thank all the reviewers who helped to shape *FOCUS* in its previous editions: Peg Adams, Northern Kentucky University; Josie Adamo, Buffalo State College; Sandy Aguilar, Florida Community College at Jacksonville-Kent; Barbara Anderson, Midlands Technical College; Jon Aoki, University of Houston-Downtown; Andrew J. Armijo, University of New Mexico; Marinda Ashman, Utah Valley University; Mercy Azeke, Norfolk State University; Michael Becraft,

Austin Peay State University; Lynda Bennett, Blue Mountain Community College; Janet Breaker, Milwaukee Area Technical College; David Borst, Concordia University; Beverly Brucks, Illinois Central College; Toi Buchanan, Fayetteville Technical Community College; Castell Burton, Valencia Community College; David Campaigne, University of South Florida; Lea Campbell, North Harris Montgomery Community College; Barbara Chavis, Cleveland Community College; Miriam Chiza, North Hennepin Community College; G. Jay Christensen, California State University, Northridge; Regina Vincent Clark, Tennessee State University; Karen Clay, Miami Dade College; Geoff Cohen, University of California, Riverside; Carrie Cokely, Meredith College; Della Colantone, Alderson-Broaddus College; Therese Crary, Highland Community College; Kimberly Cummings, University of Tampa; Allison Cumming-McCann, Springfield College; Janice A. Daly, Florida State University; Vrita H. Delaine, The University of Southern Mississippi; Mark Demark, Alvin Community College; Gigi Derballa, Asheville-Buncombe Technical Community College; Anne Dickens, Lee College; Michael Discello, Pittsburgh Technical Institute; Carmen Etienne, Oakland University; Sally Firmin, Baylor University; Charles Frederick, Indiana University; Doug Gardner, Utah Valley University; Becky Garlick, Blinn College; Sharol Gauthier, University of South Carolina Upstate; Jayne Geissler, East Carolina University; Alice Godbey, Daytona State College; Dee Allen Goedeke, High Point University; Laura Goppold, Central Piedmont Community College; Marie Gore, University of Maryland, Baltimore County; Wendy Grace, Holmes Community College; Dawn Green, Central Texas College, Killeen; Laurie Grimes, Lorain County Community College; Rhonda Hall, West Virginia University; Tuesday Hambrick, North Lake College; Linda Hensen-Jackson, Arkansas Tech University; Valerie Hewitt, Remington College; Cynthia S. Johnson, Palm Beach Community College; Joseph Jumpeter, Pennsylvania State University, Wilkes-Barre Page Keller, College of Charleston; Amy Koning, Grand Rapids Community College; Charlene Latimer, Daytona State College; Lois Lawson-Briddell, Gloucester County College; Kelly Lee, Orange Coast College; Janet Lindner, Midlands Technical College; Jen Manson, Lake Sumter Community College; Brenda Marina, The University of Akron; Marty Marty, Missouri State University; Claudia McDade, Jacksonville State University; Michelle McDaniel, Middle Tennessee State University; Bridgett McGowen, Prairie View A&M University; Karen McKinney, Georgia Perimeter College, Clarkston Aiesha Miller, The University of Akron; Deborah Miller, Ohio State University, Newark; Brian Mitchell, Gibbs College of Boston; Karen Mitchell, Northern Essex Community College; Kelly Morales, University of Texas-Pan American; Gail Muse, Holmes Community College; Harriet Napierkowski, University of Colorado; Bonnie Porter Pajka, Luzerne County; Community College; Kate Pandolpho, Ocean County College; Stan Parker, Charleston Southern University; James Penven, Virginia Polytechnic Institute and State University; Karla Pierce, Florida Community College at Jacksonville; Mia Pierre, Valencia Community College; Jeanne Pettit, Northern Kentucky University; Joni Webb Petschauer, Appalachian State University; Amy Poland, Buena Vista University; Margaret Puckett, North Central State College; Terry Rafter-Carles, Valencia Community College; Melanie Rago, Indiana University; Margaret Rapp, Tyler Junior College; Rebecca Reed, Johnson & Wales University; Virginia Reilly, Ocean County College; Saundra

Richardson, University of North Carolina at Pembroke; Chuck Rhodes, Sonoma State University; Jennifer Rockwood, The University of Toledo; Lawrence Rodriguez, Palo Alto College; Bea Rogers, Monmouth University; Keri Rogers, Sam Houston State University; Tara Ross, Keiser College; Patty Santoianni, Sinclair Community College; Alan Schlossman, Daytona State College; Cathy Seyler, Palm Beach Community College; Sarah Shutt, J. Sargeant Reynolds Community College; Phebe Simmons, Blinn College; Brenda A. Smith, Norfolk State University; Kim Smokowski, Bergen Community College; Marilyn Starkes, Thomas Nelson Community College; Angie Walston, Barton College; Janice Waltz, Harrisburg Area Community College; Jodi Webb, Bowling Green State University; Jill Wilks, Southern Utah University; Shane Williamson, Lindenwood University.

The Cengage Team   No book, of course, gets very far without a publisher, and *FOCUS* has had the best publishing team imaginable: the dynamic, highly people-skilled Annie Todd, Product Director; the best-in-the-industry, innovative, energetic Shani Fisher, Senior Product Manager; the meticulous, and multi-talented Damaris Curran Herlihy, Content Developer; true professionals who combed pages and probably did more than I'll ever know, Jessica Rassile, Content Project Manager; Content Coordinator, Rebecca Donahue, for her work on all the outstanding supplements to *FOCUS*; the obviously talented Art Director, Pam Galbreath; and Ed Dionne, Project Manager at MPS Limited. I'd like to especially thank Larry Harwood, the master photographer who took photos of the *FOCUS* cast on the University of Colorado at Colorado Springs campus. And heartfelt thanks to Annie Mitchell and Sean Wakely, who believed in this project from the very start at Wadsworth; Sylvia Shepherd, whose creative vision shaped much of the first *FOCUS* book, and Lauren Larsen, whose wit and wisdom formed the basis for several of the original early chapters.

Other Contributors   I'd also particularly like to thank the "*FOCUS* All-Stars," as I call them, my students who modeled for the photo shoots and starred in the "Inside the FOCUS Studio" videos. I'd also like to thank my colleagues at UCCS who have helped me develop many of the ideas in this book, whether they know it or not—all the Freshman Seminar faculty past and present. I also can't go without thanking the many authors who granted me permission to use their work, and four essential scholars who allowed me to use, apply, and extend their instruments throughout the book: Neil Fleming, Brian French, John Bransford, and John Pelley. And thanks to my expert student research assistants: Phil Wilburn, Sarah Snyder, Jessica Smith, and Lindsey McCormick, and my best buddy Liz for all her encouraging words. I'd like to give a special thanks to Aren Moore who worked closely with me to create *FOCUS*Points, the interactive, multimedia PowerPoint designed for *FOCUS*. And finally, I'd like to thank Matt McClain, the comedy writer who brought his innovative humor to the learning process through podcast summaries of the chapters and television scripts for the website TV shows. He took the "big ideas" from *FOCUS* chapters and made them memorable to students by using their own best-loved media.

Above all, *FOCUS* has taught me truly to focus. Writing a book takes the same kind of endurance and determination that it takes to get a college degree. My empathy level for my students has, if anything, increased—and I am thankful for all I've learned while writing. It has been a cathartic experience to see what has filled each computer screen as I've tapped, tapped, tapped away. Ultimately, what I have chosen to put into each chapter has told me a great deal about who I am, what I know (and don't), and what I value. There's no doubt: I am a better teacher for having written this book. May all my readers grow through their *FOCUS* experience, too.

Meet the Cast

Chapter 1: Carson Reed / Dan

Hometown: Highlands Ranch, Colorado.

Major: Business

Lessons Learned: Dan realized that he had to learn how to motivate himself, especially when it came to studying, because no one was telling him he had to do it. He also realized how important it is to get to know people in his classes. "This helps because if you can't show up to class…you can always get the notes from a friend, and you can gather your friends to make study groups to help ace those tests."

Toughest First-Year Class: World Politics. In every other class, Dan had some prior knowledge about the subject, but everything about World Politics was brand new. Dan says this made the class enjoyable!

Advice to New Students: "Take good notes. Your test grade does in fact reflect your note-taking capability. If just taking bullet point notes isn't your style, try using different note-taking techniques."

Free Time: Play basketball, go to the gym, play video games, hang with friends.

Chapter 2: Sylvia Sanchez / Alycia

Hometown: I've lived all over Colorado. I consider the whole state to be my home town!

Major: Nursing with a minor in psychology

Lessons Learned: Alycia is still learning lessons about college. She keeps growing and discovering new things about herself and has made life-long friends. She plans to remember college as the best years of her life!

Toughest First-Year Class: Anatomy . . . It was hard to study ALL the time.

Advice to New Students: "Listen to your heart; it will lead you to the right place. Take every opportunity that comes to you because college is about finding out who you are and what you want from life."

Chapter 3: Tammy Ko / Jessica

Hometown: Manitou Springs, Colorado

Major: Marketing

Lessons Learned: Juggling a part-time job while in school, Jessica loved living on campus her first term and meeting new people, but she regretted not talking to other students about which professors and courses to take towards her marketing major. In order to succeed, she says, you've "gotta give it all you've got!"

Toughest First-Year Class: Microeconomics because it wasn't like high school courses that just required memorizing a lot of facts.

Advice to New Students: "Talk to other students to learn about the best professors, and make sure you are studying something that you are truly interested in."

Chapter 4: Derek Johnson / Derrick

Hometown: Colorado Springs, Colorado

Major: Communications/Recording Arts

Lessons Learned: Even though he's not married and has no children, Derrick and his case study character have much in common—too much to do and too little time! Derrick felt his biggest mistake his first year was not asking enough questions in class. He knows now he should have asked for clarity on content or assignments he didn't understand.

Toughest First-Year Class: English because he and his instructor had differing opinions, but he communicated through the tough spots and earned an "A".

Advice to New Students: "Surround yourself with positive people. As the saying goes, 'you are the company you keep.' I've seen many of my friends drop out because the people they called friends were holding them back from their full potential. Now that I have graduated, I look back at all the people I hold close and know that I wouldn't have made it without them."

Free Time: composing music and producing films

Chapter 5: Annie Miller / Meagan

Hometown: Albuquerque, New Mexico

Major: Nursing

Lessons Learned: Meagan admits that her biggest mistake her first term was not asking anyone for help with anything. But she enjoyed moving away from home and being more independent, meeting new people, and having a more laid-back academic schedule than her high school schedule had been.

Toughest First-Year Course: Calculus because she was overconfident and didn't study for exams.

Advice to New Students: "Don't give up! College is amazing! Oh, and don't spend all of your money on food." Restaurant bills and snacks add up!

Free Time: biking, hiking, playing Ultimate Frisbee, and giving campus tours

Chapter 6: Dario Jones / Orlando

Hometown: Fountain, Colorado

Major: MA, Communication

Lessons Learned: Start strong, work hard, and finish strong

Toughest First-Year Course: Math 099

Advice to New Students: "Get to know your instructors and fellow classmates. Ask questions in class when you're not sure about something."

Free Time: What free time? To relax, I listen to jazz or classical music, or I'll channel surf until I find something interesting to watch.

Chapter 7: Lindsey Collier / Heather

Hometown: Her parents have moved several times while she's been in college—so where is home?

Major: Nursing

Lessons Learned: Heather made the mistake of not making academics her first priority, but she learned from her first-year seminar course that she needed to be willing to sacrifice social time for study time.

Advice to New Students: "College isn't like high school—you do actually have to study three times as much for any course. No matter what course it is, study for it. You'll feel much better about receiving high marks than about partying with friends. And get involved on your campus. It's your home away from home, so why not make the most of it?"

Free Time: College Step and Dance Team

Chapter 8: Katie Alexander / Christina

Hometown: Colorado Springs, Colorado. Since she went to college in her hometown, Christina really enjoyed the opportunity college provided to meet new people.

Major: Nursing

Lessons Learned: Spending her free time with her friends watching movies, going bowling or dancing, and just hanging out, Christina found that like her FOCUS Challenge Case character, she, too, would make up excuses to get out of studying and doing her homework. She quickly learned the importance of reading and taking notes. "As weird as it may sound, reading cuts your end study time by more than half. Reading the material ahead of time helps you understand everything so much better."

Advice to New Students: "Stay motivated. College is going to FLY by! If you stay motivated and get good grades, it really will be over before you know it."

Chapter 9: Darnell Williams / Calil

Hometown: Colorado Springs, Colorado

Major: History with a secondary education emphasis

Lessons Learned: Calil noticed many similarities between himself and the FOCUS Challenge Case character he portrayed, besides playing football and watching movies. Calil, too, had problems with the transition from high school to college. He admits he was a student who "coasted" through his senior year of high school, which made his first year of college more difficult. He didn't study as hard as he should have as a first-year student.

Toughest First-Year Class: English, because he wasn't fully aware of the instructor's expectations.

Advice to New Students: "Determination is the key to success. If you are determined, there is nothing in the world that can stop you."

Chapter 10: Serena Jackson / Queen

Hometown: Denver, Colorado

Major: Nursing

Toughest First-Year Course: Biology because the way the class was taught in college (lecture-based) was very different than the way classes were taught in high school. She had to learn on her own what material was most important to study.

Lessons Learned: Queen wishes she had gone to more study groups and devoted more of her time to subjects that she struggled with in order to be more successful. She also would have asked for help from professors since she now realizes they are fully ready to help a student become better in their class.

Advice to New Students: "Make the most out of your college years. Make new friends because they could be great resources in the future. Also, if your professor tells you to read something, make sure you read the entire thing and you are able to teach it back to them because that will help your grade."

Free Time: Hanging out with friends, participating in club events, and volunteering.

Helpful Study Apps: Quizlet, Learnsmart, and Study Blue help Queen study for upcoming quizzes and exams.

Chapter 11: Anthony Lopez / Luis

Hometown: Aguascalientes, Mexico

Major: Spanish with an emphasis in secondary education

Lessons Learned: Luis is extremely involved on campus and within his community—he is President of the Association of Future Teachers, sings with his church choir, plays intramural soccer, and works for the Air Force on weekends—and as a first-year student, in order to cope with stress on a few occasions, he found himself doing the same things his FOCUS case study character did—partying too much. Luis thinks one mistake he made in his first term was that he procrastinated with homework because his new freedom let him think he could have fun first and study later, but he quickly learned he was wrong.

Advice to New Students: "Be smart and get involved, but always do your homework first. If you are involved on campus, you will meet people that will help make your college experience easier and more fun."

Chapter 12: Ethan Cole / Josh

Hometown: Fort Morgan, Colorado

Major: Sociology

Lessons Learned: Like his FOCUS Challenge Case character, Josh noticed that he, too, didn't always push himself to reach his potential. But he learned through his first-year seminar course that he is responsible for himself and that professors aren't like high school teachers. They will let you fail a class if you don't do what you need to. It's up to you.

Advice to New Students: "Not only did getting involved on campus help me have more fun in school, but it has also helped me academically. It has taught me how to manage my time and has made it so much easier for me to participate with confidence in class. Just make sure you get what you need to do done, and you will enjoy your college experience so much more."

Free Time: "Free time? What's that?! I'm too busy to have free time!" (But he secretly admits he snowboards, plays guitar, draws, and spends time with friends.)

MEET THE AUTHOR: Constance Staley

Hometown: Pittsburgh, Pennsylvania (although she never actually lived there. Instead, she lived all over the world and went to ten schools in twelve years.)

Background: Connie has taught at the University of Colorado at Colorado Springs for more than thirty five years after getting a bachelor's degree in education, a master's degree in linguistics, and a Ph.D. in communication.

College Memories: Connie remembers loving her public speaking class as a first-year student and having tons of friends, but being extremely homesick for her family.

Advice to New Students: "Earning a college degree is hard work, takes a long time, and requires a substantial investment of your time, energy, and resources. But it's the best investment you can make in your own future—one you'll never regret."

Free Time: Spending time with her husband, her two daughters, and her boy-girl grandtwins; relaxing at her cabin in the mountains; and traveling around the country to speak to other professors who also care about first-year students and their success.

Introduction to Students

Dear Reader,

This book is different. It won't coerce, coddle, caution, or coax you. Instead, it will give you the tools you need to coach yourself. Ultimately, this book is about you, your college career, and your career beyond college. It's about the future you will create for yourself.

FOCUS on College Success stars a cast of twelve of my own students, like a stage play. One student "actor" is featured in each chapter's opening case study. All twelve cast members reappear throughout the book, so that you'll get to know them as you read. I've been teaching for almost forty years now and worked with thousands of students. Each case study is about a real student (with a fictitious name) that I've worked with or a composite of several students. You may find you have some things in common with them. But whether you do or not, I hope they will make this book come to life for you. You'll also be able to meet these "actors" electronically in videos.

I love what I do, and I care deeply about students. I hope that comes through to you as a reader. You'll see that I've inserted some of my personality, had a bit of fun at times, and tried to create a new kind of textbook for you. In my view, learning should be engaging, personal, memorable, challenging, and fun.

Most importantly, I know that these next few years hold the key to unlock much of what you want from your life. And from all my years of experience and research, I can tell you straightforwardly that what you read in this book works. It gets results. It can turn you into a better, faster learner. Really? you ask. Really! The only thing you have to do is put all the words in this book into action. That's where the challenge comes in.

Getting a college degree takes time, energy, resources, and focus. At times, it may mean shutting down the six windows you have open on your computer, and directing all your attention to one thing in laser-like fashion. It may mean disciplining yourself to dig in and stick with something until you've nailed it. Can you do it? I'm betting you can, or I wouldn't have written this book. Invest yourself fully in what you read here, and then decide to incorporate it into your life. If there's one secret to college success, that's it.

So, you're off! You're about to begin one of the most fascinating, liberating, challenging, and adventure-filled times of your life. I may not be able to meet each one of you personally, but I can wish you well, wherever you are. I hope this book helps you on your journey.

Constance Staley

Readiness FOCUS
Entrance Interview

"Although you may not have experienced life as a new college student for long, we're interested in how you expect to spend your time, what challenges you think you'll face, what strengths you can build on, and your general views of what you think college will be like. Please answer thoughtfully."

INFORMATION ABOUT YOU

Name _____

Student Number _____ Course/Section _____

Instructor _____

Gender _____ Age _____

Entrance Exam

Your Background

1. **Ethnic Identification (check all that apply):**

_____ American Indian or Alaska Native   _____ Native Hawaiian or Other Pacific Islander   _____ Asian

_____ Hispanic/Latino   _____ Black or African American   _____ White

_____ Mixed Race (for example, one Caucasian parent and one Asian)   _____ Prefer not to answer

2. **Is English your first (native) language?**

___ yes   ___ no

3. **Did your parents graduate from college?**

_____ yes, both _____ yes, father only _____ yes, mother only _____ neither _____ not sure

Your High School Experience

4. **If you are entering college soon after completing high school, on average, how many total hours per week did you spend studying outside of class in high school?**

_____ 0–5   _____ 6–10   _____ 11–15   _____ 16–20   _____ 21–25

_____ 26–30   _____ 31–35   _____ 36–40   _____ 40+   _____ I am a returning student and attended high school some time ago.

5. **What was your high school grade point average when you graduated?**

_____ A+   _____ A   _____ A–   _____ B+   _____ B

_____ B–   _____ C+   _____ C   _____ C–   _____ D or lower

_____ I don't remember.   _____ I earned a GED.

Information About This Semester/Quarter

6. How many credit hours are you taking this term?

____ 6 or fewer   ____ 7–11   ____ 12–14   ____ 15–16   ____ 17 or more

7. Where are you living this term?

____ in campus housing   ____ with my immediate family   ____ with a relative other than my immediate family

____ on my own   ____ other (please explain)

Working While in College

8. In addition to going to college, do you expect to work for pay at a job (or jobs) this term?

____ yes   ____ no

9. If so, how many hours per week do you expect to work?

____ 1–10   ____ 11–20   ____ 21–30   ____ 31–40   ____ 40+

10. If you plan to work for pay, where will you work?

____ on campus   ____ off campus   ____ at more than one job

YOUR COLLEGE EXPECTATIONS

Your Reasons and Predictions

11. Why did you decide to go to college? (Check all that apply.)

____ because I want to build a better life for myself.   ____ because I want to build a better life for my family.

____ because I want to be well off financially in the future.   ____ because I need a college education to achieve my dreams.

____ because my friends were going to college.   ____ because my family encouraged me to go.

____ because it was expected of me.   ____ because I was recruited for athletics.

____ because I want to continue learning.   ____ because the career I am pursuing requires a degree.

____ because I was unsure of what I might do instead.   ____ other (please explain) _____

12. How do you expect to learn best in college? (Check all that apply.)

____ by looking at charts, maps, graphs   ____ by looking at color-coded information   ____ by looking at symbols and graphics

____ by listening to instructors' lectures   ____ by listening to other students during in-class discussions   ____ by talking about course content with friends or roommates

____ by reading books   ____ by writing papers   ____ by taking notes

____ by going on field trips   ____ by engaging in activities   ____ by actually doing things

13. The following sets of opposite descriptive phrases are separated by five blank lines. Put an X on the line between the two that best

represent your response, like this: For me, high school was easy ____:__X__:____:____:____ hard

I expect my first term of college to:

challenge me academically	____:____:____:____:____	be easy
be very different from high school	____:____:____:____:____	be a lot like high school
be exciting	____:____:____:____:____	be dull
be interesting	____:____:____:____:____	be uninteresting
motivate me to continue	____:____:____:____:____	discourage me
be fun	____:____:____:____:____	be boring
help me feel a part of this campus	____:____:____:____:____	make me feel like an outsider

14. How many total hours per week do you expect to study outside of class for your college courses?

_____ 0–5	_____ 6–10	_____ 11–15	_____ 16–20	_____ 21–25
_____ 26–30	_____ 31–35	_____ 36–40	_____ 40+	

15. What do you expect your grade point average to be at the end of your first term of college?

_____ A+	_____ A	_____ A–	_____ B+	_____ B
_____ B–	_____ C+	_____ C	_____ C–	_____ D or lower

Your Strengths, Personality, and Interests

16. Please identify your *strengths*—personal characteristics that will contribute to your college success. (Check all that apply.)

_____ a. I am good at building relationships.

_____ b. I can usually convince others to follow my plan.

_____ c. I like to win.

_____ d. I work toward future goals.

_____ e. I like to be productive and get things done.

_____ f. I have a positive outlook on life.

_____ g. I'm usually the person who gets things going.

_____ h. I enjoy the challenge of learning new things.

_____ i. I am focused.

_____ j. I can usually look at a problem and figure out a plan of action.

_____ k. I work to keep everyone happy.

_____ l. I'm a take-charge kind of person.

_____ m. I help other people develop their talents and skills.

_____ n. I'm a very responsible person.

_____ o. I can analyze a situation and see various ways things might work out.

_____ p. I usually give tasks my best effort.

17. How confident are you in yourself in each of the following areas? (1 = very confident, 5 = not at all confident)

_____ overall academic ability

_____ mathematical skills

_____ leadership ability

_____ reading skills

_____ public speaking skills

_____ study skills

_____ technology skills

_____ physical well being

_____ writing skills

_____ social skills

_____ emotional well being

_____ teamwork skills

18. For each of the following pairs of descriptors, which set sounds most like you? (Please choose between the two options on each line and place a check mark by your choice.)

_____ Extraverted and outgoing	or	_____ Introverted and quiet
_____ Detail-oriented and practical	or	_____ Big-picture and future-oriented
_____ Rational and truthful	or	_____ People-oriented and tactful
_____ Organized and self-disciplined	or	_____ Spontaneous and flexible

19. *FOCUS* is about 12 different aspects of college life. Which are you most interested in applying to yourself in your academic work? (Check all that apply.)

_____ Starting strong, building resilience

_____ Setting goals, achieving dreams

_____ Managing your time, energy, and money

_____ Learning online

_____ Developing memory, taking tests

_____ Communicating in groups, valuing diversity

_____ Choosing a college major and career

_____ Learning styles and studying

_____ Thinking critically and creatively

_____ Engaging, listening, and note-taking in class

_____ Reading, writing, and presenting

_____ Working toward wellness

Your Challenges

20. Of the 12 aspects of college life identified in the previous question, which do you expect to be most challenging to apply to yourself in your academic work? (Check all that apply.)

_____ Starting strong, building resilience

_____ Setting goals, achieving dreams

_____ Managing your time, energy, and money

_____ Learning online

_____ Developing memory, taking tests

_____ Communicating in groups, valuing diversity

_____ Choosing a college major and career

_____ Learning styles and studying

_____ Thinking critically and creatively

_____ Engaging, listening, and note-taking in class

_____ Reading, writing, and presenting

_____ Working toward wellness

21. Which one of your current classes do you expect to find most challenging this term and why?

Which class? (course title or department and course number) _____

Why? _____

Do you expect to succeed in this course?   _____ yes   _____ no _____ Perhaps (please explain): _____

22. Please mark your *top three areas of concern* relating to your first term of college by placing 1, 2, and 3 next to the items you choose (with 1 representing your top concern).

_____ I might not fit in.

_____ I might not be academically successful.

_____ I'm not sure I can handle the stress.

_____ I might overextend myself and try to do too much.

_____ I might not reach out for help when I need it.

_____ I might not put in enough time to be academically successful.

_____ I might be tempted to drop out.

_____ I might not be organized enough.

_____ I may be distracted by other things, like spending too much time online.

_____ Other (please explain) _____

_____ I might have difficulty making friends.

_____ My grades might disappoint my family.

_____ I may have financial problems.

_____ I might cut class frequently.

_____ I tend to procrastinate on assignments.

_____ My professors might be hard to communicate with.

_____ I might be homesick.

_____ I might be bored in my classes.

_____ My job(s) outside of school might interfere with my studies.

Your Future

23. How certain are you now of the following (1 = totally sure, 5 = totally unsure)?

_____ Finishing your degree

_____ Choosing your major

_____ Deciding on a career

_____ Completing your degree at this school

_____ Continuing on to work toward an advanced degree after college

24. What are you most looking forward to in college?

25. Describe the best outcomes you hope for at the end of this first semester/quarter. Do you expect to achieve them? Why or why not?

1 Starting Strong, Building Resilience

How this chapter relates to YOU

1. When it comes to getting the right start in college and sticking with it, what are you most unsure about, if anything?

Whether college is right for me

What academic professionalism means

What instructors expect

What it takes to succeed in college

How to deal with hurdles along the way

2. What is most likely to be your response? Circle it.

I'll check with my instructors.	I'll ask my classmates.	I'll see how things go and adjust.	I'll wait and eventually figure it out.

3. What would you have to do to increase your likelihood of success? Will you do it this quarter or semester?

_____

_____

_____

How YOU will relate to this chapter

What are you most interested in learning about? Put check marks by those topics.

☐ Why college is important
☐ How college works
☐ How to display academic professionalism
☐ What obstacles you may face
☐ What benefits await you
☐ What resilience is and why you need it

● How motivated are you to learn more about getting the right start and building resilience in college?
(5 = high, 1 = low) _____

● How ready are you to read now? _____

(If something is in your way, take care of it if you can. Zero in and focus.)

● How long do you think it will take you to complete this chapter? If you start and stop, keep track of your overall time.
_____ Hour(s) _____ Minutes

1

challenge

Carson Reed

After all the boxes were unloaded in his dorm room, and they finally said a sweaty goodbye—hugs all around—Carson couldn't help but wonder. Would he appreciate being on his own or eventually become home-sick—or both? He and his family were close. They texted back and forth all day, and talked on the phone frequently. As they said goodbye, he realized that his sister Aillie's hug lasted a little longer. He knew she'd miss him terribly. Even though she was five years younger, they were good buddies—hanging out together sometimes on week-ends, watching movies, popping popcorn, or finishing off a carton of ice cream by themselves.

But still he had to admit that knowing he was on his own now felt really good right. Better than good, actually. His family decided to check

into a local motel for a few days to make sure he was settling in, and that was fine with him. At least he'd prob-ably get some good restaurant meals out of the deal. To them, he was a rock star for getting into a very good university. They were so proud of him.

Confidence was something Carson had never been short on. His bedroom at home was wall-to-wall trophies. He hadn't actually won any awards, but he had earned trophies for

competing in the science fair and the history fair, and for being on the debate team all through high school. He was on the tennis team, the track team, and he'd been playing soccer since he was five. College would just

be an extension of his past successes, he predicted. *No big deal.* So when Labor Day vacation rolled around, he opted out of going home, despite his parents' pleas, and stayed on campus so that he wouldn't miss anything.

His classes got off to a remarkably good start. They were easy, in fact, just reviews of what he had learned in high school. He was meeting some great people, including his two roommates who liked the same movies and video games. They took up much of his time, especially late at night, so much so that they were all missing some of their morning classes. He worked as a server three nights a week and weekends at a local chain restaurant to help pay for his loans, so finding study time was a challenge. But he figured everything

would work out as it always had. But as the weeks went by, Carson noticed that the pace was picking up quickly in his classes. Sooner or later, he'd have to buckle down and think about what kind of job he wanted after college, if he could even find a good job after he graduated.

But around the middle of the semester, Carson got a shocking reality check. It came in the form of an F on his third English paper. He couldn't believe it. He'd gotten a B on the first one, a C+ on the second one, and now an F. An F! Some students hadn't even turned in a paper; at least he should get some credit for that. Carson had never gotten an F in his life—on any assignment in any class—ever. The F on his English paper made him begin

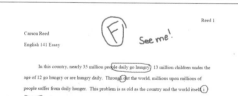

to wonder about his grades in all his classes. He was right: he got a D on his history midterm and his biology professor had mentioned the words "early alert," which meant that he was turning in Carson's name to the Student Support Center because his grade was at risk. He had been trying to slide by, and things were now totally out of control. What was strange was how quickly it happened! Major stress!

Carson was stunned. He'd never expected anything like this to happen, especially when things had gotten off to such a great start. He had always thought of himself as a winner, but now he was beginning to feel like a loser, and he didn't like the feeling at all. He had to face the music and, more importantly, face his parents, who were considering taking out a second mortgage on the house to help pay his way. He felt guilty and angry with himself for letting things go wrong. The questions began to mount: Did he belong in college? Was he smart enough? Should he drop his English class? And why did he have to take classes like history and biology, anyway? What would they possibly have to do with his future? Should he call his parents and tell them he wanted to quit school? Or should he just wait and see and keep quiet for now? College was much more stressful than he expected, and he was tempted to try another school or just give up altogether. To him, right now, he wasn't sure it was worth the stress or the money.

❶ Why aren't things going the way Carson expected in college? Identify three reasons and explain them.
❷ What should Carson do to get his college career on track? If he were your friend, what advice would you give him?
❸ In your view, will Carson be successful in college? Why or why not?
❹ It seems that Carson doesn't know much about being a college student. What is he missing? Can you identify what being a "professional" college student entails?

You're in College Now

Teachable Moment There is more to a first-year seminar course than skill development. This book (and the class itself) will also focus on values, positive psychology, and character development—to the extent that these qualities foster academic success. For most entering students, the first year is a time of accelerated self-exploration and growth.

Congratulations! You're in college. You've just joined nearly 16 million other students attending U.S. colleges and universities. As the saying goes, "The first step toward getting somewhere is to decide that you are not going to stay where you are." In choosing to go to college, that's what you've decided. You're *not* going to stay where you are. Your journey has begun.

As a new college student, you may be feeling competing emotions: excitement *and* anxiety, happiness *and* sadness, exhilaration *and* fear. That's natural; your life is about to change forever. But as motivational speaker Tony Robbins says, "Change is inevitable." But, he quickly adds, "Progress is optional." Progress, specifically progress toward the future you want for yourself, is your goal, and that's what *FOCUS* is about—helping you make actual, steady, undeniable progress. This chapter will launch you on your journey by discussing essential elements of college life that make or break many students. You'll read about starting strong and keeping your focus, even when challenges present themselves. This book and this class can make all the difference, but only on one condition: *You* have to keep *your* part of the bargain.

Admittedly, we live in a fast-paced society. We've become accustomed to instant gratification, as it's called. We want what we want, and we want it right now! But earning a college degree takes time, commitment, and determination. It won't happen overnight and it won't happen automatically. Unlike almost anything else you can buy, you must invest more than money to become truly

> **"**
> The trouble with not having a goal is that you can spend your life running up and down the field and never score.
> **"**
>
> *Bill Copeland, Australian cricket umpire, 1929-2011*

Ian Wilson/Photos.com

educated. If you're like most students, there will be times along the way when you're tempted to throw in the towel. Some students do. But if you read this book carefully and follow its advice, you will become the best student you can possibly be. You will read about practical tools to help you manage your life, and the advice here will take you beyond college into your career. And most of all, it will encourage you to become a true scholar, someone for whom learning is a priority—someone with goals to achieve and self-expectations to live up to. That is this book's challenge to you as you begin your college experience.

Teachable Moment Now, at the beginning of this course, is a good time to talk with your students about why they're in college. Was it their own decision? Did a family member recommend college or insist on it, or did their friends decide to go to college, so they simply followed suit? Explore the reasons at the outset of the course to set up a discussion later about *internal* and *external* motivation and what works best.

Why Is College Important?

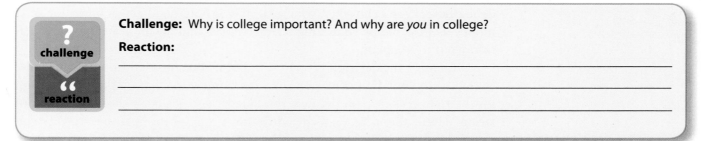

Challenge: Why is college important? And why are *you* in college?

Reaction:

_____

_____

_____

In today's economy, many students wonder if the decision to earn a college degree is a good one. Tuition is expensive, and there are no promises that the job market will rebound dramatically by the time graduation rolls around. The prospect of working hard now so that you get a payoff later is more elusive than it may have been for past college graduates. (On the other hand, a college education is and always has been a *tool*, not a *guarantee*.) As you researched which college to attend, you probably ran across articles with titles like "Who Really Needs a College Degree?" or "Newsflash: College Dropouts *Can* Get Rich." Perhaps, as you read, thoughts like these popped into your head:

Activity Option Divide the class in half, with one side brainstorming the pro's of getting a college degree, and one side identifying the con's. If students generate these lists themselves, they are more likely to understand the cost-benefit ratio than they would be by simply reading about them. Note, however, that all costs and benefits are not created equal. One benefit may outweigh many costs, as is always the case with this type of analysis.

> I'm going to run up quite a tab here, and someday I'll have to pay all these loans back. How will I do that?

> Will I get a better job with a college degree? Maybe I should just pick a career that doesn't require one.

> Should I really be going to college when my parents are struggling financially? They're sacrificing on my behalf, and I feel guilty.

> How can I keep my grades up and still earn enough money to work my way through college?

> Is all this stress really worth it?

These questions are the exact ones going through my head right now …

These are perfectly legitimate questions, and you're not alone in asking them. It's important to research colleges, majors, careers, finances, and options that will work for you. You should be reassured, however, by the results of recent national surveys involving hundreds of college graduates:

1. College graduates (86 percent) say that "college has been a good investment for them personally."[1]

2. College graduates believe that, on average, they make $20,000 per year more than their counterparts without college degrees. These beliefs are confirmed by actual salary data (although exact amounts vary by type of

career). In terms of lifetime earnings, college graduates earn 1.3 million dollars more than their non-degreed peers.[2]

3. The current job market for college graduates is tight right now, but it's even tighter for non-college graduates. Recent high school graduates who don't continue on to college are unemployed at a rate of nearly 24 percent.[3]

College is a good investment for most graduates—some might say now more than ever—and an overwhelming majority of graduates are glad they went to college. In one recent study, only 4 percent of college grads said they wish they hadn't gone. A college degree makes it easier to find a job and keep one.[4]

Of course, choosing a college you can afford is important, as is deciding how much debt you can afford (and from where), and learning how to manage debt after college.[5] However, your goal now should be to get as much for your money as possible by squeezing all the value—and all the learning—you can from your investment.

Ultimately, the decision is up to you. But if you consider dropping out some time during your first semester, do your homework first. Make the decision for the right reasons, not because you failed a test, dislike a class, or ran out of steam. Think about it: A college education is one of the best investments you can make. Once you've earned a college degree, it's yours forever. Someone can steal your car, walk away with your cell phone, or carry off your iPad, but once you've earned a college degree, no one can ever take it from you. Your choice to be a college graduate will pay off in many ways. So even if you aren't sure exactly how you want to spend the rest of your life right now, you can't go wrong by investing in your own future. A college education has the power to create a better life for you, and in the opinion of many people who look back on theirs, it's possibly the best thing they've ever done.

Understanding Where *Your* College "Fits"

There's no doubt about it: Where you choose to go to college and why are important decisions. What type of college did you choose to attend? What's the "feel" of the campus itself? Each individual campus has a different culture. Finding the right fit is important, just like finding the right place to work or finding the right life partner.

Four-Year College or University

Many colleges and universities offer a traditional college experience, one that includes student life, residence halls, sports events, student clubs, sorority or fraternity membership, and face-to-face collaboration with professors and peers. Four-year schools can be small, medium, or large, public or private. Major **research universities** provide particular advantages, like an opportunity to learn from leading experts, collaborate with professors on research, and interact with graduate students; they also tend to give you expanded opportunities in choosing a major—including unusual majors like Genetics, Immunology, Demography, Folklore, and Lesbian/Gay/Bisexual and Transgender Studies.[6] But with these opportunities come major responsibilities. Your professors will expect you to adhere to rigorous standards; demonstrate a mature work ethic; and read, write, and think at a high level. If you want to be successful, you'll find that every recommendation in this book is essential.

Teaching with Technology Google Rampell's article in endnote 4 ("Once Again, Is College Worth It?") and show your students the charts that are included. They make some strong points, visually, about the value of a college degree.

I need to think about this!

I've wanted to go to one school for as long as I can remember. I'm hoping it's right for me...

Community College

Some students want to earn an associate's degree or certificate for a particular degree, test the waters to see if college is right for them, or save money on their first year or two of college. Perhaps they plan to attend school part-time, support themselves, work full-time, are single parents, waited to go to college, are returning to college to retool, or got their high school degrees in nonstandard ways.[7] Typically, community colleges provide smaller classes, specialized degrees, faster career preparation, specific certificate programs, more hands-on classes, and more flexible schedules. More than 8 million college students in America choose to go to community colleges.[8] They can be great places to launch your college education if you want the convenience of going to college right in your own community and if any of the descriptors above fit you.

Career or Technical College

If you want special preparation for a specific career, or you're an older adult who wants to change careers, you may have chosen a career or technical college. Sometimes these schools are called "click" institutions, rather than "brick" institutions, because they emphasize technology and don't have large, sprawling campuses with dozens of buildings. If you have specific career goals and want hands-on training, job placement, and a quick jump-start to a career, a career or technical college might fit.[9]

No matter which type of institution you have chosen to attend, you have made a pact—with the institution itself, with the people who are supporting you, and with yourself. As this chapter's title suggests, start strong and keep going. Although Steven Spielberg, self-made billionaire in the film industry and winner of Academy Awards for directing the films *Schindler's List* and *Saving Private Ryan,* didn't complete the college degree he started, he went back to college more than thirty years later—after he had already achieved world fame. He felt the need to finish the college degree he had started and keep the promise he had made to himself. "I wanted to accomplish this for many years as a 'thank you' to my parents for giving me the opportunity for an education and a career, and as a personal note for my own family—and young people everywhere—about

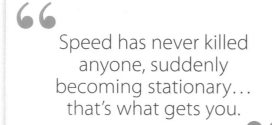

> Speed has never killed anyone, suddenly becoming stationary… that's what gets you.

Jeremy Clarkson, British racing broadcaster and star of the television show Top Gear

Oscar Calero/Photos.com

Take a few minutes to finish the following statements. Think about what each sentence says about you. Use your responses to introduce yourself to the class or form pairs, talk over your responses together, and use your partner's answers to introduce him or her to the class.

1. I'm happiest when _____.

2. I'm disappointed when _____.

3. If I had an extra $100, I'd _____.

4. The thing I'm most proud of is _____.

5. Once people get to know me, they're probably surprised to find I'm _____
_____.

6. My family wants me to _____.

7. I'd really like to become _____.

8. My friends enjoy me because _____.

9. I've been known to consume large quantities of _____.

10. I'd rather be _____ than _____.

11. When I'm under stress, _____.

12. My best quality is _____.

13. My worst quality is _____.

14. The academic skill I'd most like to develop is _____.

15. One thing I'd like to figure out about myself is _____.

Teaching with Technology As an alternative to this exercise (or in addition to it or one like it), consider asking students to create posters about themselves, using images, text, videos, and music on glogster.com or a similar online tool and present them in class.

the importance of achieving their college education goals," he said. "But I hope they get there quicker than I did. Completing the requirements for my degree 33 years after finishing my principal education marks my longest 'post-production schedule.'"[10]

How Does College Work?

Challenge: Some students see college as a collection of random courses; you "check off boxes" until you earn a degree. But how does college *really* work?

Reaction:

_____

_____

_____

Sometimes, especially to new students, college is confusing, even overwhelming. How does it all work? It may seem like a collection of random courses—a smattering of this and a smattering of that. And when you finally check off enough boxes, you get a degree in whatever you have the most credits in. That's not the way it's supposed to work.

Diversity Discussion While discussing how college works with your students, consider exploring how other cultures value college, or college and socioeconomic factors, ethnicities, and gender. Adding these diversity-based topics could make for a richer discussion.

College is about becoming an educated person, learning how to think, solving problems, and making decisions. College is much more than the "sum of its tests." It's about developing yourself as a person and becoming well-educated. What does it mean to be well-educated? Simply put: Being well-educated is about the pursuit of human excellence.[11]

Why do societies have colleges and universities? Why have they been around so long? Ancient Greece had Plato's Academy and Aristotle's Lyceum. The Sorbonne flourished in France in the Middle Ages. England's Cambridge and Oxford are two of the oldest English-language universities in the world. And Harvard, founded in 1636, was one of the first American institutions of higher education.

Colleges and universities help societies *preserve the past* and *create the future.* Studying the history of the U.S. Constitution in a political science course (past) as opposed to studying potential cures for cancer in a cell biology course (future) are concrete examples. Colleges and universities help us look back (preserve the past) and look ahead (create the future).

College in a Box?

Have you ever thought about the fact that college courses appear to exist in discrete "boxes"? Schools tend to place courses in academic departments, and your class schedule reflects these divisions. For example, your schedule this term might look something like the one in Figure 1.1.

This organizing system helps you keep things straight in your head, and it also helps your school organize a complex institution. The English department's budget is separate from the physics department's budget. Professors normally work in one department or another. And classes are categorized into particular academic disciplines.

That's the bottom line. But something first-year students often wonder about is how to connect the dots. What's the big picture? Knowledge isn't quite as neat as departments and boxes; it's messy. It overlaps and converges. Despite

	M	T	W	Th	F
9–10	ENG			SOC	
10–11		PHY			
11–12			PSCI		PSCI

FIGURE 1.1
Most Schools Compartmentalize Learning

huh . . . never thought of it like that!

the convenient institutional compartmentalization of knowledge on a college campus, you might be able to take a somewhat similar course in visual art from the art department, the computer science department, or the communication department. You've probably heard something in one of your classes that's also being discussed in another one. Knowledge is interconnected. College in a Box isn't an accurate way of looking at things.

Even though each discipline has its own history and identity and way of asking questions and finding answers, the disciplines aren't as distinct as your class schedule might lead you to believe. Let's explore how academic disciplines interrelate.

How Do the Disciplines Connect?

The Circle of Learning (see Figure 1.2) illustrates the interconnectedness of knowledge. Although this circle could be drawn in many different ways, using many different traditional academic disciplines, here is an example to get you thinking.[12]

It works like this. Let's start at the top of the circle with *math,* which is a basic "language" with rules and conventions, just like spoken language. You manipulate numbers and operations and functions, just as you manipulate sounds and words and sentences. Now, move clockwise around the circle.

Activity Option Draw the Circle of Learning on the board and ask for several student volunteers to talk through their courses this term and how they connect.

FIGURE 1.2
- - - - - - - - - - - - -
The Circle of Learning

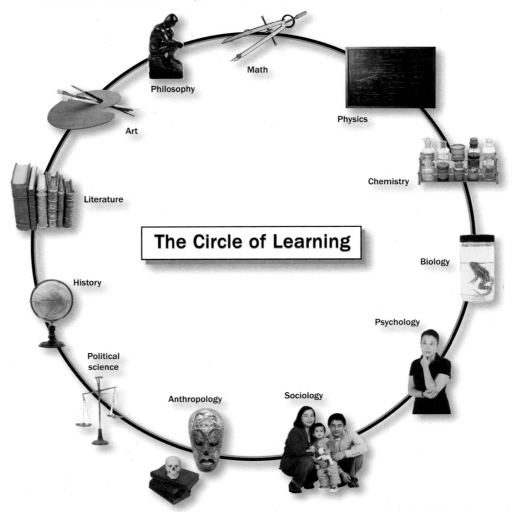

Really cool!
Let me try with
my courses . . .

(clockwise from top center): © Travis Klein/Shutterstock.com; Image Source/Jupiter Images; Hemera Technologies/PhotoObjects.net/ Jupiter Images; Hemera Technologies/PhotoObjects.net/Jupiter Images; PhotoObjects.net/Hemera Technologies/Getty Images; PhotoObjects.net/Getty Images/Jupiter Images; © OlegD/Shutterstock.com; © Sebastian Kaulitzki/Shutterstock.com; © Sebastian Kaulitzki/Shutterstock.com; Photos.com Select/Index Open/PhotostoGo; © originalpunkt/Shutterstock.com; © aquatic creature/ Shutterstock.com

Math is the fundamental language of *physics*, the study of atomic and subatomic particles. When atoms combine into elements, such as carbon and oxygen, the academic discipline is called *chemistry*. Chemicals combine to create living organisms studied in *biology* courses. Living organisms don't just exist, they think and behave, leading to the study of *psychology*. They also interact in groups, families, and organizations, which you study in *sociology*. You can also study units of living beings throughout time and across cultures in the discipline of *anthropology*. These units—people—who live and work together are typically governed or govern themselves, leading to *political science*. Let's keep going.

When an account of peoples and countries and their rulers is recorded, you study *history*. These written accounts, sometimes factual or sometimes fictional (for pleasure or intrigue) comprise the study of *literature*. Literature is one way to record impressions and provoke reactions—poetry is a good example—through the use of words. But images and symbols can do the same things—enter *art*. A particular question artists ask is "What is beauty?" otherwise known as *aesthetics*, which is also a particular topic of study in *philosophy*. Philosophy also includes another subspecialty called *number theory*, one of the earliest branches of pure mathematics. And now we're all the way around the Circle of Learning, arriving right back at *math*.

That's a quick rundown. Of course, many academic disciplines don't appear on this chart, but they could and should. A philosophy major might see her discipline at the center of the circle, or a geography major might say, "Hey, where's geography on this chart?" The circle, as it appears here, is representative. The point isn't which disciplines are represented. Instead, the Circle of Learning demonstrates that academic disciplines are interconnected because knowledge itself is interconnected. *Anthropology* (understanding people throughout time and across cultures) can provide an important foundation for *political science* (how people are governed or govern themselves), and *history* (a record of peoples and countries and rulers) can easily be the basis for *literature*. Capitalizing on what you're learning in one discipline can lead to deeper understanding in another.

In your career, you'll need to use knowledge without necessarily remembering in which course you learned it. You'll be thinking critically and creatively, solving problems, and calling upon all the skills you're cultivating in all the courses you're studying in college. The bottom line is that connections count. Recognize them, use them, and strengthen them to reinforce your learning.

> ❝ No one can become really educated without having pursued some study in which he took no interest. ❞
>
> *T. S. Eliot, American-born poet*
> *(1888–1965)*

Maybe… but biology and history? I need to keep the Circle of Learning in mind.

Academic Professionalism: What Instructors Will Expect from You

Challenge: What is academic professionalism? How is it displayed?

Reaction:

_____

_____

_____

Teaching with Technology Ask students to search online for research about employers' concerns that college graduates are not ready for the workplace, a popular topic these days. Ask your students how these findings can motivate, rather than *discourage*, new college students like themselves.

Let us not look back in anger, nor forward in fear, but around in awareness.

James Thurber, American author (1894–1961)

Activity Option Have students ask a senior or graduate student to identify which of these 10 items caught them off guard as a first year student. Have students discuss their findings in class.

The way to start strong in college can be summed up in these two words: Academic Professionalism. Here's what the term means, and using a comparison may help to explain it. Imagine this: You've just landed a new job, and it's a good one, one you really wanted. How do you know what to do and how to act? What will your boss expect from you? Should you just show up whenever it's convenient, take on this job on top of others you already have, and start firing off casual e-mails and texts about business? ("what up with the johnson report i thought max was gonna write that") Probably not—at least not if you want to be successful. You'll want to display workplace professionalism by noting how professionalism is defined in your new organization, and then start doing those things right away. The same thing is true in college: If you want to be successful, you must display academic professionalism. It's a set of behaviors you start now and carry with you into your career.

Hiring experts in the workplace identify three areas in which they believe college graduates are not as well prepared as they should be. They expect college graduates to have **oral and written communication skills, a positive attitude and strong work ethic**, and the ability **to work in groups and teams**.[13] You'll see that these three things, among others, are emphasized throughout *FOCUS*. You may be thinking, *"But wait a minute…I just started college!"* True, but considering how competitive the job market is these days, why not start preparing for it *now*? You'll gain a major advantage over other applicants—college graduates, or not. The academic professionalism you cultivate early in your college career can translate into career professionalism later. Or if you decide to continue for an advanced degree, all the academic strengths you begin honing from your first year on will serve you well when graduate school requires even more of you.

So how is academic professionalism defined, specifically, and what's required? If you surveyed college instructors across the country, they'd give you advice like this:

1. **Don't just pile on.** Ever see the winning team "pile on" after a big football game? When one too many players jumps on top of the one unfortunate person at the bottom, the whole pile collapses. Some students hope they'll be able to just add college to an already-long list of

obligations. But when they add one more thing, the entire stack crumbles. College isn't just "one more thing" to fit into the daily agenda of your life. Like many students, you may have to work to afford tuition, or you may want to keep up the demanding social life you had in high school. But being successful in college may mean that you must give something up (like the temptation to OD on video games or Facebook) to give school the attention it needs. Something in your life will need adjusting to make room for college classes. You may have to reduce your hours at work once you get a sense of your academic workload, or tell your roommate who has to miss class because she has the flu that you can't stay and keep her company because you have class, too. Put college at the top of your list of obligations.

2. **Choose to go to class.** Let's face it: life is complicated. It involves overlapping demands and minute-by-minute decisions. Your boss wants a piece of you, your friends want your attention while you try to study, your romantic partner wants to go to the movies the night before your midterm exam, the bills keep mounting—and on and on. Some students choose to miss class to pick up a relative at the airport or shop with a friend who's in town, for example. Sometimes true emergencies in your personal life will interfere with your academic life. If you're ill, for example, call or e-mail your instructor beforehand, if for no other reason than to be courteous. But your instructors will expect you to plan non-emergencies around your already scheduled (and paid-for!) classes. Many things in your life are important—it's true—but while you're in school, going to class and doing your coursework should be at the top of your to-do list.

Here's one place I messed up. I didn't realize how important it is.

Activity Option Ask students to look at these 10 items from an instructor's point of view. Which of the items would be disturbing to instructors who are really working to help their students succeed?

3. **Don't be an ostrich!** Some students fall prey to "the Ostrich Syndrome." If reading or homework assignments seem too hard or feel like busywork, they just don't do them. Instead, they bury their heads in the sand and pretend like nothing's at stake. Somehow they may even think that they can't get a bad grade if they don't turn in an assignment for the instructor to grade. It goes without saying (but here it is, anyway) that "ostriching" is the opposite of academic professionalism, and your instructors will *not* be impressed. Always do your best work and submit it on time. If the

My roommates are in this category!

An ostrich with its head in the sand is just as blind to opportunity as to disaster.

Anonymous

Juniors Bildarchiv/Age Fotostock

assignment is due on October 1, it's due on October 1. Familiarize yourself with each syllabus since it will outline what's due and when for every one of your classes. Honest-to-goodness realism and continuous upkeep in your courses work wonders in college, just as they do in the workplace.

4. **Show respect.** One thing instructors dislike is getting a sense from students that school isn't a top priority. Dress like you're a serious student who's there to learn. Leave the muscle tanks and halter tops for truly informal occasions. You're not in college to score fashion points, draw attention to your tattoos, or define your personality with your baseball cap. That doesn't mean you can't be yourself, but it does mean that you should use good judgment. And when you breeze in late or sneak out early, you're communicating that you don't value school, your instructor, and your classmates, whether you realize it or not. If you criticize a classmate or your instructor in public—even if you think it's constructive—that's disrespectful, too. And when you whip out your cell phone to see how many "likes" you have in response to your latest Facebook post, or text your boyfriend about where to go for dinner, everyone knows where your head is. When you're in class, be in class.

5. **Know the rules.** Your college and your professors have policies you need to know about up front. What constitutes cheating? How can you avoid plagiarism? Who should you talk to if you have a concern about your grade? Do instructors accept texts and cell phone calls? What kind of writing will they expect in e-mails? Even when it comes to everyday things—like weather cancellations—your college and instructors have policies and procedures to guide you. Don't leave yourself in the dark when it comes to important rules that affect you.

6. **Take charge.** When it comes right down to it, who is responsible for your success? None other than you! Even though you may be afraid to speak up or not want to admit that you're fuzzy about something, your instructors will rely on *you* to let them know that. They aren't mind readers. Do what you need to do: get help, take advantage of instructors' office hours, or hire a tutor. Don't sit idly by while success drifts away.

7. **Invest enough time.** In high school you may have done well without trying very hard. A teacher may have forgiven a late assignment, provided opportunities for extra credit, or graded on a curve so that everyone passed. But college is different. In college, it's important to get ready for class beforehand by reading and doing assignments, and then jump in once you're there. Bring your books, notebook, and pen, and sit up straight, too, just like mom always used to say. College isn't a place to just slide by or wing it. It's a place to put your best foot forward. That may mean rewriting a paper three times or rereading a textbook chapter more than once. Academic professionalism requires you to invest as much time as it takes.

8. **Learn to work in groups.** Your instructors know the value of teamwork later in your career, so they'll expect you to work with your classmates in class, outside of class, or online. They may even think it's important enough to assign points for group projects in the course syllabus. Even though you may prefer to work alone, teamwork skills are highly valued

Teachable Moment Item five makes for a good discussion topic. What differences are students finding among their instructors? Are some professors more casual and others more formal in terms of the class climate they create? Talk with your students about the importance of "discerning" the rules in every class, even if they aren't clarified, based on the instructor's communication style, the format and appearance of the syllabus, etc.

How come nobody told me this? I wrote that "F" essay at midnight in half an hour, and I thought it was pretty good.

> **"** No one can whistle a symphony. It takes a whole orchestra to play it. **"**

H. E. Luccock, 1885-1961, Professor, Yale Divinity School

in today's workplace, and you'll learn things from other students that you might not learn from your instructor.

9. **Check your e-mail regularly.** Sure, you can talk to an instructor in person or on the phone, or text a classmate with a question about an assignment. But the primary means of communication in college is e-mail. Most colleges will send all "official correspondence" (like bills) this way, and many professors will use campus e-mail to communicate with you. If you never check your school e-mail account, but instead only use your personal account, you'll miss important information. ("What? The instructor's sick today? I broke my neck to get here!") Your campus IT department or an online helpsheet can tell you how to forward one e-mail account to the other so that you're always up to speed. Believe it or not, this one simple thing trips up more students than you would ever imagine!

10. **Engage!** Students who soak up all they can enjoy college most. When they're in class, they're tuned in. Sure, Professor Whoever may not be quite as funny as your favorite late-night TV comedian, and going to class isn't like going to see the latest box office smash hit. But college is about becoming an *educated* person, not an *entertained* one. If you follow all the advice offered in these ten recommendations, you'll display academic professionalism and reach your goal—to start strong.

Teachable Moment Make sure every one of your students is using your school's email or forwarding his or her school account to a personal account. You might even "test" them by sending an email with important or incorrect information (like, class will start a half hour early this week...) and then checking to see who missed it.

> **"** We are what we repeatedly do. Excellence, then, is not an act, but a habit. **"**

Aristotle, Greek philosopher (384–322 B.C.)

Academic Professionalism: How to Help Yourself Succeed

What does it mean to succeed? Actually, success is difficult to define, and different people define success differently. Right now in college, you may think of success in terms of your future income. But is success simply about material wealth? Is it about fame? Status?

According to motivational author Robert Collier, "Success is the sum of small efforts, repeated day in and day out." Perhaps to you, success is somewhere off in the distant future, and it happens more or less suddenly, like winning the lottery. Actually, success begins right now. You should be the one to define what success will look like in your life, but generally, success is *setting out to do something that's personally meaningful, and then being fully engaged while doing it.* It's that simple. And it applies to your college experience as well. It starts now.

In order to understand your own definition of success in college, first you need to ask yourself why you're here. Why *did* you come—or return—to college, anyway? Do you want to develop into a more interesting, well-rounded, educated human being? Are you working toward a degree that leads to a specific career? Do you have children and want an education in order give them a better life? Did your mom or dad tell you that college wasn't optional?

We will assume that part of your definition of succeeding in college includes *graduating* from college. This book will provide you with an honest look at what that takes, including many opportunities to assess yourself in these areas. It will also offer an array of tools you can use throughout your college career and carry into your life beyond college.

The Inside Word: What It Takes

Many people falsely assume that the best indicator of whether or not you will graduate from college has to do with the brain matter found between your ears. Wrong! Brainpower alone—especially brains measured by your high school grade point average or even your SAT or ACT score—is no guarantee that you'll earn a college degree. Exactly what does it take?

Believe it or not, many of the traits required for college success aren't traits you have to be born with. That's the good news. Factors that support your goal of graduating from college are things you can become better at if you are committed to doing so. And in making commitments to improving these factors *now*, you are making a commitment to graduating from college *later.*

66 Though no one can go back and make a brand new start, anyone can start from now and make a brand-new ending. 99

Carl Bard

Ryan McVay/Photodisc/Getty Images

Challenge: What does it take to succeed in college?

Reaction: Multiple factors (besides past grades and entrance test scores) impact your success in college. Read down this list and ask yourself how you measure up in each of these areas. Mark an honest response from 1 to 7. If you're just beginning college and you're unsure about how you'll do, use your habits in the past to gauge your responses.

Exercise 1.2	College Success Factors

1	2	3	4	5	6	7
NO!	NO	No	Maybe/ Sometimes	Yes	YES	YES!

_____ **Ability to adapt.** Are you the type of person who thrives in new environments? Do you enjoy meeting new classmates, new professors, and new counselors? In general, do you like—and do well—with change?

_____ **Attitude.** Do you have a positive attitude toward your education? Do you want to be here? Are you motivated to learn and grow? Are you confident that you can do well in school? Are you willing to do the hard work involved in earning a college degree?

_____ **Maturity.** Are you emotionally mature? Are you willing to display the level of maturity required to manage your college education over time and earn a degree?

Maybe I should work on my score on this one.

_____ **Class attendance.** Do you have a good track record of attending class in the past? Are you willing to commit to attending each of your college classes regularly, regardless of whether or not you actually *feel* like attending on a particular day? Did you know that class attendance is a major predictor of college success?

_____ **Study habits.** Do you spend enough time studying? Do you study until you understand the material or do you simply study until you're out of time or need to move on to the next thing? Are you willing to make the necessary commitment to time spent studying even if it takes more time than you're planning on?

_____ **Note-taking skills.** Note-taking is not an ability we're born with. It's a skill that must be learned and can be taught to just about anyone. Many of your professors will expect you to learn through lectures. How complete and comprehensive are your notes? Do you work with them after class (color-coding, typing up, and so on)?

_____ **Academic support services.** Do you know what resources are available on campus to help you with academic issues? Are you willing to use a tutor or a campus learning center to help with a particular course that overwhelms you?

Yes, my family is pretty great.

_____ **Personal support system.** How strong is your personal support system? Who cares about your success in college? Do you have parents, siblings, and friends who support you, encourage you, and ask how you're doing?

_____ **Faculty connections.** Are you interested in knowing more about your professors, their backgrounds, and their academic interests beyond the particular class you're taking with them? Are you willing to visit your instructors during their office hours if you are having difficulty with a class?

_____ **Campus connection.** Do you plan to participate in or attend on-campus events?

(continued on next page)

Sometimes students unknowingly fall prey to the PCP (parking lot, class, parking lot) syndrome. They're only on campus for their classes, and as soon as class is over, they're outta there. Believe it or not, connecting to your campus, other students, and your instructors is critical to your success.

_____ **Time management skills.** Are you capable of managing your time effectively so that the important things—not necessarily just the urgent or exciting, fun things—get completed? Do you use a specific system for time management? Are you willing to learn these skills?

_____ **Money management skills.** How good are you at managing your money? Some students fall into the trap of using their school loans or grants to pay off credit card debt. Or they work far too many hours, which takes time away from their studies and makes academic success difficult to achieve. While managing your money isn't an academic skill, per se, not knowing how to do it can substantially impact your college career.

Now add up your scores on each item for a final tally. While this list isn't exhaustive, these factors are vital to college success. If your score was 60 or higher, you're in good shape. If not, take a close look at the areas that could affect your college success, read more about them in this book, and develop insights that lead to more effective action.

The Bad News: Obstacles along the Way

challenge

reaction

Challenge: Can you identify the five most common mistakes new college students make?

Reaction:

_____

_____

_____

Wow! I didn't know these statistics.

Getting accepted to college is a good thing! You should feel proud. According to the Bureau of Labor Statistics, over 66 percent of high school graduates go on to college.[14] While everybody's doing it, or so it seems, not everyone is doing it successfully. "Only about 33 percent of young adults get a four-year degree today, while another 10 percent receive a two-year degree"[15]

Realistically, the distance between getting accepted to college and graduating from college is considerable, and the journey can be both exhilarating and discouraging at times. Of all the college students who began as first-time, full-time students in 2004, only 58 percent had graduated six years later.[16]

Risk factors include working more than thirty hours per week, going to school part-time, being a single parent or having children at home, experiencing financial difficulties, being academically underprepared, and being a first-generation college student.[17] The important thing to keep in mind as you think about risk factors is that they alone cannot determine your ultimate level of success. Don't throw in the towel now if you had a child at age sixteen or are working thirty-five hours per week off campus. These factors are presented merely as information to assist you on your journey. They are simply *predictors*—not *determiners*. Only you can determine your outcomes in life, and that includes college.

It's worth taking a close look at these success inhibitors now, rather than becoming a statistic yourself later. Your effort, attitude, and willingness to get any help you need to succeed are all vital. Henry Ford was right: "Whether you think you can or you can't, you're right."

Box 1.1 Five Mistakes That Can Cost You Big Time!

Every year, more than 3 million first-year students begin college. Here are the five most common mistakes they make—so you can avoid them.[18]

MISTAKE 1: CUTTING CLASSES.

Going to every class session gives you a real advantage; cutting class is a predictor of how well you won't do. If you think about how much each class session has already cost you in tuition, you'll realize that class is an investment you can't afford to blow off. If you're taking an online class, don't put off the work until the end of the semester. Keep up on a regular basis, just as you would by physically going to class.

MISTAKE 2: OVERLOADING.

Some students think it's to their advantage to take as many classes as possible their first semester—even if they're working full or part-time. "Suffering" gives them bragging rights. College isn't something you can just "pile on" to an already very busy life and be successful without putting yourself through some serious stress.

MISTAKE 3: OVERMEDIA-ING.

If you spend hours and hours a day on Facebook, Twitter, and YouTube, or playing video games, obviously, you aren't studying. It may take an hour or more to read a chapter of your textbook, but when you've been jumping between bits and bytes, it may take even longer. Rather than stressing out about how little time you have to study, train yourself to set aside some "media-free" time just for schoolwork, and then reward yourself with the social media fun that's an important part of your life, too.

MISTAKE 4: PROCRASTINATING.

Many students say they can't get serious about their assignments until the adrenaline kicks in at the last minute. What they don't think about is what will happen during a "peak week" when four papers, three presentations, and two exams hit at once. You can do a great deal to pre-manage your own stress level with regular upkeep—like taking care of your car or your relationships. It's your college education, after all, and you're in charge.

MISTAKE 5: GOING IT ALONE.

Many students think sending a professor an e-mail or showing up during her office hours is intimidating or an obvious sign of weakness. Professors have office hours because they *want* you to stop in; they don't want to just sit there, waiting for students to show up. Most instructors actually want to get to know you, and they're pleased when you show an interest in their course content. Use *their* office hours to *your* advantage.

Memorize these five mistakes and take them seriously so that you get off to the best start possible!

Source: Jacobs, L.F. and Hyman, J.S., "The 5 Biggest Mistakes College Students Make." *U.S. News and World Report,* September 1, 2010.

The Good News: Benefits at the End of the Road

Regardless of how you choose to define success as it pertains to your college experience, it's a fact that there are plenty of benefits to graduating from a college or university. According to a recent study, "The evidence is overwhelming that college is a better investment for most graduates than in the past . . ." even for people in jobs that don't require a degree, like secretaries, plumbers, and cashiers. "And, beyond money, education seems to make people happier and healthier."[19] Here's a quick look at some of them:

1. **Higher earning potential.** Some studies show that college graduates earn twice as much income as their peers with only a high school diploma (see Figure 1.3).[20]

2. **Lower unemployment rates.** College graduates are more employable than their non-degreed peers. This is especially helpful during cyclic downturns in the economy, when many people—even talented and committed employees—find themselves out of work.

3. **Wisdom.** College students have the opportunity to gain understanding about a broad range of topics—politics, sociology, and history, to name a few. A well-educated person knows Sigmund Freud's contribution to

Box 1.2   Campus Resources: HELP Is Not a Four-Letter Word

It's not uncommon for new college students to feel isolated, even at a small school. Everything about your college experience is new, and you're adjusting gradually. As you adjust, remember that everyone needs a little help sometimes. Whatever the problem, your campus has all kinds of resources available for the taking, but you must take them. They won't come to you.

SOCIAL CONNECTIONS

How can I meet other students? Does your campus have a Student or University Center? Take advantage of favorite gathering spots on campus. Not only can you meet people, but you can also scan the bulletin boards for information. If you're finding it hard to meet people, could it be because you're not around? To meet people, it helps to be where they are.

ACADEMIC RESOURCES

How can I learn more about how I learn? Check to see if your campus has a Learning Center, an office that helps with learning disabilities, or a place you can go to fill out a learning style instrument. If writing is a struggle, look for your campus's Writing Center. If your calculus class is giving you fits, find the Math Learning Center. Or particular courses may offer what's called Supplemental Instruction, extra help beyond class sessions with basic principles or homework assignments. And get to know your academic advisor as if she or he were your best friend. That person can save you time and money and steer you toward classes in which you're most likely to be successful.

ADJUSTMENT

What if I need a counselor? College is a time of accelerated personal development and wonderful discoveries. But it may also be a time when you face challenging issues, such as leaving the comfort zone of your family; breaking up or beginning a new romance; or dealing with feelings of anxiety, isolation, or depression. The Counseling Center on your campus can help you work through a variety of issues. Many students—more than ever, many colleges report—are taking advantage of what Counseling Centers have to offer. And if you find yourself in the middle of a real crisis, call the campus hotline for immediate help.

FINANCES

Where can I find information about financial aid or get help with money problems? Your campus Financial Aid Office can help with loans, scholarships, and grants to pay for college. If you have a financial emergency—you lost the lease on an apartment, the residence halls are full, and you'll be living out of your car—help is available from the Red Cross or Salvation Army. If it's a matter of just blowing your budget, you can find advice, often free, from consumer credit agencies. Your campus may also offer free workshops on managing your money through a Learning Center or Student Success Center.

TECHNOLOGY

What if I have a technology meltdown? The new version of the old "my dog ate my homework" story relates to numerous variations on a theme: technology crashing. Your campus may not have round-the-clock advice from techies, but the Computer Help Desk can often solve what sounds like a complicated problem with simple advice. Also, use the campus computer labs. You can make good use of short blocks of time—or long ones—between classes.

HEALTH

Are health services available to students? Many campuses have a Student Health Center where you can find a range of free or inexpensive services—everything from flu shots to strep throat tests to birth control advice if you're sexually active. Join the recreation center, if your campus has one, or an intramural team, coach a children's soccer team, or devote some time to exercise each day to stay healthy.

MAJORS AND CAREERS

What do I want to be when I grow up? Thinking ahead to a career is sometimes difficult when so much is going on. Sometimes a career is nothing like you imagined—or preparing for one entails much more than you'd predict. Become an intern to try out a career or visit your campus's Career Center. Experts there can give you diagnostic tests to help you discover a major and career for which you are well-suited.

ET CETERA

Where can I buy my books? Textbooks are part of your college investment, and it's important to buy the right editions for your classes. Often you can also rent textbooks or buy e-books instead of print copies. Buying books online may save you money, although you'll have to wait for shipment. The bookstore is a much quicker option, and it's a good idea to find out where it is, no matter where you buy your books. You'll most likely need it for other school supplies.

What if I'm in need of Campus Security? If you feel unsafe walking to your car late at night or you need information about parking permits on campus, check with the Campus Security or Public Safety Office. They're there for your protection.

What's the bottom line? Get to know your campus and its full range of offerings—and take advantage of everything that's in place for your success.

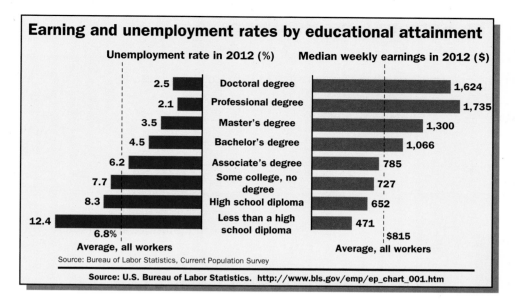

Earning and unemployment rates by educational attainment

Unemployment rate in 2012 (%)		Median weekly earnings in 2012 ($)
2.5	Doctoral degree	1,624
2.1	Professional degree	1,735
3.5	Master's degree	1,300
4.5	Bachelor's degree	1,066
6.2	Associate's degree	785
7.7	Some college, no degree	727
8.3	High school diploma	652
12.4	Less than a high school diploma	471
6.8%		$815
Average, all workers		**Average, all workers**

Source: Bureau of Labor Statistics, Current Population Survey

Source: U.S. Bureau of Labor Statistics. http://www.bls.gov/emp/ep_chart_001.htm

FIGURE 1.3

Education, Earnings, and Employment: The Quantifiable Value of a College Degree

Source: Bureau of Labor Statistics, Current Population Survey.

psychological theory, Charles Darwin's contribution to evolutionary theory, and Adam Smith's contribution to economic theory. But beyond theories, facts, and dates, a well-educated person knows how to think critically, contribute to society, and manage his or her life.

4. **Insight.** College students have the opportunity to understand themselves better as they participate in the academic, social, and co-curricular opportunities of higher education.

5. **True scholarship.** College students have the opportunity to become lifelong learners. True scholarship is not about making the grade. It's about becoming the best student-learner you can be—inside or outside of the classroom. The value of this benefit is beyond measure and will serve you throughout your life as career fields morph and new careers emerge.

6. **Lifelong friendships.** Many college graduates report that some of their strongest lifelong relationships were formed during their time at college. Choosing to attend college and choosing a specific major puts you in touch with a network of people who share your specific interests.

Losers make excuses; winners make progress.

Brian Tracy

The Bottom Line: Resilience

Challenge: What is *resilience*? Why is it important to you and your college success?

Reaction:

_____

_____

_____

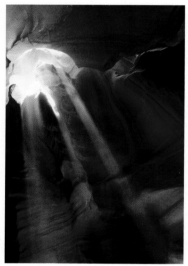

John W. Warden/Aflo/Visualphotos

> "
> There's a crack in everything. That's how the light gets in.
> "

Leonard Cohen, Canadian singer-songwriter, poet, and novelist

Let's face it: Life Happens. Although some bumper stickers may substitute another less polite word for "life," it's true. Everyone faces tough challenges, and college students aren't exempt. In fact, sometimes life's challenges are more than bumps in the road. They're major setbacks, personal tragedies, or even natural (or unnatural) disasters. If someone's home on the beach is destroyed by a hurricane, or the family dog is diagnosed with an irreversible disease, devastation is a natural response. Some students only find out about their parents' plans to divorce after they leave for college, and the shock sends them reeling.[21] Veterans who recently served in combat may have witnessed unforgettable atrocities and still feel the effects. Serious circumstances like these cause great distress, and one possible reaction is to think "Why me? I feel like a helpless victim in a cruel world." You can probably think of examples in your own life before college—times when you faced shock, grief, or a major disappointment. What's in question is not whether adversity will intrude, but rather how you handle it.

Interestingly, people handle tough situations differently. Some succumb to "give-up-itis" immediately. But after the same initial adverse reaction, eventually, other people see disasters as challenges. You may not believe the following paragraph, and if you don't already know who it's about, you may not be able to guess:

> A five-year old boy watched helplessly as his younger brother drowned. In the same year, glaucoma began to darken his world, and his family was too poor to afford the medical help that might have saved his sight. Both of his parents died during his teens. Eventually he was sent to a state institution for the blind. Because he was an African-American he was not permitted access to any activities, including music. Given the obstacles he faced, one could not have predicted that he would someday become a world-renowned musician.[22]

Ray Charles endured more challenges than anyone could possibly imagine, yet he overcame the odds. Although resilience is a term we usually reserve for people like Ray Charles, it applies to all of us. Psychologists don't fully understand why people react differently, but two words come to mind: "True Grit." Besides being the title of a famous novel and award-winning movie, what does it have to do with you as a new college student? Fill out the instrument in Exercise 1.3 to begin thinking about your own resilience potential in college.

Please read the following statements. To the right of each you will find seven numbers, ranging from "I" (Strongly Disagree) on the left to "7" (Strongly Agree) on the right. Circle the number which best indicates your feelings about that statement. For example, if you strongly disagree with a statement, circle"I." If you are neutral, circle "4," and if you strongly agree, circle "7," and so on.

	Strongly Disagree						Strongly Agree
1. I usually manage one way or another.	1	2	3	4	5	6	7
2. I feel proud that I have accomplished things in life.	1	2	3	4	5	6	7
3. I usually take things in stride.	1	2	3	4	5	6	7
4. I am friends with myself.	1	2	3	4	5	6	7
5. I feel that I can handle many things at a time.	1	2	3	4	5	6	7
6. I am determined.	1	2	3	4	5	6	7
7. I can get through difficult times because I've experienced difficulty before.	1	2	3	4	5	6	7
8. I have self-discipline.	1	2	3	4	5	6	7
9. I keep interested in things.	1	2	3	4	5	6	7
10. I can usually find something to laugh about.	1	2	3	4	5	6	7
11. My belief in myself gets me through hard times.	1	2	3	4	5	6	7
12. In an emergency, I'm someone people can generally rely on.	1	2	3	4	5	6	7
13. My life has meaning.	1	2	3	4	5	6	7
14. When I'm in a difficult situation, I can usually find my way out of it.	1	2	3	4	5	6	7

Now total your response on the 14 items of "The 14-Item Resilience Scale™ (RS-14™)." If your resilience level is high, you are doing very well in almost all aspects of resilience. Others with your score report that they are rarely if ever depressed or anxious about their lives. Stress is manageable. Anxiety is low. Life is good. You will want to keep your resilience strong; it takes practice. If your resilience level is low, that doesn't mean you have no resilience at all. Everyone is resilient to some degree. Others with your score have reported depression, anxiety, unmanaged stress, lack of self-confidence and discouragement. However, you can strengthen your resilience and doing so will make a significant and positive change in your life.

Very Low	Low	Mod. Low	Mod. High	High	Very High
14–56	57–64	65–73	74–81	82–90	91–98

© 1987 Gail M. Wagnild & Heather M. Young. Used by permission. All rights reserved. "The Resilience Scale" is an international trademark of Gail M. Wagnild & Heather M. Young.

Teachable Moment Resilience is a "hot topic" these days—in industry, the military, and on college campuses. It is a major key to persistence and retention. Generally, students are intrigued by the topic and recognize its importance. Their interest and personal experiences may become "fodder" for a meaningful, memorable discussion.

If you look up the word *grit*, you'll find this definition: "firmness of character; indomitable spirit; pluck."[23] People with grit have what it takes to hang in there. They tough things out, despite huge obstacles that get thrown in their way. They bounce back stronger than before. If someone you know says you have true grit, that's a compliment. "Grit is a willingness to commit to long-term goals, and to persist in the face of difficulty. Studies show that gritty people obtain more education in their lifetime, and earn higher college GPAs. Grit predicts which cadets will stick out their first grueling year at West Point. In fact, grit even predicts which round contestants will make it to at the Scripps National Spelling Bee."[24]

Think of it this way: in college, grit explains the difference between three students who fail the same calculus test but respond very differently. One decides to drop out of college: "I knew this was a bad idea. I just can't hack it, and I might as well admit it now." One throws the exam in the trash can on the way out of the lecture hall and refuses to ever crack open the textbook again. The other vows to study differently and spend more time doing it. "I'm not going to let calculus *get the better of me*. I'm going to take control of my learning so that it gets the *best* from me!" See the difference? After college, in the workplace, grit has to do with how you react to being treated unfairly or badly—like being shocked because you're laid off just when you thought your job was going particularly well. Some people give up; others dig in to beat the challenge.

Psychologists have been interested in grit (also called *resilience* or *hardiness*) for years, harkening back to a major study conducted when the government deregulated the telephone business. Half of the employees at AT&T were laid off. Two-thirds of these people simply couldn't cope. They died of heart attacks or strokes, engaged in violence, got divorces, or suffered from mental health issues. The lives of the other third actually improved. They got better jobs, deepened their relationships, and launched highly successful lives. When all was said and done, psychologists believed that it had to do with three "Cs": **c**ommitment, **c**ontrol, and **c**hallenge.[25] They were **c**ommitted to turning a bad situation around, they took **c**ontrol of their lives, and they saw adversity as a **c**hallenge to overcome. The good news is that if you're short on grit, you can get more. Increasing your self-awareness, especially with help from experts, is the way to start. Also consider these five suggestions:

1. **Cultivate "realistic optimism."** "Realistic optimism" isn't blind faith or false hope; it's looking for the best in things and then working to make them happen. It's accepting what's going on around you, but at the same time admitting what needs to be changed. It's about resilience, "getting back on the horse," and trotting on. It's a productive pattern of thinking. If a particular course isn't going well for you, realistic optimism means admitting it and moving ahead full throttle to reverse the situation. Some students just throw up their hands and decide a particularly challenging course is a waste of their time. Instead, invest *more* time to prove you can do it.

2. **Fail forward.** Have you ever thought about the positive consequences of tough challenges? "J.K. Rowling described to a Harvard graduating class a

perfect storm of failure—broken marriage, disapproval from her parents, poverty that bordered on homelessness—that sent her back to her first dream of writing because she had nothing left to lose. 'Failure stripped away everything inessential,' she said. 'It taught me things about myself I could have learned no other way.'"[26] Dilbert cartoonist Scott Adams says, "If you're taking risks, and you probably should, you can find yourself failing 90% of the time. The trick is to get paid while you're doing the failing and to use the experience to gain skills that will be useful later. I failed at my first career in banking. I failed at my second career with the phone company. But you'd be surprised at how many of the skills I learned in those careers can be applied to almost any field, including cartooning… failure is a process, not an obstacle."[27] Many people picture failures as "crash and burn" scenarios. Try picturing failure as "forward progress." When you trip and fall, can you come out ahead in the long run?

3. **Realize that becoming resilient is a process.** Some people think that the natural response to a stressful triggering event is depression. Depression is a possible response, but it's only part of the picture. Becoming resilient is a process that involves passing through seven stages. When adversity strikes, imagine someone beginning in the upper-left quadrant of Figure 1.4 with 1) *shock* and 2) *guilt*, then descending into the negativity of 3) *anger* and 4) *depression*, and then rounding the corner to move up through 5) *exploration* and 6) *action* to reach 7) positive *change*. Psychologists tell us we can't jump right from 1) shock to 7) change. We must pass through these various stages—sometimes through the depths of despair—to reach an eventual healthy response. Think back to a time in your life when you showed resilience during adversity and imagine yourself going through the seven stages when faced with a tough academic problem, for example, in college.

Sensitive Situation See if you can find a current event or local news story to use as an example and talk with your students about the seven stages. This could be a difficult discussion, and not really feasible if it hits too close to home, but even a fictitious example may help them understand the model. You might start by asking if they think Carson is displaying a particular stage in the case study. What would it take for him to move forward from that stage?

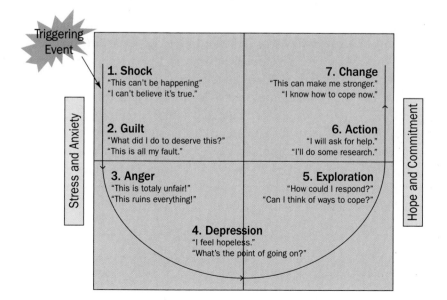

FIGURE 1.4

The Seven Stages of Resilience

Triggering Event

Stress and Anxiety

Hope and Commitment

1. Shock
"This can't be happening"
"I can't believe it's true."

2. Guilt
"What did I do to deserve this?"
"This is all my fault."

3. Anger
"This is totaly unfair!"
"This ruins everything!"

4. Depression
"I feel hopeless."
"What's the point of going on?"

5. Exploration
"How could I respond?"
"Can I think of ways to cope?"

6. Action
"I will ask for help."
"I'll do some research."

7. Change
"This can make me stronger."
"I know how to cope now."

4. **Recognize how you contribute to your own need for resilience.** You can't snap your fingers and control everything. But you *are* the author of your own life—not your parents or teachers or even your friends. If you run into bureaucratic red tape in college, find out how to cut through it and pursue answers yourself. If you tend to procrastinate with a capital "P," take command and get your work done. If the temptation of technology overwhelms you, zero in and focus. If you'd like to improve your performance in a course, find a resource to help you. Leaving problems to someone else to solve for you (like your Mom) or hoping they'll resolve on their own can cause your stress level (and your need for resilience) to skyrocket.[28]

5. **Look around.** Daniel Goleman, expert on emotional intelligence, says this, "Self-absorption in all its forms kills empathy, let alone compassion. When we focus on ourselves, our world contracts as our problems and preoccupations loom large. But when we focus on others, our world expands."[29] Sometimes reaching out to someone else who is also dealing with adversity puts things in perspective, and helping someone else develop resilience helps you develop more.

So when unexpected challenges surface—and they surely will—remember the quote above: "There's a crack in everything. That's how the light gets in." Cracks are just cracks. They don't have to become breaks. And they can shed light on an otherwise dark situation. It's not the challenge itself that counts; it's how you respond to it. When adversity strikes, remember the three "C's," see the light, and get truly gritty.

This Course Has a Proven Track Record

If you're reading this book, there's a good chance you're enrolled in a first-year seminar course. It may be called "Freshman Seminar," "First-Year Forum," "University 101," "First-Year Experience," "College Success," "A Learning Community," or any of a host of other names. These courses are designed to introduce you to college life, familiarize you with your own campus, and help you refine your academic skills. Do they work? According to experts, "In short, the weight of evidence indicates that FYS [first-year seminar] participation has statistically significant and substantial, positive effects on a student's successful transition to college…. And on a considerable array of other college experiences known to be related directly and indirectly to bachelor's degree completion."[30] Of course, you have to keep your part of the bargain, but in general, students who participate in first-year seminars complete more credit hours, adjust to college more quickly, become more involved in campus life, view themselves and their skills more accurately, enjoy and appreciate their college experience, and ultimately, graduate. That's what this course is about. Your instructor and your classmates are rooting for you. Now it's up to you!

I guess so...

How Do I Want to Be Different When I'm Done?

One thing is sure: College will change you. Most every high-intensity experience full of opportunities does. Take advantage, meet new people, and stretch yourself. You may notice that as a result of your college experience, your old relationships may "fit" differently. Your romantic partner may brag about you or secretly envy you. Your family may praise your efforts or hardly notice. But you will. If you finish what you've begun, you will watch yourself become a more sophisticated, more knowledgeable, more confident person. You can't help but be. Ask yourself now, at the beginning of your college experience, just how you'd like to change, and make it happen.

Now What Do You Think?

insight

action

❶ At the beginning of this chapter, Carson Reed, a new college student, was about to begin his college career. Now after reading this chapter, would you respond differently to any of the questions you answered about the "FOCUS Challenge Case"? Knowing what you know now, how would you advise him? Write a paragraph ending to the story, incorporating your best advice.

❷ Why did you choose to attend college? Be as specific as you can in listing the reason(s). Review your list and put an asterisk next to the most positive, goal-oriented reasons. After reading this chapter, can you identify your greatest challenges and what you'll do to overcome them?

❸ Do you agree with the principles of academic professionalism outlined in this chapter? Do they make sense to you, and do they seem important? Why or why not?

❹ If you are comfortable writing about the subject of resilience in yourself or others, describe a time when you witnessed its importance. How does the event you're writing about relate to earning a college degree? What steps, specifically, will you take to get there?

❺ How *do* you want to be different when you're done with college? Describe yourself in five years or so, what you will be like, and what you expect the future to hold for you.

Reality Check

On a scale of 1 to 10, answer the following questions now that you've completed the chapter.

low   1   2   3   4   5   6   7   8   9   10   high

In hindsight, how much did you already know about this subject before reading the chapter?

Can you answer these questions about starting strong and building resilience more fully now that you've read the chapter?

❶ What does "The Circle of Learning" demonstrate?

❷ What does the term *academic professionalism* mean?

❸ Define the concept of *resilience*.

How useful might the information in this chapter be to you? How much do you think this information might affect your success overall? _____

How much energy did you put into reading this chapter? _____

How long did it actually take you to complete (both the reading and writing tasks)? _____ Hour(s) _____ Minutes

Did you finish reading this chapter? _____

Did you intend to when you started? _____

If you meant to but didn't, what stopped you? _____

Take a minute to compare these answers to your answers from the "Readiness Check" at the beginning of this chapter. What gaps exist between the similar questions? How might these gaps between what you thought before starting the chapter and what you now think after completing the chapter affect how you approach the next chapter in this book?

2 Setting Goals, Achieving Dreams

How this chapter relates to **YOU**

1. When it comes to dreams, goals, and your own future, what are you most unsure about, if anything?

What I really want to do with my life

What motivates me to succeed

What my values are

Whether my dreams are achievable

How to set realistic goals

2. What is most likely to be your response? Circle it.

I'll keep thinking about it.	I'll ask for guidance from an expert on campus.	I'll see which courses really interest me.	I'll figure it out on my own.

3. What would you have to do to increase your likelihood of success? Will you do it this quarter or semester?

_____

_____

_____

How **YOU** will relate to this chapter

What are you most interested in learning about? Put check marks by those topics.

☐ How this book will help you learn

☐ What motivates you

☐ How negativity can sabotage you

☐ What distinguishes *performers* and *learners*

☐ How to understand your values, dreams, and goals

☐ How to develop *goals* to help you achieve your *dreams*

● How motivated are you to learn more about setting goals and achieving dreams? (5 = high, 1 = low) _____

● How ready are you to read now? _____ (If something is in your way, take care of it if you can, zero in and focus.)

● How long do you think it will take you to complete this chapter? If you start and stop, keep track of your overall time. _____ Hour(s) _____ Minutes

Sylvia Sanchez

© Larry Harwood Photography. Property of Cengage Learning

College—finally! As Sylvia opened the new package of turquoise sheets for the bed in her dorm room, she felt excited but at the same time, amazingly calm. Sylvia had been counting off the days all summer, and frankly, it felt good to be on her own. No younger brothers and sisters squawking, no parents breathing down her neck, no grand-parents expecting regular visits, and no lame boyfriend hanging around all the time. She stopped to check her cell phone—four new texts, probably all from him.

And all those pictures of her he had posted on Facebook this morn-ing! She wanted to write back and tell him to get over it, but she thought she'd better wait awhile for that. *Let's just see what college has to offer. That's smarter,* she admitted. Her three suite-mates hadn't arrived yet, so naturally Sylvia claimed the best bedroom. *They'd probably have done the same thing,* she reassured herself. *They should have gotten here earlier.*

© Artmim/Shutterstock.com

Sylvia had always been smart—not brilliant, but smart enough to know how to play the game. She was always rushing around, doing a hundred things at once. Focusing wasn't her strong point, and multitasking didn't always get her the best grades, but truthfully, she'd never even cracked a book during her senior year and still earned all A's and B's, even in AP and IB classes. College, she imagined, would be a slightly harder ver-sion of high school. It couldn't be as hard as her parents had warned. She remembered their threats when she brought home a bad grade in high school: *You just wait until you get to col-lege!* How would they know? They'd never even been to college themselves. If all that propaganda from parents and high school teachers were really true, no one would go to

Mom & Dad – last summer

© Andy Dean Photography/Shutterstock.com

Google.com

SDV 101: Academic Fitness
Focus on College Success

CHECK IT OUT!

"Excellence is achieved by the mastery of fundamentals"
Vince Lombardi

The introductory class will meet on **Saturday, August 29** from 10 a.m. to 2 p.m. in **Main Hall 412.** Following this introductory class session, students will meet with their instructor and classmates one hour every week.

In this required course,

Contacts:

college! *How hard can it possibly be?* she asked herself. Her parents were helping with the finances, but they weren't able to afford much. "And we're not paying for anything below a B!" her father had insisted. She just had to keep her grades up enough to hold onto her financial aid, and if she could manage to impress her parents, that wouldn't hurt, either.

Of her four new college courses, Sylvia was least worried about her college success class. *Automatic A*, she predicted. *Everyone knows how to study. It's just common sense*, she thought to herself. But whether studying enough to "live up to her potential" was on her agenda was another thing. The thought of writing an essay every week for her English Composition class brought on major dread; in fact, she wasn't all that excited about any of her classes. There might be other, more compelling pursuits that took up her time in college, like meeting interesting people and finishing her demo CD.

The one thing Sylvia knew for sure was that she desperately wanted to major in music, and her parents desperately wanted her to major in

business. "Who gets a job with a music degree?" they would ask. Her Dad was always sending her links to job ads in business. "There are all kinds of possible careers if you earn a business degree, but only one music teacher per school. And when budget cuts come around, it's the arts that always go first. How about paying for a music degree on your own? Your mother and I never had the chance; don't blow this opportunity!" "Yeah, whatever . . ." was her usual retort.

But all Sylvia really wanted in life was to be behind a microphone in front of an audience. And the bigger the audience, the better. Someday—she just knew it—she'd sign a recording contract with a major record label. All her friends told her how good she was. They'd even encouraged her to try out for a TV singing competition. Imagine—fame and fortune. *Sylvia Sanchez, recording artist . . .* even her name had the right ring to it and eventually, everyone would recognize it. They'd download her top hits, and she'd have the clothes, hair, make-up, and money she'd always wanted.

As she stood at the foot of the bed, admiring her new sheets, Sylvia caught a glimpse of herself in the mirror on the wall. "Looking good!"

she whispered. Was she referring to her how her new bedroom was shaping up or how she'd made the right decision on what to wear?

Suddenly, Sylvia heard laughter in the hallway and realized she was just about to meet her new suite-mates. What would they be like? Would she like them? Would they like her? Deep down, Sylvia realized she really did want to be successful in college. She wanted to live her own life and do her own thing. Still, she rationalized, *If this whole college thing doesn't work out, I'll go back home, pick up where I left off, get back my old job at the mall, and wait for the future I really want.*

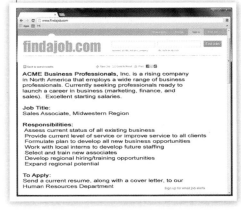

findajob.com

ACME Business Professionals, Inc. is a rising company in North America that employs a wide range of business professionals. Currently seeking professionals ready to launch a career in business (marketing, finance, and sales). Excellent starting salaries.

Job Title:
Sales Associate, Midwestern Region

Responsibilities:
Assess current status of all existing business
Provide current level of service or improve service to all clients
Formulate plan to develop all new business opportunities
Work with local interns to develop future staffing
Select and train new associates
Develop regional hiring/training opportunities
Expand regional potential

To Apply:
Send a current resume, along with a cover letter, to our Human Resources Department

Course Schedule
Main Campus
State College

FALL SEMESTER

Student: Sanchez, Sylvia

Course ID	Course Title	Hrs	
PSYCH 100	INTRO TO PSYCH	3.0	
ENGL 130	ENGLISH COMP	3.0	
UNIV 101	COLLEGE SUCCESS	3.0	
PHIL 102	PHIL	3.0	
	Credit Load:	12	

Work Schedule Week # 46   **Chique Street South Mall**

	Sunday	Monday	Tuesday	Wednesday	Thursday	Friday	Saturday
Abel, Nora	8-5	2-CL			8-5	9-6	8-5
Collins, Becky	2-CL		9-6	2-CL		2-CL	9-6
Sanchez, Sylvia		8-5	2-CL		9-6	8-5	10-7
Harper, Alex			9-6	8-5	10-7	2-CL	9-6
Monahan, Zoe		10-7		2-CL		8-5	9-6
Parker, Patricia	9-6	8.5	10-7	2-CL			

challenge

" **reaction**

❶ Is Sylvia sufficiently motivated to succeed in college? Why or why not?
❷ Describe Sylvia's beliefs about her intelligence. Does she think college is mostly about effort or about ability? Is Sylvia a *learner* or a *performer*?
❸ Is Sylvia's vision of becoming a famous singer a goal or a dream? Why?
❹ Identify three things that show focus a nd might help Sylvia make good life management choices.
❺ Are any elements of Sylvia's situation similar to your own college experience thus far?

Who Are You?
And What Do You Want?

Teachable Moment The students depicted in the case studies throughout this text are based on real students the author has worked with over the years. They face challenges that many college students face. Case studies are a good way of discussing issues that students may have themselves in a safe, nonthreatening way. It's easy to talk about someone else, rather than oneself. Take advantage of every opportunity to constructively criticize, challenge, and compliment Sylvia, and all of the students you will meet in this text.

Yeah, but maybe with some luck I won't really need a degree . . .

❝

It's always smart to learn from your mistakes. It's smarter to learn from the mistakes of others.

❞

Hillel Segal and Jesse Berst, computer experts

Activity Option Give each student ten sticky notes. Ask students to write one word on each note to fill in the blank: Successful students _____. Repeat this phrase ten times, each time giving the students only seconds to fill in the blank. On the board, write "Student has control" on one side and "Student has no control" on the other. Have students put each sticky note under the heading they believe is true of their statement. Some students believe that they have no control over issues that they really do. Let students lead the discussion.

Imagine this voicemail greeting: "Hi. At the tone, please answer two of life's most important questions. Who are you? And what do you want?" Beep. Very clever, don't you think? Can you answer these questions right now? Have you thought much about them? How much do you really know about yourself and what you want from this life of yours?

Don't worry. These aren't trick questions and there are no wrong answers. But there are some answers that are more right for you than others. College is a great time to think about who you are and what you want. In addition to learning about biology or history or business—whatever you choose for a major—college will be a time to learn about yourself: your motivation, values, dreams, and goals. College is a time when you'll make some of the most important choices of your life. Which major will you choose? Which career will you aim for? How many lifelong friends will you make? From this point on, it's up to you. Have you ever heard this phrase with ten two-letter words: "If it is to be, it is up to me"? It's true.

This book starts with the big picture: your life. It's about managing your life, being fully invested in what you're doing, and using your abilities to their utmost. Notice the phrase "managing your life"—not *controlling* your life. Let's face it: many things in life are beyond our control. We can't control international politics, set tuition rates, or advise characters in our favorite movies about what to do next. But you can manage your life by making smart choices, setting realistic goals, monitoring your time and energy, motivating yourself, and ultimately creating your own future. As the title of this book states boldly, it's about focus.

Zoom In and Focus

As you're starting college, two things will be important—zooming in and zooming out. The ability to zoom in on your academic work is critical, but for many of us, focusing is a challenge. We work too many hours, crowd our lives with obligations, and rush from one thing to the next. We think we're good at multitasking. We can surf the Internet, listen to music, watch a DVD, and read this chapter—all at the same time, right? But think about Gandhi's wise words applied to today's lifestyle: "There is more to life than increasing its speed." In

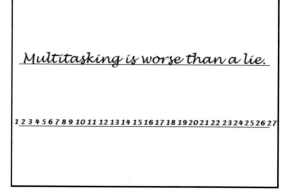

FIGURE 2.1

----

30 seconds for trial 1 and 55 seconds for trial 2! Twice as long when I try to multitask!!!

fact, there's evidence that when we "switch-task," it slows us down considerably. Try the experiment described below (and shown in Figure 2.1) while timing yourself with your cell phone stopwatch or the second hand on your wristwatch for both trial one and trial two.[1]

Trial 1: Draw two lines across a page as shown. The first time through this brief activity, write "Multitasking is worse than a lie" on line one and the numbers 1 through 27 on line two. Record how many seconds it took you to write on the two lines.

Trial 2: Draw two more lines. This time, write the same thing on each line, but alternate between lines—M, 1; u, 2; and so forth, going back and forth between each letter and number. Record your time again when you've finished. If you are like most people, it will take you approximately twice as long to multitask.

> "The biggest impediment to concentration is your computer's ecosystem of interruption technologies."
>
> *Cory Doctorow, science fiction writer and blogger*

Teaching with Technology Have your students visit the *New York Times* interactive sites, "Test Your Focus," "Gauge Your Distractions," or "Test How Fast You Juggle Tasks." These activities will make for a live demonstration of what this section of the chapter is about.

Activity Option If students have not tried this experiment on their own during their reading, do it in class and time both trials. It is a convincing example of the down side of trying to multitask. If they practiced trial 2 over and over, they could improve; however, repeated attempts at multitasking reduce our ability to focus over time.

Our brains are adaptable, a characteristic scientists call "plasticity." In other words, if you practiced this activity over and over again, you would get better at it. Your brain would be able to switch between tasks more quickly, and you could concentrate less and make fewer mistakes. But the truth is, the more you try to multitask, the more you end up sacrificing the self-discipline required for in-depth study. Recent research indicates that multitasking hurts your brain's ability to learn, and that it's harder to make meaning of what you're trying to learn while you're distracted.[2] In fact, even though technology gives you new access and abilities, according to one study, when you're distracted by e-mail or phone calls, your IQ drops by 10 points.[3] Technology's stimulation gives your brain a squirt of dopamine, which can actually be addictive, and research shows that being constantly connected can cause brain fatigue.[4] Many experts say that multitasking causes a brownout in your brain; there's just not enough power to go around. Your stress level can skyrocket when you "fragment" your attention in dozens of directions at the same time, and nothing actually gets done. And "rebooting" after you've interrupted yourself to bounce out to something else can take from seconds to hours.[5]

Picture yourself working on a complex math homework problem and getting close to a solution, but suddenly stopping to check a text "bing" or see who's replied to your Facebook post. When you get back to the math problem, you have to reconstruct what you had figured out before you "left." That could

Dieter Hawlan/Photos.com

> ❝ Furious activity is no substitute for understanding. ❞
>
> *H. H. Williams,*
> *British poet and playwright*

Activity Option Have students try to count backwards from 20 aloud while copying this paragraph into their notebooks. You can design any one of a number of similar experiments to illustrate the point made in this section.

take a little time or a great deal of time—and if you bounced back and forth constantly while working on all of your assignments, you might never finish any of them. At the very least, it might take you twice as long. Students who can zoom in and focus make greater, faster gains.

Zoom Out and Wander

At the beginning of your college career, you may not know the answers to the questions "Who are you?" and "What do you want?" *I have no idea right now. I'm taking it one step at a time,* you may be thinking. That's a perfectly legitimate response. College is a time of discovery for many students, a time to wander. You'll hear this piece of advice: follow your passions. You may take courses in areas you're totally unfamiliar with and discover a hidden passion. You may find that a particular instructor's enthusiasm for his discipline is contagious. It lights a fire in you. But just starting college as you are now, you may be unsure, open to all kinds of options. As Tolkien wisely observed, wandering doesn't necessarily mean you're lost; you're exploring, and that can be a very good thing in the long run. But finding some sense of direction early on can also be motivating.

Teachable Moment Many students believe that they should have had a major in mind before they even arrive at college. While it's true that deciding can help students focus, it's also true that taking time to explore may lead to a better result. Reassure them of this, if they express anxiety about not knowing yet.

Stephen Strathdee/Photos.com

> ❝ Not all who wander are lost. ❞
>
> *J. R. R. Tolkien,*
> *English author (1892–1973)*

So just how to do you discover your passions? Do you examine your habits? (You watch football on television on Sunday afternoons and Monday nights, so you should be a football player, right?) Your easily identified "likes"? (You're crazy about ice cream; therefore you should open your own store so you can eat all you want?) Or do you simply list all the things you hate and then think of their opposites? Hmmm…

Try this method instead, created by Katharine Brooks, the author of *You Majored in What?* She calls it "a wandering map." It's a way to meander through people, places, and things, connect the dots in your life, and discover themes that are important to you (and your eventual career). Take a look at the wandering map created by a hypothetical student named Bill. He listed things that seemed significant—memories, past experiences, preferences, traits—and then he connected them. The process helped him discover themes that are probably very important about himself.

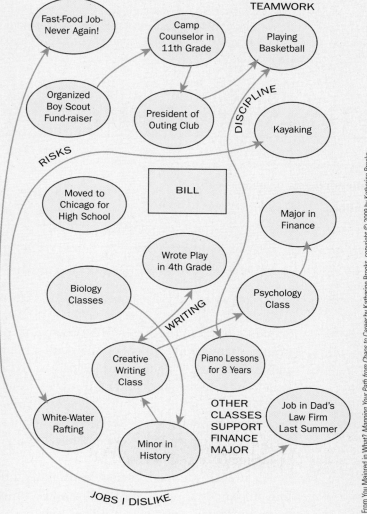

From *You Majored in What? Mapping Your Path from Chaos to Career* by Katharine Brooks, copyright © 2009 by Katharine Brooks. Used by permission of Viking Penguin, a division of Penguin Group (USA) Inc.

He identifies connections and labels them, and it's easy to see themes that stand out:

1. He seems to like creative pursuits, like writing and music.

2. He likes exciting things, rather than routine, boring ones.

3. He likes to work with people, organize, and lead.

(continued on next page)

Who are you? And what do you want? **35**

Now get a large sheet of blank paper and try it for yourself. First, list all the things that seem significant in <u>your</u> life—memories, past experiences, dreams, preferences, skills, objects, traits—and place them on a large sheet of paper in any order. Then start linking these individual items as connections begin to make sense to you. Once you've completed the linking arrows (as Bill did), then list the themes you discover here.

1.

2.

3.

Once you have identified your three personal themes, start pondering which sorts of career choices would match up best with your themes, and preferably with *all* your themes. Can you think of career options that would be ideal for Bill? If you can't think of a career that satisfies all your themes, zero in on one important one. If you remembered building model cars, for example, entering a soap-box derby, and reading automotive magazines, you might realize that one theme in your life has been a love of cars. From this realization, you might identify an engineering career in automotive design. Try it, and map career possibilities that capitalize on what you're already passionate about.

Spending Time "in the System"

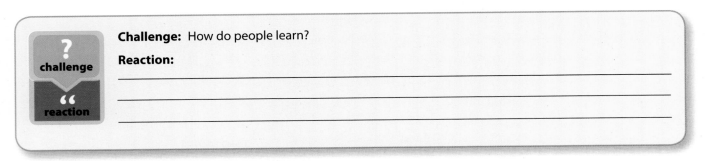

Challenge: How do people learn?

Reaction:
_____
_____
_____

Teachable Moment Some students see college as a "necessary evil"—something they must endure on the way to a career that pays well. Those students may be less interested in college as a *process*, and more interested in the *product*—a diploma. Explain that the most successful students are those who take responsibility for their own learning. As an instructor, your job is to help students clearly understand what they need to do and when it needs to be completed. Make sure they know that each assignment is a class requirement and that you expect them to complete it—on time and with their best effort. Emphasize that this course is not about you proving to them how much you know. Rather it is about them and how much they can learn.

Spending time "in the system"? No, being in college isn't like being in jail—far from it. Many people reflect on their college days as one of the most enjoyable, active, and interesting times of their lives. Get involved on campus, make lifelong friends, and gain as much as you can from your college experience.

"The system" is the approach used in this book to structure productive learning: the Challenge → Reaction → Insight → Action system. It is based on the work of Dr. John Bransford and his colleagues, who together wrote an influential book called *How People Learn*.

Figure 2.2 summarizes how learning requires focus, and focus involves the four steps in this system. Ideally, it would be interesting to hear the conversation going on in your head as you learn—what's called metacognition, or knowing how you come to know something. But because that's impossible, this book asks you to write and discuss things along the way: your reactions, your insights, and the actions you plan to take. You'll come to realize things about yourself. This book's goal for you is *transformative learning*: "a process of examining, questioning, validating, and revising [your] perceptions."[7] What you'll learn by reading it has the potential to *transform*, or *change* you, so that you're ready to

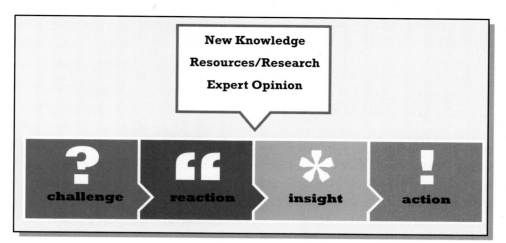

FIGURE 2.2

How People Learn

Source: Based on J. Bransford, et al. (2000). *How People Learn: Brain, Mind, Experience, and School.* Washington, DC: National Academy Press.

Teachable Moment The Challenge → Reaction → Insight → Action system is a very important feature of this text. The cycle is to react to a presented challenge, for students to find out how much they already know, use the new knowledge provided to gain insight, and then turn that insight into action. Keep reminding students about this chain reaction.

meet the many challenges that await you in college and in life. Here's a step-by-step explanation of the learning system used in this book.

STEP 1: Accept the FOCUS challenge. Every time you study a new subject or take a new course, you are challenged, right? Within each chapter of this book, you'll be presented with challenges, beginning with a case study about a college student—perhaps someone like you or a friend—who is experiencing something new and difficult. Research shows that people can learn more from examples of things going wrong than they can from examples of things going perfectly smoothly. As you continue to read, you'll be presented with additional challenges related to the chapter's content to pique your curiosity, motivate you to keep reading, and

I hope things go right for me!

❝ Surround yourself with people who take their work seriously, but not themselves, those who work hard and play hard. ❞

Colin Powell, former U.S. Secretary of State

start a learning chain reaction. Don't skip over this step; it's an important part of the learning process. Challenge yourself!

STEP 2: React to the challenge. Whenever you're learning something new, the best place to start is by figuring out what you think you already know—let's call it your gut reaction. You're a novice to any new field you're studying, not an expert, but you bring with you to the learning process a set of preconceptions, assumptions, sometimes biases or misperceptions, and of course, all your previous experiences. Your reaction to each challenge in *FOCUS* chapters will tell you what you think you already know. If you come across an unfamiliar term, look it up in the dictionary. Of course, you won't know everything there is to know in reacting to the challenge yet. But you'll find out what you do know and what you don't, and by the end of the chapter, you'll know more about all the challenges you've encountered throughout your reading. Stop and fill in your reactions to the Challenge questions. What *do* you already know? Check yourself and see. The goal of this book is to help you become a deep learner, as opposed to skimming the surface and simply rushing on to the next assignment and the next course—as many college students do. It will ask you to pause, take stock, focus, and think.

STEP 3: Use new knowledge to gain insights. After your initial reaction, you must pay attention to your inner voice—insights you've gained from new knowledge. An "Insight → Action" activity at the end of every chapter will help you keep track of them. Your instructor may ask you to record your answers online or in a notebook, or you may discuss these questions in class. Let's say, for example, that you read later in this chapter about goal setting. When you first thought about it, the whole idea of setting goals seemed simple, but after reading about it, you decide you really hadn't ever thought about it very deeply and hadn't thought much at all about setting your own goals. The difference between step 2 (whatever reaction you provided to the challenge) and step 3 (the insights you've gained) demonstrates that learning is taking place.

STEP 4: Use your insights to propel you toward action. Insights have no impact unless they become integrated into your life, unless they lead to change. Decide how an insight affects your existing beliefs, how it changes them, and, therefore, what you've learned. Your insights may lead you to change your behavior, develop an informed opinion, or make choices about your education, your job, your family, or your life. The bottom line is: You must use your insights to take action. To become real, new knowledge must lead to personal insights that result in action.

Each step in this four-part system is important. For example, if you skip step 2, *react to the challenge,* by identifying what you *think* you know, you may assume you already know all the new information you're reading or hearing. You may think, "Sure, of course, that makes sense. I already knew that," when you really didn't. Realizing there's a gap between steps 2 and 3—what you thought you knew and the insights you've gained from new knowledge—is important. And actually putting the insights you gain into real, live, honest-to-goodness action is vital.

Talk about insight and action—my bathroom scale gave me an insight this morning. I need to lose five pounds, but will I follow through with action? That's another question!

Right! Maybe I'm just recognizing that what I'm reading sounds right. I guess I really didn't know all these things beforehand.

As you work through this book, the Challenge → Reaction → Insight → Action system will continue cycling back to step 1, presenting you with new challenges. If you follow the system built into this book and integrate it into your other academic pursuits, you can become a lifelong learner. Thinking in terms of the learning cycle will become ingrained. Someone once said that change is accelerating in such mind-boggling ways today that "Learning is what most adults will do for a living in the 21st century." Life management is about knowing how to learn.

How Motivated *Are* You and *How* Are You Motivated?

Challenge: How intrinsically motivated do you think you are on a scale of 1 to 10 with 10 meaning EXTREMELY ACADEMICALLY MOTIVATED and 1 meaning NOT VERY MOTIVATED AT ALL? Why does this number seem right to you?

Reaction: _____

I'd say 5 for me. I just want to get to the best part—my singing career!

Let's get serious. When it comes to getting a college education, where does motivation come into the picture? In general, motivation is your desire to engage and put forth effort, even when the going gets rough. The word *motivation* comes from Medieval Latin, *motivus*, meaning moving or impelling. What moves you to learn? There are many ways to define motivation, and different people are motivated by different things.

How motivated would you be to learn something difficult, such as a new language, one you'd never studied before? Let's say that you were offered a chance to learn Finnish, a challenging language that is not related to English. For example, in Finnish *Kiitoksia oikein paljon* means "thank you very much." Finnish would be a challenge to learn. To determine your level of motivation, it would help to know your attitude toward Finland and Finnish people, whether you needed to learn Finnish for some reason, how you felt about learning it, if you thought you could learn it successfully, if you were reinforced in some way for learning it, and just how stimulating you found the learning process to be.[8] In other words, your motivation level depends on many factors, right?

You'd probably be more motivated to learn Finnish if these sorts of things were part of the picture: (a) you were going to visit relatives in Finland and were excited about it, (b) you'd always excelled at learning foreign languages and you expected to learn this one easily, (c) your boss was planning to transfer you to Helsinki as part of a big promotion, or (d) you enjoyed your Finnish language class, thought the instructor was a gifted teacher, and found the other students to be as motivated as you were. So, whose job is it to motivate

> "In the new economy, information, education, and motivation are everything."

William J. Clinton, 42nd President of the United States

Teachable Moment Although the majority of the statements in Exercise 2.2 are "I" statements, consider pairing students with a partner to discuss their answers. For example, the responses to question 3, "I determine my career goals," may vary. Some students think that a strict teacher should determine students' goals when they don't pass a math class. But students can keep each other on task and help each other solve problem situations. According to J. W. Atkinson, "Achievement is a we thing, not a me thing, always the product of many heads and hands." Ask students how we, the class, can help each other succeed. Make a list and agree on some things the class, and you, can do to help each other.

Read each of the following statements and circle the number beside each statement that most accurately represents your views about yourself.

	Completely Not True	Somewhat Not True	Neutral	Somewhat True	Completely True
1. I have academic goals.	1	2	3	4	5
2. I am confident I can complete my degree.	1	2	3	4	5
3. I determine my career goals.	1	2	3	4	5
4. I enjoy solving challenging, difficult problems.	1	2	3	4	5
5. I work on an assignment until I understand it.	1	2	3	4	5
6. I am confident I will graduate from college.	1	2	3	4	5
7. I determine the quality of my academic work.	1	2	3	4	5
8. I am pursuing a college degree because I value education.	1	2	3	4	5
9. I feel good knowing that I determine how my academic career develops.	1	2	3	4	5
10. I have high standards for academic work.	1	2	3	4	5
11. Staying in college is my decision.	1	2	3	4	5
12. I study because I like to learn new things.	1	2	3	4	5
13. I enjoy doing outside readings in connection to my future coursework.	1	2	3	4	5
14. I am intrigued by the different topics introduced in my courses.	1	2	3	4	5
15. I study because I am curious.	1	2	3	4	5
16. I look forward to going to class.	1	2	3	4	5
17. I am excited to take more courses within my major.	1	2	3	4	5

(continued)

		1	2	3	4	5
18.	I enjoy learning more within my field of study.	1	2	3	4	5
19.	I like to find answers to questions about material I am learning.	1	2	3	4	5
20.	I enjoy studying.	1	2	3	4	5
21.	I have pictured myself in a profession after college.	1	2	3	4	5
22.	I am excited about the job opportunities I will have when I graduate.	1	2	3	4	5
23.	I have pictured myself being successful in my chosen profession.	1	2	3	4	5
24.	I believe I will make a substantial contribution to my chosen profession.	1	2	3	4	5
25.	I feel good knowing I will be a member of the professional community in my area of study.	1	2	3	4	5

Total each column, then add your scores across.

_____ + _____ + _____ + _____ + _____ = _____ OVERALL SCORE

Continue reading to find out what your overall score means.

Source: French, F.B., & Oakes, W. (2003). Measuring academic intrinsic motivation in the first year of college: Reliability and validity evidence for a new instrument. *Journal of the First Year Experience 15*(1), 83–102.

you? Your instructor's? Your parents'? This book's? Yours? *Can* anyone else besides you motivate you? This book will ask you: how motivated *are* you to succeed in college? And *how* are you motivated?

To assess your own motivation, it's important to understand the difference between (extrinsic) and (intrinsic) motivation.[9] People who are *extrinsically,* or externally, motivated learn in order to get a grade, earn credits, or complete a requirement, for example. They are motivated by things outside themselves. People who are *intrinsically,* or internally, motivated learn because they're curious, fascinated, challenged, or because they truly want to master a subject. They are motivated from within. Let's be realistic, however. Extrinsic motivation is real and important. You need a particular number of credit hours to graduate. You'd rather get A's than F's. But how intrinsically motivated you are in college will have a great deal to do with just how successful you are. The motivation to become truly educated must come from within you.

Look at Figure 2.3 and circle the three boxes (and only three) that most accurately describe your overall current motivation to attend college. Does your motivation vary in the different courses you're taking? When you think about why you're in college, are you generally on the extrinsic side or the intrinsic

Good point. Is it <u>my</u> motivation or my parents'?

Extrinsic Motivation

Grades

Credits

Pay

Parents

Intrinsic Motivation

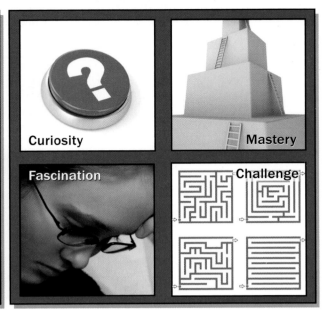

Curiosity

Mastery

Fascination

Challenge

FIGURE 2.3

Extrinsic versus Intrinsic Motivation

side—or both? Your instructor may wish to generate a discussion about these questions in class.

You completed the Academic Intrinsic Motivation Scale (AIMS) in the previous exercise, which is designed to measure your intrinsic, or internal, motivation to succeed in college in terms of these four C-Factors. You'll see these C-Factors reappear throughout the book to boost your intrinsic motivation:

 CURIOSITY Do you want to learn new things? Are you truly interested in what you're learning? Do you ask questions? Do you allow your curiosity to propel your learning? Many chapters include a short article based on current research, a *New York Times* bestseller, an upcoming trend, or a new way of looking at what's needed to succeed in college. You'll read cutting-edge information that may pique your curiosity and lead you to consider exploring the original source or related material on your own.

 CONTROL Do you think the academic investment you make will lead to successful outcomes? Do you believe you can control how successful you'll be? You are encouraged throughout this book to apply what you are reading about to your most challenging class this term and to take charge of your own learning. The challenge in your chosen class may be due to the level, for example—either too high level because the material is extremely difficult (a killer course) or too low level (a no-brainer, boring course). This book will help you succeed in your chosen class by prompting you to work with your instructor through an office hours visit or e-mail, for example. Taking charge of your own learning is vital to college success.

 CAREER OUTLOOK Are you goal oriented? Are you future oriented? Can you imagine yourself graduating and getting a job you want? *FOCUS* includes some extremely useful advice about career prospects, perceptions, progress, priorities, or professionalism that will put you ahead of the game by the time you launch your career. (Much of the

Activity Option Before class, write on index cards something that might cause a student to lose focus in school (i.e., your roommate blasts music all day, your grandmother is ill, your computer cost more money than you expected, your job is cut). Make as many cards as you need for the size and composition of your class. Pass out the cards, one per student, and as each student holds up his or her card, ask the class whether it's possible to exert some control over the situation, and if so, how.

I'm goal oriented, but I'm just not sure what it will take . . .

advice works for your college career, too.) Looking ahead now can do you a world of good later. Employers say that many college graduates are ready in theory, but not in practice. They have the knowledge they've gained while studying for a college degree, but not necessarily the ability to put that knowledge into practice. As Yogi Berra says, "In theory there is no difference between theory and practice. In practice there is." It's time to start practicing for your career now!

CHALLENGE Does your college coursework challenge you appropriately? Too much challenge can cause you to become frustrated and give up. Not enough challenge can cause you to lose interest.[10] In general, if a course is too challenging, you may be tempted to give up. If it's too easy, you may lose interest. Adjusting the level of challenge to one that's right for you is key to keeping yourself motivated to learn, and that's up to you. No one else. Online quizzes for each chapter will challenge you so that you can work at your best. For more practice online, go to www.cengagebrain.com to take the Challenge Yourself online quizzes.

Activity Option Ask students to call out loud the names of their most challenging courses. Make a list of the top five most challenging courses in the group. Ask for suggestions on how the C-Factors and intrinsic motivation apply. Have students share what they plan to do to be motivated in these challenging courses. Remind students that planning and follow-through are the key words. Remind them that academic success requires a serious investment.

CONTROL: Your Toughest Class

Think about all the courses you're enrolled in this term. Use the following matrix to analyze your C-Factors for these courses. Describe each course in terms of its *challenge* level, your *curiosity* about the subject, how much *control* you believe you have to succeed, and the way each class impacts your *career outlook*. (Keep in mind that many first-year introductory courses are broad-based. They may seem less directly related to your career than later classes in your major, but it's still important to consider what skills you can gain that will lead to a more successful career.) Once you've determined the levels of challenge, curiosity, control, and career outlook you perceive in your courses, remember that it's your responsibility to adjust them. Instructors can't always meet the differing requirements of each student in a class. But *you* can make your own adjustments to gain as much as possible from each of your courses. Assess your C-Factors in each of your classes, and consider the adjustments you need to make.

Course Title	Challenge	Curiosity	Control	Career Outlook	Adjustments Required
Composition	Very High: never been good at writing	Very Low: had a discouraging teacher in H.S.	Moderate: probably higher than it feels to me	Will need to know how to write in any job	Need to spend more time pre-writing and going to the campus Writing Center for help

Which of the classes you listed will be your most challenging this term? What is the relationship between the four C-Factors and your intrinsic motivation to learn in each one of these courses? What can you do to increase your intrinsic motivation and become more successful?

Stop Tweeting. Close your Facebook. Turn off your smartphone. Crank down the iTunes, and listen up. Attention is a hot new topic that neuroscientists are focusing on.

According to attention expert Winifred Gallagher in her book *Rapt: Attention and the Focused Life,* today we live in a distraction-rich world. Stimulation overload is an ever-present danger, and everybody and everything want your attention. "People don't understand that attention is a finite resource, like money. Do you want to invest your cognitive cash on endless Twittering or Net surfing or couch potatoing? You're constantly making choices, and your choices determine your experience." "Multitasking is a myth. You cannot do two things at once. It's either this or that," Gallagher claims.

You can always tell when people are trying to multitask while you're on the phone with them, for example. Apart from the tapping of keys in the background, there's silence after you ask a question. "Are you still there?" you ask. They're making choices, and at the moment they're choosing something else over talking on the phone with you. According to one expert, most office workers keep eight windows open on their computers at once and skip between them every 20 seconds. Our brains can switch between tasks at astonishing speed, and switching makes us feel efficient.

But try this experiment: read this section out loud while you type something else. Just how efficient are you?

Here's a fascinating notion of Gallagher's. If you look back at your life, you'll see that who you are is based largely on what you've chosen to pay attention to. In what ways might that be true for you? If you took countless piano lessons as a kid and spent endless hours practicing the piano, music may matter to you now in ways that other people can't begin to understand. You probably also learned some important lessons about focus. If piano hadn't been your thing, but you'd put the same amount of attention into baseball, you might be a different person with another reality. Your life, Gallagher says, is the sum of what you focus on.

In the "Age of Distraction," is it possible to lead a focused life? Learning how to focus—really focus—like any other skill takes discipline and effort. It takes tremendous brain power to ignore all the "incomings" that hit us every day. We must learn to deliberately create our own "distraction-proof personal pods" to do it. Her recommendation? Spend the first ninety minutes of every day concentrating on your most important task. During that time, don't answer e-mails, don't Google, don't text, don't make phone calls—just focus. Paying attention to how you pay attention leads to a fuller, richer, more successful life.[11]

If your overall score on the AIMS in Exercise 2.2 was 100–125, you're intrinsically motivated at a high level. If you scored between 75 and 99, you're intrinsically motivated at a moderate level, but increasing your intrinsic motivation may help you achieve more. If you scored below 75, a lack of intrinsic

> " People often say that motivation doesn't last. Well, neither does bathing—that's why we recommend it daily. "
>
> *- Zig Ziglar,*
> ***American motivational speaker and author***

motivation could interfere with your college success. If you're intrinsically motivated, you'll accept challenges, react to them by identifying what you already know, seek insights from new knowledge, and take action based on what you've learned. If your score is below 75, you may need a reality check about why you're in college in the first place, or at the very least, an attitude adjustment.

Positivity Pays Off

There's a difference of opinion on the subject of attitude. Some people say attitude is not all that important. Attitude-schmattitude, they say. Others say that *attitude* is more important than *aptitude*. Some even say attitude is everything—and attitude can be improved. What do you think? Being truly motivated for the challenges of college may require that you tweak your attitude. How would you rate your attitude right now—positive, negative, or somewhere in between?

According to happiness expert Shawn Achor and dozens of other researchers, you can actually train your brain to become happier and more positive.[12] Research indicates that happier people perform better; they're more creative, more productive, and more engaged. Achor works with employees in organizations to train them to be happier, better performers. He asks them to do simple tasks that can become habits, like these. Every day for three weeks, he asks them to do one of the following activities:

1. Jot down three things you are grateful for.
2. Write a positive message to someone in your social support network.
3. Meditate at your desk for two minutes.
4. Exercise for 10 minutes.
5. Take two minutes to describe in a journal the most meaningful experience of the past twenty-four hours.

1. Mom, Dad, Grandma

2. Mom, thanks for your text today. I had just gotten out of a tough exam, and you made me laugh!

3. Can I do this?!

4. Time to visit the campus Rec Center!

5. This would require some thought, but it's an interesting idea

His results are impressive, and they appeared to be long-lasting. Happiness had become a habit. Four months later, the effects of their chosen daily happiness activity were still present when he retested the group on the Life Satisfaction Scale, a well-respected measure, and compared the results with a control group who hadn't completed the daily happiness activity for three weeks.

Honestly, many people chase happiness. ("If I can just get past next Thursday, I'll be happy." "If I can just achieve my dream, I'll finally be happy.") Often, we blame unhappiness on genetics or our environments—and those things do have an impact—or we compare ourselves to others and don't like the results. There's even evidence that other people's happy Facebook photos can make us sad.[13] And many college students do discover that they have tough issues to work through, sometimes with the aid of college counselors.[14] But the good news is that we have more control over our own happiness than we realize.[15] Think about it!

When it comes to academic success, positivity has payoffs. In one study, students who were hopeful graduated at rates 16 percent higher than non-hopeful students. New research indicates that hopefulness may predict academic success more accurately than standardized test scores, intelligence, personality, or past academic record. What is hope? Hope is a belief that your future will be better than your present, and that you—yourself—can help make that happen. Hope is powerful, and a positive attitude will give you a better shot at college and career success.[16]

> "You are never given a wish without the power to make it come true. You may have to work for it, however."
>
> **Richard Bach, from Illusions**

Eight Ways to Adjust Your Attitude

The good thing about attitude is that you can change it yourself. In fact, you can give yourself an overall attitude adjustment, which can lead to better control over your learning and deeper investment in your own education. As you think about the benefits of developing a more positive attitude, keep these eight recommendations in mind:

1. **Know that you always have choices.** Regardless of circumstances—your income, your background, or your prior academic record—you always have a choice, even if it's limited to how you choose to perceive your current situation.

2. **Take responsibility for your own outcomes.** Coach Vince Lombardi used to have his players look in a mirror before every game and ask themselves, "Am I looking at the person who is helping me win or the one who is holding me back?" Blaming others simply reduces your own power to work toward constructive responses to challenges.

3. **Convert turning points into learning points.** Instead of beating yourself up when things don't go well, figure out why. See what you can learn from the experience and then move on. As Henry Ford once said, "Failure is the opportunity to begin again, more intelligently."

4. **Choose your words carefully.** "Can't" and "won't" are two of the biggest inhibitors to a healthy attitude. Also pay attention to how you describe things. Is the cup half empty or half full? State things in the positive rather than the negative (for example, "stay healthy" rather than "don't get sick"). Language is a reflection of attitude.

> "A positive attitude is your most priceless possession, one of your most valuable assets. To a great extent, it determines the overall quality of your life."
>
> **Keith Harrell, from Attitude Is Everything**

5. **Fill your mind with messages about the attitude you want to have.** The old saying, "garbage in, garbage out," applies to attitudes as well. There are countless books, CDs, and films that offer positive, motivating messages. Paying attention to role models whose traits you admire is also a great way to bolster your outlook.

6. **Remember that negative experiences can be great teachers.** Have you ever watched someone do something so badly that you've said to yourself, "I'm never going to do that! I'm going to do it differently!"? You can also choose to learn from your own mistakes and setbacks. They all offer some sort of lesson—be it greater clarity, personal growth, or a new vision—even if it takes a bit of distance from the event to see what you can learn. It's hard to believe, but Michael Jordan was cut from his high school basketball team. He once observed, "I've failed over and over again in my life. That is why I succeed."

7. **Offer help without expecting something in return.** Give freely of yourself, with no expectations of *quid pro quo*, and life will reward you in unexpected ways—not the least of which is a positive outlook. Offer to help someone study for a test or suggest that a classmate practice a presentation for class in front of you, for example. Engage in random acts of kindness; it'll do amazing things for your attitude.

8. **Acknowledge your blessings.** Taking time at the end of each day to recognize and feel gratitude for the blessings in your life—no matter how large or small—is a great way to amplify a positive attitude.

> *Maybe I do need an attitude adjustment. There are some good points here that I've never thought about . . .*

Activity Option Divide students up so that at least two students are assigned to each of the eight ways to adjust attitude. Ask students to describe a real-life example related to the numbered point they have been assigned.

> "If you don't like something, change it. If you can't change it, change your attitude."
>
> *Maya Angelou, American author and poet*

Statements That Ought to Be Outlawed in College . . . and Why

Because words reflect attitudes (and help shape them), listen for statements like these escaping from your mouth. They can negatively affect your attitude and therefore your learning:

> *I can agree with that! But I'm starting to get interested in some of them.*

➤ **"I thought college classes would be more interesting than they are."** Some students, especially those who didn't find high school classes particularly interesting, expect something different in college. *Interesting* is in the mind of the beholder. You may not, but your professors think chemistry, calculus, and psychology are the most interesting things on the planet. It's up to *you* to generate your own enthusiasm for learning, rather than expecting your instructors to do it for you. Not all college classes will be naturally interesting to you, but you'll be much more successful if you decide to learn all you can, regardless of the wow factor.

➤ **"I didn't learn a thing in that class."** This statement may say more about you than it does about the quality of the instructor, teaching assistant, or course content. Actively search for what you can take away from a class, even if it didn't quite meet your expectations. When you play the blame game, you lose.

Teaching with Technology As a brief homework assignment, ask students to send you a text message or e-mail with a statement *THEY* think ought to be outlawed in college. During the next class, choose a few of the statements and have students explain their responses. Why do they think this statement should be outlawed? Do they have any examples of problems this statement might cause? This activity not only opens new channels of communication between you and your students, but it allows you to bridge material from the previous class session into the next.

> *There is only one success—to be able to spend your life in your own way.*

Christopher Morley (1890 -1957), American journalist, novelist, essayist and poet

Expectations. They play a big role in our lives. Your teachers expect you to work up to your full potential. Your grandparents expect you to marry someone who's "good enough" for you. Your parents expect you to give college your best shot. Sometimes it can seem as if you have less input than you should. Although they have your best interests at heart, it is *your* life, after all.

It's true about careers, too. Perhaps your family has talked about it for years: "Our Gabe is going to be a doctor. We've known it since we watched him play with his toy doctor's kit as a little kid." The story has been repeated so many times that it's now turned into a real expectation your family has for you. Or perhaps your parents have decided on a major for you based on economics, despite the fact that you have other interests. "We're not paying tuition for any major that won't lead to a real career with good job prospects. It's just not worth it."

But here's an important question: What do *you* want to do with your life? While your parents will most likely have an important perspective, figuring this out for yourself is one of the most important questions you will begin to answer in college.

Think of it this way: Before you take a road trip, you don't just close your eyes and point to a place on the map, do you? You don't automatically take someone else's recommendation. And you don't just start driving and hope to end up someplace interesting. You take your time and figure things out, realizing that you may end up taking an unexpected detour along the way. That's an important comparison.

Most college students change their majors at least once, and many adults change their careers, too. Our fictitious Gabe above, whose family has decided should be a doctor, may actually become one. But instead, he may eventually decide to head up the hospital as a businessman, rather than practice medicine, or open an emergi-care franchise as an entrepreneur. He may (or may not) choose something related to medicine, but not actually practice it.

Begin your journey with this advice in mind: Don't panic, but do start discovering your own expectations of yourself now. Use college as an opportunity to truly get to know yourself. Pay attention to which disciplines fascinate you as a learner. Make decisions for the right reasons. A career that pays well but holds no real appeal for you may result in major dissatisfaction later on. Project some alternative futures for yourself based on various career possibilities. Imagine yourself wearing different career "hats." As a French Pulitzer-prize winning author once said, "Be faithful to that which exists nowhere but in yourself." And set *your own* course.

Think Ahead Why are you going to college? Who among your family members or friends has communicated their expectations for your future career? If so, is it a future you really want?

Cast on Careers

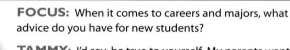

Yikes! This is about me!

© Larry Harwood Photography. Property of Cengage Learning.

FOCUS: When it comes to careers and majors, what advice do you have for new students?

TAMMY: I'd say, be true to yourself. My parents wanted me to major in accounting because they own a family-run business, but I just didn't have any interest in numbers. And sitting behind a desk all day held no appeal at all. Eventually, I convinced them that it was a better idea to major in business, rather than specialize in accounting. But it took me a semester of mediocre grades to get there.

FOCUS: How can new students be true to themselves when they don't know what they want?

TAMMY YO: For me, it was important to "go with my gut." I knew myself well enough to know what energized me and which classes I looked forward to, beyond just liking the instructor. I was genuinely interested in the content. Don't worry if you don't have it all figured out right away. Eventually, things will come into FOCUS!

Yes, I totally get this!

> **"The textbook is really dull. Why bother reading it?"** This question is about personal responsibility, too. Hey, it's your college experience. If you choose not to learn because the written material doesn't meet your entertainment criteria, how sad is that?

> **"The professor is soooo-o-o boring."** Again—it's your choice. Life isn't all Comedy Central. In your career, you'll be interacting with many different types of personalities, so it's good to begin now to appreciate that different people communicate differently. Get beneath the surface and you'll be amazed at how much you can learn.

> **"Why do I have to take this required course? What's the point?"** The point is to broaden your horizons, expand your skills as a critical thinker, and become a lifelong scholar. Care enough to give yourself every opportunity to do your best. And, yes, every class, every situation in life, is an opportunity. You're worth it.[17]

> **I can tell that my instructor doesn't like me.** The instructor may or may not like you (and you may or may not like him or her). That's not really the point. He may be focused on the course content, or she may just be introverted. Even if it were true, you'll still want to give it your best shot.

Self-Motivation Works Best

Imagine this: Two students volunteer to take part in an experiment: Student A and Student B. Both are tasked with learning some new material in fifteen minutes. Student A reads and rereads the material until it's virtually memorized. Student B tries to figure out what the material means by looking for patterns, connections, and themes. Both students use their fifteen minutes, but Student B vastly outperforms Student A on a test that follows. Why? Student B was motivated to actually learn the material; Student A was motivated to get through the experiment. Even though you could say that the two students came to the task with roughly the same *amount* of motivation, the *type* of motivation they each had was very different. To better understand motivation, think about these two factors—amount and type.[18]

Think, too, about these three additional factors that explain how and why people are motivated—autonomy, value, and competence.[19] Let's take a look at what these terms mean, especially as they relate to you as a college student.

Autonomy. When all is said and done, the kind of motivation that gets the best from you has to *come from you.* Remember this old fable? If you want your stubborn donkey to move, you can do one of two things: dangle a *carrot* in front of him or beat his back side with a *stick.* Heads or tails. These two options relate to positive or negative reinforcement, and the donkey will usually move either way.

Now think about that analogy in terms of human beings. Your parents agree to pay double tuition for any course in which you earn an "A" (a "carrot" approach) or refuse to pay for any course in which you earn lower than a "B" (a "stick" approach). Your English instructor says, "The first person to submit a good essay this week will earn five extra points!" ("carrot") or, "I won't give you an opportunity to rewrite your next essay, so turn in your best work or suffer the consequences!" ("stick"). You might be motivated by either

Teaching with Technology Online resources can be a valuable source of ideas and information. www.teachertube.com is a free resource for teachers and students that allows users to view multimedia content about lesson plans, teaching strategies, projects, and more. It can be used to supplement in-class discussions, to enhance class activities, or as a resource for students outside of class.

Singers don't need to be critical thinkers . . . or do they?

❝ Ability is what you're capable of doing. Motivation determines what you do. Attitude determines how well you do it. ❞

Lou Holtz, former college football coach and ESPN sports analyst

Teachable Moment Motivation and optimism are connected. If you are not very optimistic about the outcome of something and have an "I can't" attitude, motivation will be minimized. Why do something if you think you will fail? Make sure students understand this relationship, and focus on their control of their own learning.

> **66**
> There's more to motivation
> than carrots and sticks.
> **99**
>
> *Anonymous*

of these two strategies, but the motivation would be short-lived in the first case and stressful in the second. Autonomy means asking: Can I generate the energy required for action on my own? If *you* are motivated to do something, you're eager and energetic. If someone else wants you to do something you really don't particularly care about, you're bothered and bored. The truth is, the best motivation for writing an excellent essay must come from within you. To the extent you're able, choose an assignment that fires you up or a major for which you have real passion.[20] If you don't know what that is yet, be on the lookout. You'll find it.

Value. It's much easier to motivate yourself if you think whatever you need to do is worthwhile. Picture two men. Both are picking up bits of paper along a highway. One is doing penance for a DUI; the other is looking for a winning lottery ticket that blew out of the car window. The difference in value is obvious. In college, you may think to yourself, *What? An essay every week?* Interestingly, we don't respond the same way to other stiff requirements, *What? Three meals every day?* The difference, of course, is that food is vital; essays aren't, or so we seem to think. If you didn't eat for four weeks, you might die. If you didn't write essays for four weeks, you'd have more time for flag football. But essays are in fact essential for several reasons: they give us an opportunity to reflect and record what we think. They give us practice in a life skill that—believe it or not—may make or break our careers. But the value is s-t-r-e-t-c-h-e-d out. In college, your instructors will value everything they ask you to read or write about. They'll value every class or online session; otherwise, they wouldn't include these things in the course. You, on the other hand, may have to recognize or search for value. Make a list of all the reasons math homework or research skills are important. Convince yourself to look for the value in every individual course, and remind yourself continually of the long-term value of your overall college degree. It's your future, after all, and you want to be ready for it.

> **66**
> Nobody's a natural. You work
> hard to get good and then work
> to get better.
> **99**
>
> *Paul Coffey, Retired Professional Hall of Fame Ice Hockey Defenseman*

Competence. It's easier to find motivation when you think you're good at something than when you think you aren't. To conjure up a ridiculous but memorable image, picture this. Imagine challenging yourself to swim the English Channel when you can barely dog paddle. But if you've put in countless hours refining your swimming skills and you've developed confidence based on that hard work, you might just give it (or something like it) a go. The same thing is true in college. The more you work to develop your calculus skills, the better you get at doing calculus, and the more motivated you are to keep getting better. In your introductory courses, commit to working hard, so that when the challenges really hit later, you've already developed the competence you need to do well.

One last thought. Is it really motivation you're lacking, or is it follow-through?[21] It's easy to sit on the couch and say, "I really should be reading my psychology chapter right now" after every consecutive television show ends but never actually get up and get the book out of your backpack. You ask your Mom or your roommate, "How can I get myself out of this chair to do my homework?" You text your best friend, "I'm just not motivated to read that psych chapter. Have *you* read it?" What's interesting is this thought: You may actually be motivated to read; what you're lacking is follow-through. If you weren't motivated, you wouldn't necessarily bother to ask other people for advice. You'd just skip it. Motivation is in your head; follow-through is in your actions. Here are some ideas that may help with both:

Wow, I've never thought about it this way!

1. Create an environment for follow-through. Being sunk into a cushy chair with pillows all around you may not be conducive to reading with alertness and comprehension.

2. Make a deal with someone else who is in the same situation. Give yourselves an hour to complete the task, and then check in with each other. Accountability is important.

3. Develop a concrete plan. "I'll read my psychology chapter at my desk from seven to eight o'clock, right after dinner tonight."

4. Get over the hump. Realize that once you get started, you've just jumped over the hurdle of getting started. Things will get much easier.

5. Remember this moment. You did it. You won! The next time your mind starts to argue with you, ignore it. "You're smarter than your mind. You can see right through it."[22] Take this advice to heart, and remember: The choice to motivate yourself (and follow-through) is always yours.

> **❝**
> I do not try to dance better than anyone else. I only try to dance better than myself.
> **❞**
> *Mikhail Baryshnikov, Russian American ballet dancer and choreographer*

Ability versus Effort: What's More Important?

Successful people have several things in common: they love learning, seek challenges, value effort, and persevere even when things become difficult.[23] They demonstrate both ability and effort. These two things are the basic requirements for success.

> **Only the curious will learn and only the resolute overcome the obstacles to learning. The quest quotient has always excited me more than the intelligence quotient.**
>
> *Eugene S. Wilson, former Dean of Admissions, Amherst College*

Many people think ability is more important than effort. Either you have it or you don't. But here's a new way of thinking about the question. Take the notion of genius, for example. Experts used to think that a genius was someone born with extraordinary talent, like Mozart. From an early age, geniuses demonstrate exceptional natural abilities, they thought. But experts have changed their thinking: "What Mozart had, we now believe, was ... the ability to focus for long periods of time. The key factor separating geniuses from the merely accomplished is not a divine spark.... It's deliberate practice. Top performers spend more hours (many more hours) rigorously practicing their craft." A master violinist once said, "I practice the violin eight hours a day for 40 years, and they call me a genius?" Effort counts much more than you might think.[24]

That said, think about some of the possible combinations of ability and effort. If you have high ability and exert great effort, you'll most likely succeed. If you have high ability and exert little effort, and still succeed, you've just proved how smart you must be! But if you have high ability and exert little effort and fail, you can always claim you didn't have the time to invest or you didn't care, right? You can always say that you could have done well if you'd tried harder. Rationalizing can lead to a dangerous strategy, one that's called "self-handicapping."[25] Some college students actually consciously or unconsciously apply this strategy. They exert little effort, perhaps because they have no confidence in themselves or because they fear failure, and then they rationalize when they don't do well.

Research shows that what you *believe* about your own intelligence—your *mindset*—can make a difference in how successful you'll be in college. At first glance this statement seems absurd. What does what you believe about intelligence have to do with how smart you really are?

The scaled questions demonstrate that there are two basic ways to define intelligence. Some of us are *performers*, who agree with statements 1 and 2, while others of us are *learners*, who agree more with statements 3 and 4.

Diversity Discussion You may wish to make diversity a running theme in your course. If so, work with your students early on to define all the various aspects of the term, so that you have laid the groundwork. In a study by James Flynn in *Asian American Achievement: Beyond IQ* (1991), Flynn reports that Asian-American students with similar IQs to their Caucasian counterparts do better in school. He attributes this to higher motivation and persistence. In part, effort may be a culturally derived variable. If students have traveled or have friends from other cultures, use this topic to generate an interesting in-class or online discussion.

Exercise 2.3 | Theories of Intelligence Scale

Using the following scale, indicate the extent to which you agree or disagree with each of the following statements by writing the number that corresponds to your opinion in the space next to each statement. There are no right or wrong answers.

1	2	3	4	5	6
Strongly Agree	Mostly Agree	Agree	Disagree	Mostly Disagree	Strongly Disagree

_____ 1. You have a certain amount of intelligence, and you can't really do much to change it.

_____ 2. You can learn new things, but you can't really change your basic intelligence.

_____ 3. You can always substantially change how intelligent you are.

_____ 4. No matter how much intelligence you have, you can always change it quite a bit.

challenge

" reaction

Challenge: What is intelligence? Where does it come from? How do your views of intelligence affect you and your learning?

Reaction:

_____

_____

_____

Performers believe that intelligence is a fixed trait that cannot be changed. From the moment you're born, you have a certain amount of intelligence that's been allotted to you, and that's that. *Learners*, on the other hand, believe you can grow your intelligence if you capitalize on opportunities to learn. Whenever you tackle a tough challenge, you learn from it. The more you learn, the more intelligent you can become. Understanding which view of intelligence you endorse will make a difference in how you approach your college classes, as well as the outcomes—both positive and negative—that you'll achieve.

These two contrasting views of intelligence have been revealed through the research of Dr. Carol Dweck of Stanford University, her graduate students, and other social psychologists. Some of their original work began with children, who were first asked to agree or disagree with questions similar to those you just answered to determine which view of intelligence they held. Afterward, they were given eight conceptual problems to solve, problems that were appropriate for their grade level. As they worked on the problems, the researchers asked them to talk aloud about whatever was on their minds, even if it was unrelated to the actual problems. After they had solved the first eight problems successfully, they were given four additional problems that were far too difficult for them to solve. This is where their views about the nature of intelligence made a difference.

Diversity Discussion You may wish to generate a discussion about the fact that first-generation students may feel pressure to *perform* as opposed to *learn* because they are being "watched" by family members who have never gone to college. Ask students if the *performer* versus *learner* scale has components that could relate to some aspects of diversity.

Ho imparato che niente e impossibile, e anche che quasi niente e facile . . . (I've learned that nothing is impossible, and that almost nothing is easy . . .)

Articolo 31 (Italian rap group)

I'm really glad this was early in the book because it's about me, and I hadn't really thought about any of this.

Box 2.1 — Generation 1: First in the Family?

Did both your parents graduate from a four-year college? If not, you are a "first-generation college student." Quite an impressive title, isn't it? Being first at something has some definite pros. You're a trailblazer, a pioneer, someone to be looked up to. "Imagine, our son Dion with a college degree? Isn't that something?" But along with pros come potential challenges. Who will you go to for advice? Will your family understand what it takes? Will they support your efforts? At moments when your confidence is shaken, you may wonder: *can* a first-generation student be successful? The answer? Of course! (Your author is a first-generation college graduate!) In the end, your success is up to you. As you begin your college career, take these suggestions to heart:

1. **Communicate with your family.** Research shows that the *quality* and *quantity* of communication about college that you engage in with your family is key to your success. While they can't empathize because they haven't been there and done that, they can listen and encourage you. Talk to them openly about your college experience.[26]

2. **Keep your stress level in check.** If your family puts extra pressure on you to perform, your stress level may increase dramatically. But stress isn't the best motivator. This is something you want to do, so hone in and hunker down. Pay particular attention to your instructors, keep track of due dates, and focus. All you can do is your best. Think of it this way: you're "demystifying" college. You may just inspire Mom or Dad or your little brother to go to college one day, too.[27]

3. **Get going.** Remember this: when the going gets tough, the tough get going. Sometimes first-generation students are tempted to drop out, scale back (from four classes to three, for example), avoid assessment (thinking, oddly, "If I don't hand my paper in, I can't get a bad grade on it"), or lower their own expectations ("I was hoping for a 4.0 GPA, but maybe a 2.0 will do"). While sometimes these options may be the right ones, sabotaging your own efforts is never a good idea. Keep your eye on the prize—that degree you'll be the first one to earn in your family.[28]

4. **Find a true mentor.** Look for a particular professor or advisor to serve as a mentor—someone you can go to for advice and support. Just knowing that someone cares can be a powerful motivator. Ask this person to help you through rough patches or go to her to get recharged when your "academic batteries" are low.

5. **Get involved.** College may feel like a "foreign" culture to you. You may have conflicting emotions: excitement, confusion, and anxiety. You may not understand what instructors expect, how to fit in, or how to get it all done. But you won't learn these things if you aren't around. If you breeze in for your classes and bolt afterwards, it will be harder to adjust to your new role. Ease into the campus culture and take full advantage of what it means to be in college. Make friends and feel the beat of campus life.[29]

If you follow this advice, you *can* be successful! If you're a first-generation college student, dogear the corner of this page, and refer back to it whenever you need to.

I'm not sure I'm really a learner . . .

As they tried to tackle the problems that were too difficult for them, the *performers* talked about feeling helpless. They became discouraged and anxious, forgot that they had solved the first eight problems successfully, and told themselves they weren't very smart. The *learners*, on the other hand, coached themselves on how to do better, remained optimistic, and actually improved their problem-solving strategies. They wanted to master what they were working on. To *learners*, academic challenges were opportunities for growth; to *performers*, academic challenges were threats that might reveal their deficiencies. Performance is about measuring ability, "trying to convince yourself and others that you have a royal flush when you're secretly worried it's a pair of tens."[30] Learning is about investing the effort required to master new things: "Why waste time proving over and over how great you are, when you could be getting better?"[31]

Sometimes students who are highly confident are *performers*. They've always been told they're smart, and they have an image to protect. They become focused on the possibility of failure, which they need to avoid at all costs, instead of developing strategies to help them succeed. If you believe you only have a certain amount of intelligence, whether you realize it or not, your goal in college may be to prove you have enough. When you come to a tough course, you think, "If I have to work hard at this, I must not be very good at it." But if you believe you can develop your intelligence through learning, your goal will be to increase your ability: "If I have to work hard at this, eventually I'll become *very* good at it." Note that the research is not claiming that everyone is equally intelligent. That's not true, but what is true is that for any given individual, intellectual capacity can be increased with effort and guidance. Think of college as your opportunity to do that. According to Dweck, just learning about the importance of mindset can make a difference. Truly mastering something takes more sustained effort; performing can simply be an easy out. Learners are more likely to be intrinsically motivated; performers love the "cheering of the crowd"—external approval. Mindset matters, perhaps more than you've ever even considered.

Let's admit it: We live in a performance-based society. Getting good grades is what it's all about, we're told. We all want to do well, look good, appear smart, and impress others. Did your previous schooling emphasize the performance mindset? Do you come from a family that overemphasizes grades? Are your parents putting extra pressure on you because they never had the chance to go to college? Are you from an underrepresented population on campus and because of this you feel performance pressure to succeed?[32] That's normal, but your view of intelligence can be changed, and changing it may be your key to academic success. There is evidence that students who are taught the value of a learning mindset over a performance mindset can actually achieve more than students who aren't.[33]

Like mine?!

Regardless of what you believe about your precise intelligence level, the fact is this: *intelligence can be cultivated through learning.* And people's theories about their intelligence levels can be shifted.

What Drives You? Values, Dreams, and Goals

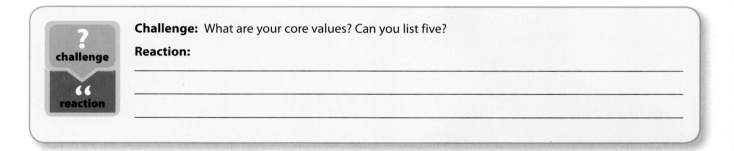

Challenge: What are your core values? Can you list five?

Reaction:

_____

_____

_____

Before tackling the big questions about what you want to create with your life, it's important to first take a close look in the mirror. Who are you? What makes you tick? What do you value? Where will your dreams take you? What short and long-term goals will help you get there? How motivated are you to get there? How will your attitude affect your journey? How much effort versus ability will it take? Everything you've read about so far in this chapter fits into the future you're creating for yourself.

Review the following list and check off the items that you value. Don't spend too much time thinking about each one; just go with your initial gut reaction. For each item, ask yourself "Is this something that's important to me?"

_____ Health
_____ Fitness/Physical strength
_____ Loyalty
_____ Academic achievement
_____ Success
_____ Happiness
_____ Social life
_____ Athletics
_____ Creativity
_____ Meaningful work
_____ Adventure

_____ Fame
_____ Independence
_____ Honesty
_____ Children
_____ Leadership
_____ Family
_____ Marriage/Partnership
_____ Spirituality
_____ Variety
_____ Challenge
_____ Personal growth

_____ Financial wealth
_____ Commitment
_____ Compassion
_____ Leisure time
_____ Balance
_____ Friendship
_____ Recognition
_____ Status
_____ Wisdom
_____ Time spent alone
_____ Other (list here)

For me, it's about fame, success, happiness, creativity and wealth!

Now review all of the items you checked off and circle the five that are most important to you at this point in your life. Then rank them by putting a number next to each of the five circled values with number one as your top priority. Finally, take stock. Is this the person you want to be? Is there anything about your values that you would like to change? If so, why not go ahead and do it?

Teachable Moment Students need to understand that individuals have different values. However, if you ask members of the class to list their top five values, you should find some similarities. Research shows that attaining great wealth may be important to many of today's students, but things like friendship may rise to the top, too. Students should discuss why they think their values are important to them. Where did their values originate?

Values at the Core

One way to gain some insights about who you are is to look at your core values. So what do you value in life? By taking time to examine your personal values, managing your life will become easier and make more sense. Values can be intangible concepts such as love or respect, or tangible things such as family or money, and understanding how they motivate you isn't as simple as it might seem.

Values can change as you go through life. For example, if you're single now, you may value the freedom to meet a variety of potential romantic partners. Just get to know people and have fun, that's all. Later, however, you may want a committed relationship because you value companionship and stability more than you used to. For this reason, it's important to reassess your values from time to time and reprioritize them.

Another complicating factor is that values can conflict with one another. Suppose that you value honesty and kindness, and you are at a party and a friend asks you what you think of her new hair color. You honestly think it's hideous, but telling her so would hurt her feelings, thus violating your value of being kind. How do you respond? That would depend on which value

> It is our choices that show what we truly are far more than our abilities.
>
> *Albus Dumbledore,*
> *Harry Potter and the Prisoner of Azkaban*

> Self-knowledge is far more important than self-confidence.

Simon Cowell, long-time American Idol judge, *from* I Don't Mean to Be Rude, But . . .

Patrik Giardino/Crush/Corbis

is a higher priority for you. You have to make an on-the-spot decision about which value to tap. Once you define your values, however, they can serve as guideposts in helping you make choices every day—everything from the insignificant day-to-day choices to more significant ones such as which major to pursue in college.

In the Challenge → Reaction → Insight → Action system, knowing your values in life is key to understanding your reaction. Once you've defined your values, you can use them in your daily life to guide your actions. For example, if academic achievement is one of your top values, the next time you have the urge to cut class, consider the impact that choice would have on your value system. There is a great inner satisfaction that comes from living a life tied to core values.

Dreams versus Goals

Do you agree or disagree with this statement: "I can be anything I want to be"? If you are like most students, people have probably told you this all your life. Your parents and teachers all want you to have positive self-esteem, and certainly there are many career options available today. But is it true? Can you be *anything* you want to be? What's the difference between a dream and a goal?

As a college student, you may dream of being a famous doctor or a famous athlete or just plain famous. That's the beauty of dreams—you can imagine yourself in any career, any circumstances. When you're dreaming, you don't even have to play by the rules of reality. Dreams are fantasy-based—*you* in a perfect world. But when it's time to come back to reality, you discover that there are, in fact, rules. You may have dreamed of becoming a top-earning NBA player or a top fashion model when you were a child, but you have grown up to be the same height as Uncle Al or Aunt Sue—and that's not tall enough.

Dreams alone are not enough when it comes to "creating the future." As professional life coach Diana Robinson says, "A dream is a goal without legs."

Activity Option Ask students to answer the following question: "If I could spend one day with someone who has died, who would it be?" Have students share their choice and explain why. This activity demonstrates what values really seem to be important to that individual. Suggest reading Mitch Albom's book *For One More Day*.

> The best way to predict the future is to create it.

Peter Drucker, management expert (1909–2005)

I wonder how I can start doing that . . .

Activity Option Put students in groups of three or four and assign each group two letters of the word FOCUS. Ask students to think of successful student behaviors that begin with the letters they are assigned. Ask them how these behaviors connect to goal-setting.

Maybe I should audition for that new vocal group on campus that I've heard about.

And without legs, that goal is going nowhere. Dreaming is the first step to creating the future you want, but making dreams come true requires planning and hard work. Suppose you want to become a fashion designer because you like clothes and people always tell you you look good. As you continue through college, however, you will come to understand the nuts and bolts of the fashion design business. Perhaps you'll learn that famous fashion designer Yves Saint Laurent got his first fashion designer job with Christian Dior after winning an International Wool Secretariat design competition. The fashion industry might be challenging to break into, but that doesn't mean you should abandon your dream. Instead, you must realize that dreams and goals are not the same thing. You must find a reality-based path to help you develop actual goals that help you reach your dreams. Just dreaming isn't enough.

Dreams are exciting; you can let your imagination run wild. Goals are real; you must work out how to actually achieve your dreams. Goal setting is an important part of the life management skills this book will help you develop. Your goals may not seem at all clear to you right now, but the important thing is to learn that there's a right way and a wrong way to go about goal setting. The best way to ensure that the goals you set will serve you well is to make sure you FOCUS. Here's a brief overview of what that means.

F   Fit. Your goal must fit your values, your character, and who you are as a person. Goals that conflict with any of these things will not only be difficult to accomplish, but they just won't work. If your goal is to become a writer for a travel magazine because you love adventure, but you have a fear of flying, you're in trouble.

O   Ownership. You must own your goals. In other words, you've got to see it, taste it, want it! It must be your goal, not someone else's goal for you. Ask yourself: Does the thought of achieving this goal get me fired up? Do I genuinely own this goal or do I feel I ought to have this goal because it sounds good or pleases someone else?

C   Concreteness. For any goal to be effective, it must be real. In other words, you must be able to describe your goal—and it's ultimate outcome—in complete and specific detail, including your deadline for accomplishing it. "To run a mile in less than six minutes by March 4th" is much more concrete than "to eventually run faster." The more concrete, the better.

U   Usefulness. Goals must have utility, or usefulness. They must serve a purpose, and that purpose should be tied to your long-term vision of the person you want to become. For example, if you want to work for an international corporation some day, it would be useful to begin studying a foreign language now.

S   Stretch. In the business world, people talk about stretch goals. These are goals that require employees to stretch beyond their usual limits to achieve something more challenging. The key to stretching is to find a good balance between being realistic and being challenged. Realistic goals are those

> " What you get by achieving your goals is not as important as what you become by achieving your goals. "
>
> *Zig Ziglar, Motivational speaker, writer, and trainer*

whose outcomes are within your control. (Winning the lottery, for example, is beyond your control, and therefore not a very realistic goal.) Goals must be based in reality, but also offer you a chance to grow beyond the person you currently are.

Goals should be set for different time frames in your life to include both short- and long-term goals. Once your long-term goals are set (though they may shift over time as *you* shift over time), you will then want to set some short-term goals, which act as intermediate steps to achieving your long-term goals.

Activity Option Have students write a letter to themselves, their parents, loved ones, or a friend listing their goals for the semester and what they will do to meet them. Provide envelopes for students and seal their letters and return these to your students at the end of the term to see if they met their goals. Have them write a paragraph about why they did or did not meet their goals when they get their letters back.

Long-Term Goals What do I want to accomplish . . .	Short-Term Goals What do I want to accomplish . . .
In my lifetime?	This year?
In the next twenty years?	This month?
In the next ten years?	This week?
In the next three to five years?	Today?

Fame! Grammy award Platinuum album Viral music video

GPA+++ Try hard Turn everything in Go to class!

College is a time to clarify your motivation, values, dreams, and goals as part of answering the two questions at the beginning of this chapter: Who are you? And What do you want? You've begun your journey; you're on your way!

Box 2.2　How to Read A Case Study

Each chapter of *FOCUS* begins with a case study about a real student, portrayed by a member of the *FOCUS* cast. (You'll see the cast members in photos throughout the book—and you may almost feel you know them all by the end.) As you read the FOCUS Challenge Case, you may think: *Hmmm . . . this is an interesting story, but what does it have to do with me?* Make the most out of these case studies by following these suggestions:

- **Make a connection.** Although you may be a different age, gender, or ethnicity, look at the issues beneath the surface. Actually, you may have some things in common with the case study character, or you may know someone else who does. Are you tempted to make some of the mistakes Sylvia is making? Is your best friend worried about similar issues? Did your sister, who was in college before you, struggle with her dreams and goals, as Sylvia does?

- **Get engaged.** The case studies are designed to be a fully interactive and visual experience for you. You can gain a complete picture of the case study students by reading their stories *and* looking closely at the photos and visual examples. Learn even more about these stu-

dents by looking at sample emails, notes, text messages, Facebook profiles, and other key visual examples of their lives. You'll also learn more about them as you read their own words in the "Cast on Careers" section of every chapter's Career Outlook.

- **Think critically.** Imagine yourself in a conversation with the case study students. What advice would you give them? How would you help them solve their problems? Becoming an active reader and critical thinker will help you build skills that will contribute to your success as a college student.

- **Prepare to learn.** The case study will preview all the topics you'll read about in the chapter. The chapters will provide you with strategies to deal with these challenges. Make sure you read each case thoroughly, watch for things you will learn in the chapter itself, and then answer the Reaction questions that appear after each case.

If you follow them through the book, these featured students will lead you into a rich, "FOCUSed" learning experience!

Everyone has a story. This is your opportunity to tell yours! Start by flipping through *FOCUS* and skimming the other Challenge cases. Perhaps your biggest challenge will be something like those facing Katie Alexander or Derek Johnson, or maybe your particular challenge doesn't appear in this book. (*If you expect everything to be "smooth sailing" for you, you may prefer to write about a friend or relative beginning college, and that's acceptable too.*) This exercise will allow you to personalize what you will learn in this class and identify possible issues that may interfere with your success in college early on. Here are the steps you will follow:

1. First, write your *CHALLENGE* story. Your instructor will give you specific guidelines, but in general, write a two-page case study that highlights your previous learning experiences, your expectations for college, key pieces of your life outside of college that may interfere with your success, and the top challenges you are facing right now in college. (At some gut level, you probably know what your challenges will be.) You should write your story in the third person, and you may give yourself a fictional (but real-sounding) name. You may write, for example, "It was her first day of college, and the temperature outside had reached a record high. She rushed into the building from the parking lot so that the air conditioning would start cooling her down right away. But she had more than the temperature outside on her mind. She was nervous. No one from her family had ever gone to college, and suddenly she felt pressure to impress them"—or whatever was true for you. Remember to leave things "up in the air" at the end of your case study so that readers can speculate about how things will turn out.

2. Choose personalized images to illustrate your story—a photo of you, other photos of people in the story, images that relate to the case, whatever you wish—and intersperse them in the story.

(Go to an online site that has free images you can choose from or download photos from your Facebook page, if you have one.) Your case should look something like one of the ones in *FOCUS*. You may use whatever e-tool you wish to create your case (PowerPoint or Word, for example), but your instructor may want you to turn in a paper copy. This part of the assignment should be two (facing) pages.

3. Write three to five *REACTION* questions to go along with your case. Start by thinking about issues where you need the most advice, and build your questions around those. You may want to ask your reader, "What's the primary challenge facing this new student? Describe it in your own words." or "Why is this issue (whatever it is) something that could interfere with college success?" Your instructor may ask you to answer these questions yourself or swap your case with a classmate and answer his or her questions. At the end of this course, you will look back at your beginning case study (CHALLENGE→REACTION) and write about the INSIGHT→ACTION learning that has taken place for you along the way.

Now What Do You Think?

❶ At the beginning of this chapter, Sylvia Sanchez, an ambivalent student, was about to begin her college career. Now after reading this chapter, would you respond differently to any of the questions you answered about the "FOCUS Challenge Case"? Knowing what you know now, how would you advise her? Write a paragraph ending to the story, incorporating your best advice.

❷ What do you think about the Challenge→ Reaction → Insight → Action system? Does it make sense? Do you understand how it works? Write a few paragraphs describing it in your own words.

❸ What types of things fascinate you and fire up your intrinsic motivation? Why are they intrinsic motivators for you?

❹ What actions can you take to become more of a *learner* and less of a *performer,* particularly in your most challenging class this term?

❺ Think about one of your goals for the future. Run it through a quick check to ensure that it's a FOCUS goal. Circle the appropriate answer:

• Does this goal fit me?	Yes	No
• Do I really want this goal? Do I own it?	Yes	No
• Does my goal have concrete details and deadlines?	Yes	No
• Is this goal useful to me? Does it serve a purpose?	Yes	No
• Does this goal stretch me? Is it challenging, yet achievable?	Yes	No

If you answered "no" to any of the previous questions, your goal needs to be more *FOCUS*ed. What must you do to make that happen?

What did you LEARN?

On a scale of 1 to 10, answer the following questions now that you've completed the chapter.

 low   1   2   3   4   5   6   7   8   9   10   high

In hindsight, how much did you already know about this subject before reading the chapter?

Can you answer these questions about goals and dreams more fully now that you've read the chapter?

❶ What is the difference between a learner and a performer?

❷ What is the difference between intrinsic and extrinsic motivation?

❸ Which four factors—all beginning with the letter "C"—are a part of intrinsic motivation—and your college success?

How useful might the information in this chapter be to you? How much do you think this information might affect your success overall? _____

How much energy did you put into reading this chapter? _____

How long did it actually take you to complete (both the reading and writing tasks)? _____ Hour(s) _____ Minutes

Did you finish reading this chapter? _____

Did you intend to when you started? _____

If you meant to but didn't, what stopped you? _____

Take a minute to compare these answers to your answers from the "Readiness Check" at the beginning of this chapter. What gaps exist between the similar questions? How might these gaps between what you thought before starting the chapter and what you now think after completing the chapter affect how you approach the next chapter in this book?

3 Learning Styles and Studying

How this chapter relates to YOU

1. When it comes to learning and studying in college, what are you most unsure about, if anything?

Whether I can find enough time

Whether I really know how

How I learn best

How to study different subjects

How to make myself study when I don't want to

2. What is most likely to be your response? Circle it.

| I'll ask my instructors for suggestions. | I'll ask my classmates what they do. | I'll see how things go and adjust. | I'll probably just figure it out somehow. |

3. What would you have to do to increase your likelihood of success? Will you do it this quarter or semester?

_____

_____

_____

How YOU will relate to this chapter

What are you most interested in learning about? Put check marks by those topics.

☐ How learning changes your brain

☐ How people are intelligent in different ways

☐ How you learn through your senses

☐ How your personality type can affect your learning style

☐ What metacognition is and how it can help you

☐ How to apply your learning style to your study style

☐ How to become an intentional learner and make a master study plan

● How motivated are you to learn more about learning styles and studying in college? (5 = high, 1 = low) ____

● How ready are you to read now? ____ (If something is in your way, take care of it if you can, zero in and focus.)

● How long do you think it will take you to complete this chapter? If you start and stop, keep track of your overall time.
____ Hour(s) ____ Minutes

63

challenge ?

TAMMY KO

As she walked out of her "Introduction to Criminology" class with her classmate Sam on a dark rainy afternoon, Tammy Ko noticed that her mood was in sync with the weather. "I had no idea what I was getting into," she confessed to Sam. It was obvious to Sam that Tammy and their professor lived in different worlds. Hers was filled with people and excitement. His was filled with dull lecture notes and complex theories in books.

Tammy was a first-semester student at a large state campus several hours from her tiny hometown, where she'd been a popular student. If you went through her high school yearbook, you'd see Tammy's picture everywhere. There Tammy had been a big fish in a small pond, but now it was the other way around.

Even though she found college life at the large state university overwhelming, Tammy was excited about her major, forensic chemistry. The crime shows on TV were her favorites. She watched them all each week. She rationalized how much time it took by thinking of it as career development.

The fun was picturing herself as an investigator solving headline cases: "Man Slain, Found in City Park" or "Modern Day 'Jack the Ripper' Terrorizes Las Vegas." She could envision herself hunched over laboratory equipment, testing intently for fibers or DNA, and actually breaking the case.

When she registered for classes, her academic advisor had told her that taking an "Introduction to Criminology" course from the sociology department would be a good idea. "It'll teach you how to think," he'd said, "and it'll give you the background you need to understand the criminal mind. At the end of this class," he said, "you'll

Pleasantville High School Yearbook 2013

© Boris Vian/Shutterstock.com

University Program Description:

FORENSIC CHEMISTRY

Any science used for the purpose of law is forensic science. Forensic Scientists use empirical methods to gain objective data for use in a court of law. Forensic Chemistry focuses specifically on the composition, structure, and properties of matter, as well as the study of chemical reactions. This field of the Forensic discipline includes studies of DNA and other complex chemical compounds.

Forensic Chemistry is a rapidly growing field of study, and has many possible career options, including: Crime Scene Investigator, Detective, Clinical Lab Technologist/Technicians, Forensic Science Technician, Analyst, Medical Examiner, Toxicologist Forensic, Pathologist, Forensic Anthropologist, Fingerprint Examiner, Laboratory Director, and Professor.

Course Work

Freshman Year
CHEM 103 - General Chemistry I
CHEM 106 - General Chemistry II
CHEM 108 - Introduction to Chemistry Lab Research
Soc 150 Introduction to Criminology
MATH 135 - Calculus I
MATH 136 - Calculus II
BIOL 121 - General Biology I
Elective - 3 credits

Sophomore Year
CHEM 331 - Organic Chemistry I
CHEM 332 - Organic Chemistry II
CHEM 337 - Practical Organic Chemistry I
CHEM 338 - Practical Organic Chemistry II
CJ 215 - Statistics for Criminal Justice
CJ 225 - Violence in Society
MATH 235 - Calculus III
Electives - 6 credits

Junior Year
CHEM 417 - Analytical Chemistry I
CHEM 418 - Analytical Chemistry II
CHEM 420 - Practical Instrumental Analysis
CHEM 451 - Physical Chemistry I
CHEM 452 - Physical Chemistry II
CHEM 455 - Experimental Physical Chemistry
CHEM 483 - Biochemistry Principles
PES 213 - General Physics III
Electives - 6 credits

Senior Year
CHEM 401 - Inorganic Chemistry I
CHEM 402 - Inorganic Chemistry Laboratory
CHEM 495 - Chemistry Seminar I
CHEM 496 - Chemistry Seminar II
Chemistry electives (upper division) - 9 credits
Electives - 12 credits

ELECTIVES
CSI: Fact or Fantasy?
Interview and Interrogation Techniques
Professionalism and Ethics
Investigation of Injury and Death
Crime Scene & Crime Lab
Psychosocial of Forensic Science
Legal Aspects of Forensic Science

-166-

© Cengage Learning

© Larry Harwood Photograph. Property of Cengage Learning.

© Larry Harwood Photograph. Property of Cengage Learning.

tangents. Tammy had always preferred teachers who created exciting things to do in class over teachers who went completely by the book.

Tammy's biggest complaint about Professor Caldwell was that he only talked about *theories* of criminology. When was he ever going to get to the hands-on part of the course? She couldn't help thinking, *When will we stop talking about theories and start working on real cases—like the ones on all those TV shows?*

preferred talking about things to doing things. They seemed to take more interest in theories than in the real world. *Too bad, she thought, the real world is where exciting things happen.* Although she hated to admit it, sometimes Tammy couldn't wait for her college career to be over so that she could begin her real career.

A few of Tammy's other friends had taken Professor Caldwell's classes. "Just try and memorize the stuff; that's all you can do," they'd advised her. Regardless of what they happened to be talking about, somehow the conversation always came around to stress, Professor Caldwell, and how impossible it was to learn in his classes.

know if you really want to pursue a career in forensics." *Maybe it would teach me how to think,* Tammy thought to herself now that the term was underway, *if only I could understand the professor. Forget understanding the criminal mind—I'd just like a glimpse into his!* Most of the time, Sam agreed with her just to keep the peace although he always aced everything.

Professor Caldwell was quiet and reserved, and he seemed a bit out of touch. He dressed as if he hadn't bought a new piece of clothing in as many years as he'd been at the university. In class, he was very articulate, knowledgeable, and organized with his handouts neatly piled on the desk, and he covered each day's material methodically point by point. Tammy wished he'd leave his notes occasionally to explore fascinating, related

To make matters worse, learning from lectures was not Tammy's strong suit. She hadn't done well on the first exam because she'd had to resort to memorizing things that didn't make much sense to her, and her D grade showed it. The exam consisted of one question: "Compare and contrast two theories of criminology discussed in class thus far." Tammy hated essay tests. She was at her best on tests with right or wrong answers, like true-false or multiple-choice questions. Making sense out of spoken words that go by very quickly during a lecture and trying to psych out professors' preferred answers on essay tests were challenges to her.

But her "Introduction to Criminology" class was far from hands-on. In fact, Tammy had noticed that many of her teachers

Name: TAMMY KO

ESSAY TEST
INTRO TO CRIMINOLOGY
DR. CALDWELL

65% D

QUESTION: COMPARE AND CONTRAST TWO THEORIES OF CRIMINOLOGY DISCUSSED IN CLASS THUS FAR

Classical Theory was first developed by Cesar Beccaria in the X century. Classical theory says that people engage in a social deal. They must balance between freedom and happiness. Classical theory also describes special and general deterrence. General deterrence is punishing a person for a crime. Special deterrence is making examples of people so that others don't do the same thing. Neoclassical theory was developed in the X century and includes the concepts of free will and penitentiaries. These systems are the basis for the US Government system of justice. The positivist approach includes the ideas of free will and determinism. It says that there is a fundamental difference between criminals and non-criminals. It also says that there are many factors that contribute to crime. The positivist approach also suggests that there is subjectivism in social science. In other words social science is based on the viewpoint of each individual, not specific facts or data. Finally the biological theories suggest that criminals are biologically superior to non-criminals.

❶ Why is Tammy having difficulty learning in her "Introduction to Criminology" class?

❷ Is Tammy smart? If so, in what ways? What sensory modality does Tammy prefer for taking in information? Does she learn best by watching, listening, reading and writing, or doing?

❸ What do you think Tammy's personality type is? How does her personality type relate to her learning style?

❹ How would you describe Professor Caldwell's teaching style? His personality type? How does his personality type relate to his teaching style?

❺ What should Tammy do to become a better learner in Professor Caldwell's class?

Go to the HEAD of the Class: Learning and the Brain

Challenge: What is learning? Can you explain the process?

Reaction:

_____

_____

_____

Exercise 3.1   Assessing Your Views on Learning

The following statements represent common student views on learning. Think about each statement, and mark it true or false based on your honest opinion.

_____ 1. Learning is often hard work and really not all that enjoyable.

_____ 2. Memorization and learning are basically the same thing.

_____ 3. The learning done in school is often gone in a few weeks or months.

_____ 4. In college, most learning takes place in class.

_____ 5. Learning is usually the result of listening to an instructor lecture or reading a textbook.

_____ 6. The best way to learn is by working alone.

_____ 7. Most students know intuitively how they learn best.

_____ 8. Teachers control what students learn.

_____ 9. Learning only deals with subjects taught in school.

_____10. The learning pace is controlled by the slowest learner in the class.

I'D SAY NUMBER 3 IS DEFINITELY TRUE— AT LEAST FOR ME!

You probably noticed that many of these statements attempt to put learning in a negative light. How many did you mark true? This chapter will help you understand more about learning as a process and about yourself as a learner. As you read, your goal should be to use the insights you gain to become a better learner.

Let's start our exploration of the learning process close to home—in our own heads. What's going on up there, anyway? While your hands are busy manipulating test tubes in chemistry lab, or your eyes are watching your psychology professor's PowerPoint presentation, or your ears are taking in a lecture on American politics, what's your brain up to? The answer? Plenty.

This chapter will help you understand how you learn best. In some ways, learning is learning—everyone learns according to the same general principles. For example, new research shows that in many ways, the old one-two-three method still works best: read, close the book, and write down what you remember. Amazingly, it works like a charm. You just have to discipline yourself to do it, and then go back to the book and continue to fill in the gaps.[1]

In other ways, however, you have your own distinct learning preferences. Perhaps you catch on quickly and prefer that teachers clip right along. Or maybe you like chewing over material at a slower pace, especially if it's complex. Maybe you consider yourself to be a (hands-on learner.) You learn best when someone gives you some guidance, hands over the controls, and lets you have at it. Many students find it easier to learn by doing things themselves, rather than by watching their instructors do things. Math can be a good example. If that's the case for you, you'll have to create hands-on ways to reinforce your learning either in class or outside of class. This chapter will help you find ways to do that.

Use It or Lose It

The human brain consists of a complex web of connections between neurons. This web grows in complexity as it incorporates new knowledge. But if the connections are not reinforced frequently, they degenerate. As you learn new things, you work to hardwire these connections, making them less susceptible to degeneration. When your professors repeat portions of the previous week's lecture or assign follow-up homework to practice material covered in class, they're helping you to form connections between neurons through repeated use—or, in other words, to learn. Repetition is vital to learning. You must use and reuse information in order to hardwire it. Think of it this way: People say that practice makes perfect. But practice also makes learning "permanent, automatic and transferable to new situations."[2]

Giving your brain the exercise it needs—now and in your years after college—will help you form connections between neurons that, if you keep using them, will last a lifetime. From a biological point of view, that's what being a lifelong learner means. New research shows that your brain is "competitively plastic." You get better at what you practice, and you lose what you don't use.[3] The age-old advice "use it or lose it" is true when it comes to learning.

Ask Questions and Hardwire Your Connections

Your professors have been studying their disciplines for years, perhaps decades. They have developed extensive hardwired connections between their brain neurons. They are *experts*. Woodrow Wilson once said, "I not only use all the brains I have, but all that I can borrow." Think of college as an ideal time to borrow some excellent brains—your professors'!

THIS SOUNDS EXACTLY LIKE ME!

> The art and science of asking questions is the source of all knowledge.

Thomas Berger, American novelist

© Larry Harwood Photograph. Property of Cengage Learning.

By contrast, you are a *novice* to whatever discipline you're studying. You've not yet developed the brain circuitry that your professors have developed. This realization points to a potential problem. Sometimes professors are so familiar with what they already know from years of traveling the same neuron paths that what you're learning for the first time seems obvious to them. Without even realizing it, they can expect what is familiar to them to be obvious to you. Sometimes, it isn't obvious at all. One learning expert says this: "The best learners . . . often make the worst teachers. They are, in a very real sense, perceptually challenged. They cannot imagine what it must be like to struggle to learn something that comes so naturally to them."[4] Think of how challenging it is when you try to teach something that you understand thoroughly to another person who doesn't, like teaching someone who has never used a computer before how to upload an assignment.

[handwritten note: DEFINITELY PROFESSOR CALDWELL!]

Teaching with Technology The Internet has countless resources for students who are intrinsically motivated to learn. AcademicEarth.org and Ted Talks at www.ted.com are websites that allows users to access hundreds of free college-level video lectures on a variety of topics. These resources can be used by instructors and students to supplement their knowledge for a particular class, or by those who want to expand their knowledge about a subject.

Since you're a novice, you may not understand everything your professors say. Ask questions, check, clarify, probe, and persist until you do understand. Sometimes your confusion is not due to a lack of knowledge, but a lack of the *correct* knowledge. You may be getting interference from misinformation or unproductive habits of thinking and learning that have become hardwired in your brain. For example, you may study for a test by doing only one thing—reading and re-reading the textbook when you actually need to do more than that. It's important to be familiar with an array of study tools and choose the ones that work best for you and the subject matter you're trying to learn.

Think of it this way. Learning often involves "messy journeys back, forth and across" new territory.[5] Some of the neural connections you brought with you to college are positive and useful, and some are counterproductive. When you learn, you not only add new connections, but you rewire some old connections. While you're in college, you're under construction![6]

Take Charge and Create the Best Conditions for Learning

Throughout this discussion, we've been talking about internal processes in your brain. *Your* brain, not anyone else's. The bottom line is this: Learning must be *internally initiated*—by you. It can only be *externally encouraged*—by someone else. You're in charge of your own learning. Learning changes your brain.

Let's look at food as an analogy: If learning is a process that is as biological as digestion, then no one can learn for you, in the same way that no one can eat for you. The food in the refrigerator doesn't do you a bit of good unless you walk over, open the door, remove it, and start eating. It's there for the taking, but you must make that happen. To carry the analogy further, you eat on a daily basis, right? "No thanks, I ate last week" is a silly statement. Learning does for your brain what food does for your body. Nourish yourself!

Brain researchers tell us the best state for learning has many dimensions. Let's look at some of the most important ones.

1. **You're intrinsically motivated (from within yourself) to learn material that is appropriately challenging.**

   ➤ **Examine where your motivation to learn comes from.** Are you *internally* motivated because you're curious about the subject and want to learn about it or *externally* motivated to get an A or avoid an F? Can you generate your own internal motivation? This book has built-in reminders to boost your intrinsic motivation. Use them to your advantage as a learner.

   ➤ **Adjust the level of challenge yourself.** You might think that instructors should be the ones to adjust the level of challenge—to pay attention to what's called "The Goldilocks Principle." But in college, it's your responsibility to get the challenge level "just right" for you.[7] If you're too challenged in a class, you become nervous. Make sure you're keeping up with the workload and that you've completed the prerequisites. In many classes, you must know the fundamentals before tackling more advanced concepts. If you're not challenged enough, you can become bored and tune out. Your instructor will provide one level of challenge for everyone in the class. But it's up to you to fine-tune that challenge for yourself. Get extra help if you aren't quite up to the task, or bump up the challenge a notch or two if you're ahead of the game so that you're continually motivated to learn. Go further than you're expected to and learn as much as you can or help teach other students who are struggling so that you're continually motivated to learn.

When we come to know something, we have performed an act that is as biological as when we digest something.

Henry Plotkin, Darwin Machines and the Nature of Knowledge (1994)

© Colin Anderson/Blend Images/CORBIS

2. **You're appropriately stressed, but generally relaxed.**

   ➤ **Assess your stress.** According to researchers, you learn best in a state of *relaxed alertness,* a state of high challenge and low threat.[8] Although relaxed alertness may sound impossible, it can be achieved. No stress at all is what you'd find in a no-brainer course. Some stress is useful; it helps you learn. Stress can heighten your alertness and help you focus. How stressed are you—and why—when you get to class? Are you overstressed because you've rushed from your last class, you're late because you stopped for coffee, or because you haven't done the reading and hope you won't be called on? Prepare for class so that you're ready to jump in. Or instead of too much stress, are you understressed because you don't value the course material? Consider how the information can be useful to you— perhaps in ways you've never even thought of. Here's the vital question to ask yourself: How much stress do I need in order to trigger my best effort?

   ➤ **Pay attention to your overall physical state.** Are you taking care of your physical needs so that you can stay alert, keep up with the lecture, and participate in the discussion?

3. **You're curious about what you're learning, and you look forward to learning it.**

   ➤ **Get ready to learn by looking back and by looking ahead.** When you're about to cross the street, you must look both ways, right? Keep

Activity Option Divide students into groups, and ask students to make a list of the conditions they think are necessary for learning. Then have the students read over this section to see whether their conditions for learning are represented in the list here.

Teachable Moment Ask students to raise their hands if they've ever felt "lost" in a class. Count the total and write it on the board. Ask students to raise their hands if they did not seek help. Ask them why they did not get help and what the consequences were. Then ask students to raise their hands if they did seek help and what kind of help they sought out. You hope that those students who did not seek help can learn from those who took the initiative to get help.

Don't look now, but you're a very busy person! If you were watching a movie of your life at this moment, what would the scene look like? A cell phone in your hand, a website open on your computer screen, your earbuds plugged in, and this book propped in your lap? So much to do, so little time! All we can hope for is that some scientist somewhere will invent a way to get a bigger, better brain! But let's face it: brain enhancement surgery won't be available any time soon.

Even so, scientists have been busy recently learning more about this heady organ of ours. From birth to adolescence, we lay the brain's basic circuitry. Stimulation is critical. When children grow up in isolated, sterile environments, their brains suffer. But when they grow up in fertile, rich environments, their brains thrive. The more our moms and dads read to us and play learning games with us, the better. Scientists used to think that our basic circuitry is hardwired for life by the time we're adults. But new brain research focuses on *neuroplasticity*. It is possible to build a better brain, especially after traumatic injury, because the brain is more "plastic" than previously thought—not plastic like a Barbie doll, but plastic in that it can "reshape" itself, based on what science has discovered. In a fascinating new book, *The Brain That Changes Itself*, Dr. Norman Doidge recounts miraculous stories of patients whose injured brains have been rewired to work better. If you want some interesting reading, take a look.[9]

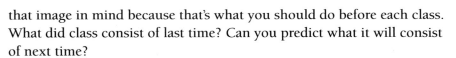

© iStockphoto.com/Vladislav Ociacia

What's the secret to a healthy brain? When we think of fitness, most of us think from the neck down—strong abs, bulging pecs, and tight glutes. But brain health tops them all. New evidence shows that physical exercise helps our brains shrug off damage, reinforce old neural networks, forge new ones, and ultimately result in a better brain![10]

Current research focuses on a protein called BDNF (for brain-derived neurotrophic factor). BDNF, sometimes referred to as "Miracle-Gro" for the brain, helps nerve cells in our brains grow and connect, is important for development in the womb, but it's also important in adult brains. Simply put: it helps us learn. According to researchers, rats that eat a high-calorie, fast-food diet and have a couch-potato lifestyle have less BDNF in their brains. Omega-3 fatty acids found in fish normalize BDNF levels and counteract learning disabilities in rats with brain injuries. Scientists are working to see if the same thing may be true for humans.[11]

"Exercise your brain. Nourish it well. And the earlier you start the better," scientists tell us.[12] New research indicates that education is a great way to nourish our brains. People who are less educated have twice the risk of getting Alzheimer's disease in later life, and less educated people who have ho-hum, nonchallenging jobs have three to four times the risk. According to researchers, "College seems to pay off well into retirement."[13] It can help you build a better brain!

that image in mind because that's what you should do before each class. What did class consist of last time? Can you predict what it will consist of next time?

> **Focus on substance, not style.** Despite society's obsession with attractiveness, grooming, and fashion, a student's job is to ask, "What can I learn from this person?" Deciding an instructor isn't worth paying attention to because he doesn't dress well or because his hair style is outdated is just an excuse not to learn.

4. **You search for personal meaning and patterns.**

> **Ask yourself: What's in it for me?** Why is knowing this important? <u>How can I use this information in the future?</u> Instead of dismissing material that appears unrelated to your life, try figuring out how it *could* relate. You may be surprised!

RIGHT, BUT CALDWELL NEEDS A MAJOR MAKEOVER!

IF I DO BECOME A CSI, I GUESS I MIGHT HAVE TO KNOW SOME THINGS ABOUT THE CRIMINAL MIND.

> Learning is not so much an additive process, with new learning simply piling up on top of existing knowledge, as it is an active, dynamic process in which the connections are constantly changing and the structure reformatted.

K. Patricia Cross, Professor Emerita of Higher Education, University of California, Berkeley

> ➤ **Think about how courses relate to one another.** How does this new knowledge relate to things you're learning in other courses? Does sociology have anything to do with history? Psychology with economics?

5. **Your emotions are involved, not just your mind.**

> ➤ **Evaluate your attitudes and feelings.** Do you like the subject matter? Do you admire the teacher? Remember your high school teacher, Mr. Brown, whose class you just couldn't stand? Not every class will be your favorite. That's natural. But if a class turns you off as a learner, instead of allowing your emotions to take over, ask why and whether your feelings are in your best interest.

> ➤ **Make a deliberate decision to change negative feelings.** Fortunately, feelings can be changed. Hating a course or disliking a professor can only build resentment and threaten your success. It's possible to do a 180–degree turn and transform your negative emotions into positive energy.

6. **You realize that as a learner you use what you already know in constructing new knowledge.**[14]

> ➤ **Remember that passive learning is impossible.** When it comes to learning, you are the construction foreman, building on what you already know to construct new knowledge. You're not just memorizing facts someone else wants you to learn. You're a full partner in the learning process!

> ➤ **Remind yourself that constructing knowledge takes work.** No one ever built a house by simply sitting back or just hanging out. Builders work hard, but in the end they have something to show for their efforts. In your college courses, identify what you already know, and blend new knowledge into the framework you've built in your mind. By constructing new knowledge, you are building yourself into a more sophisticated, more polished, and most certainly more educated person.

7. **You're given a degree of choice in terms of what you learn, how you do it, and feedback on how you're doing.**

> ➤ **Make the most of the choices you're given.** College isn't a free-for-all in which you can take any classes you like toward earning a degree. However, which electives you choose will be up to you. Or in a particular course, if your instructor allows you to write a paper or shoot

Teachable Moment Take this opportunity to share some basic campus resources with the group. Students may discuss difficult courses, and if students don't suggest an action, like going to the learning or tutoring center, suggest it to students now. Consider building a visit to your learning center into a class activity so students begin to feel more comfortable with going there for help.

GUESS I SHOULD...

Activity Option Ask students to work in teams to build a learning tower. Draw a tower consisting of four blocks on the bottom row, three on the third, two on the second, and one at the top. The top block should be labeled "Successful Student." Students are to fill in what they need to know first before they can become successful students. Each row should be a prerequisite to the next row.

Sensitive Situation Giving or getting feedback can be a very sensitive situation. Instructors must be aware that some students see feedback as negative and never get beyond that. Always say something positive to students about their work whenever possible, while still providing the constructive criticism they need to improve. Remind students that not every instructor will have positive things to say and that they have to look for what they can learn from the feedback, instead of concentrating on the negative. Share your own experiences. Point out that some professions require feedback to produce quality work. For example, writers have many editors who give plenty of feedback before the final product is complete.

Teachable Moment Remind students that they do have choices. They have the choice to focus or allow distractions, to come to class or not, to do the homework or skip it, and to do their best work or not. It's their choice, and choices have consequences.

> 66
> It ain't what you know that gets you into trouble. It's what you know for sure that just ain't so.
> 99
>
> *Mark Twain*

Teachable Moment Research shows that when people are told they belong to a group that does very well, as opposed to being told that they belong to a group that does poorly, their brains are flooded with cortisol and dopamine, both of which provide a surge of motivation. Telling your students about what they do well and that you believe they can succeed can inspire them to learn.

Activity Option Determine whether there are any commonalities among the students' responses to this "Control" exercise. Which courses do most students find the easiest? Which are the most difficult? Which are the least interesting? Have students share their responses so they can learn from their peers. (The only caution is to make sure that instructors' names are left out of the discussion, so that a particular professor isn't "bashed.")

a video, choose the option that will be more motivating for you. When you receive an assignment, select a topic that fires you up. It's easier to generate energy to put toward choices you've made yourself.

➤ **Use feedback to improve, and if feedback is not given, ask for it.** It's possible to get really good at doing something the wrong way. Take a golf swing or a swimming stroke, for example. Without someone intervening to give you feedback, it may be difficult to know how to improve. Your instructors will most likely write comments on your assignments to explain their grades. Evaluating your work is their job; it's what they must do to help you improve. Take their suggestions to heart and try them out.

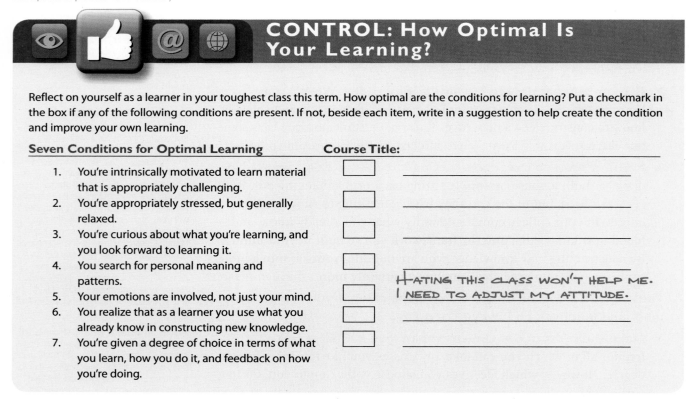

CONTROL: How Optimal Is Your Learning?

Reflect on yourself as a learner in your toughest class this term. How optimal are the conditions for learning? Put a checkmark in the box if any of the following conditions are present. If not, beside each item, write in a suggestion to help create the condition and improve your own learning.

Seven Conditions for Optimal Learning   **Course Title:** _____

1. You're intrinsically motivated to learn material that is appropriately challenging. ☐ _____
2. You're appropriately stressed, but generally relaxed. ☐ _____
3. You're curious about what you're learning, and you look forward to learning it. ☐ _____
4. You search for personal meaning and patterns. ☐ _____
5. Your emotions are involved, not just your mind. ☐ _HATING THIS CLASS WON'T HELP ME. I NEED TO ADJUST MY ATTITUDE._
6. You realize that as a learner you use what you already know in constructing new knowledge. ☐ _____
7. You're given a degree of choice in terms of what you learn, how you do it, and feedback on how you're doing. ☐ _____

All of us are already good learners in some situations. Let's say you're drawn to technology, for example. You're totally engrossed in computers and eagerly learn everything you can from books, classes, and online sources—and you sometimes totally lose yourself in a flow state as you're learning. No one has to force you to practice your technology skills or pick up an issue of *Wired* or *PC World*. You do it because you want to. In this case, you're self-motivated and therefore learning is easy. This chapter provides several different tools to help you understand your own personal profile as a learner so that you can try to learn at your best in *all* situations.

The purpose of learning is growth, and our minds, unlike our bodies, can continue growing as long as we live.

Mortimer Adler, American philosopher, educator, and editor (1902–2001)

Multiple Intelligences: *How* Are You Smart?

?
challenge

"
reaction

Challenge: Are people smart in different ways? How so?

Reaction:
_____
_____
_____

Exercise 3.2 | **Multiple Intelligences Self-Assessment**

On each line, put check marks next to all the statements that best describe you.

Linguistic Intelligence: **The capacity to use language to express what's on your mind and understand others ("word smart")**

_____ I'm a good storyteller.

_____ I enjoy word games, puns, and tongue twisters.

_____ I'd rather listen to the radio than watch TV.

_____ I've recently written something I'm proud of.

_____ I can hear words in my head before I say or write them.

_____ When riding in the car, I sometimes pay more attention to words on billboards than I do to the scenery.

_____ In high school, I did better in English, history, or social studies than I did in math and science.

_____ I enjoy reading.

_____ TOTAL check marks

Logical-Mathematical Intelligence: **The capacity to understand cause/effect relationships and to manipulate numbers ("number/reasoning smart")**

_____ I can easily do math in my head.

_____ I enjoy brainteasers or puzzles.

_____ I like it when things can be counted or analyzed.

(continued on next page)

_____ I can easily find logical flaws in what others do or say.

_____ I think most things have rational explanations.

_____ Math and science were my favorite subjects in high school.

_____ I like to put things into categories.

_____ I'm interested in new scientific advances.

_____ TOTAL check marks

Spatial Intelligence: The capacity to represent the world visually or graphically ("picture smart")

_____ I like to take pictures of what I see around me.

_____ I'm sensitive to colors.

_____ My dreams at night are vivid.

_____ I like to doodle or draw.

_____ I'm good at navigating with a map.

_____ I can picture what something will look like before it's finished.

_____ In school, I preferred geometry to algebra.

_____ I often make my point by drawing a picture or diagram.

_____ TOTAL check marks

Bodily-Kinesthetic Intelligence: The capacity to use your whole body or parts of it to solve a problem, make something, or put on a production ("body smart")

_____ I regularly engage in sports or physical activities.

_____ I get fidgety (tap my foot, etc.) when asked to sit for long periods of time.

_____ I get some of my best ideas while I'm engaged in a physical activity.

_____ I need to practice a skill in order to learn it, rather than just reading or watching a video about it.

_____ I enjoy being a daredevil.

_____ I'm a well-coordinated person.

_____ I like to think through things while I'm doing something else like running or walking.

_____ I like to spend my free time outdoors.

_____ TOTAL check marks

Musical Intelligence: The capacity to think in music; hear patterns; and recognize, remember, and perhaps manipulate them ("music smart")

_____ I can tell when a musical note is flat or sharp.

_____ I play a musical instrument.

_____ I often hear music playing in my head.

_____ I can listen to a piece of music once or twice, and then sing it back accurately.

_____ I often sing or hum while working.

_____ I like music playing while I'm doing things.

_____ I'm good at keeping time to a piece of music.

_____ I consider music an important part of my life.

_____ TOTAL check marks

I CAN TELL I'M GOING TO SHINE HERE!

Interpersonal Intelligence: The capacity to understand other people ("people smart")

_____ I prefer group activities to solo activities.

_____ Others think of me as a leader.

_____ I enjoy the challenge of teaching others something I like to do.

_____ I like to get involved in social activities at school, church, or work.

_____ If I have a problem, I'm more likely to get help than tough it out alone.

_____ I feel comfortable in a crowd of people.

_____ I have several close friends.

_____ I'm the sort of person others come to for advice about their problems.

_____ TOTAL check marks

Intrapersonal Intelligence: **The capacity to understand yourself, who you are, and what you can do ("self-smart")**

_____ I like to spend time alone thinking about important questions in life.

_____ I have invested time in learning more about myself.

_____ I consider myself to be independent minded.

_____ I keep a journal of my inner thoughts.

_____ I'd rather spend a weekend alone than at a place with a lot of other people around.

_____ I've thought seriously about starting a business of my own.

_____ I'm realistic about my own strengths and weaknesses.

_____ I have goals for my life that I'm working on.

_____ TOTAL check marks

Naturalistic Intelligence: **The capacity to discriminate between living things and show sensitivity toward the natural world ("nature smart")**

_____ Environmental problems bother me.

_____ In school, I always enjoyed field trips to places in nature or away from class.

_____ I enjoy studying nature, plants, or animals.

_____ I've always done well on projects involving living systems.

_____ I enjoy pets.

_____ I notice signs of wildlife when I'm on a walk or hike.

_____ I can recognize types of plants, trees, rocks, birds, and so on.

_____ I enjoy learning about environmental issues.

_____ TOTAL check marks

Which intelligences have the most check marks? Write in the three intelligences in which you had the most number of check marks.

_____   _____   _____

Although this is an informal instrument, it can help you think about the concept of multiple intelligences, or MI. How are you smart?

Based on Armstrong, T. (1994). *Multiple intelligences in the classroom.* Alexandria, VA: Association for Supervision and Curriculum Development, pp. 18–20.

Activity Option Have students tally the number of checks in each category. Then group students according to their highest numbers. Give each group five minutes to share with each other their favorite classes (present or past). Ask students whether the types of intelligences they scored highest in were related to their favorite classes. Have the students consider the classes they found uninteresting or difficult. Ask students whether the types of intelligences they scored lowest in related to their class problems. Have students determine what steps should be taken when faced with this type of class in the future.

Have you ever noticed that people are smart in different ways? Consider the musical genius of Mozart, who published his first piano pieces at the age of five. Olympic Gold Medalist Lindsey Vonn started skiing when she was two years old. Not many of us are as musically gifted as Mozart or as physically gifted as Lindsey Vonn, but we all have strengths. You may earn top grades in math, and not-so-top grades in English, and your best friend's grades may be just the opposite.

FIGURE 3.1

Multiple Intelligences

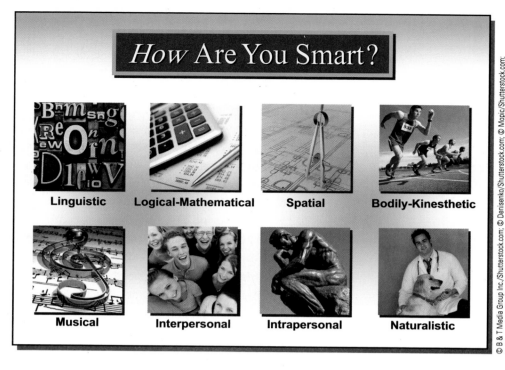

How Are You Smart?

Linguistic   Logical-Mathematical   Spatial   Bodily-Kinesthetic

Musical   Interpersonal   Intrapersonal   Naturalistic

© B & T Media Group Inc./Shutterstock.com; © Denisenko/Shutterstock.com; © Mopic/Shutterstock.com;
© Morgan Lane Photography/Shutterstock.com; © YAKOBCHUK VASYL/Shutterstock.com;
© Yuri Arcurs/Shutterstock.com; © Sean Nel/Shutterstock.com; © william casey/Shutterstock.com

According to Harvard psychologist Howard Gardner, people can be smart in the eight different categories you saw in Exercise 3.2. Most schools focus on particular types of intelligence, linguistic and logical-mathematical intelligence, reflecting the three R's: reading, writing, and 'rithmetic. But Gardner claims there are many different types of intelligence that can't be measured by traditional one-dimensional standardized IQ tests and represented by a three-digit number: 100 (average), 130 (gifted), or 150 (genius). Gardner defines intelligence as "the ability to find and solve problems and create products of value in one or more cultural settings."[15] Although we all have ability in all eight intelligences, most of us, he claims, are strong in two or three.[16] What are yours?

So instead of asking the traditional question "How smart are you?" a better question is "How are you smart?" The idea is to find out how, and then apply this understanding of yourself to your academic work in order to achieve your best results.

Use Intelligence-Oriented Study Techniques

Do you sometimes wonder why you can't remember things for exams? Some learning experts believe that memory is intelligence-specific. You may have a good memory for people's faces but a bad memory for their names. You may be able to remember the words of a country-western hit, but not the dance steps that go with it. The Theory of Multiple Intelligences may explain why.[17]

Examine your own behaviors in class. If your instructors use their linguistic intelligence to teach, as many do, and your intelligences lie elsewhere, can you observe telltale signs of your frustration? Instead of zeroing in on the lecture, do you fidget (bodily-kinesthetic), doodle (spatial), or socialize

Teaching with Technology If you'd like your students to take an MI instrument online, consider taking them to "Multiple Intelligences for Adult Literacy and Education" or to Edutopia's multiple intelligence quiz. (You can find them by Googling). These informal instruments will compute their scores and provide immediate feedback.

Diversity Discussion You may wish to introduce the idea that the Multiple Intelligences are a form of diversity. Sometimes students (or teachers) with a certain type of intelligence (like logical-mathematical, for example) can't understand why those with less developed intelligence in that area "just don't get it." It's the particular combination of intelligences in each of us that makes us unique.

Activity Option Have students read through the Intelligence-Oriented Study Techniques. Ask them to highlight the techniques that they currently use and circle the ones they would like to try. Did they all fall into one intelligence type? Encourage students to try to develop other intelligences that they may not be strong in. Developing other intelligences will help them adapt to different courses and teaching styles.

(interpersonal)? You may need to translate the information into your own personal intelligences, just as you would if your professor speaks French and you speak English. If you're having learning problems in one of your classes, it may be partially due to a case of mismatched intelligences between yours and your instructor's. Take a look at the following chart of intelligence-based study techniques. Based on your own specific intelligences, you may need to go beyond reading and create flash cards or talk over the material with someone else. Translating material into your own intelligences and tweaking the way you study can make a world of difference.

Since my highest intelligence is interpersonal, I should probably study for Professor Caldwell's class with someone else. Talking about things would help. Maybe Sam??

Linguistic ---->	1. Rewrite your class notes. 2. Record yourself reading through your class notes, and play the recording as you study. 3. Read the textbook chapter aloud.
Logical Mathematical ---->	1. Create hypothetical conceptual problems to solve. 2. Organize chapter or lecture notes into a logical flow. 3. Analyze how the textbook chapter is organized and why.
Spatial ---->	1. Draw a map that demonstrates your thinking on course material. 2. Illustrate your notes by drawing diagrams and charts. 3. Mark up your textbook to show relationships among concepts.
Bodily–Kinesthetic ---->	1. Study course material while engaged in physical activity. 2. Practice skills introduced in class or in the text. 3. Act out a scene based on chapter content.
Musical ---->	1. Create musical memory devices by putting words into well-known melodies. 2. Listen to music while you're studying. 3. Sing or hum as you work.
Interpersonal ---->	1. Discuss course material with your classmates. 2. Organize a study group that meets regularly. 3. Meet a classmate before or after class for coffee and class conversation.
Intrapersonal ---->	1. Keep a journal to track your personal reactions to course material. 2. Study alone and engage in internal dialogue about course content. 3. Coach yourself on how to best study for a challenging class.
Naturalistic ---->	1. Search for applications of course content in the natural world. 2. Study outside (if weather permits and you can resist distractions). 3. Go to a physical location that exemplifies course material (for example, a park for your geology course).

Develop Your Weaker Intelligences

It's important to cultivate your weaker intelligences. Why? Because life isn't geared to one kind of intelligence. It's complex. A photo journalist for *National Geographic,* for example, might need linguistic intelligence, spatial intelligence, interpersonal intelligence, and naturalistic intelligence. Being well-rounded, as the expression goes, is truly a good thing. Artist Pablo Picasso once said, "I am always doing that which I cannot do, in order that I may learn how to do it."

Use your multiple intelligences to multiply your success. Remember that no one is naturally intelligent in all eight areas. Each individual is a unique blend of intelligences. But the Theory of Multiple Intelligences claims that we all have the capacity to develop all of our eight intelligences further. That's good news! Howard Gardner puts it this way: "We can all get better at each of the intelligences, although some people will improve in an intelligence area more readily than others, either because biology gave them a better brain for that intelligence or because their culture gave them a better teacher."[18]

CSI's PROBABLY NEED OTHER KINDS OF INTELLIGENCE, TOO, LIKE LOGICAL-MATHEMATICAL TO RUN TESTS ON EVIDENCE AND FIGURE OUT WHAT IT MEANS.

How Do You Perceive and Process Information?

Challenge: You've lived with yourself for many years now, but how well do you know yourself as a learner?

Reaction: List as many descriptive phrases about your learning preferences as you can. For example, you might write, "I learn best when I listen to an instructor lecture" or "I learn best when I make color-coded binders for each class." Use this activity to discover some specifics about your learning style.

_____

_____

_____

I LEARN BEST WHEN I'M ACTIVELY INVOLVED. I LEARN BEST WHEN I WORK WITH OTHER PEOPLE. I LEARN BEST WHEN I CAN UNDERSTAND THE PROFESSOR!

Style—we all have it, right? What's yours? Baggy jeans and a T-shirt? Sandals, even in the middle of winter? A stocking cap that translates into I-just-rolled-out-of-bed-before-class? When it comes to appearance, you have your own style.

Think about how your mind works. For example, how do you decide what to wear in the morning? Do you turn on the radio or TV for the weather forecast? Jump on the Internet? Stick your head out the front door? Throw on whatever happens to be clean? We all have different styles, don't we?

So what's a learning style? A learning style is defined as your "characteristic and preferred way of gathering, interpreting, organizing, and thinking about information."[19] The way you perceive information and the way you process it—your perceiving/processing preferences—are based in part on your senses. Which sensory modalities do you prefer to use to take in information—your eyes (visual-graphic or visual-words), your ears (aural), or all your senses using your whole body (kinesthetic)? Which type of information sinks in best? Do you prefer teachers who lecture? Teachers who use visuals such as charts, web pages, and diagrams to explain things? Or teachers who plan field trips, use role-plays, and create simulations?

To further understand your preferred sensory channel, let's take this example. You decide to buy a new car and you must first answer many questions: What kind of car do you want to buy—an SUV, a sedan, a sports car, a van, or a truck? What are the differences between various makes and models? How do prices, comfort, gas mileage, and safety compare? Who provides the best warranty? Which car do consumers rate highest? How would you go about learning the answers to all these questions?

Which would you be most likely do to?

a) Look up charts that compare different makes and models by cost, gas mileage, buyer satisfaction, and so forth, visually. (V)

b) Ask friends and relatives to tell you how satisfied they are with the last car they bought or listen to various pitches made by salespeople. (A)

c) Buy a copy of Consumer Guide's annual edition on autos or read magazines like *Car and Driver*. (R/W)

d) Go to various showrooms and test drive different makes and models. (K)

Eventually, as you're deciding which vehicle to buy, you might do all these things, and do them more than once. But learning style theory says we all have preferences in terms of how we perceive and process information.

After reading the car-buying description, you probably have a gut feeling about your own style. However, take a few minutes to answer the questions about yourself in Exercise 3.3—for confirmation or revelation—to verify your hunches or to learn something new about yourself.

You can take the VARK online at http://www.vark-learn.com/english/page.asp?p=questionnaire and your results will be tabulated for you.

Now that you've calculated your scores, do they match your perceptions of yourself as a learner? Could you have predicted them? The VARK's creators believe that *you* are best qualified to verify and interpret your own results.[20]

© iStockphoto.com/Marcela Barsse; Johanna Goodyear/Dreamstime.com;
© iStockphoto.com/Nadezda Firsova; © iStockphoto.com/Pascal Genest

Activity Option Ask students to have someone who knows them well fill out the same "Challenge → Reaction" about them. Does their roommate or friend know that they must have total silence to study, for example? Encourage students to share their preferences with roommates and family members who may have a different style. The responses will help students see how others perceive them as well.

I wish we'd take a field trip to the county jail or a real crime lab as part of class!

Teachable Moment Ask students to help you think of real-life examples of learning style preferences. For instance, if they have a tech problem, would they prefer to first a) find a troubleshooting chart, b) call the Help Desk for advice, c) look through the hardware or software manual, or d) keep trying things until something works?.

Teaching with Technology Give an assignment with different options for completion based on a preferred learning style, and use technology to enhance learning. Aural learners may want to complete an assignment by making a podcast, while visual learners may want to create a PowerPoint presentation. Allow students to adapt the assignment to their own learning style; then discuss how this affected the way they learned.

Sensitive Situation Keep in mind that you may have some students in your class with either disclosed or undisclosed disabilities. Open up the door for this kind of discussion and encourage students to learn more about themselves, and share their needs with their instructors, especially if they have a learning disability, a hearing loss, low vision, ADHD, or any other unique need.

My VARK scores are K = 14, A = 6, V = 5, R = 4 Since I prefer my chem lab over lecture classes, I'm not surprised at that high kinesthetic score!

Holger Winkler/Cusp/Corbis

> 66 Learning how to learn is life's most important skill. 99
>
> **Tony Buzan, memory expert**

Exercise 3.3 | VARK Learning Styles Assessment

Choose the answer that best explains your preference and circle the letter. Please select more than one response if a single answer does not match your perception. Leave blank any question that does not apply.

1. You are helping someone who wants to go downtown, find your airport or locate the bus station. You would:
   a) draw or give her a map.
   b) tell her the directions.
   c) write down the directions (without a map).
   d) go with her.

2. You are not sure whether a word should be spelled "dependent" or "dependant." You would:
   a) see the word in your mind and choose by the way different versions look.
   b) think about how each word sounds and choose one.
   c) find it in a dictionary.
   d) write both words on paper and choose one.

3. You are planning a group vacation. You want some feedback from your friends about your plans. You would:
   a) use a map or website to show them the places.
   b) phone, text or e-mail them.
   c) give them a copy of the printed itinerary.
   d) describe some of the highlights.

4. You are going to cook something as a special treat for your family. You would:
   a) look through the cookbook for ideas from the pictures.
   b) ask friends for suggestions.
   c) use a cookbook where you know there is a good recipe.
   d) cook something you know without the need for instructions.

5. A group of tourists wants to learn about the parks or wildlife reserves in your area. You would:
   a) show them Internet pictures, photographs or picture books.
   b) talk about, or arrange a talk for them on parks or wildlife reserves.

    c) give them a book or pamphlets about the parks or wildlife reserves.

    d) take them to a park or wildlife reserve and walk with them.

6. You are about to purchase a digital camera or cell phone. Other than price, what would most influence your decision?
    a) Its attractive design that looks good.
    b) The salesperson telling me about its features.
    c) Reading the details about its features.
    d) Trying or testing it.

7. Remember a time when you learned how to do something new. Try to avoid choosing a physical skill, like riding a bike. You learned best by:
    a) diagrams and charts—visual clues.
    b) listening to somebody explaining it and asking questions.
    c) written instructions—e.g. a manual or textbook.
    d) watching a demonstration.

8. You have a problem with your heart. You would prefer that the doctor:
    a) showed you a diagram of what was wrong.
    b) described what was wrong.
    c) gave you something to read to explain what was wrong.
    d) used a plastic model to show what was wrong.

9. You want to learn a new software program, skill or game on a computer. You would:
    a) follow the diagrams in the book that came with it.
    b) talk with people who know about the program.
    c) read the written instructions that came with the program.
    d) use the controls or keyboard and try things out.

10. I like websites that have:
    a) interesting design and visual features.
    b) audio channels where I can hear music, radio programs or interviews.
    c) interesting written descriptions, lists and explanations.
    d) things I can click on or try out.

11. Other than price, what would most influence your decision to buy a new non-fiction book?
    a) The way it looks is appealing.
    b) A friend talks about it and recommends it.
    c) You'd quickly read parts of it.
    d) It contains real-life stories, experiences and examples.

12. You are using a book, CD or website to learn how to take photos with your new digital camera. You would like to have:
    a) diagrams showing the camera and what each part does.
    b) a chance to ask questions and talk about the camera and its features.
    c) clear written instructions with lists and bullet points about what to do.
    d) many examples of good and poor photos and how to improve them.

13. Do you prefer a teacher or a presenter who uses:
    a) diagrams, charts or graphs?
    b) question and answer, talk, group discussion or guest speakers?
    c) handouts, books or readings?
    d) demonstrations, models, field trips, role plays or practical exercises?

14. You have finished a competition or test and would like some feedback. You would like to have feedback:
    a) using graphs showing what you had achieved.
    b) from somebody who talks it through with you.

(continued on next page)

c) in a written format, describing your results.

d) using examples from what you have done.

15. You are going to choose food at a restaurant or cafe. You would:
   a) look at what others are eating or look at pictures of each dish.
   b) ask the server or friends to recommend choices.
   c) choose from the written descriptions in the menu.
   d) choose something that you have had there before.

16. You have to give an important speech at a conference or special occasion. You would:
   a) make diagrams or create graphs to help explain things.
   b) write a few key words and practice your speech over and over.
   c) write out your speech and learn from reading it over several times.
   d) gather many examples and stories to make the talk real and practical.

Source: N. Fleming. (2001–2011). *VARK, a Guide to Learning Styles.* Version 7.1. Available at http://www.vark-learn.com/english/page.asp?p=questionnaire. Used with permission from Neil Fleming.

Scoring the VARK

Let's tabulate your results.

Count your choices in each of the four VARK categories.	(a)	(b)	(c)	(d)
	Visual	Aural	Read/Write	Kinesthetic

Using Your VARK Preferences

Knowing your preferences can help you in your academic coursework for reasons like these:

1. You can use your preferences to get the best results.

2. You can pay attention to how you study, not just what you study.

3. You can make conscious choices that positively affect your overall college success.

Activity Option On the board or on a large piece of poster board, list the four modalities (Visual, Aural, Read/Write, and Kinesthetic) and have students write their name and score of their top two modalities. For example, a student might put her name and a 10 under Visual and her name and an 8 under Aural. Are there similarities in the class? Do these students enjoy the same classes? Now ask students to put their dominant multiple intelligence next to their name. Are there any patterns? Ask each student to describe one way in which they can use their dominant learning style and strong intelligence to help them in college (if there is not enough time in class, they can e-mail the class with their answer, or bring their response to the next class).

If your highest score (by 4 or 5 points) is in one of the four VARK modalities, that particular learning modality is your preferred one.[21] If your scores are more or less even between several or all four modalities, these scores mean that you don't have a strong preference for any single modality. It's estimated that 60 percent of the population is multimodal, which gives most of us flexibility in the way we learn.[22] A lower score in a preference simply means that you are more comfortable using other styles. If your VARK results contain a zero in a particular learning modality, you may realize that you do indeed dislike this mode or find it unhelpful. "Why would anyone want to use *that* mode?" you may have asked yourself in the past. It may be helpful to reflect on why you omit this learning modality. To learn more about your results and suggestions for applying them, see Figure 3.2 for your preferred modality.

	Everyday Study Strategies	Exam Preparation Strategies
VISUAL	• Convert your lecture notes to a visual format. • Study the placement of items, colors, and shapes in your textbook. • Put complex concepts into flowcharts or graphs. • Redraw ideas you create from memory.	• Practice turning your visuals back into words. • Practice writing out exam answers. • Recall the pictures you made of the pages you studied. • Use diagrams to answer exam questions, if your instructor will allow it.
AURAL	• Read your notes aloud. • Explain your notes to another auditory learner. • Ask others to "hear" you understanding of the material. • Record your notes or listen to your instructors' podcasts. • Realize that your lecture notes may be incomplete. You may have become so involved in listening that you stopped writing. Fill your notes in later by talking with other students or getting material from the textbook.	• Practice by speaking your answers aloud. • Listen to your own voice as you answer questions. • Opt for an oral exam if allowed. • Imagine you are talking with the teacher as you answer questions.
READ/WRITE	• Write out your lecture notes again and again. • Read your notes (silently) again and again. • Put ideas and principles into different words. • Translate diagrams, graphs, etc., into text. • Rearrange words and "play"with wording. • Turn diagrams and charts into words.	• Write out potential exam answers. • Practice creating and taking exams. • Type out your answers to potential test questions. • Organize your notes into lists or bullets. • Write practice paragraphs, particularly beginnings and endings.
KINESTHETIC	• Recall experiments, field trips, etc. Remember the real things that happened. • Talk over your notes with another "K" person. • Use photos and pictures that make ideas come to life. • Go back to the lab, your manual, or your notes that include real examples. • Remember that your lecture notes will have gaps if topics weren't concrete or relevant for you. • Use case studies to help you learn abstract principles.	• Role-play the exam situation in your room (or the actual classroom). • Put plenty of examples into your answers. • Write practice answers and sample paragraphs. • Give yourself practice tests.

Your highest score represents your preferred learning style; your lowest score, your least preferred. Most college classes emphasize reading and writing; however, if your lowest score is in the read/write modality, don't assume you're academically doomed. VARK can help you discover alternative, more productive ways to learn the same course material. As Fleming writes, knowing your VARK scores doesn't naturally help you become a better learner any more than jumping on a scale helps you slim down. You must take the next step and do something about it![23]

Learning style descriptions aren't meant to put you into a cubbyhole or stereotype you. And they certainly aren't meant to give you an excuse when you don't like a particular assignment. You may learn to adapt naturally to a particular instructor or discipline's preferences, using a visual modality in your economics class to interpret graphs and a kinesthetic modality in your chemistry lab to conduct experiments.

FIGURE 3.2

Visual, Aural, Read/Write, and Kinesthetic Learning Strategies

That's right. I can't change the way Professor Caldwell teaches. I'll guess I'll just have to change the way I study.

> ❝ Our lives have been divided into smaller and smaller increments of focus. We do more things than ever, but we've lost control of our attention. ❞
>
> *Tony Schwartz,*
> *The Way We're Working Isn't Working*

Multitasking. It's quickly becoming one of the most popular words in the English language. In whatever career you enter, you'll be expected to juggle many things at once. You'll get a phone call while answering one of the two billions e-mails sent daily in the U.S. and at the same time be conducting online research for your boss. Reportedly, the average worker spends 11 minutes at a time on any given project, switching between different aspects of it every three minutes.[24] The odd thing about our so-called ability to multitask is that it makes us feel productive, powerful, and prolific. But not only do interruptions break our focus, they also increase the number of mistakes we make, and often actually *cost*—rather than *save*—us time. This of it this way: would you really want a brain surgeon to stop your operation to check her Facebook wall or answer texts from her kids every so often? Probably not.

To help you get the picture, visualize the prefrontal cortex of your brain as a stage. Instead of allowing any actor on stage who wants some attention, be selective. ("Not now; wait for Act 3, Scene 2!") The stage is only so big; every actor in the play can't fit on it at once.[25] Pulling off an entire production requires maximum effort, and some scenes require an actor doing a monologue, instead of different actors entering "stage left" or "stage right" constantly and chaotically.

To make things even more challenging, we may be tempted to "stray" by our learning style preferences. Someone who prefers an aural modality, for example, may want to discuss everything fully just to hear the sound of his own and others' voices, when a quick "executive decision" would be more appropriate. A reserved, introverted person may prefer texting over facing a live human being, even when sensitive issues are at stake. Your learning style preferences could actually jeopardize your ability to focus on one thing when the right decision might be to choose the best modality for that thing, and get it done.

Instead of multi-tasking, try uni-tasking. When a task is both urgent *and* important, put on your blinders. As Jason Fried and David Heinemeier Hansson, the authors of *Rework,* wisely claim, "Interruption is the enemy of productivity. You can't get meaningful things done when you're constantly going start, stop, start, stop. Instead, you should get in the alone zone. Long stretches of alone time are when you're most productive. When you don't have to mind-shift between various tasks, you get a boatload done."[26] So close your office door, zero in, and stick to one thing until you're actually finished— or you've gone as far as you can. Oh, and it works in college, too.

Think Ahead In whatever career you're thinking of for yourself, what do you expect will be the most challenging, competing tasks? What sorts of things might you be juggling? How well does multitasking work for you now? How well might it work for you then, and what will you do to manage?

Cast on Careers

I CAN FOCUS, BUT ONLY ON THINGS I LIKE . . .

© Larry Harwood Photograph.
Property of Cengage Learning

FOCUS: Describe your ability to focus. Are you good at it?

ETHAN: As a brand new student, I was horrible at it. I wanted to jump into everything, and I was so excited by all the new friends I made that I didn't really focus on schoolwork much at all. I'm very extraverted; people matter to me. My residence hall door was always open, and other students came and went at all hours of the day and night. And I'm a kinesthetic learner, so I wanted to "do it all"! Unfortunately, all those things caught up with me and the result was major stress! I'm getting better at it though, and *FOCUS* has helped.

FOCUS: What career plans do you have right now? Is multitasking likely to be an issue?

ETHAN: I have two long-term goals: I'd like to become a teacher, and I'd like to travel internationally. Put those two together, and I can see myself teaching somewhere like New Zealand or Korea after I graduate. If I do that, not only will I have to pay attention to each one of my students, but I'll have to learn a new culture. But I can't wait for those career challenges!

Of course, you'll be required to use all four modalities in college. You'll have to read your literature assignments and write your English papers, even if read/write isn't your preferred style. Different disciplines require different kinds of information access. As one skeptic of learning styles writes, "At some point, no amount of dancing will help you learn more algebra." Actually, some teachers do use dance to help students learn math, and there are plenty of other kinesthetic techniques that work well, like solving actual problems, rather than simply re-reading a chapter in your math book.[27]

Regardless, you may also find that you need to deliberately and strategically re-route your learning methods in some of your classes, and knowing your VARK preferences can help you do that. Learning to capitalize on your preferences and translate challenging course material into your preferred modality may serve you well.

What Role Does Your Personality Play?

Challenge: How does your personality affect your learning style?

Reaction:
_____
_____
_____

One of the best things about college is having a chance to meet so many different types of people. At times you may find these differences intriguing. At other times, they may baffle you. Look around and listen to other students, and you'll start to notice. Have you heard students saying totally opposite things such as those listed here?

"There's no way I can study at home. It's way too noisy."

"There's no way I can study in the library. It's way too quiet."

"I'm so glad I've already decided on a major. Now I can go full steam ahead."

"I have no idea what to major in. I can think of six different majors I'd like to choose."

"My sociology instructor is great. She talks about all kinds of things in class, and her essay tests are actually fun!"

"My sociology instructor is so confusing. She talks about so many different things in class. How am I supposed to know what to study for her tests?"[28]

You're likely to run into all kinds of viewpoints and all types of people, but differences make life much more interesting! We're each unique. Perhaps your friends comment on your personality by saying, "She's really quiet," or "He's a 'party animal'," or "He's incredibly logical," or "She trusts her gut feelings." What you may not know is how big a role your personality plays in how you prefer to learn.

The Myers-Briggs Type Indicator® (MBTI) is the most well-known personality assessment instrument in the world. Each year, approximately 2 million people worldwide get a look into their personalities, their career choices, their interaction with others, and their learning styles by completing it. If you are able to complete the full Myers-Briggs Type Indicator in the class for which you're using this textbook, or through your college counseling center or learning center, do so. You'll learn a great deal about yourself.

The Myers-Briggs Type Indicator shows you your preferences in four areas (see also Figure 3.3):

E or I **What energizes you and where do you direct energy?** Do you get energy from other people (Extravert) or do you go within yourself to find strength (Introvert)?

S or N **How do you gather information and what kind of information do you trust?** Do you trust your senses and factually based information (Sensor) or do you trust your gut feelings (iNtuition)?

T or F **How do you make decisions, arrive at conclusions, and make judgments?** Do you think things through logically (Thinker) or do you care about how others react and feel (Feeler)?

J or P **How do you relate to the outer world?** Do you prefer organization and structure (Judging) or do you like spontaneity and going with the flow (Perceiver)?

If you take the Myers-Briggs Type Indicator you should realize that it isn't about what you can do. It's about what you prefer to do. Here's an illustration. Write your name on the first line.

_____

_____

Each person is an exception to the rule.

Carl Jung, psychiatrist (1875–1961)

Extravert (E)

"How do you recharge your batteries"? Students who prefer extraversion pay attention to people and things around them. That's also where they get their energy. As learners, they:

- Learn best when actively involved
- Like to study with others
- Like background noise while studying
- Don't particularly enjoy writing papers
- Want teachers to encourage discussion in class

Introvert (I)

Students who prefer introversion focus on the world inside their heads. They pay attention to their own thoughts, feelings, and ideas, and draw energy from their inner experience. As learners, they:

- Learn best by pausing to think
- Like to study alone
- Say they aren't good public speakers
- Need to study in quiet
- Want teachers to give clear lectures

Sensing (S)

What kind of information do you rely on? Students who are sensors become aware of things that are real through their senses: sound, touch, taste, feel, and smell. They focus on what is happening in the here and now. As learners, they:

- Look for specific information
- Memorize facts
- Follow instructions
- Like hands-on experiences
- Want teachers to give clear assignments

Intuition (N)

Students who trust their intuition, or sixth sense, look for patterns, possibilities, and the big picture. As learners, they:

- Look for quick insights
- Like theories and abstract thinking
- Read between the lines
- Create their own directions
- Want teachers to encourage independent thinking

Thinking (T)

Students who are thinkers like to make decisions objectively using logic, principles, and analysis. They weigh evidence in a detached manner. As learners, they:

- Use logic to guide their learning
- Like to critique ideas
- Learn through challenge and debate
- Can find flaws in an argument
- Want teachers to present logically

Feeling (F)

Students who are feelers value harmony and focus on what is important to them or to others when they make decisions. As learners, they:

- Want information to apply to them personally
- Like to please their teachers
- Find value or good in things
- Learn when they are supported or appreciated
- Want teachers to establish rapport with students

Judging (J)

Students who are judgers like to make quick decisions, settle things, and structure and organize their worlds. As learners, they:

- Like more formal class structures
- Plan their work in advance
- Work steadily toward their goals
- Like to be in charge
- Want teachers to be organized

Perceiving (P)

Students who are perceivers want to adapt to the world around them. They don't like to close off options; instead they'd rather experience whatever comes up. As learners, they:

- Like informal learning situations
- Enjoy spontaneity
- Stay open to new information
- Work in energy bursts
- Want teachers to entertain and inspire

Teaching with Technology The Internet has a wealth of additional information about the MBTI. Websites such as MyersBriggs.org contain general overviews about the instrument and more specific information about each type. There are also several videos that help further explain MBTI. Try searching for MBTI on youtube.com.

Teaching with Technology Take your students to www.typecan.com for an enjoyable way to explore the subject of psychological types. "Those Talking Letters" is particularly fun. The website was developed by the Center for Applications of Psychological Type.

Activity Option If you incorporate the MBTI into your class, before they actually fill out the instrument, have students guess their type. Let them know that an "E" learns from doing, an "I" prefers studying in quiet, an "S" likes to memorize, "N's" like to think about the big picture, "F's" relate information to people, while "T's" are logical, "J's" love organized classrooms and clear syllabi, and "P's" don't mind change and going with the flow. After the assessment, see if they were correct on any of the indicators.

[handwritten note] A-HA! HERE'S THE BIGGEST PROBLEM! I'M AN ESFP, AND I'LL BET PROFESSOR CALDWELL IS AN INTJ. WE COULDN'T BE MORE OPPOSITE!

FIGURE 3.3

Learning Style Preferences

Source: Based on J. K. DiTiberio & A. L. Hammer. (1993). *Introduction to Type in College.* Palo Alto, CA: Consulting Psychologists Press.

Now put the pen in your other hand, and try writing your name on the second line. What was different the second time around? For most people, the second try takes longer, is messier, probably feels strange, and requires more concentration. But could you do it? Yes. It's just that you prefer doing it the first way. The first way is easier and more natural; the second way makes a simple task seem like hard work! It's possible that you might have to try "writing with your other hand" in college—doing things that don't come naturally.

Throughout this book, you will find "Your Type Is Showing" features. These short articles summarize MBTI research that investigates the chapter's topic. They are intended to pique your interest and invite you to go beyond what you see in the chapter. Chances are you'll be fascinated by what you can learn about yourself through the MBTI.

This chapter has covered learning from several different perspectives, and you now know more about yourself as a learner than you did before you read it. But you may be wondering: So how do Multiple Intelligences, VARK preferences, and personality traits (MBTI) work together to produce a unique learner? Although the three perspectives aren't intended to connect, let's look at this example to help you understand how each one would explain how people learn.

Let's say the person you sit by in your math class always asks you whether you want to join his study group. Based on what you've learned in this chapter, you'd be more likely to say yes if you:

1. **MI:** have *interpersonal* (or social) intelligence

2. **VARK:** are an *aural* learner who likes to discuss things

3. **MBTI:** are *extraverted* (you get energy from other people).

The three perspectives don't overlap; they're different. That's why this chapter presents all three. Each perspective explains how people learn in a different way.

Although simply knowing about these three perspectives is good, it's important to go further and act on that knowledge. As a single learner in a larger class, you will need to adjust to the teaching style of your instructor in ways such as the following:

> **Translate for maximum comfort.** The way to maximize your comfort as a learner is to find ways to translate from your instructor's preferences to yours. If you know that you prefer feeling over thinking, and your instructor's style is based on thinking, make the course material come alive by personalizing it. How does the topic relate to you, your lifestyle, your family, and your future choices?

> **Make strategic choices.** Although learning preferences can help explain your academic successes, it's also important not to use them to rationalize your nonsuccesses. An introvert could say, "I could have aced that assignment if the instructor had let me work alone! I hate group projects." Become the best learner you can be at what you're naturally good at. But also realize that you'll need to become more versatile over time. In the workforce, you will not always be able to choose what you do and how you do it. Actively choose your learning strategies rather than simply hoping for the best. Remember: No one can learn for you, just as no one can eat for you.

> **Take full advantage.** College will present you with an extensive menu of learning opportunities. You will also build on your learning as you move beyond your general, introductory classes into courses in your

SHOULD I GO TO HIM FOR HELP IN MAKING CONNECTIONS BETWEEN THEORIES AND THE REAL WORLD? MAYBE WE WATCH THE SAME TV SHOWS AND WE CAN TALK ABOUT HOW TRUE TO LIFE THEY ARE—OR AREN'T.

Box 3.1 Learning Disability? Five Ways to Help Yourself

Perhaps you were diagnosed with Attention-Deficit/Hyperactivity Disorder (ADHD) or dyslexia as a young child. If you're beginning your college career with a learning disability (LD), you're not alone. In a college or university with an enrollment of 25,000 students, for example, approximately 550 of those students have learning disabilities.[29] By some estimates, two-thirds of students with diagnosed LDs continue on to college after high school.[30] Does a learning disability mean all the odds are against you? No, but there are some important steps you must take to help yourself. Successful college students with LDs recognize, understand, and accept these steps, and develop compensating strategies to offset their LDs.

1. If you've been previously diagnosed with a learning disability, bring a copy of your evaluation or Individualized Education Plan (IEP) with you to campus. Some schools require documentation in order to use the institution's support services.

2. Locate the support services office on your campus and use it. These services are free and can make all the difference in your success.

3. Learn more about your specific LD. Read about it. Visit credible websites. Understanding the ins and outs of what you're up against is important.

4. If you need special accommodations such as taking exams somewhere other than the classroom, schedule an appointment with your instructors early in the term to let them know. Having a learning disability doesn't mean you're required to do less work, but you'll get the support you need in order to do your best.

5. Remember that the advice in this book, which is helpful to all college students, can be even more useful to anyone with a learning disability. Time management strategies and study skills tailored to your specific LD are key.

Don't let fear of failure immobilize you. Instead, keep your eye on the goal and take charge of your own learning.[31]

chosen major—and across and between classes. Don't fall victim to the temptation to make excuses as some students do ("I could have been more successful in college if . . . I hadn't had to work so many hours . . . I hadn't had a family to support . . . my instructors had been more supportive. . . ." If, if, if. College may well be the most concentrated and potentially powerful learning opportunity you'll ever have. Ultimately, learning at your best is up to you.

Metacognition: Take Charge of How You Study

Exercise 3.4 Study Habit Self-Assessment

To what extent do these ten statements apply to you? Write the number for each statement on the line preceding it.

	Never		Sometimes		Always
	1	2	3	4	5

34

I GOTTA WORK ON THIS!

_____ 1. I keep going with things I have to learn rather than skipping over what I don't understand.

_____ 2. When I'm studying something difficult, I realize when I'm stuck and ask for help.

_____ 3. I make a study plan and stick to it in order to master class material.

_____ 4. I quiz myself as I'm studying to see what I understand and what I don't.

_____ 5. I talk through my problems, understanding things while I study.

_____ 6. After I study something, I think about how well it went.

_____ 7. I know when I learn best: morning, afternoon, or evening, for example.

(continued on next page)

_____ 8. I know how I study best: alone, with one other person, in a group, etc.

_____ 9. I know where I study best: at home, at the library, at my computer, etc.

_____ 10. I believe I'm in control of my own learning.

Now tally your scores on this informal instrument. If you scored between 40 and 50 total points, you have excellent metacognitive skills. If you scored between 30 and 40 points, your skills are probably average. However, note any items you rated down in the 1 to 2 range, and then continue reading this section of the chapter carefully.

Talk about needing to use a dictionary! What does the word *metacognition* mean? *Meta* is an ancient Greek prefix that is often used to mean *about*. For example, metacommunication is communicating *about* the way you communicate. ("I feel humiliated when you tease me in front of other people. Can you *not* do that?")

Being busy does not always mean real work. The object of all work is production or accomplishment and to either of these ends there must be forethought, system, planning, intelligence, and honest purpose, as well as perspiration. Seeming to do is not doing.

Thomas Edison, American inventor (1847–1931)

Because cognition means thinking and learning, metacognition is thinking about your thinking and learning about your learning. It's about identifying your learning goals, monitoring your progress, backing up or getting help when you're stuck, forging ahead when you're in the groove, and evaluating your results. Metacognition is about knowing yourself as a learner and about your ability (and motivation) to control your own learning. Some things are easy for you to learn; others are hard. What do you know about yourself as a learner, and do you use that awareness intentionally to learn at your best?[32] When your instructor says, "Study hard for the test!" what does that mean to you?

These questions may seem simple, but how do you know:

1. When you've finished a reading assignment?

2. When your paper is ready to turn in?

3. When you've finished studying for an exam?

When you're eating a meal, you know when you're full, right? But when it comes to academic work, how do you know when you're done? Some students resort to answers like this to the question "How do you know when you're done?" Look at the range of students' answers:

➤ I just do.

➤ I trust in God.

➤ My eyelids get too heavy.

➤ I've been at it for a long time.

➤ My mom tells me to go to bed.

➤ I understand everything.

➤ I can write everything down without looking at the textbook or my notes.

[handwritten notes:] ? ? When I've gotten to the end? Whenever the due date is? When it's late at night?

> 66 Striving for success without hard work is like trying to harvest where you haven't planted. 99

David Bly, Minnesota politician

➤ I've created a practice quiz for myself and get all the answers right.

➤ When my wife or girlfriend drills me and I know all the answers.

➤ When I can teach my husband everything I've learned.

➤ When I've highlighted, recopied my notes, made flash cards, written sample questions, tested myself, and so on.

You can see that their answers become increasingly reliable as you progress down the list.[33]

Metacognition is about having an "awareness of [your] own cognitive machinery and how the machinery works."[34] It's about knowing the limits of your own learning and memory capabilities, knowing how much you can accomplish within a certain amount of time, and knowing what learning strategies work for you.[35] Know your limits, but at the same time, stretch.

Teachable Moment Ask your students which of these answers sounds about right for them. Discuss the value of moving down the list to improve results.

Teachable Moment Encourage students to give themselves little rewards. If they stay on task for a specific amount of time, they should reward themselves by taking a quick walk or calling a friend (nothing that will break the work flow, though!). For longer projects that they complete, students can give themselves a bigger reward—going to a movie with friends, for example. Encourage students to break up big tasks into small chunks and reward themselves along the way (even if it's only a pat on the back).

Apply Your Learning Style to Your Study Style

Now that you've gained some insight into how you prefer to learn, it's time to apply those preferences to how you study. Are you the kind of student who re-reads a textbook page five times without having the information sink in? Do you procrastinate when it comes to reading assignments for your classes?

> 66 The more I want to get something done, the less I call it work. 99

Richard Bach, American author, (1936–)

If so, through this chapter, you may have discovered why. Perhaps your linguistic intelligence is relatively low. Perhaps Read/Write is your least preferred VARK modality. Perhaps your off-the-charts extraverted personality enjoys the company of others, not a book.

Metacognition means thinking about your thinking and learning about your learning—taking charge of your own learning—and maybe that's exactly what you need to do. Early on, this chapter advised you about "Creating the Best Conditions for Learning." Monitoring how you study and how well it's working is at the top of the list. You may just see an improvement!

Becoming an Intentional Learner:
Make a Master Study Plan

"
'Tis not in mortals to command success, but we'll do more ... we'll deserve it.
"

Joseph Addison,
English politician and writer
(1672–1719)

Dann Tardif/Cusp/LWA/Corbis

What's your favorite class this term? Or let's turn the question around: What's your least favorite class? Becoming an educated person may well require you to study things you wouldn't *choose* to study. Considering all you have to do, including your most and least favorite classes, what would making a master study plan look like? You've "been there, done that" all through your schooling, but do you *really* know how to study?

To begin, think about what you have to think about. What's your goal? Is it to finish your English essay by 10:00 P.M. so that you can start your algebra homework? Or is it to write the best essay you can possibly write? If you've allowed yourself one hour to read this chapter, but after an hour you're still not finished, you have three choices: keep reading, finish later, or give up entirely. What's in your best interest, honestly? See whether you find the following planning strategies helpful.

1. **Make sure you understand your assignments.** Understanding is critical to making a master plan. You can actually waste a great deal of time trying to read your instructor's mind after the fact: "Did she want us to *analyze* the play or *summarize* it?" When you leave class, make sure you're clear on what's been assigned.

2. **Schedule yourself to be three places at once.** Making a master plan requires you to think simultaneously about three different time zones:

The past: Ask yourself what you already know. Is this a subject you've studied before? Have your study habits worked well for you in the past? How have you done your best work—in papers, on exams, on projects?

The present: Ask yourself what you need to learn now. How interested are you in this material? How motivated are you to learn it? How much time will you devote to it?

The future: Ask yourself how you'll go about learning it. Will you learn it using the strategies that work best for you? Which learning factors will you control? Will you do what you can to change what's not working?[36]

3. **Talk through your learning challenges.** There's good evidence that talking to yourself while you're studying is a good thing. Researchers find it helps you figure things out: *Okay, I understand the difference between a neurosis and a psychosis, but I'm not sure I can provide examples on my psychology test.* Once you've heard yourself admit that, you know where to focus your efforts next.[37] Or consider the possibility on "talking online" to other students worldwide at openstudy.com.

4. **Be a stickler.** Sticklers pay attention to details. They want to make sure everything is absolutely right. Have you ever thought about how important accuracy is? For example, if you were 99 instead of 100 percent accurate, that would mean that:

   ➤ 500 airplanes in U.S. skies each day wouldn't be directed by air traffic controllers.[38] Disastrous!

As you read and study, remember this example. Be thorough. Read the entire assignment. Pay attention to details. If you make a mistake, for example in solving a math problem, figure out exactly what went wrong so that you don't hold on to a bad academic habit. Rework the problem at least twice, write a few sentences describing the right way to solve it, and try another problem similar to it to see whether you really understand.[39] Accuracy counts!

5. **Take study breaks.** The human attention span is limited, and according to some researchers, it's shrinking, rather than expanding.[40] Plan to take brief scheduled breaks to stretch, walk around, or grab a light snack every half hour during study sessions. Of course, it's important to sit down and get back to work again. Don't let a quick study break to get a snack multiply into several hours of television viewing that wasn't in the plan.

6. **Mix it up.** Put a little variety into your study sessions by switching from one subject to another or from one mode of studying—for example, reading, self-quizzing, writing—to another. Variety helps you fight boredom and stay fresh (unless, of course, you're on the verge of a breakthrough). Even changing locations from time to time, rather than always studying in one place, stimulates your brain to reboot.[41]

Concentrate all your thoughts upon the work at hand. The sun's rays do not burn until brought to a focus.

Alexander Graham Bell, inventor, scientist, and engineer (1847–1922)

© Larry Harwood Photography. Property of Cengage Learning.

Teachable Moment Encourage students to use a planner and record their assignments and upcoming tests. Explain to students that the time to ask for clarification on how to do an assignment or what material will be covered on the test is before they leave the classroom.

Teachable Moment Recitation is an important part of learning: Whether you recite out loud or subconsciously hear the information over and over again, either helps you to retain it. Reciting into a recorder and playing it back, working in a study group, or just letting someone quiz you are all effective study practices.

7. **Estimate how long it will take.** Before starting an assignment, estimate the amount of time you will need to complete that assignment (just as you do at the start of each chapter of this book), and then compare that estimate with the actual amount of time the assignment took to complete. Getting into this habit helps you develop realistic schedules for future projects.

8. **Vary your study techniques by course content.** Studying productively is more than just learning a few general rules that apply to any type of subject matter. You need to zoom in on whatever subject or discipline it is that you're studying. Look over the pages of your textbook. Does the material synch with your learning style? Is it text-heavy (read/write)? Do graphs or charts explain the text and seem important? Are color-coding or bulleting used to call your attention to particular items (visual)? If the material isn't presented as you'd prefer, what can you do to "translate"? For example, if you're a kinesthetic learner, can you make flash cards? Can you create and complete practice tests? If you learn by listening, can you read the material aloud (aural)? And finally, what kind of exam (multiple-choice, essay, problem sets, etc.) does the material lend itself to? What are you likely to need to know, and what will you be asked to do on an exam? When you study math, it's important to do more than read. Working problem sets helps you actually develop the skills you need. When you study history, you study differently. You might draw a timeline of the events leading up to World War I, for example.[42]

9. **Study earlier, rather than later.** Whenever possible, study during the daytime, rather than waiting until evening. Research shows that each hour used for study during the day is equal to one and a half hours at night. Another major study showed that students who study between 6:00 P.M. and midnight are twice as likely to earn A's as students who put off their studying until after midnight.[43] And simply getting enough sleep can help you rachet up your GPA more than you'd expect.

10. **Create artificial deadlines for yourself.** Even though your instructors will have set deadlines for various assignments, create your own deadlines that precede the ones they set. Finish early, and you'll save yourself from any last minute emergencies that may come up, like crashed hard drives or empty printer cartridges.

Assume you are taking a class in calculus and a class in music theory this term. Look at the excerpts from the textbooks you're assigned to read, and describe how you would go about studying the material, based on what the content in these three subjects requires. Among other things, which particular VARK learning style preferences should be used: V, A, R, and/or K? Fill in specifics about how you would study each subject's textbook page. It's also important to annotate as you read, as shown here. Make notes to yourself in the margins or on sticky notes, reacting, explaining, or summarizing what you've learned or what is still fuzzy. In doing so, you'll be interacting with the material and personalizing it. Make connections; don't just let information float by and hope that something sticks. After you're done, compare notes with your classmates.

---

2   **Chapter P**   Preparation for Calculus

P.1   Graphs and Models

- Sketch the graph of an equation.
- Find the intercepts of a graph.
- Test a graph for symmetry with respect to an axis and the origin.
- Find the points of intersection of two graphs.
- Interpret mathematical models for real-life data.

The Graph of an Equation

In 1637 the French mathematician René Descartes revolutionized the study of mathematics by joining its two major fields—algebra and geometry. With Descartes's coordinate plane, geometric concepts could be formulated analytically and algebraic concepts could be viewed graphically. The power of this approach was such that within a century of its introduction, much of calculus had been developed.

The same approach can be followed in your study of calculus. That is, by viewing calculus from multiple perspectives—*graphically*, *analytically*, and *numerically*—you will increase your understanding of core concepts.

Consider the equation $3x + y = 7$. The point $(2, 1)$ is a **solution point** of the equation because the equation is satisfied (is true) when 2 is substituted for x and 1 is substituted for y. This equation has many other solutions, such as $(1, 4)$ and $(0, 7)$. To find other solutions systematically, solve the original equation for y.

$$y = 7 - 3x \qquad \text{Analytic approach}$$

Then construct a **table of values** by substituting several values of x.

x	0	1	2	3	4
y	7	4	1	-2	-5

Numerical approach

From the table, you can see that $(0, 7)$, $(1, 4)$, $(2, 1)$, $(3, -2)$, and $(4, -5)$ are solutions of the original equation $3x + y = 7$. Like many equations, this equation has an infinite number of solutions. The set of all solution points is the **graph** of the equation, as shown in Figure P.1.

> **NOTE** en though we refer to the sketch shown in Figure P.1 as the graph of $3x + y = 7$, it really represents only a *portion* of the graph. The entire graph would extend beyond the page. ∎

In this course, you will study many sketching techniques. The simplest is point plotting—that is, you plot points until the basic shape of the graph seems apparent.

EXAMPLE 1   Sketching a Graph by Point Plotting

Sketch the graph of $y = x^2 - 2$.

Solution   First construct a table of values. Then plot the points shown in the table.

x	-2	-1	0	1	2	3
y	2	-1	-2	-1	2	7

Finally, connect the points with a *smooth curve*, as shown in Figure P.2. This graph is a **parabola.** It is one of the conics you will study in Chapter 10. ∎

RENÉ DESCARTES (1596–1650)

Descartes made many contributions to philosophy, science, and mathematics. The idea of representing points in the plane by pairs of real numbers and representing curves in the plane by equations was described by Descartes in his book *La Géométrie*, published in 1637.

Graphical approach: $3x + y = 7$
Figure P.1

The parabola $y = x^2 - 2$
Figure P.2

3x + y = 7

y = x² − 2

How would you study this? *Calculus, 9th Edition, by Ron Larson and Bruce H. Edwards.*

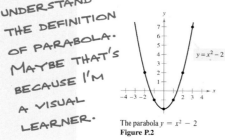

Measures

As you performed the different meters, you may have lost your place momentarily. Even if you didn't, you can see that it would be difficult to play a long piece of music without losing one's place. For this reason, music is divided into **measures** with vertical lines called **bar lines**.

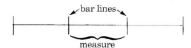

A bar line occurs immediately before an accented pulse. Thus, duple meter has two pulses per measure, triple meter has three pulses per measure, and quadruple meter has four pulses per measure. The following example shows the common meters again, this time with bar lines included. Notice how much easier it is to read and perform the meter when it is written this way.

duple meter

triple meter

quadruple meter

Double bar lines have a special meaning: Their two most common uses are to signal the beginning of a new section in a large work and to mark the end of a work. Put double bar lines at the end of any exercises or pieces you write.

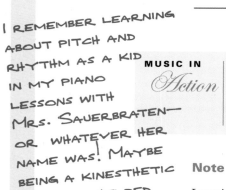

I REMEMBER LEARNING ABOUT PITCH AND RHYTHM AS A KID IN MY PIANO LESSONS WITH MRS. SAUERBRATEN— OR WHATEVER HER NAME WAS! MAYBE BEING A KINESTHETIC LEARNER HELPED ME MEMORIZE THE HAND MOTIONS OF A SONG? ? ?

MUSIC IN *Action*

Hearing Pulse and Meter

As members of the class listen, clap a steady pulse without any noticeable accents. Slowly change the pulse to duple, triple, or quadruple meter. You may want to have a contest to see how quickly members of the class can detect the shift to a measured pulse.

Note Values

Learning to read music involves mastering two different musical subsystems: pitch notation and rhythmic notation. Pitch is indicated by the placement of a note on a five-line staff (the higher the note on the staff, the higher the pitch). You will learn about that later in this chapter. Rhythm, on the other hand, is written with

How would you study this? *A Creative Approach to Music Fundamentals, 10th Edition, by William Duckworth.*

_____

_____

Finally, what have you learned about studying and about yourself as a learner by completing this exercise?

11. **Treat school as a job.** If you consider the amount of study time you need to budget for each hour of class time, and you're taking 12–15 credits, then essentially you're working a 36–45 hour/week job on campus. Arrive at "work" early and get your tasks done during "business hours" so you have more leisure time in the evenings.

12. **Show up.** Once you've decided to sit down to study, really commit yourself to showing up—being present emotionally and intellectually, not just physically. If you're committed to getting a college education, then give it all you've got! Get help if you need it. If you have a diagnosed learning disability, or believe you might, find out where help is available on your campus. One of the best ways to compensate for a learning disability is by relying on metacognition. In other words, consciously controlling what isn't happening automatically is vital to your success.[44]

Sprinting to the Finish Line: How to Study When the Heat Is On

Let's be realistic. Planning is important, but there will be the occasional time when you'll have to find some creative ways to survive the onslaught of all you have to study. You'll need to prioritize your time and make decisions about what to study. When you do need to find a way to accomplish more than is humanly possible, keep these "emergency preparedness" suggestions in mind:

1. **Triage.** With little time to spare, you must be efficient. Consider this analogy: If you're the physician on duty in the ER, and three patients come in at once, who will you take care of first: the fellow with strep throat, the woman with a sprained wrist, or the heart attack victim who needs CPR? Making decisions about priorities is called triage. Of all the material you need to study, ask what is most important, moderately important, and least important. For example, if you are earning an A− in art history, a B+ in geography, and a C− in math, you know which course most needs your attention. Evaluate the material and ask yourself which topics have received the most attention in class and in the textbook. Then focus your study time on those topics, rather than trying to study everything.

2. **Use every spare moment to study.** If flashcards work for you, take your flashcards with you everywhere, like on your daily bus ride or to the laundromat, for example. Organize your essay answer in your head while you're filling up at the pump. It's surprising: Small amounts of focused time do add up.

3. **Give it the old one-two-three-four punch.** Immerse all your senses in the precious little amount of time you have to study: *read, write, listen,* and *speak* the material.

Teaching with Technology Technology has made studying on-the-go even easier. Today, you don't need to be in the library, in front of a book, or even in front of a computer screen to be able to study effectively. Encourage students to be creative when it comes to sneaking in a few extra minutes of studying. They could send themselves a voicemail or text message, record some information to their iPod, or even Tweet some last-minute study info from their cell phone.

Teachable Moment Explain to students that the more senses they can incorporate when studying, the better. Visually seeing the information, using different colors, graphic organizers, charts or graphs; hearing the information, using an iPod, tape recorder, or study group; or tactilely writing out notes, manipulating items, or using flash cards are all ways to incorporate all of the senses into your study sessions.

© iStockphoto.com/Jacob Wackerhausen

> "It's not that I'm so smart, it's just that I stay with problems longer."
>
> *Albert Einstein, American theoretical physicist (1879–1955)*

4. **Get a grip on your gaps.** Honesty is the best policy. Rather than glossing over what you don't know, assess your knowledge as accurately as possible, and fill in the gaps. The question is: what's the best way to do that? If you're completely honest, you may not know, exactly. Perhaps you didn't do much studying in high school because you didn't need to. If you had to choose an adjective to describe your attitude toward school then, you may come up with "relaxed, "apathetic," or even "bored." The challenges weren't high, so your study skills didn't matter much. But now that you're in college, stress, worry, and anxiety can escalate because the academic challenges you're facing demand much more. This chapter's goal is to help you rise to the challenge!

5. **Cram, but only as the very last resort.** If you're ultrashort on time due to a real emergency, and you have studying to do for several classes, focus on one class at a time. Be aware: If you learn new information that is similar to something you already know, the old information can interfere. So if you're studying for a psychology test that contains some overlap with your sociology test, separate the study sessions by a day. Studies also show that cramming up to one hour before sleeping can help to minimize interference.[45] Nevertheless, continually remind yourself: What's my goal here? Is it to just get through twenty-five pages or is it to truly understand?

A final word about learning and studying: Albert Einstein said this: "Never regard study as a duty, but as the enviable opportunity to learn . . ." Studying and learning are what college is all about. Take his advice: Consider the opportunities before you to become an educated person, and take advantage of them all.

VARK It!

Complete the recommended activity for your preferred VARK learning modality. If you are multimodal, select more than one activity. Your instructor may ask you to (a) give an oral report on your results in class, (b) send your results to him or her via e-mail, or (c) post them online.

 Visual: Look back over this chapter to see which photos (and quotes) remind you of yourself and your learning. Mark the photo and write an explanation.

 Aural: Discuss your 1) multiple intelligences, 2) VARK preferences, or 3) personality factors that affect learning with your friends or family. Do your results make sense to them? Why or why not?

 Read/Write: Choose one major section of this chapter that made an impact on you, and write a paragraph summary about your own learning.

 Kinesthetic: Do your own online research to further your understanding of how the three self-assessment tools in this chapter impact you or change the way you think of yourself as a learner.

Now What Do You Think?

insight

action

❶ At the beginning of this chapter, Tammy Ko, a frustrated and disgruntled student, faced a challenge. Now after reading this chapter, would you respond differently to any of the questions you answered about the "FOCUS Challenge Case"? Knowing what you know now, how would you advise her? Write a paragraph ending to the story, incorporating your best advice.

❷ What are your most developed intelligences? Describe a situation in which you excelled as a learner and how the Theory of Multiple Intelligences helps explain your success.

❸ What is or are your VARK preferences? Are they what you predicted? How will you capitalize on them to learn at your best?

❹ How does your personality affect your learning? Provide an example of how you can make the best use of what you know now about your approach to learning based on your personality type.

❺ This chapter asked you to assess your learning in three different ways by thinking about your multiple intelligences, sensory modalities, and personality. We learned from Tammy's notes that she has high Interpersonal Intelligence, is a kinesthetic learner according to the VARK, and that her personality type is ESFP (while Professor Caldwell's is probably INTJ). How do these three assessments fit together for her? How do your three assessments fit together for you? How is the new picture of yourself as a learner similar to or different from what you used to think about yourself? How will it change the way you approach learning in the future?

Reality Check

On a scale of 1 to 10, answer the following questions now that you've completed the chapter.

 low   1   2   3   4   5   6   7   8   9   10   high

In hindsight, how much did you already know about learning styles and studying before reading the chapter?

Can you answer these questions about learning more fully now that you've read the chapter?

❶ What does the term "multiple intelligences" mean? Can you name three different types of intelligences?

❷ What does VARK stand for? Can you identify the letters as they relate to students' preferences for taking in information?

❸ What does your personality have to do with how you learn? Give several examples.

How useful might the information in this chapter be to you? How much do you think this information might affect your success in college? _____

How much energy did you put into reading this chapter? _____

How long did it actually take you to complete this chapter (both the reading and writing tasks)? _____ Hour(s) _____ Minutes

Did you finish reading this chapter? _____
Did you intend to when you started? _____
If you meant to but didn't, what stopped you? _____

Activity Option Ask students to summarize their responses to the "Reality Check" and send it to you via e-mail. In addition, ask them to tell you the most significant thing they learned about themselves and give a specific example of how they will use what they've learned to prepare for an exam.

Take a minute to compare these answers to your answers from the "Readiness Check" at the beginning of this chapter. What gaps exist between the similar questions? How might these gaps between what you thought before starting the chapter and what you now think after completing the chapter affect how you approach the next chapter in this book?

4 Managing Your Time, Energy, and Money

Larry Harwood Photography. Property of Cengage Learning.

How this chapter relates to YOU

1. When your time is limited, and you should be using it to study, what is most likely to derail you, if anything? Please circle one or more responses, if any are generally true for you.

People needing my attention

My job getting in the way

Spending time online

Watching TV or movies

Having responsibilities at home

2. What is most likely to be your response? Circle it.

| I have strong will power and focus no matter what. | Even though it's hard, eventually I settle in and focus. | I try to focus, but I can't seem to do it for long. | I give in to the urge to do something else and procrastinate. |

3. What would you have to do to increase your likelihood of success? Will you do it?

_____

_____

_____

How YOU will relate to this chapter

What are you most interested in learning about? Put check marks by those topics.

☐ Why time management alone doesn't work

☐ How time management differs from energy management

☐ How to schedule your way to success

☐ How the P word can derail you

☐ How to realistically balance work, school, and your personal life

☐ How to manage your money

● How motivated are you to learn more about managing your time, energy, and money in college?
(5 = high, 1 = low) _____

● How ready are you to read now? _____
(If something is in your way, take care of it if you can, zero in and focus.)

● How long do you think it will take you to complete this chapter? If you start and stop, keep track of your overall time.
_____ Hour(s) _____ Minutes

DƐƦƐk Johnson

As Derek Johnson walked out of his World History class on Wednesday evening, he felt panicked. The professor had just assigned a twelve-page paper, due one month from today. *How could she?* Derek thought. *Doesn't she realize how busy I am?* The syllabus mentioned a paper, but twelve pages was downright excessive. He sent a tweet complaining about it from his phone on his way to his next class. Twitter was quickly becoming Derek's favorite way to communicate. Writing short tweets was certainly better than dragging something out over twelve pages!

MAKE TO-DO LIST!?

REMEMBER TO BUY MOM A BIRTHDAY GIFT!!!

REMEMBER: COMPUTER TRAINING CLASS FOR WORK ON WEDNESDAY!

When Derek had decided to go to college after working for a year after high school, he hadn't quite realized what a juggling act it would require. First, there was his family—his Mom and stepdad, his five-year-old sister, Taura, and three other stepbrothers and stepsisters on his Dad's side. Then there was his full-time job, which was really quite demanding for an administrative assistant. He hoped that a degree in business would help him move into the management ranks, where the salaries were higher. No matter what, Derek always ran out of money before the end

of the month. Besides his job, there was singing in his church choir, coaching the youth soccer league, competing in cycling races, and working out every morning at the gym. Derek had been a high school athlete, and physical fitness was a priority for him.

His head began to swim as he thought about all his upcoming obligations: his mother's birthday next week, the dog's vet appointment, his stepbrother coming to town for a visit, the mandatory training

Community Center
Gym Schedule

Monday	Tuesday	Wednesday	Thursday	Friday
Open Gym 6:30-8:30	Open Gym 6:30-8:30	Open Gym 6:30-8:30	Open Gym 6:30-8:30	Open Gym 6:30-8:30
Cycling Class 9:00-10:00	Taekwondo Class 9:00-10:00	Taekwondo Class 9:00-10:00	Kick Boxing 9:00-10:00	Cycling Class 9:00-10:00
Taekwondo Class	Yoga Class 12:00-1:00	Yoga Class 12:00-1:00	Yoga Class 12:00-1:00	Taekwondo Class

Mᴇᴛᴇᴏʀ Wᴏʀʟᴅᴡɪᴅᴇ Mᴀʀᴋᴇᴛɪɴɢ

DEREK JOHNSON
Administrative Assistant

www.MWM.com
(o) 212-555-9865
(c) 212-555-6545
D.Johnson@mwm.com

class for work. Something had to go, but he couldn't think of anything he could sacrifice to make time for a twelve-page paper. Maybe he'd have to break down and buy one of those planners, but weren't most people who use those slightly, well . . . compulsive?

Still, the paper was to count as 25 percent of his final grade in the course. He decided he'd try and think of a topic for the paper on his way home. But then he remembered that his mom had asked him to stop at the store to pick up groceries. Somewhere on aisle 12, between the frozen pizza and the frozen yogurt, Derek's thoughts about his research paper vanished.

The following week, the professor asked the students in the class how their papers were coming along. Some students gave long accounts of their research progress, the wealth of sources they'd found, and the detailed outlines they'd put together. Derek didn't raise his hand.

A whole week has gone by, Derek thought on his way back to his car after class. *I have to get going!* Writing

had never exactly been Derek's strong suit. Through a great deal of hard work, he had managed to earn a 3.8 GPA in high school—a record he planned to continue. A course in World History—not even in his intended major—was *not* going to ruin things! The week had absolutely flown by, and there were plenty of good reasons why his paper was getting off to such a slow start.

It was true that Derek rarely wasted time, except for occasionally watching his favorite TV shows. But then again, with such a jam-packed schedule, he really felt the need to unwind once in a while. Regardless, he rarely missed his nightly study time from 11:00 P.M. to 1:00 A.M. Those two hours were reserved for homework, no matter what.

At the end of class two weeks later, Derek noticed that several students lined up to show the professor the first drafts of their papers. *That's it!* Derek thought to himself. *The paper is due next Wednesday. I'll spend Monday night, my only free night of the week, in the library. I can get there right after work and stay until 11:00 or so. That'll be five hours of concentrated time. I should be able to write it then.*

Despite his good intentions, Derek didn't arrive at the library until nearly 8:00 p.m., and his work session wasn't all

that productive. As he sat at his library computer, he found himself obsessing about things that were bothering him at work. His boss was being difficult, and his team of coworkers argued

contantly about their current project. Finally, when he glanced at his watch, he was shocked to see that it was already midnight! The library was closing, and he'd only written three pages. Where had the time gone?

On his way out to the car, his cell phone rang. It was his Mom, wondering if he could watch Taura tomorrow night. She was running a fever. Oh, and his boss had called about an emergency meeting at 7:00 a.m. *If one more thing goes wrong . . .* , Derek thought to himself. His twelve-page paper was due in two days.

University Library

FALL SEMESTER HOURS
Monday – Thursday: 8 am – Midnight
Friday – Saturday: 8 am – 8 pm
Sunday: 10 am – 4 pm

LIBRARY SERVICES:
- Computer Access
- Internet Access and Wi-Fi
- Photo Copying
- Interlibrary Loan
- Email and Tech Support
- Book, Journal, and Media Collections
- Expert Research Help

WORLD HISTORY
Fall Semester Syllabus

Instructor: Julia Alexander
Office: Main Hall 320
Email: Julia.Alexander@campusmail.edu
Phone: 555-3424
Office Hours: 12:30-3pm daily

Required Textbook:
World History, 6th Edition. By William J. Duiker and Jackson J. Spielvogel ISBN: 0495569011

Grading:

Quizzes:	10 @ 10 points each	100pts
Midterm Exam:		100pts
Cultural Analysis:		50pts
Course Essay:		150pts
Final Exam:		100pts
TOTAL:		500pts

What Do *You* Think?

challenge

" reaction

❶ Describe Derek's time management strategies. Are they working? Is time management Derek's only problem?
❷ Identify the time-wasters that are a part of Derek's schedule. Do you think procrastination is an issue for Derek? What's behind his failure to make progress on his paper?
❸ Suggest three realistic ways for Derek to balance work, school, and his personal life.
❹ What aspects of Derek's situation can you relate to personally? Besides time management challenges, are you experiencing money management issues as he is in your life right now?

Teachable Moment Now that students have been introduced to the VARK, "VARK It!" activities will appear at the beginning of each chapter. Students will be able to *use* the suggestions as they read, rather than completing them afterwards as assignments that could be perceived as busywork.

VARK It!

Complete the recommended activity for your preferred VARK learning modality. If you are multimodal, select more than one activity. Your instructor may ask you to (a) give an oral report on your results in class, (b) send your results to him or her via e-mail, or (c) post them online.

 Visual: Buy a set of adhesive colored dots from a local office supply store. As you go through this chapter, put red dots by things you'll try right away, yellow dots by things that sound like a good idea, and green dots by things you're already doing well.

 Aural: Listen to the mp3 summary at www.cengagebrain.com for this chapter before you read further. As soon as you've finished, write down three ideas you'll watch for as you read.

 Read/Write: Write a paragraph about yourself and your time management challenges over the last week, and watch for suggestions that come up that apply to you as you read.

 Kinesthetic: Find a YouTube or other online resource on time management that adds to this chapter. Show your YouTube or "compete" with other "K" students to show the best one in class as you begin discussing this chapter.

Time Management Isn't Enough

challenge

" reaction

Challenge: What is the difference between managing your time and managing your attention?

Reaction:

_____

_____

_____

Teachable Moment This chapter is about one of the "hottest" topics in student success courses. Students and instructors talk about managing time, but not much about managing oneself and one's energy. Let students know that there is no "one size fits all" approach to figuring out how to stay on top of things; they need to factor in their strengths and challenges when learning about managing time and energy and ultimately themselves!

Years ago, the Rolling Stones first belted out these lyrics: "Time is on my side—yes, it is." The song was optimistic. It predicted that some fictitious woman would get tired of her new love and eventually come "runnin' back."

Today, many of us are pessimistic about time. We feel that time is working against us. We are overwhelmed—school, job, family, friends. The list goes on and on, specific to each of us, but lengthy for all of us. How can we get it all done?

In college and in your career, time management will be one of your greatest challenges. Why? The pace of life is accelerating. Today's world is about high-speed technology, rapid transit, information overload, and a frenetic lifestyle. Leisurely fine dining or family meals around the table have deteriorated into grabbing fast food on the run. Many of us try to cram more into our lives: one more activity, one more experience, one more obligation. As one time management expert notes, "You can be so busy that you don't even take the time to decide what actually does matter most to you, let alone make the time to do it."[1]

Sometimes we'd like to be able to just hit "insert" on the toolbar, and click on "hours." But when it comes to real-time time management, we're all dealt the same hand. No matter who you are, you have the same 24 precious hours in a day, 168 jam-packed hours in a week as everyone else. We may not be able to change the natural laws of the universe, but we can learn more about making conscious, productive decisions, and—at the same time—finding the key to balance in our lives.

First, let's really understand what we mean by effective time management. It's simply planning, scheduling, and structuring your time to complete tasks you're responsible for efficiently and effectively. Perhaps you're a natural planner. You crave structure and welcome organizing strategies. Or you may be a person who despises the idea of restricting yourself to a schedule. But no matter which of these categories you fall into, you can improve your time management skills.

Before delving into the details of time management skills, however, let's clarify one important point. There's a sense in which the phrase *time management* is misleading. Let's say you decide to spend an hour reading the assigned short story for your literature class. You may sit in the library with your book propped open in front of you from 3:00 to 4:00 o'clock on the dot. But you may not digest

In truth, people can generally make time for what they choose to do; it is not really the time but the will that is lacking.

Sir John Lubbock, British banker, politician, and archaeologist (1834–1913)

Teaching with Technology Consider Googling to find and showing your students the RSAnimates, "The Secret Powers of Time". The video (as well as other research about college students) emphasizes that success is generally related to future-orientation. Use it to jumpstart the chapter or create a worksheet for small groups to fill out after watching it to get a discussion going.

Sensitive Situation Keep in mind that Derek's hectic life is much like the lives of many of your students. Today 80 percent of college students work at least part-time while attending school. Time management—and devoting enough time to be successful—is perhaps their greatest challenge in college.

Don't confuse activity with accomplishment. 'Time = Success' is a myth.

Dr. Constance Staley, University of Colorado, Colorado Springs

Digital Vision/Getty Images

a single word you're reading. You may be going through the motions, reading on autopilot. Have you managed your time? Technically, yes. Your planner says, "Library, short story for Lit 101, 3:00–4:00 p.m." But did you get results? The quality of what you do is as or more important than the fact that you did it. Time management expert Jeffrey Mayer asks provactively in the title of his book: *If You Haven't Got the Time to Do It Right, When Will You Find The Time to Do It Over?*. Now that's a good question!

No kidding!

It's not just about managing your time, it's about managing your attention. Attention management is the ability to focus your attention, not just your time, toward a designated activity so that you produce a desired result. Time management may get you through reading a chapter of your chemistry textbook, but attention management will ensure that you understand what you're reading. It's about *focus*. Without attention management, time management is pointless.

Succeeding in school, at work, and in life is not just about what you do. It's about what gets done. You can argue about the effort you put into an assignment all you want, but it's doubtful your professor will say, "You know what? You're right. You deserve an A just for staying up late last night working on this paper." Activity and accomplishment aren't the same thing. Neither are quantity and quality. Results count. So don't confuse being busy with being successful. Staying busy isn't much of a challenge; being successful is.

Here's a list of preliminary academic time-saving tips. However, remember that these suggestions won't give you a surefire recipe for academic success. To manage your time, you must also manage yourself: your energy, your behavior, your attention, your attitudes, *you*. Once you know how to manage all that, managing your time begins to work. Here are some suggestions worth trying:

Teaching with Technology Consider showing your students all or part of the TEDTalk by Andy Puddicombe, "All it takes is 10 mindful minutes," about taking 10 minutes each day to do nothing, recollect our thoughts, and thereby reboot our brains. His "juggling exercise" in the video is a memorable object lesson for students.

Teachable Moment Share some of the excuses you have heard from students. Is there really a good excuse? Attendance policies may vary from teacher to teacher, but remind students to plan ahead if they know they will miss a class. For example, maybe they can't miss the rehearsal for a sister's wedding, but if they plan and communicate with their instructors, they're showing they are on top of things, and they will ultimately reduce stress and enjoy the wedding.

Activity Option Have students put their tasks for tomorrow on sticky notes and arrange them in some kind of chronological order. Then have them try moving the sticky notes around to make for the best use of their time.

> **Have a plan for your study session; include time allotments for each topic or task.** Build predictions of how much time you think each assignment will need into your plan, but make adjustments if you get hung up.

> **Capture killer B's.** You're working on Task A and Task B presents itself—perhaps it's a text or an e-mail, something that seems important at the time. Immediately capture the threatening "Killer B" by writing it in a paper notebook that's always by your side. Why paper? If you use an online journal, you'll be tempted to wander further online. You may end up in Timbuktu.com and make countless stops along the way.[2]

Twitter??

> **Keep track of what derails you.** If you come to understand your patterns, you may be better able to control them: *Oops, there I go again. I'm not going to give in to that temptation!* For example, one new pilot study reports that spending too much time on Facebook highjacks valuable study time and impacts your grades. That makes sense; you only have so much attention to spread around.[3]

> **Create activation triggers to eliminate your time-wasters.** If your cell phone is the culprit you turn to whenever you're bored (that is, your schoolwork seems uninteresting or unimportant), move it to another room while you work. When you find yourself bored, you may not want to walk all the way to the other room to get it. You may decide to

continue working instead. It takes three to four weeks to change a habit, experts say, but you have to create the activation triggers.[4]

➤ **If you're working on your computer, work offline whenever possible.** If you must be online to check sources frequently, don't give in to the temptation to check your social networking account or e-mail every ten minutes. Even though you may feel you're being highly productive by taking care of all of your online business at once, you'll end up wasting time in the long run.

➤ **Take two minutes to organize your workspace before beginning.** Having the resources you need at your fingertips makes the session go much more smoothly, and you won't waste time searching for things you need. Be merciless about this one thing, and watch the difference it makes.

➤ **Learn to say no.** Saying no to someone, especially someone you care about, can feel awkward at first, but people close to you will understand that you can't do everything. Life is about choices, and choosing requires the use of the word no. When you face an added task, ask these three questions: Does what you're being asked to do align with your core values? Does it tap into your strengths?[5] Can you actually fit it into your schedule? If not, practice now: "No, thanks." "Sorry, can't do it this time." See? It's not that hard.

I need to work on this!

➤ **Slow down.** As they say, "haste makes waste." Working at something a million miles a minute will most likely result in mistakes, superficial thinking, and poor decisions. Ironically, if you rush, you may run out of time and end up settling for less than your best.

➤ **Actually use a timer.** Forty minutes is thought by some experts to be the optimum amount of time to focus on something before taking a break. It takes thirty minutes to really get in gear, and then you arrive at another ten minutes of optimal productivity. If you aim for more than that, tedium can set in. And use a real, physical countdown timer. When

Never thought of this idea! Check to see if we have one in the kitchen.

> 66
> Speed is the blessing (and the curse) of the modern age. It is our drug of choice. 99

Edward M. Hallowell, M.D.,
Crazy Busy

© 2013 Clayton J. Price.

you hear the "ding," you get a real feeling of accomplishment and a bit of relief from stress. Online timing tools can get buried under layers of other software applications. A real-life timer can force you to face the challenge.[6]

> **Monitor how your life works.** There are different ways to manage time, and different ways work best for different people. Think of this analogy: Is time like ice or like water? A hard copy planner is a day-by-day record of solid blocks of time. But in today's world, solid blocks can melt away in seconds as events around us change. Managing time may be less like moving around chunks of ice, and more like "going with the flow."[7] Or it may work to think of time management as having a realistic "if-then" component: "If I'm still working on my English paper at 3, I'll stop and start on my biology lab."[8] Remember that many dynamic e-tools are also available to help you on a minute-by-minute basis, to help you stay on top of how time flows in your life. Whether it's an automatic, audible reminder from something you've entered into your Google calendar or an electronic "personal assistant" like Siri via your iPhone, these reminder systems can help you manage your obligations.[9]

Energy, Our Most Precious Resource

Challenge: What are ways you can increase your energy throughout the day?

Reaction:

_____

_____

_____

challenge

reaction

Teachable Moment Ask students to give examples of the differences between time management, attention management, and energy management. How are these three things related and how are they different? For example, compare a hypothetical student who a) doesn't plan and runs out of time to write an essay, b) a student who is distracted by a relationship breakup and can't finish an essay c) and a student who stays up all night playing computer games with friends and is too tired to write an essay. All three will be non-productive but for different reasons: time, attention, and energy.

"We live in a digital time. Our rhythms are rushed, rapid-fire and relentless, our days carved up into bits and bytes. . . . We're wired up but we're melting down." So begins a bestselling book, *The Power of Full Engagement: Managing Energy, Not Time, Is the Key to High Performance and Personal Renewal.* The authors, Jim Loehr and Tony Schwartz, have replaced the term *time management* with the term *energy management.* Their shift makes sense. Since most of us are operating in overdrive most of the time, energy is our most precious resource.

Energy management experts say you can't control time—everyone has a fixed amount—but you can manage your energy. And in fact, it's your responsibility to do so. Once a day is gone, it's gone. But your energy can be renewed. It's not just about managing your time or your attention, it's about having enough energy to do what you need to do.

It's clear that some things are energy *drains,* zapping your drive: bad news, illness, interpersonal conflict, bureaucratic hassles, a heavy meal, rainy days. Likewise, some things are energy *gains,* giving you a surge of fresh vitality: a new job, good friends, music, laughter, fruit, coffee. It's a good idea to recognize your own personal energy drains and gains so that you know how and when to

Energy gains:
• working out
• Music
• Taura!!

replenish your supply.[10] Energy management experts say it's not just about *spending time*, it's about *expending energy*:

> *physical* energy
> *mental* energy

> *emotional* energy
> *spiritual* energy

Energy is multi-faceted. Winning a 100-mile cycling competition would leave you physically drained, but mentally sharp and emotionally charged, right?

Of the four dimensions of energy, let's take a closer look at the first two. To do your very best academically, it helps to be *physically* energized and *emotionally* connected. Physical energy is measured in terms of *quantity*. How much energy do you have—a lot or a little? Emotional energy, on the other hand, is measured by *quality*. What kind of energy do you have—positive or negative? If you put them together into a two-dimensional chart with *quantity* as the vertical axis and *quality* as the horizontal axis, you get something like Figure 4.1.

When you're operating in the upper-right quadrant with high, positive energy, you're most productive, which makes sense. The question is: How do you get there? How do you make certain you're physically energized and emotionally connected so that you can do your best, academically?

Get Physically Energized

To make sure you're physically energized, try these suggestions.

1. **Go with the flow.** Have you noticed times of the day when it's easier to concentrate than others? Perhaps you regularly crash in the middle of the afternoon, for example. This is partly due to the patterns of electrical impulses in your brain, alpha rhythms that are unique to each individual.

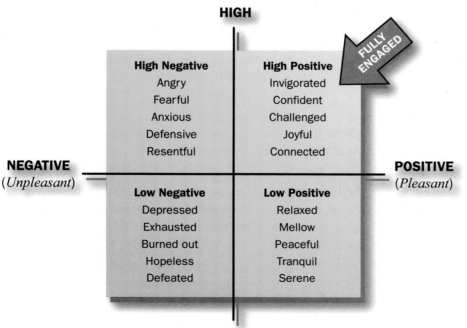

FIGURE 4.1

The Dynamics of Energy[11]

I'm either burned out or zoned out too often in class. I think both of those would be on the low half of this chart . . .

© Larry Harwood Photography, Property of Cengage Learning

> " Performance, health and happiness are grounded in the skillful management of energy. "

**Jim Loehr and Tony Schwartz,
from The Power of Full Engagement**

In other words, everyone has a biological clock. Paying attention to your body's natural rhythms is important. Plan to do activities that require you to be alert during your natural productivity peaks. That's better than plodding through a tough assignment when the energy just isn't there. Use low energy times to take care of mindless chores that require little to no brainpower.[12]

2. **Up and at 'em.** What about 8:00 a.m. classes? Don't use your body's natural rhythms as an excuse to sleep through class! ("I'm just not a morning person. . . .") If you're truly not a morning person, don't sign up for early morning classes. Some students get into the *social* habit of staying up late into the wee, small hours, and then they just can't get up in the morning. Sleeping through your obligations won't do much for your success—and you'll be playing a continual game of catch-up, which takes even more time.

3. **Sleep at night, study during the day.** Burning the midnight oil and pulling all-nighters aren't the best ideas, either. It only takes one all-nighter to help you realize that a lack of sleep translates into a plunge in performance. Without proper sleep, your ability to understand and remember course material is impaired. Research shows that the average adult requires seven to eight hours of sleep each night. If you can't get that much for whatever reason, take a short afternoon nap. Did you know that the Three Mile Island nuclear meltdown in Pennsylvania in 1979 and the Chernobyl disaster in the Ukraine in 1986 took place at 4 a.m. and 1:23 a.m., respectively? Experts believe it's no coincidence that both these events took place when workers would normally be sleeping.[13]

4. **"Prime the pump."** You've heard it before: Food is the fuel that makes us run. The better the fuel, the smoother we run. It's that simple. A solid diet of carbs—pizza, chips, and cookies—jammed into the fuel tank of your car would certainly gum up the works! When the demands on your energy are high, such as exam week, use premium fuel. If you don't believe it, take a look at how many of your classmates get sick during midterms and finals. Watch what they're eating and note how much sleep they're getting, and you'll get some clues about why they're hacking and coughing their way through exams—or in bed missing them altogether.

Get Emotionally Connected

Physical needs count, to be sure, but emotional connections are part of the picture, too. See if you agree with these suggestions.

1. **Communicate like it matters.** Sometimes we save our best communicating for people we think we have to impress: teachers, bosses, or clients, for example. But what about the people we care about most in our lives? Sometimes these people get the leftovers after all the "important" communicating has been done for the day. Sometimes we're so comfortable with these people that we think we can let it all hang out, even when doing so is *not* a pretty sight. Vow to learn more about communicating at your best in valued personal relationships, and then do it. Communicate as if everything you said would actually come true—"Just drop dead," for instance—and watch the difference! Communicating with people we care about is one of our primary vehicles for personal renewal.

2. **Choose how you renew.** Finish this analogy: junk food is to physical energy as _____ is to emotional energy. If you answered ⟨TV,⟩ you're absolutely right. Most people use television as their primary form of emotional renewal, but, like junk food, it's not that nutritious and it's easy to consume too much. Perhaps for you, it's Facebook or surfing the Internet, rather than TV. Try more engaging activities that affirm you: singing or reading or playing a sport.[14]

3. **Let others renew you.** Remember that people don't just make demands on your time, they can provide emotional renewal. There's pure joy in a child's laugh, a friend's smile, a father's pat on the back. These small pleasures in life are priceless—prize them!

Guess I could cut back.

Teachable Moment Research indicates that between watching TV, recreational reading, academic reading, and Internet use, the Internet is traditional students' preferred way to spend time. Find out which of the four categories your students prefer and discuss the implications.

Manage Your Classroom Energy

Think of the implications of what you've been reading about—your energy management—on your in-class performance. When your attention meter is on empty and you can't concentrate on your instructor's presentation, energy management could be the problem—and the solution.

It's hard to manage your attention if you bring "High Negative" energy to class. Realistically, how easy is it to learn when you're feeling angry, fearful, anxious, defensive, or resentful? You may be terrified of the upcoming midterm exam or annoyed at the professor who lectures too quickly by simply reading PowerPoint slides as they whiz by. In order to confront your "High Negative" energy and regain control of your attention, you may need to talk with your instructor. Explain how the course is overwhelming you and ask what you can to do ensure success. Make sure you keep up your end of the bargain, though, and do what you can to lower your "High Negative" energy yourself. If your anxiety is stemming from your own lack of preparation, that's an issue you can fix on your own.

It's also hard to manage your attention if you bring "Low Negative" energy to class. Realistically, how easy is it to learn when you're feeling depressed, exhausted, burned out, hopeless, or defeated? In fact, these are times when some students simply don't come to class, period. But that begins a negative chain reaction. Once you get behind on course material, you become more depressed and hopeless about a positive outcome, and so begins a downward spiral. Even "Low Positive"

NEVER thought about school this way!

Teachable Moment Some students with high positive energy are successful and some are not. What is the difference? Get students talking about situations where they used their high energy to accomplish something positive related to school. Can they also give some not-so-positive examples?

© Larry Harwood Photography. Property of Cengage Learning

> ❝ Make the most of yourself, for that is all there is of you. ❞
>
> *Ralph Waldo Emerson, American author (1803–1882)*

energy can be counterproductive in class. Imagine yourself so relaxed, mellow, peaceful, tranquil, and serene that you zone out and nod off.

Is it possible to have too much "High Positive" energy? What if you're too invigorated, confident, challenged, joyful, and connected? What if you're so thrilled about some exciting news that you can't sit still? As you sit in your seat, some part of your anatomy is continuously moving because of stored-up nervous energy. Things seem to be moving too slowly, and you'd give anything to be able to get up and run around the room. Instead of running around the classroom, run to class or work out beforehand so that you use up some of your spare energy. If you're the kind of person who gets distracted easily, make sure you sit up front. Jump into the discussion by asking questions, and channel your energy into content-related, focused activities. If you find it difficult to manage your attention in a classroom full of friends, meet beforehand for coffee and compare notes on the reading assignment. Do whatever you must to manage your energy productively. It's your responsibility, and it's a vital part of the learning process.

Begin noticing your own energy patterns. Think about the requirements of each day, and the energy that you'll need as you progress from one activity to the next. Working out early in the morning may energize you for the rest of the day. Your most challenging class may temporarily drain you, but after lunch or dinner, you're refreshed and ready to go again.

Finally, although we've focused on physical and emotional energy here, remember that all four dimensions of energy—physical, emotional, mental, and spiritual—are interconnected. If you subtract one from the equation, you'll be firing on less than four cylinders. If you are fully engaged and living life to the fullest, all four dimensions of your energy equation will be in balance. Throughout this book, you'll read about all four dimensions of energy.

Activity Option Give students a chart with times for a full day (twenty-four hours). Have them quickly list their high-energy times. Come together as a group and compare. Are there common times among the group? You should see differences among the students. Now, ask students to volunteer to tell you when they typically study. Are they doing it during peak energy times?

Your TYPE is Showing

What does your psychological type say about your time management preferences? Fill in this quick assessment and find out!

4	3	2	1
Very much like me	Somewhat like me	Not much like me	Not at all like me

1. I am most motivated when I work on active tasks that let me move around or talk to people. (E) _____

2. I avoid tasks that don't fit my own personal value system. (F) _____

3. I don't get around to things I enjoy doing as often as I should. (T) _____

4. I often have to redo work, which takes time, because I've overlooked important details. (N) _____

5. I don't make a schedule; I prefer to be spontaneous. (P) _____

6. I sometimes get locked into a routine, even if it's not particularly productive. (S) _____

7. I have a fairly long attention span and don't mind reading or studying on my own. (I) _____

8. I make schedules and stick to them. (J) _____

9. I work at what's most important first, even if I'd really rather work on something I like. (T) _____

10. I tend to avoid planning and jump right into things even if I make mistakes. (E) _____

11. I like to personalize things I do on my own. (N) _____

12. I prefer e-mail to face-to-face contact when scheduling events with other people. (I) _____

13. I sometimes organize my schedule based on who I'm interacting with. (F) _____

14. I often over-obligate myself with too many commitments. (P) _____

15. I sometimes resist changing my schedule when I should because I already have it so well organized. (J) _____

16. I put-off schoolwork that seems too theoretical. (S) _____

17. I enjoy social connections made in study groups. (E) _____

18. I usually work on the things I like first even if they're not the most urgent. (F) _____

19. I tend to be good at prioritizing and construct schedules that make sense. (T) _____

20. I dislike routines. (N) _____

21. I like to think about things for a while before I get started. (I) _____

22. If I were honest, I'd say I have quite a bit to learn about scheduling and prioritizing. (P) _____

23. I sometimes get bogged down in the details of a project. (S) _____

24. I make schedules and stick to them. (J) _____

Now total your scores for each of the MBTI scales. (There are three items related to each scale.)

Totals: _____ E _____ I _____ S _____ N _____ T _____ F _____ J _____ P _____

High Preference, 12–10   Medium Preference, 9–7   Low Preference, 6 or less

Does your score on this informal time management assessment reflect your SuccessType Learning Style Type Indicator results? All aspects of psychological type can play a role in time management preferences.[15] Take a close look at your scores on the most important scale relating to time management: Judging versus Perceiving. If you scored high on the Judging scale of the MBTI or SuccessTypes Learning Style Indicator, you've probably already bought a planner and have all your upcoming commitments entered—and color-coded, no less.

If you scored high on the Perceiving scale, the words *schedule* and *prioritizing* may not be part of your vocabulary. You just do things when you need to do them, and *most* things get done. The key word in the last sentence is *most*. As you're responsible for more in demanding college classes, what about all the things that will fall into the cracks? That could be a problem, couldn't it?

It's true that some people are natural planners and some aren't. If you're high on the Perceiving scale, you'll have to develop your own coping strategies. Some P's who learn about their preferences make lists for everything. They realize that "Judging" is a requirement for success in most jobs, and they've learned coping mechanisms that serve them well. On the other hand, the spontaneity and curiosity that P's bring to the table can lead to success, too.[16] Take a look at some other possibilities if scheduling doesn't come naturally for you.

1. **Hire a personal assistant.** This advice is mostly facetious, but the principle is a good one. If something isn't a strength of yours, associate yourself with people for whom it is. A friend who can call you and say, "Don't forget that our paper is due Friday" can be a good thing. You don't want to over-rely on people, but perhaps you can learn from them.

2. **Develop a routine that works.** Instead of managing time in increments by scheduling minutes and hours, think in terms of the flow of each day. Perhaps your days go something like this: Exercise → Shower → Class → Lunch → Class → Library → Errands (saved for a low energy time of day) → Dinner → Study. For some people who think in terms of linking events and which order makes the most sense, this approach can work well. There's one caveat— you need to be able to estimate how long each event will take fairly accurately, so that the flow works and you don't run out of time.

3. **Identify one location you can always go to for reminders.** Some people use a well-located whiteboard, notes on the refrigerator, or messages taped to computer screens. Pick one place to go for reminders when you get off track. If you live with other people, you can share this space, and comment on other people's schedules, too.

"I'll Study in My Free Time" ... and When Is That?

Challenge: List all the activities you engage in during an average school day.

Reaction:

_____

_____

_____

Exercise 4.1   Self Assessment—Where Did the Time Go?

Fill in the number of hours you spend doing each of the following, then multiply your answer by the number given (7 or 5 to figure weekly amounts) where appropriate.

Number of hours per day

Sleeping: _____ × 7 = _____

Personal grooming (for example, showering, shaving, putting on makeup):   _____ × 7 = _____

Eating (meals and snacks; include preparation or driving time):   _____ × 7 = _____

Commuting during the week (to school and work):   _____ × 5 = _____

Doing errands and chores: _____ × 7 = _____

Spending time with family (parents, children, or spouse):   _____ × 7 = _____

Spending time with boyfriend or girlfriend: _____ × 7 = _____

Number of hours per week

At work: _____

In classes: _____

At regularly scheduled functions (church, clubs, etc.):   _____

Socializing, hanging out, watching TV, talking on the phone, etc.:   _____

Total = 178
This exercise explains a lot! I ended up 10 hours in the hole—with no studying!

Now add up all the numbers in the far right column and subtract that amount from 168. This is the number of hours you have remaining in your week for that ever-important task of studying.

    Is the number you arrived at too low? Are you already below zero? Start over on this chart, and write in studying first (above the first item—sleeping), before anything else. Then make adjustments elsewhere. How many hours per day should you study, based on how many courses you are taking and how challenging they are? Achieving real success in college takes time!

Ask ten students when they study, and chances are at least eight will reply, "in my free time." The irony in this statement is that if you actually waited until you had free time to study, you probably never would. Truthfully, some students are amazed at how easily a day can race by without ever thinking about cracking a book. This is why you should actually *schedule* your study time, but to do that, you should first be aware of how you're currently spending those twenty-four hours of each day.

Notice that the Exercise you just completed places studying at the bottom of the list, even though it's vital to your success in college. It reflects a common attitude among college students, namely that studying is what takes place after everything else gets done. Where does schoolwork rank on *your* list of priorities?

If succeeding in college is a top priority for you, then make sure that you're devoting enough time to schoolwork outside the classroom. Most instructors expect you to study two to three hours outside of class for every hour spent in class. If it's a particularly challenging class, you may need even more study time. You can use the following chart to calculate the total number of hours you ought to expect to study—effectively—each week:

Credit hours for less demanding classes: _____ × 2 hours = _____ hours

Credit hours for typical/average classes: _____ × 3 hours = _____ hours

Credit hours for more challenging classes: _____ × 4 hours = _____ hours

Expected total study time per week = _____ hours

Remember, just putting in the time won't guarantee that you'll truly *understand* what you're studying. You need to ensure that your study time is productive by focusing your attention and strategically selecting study techniques that work best for you. Even though you're a busy person, like everyone else, remember that truly mastering course material takes time.

[handwritten note in right margin:] World History is my hardest class. Does this mean I should be studying history at least 12 hours per week? Man!

Teachable Moment Increasingly, a time monitor chart such as the one on p. 116 is difficult for students to complete accurately because they spend so much time multitasking. While they may list the primary activity as doing homework, there is great likelihood that they are also checking their Facebook accounts, reading emails, listening to music on their iPods, and texting friends. This exercise may provide a good opportunity to discuss multitasking with your class once again.

Box 4.1   "It's Too Darn Nice Outside" (and Other Lame Excuses for Blowing Off Class)

Do you find yourself skipping class at times in order to do something else: getting an oil change for your car, soaking up the sun's rays, or socializing with some friends you ran into on the way to class? If so, ask yourself this: Would you walk into a gas station, put three $20 bills down on the counter to prepay for a tank of gas, and then put in a dollar's worth and drive off? Absolutely not, you say?

Would you buy a plane ticket for several hundred dollars to see a friend and then just not go because you decided you'd rather do something else instead? No way!

Why, then, would you purchase much more expensive "tickets" to class—the average cost of an hour in class is roughly upwards of $200 per hour—and then toss them in the trash by not attending? Don't you value your money more than that? More importantly, don't you value *yourself* more than that?

The next time you're tempted to opt out of your scheduled classes, ask yourself if you really want to throw away money, in addition to the opportunity. Check your priorities, then put one foot in front of the other and walk into that classroom. In the long run, it's the best investment in your own future.

Schedule Your Way to Success

There is no one right way to schedule your time, but if you experiment with the system presented in this book, you'll be on the right path. Eventually, you can tweak the system to make it uniquely your own. Take an honest assessment of how you currently spend your time and then try following the eight steps to schedule your way into success!

STEP 1: Fill out a "Term on a Page" calendar. There's value in having your entire semester or quarter visible on one single page. You can see where things "clump" together around midterms and finals, and when you'll have extra time to work on larger-scale, longer-term projects. Right up front, create a "Term on a Page" calendar that shows the entire school term on one page. (See Exercise 4.3.) You will need to have the syllabus from each of your classes and your school's course schedule to do this step properly. The following items should be transferred onto your "Term on a Page" calendar:

> Holidays when your school is closed

> Exam and quiz dates from your syllabi

Exercise 4.2 Time Monitor

Can you remember how you spent all your time yesterday? Using the following Time Monitor, fill in as much as you can remember about how you spent your time yesterday from 7:00 a.m. to 10:00 p.m. Be as detailed as possible, right down to thirty-minute segments.

7:00 gym	12:00	5:00
7:30 gym	12:30	5:30
8:00 gym	1:00	6:00
8:30 work	1:30	6:30
9:00	2:00	7:00
9:30	2:30	7:30
10:00	3:00	8:00
10:30	3:30	8:30
11:00	4:00	9:00
11:30	4:30	9:30

Now monitor how you use your time today (or tomorrow if you're reading this at night) on the following Time Monitor. Again, be very specific. You will refer back to this exercise later in this chapter.

7:00	12:00	5:00
7:30	12:30	5:30
8:00	1:00	6:00
8:30	1:30	6:30
9:00	2:00	7:00
9:30	2:30	7:30
10:00	3:00	8:00
10:30	3:30	8:30
11:00	4:00	9:00
11:30	4:30	9:30

Have you ever thought about how many dozens, if not hundreds, of choices you make each day? From the second you wake up, you're making decisions, even about the simplest things, like whether to order a cappuccino or a latté; decaf, half-caf, or high-octane; nonfat, two-percent, or the real deal.

Psychologist and professor Barry Schwartz, in his book, *The Paradox of Choice: Why More Is Less*, believes that making nonstop choices can actually cause us to "invest time, energy, and no small amount of self-doubt, and dread." Choosing a new cell phone plan can take some people weeks while they research models of cell phones, minutes available, quotas of text messages, and Internet access, not to mention the fine print. Simply put: Being flooded with choices, while it feels luxurious, can be stressful and even unrewarding. Paralysis, anxiety, and stress rather than happiness, satisfaction, and perfection can be the result of too much "more."

Some of us, Schwartz says, are "maximizers"; we don't rest until we find the best. Others of us are "satisficers"; we're satisfied with what's good enough, based on our most important criteria. Of course, we all do some "maximizing" and some "satisficing," but generally, which are you?

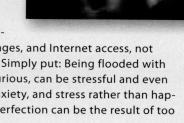

Cardinal/Corbis

Here are Schwartz's recommendations to lower our stress levels in a society where more can actually give us less, especially in terms of quality of life:

1. **Choose to choose.** Some decisions are worth lengthy deliberation; others aren't. Be conscious of the choices you make and whether they're worth the return on your investment. "Maximize" when it counts and "satisfice" when it doesn't.

2. **Remember that there's always greener grass somewhere.** Someone will always have a better job than you do, a nicer apartment, or a more attractive romantic partner. Regret or envy can eat away at you, and second-guessing can bring unsettling dissatisfaction.

3. **Regret less and appreciate more.** While green grass does abound, so do sandpits and bumpy roads. That's an important realization, too! Value the good things you already have going for you.

4. **Build bridges, not walls.** Think about the ways in which the dozens of choices you've already made as a new college student give you your own unique profile or "choice-print": where you live, which classes you take, clubs you join, campus events you attend, your small circle of friends, and on and on. Remember that, and make conscious choices that will best help you succeed.[17]

➤ Project or paper deadlines from your syllabi

➤ Relevant administrative deadlines (*e.g.*, registration for the next term, drop dates)

➤ Birthdays and anniversaries to remember

➤ Important out-of-town travel

➤ Dates that pertain to other family members, such as days that a relative will be visiting—anything that will impact your ability to attend classes or study

STEP 2: Invest in a planner. While it's good to have the big picture, you must also develop an ongoing scheduling system that works for you. Using the "It's all right up here in my head" method is a surefire way to miss an important appointment, fly past the deadline for your term paper without a clue, or lose track of the time you have left to complete multiple projects. Oops!

Teaching with Technology Many students today prefer their cell phones or online tools such as Google Calendar to a hard-copy planner. These can be excellent options. For example, after you enter your schedule into Google Calendar, you will get e-mail or sound alert reminders before each event, or you can sign up to have each day's schedule sent to you. You might consider doing an in-class activity in which students enter their academic schedule for the week into their cell phone calendars. Like any tool, however, students must use it consistently for it to work.

Take a few minutes right now to create your own Term on a Page using the charts provided.

Term _____ Year _____

	Sunday	Monday	Tuesday	Wednesday	Thursday	Friday	Saturday
Month:							

	Sunday	Monday	Tuesday	Wednesday	Thursday	Friday	Saturday
Month:							

	Sunday	Monday	Tuesday	Wednesday	Thursday	Friday	Saturday
Month:							

	Sunday	Monday	Tuesday	Wednesday	Thursday	Friday	Saturday
Month:							

	Sunday	Monday	Tuesday	Wednesday	Thursday	Friday	Saturday
Month:							

Man, I just tried this. The week of midterms is packed. I can't believe it!

> **Take care of your minutes, and the hours will take care of themselves.**
>
> *Lord Chesterfield, British statesman and diplomat (1694–1773)*

Although your instructor will typically provide you with a class syllabus that lists test dates and assignment deadlines, trying to juggle multiple syllabi—not to mention your personal and work commitments—is enough to drive you crazy. You need *one* central clearinghouse for all of your important deadlines, appointments, and commitments. This central clearinghouse could be a hard copy planner, a cell phone app, an online calendar, a web-based tool you sign up for, or something else. What's more important than what you choose is whether or not you use it faithfully! And even though it's good to have everything in one central place, redundancy can help, too. If you lose your cell phone, you don't want your entire life to fall apart! Have a scheduling back-up. Many new college students find that an ordinary paper-and-pencil daily calendar from an office supply store works best. Having a full page for each day means you can write your daily to-do list right in your planner (more on to-do lists later), and that can be a huge help.

STEP 3: Transfer important dates. The next step is to transfer important dates for the whole term from your "Term on a Page" overview to the appropriate days in your planner. This may seem repetitious, but there's a method to the madness. While it's important to be able to view all of your due dates together to create a big picture, it's equally important to have these dates recorded in your actual planner because you will use it more regularly—as the final authority on your schedule.

STEP 4: Set intermediate deadlines. After recording the important dates for the entire academic term, look at the individual due dates for major projects or papers that are assigned. Then set intermediate stepping-stone goals that will ultimately help you accomplish your final goals. Working backward

Teaching with Technology Technology can make many tasks much easier, especially when it comes to academics. Make sure students are aware of the electronic resources available on your campus, including library catalogues and research databases. Give a brief tutorial on how to access these services, and how they offer convenience and efficiency.

> The first hour is the ???? rudder of the day.
>
> **Henry Ward Beecher, 1813–1887, clergyman, social reformer, abolitionist, and speaker**

Imagine yourself off to a great start, impressing everyone, especially your boss, in your long-awaited career after college. But something is gnawing at you. You can't help but notice your stress level inching up. One day, when you power up your office computer, you immediately see 250 new e-mails that weren't there yesterday. A-a-a-a-k!!! When you have multiple projects with deadlines, the bottom line question becomes "Which task do you do first when you're totally overwhelmed?"

Workaholism—that's the answer some people come up with. They come in early, stay late, bring work home, furnish their offices with "sleep-able" sofas, and kill themselves by working around the clock. Our culture seems to admire these "heroes" who try to solve problems by throwing hours at them. But "not only is this workaholism unnecessary, it's stupid. Working more doesn't mean you care more or get more done. It just means you work more."[18]

Instead of working harder, how about working smarter? In the quote above, Beecher's claim is that the first hour sets the course for the day. A rudder is a vertical mechanism at the front of a boat that directs its course. It can either help you get where you need to go or cause you to float aimlessly—or even capsize. If that happens, at the very least, you'll feel frustrated because you don't know how to flip yourself over.

Instead of staying at the office so late that you're doubled over with hunger pangs, try putting a whiteboard on your office wall, and spending the first hour prioritizing your day. Shut the door, turn everything off, and list your goals for the day by creating small boxes to represent your three main projects. Then explore how they can be chunked into smaller

A whiteboard! i'll try it!

subprojects and look for relationships between them and patterns across them. *But then I'll never finish!* you may be thinking to yourself. Actually, you'll be able to *save* yourself time and accomplish much more. Your whiteboard will help you prioritize prioritizing (and no, that's not a typo). You're moving the process of priorizing right up to the top of your to-do list.

By prioritizing first, you're guaranteeing that you'll make greater headway than you would otherwise. You're working smarter, not harder. At the end of the day, you can look back at your "wake" in the imaginary river of your work life, satisfied with how far you've come from the shoreline. As Seneca, a wise man who—believe it or not—lived from 4 BC to 65 AD, said "Love of bustle is not industry [hard work]." We get a rush of adrenaline from the hustle-bustle. We wring our hands over the shocking amount of work we have to do. But that's not the same as the true "high" you get from actually *doing* that real, honest-to-goodness hard work. As someone once said, "Efficiency is intelligent laziness." Figure it out *now*. It's all about working smarter and getting things done.[19]

Think Ahead Why is prioritizing your workload important? What challenges do you see with prioritizing your work? How can you practice prioritizing *now* to develop the skills you'll need in your eventual career?

Cast on Careers

© Larry Harwood Photography. Property of Cengage Learning

FOCUS: How much prioritizing did you do your first semester of college?

KATIE: Oh, that's easy—none. I spent most of my time figuring out excuses for not doing assignments at all. Then I'd panic and do nothing but homework frantically to catch up. But that was an all-or-nothing strategy, alternating between being a slacker and a fanatic, that I wouldn't recommend. It seemed I had no balance whatsoever, and the result was mega stress! But I'm learning how to work smarter by prioritizing. The academic demands are heavy in my major, and you have to come up with a plan to get things done early on.

FOCUS: What are your career plans? Will you benefit from knowing how to prioritize?

KATIE: Absolutely! I'm majoring in nursing. Nurses have to pay attention to many different patients at once. They must also triage, or decide who to treat first; they make life and death decisions on a daily basis. That's just what I'm learning to do with my overwhelming workload. Deciding whether to study chemistry or pharmacology may not be a life and death decision, but it may affect my academic survival! Every day I take stock first thing, and then I feel like I'm making progress and accomplishing real goals as the day goes on.

This is one quote I have to remember...

> Hard work is often the easy work you did not do at the proper time.
>
> **Bernard Meltzer, American radio host (1916–1998)**

from the due date, choose and record deadlines for completing certain chunks of the work. For example, if you have a research paper due, you could set an intermediate deadline for completing all of your initial research or writing a first draft.

STEP 5: Schedule fixed activities for the entire term. Next you'll want to schedule in all fixed activities throughout the entire term: class meeting times and reading assignments, religious services you regularly attend, club meetings, and regular co-curricular activities such as athletics or choir.

STEP 6: Check for schedule conflicts. Now, take a final look at your planner. Do you notice any major scheduling conflicts, such as a planned trip to your sister's wedding smack dab in the middle of midterm exam week? Look for these conflicts now, when there's plenty of time to adjust your plans and talk with your instructor to see what you can work out.

STEP 7: Schedule unscheduled time. Although scheduling unscheduled time in college may seem like a contradiction of terms, it's important! You do need personal time for eating, sleeping, exercising, and other regular activities that don't have a set time frame, and you need some downtime to reenergize. Besides, despite your planner, life will happen. Several times each week, you can count on something coming up that will offer you a chance (or force you) to revise your schedule. The decision of how high the item ranks on your priority list rests with you, but the point is to leave some wiggle room in your schedule. The tech giant Google allows employees "Innovation Time Off," during which they can spend up to 20 percent of their time working on whatever they want (which has led to several great new products such as Google News and Gmail).[20]

Sensitive Situation It's important that we as instructors not tell students what we think is the best kind of planner. Some people do much better with a hard copy daily planner and others prefer the portability of a cell phone. What is important is that students have a plan that works for them and that they stick to it.

Nothing is so fatiguing as the eternal hanging on of an uncompleted task.

William James, American psychologist and philosopher (1842–1910)

Pando Hall/Photographer's Choice/Getty Images

Teachable Moment Some students may read the part about not skipping the review and revise part, and skip it anyway. Ask for some volunteers who are willing to share that they did step 8. Most likely, your J's and S's will volunteer. When students see that someone really did this, and it worked, it may motivate them to try. Another option: require students to send you an e-mail summarizing what they learned about their current time management practices and how they measure up.

STEP 8: Monitor your schedule every day. At this point, you've developed a working time management system. Now it's important to monitor your use of that system on a daily basis. Each morning, take time to preview what your planner has planned for you. Each night, take three minutes to review the day's activities. How well did you stick to your schedule? Did you accomplish the tasks you set out to do? Do you need to revise your schedule for the rest of the week based on something that happened—or didn't happen—today? Don't skip this step. Mentally playing out the day in advance and reviewing afterwards will help you internalize what must be accomplished and help you create a pace for each day. Unless you're willing to take this last step, everything else you do in steps one through seven won't matter!

To Do or Not to Do? There *Is* No Question

Part of your personal time management system should be keeping an ongoing to-do list. While the concept of a to-do list sounds relatively simple, there are a few tricks of the trade. One of the most important to-do list techniques used by top executives is not only listing what needs to be done, generally, but next to it listing the precise goal or purpose.[21] In other words, if your write "read chapter six, history text" in your planner, also write your exact goal, "pay special attention to the section on the fall of the Roman Empire for the midterm exam." The reminder may jog your memory, and you'll be more productive with your time. It's also important to prioritize your to-do list. In terms of Figure 4.2, is reading chapter six an "A," "B," or "C" priority item, especially if your current grade in history is a C- and the midterm exam is tomorrow?

Before the beginning of each school week, brainstorm all the things that you want or need to get done in the upcoming week. Using this random list of to-do items, assign a priority level next to each one. The A-B-C method is simple and easy to use:

A = 7:00 AM meeting at work

B = vet appointment, could delay

C = cycling race deadline

A = must get this done; highest priority

B = very important to get done at some point

C = must do it right away, but it's not an extremely high priority

The two factors to consider when assigning a priority level to a to-do item are *importance* and *urgency*, creating four time zones. Use Figure 4.2 as a guide.[22]

FIGURE 4.2
Time Zones

Important and Urgent: "A" Priorities	Important, but Not Urgent: "B" Priorities
Not Important, but Urgent: "C" Priorities	Not Important and Not Urgent: Scratch these off your list!

Assume this is your to-do list for today (Monday). Assign each item one of the four time zones described earlier: A, B, C (and strike through any items that are not urgent and not important). Finally, renumber the items to indicate which you would do first, which second, and so forth. Outline the criteria you used for making your decisions. For example, did you base your answers on personal priorities, locations (combining tasks based on where you need to do them), urgency/importance, or some other principle? Note that this exercise asks you to put these tasks in order, according to whatever principles from this chapter you choose—not to figure out how to multitask and accomplish several at once! If you choose to call your aunt (5) while writing your essay (11), chances are she'll hear the tapping of the keys and the breaks in the conversation and know exactly what you're doing. It's important to base your choices not only on what's quick or convenient, but also on how much people and priorities mean to you.

Start time: 9:00 a.m., Monday morning, during the second week of the fall term.

1. _____ Return Professor Jordan's call before class tomorrow. He left a message saying he wants to talk to you about some problems with your LIT 101 paper.
2. _____ Pick up your paycheck at McDonald's and get to the bank before it closes at 5:00 p.m. this afternoon.
3. _____ Call the new love interest in your life and ask about going to the party together this weekend before someone else does.
4. _____ Visit the Speech Center to get critiqued on your first speech due Friday. It's closed evenings.
5. _____ Call your favorite aunt. She lives overseas in a time zone seven hours ahead of yours. Today is her fortieth birthday.
6. _____ Stop by the Health Center to take advantage of free meningitis vaccinations today only.
7. _____ Upload the weekend's photos to your Facebook page.
8. _____ Leave a note asking your roommate to please stop leaving messes everywhere. It's really aggravating.
9. _____ Read the two chapters in your History textbook for the in-class quiz on Wednesday.
10. _____ Watch the first episode of the new reality TV show you've been waiting for at 9 p.m. tonight.
11. _____ Write a rough draft of the essay due in your composition class on Thursday.
12. _____ Check with your RA about inviting a high school friend to spend the weekend.
13. _____ Return the three library books that are a week overdue.
14. _____ Call your math Teaching Assistant and leave a message asking for an appointment during her office hours to get help with the homework due on Wednesday. Nearly everyone is confused about the assignment.
15. _____ Go to the campus Athletic Banquet tonight at 6 p.m. to receive your award.

Identify the criteria you used in making your decisions.

> 66
> To do two things at once
> is to do neither.
> 99
>
> *Publius Syrus, Maxim 7, 42 B.C.*

What can I afford to give up? Maybe not work out every day?

After you've assigned a time zone to each item, review your list of A and B priorities and ask yourself:

1. **Do any of the items fit best with a particular day of the week?** For example, donating blood may be a high priority task for you, yet you don't want to do it on a day when you have co-curricular sports planned. That might leave you with two available days in the upcoming week that you can donate blood.

2. **Can any items be grouped together for easier execution?** For example, you may have three errands to run downtown on your to-do list, so grouping them together will save you from making three separate trips.

3. **Do any A and B priorities qualify as floating tasks that can be completed anytime, anywhere?** For example, perhaps you were assigned an extra long reading assignment for one of your classes. It's both important and urgent, an A priority item. Bring your book to read while waiting at the dentist's office for your semi-annual teeth cleaning appointment, a B priority. Planning ahead can really help save time.

4. **Do any priorities need to be shifted?** As the days pass, some of your B priorities will become A priorities due to the urgency factor increasing. Or maybe an A priority will become a C priority because something changed about the task. This is normal.

As for those not-urgent, not-important to-do items, scratch them off the list right now. Life is too short to waste time on unimportant tasks. Give yourself permission to focus on what's important. Since time is a limited resource, one of the best ways to guarantee a successful college experience is to use it wisely. If you don't already use these tools on a regular basis, give them a try.

How Time Flies!

Challenge: What are the most common ways you waste time? What can be done about them?

Reaction:

_____

_____

_____

According to efficiency expert Michael Fortino, in a lifetime, the average American will spend:

> - Seven years in the bathroom
> - Six years eating
> - Five years waiting in line
> - Three years in meetings
> - Two years playing telephone tag

> ➤ Eight months opening junk mail
> ➤ And six months waiting at red lights[23]

What a waste of time! We can't do much about some of these items, but what *can* we do about other time-wasters? Plan—schedule—organize! Think about the issue of control in time management, and write in examples for the following:

1. Things you think you can't control, and you can't: _____
2. Things you think you can't control, but you can: _____
3. Things you think you can control, but you can't: _____
4. Things you think you can control, but you don't: _____
5. Things you think you can control, and you can: _____

Perhaps you wrote in something like *medical emergencies* for (1). You could have written in *family or friends barging into your room* for (2). For (4), maybe you could control your *addiction to social networking*, but you don't. And for (5), perhaps you wrote in *your attention*. You're absolutely right. But what about (3)? Did anything fit there? Are there things you think you can control, but you can't? Try and think of something that would fit into (3), and then think of creative ways you really could control this situation if you tried.[24]

A recent ad for a well-known high-tech company asserts, "You can't control your boss, your workload, your weight, your backhand, your weeds, your dog, your life. At least now you can control your cursor."[25] Actually, you can control more than you think you can control—and if not control, at least manage. Your time, attention, and energy are three of these things. Time-wasters lurk in every corner waiting to steal your scheduled time from you. Watch out! Don't let them spend your time *for* you!

> 66
> We cannot waste time. We can only waste ourselves.
> 99
>
> *George Matthew Adams, newspaper columnist (1878–1962)*

The P Word. Read This Section *Now!* . . . or Maybe Tomorrow . . . or the Next Day . . . or . . .

Challenge: What are the most common reasons you procrastinate?

Reaction:

_____
_____
_____

Picture this: You sit down to work on a challenging homework assignment. After a few minutes, you think, *Man, I'm thirsty,* so you get up and get a soda. Then you sit back down to continue your work. A few minutes later, you decide that some chips would go nicely with your soda and off you go again. Again, you sit down to face the task before you, as you concentrate more on eating than on working. Ten minutes go by and a nagging thought starts taking over: *Must do laundry*. Up you go again and throw a load of clothes in the washer. Before long you're wondering where all the time went. Since you only have an hour left before your next class, you think, *Why bother getting started now? Doing this project will take much more time than that, so I'll just start it tomorrow*. Despite good intentions at the beginning of your work session, you've just succeeded in accomplishing zip, nadda, nothing.

Congratulations! You—like thousands of other college students—have just successfully procrastinated! Researchers define procrastination as "needlessly delaying tasks to the point of experiencing subjective discomfort."[26] And according to researchers, 95 percent of college students admit to procrastinating on their assignments.[27]

You may be in the majority, but alas, in this case, there's no safety in numbers! We're all prone to procrastinate—to put things off until later—from time to time. In fact, in some instances, our society even rewards procrastination: storewide bargains for last-minute holiday shoppers and extended post office hours for income tax slowpokes on April 15, for example. You may think to yourself, if I delay long enough: someone else may do it for me, whatever it was will resolve itself, I can avoid unpleasantness (a difficult encounter with an instructor, for example), or maybe nobody else will do it either, taking some of the heat off.

But academic procrastination is a major threat to your ability to succeed in college. And procrastination in the working world can actually bring your job, and ultimately your career, to a screeching halt. Plenty of people try to rationalize their procrastination by claiming that they work better under pressure. However, the challenge in college is that during some weeks of the term, every single class will have an assignment or test due, all at once, and if you procrastinate, you'll not only generate tremendous anxiety for yourself, but you'll lower your chances of succeeding on any of them.

Before you can control the procrastination monster in your life, it's important to understand *why* you procrastinate. Why is getting started on an assignment difficult until you feel the jaws of a deadline closing down on you?[28] Procrastinators don't tend to be less smart or have a definitive psychological type. They do, however, tend to have lower self-confidence and get lost in their own thoughts.[29] In fact, according to one recent study, procrastination's root cause is a lack of confidence.[30] The reasons for procrastinating vary from person to person, but once you know your own reasons for putting things off, you'll be in a better position to address the problem from its root cause.

The next time you find yourself procrastinating, ask yourself why. Procrastination is self-handicapping: "It's like running a full race with a knapsack full of bricks on your back. When you don't win, you can say it's not that you're not a good runner, it's just that you had this sack of bricks on your back."[31] In addition to understanding why you procrastinate, try these ten procrastination busters to help you kick the habit.

1. **Keep track (of your excuses).** Write them down consistently, and soon you'll be able to recognize them for what they are. Hold yourself accountable. Own your responsibilities—in school and in the rest of your life.

2. **Break down.** No, not psychologically, though sometimes it can feel like you're headed that way. Break your project into its smaller components. A

Teaching with Technology The Internet is obviously an invaluable tool for students, but it can also be a major cause of procrastination. With the ability to check e-mail or visit a Facebook page at the click of the mouse, computers and other devices can be an easy place to get sidetracked. (Recent statistics show, however, that Facebook usage has dropped, for example, because people are realizing how much valuable time it can take up.) Have students consider whether they need to use a computer for the task at hand. If not, it might be best to keep away from it altogether. Students need to know when technology hinders as well as when it helps.

Teachable Moment Ask students to keep track of each time they procrastinate in a given day or week. They may be shocked at the results! Procrastination becomes a habit, and our brains go on autopilot, not even realizing what's going on. The study of habits has become a hot research topic among scholars and popular writers. It's important to call habits into question, and change the cue, routine, and reward cycle in order to change the habit.

Exercise 4.5   Who, Me, Procrastinate?

Procrastination is a habit. It may show up as not getting around to doing your homework (if you don't turn it in, you can't get a bad grade on it—which almost guarantees that you'll get a bad grade on it), not vacuuming the carpet because it takes too much energy to lug the machine around, or not getting to work on time because your job is boring. What about you? Think about the following ten situations, and put a check mark next to each one to indicate the degree to which you normally procrastinate:

		Always	Sometimes	Never
1.	Doing homework	____	____	____
2.	Writing a paper	____	____	____
3.	Studying for tests	____	____	____
4.	Reading class material	____	____	____
5.	Meeting with your academic advisor	____	____	____
6.	Texting/e-mailing a friend	____	____	____
7.	Playing a game/hanging out	____	____	____
8.	Going to see a movie you've heard about	____	____	____
9.	Meeting someone for dinner at a restaurant	____	____	____
10.	Watching TV	____	____	____

If you are like many students, you checked "always" or "sometimes" more often for the first five items than you did for the last five items. But procrastination isn't as simple as not procrastinating when you want to do something and procrastinating when you don't. You may actually hate vacuuming but decide to vacuum the entire house so that you don't have to face studying for a test. There are "layers" of procrastination and many reasons why people procrastinate. Which of these apply to you?

_____ Avoiding something you see as unpleasant   _____ Not realizing how important the task is

_____ Feeling overwhelmed by all you have to do   _____ Reacting to your own internal conflict

_____ Being intimidated by the task itself   _____ Protecting your self-esteem

_____ Fearing failure   _____ Waiting for a last-minute adrenaline rush

_____ Fearing success   _____ Just plain not wanting to

term paper, for example, can be broken down into the following smaller parts: prospectus, thesis, research, outline, small chunks of writing, and bibliography. Completing smaller tasks along the way is much easier than facing a daunting monster of a project.

3. **Trick yourself.** When you feel like procrastinating, pick some aspect of the project that's easy and that you would have to do anyway. If the thought of an entire paper is overwhelming you, for example, work on the bibliography to start. Starting with something—*anything*—will get you into the rhythm of the work.

Good idεa for my history papεr!

4. **Resolve issues.** If something's gnawing at you, making it difficult to concentrate, take care of it. Sometimes you must deal with a noisy room-mate, your kids vying for your attention, or something equally intrusive. Then get down to work.

> Things which matter most should never be at the mercy of things which matter least.
>
> *Johann Wolfgang von Goethe, German writer and scholar (1749–1832)*

Sensitive Situation Note that first-generation students may have serious time management conflicts because their parents do not understand their academic workload and load them up with other family obligations. When a parent asks a first-generation college student to watch a younger sibling during class time, the student is faced with a conflict of interests, and stress levels can increase sharply. Explore ways to cope with these situations with these students, if possible.

5. **Get real.** Set realistic goals for yourself. If you declare that you're going to finish a twelve-page paper in two hours, you're already doomed. Procrastinators are characteristically optimistic. They underestimate how much time something will take. Make it a habit to keep track of how long assignments take you in all your courses so that you can be increasingly realistic over time.

6. **Listen to your self-talk.** Do you say negative things like this to yourself? "I should work on my paper," "I don't want to work on my paper." "I hate having to write this paper," "My instructor is making me do this," "If I just worry about it enough, something will come to me." How much more smoothly would the process go if you said positive things like this? "I will work on my paper" or "I'm choosing to write this paper." As the saying goes, "The difference between 'I can't' and 'I can' is often 'I will.'"[32]

7. **Make a deal with yourself.** Even if it's only spending fifteen minutes on a task that day, do it so that you can see progress.

8. **Overcome fear.** Many of the reasons for procrastinating have to do with our personal fears. We may fear not doing something perfectly, or failing completely—or even the responsibility that comes with success to keep succeeding. But as Susan Jeffers, author and lecturer states, "Feel the fear, and do it anyway!"

9. **Get tough.** Sometimes projects simply require discipline. The best way to complete a daunting task is to simply dig in. Become your own taskmaster, crack the proverbial whip, and force yourself to focus on those things that are high priorities, but perhaps not your idea of fun. The thought of diving into that term paper is overwhelming to you, so you're waiting to be inspired. Bah! If you wait for inspiration, you may wait a long time.

10. **Acknowledge accomplishment.** We're not talking major shopping sprees at Neiman Marcus here. We're talking reasonable, meaningful rewards commensurate with the action completed. Go buy yourself a

Teachable Moment Generate a discussion with your students about the rewards that are most valuable to them. It may be something as simple as spending extra time with someone or having free time to de-stress.

> ❝ If we did all the things we were capable of doing, we would literally astound ourselves. ❞
>
> *Thomas Edison,*
> *American inventor (1847–1931)*

small treat, call your best friend in another state, take a relaxing soak in the bathtub, or do something to celebrate your accomplishments—big and small—along the way. Acknowledgment, from yourself or others, is a great motivator for tackling future projects.

Beyond Juggling: *Realistically* Manage Work, School, and Personal Life

challenge

❝ reaction

Challenge: How do successful people juggle work, school, and personal life?

Reaction:

_____

_____

_____

Your personal time management needs depend on who you are and how many obligations you have. Today's college students are more diverse than ever. Increasing numbers of college students are also parents, full- or part-time employees, husbands or wives, community volunteers, soccer coaches, or Sunday school teachers. How on earth can you possibly juggle it all?

Teachable Moment Keep driving home the point that we do have control of most everything and again, we do have total control of how we respond to something. When we fail, we either give up or pull ourselves up and figure out what to do about it.

The answer? You can't. According to work-life balance expert Dawn Carlson, juggling is a knee-jerk coping mechanism—the default setting when time gets tight and it seems that nothing can be put on the back burner. If you, like millions of others, feel overworked, overcommitted, and exhausted at every turn, you may have already learned that you can't juggle your way to a balanced life. It's impossible.[33]

Think about it. A professional juggler—the kind you find at a carnival—focuses every bit of his attention to keep all the balls in the air. The minute he takes his eye off the ball for even a second, down it goes. It's no surprise that you constantly hear people say, "I dropped the ball" with this or that. Not even real jugglers can maintain their trick forever. In fact, a world-record holder in juggling, Anthony Gatto, was only able to keep nine balls in the air (thrown at least twice without dropping) for a whopping fifty four seconds.[34] That's it! So why do we even try to juggle our many responsibilities 24/7? Let's face it—it's a losing battle.

Now for the good news. Balance among work, school, and personal life is possible. All of us have three primary areas of our lives that should be in balance, ideally—meaningful work (including school), satisfying relationships, and a healthy lifestyle. In addition to work and relationships, we all need to take care of ourselves. See what you think of these five rebalancing strategies. The idea is you can't have it all, but you can have it better than you do now.

1. **Alternating.** If you use this strategy, your work-life balance comes in separate, concentrated doses. You may throw yourself into your career with abandon, and then cut back or quit work altogether and focus intensely on your family. You may give your job 110 percent during the week, but devote Saturdays to physical fitness or to your family or running all the errands you've saved up during the week. Or you save Tuesdays and Thursdays for homework, and go to classes Mondays, Wednesdays, and Fridays. People who use this strategy alternate between important things, and it works for them. An alternator's motto is "I want to have it all, but just not all at once."

2. **Outsourcing.** An outsourcer's motto might be "I want to have it all, not do it all." This strategy helps you achieve work-life balance by giving someone else some of your responsibilities—usually in your personal life—to free up time for the tasks you care about most. If you have enough money, hire someone to clean the house or mow the lawn. If you don't, trade these jobs among family, friends, or neighbors who band together to help each other. Of course, there are ways this strategy could be misused by college students, like downloading your paper from the Internet with a charge card! Warning: This practice will definitely be hazardous to your academic health! In fact, your college career may be over!

3. **Bundling.** This strategy helps you rebalance your life by killing two birds with one stone. Examine your busy life and look for areas in which you can double dip, such as combining exercising with socializing. If your social life is suffering because of time constraints, take walks with a friend so that you can talk along the way. Do your laundry with your roommate so that you can chat about your classes. A bundler's motto is "I want to get more

Teaching with Technology Help students "bundle" tasks by creating content that allows them to combine studying with other activities. Instead of creating a paper handout or review sheet, make a mini-lecture podcast that students can download and listen to while at the gym, in their car, or walking to class. Mini-lectures are a way of condensing information into a "bite-size" package so that students can consume the information at any time.

Take Taura with me to the gym? :)

mileage out of the things I do by combining activities." Bundling is efficient because it allows you to do two things at once.

4. **Techflexing.** Technology allows us to work from almost anywhere, anytime, using technology. If you telecommute from home several days a week for your job, you might get up early, spend some time on e-mail, go out for a run, have breakfast with your family, and then get back on your computer. In the office, you use texting to stay connected to family members or a cell phone to call home while driving to work. Chances are you can telecommute to your campus library and do research online, check in with your professor during online office hours, register for classes online, and pay all your bills online, including tuition. You can use technology, and the flexibility it gives you, to your advantage to merge important aspects of your life. A techflexer's motto is "I want to use technology to accomplish more, not be a slave to it."

5. **Simplifying.** People who use this strategy are ready to cry uncle. They've decided they don't want it all. They've reached a point where they make a permanent commitment to stop the craziness in their lives. The benefit of simplifying is greater freedom from details, stress, and the rat race. But there are trade-offs, of course. They may have to take a significant cut in pay in order to work fewer hours or at a less demanding job. But for them, it's worth it.[35]

These five strategies, used separately or in combination, have helped many people who are dealing with work, school, and family commitments at the same time. They all require certain trade-offs. None of these strategies is a magic solution.

But the alternative to rebalancing is more stress, more physical and emotional exhaustion, more frustration, and much less personal satisfaction. If you focus on rebalancing your life—making conscious choices and course corrections as you go—small changes can have a big impact. Work-life balance isn't an all-or-nothing proposition. It's an ever-changing journey. So take it one step at a time.

> " The trouble with the rat race is that even if you win, you're still a rat. "
>
> *Lily Tomlin, comedian*

Activity Option The five strategies listed here can help students use real-life techniques to balance multiple things. Write these five techniques on index cards, one per card, and make as many sets as you need so that each student in the class has at least three cards. Hand out the cards and ask students to work in pairs or small groups to come up with real-life examples and solutions for the technique on their card to present to the class.

Sensitive Situation You might briefly discuss with your students that it's okay to delegate or ask for help. It is not a sign of weakness.

Time Is Money!

Challenge: What is your attitude toward money? Think of three ways you can get a better handle on your finances.

Reaction:

_____

_____

_____

People say that "time is money." It's true. If you're so efficient with your time that you can call more customers or sell more products, then time does equal money. If your company is the first to introduce a hot new kind of cell phone or a zippy fuel-efficient car, you win. Even if better models come out next year, they may fall flat because people have already invested.

Both time management and money management are key to your college success. Studies show that working too many hours for pay increases your chances of dropping out of college.[36] Many students find themselves working more so

Exercise 4.6 How Fiscally Fit Are You?

Before leaving the subjects of time and energy management, let's look at how you manage your money as well. How good are you at managing your finances? Check one of the three boxes for each statement to get a sense of how financially savvy you are.

	Always true of me	Sometimes true of me	Never true of me
1. At any given moment in time, I know the balance of my checking account.			
2. I use my credit card for particular types of purchases only, such as gas or food.			
3. I pay off my bills in full every month.			
4. I know the interest rate on my credit cards.			
5. I resist impulse buying and only spend when I need things.			
6. I have a budget and I follow it.			
7. I put money aside to save each month.			
8. When I get a pay raise, I increase the proportion of money I save.			
9. I keep track of my spending on a daily or weekly basis.			
10. I don't allow myself to get pressured by others into buying things I don't really need.			

Look over your responses. If you have more checks in the "Never true of me" column than you do in either of the two others, you may be able to put the information you're about to read to good use!

> ❝ I'd say it's been my biggest problem all my life . . . it's money. It takes a lot of money to make these dreams come true. ❞
>
> *Walt Disney, American animator, entrepreneur, and philanthropist (1901–1966)*

that they can spend more, which in turn takes time away from their studies. They may take a semester off from college to make a pile of money and then never come back. While there's evidence that working a moderate amount can help you polish your time and energy management skills, the real secret to financial responsibility in college is to track your habits and gain the knowledge you need to make sound financial decisions.

Exercise 4.7   Create a Spending Log

Take a look at this student's spending log, then complete one for yourself. Money has a way of slipping through our fingers. Choose one entire day that is representative of your spending, and use the chart on the next page to keep track of how you spend money. Write down everything from seemingly small, insignificant items to major purchases, and explain why you made that purchase. Your log may look something like this student's:

TIME	ITEM	LOCATION	AMOUNT	REASON
8–9 a.m.	coffee and bagel	convenience store	$3.50	overslept!
9–10 a.m.	computer paper	office supply store	$2.50	English paper due
10–11 a.m.	gas fill-up	gas station	$65.00	running on fumes!
11 a.m.–12 p.m.	burger and fries	fast-food restaurant	$6.00	lunch on the run
12–1 p.m.	toiletries, etc.	drugstore	$18.00	out of stock
1–2 p.m.	bottled water	convenience store	$2.50	forgot to bring
2–3 p.m.	supplies	bookstore	$12.00	forgot to get earlier
3–7 p.m.	WORK			
7–8 p.m.	pizza	pizza place	$12.00	meet friends
8–9 p.m.	week's groceries	grocery store	$61.50	cupboard is bare!
9–10 p.m.	library fines	campus library	$5.00	forgot!
10–11 p.m.	STUDY TIME			
11 p.m.–12 a.m.	weekend movie, online tickets, DVDs, smartphone apps	Internet retail web-sites, app store	$129.00 $20.00	friend's recommendations, need game apps

(continued on next page)

This student has spent $337 today without doing anything special! When you analyze his expenditures, you can find patterns. He seems to (1) forget to plan, so he spends money continuously throughout the day, (2) spend relatively large amounts of money online, (3) be particularly vulnerable late at night, and (4) spend money grabbing food on the run. These are patterns he should be aware of if he wants to control his spending. He could pack grocery items to save a significant amount of money, for example. Now create your own chart.

TIME	ITEM	LOCATION	AMOUNT	REASON
8–9 a.m.				
9–10 a.m.				
10–11 a.m.				
11 a.m.–12 p.m.				
12–1 p.m.				
1–2 p.m.				
2–3 p.m.				
3–4 p.m.				
4–5 p.m.				
5–6 p.m.				
6–7 p.m.				
7–8 p.m.				
8–9 p.m.				
9–10 p.m.				
10–11 p.m.				
11 p.m.–12 a.m.				

What patterns do you notice about your spending? What kinds of changes will you try to make to curb any unnecessary spending?

The Perils of Plastic

Credit cards—those attractive, little pieces of plastic that make spending money so convenient and so easy. Why go out of your way and make repeated trips to the ATM to get cash when you can just whip out your credit card instead? Now you can even customize your own with a personal photo of you and your beloved Cocker Spaniel, Rusty, or whatever your heart desires. You can spend, spend, spend until you max out. Many students today find debit cards less tempting because they tap your bank account immediately and help you keep track of your spending. But if you already have a credit card or plan to get one, keep this general advice in mind.

1. **Think about the difference between needs and wants.** You may think you need particular things so that your friends will like you ("Hey, let's stop for a burger"), so that you have a new item (like a new car you can't afford), or so that you look fabulous (like pricey manicures). Here's a rule of thumb: If buying something simply helps you move from acceptable to amazing, it's not an emergency. Do you really need a mocha latté every day? A regular old cup of coffee a day sets you back $500 per year!

2. **Leave home without it.** Don't routinely take your credit card with you. Use cash and save your credit card for true emergencies or essentials, like gas and groceries. Do you really want to risk paying interest on today's ice cream cone years from now?

3. **Don't spend money you don't have.** Only charge what you can pay for each month. Just because your credit card limit is $2,000 doesn't mean you need to spend that much each month. A vacation that costs $1,000 will take 12 years of minimal payments to pay off at an 18 percent interest rate. And that $1,000 trip will eventually cost you $2,115!

4. **Understand how credit works.** It's important to know the basics. In one study, 71 percent of new college students had no idea how much interest they were paying on their credit card bills.[37]

   Here are some terms you need to know:

   > **Credit reports.** Your credit history is based on (1) how many credit cards you owe money on, (2) how much money you owe, and (3) how many late payments you make. Bad grades on your credit report can make your life difficult later.

   > **Fees.** Credit card companies charge you in three ways: (1) annual fees (a fee you must pay every year to use the card); (2) finance charges (a charge for loaning you the money you can't pay back when your bill is due); and (3) late fees (for missing a monthly payment deadline). Think about what's most important to you—no annual fee, frequent flyer miles, lower interest rate—and shop around!

   > **The fine print.** How can you learn more? Read your credit card contract carefully. Credit card companies must give you certain important information, which is often on their website. Go to the Federal Reserve website for vital, bottom-line information, and search online to find out more.

5. **Track your expenses.** All kinds of tools—technology-based and otherwise—can help you discover where your money actually goes. To control your spending, use a credit card with caution or use a debit card.

6. **If you're already in financial trouble, ask for help.** Talk to an expert who can help you figure out what to do.[38]

Box 4.2 — Top Ten Financial Aid FAQs

Financial aid. Like all good things, you have to know how it works. You can think of financial aid as complicated and time-consuming, or it can be the one thing that keeps you in school. Take a look at these questions students often ask about the mysteries of financial aid. Most students need financial help of some kind to earn a college degree. Here is some information to help you navigate your way financially.[39]

1. **Who qualifies for financial aid? Almost everyone!** You may not think you qualify for financial aid, but it's a good idea to apply anyway. You won't know until you apply, and some types of aid are based on criteria other than your income and assets.

2. **What does FAFSA stand for?** FAFSA stands for Free Application for Federal Student Aid. You apply online at fafsa.gov, or you can get a copy of the application by calling 1-800-4-FED-AID.

3. **What types of financial aid exist?** You can receive financial aid in the form of scholarships, fellowships, loans, grants, or work-study awards. Generally, scholarships and fellowships are for students with special academic, artistic, or athletic abilities; students with interests in specialized fields; students from particular parts of the country; or students from minority groups. Typically, you don't repay them. Loans and grants come in a variety of forms and from several possible sources, either federal or state government or private organizations. Loans must be repaid, but there are many loan programs to pay down your student loans if you pursue fields such as teaching, nursing, or public service. In addition, if you qualify for a need-based work-study job on or off campus, you can earn an hourly wage to assist in your educational expenses.

4. **When should I apply?** You can apply for financial aid any time after January 1 of the year you intend to go to college, but be mindful of your school's priority filing date to ensure you meet that deadline, as grant funds are limited. The FAFSA will require tax information from the previous year. Remember, you must be enrolled by the start of classes to receive funds.

5. **Do I have to reapply every year?** Yes. Your financial situation can change over time. Your brothers or sisters may start college while you're in school, for example, which can change your family's status.

6. **How can I keep my financial aid over my college years?** Assuming your financial situation remains fairly similar from year to year, you must demonstrate that you're making progress toward a degree in terms of credits and a minimum GPA. Remember that if you drop courses, your financial aid may be affected based on whether you're considered to be a full-time or part-time student.

7. **Who's responsible for paying back my loans?** You are. Others can help you, but ultimately the responsibility is yours and yours alone. If your parents forget to make a payment or don't pay a bill on time, you will be held responsible.

8. **If I leave school for a time, do I have to start repaying my loans right away?** Most loans have a grace period of six or nine months before you must begin repayment. You can request a forbearance or deferment if you need to postpone payments beyond your grace period.

9. **If I get an outside scholarship, should I report it to the Financial Aid office on campus?** Yes. They'll adjust your financial aid package if necessary, but the rules require that scholarships must be processed through the financial aid office.

10. **Where can I find out more?** Your best source of information is in the Office of Financial Aid right on your own campus. Or you can get information online at studentaid.ed.gov. Or call the Federal Student Aid Information Center at 1–800–433–3243, and ask for a free copy of *The Student Guide: Financial Aid* from the U.S. Department of Education.

Now What Do You Think?

insight

action

❶ At the beginning of this chapter, Derek Johnson, a frustrated and disgruntled student, faced a challenge. Now after reading this chapter, would you respond differently to any of the questions you answered about the "FOCUS Challenge Case"? Knowing what you know now, how would you advise him? Write a paragraph ending to the story, incorporating your best advice.

❷ Do you feel that your energy fluctuates throughout an average day? Describe your biological clock. What actions can you take to regulate your physical and emotional energy for the sake of your own productivity?

❸ Here is a list of some of the most common ways students waste time. As you read through the list, check off those that occur in your life most frequently.

___ Unscheduled visitors
___ Phone or text interruptions
___ E-mail obsession
___ Social networking
___ Disorganized workspace/lost items
___ Inability to say no
___ Lack of focus
___ Moving too quickly
___ Procrastination
___ Poor choices
___ Haphazard or, worse yet, a complete lack of scheduling
___ Other people's "emergencies"

If you think time management isn't all that important, but you checked three or more boxes, perhaps the notion of scheduling is sounding more useful. What actions can you take to deal with the issues you marked?

❹ If you feel the need to rebalance your life due to the pressures of managing work, school, family, and friends at the same time, take some time to work through the following Rebalancing Plan worksheet.[40]

Why do I need to rebalance? _____

What rebalancing strategies will I use? _____

How will I do it? _____

How will I let go of _____ ? _____

Tasks that I should completely eliminate: _____

Tasks that I can outsource or give to others: _____

Expectations of others that affect me: _____

Time-consuming possessions or relationships that bring little value to me: _____

❺ Describe your "fiscal fitness." Among the following, which issue do you find most challenging: creating and sticking to a budget, spending money on impulse, digging a credit card hole for yourself, or working too much so that you can spend more? What's your best advice to yourself?

Adapted from K. Sandholtz, B. Derr, F. Buckner, D. Carlson (2002). *Beyond Juggling: Rebalancing Your Busy Life.* San Francisco: Berrett-Hoehler Publishing.

What did you LEARN?

Reality Check

On a scale of 1 to 10, answer the following questions now that you've completed the chapter.

 low   1   2   3   4   5   6   7   8   9   10   high

In hindsight, how much did you already know about this subject before reading the chapter?

Can you answer these questions about managing time, energy, and money more fully now that you've read the chapter?

❶ What's the difference between time management, attention management, and energy management? How are they different, and what do they have in common?

❷ What percentage of college students admit to procrastinating on assignments? Why do they procrastinate?

❸ What percentage of college students with credit cards have no idea how much interest they pay on their credit card bills?

How useful might the information in this chapter be to you? How much do you think this information might affect your success in college? _____

How much energy did you put into reading this chapter? _____

How long did it actually take you to complete this chapter (both the reading and writing tasks)? _____ Hour(s) _____ Minutes

Did you finish reading this chapter? _____
Did you intend to when you started? _____
If you meant to but didn't, what stopped you? _____

Take a minute to compare these answers to your answers from the "Readiness Check" at the beginning of this chapter. What gaps exist between the similar questions? How might these gaps between what you thought before starting the chapter and what you now think after completing the chapter affect how you approach the next chapter in this book?

5 Thinking Critically and Creatively

How this chapter relates to **YOU**

Readiness Check

1. When it comes to thinking critically and creatively in your college classes, what do you find the most challenging, if anything?

Understanding what critical thinking is

Preferring to just Google quick answers

Solving problems

Making decisions

Seeing myself as a creative thinker

2. What is most likely to be your response? Circle it.

| I'll try to learn more about critical and creative thinking. | I'll wait and see how much of this chapter I understand. | I'll actively look for ways to improve my own critical and creative thinking. | Eventually, I'll just figure it out. |

3. What would you have to do to increase your likelihood of success? Will you do it this quarter or semester?

_____

_____

_____

How **YOU** will relate to this chapter

What are you most interested in learning about? Put check marks by those topics.

☐ How critical thinking and creative thinking are defined

☐ How a four-part model of critical thinking works

☐ How to analyze arguments, assess assumptions, and consider claims

☐ How to avoid mistakes in reasoning

☐ How to become a better critical thinker

☐ How to become a more creative thinker

● How motivated are you to learn more about critical and creative thinking in college? (5 = high, 1 = low) _____

● How ready are you to read now? _____ (If something is in your way, take care of it if you can, zero in and focus.)

● How long do you think it will take you to complete this chapter? If you start and stop, keep track of your overall time. _____ Hour(s) _____ Minutes

139

ANNIE MILLER

© Larry Harwood Photography. Property of Cengage Learning

Growing up in a big city was definitely a good thing. So Annie Miller thought, anyway. Every day that went by, she missed L.A. more and more. She missed the fast pace, the diversity, the lifestyle. Why had she decided to go to such a small college after growing up in such a large city? She knew that it was because she wanted every aspect of her life at college to be different. She wanted to live on a different coast, have new friends, and study something exciting. Her huge high school had been amazing in its own way, but now she wanted a more personal education at a place where everyone knew everyone, like at the small liberal arts college she had chosen on the East Coast. When she finally arrived, eager to begin her new life there, she literally jumped for joy!

Her first semester of classes consisted of a college success course, an English composition class, Introduction to Poetry, and Philosophy 100. She was excited by the idea of learning in small classes with wise and learned professors. But Philosophy 100 had turned out to be a very challenging course. Professor Courtney had announced on the first day of class that he believed in the Socratic method of teaching. He taught by asking questions of students instead of lecturing. "Socrates, perhaps the greatest philosopher of all time," he announced the first day, "is the father of critical thinking. In this class, you'll learn to think critically. *That* is what college is all about."

Professor Courtney began every class session with a hypothetical situation and always randomly chose a student to respond. His opening went something like this:

Assume it's Valentine's Day. A young man

© Dan Breckwoort/Shutterstock.com

Philosophy 100 Syllabus

Professor: Dr. Samuel Courtney
Email Address: S.Courtney@univmail.edu
Office Hours: MWF 8am-10am
Office Location: University Hall 1020
Text: "The Big Questions" (7th edition), by Robert C. Solomon and Kathleen M. Higgins

Class Content: As our text suggests, this course will seek to answer some of the "big questions". We will explore ideas about the nature of knowing, free will, logic, and critical and reflective thinking. During this course I encourage you to ask questions and think critically. There is no such thing as a stupid question.

Class Method: Since this is a philosophy class, for our class method we will turn to one of the founding fathers of critical and philosophical thinking: Socrates. Consequently, we will be using the 'Socratic method' when approaching course material. This means that instead of giving a lecture, I will ask you, the students, questions in order to create a lively discussion.

Grading: This course will include 3 exams, each worth 20% of your overall grade. There will also be 5 quizzes during the semester, all of which contribute to another 20% of your grade. Finally, class participation will count for the final 20% of your grade. It is imperative that you attend every class session, and that you are actively participating in class discussions.

Course Outline:
Instead of giving a week-by-week overview of the class, here is a list of the topics we'll be discussing. This way, we can move at our own pace▯ talking in-depth about topics in which we find more interest, and quickly moving past those in which we don't.

- What Philosophy Is
- Greek Philosophy
- Chinese Philosophy
- Ethics
- Enlightenment
- Knowledge
- Skepticism
- Rationalism
- Empiricism
- Idealism and Realism
- Truth

© Cengage Learning

makes a trip to the biggest jewelry store in the mall to buy his fiancée a gift. He's saved up for a long time to afford 24 karat gold earrings and he's ready to choose the best money can buy. He finds the perfect pair and hands over his credit card. But when the salesclerk brings the receipt for him to sign, he notices that instead of $300, she has missed a digit, and the receipt reads $30. He now faces a dilemma: Does he sign and say nothing, or point out the error and pay the full amount? What should he do?

One student responded with, "He should sign his name and then take off quickly. This mistake was the clerk's, not his. If someone catches the mistake later, he can just claim he didn't notice. Maybe no one will ever figure it out, and he'll be $270 richer!" Professor Courtney continued, "On what ethical principle do you base your response?" The student faltered, and the professor moved on to someone else, raising other points that hadn't been considered.

"But what if his fiancée decides to exchange the earrings for another pair? What if the clerk is fired for making a $270 mistake? What if the clerk were your sister or your best friend? What if the hero of a movie did what you're proposing? What if the clerk were you?" he continued. "What would Socrates say about what you should do? According to Socrates, no one errs intentionally. This means that whenever we do something wrong—including something *morally* wrong—it is out of ignorance rather than evil motives. If the young man decides to capitalize on the clerk's error, what are

his motives—and are they evil? What would be the *right* thing to do?"

Professor Courtney continued putting students on the spot and raising questions posed by other philosophers they were studying. The questions seemed endless. Annie found herself listening more carefully than in her other classes so that she would be ready to jump in if called upon. And she silently thought through others' answers, too. Even though she had to admit that the learning environment was stimulating, speaking in front of other students made Annie nervous.

"There aren't always right answers," Professor Courtney told them. "What's important is thinking through the problem. The process of learning to think can be more important than the answer itself."

Frankly, that explanation didn't sit well with Annie. *If there aren't right answers, what am I doing in college? Things should be black and white, true or false, right or wrong. I'm paying tuition to hear what the professor thinks, not all the other students in class. He knows the right answers. Why doesn't he just tell us?*

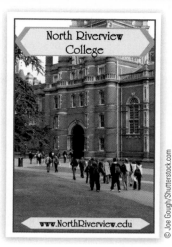

Without fail, Annie always left Professor Courtney's class with a headache from thinking so hard. Her best friend Hannah suggested that she look up his online ratings to find out what other students had said about him. "If his ratings are bad," she said, "just drop the course. At the very least you'll find out if there are secrets to getting an A in his class." But when Annie did that, she found mostly glowing praise: "I thought he was an impossible teacher at the time," wrote one student, "but he really taught me to think. Now I'm grateful!"

Compared to Philosophy 100, all her other classes seemed effortless. She had to admit that she much preferred classes in which she could express herself creatively, like Introduction to Poetry.

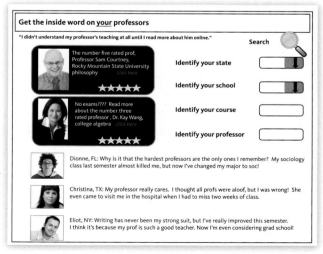

❶ Do you agree with Professor Courtney's statement that "there aren't always right answers"? If that's true, why is getting a college education so important?

❷ Even though Professor Courtney's teaching methods made her nervous, why did Annie find the learning environment in his class to be stimulating?

❸ Annie says she prefers creative thinking to critical thinking. Are they two different things? Why or why not?

❹ Identify three things Annie should do to get the most from Professor Courtney's class.

Rethinking Thinking

Challenge: What's the difference between thinking and critical thinking?

Reaction:

_____

_____

_____

Activity Option Robert Sternberg defines four kinds of thinking that college students need to develop: analytical, creative, practical, and wise and ethical. "Individuals need creative thinking to generate new ideas, analytical thinking to ascertain whether their ideas are good ideas, practical thinking to implement their ideas and convince others of their value, and wise and ethical thinking to ensure that their ideas help to achieve a common good." If you want to take this chapter further, discuss all four and decide which ones are introduced in Annie Miller's case study. Or write short scenarios college students may face on index cards and ask students to work in groups to put them into the four categories.

Teachable Moment The book, *Academically Adrift*, reports that most college students make little progress in their critical thinking skills from entry to graduation. Although some experts argue with the authors' methodology and results, you might pose this controversy to your students. Do they expect college to sharpen their critical thinking skills? How will they know whether their critical thinking skills are improving? Can they provide any examples?

Thinking is a natural, ongoing, everyday process we all engage in. In fact, we can't really turn it off, even if we try. We're always on. Some of your college instructors will claim that higher education will teach you to think. But what do they mean? Everyone thinks all the time, right? It happens any time you talk to yourself, doesn't it? However, some experts say school teaches us how to regurgitate, not how to think. Perhaps your instructors are onto something.

Picture this: You're in the library. It's late, and you're tired. You're supposed to be studying for your political science test, but instead of thinking about foreign policy, your mind begins drifting toward the foreign vacation you took last summer, how tan you were when you returned, how much fun it was to be with your best friends, and where you'd like to visit next.

Would the mental process you're engaging in while sitting in the library be called *thinking*? For our purposes in this chapter, the answer is no. Here thinking is defined as a focused cognitive activity you engage in for a reason. You direct your thoughts toward a particular topic. You're the *active* thinker, not the *passive* daydreamer who is the victim of a wandering mind. Focused thinking is deliberate and intentional, not haphazard or accidental. You choose to do it for a reason.

Did you know that developing your critical thinking skills goes hand in hand with developing overall academic abilities as a college student? According

'Knowledge is power.' Rather, knowledge is happiness. To have knowledge, deep broad knowledge, is to know truth from false and lofty things from low.

Helen Keller, American author, activist, and lecturer (1880–1968)

to thinking experts like William Perry, who interviewed 400 men in academic difficulty at Harvard roughly fifty years ago, students develop intellectually along a scale. Early on, most students view the world in terms of right or wrong, good or bad, black or white. They see teachers as having the right answers, and students getting the right answers from teachers.

Later they come to understand that knowledge depends on many factors. They no longer wait for the "truth" to be handed down by instructors. Instead, they begin to value their own and others' opinions and perceive multiple points of view as valid. Toward the end of their college careers or in graduate school, students develop their own personal values, recognize that not all views are equal (some are better than others), and learn how to select the best alternative. The point is that your critical thinking skills are developing as you go. Rarely does anyone have already fully developed critical thinking skills as a new college student.[1]

Focused thinking is like a two-sided coin. Sometimes when you think, you *evaluate* ideas—your own or someone else's. That's *critical* thinking. The word critical comes from the Greek word for *critic (kritikos)*, meaning "to question or analyze." The other side of thinking comes when you *produce* ideas. That's what this chapter calls *creative* thinking, and that's something we'll deal with later. When you're thinking critically, you're asking questions, analyzing arguments, assessing assumptions, considering claims, avoiding mistakes in reasoning, problem solving, decision making, and all the while, thinking about your thinking. Which type of thinking is most important, not only to your college success but also to your career success in the future: critical or creative? The answer is both!

Teaching with Technology For an array of complimentary teaching resources about critical thinking, go to the college and university faculty page of the "Critical Thinking Community" website. Also check out Idea Paper #37 from The Idea Center, a non-profit organization (originally connected to Kansas State University) with many online faculty development resources for in-class applications.

Diversity Discussion To some students, the word "critical" implies judging. Movie critics, for example, judge whether or not a movie is worth seeing. Discuss the actual meaning of "critical" in this context—that it doesn't mean looking down on individuals, particularly those with different backgrounds, ethnicities, religious views, or sexual orientations, for example, and then being able to "defend" your views with some sort of evidence. It's important that they fully understand the meaning of the term "critical" in order to gain as much as possible from this chapter.

> 66
> What we need is not the will to believe, but the will to find out.
> 99

Bertrand Russell, British philosopher, logician, and mathematician (1872–1970)

I KEEP HEARING ABOUT CRITICAL THINKING IN ALL MY CLASSES, BUT I HAVE NO IDEA WHAT IT IS!

What Is Critical Thinking?

Teaching with Technology You might want to show a portion of Michael Shermer's highly provocative TED TALK presentation: Why People Believe Strange Things.

Teachable Moment Ask students if they believe in ESP, astrology, UFOs, or lucky numbers, for example. If so, why do they? How did they come to trust these things? What evidence do they have? Suggest to students that these are some good topics for research papers, and how they might want to explore more. Don't assume that you, or they, really know the answers without fully researching and critically examining the arguments.

Sensitive Situation Keep in mind that we are all products of our environments. Students who have less tolerance for differences, for example, have most likely been raised in homes where there is little tolerance. As instructors, it is not our job to judge, but to help students open their minds to broader ways of thinking.

YEAH, I CAN'T BELIEVE HOW SUPERSTITIOUS SOME PEOPLE ARE!

Teachable Moment Remind students that if they had graduated five years ago with a degree in computer science, for example—or even art—what they learned then would have changed or would be enriched by new knowledge now. Learning how to think allows individuals to be lifelong learners who can take new knowledge and figure out how to combine it with knowledge they already have.

Critical thinking is a particular kind of focused thinking. It is purposeful, reasoned, and goal-directed. It's thinking that aims to solve problems, calculate likelihood, weigh evidence, and make decisions.[2] In that sense, movie critics are critical thinkers because they look at a variety of standards (screenplay, acting, production quality, costumes, and so forth) and then decide how a movie measures up. When you're thinking critically, you're not just being critical. You're on the lookout for both faults and strengths. You're looking at how things measure up.[3]

Critical thinkers develop standards they can use to judge advertisements, political speeches, sales pitches, movies—you name it.[4] Critical thinking is not jumping to conclusions; buying arguments lock, stock, and barrel; accepting controversial ideas no matter what; or ignoring the facts.

Unfortunately, some people are noncritical thinkers. They may be biased or closed-minded. Other people are *selective* critical thinkers. When it comes to one particular subject, they shut down their minds. They can't explain their views, they're emotional about them, and they refuse to acknowledge any other position. Why do they believe these things? Only if they understand the *why*, can they explain their views to someone else or defend them under fire. The importance of *why* can't be overstated. Some people, of course, have already thought through their beliefs, and they understand their positions and the reasons for them very well. Arriving at that point is the goal of anyone who wants to become a better critical thinker.

In order to develop your critical thinking skills, you must pay attention to the processes and products of your own thoughts. You must become conscious of the way you think and develop a habit of examining the decisions you come to.[5] When your critical thinking skills are well developed, they actually play a role in everything you do. You exist in a state of "critical being."[6]

Here is a list of reasons why it's important to improve your critical thinking skills. Beside each entry, mark the degree to which you'd like to concentrate your efforts as a college student, soon ready to enter a new career path. Then read on for more strategies to incorporate critical thinking into your life. On a scale from 1 to 10 with 10 representing the highest degree, would you like to:

Activity Option Before discussing this exercise in class, give students five minutes to write down this sentence: Thinking critically is "critical" to lifelong success because _____. Have students fill in the blank. Make a class list and come to some conclusions about why critical thinking is important—it's really connected to lifelong, self-directed (*I figured it out!*) learning.

I PUT 10's ON EVERYTHING, BUT I REALLY THINK 1 AND 5 ARE IMPORTANT.

Teaching with Technology As an information "consumer," learning to interpret the Internet can include more than standard websites. Have students look at blogs, videos, podcasts, or even social networking pages. How are these sources different from traditional text-based websites? How might the entertainment value of a source affect credibility? Have students think about the pros and cons of these different types of Internet media.

Teachable Moment Keep in mind that students may put 10's next to all of these because they sound like good ideas. Regardless, generate a discussion of why they value some results of good critical thinking over others, especially at this particular point in their lives.

1. _____ **Become a more successful college student?** Most college courses require you to think critically (in answering essay questions, for example). In one study of over 1,100 college students, higher scores on critical thinking skills tests correlated highly with better grades.[7] Another study indicates that the more control you believe you have over your academic success, the more likely you are to use your critical thinking skills—and vice versa.[8] There's even evidence that interaction with other students in co-curricular activities can help you develop as a critical thinker.[9] If you participate in a debate, serve as a panelist, organize a campus event, work on a campaign—all experiences outside the classroom—you can sharpen your ability to think critically, too.

2. _____ **Become a better citizen?** Critical thinking is the foundation of a strong democracy. Voters must think critically about candidates' messages and their likelihood of keeping campaign promises. It's easy to talk about balancing the budget, or improving education, but the truth is these highly complex tasks are very challenging to carry out. The American public must sift through information and examine the soundness of politicians' arguments in order to keep our democracy strong.

3. _____ **Become a better employee?** A workforce of critical—and creative—thinkers helps the American economy thrive and individuals become more successful. The U.S. Department of Labor reports that today's jobs require employees who can deal with complexity, learn and perform multiple tasks, analyze and deal with a wide variety of options, identify problems, perceive alternative approaches, and select the best approach.[10] Employers are "practically begging" for employees who can "think, collaborate, communicate, coordinate, and create."[11]

4. _____ **Become a more savvy consumer?** In today's marketplace, everyone wants your dollars. If you acted on every ad you see on the Internet or watch on television, you'd run out of money very quickly. You're told you need whitened teeth, colored hair, softened skin, strong mouthwash, and a host of other things in order to be attractive. Critical thinking will help you evaluate offers, avoid slick come-ons, and buy responsibly.

5. _____ **Build stronger relationships?** Critical thinking helps us understand our own and others' actions and become more responsible communicators. Whether with friends or romantic partners, relationships take work. Sometimes you have to figure out what your partner really means or listen between the lines for important clues. You have to persuade your partner that you're right about something or convince him or her to act on a request. Actually, critical thinking is at the heart of every relationship you care about.

6. _____ **Become a lifelong learner?** Your education doesn't end when you get your diploma. In many ways the real exams begin afterward when you put your classroom learning to the test. And in today's world you must continue to learn as you transition through jobs to give your life more meaning—personally and professionally. You'll need to keep expanding your skills, no matter what your career is. Innovation and change are the watchwords of today's workplace, and continual learning is the only way to survive and thrive.

Box 5.1 **Asking Questions: Inquiring Minds Want to Know**

Here's something worth knowing: Good thinkers are good questioners. They're always asking, "who," "what," "why," and "how." "Who says so?" "What is he trying to convince me of?" "Why is he trying to influence me?" "How is he trying to do it?" Critical thinkers know how to uncover the truth by asking questions, and they realize that the kind of questions they ask is important. They move beyond the most basic, most obvious questions and stretch their minds to maximize their learning.

The Question Pyramid is an interesting way of looking at focused thinking (see Figure 5.1). As you move up the pyramid, formulating and answering questions become increasingly difficult.

> Level 1 questions are observable, obvious, and one-dimensional. They can be answered with a yes or no answer: "Do philosophers study critical thinking?" Not too challenging.

> Level 2 questions are slightly more challenging. They consist of the standard who and what questions, like, "What is critical thinking?" Level 2 questions are straightforward. They could be answered by memorizing a section of the textbook or Googling the answer.

> Level 3 questions require actual critical thinking, "Why is critical thinking studied by philosophers?" You'd need to develop your answer by thinking about possibilities, selecting a response, and backing it up with evidence.

> Level 4 questions require creative thinking, a subject for discussion later in this chapter, "What if no one could think critically? What would societies be like?" "How do you balance critical thinking and creative thinking?" Formulating answers to level 4 questions requires you to think for yourself and come up with your own unique, creative responses.

When you're asking questions instead of answering them, it's easy to get stuck at level 1 or 2, but with effort and a true understanding of how to ask questions, you can challenge yourself to learn more. In fact, most of your college courses will require this of you. So get a head start: After listening to a lecture, create a list of questions to see if you really understand the material. After reading an assigned chapter, create a list of questions to see how much you've digested. Understand the kind of questions you're asking, and move up the pyramid to improve your thinking skills.[12]

LEVEL 4 QUESTIONS SOUND HARD, BUT ACTUALLY PRETTY INTERESTING . . .

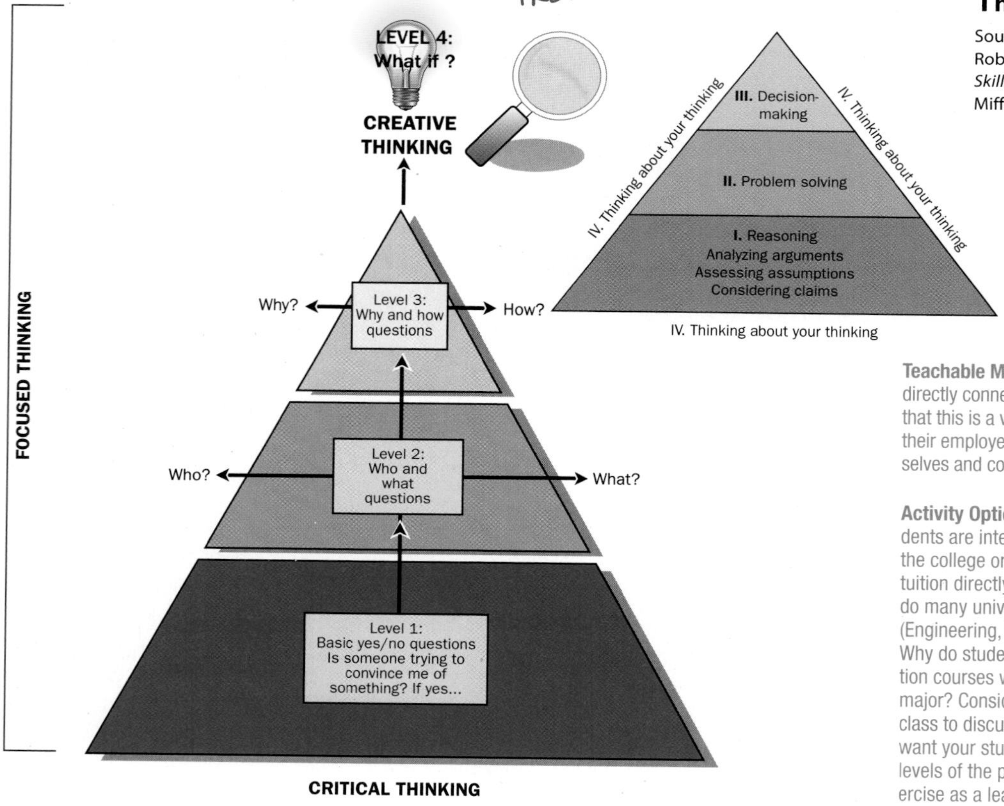

FIGURE 5.1

The Question Pyramid

Source: Adapted from Hellyer, R., Robinson, C., & Sherwood, P. (1998). *Study Skills for Learning Power*, p. 18. Houghton Mifflin Company.

Teachable Moment Level 3 and 4 questions are directly connected to lifelong learning. Remember that this is a vital skill that employers want from their employees—the ability to think for themselves and come up with creative alternatives!

Activity Option One thing some first-year students are interested in is the inner workings of the college or university they're attending. Does tuition directly pay instructors' salaries? Why do many universities include different colleges (Engineering, Education, Arts and Sciences, etc.)? Why do students have to take General Education courses when they are there for a particular major? Consider inviting a top administrator to class to discuss questions like these. You may want your students to create questions at all levels of the pyramid and use this hands-on exercise as a learning tool.

A Four-Part Model of Critical Thinking

Like your writing or speaking skills, well-cultivated critical thinking skills can serve as the infrastructure for taking on all of your academic challenges. But let's ask an important question: How do you do it? We'll look at the four primary components of critical thinking, and later in this chapter, we'll use a realistic news story, one that is relevant to many college campuses, to allow you to apply what you've learned and provide a memorable example. Take a look at Figure 5.2 to preview the four-part model of critical thinking.

I. Reasoning: The Foundation of Critical Thinking

Reasoning, the foundation of critical thinking, is the ability to come to a conclusion based on one or more arguments. A strong argument is convincing because it backs up its claim with evidence. If no one would disagree with what you're saying, it's not an argument. It's self-evident. "Grass is green" is not an argument. But "Cows that are grass-fed make the best meat" (if supporting

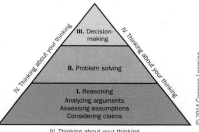

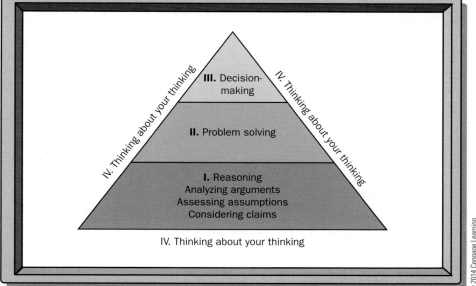

FIGURE 5.2

Critical Thinking Is Focused

Here's a four-part model of critical thinking. Your reasoning skills underlie everything. They are the foundation upon which your problem-solving and decision-making skills rest, and your metacognitive skills, or thinking about your thinking, surround all the focused thinking you do.

> ❝ The important thing is not to stop questioning. ❞

Albert Einstein, theoretical physicist (1879–1955)

evidence is provided) is. Do you see the difference? Because reasoning is the foundation for critical thinking, we'll concentrate much of our discussion there.

How good are you at creating a sound argument? Let's say that you're trying to convince your roommate to stop inviting people into your room while you're studying for major exams. What evidence would you use to convince her? How good are you at evaluating someone else's argument? For example, you're trying to decide whether an online discount is really a good deal. Would you take the advertiser's word for it or do some research to compare prices on your own? Throughout the rest of this chapter, ask yourself: Are there ways I can improve my reasoning skills?

Analyzing Arguments

challenge

❝ **reaction**

Challenge: What does the term *argument* have to do with critical thinking? Give an example of a "sound" and an "unsound" argument you have heard or read recently.

Reaction:

_____

_____

_____

I LOVE THIS YOUTUBE VID!

Teaching with Technology Watch the YouTube of this *Monty Python* sketch in class. After viewing it, divide the class into two groups to discuss the difference between an argument as defined in this chapter and a contradiction.

Activity Option Play the "How Do I Know This Is True?" game. Bring in some headlines from the student or local newspaper. Put them on a PowerPoint slide or overhead, and show them to the class. Go around the room and have students fill in the following: I know this is true because _____. Any student can say "NOT" and then explain why it is not true. If it is true, and no one challenges, students just keep adding to why it's true.

Have you ever seen the *Monty Python Flying Circus* "Argument Clinic Sketch"? In this bizarre skit a man comes to an "argument clinic" to buy an argument. The two arguers—"professional" and customer—engage in an interminably long, "yes, it is" "no, it isn't" squabble.

Critical thinking is about arguments. But when most of us think of an argument, that's the kind of bickering we think of, and having a negative view of what the term "argument" means can actually impair your critical thinking skills.[13] In the middle of the "Argument Clinic" sketch, however, the customer actually makes an important point. He protests that they're not really arguing; they're just contradicting each other. He continues, "An argument is a connected series of statements intended to establish a proposition." That's the kind of argument that's related to critical thinking.

Critical thinking is about an argument that *one* person puts forth. Attorneys—for both the prosecution and defense—put forth their closing arguments at the end of a trial. A politician puts forth an argument about where he stands on the issues. A professor puts forth an argument to persuade her class to learn important content in her discipline.

> Everyone is entitled to their own opinion, but not their own facts.

Senator Daniel Patrick Moynihan (1927–2003)

Arguments are said to be inductive or deductive. *Inductive* arguments go from specific observations to general conclusions. In criminal trials, the prosecution puts together individual pieces of evidence to prove that the defendant is guilty: eyewitnesses put him at the scene, the gun store salesman remembers selling him a pistol, and his fingerprints are on the weapon. Therefore, the prosecutor argues that the defendant is guilty. Other arguments are said to be *deductive*, meaning they go from broad generalizations to specific conclusions. All serial killers have a particular psychological profile. The defendant has this psychological profile. Therefore the defendant is the killer.

What do arguments do? They try to persuade. Arguments contain clear reasons to believe someone or something. Once you understand what an argument is, you must also understand that arguments can be sound or unsound. If I tell you that two plus two equals four, chances are good that you'll believe me. If, on the other hand, I tell you two plus two equals five, you'll flatly deny it. If I say "Cats have fur." "Dogs have fur." "Therefore dogs are cats," you'll tell me I'm crazy—because it's an unsound argument.

The standard we use to test the soundness of arguments is logic, which is a fairly extensive topic. Let's just say for our purposes here that arguments are sound when the evidence to support them is reasonable, more reasonable than the evidence supporting other opinions. The important point is that a sound argument provides at least one good reason to believe. Let's look at an example:

> I don't see why all first-year students have to take Freshman Composition. It's a free country. Students shouldn't have to take courses they don't want to take.

Based on our definition, is this example an argument? Why or why not? Is the statement "It's a free country" relevant? What does living in a free country have to do with the curricula in colleges and universities? Nothing. *Relevancy* is a condition needed for a sound argument.

Sensitive Situation Students who are not very assertive may not like the word *argument* and see all arguments as confrontational. Help students see that it is really okay to persuade or challenge and that it is one of the hallmarks of good thinking.

> Only when we know a little do we know anything; doubt grows with knowledge.

Johann Wolfgang von Goethe, German writer and scholar (1749–1832)

Now look at this example:

I don't see why all first-year students have to take Freshman Composition. Many students developed good writing skills in high school, and their Verbal SAT scores are 600 or higher.

Is this second example an argument? Why or why not? The first example doesn't give you a good reason to believe the argument; the second example does. A true argument must contain at least one reason for you to believe it.

Here's another warning. Not everything that sounds like an argument is one. Look at this example:

Everyone taking Calculus 100 failed the test last Friday. I took the test last Friday. Therefore, I will probably get an F in the course.

Is that a sound argument—or is something missing? Even though all three sentences may be true, they don't constitute a sound argument. What grade has this student earned on earlier calculus tests? How many tests are left in the course? The information present may not be adequate or enough to predict an F in the course. *Adequacy* is another condition needed for a sound argument. This alternative, on the other hand, is a sound argument:

Everyone taking Calculus 100 failed the test last Friday. I took the test last Friday. Therefore, I earned an F on the test.

When you're deciding on the soundness of an argument, you must look for two things: *relevance* and *adequacy*.[14]

Not all arguments are sound. Have you ever heard this tale? A scientist decided to begin a new study to find out what makes people drunk. He planned an orderly, methodical experiment. On Monday night, he drank three tall glasses filled half and half with scotch and water. The next morning, he recorded his results: intoxication. On Tuesday night, he drank three tall glasses of whiskey and water. On Wednesday night, he drank three tall glasses of rum and water. On Thursday night, he drank three tall glasses of vodka and water. Each morning, the results he recorded were identical. He had become highly intoxicated. His faulty conclusion? Water makes people drunk.

Not only is it important to be able to construct sound arguments, but it's also important to be able to recognize them. As a consumer in today's information society, you must know when to buy into an argument, and when not to.

Assessing Assumptions

Posing as an addled social critic, Jonathan Swift wrote the words you see to the left centuries ago, even though they sound as if they could have been written now. Intellectual laziness among some people continues to be a problem even today.

When you're thinking critically, one of the most important kinds of questions you can ask is about the *assumptions* you or someone else are making, perhaps without even realizing it. Assumptions can limit our thinking. Consider these three well-known

> " Few people think more than two or three times a year. I have made an international reputation for myself by thinking once or twice a week. "

George Bernard Shaw, Irish literary critic, playwright, and essayist, 1925 Nobel Prize for Literature (1856–1950)

FUNNY EXAMPLE OF AN UNSOUND ARGUMENT!

> " We of this age have discovered a shorter and more prudent method to become scholars and wits, without the fatigue of reading or of thinking. "

Jonathan Swift, from A Tale of a Tub, 1704

puzzles, and afterward, examine how your assumptions may have interfered with solving them.

Teachable Moment Students love challenging logic puzzles like these. Ask students if they have any to share. Offer extra credit to any student who brings in one for the next class.

1. One day Kerry celebrated her birthday. Two days later her older twin brother, Harry, celebrated his birthday. How could that be?

2. A boy and his father are injured in a car accident. They're both rushed to the hospital, but the father dies. The boy needs surgery, so a physician is called in. The surgeon rushes into the operating room, takes one look at the boy, and gasps. "I can't operate on this boy," the surgeon says. "He's my son." How can this be?

3. A woman from New York married ten different men from that city, yet she did not break any laws. None of these men died, and she never divorced. How was this possible? *??? Got me on this one . . .*

You may have solved these puzzles if you were willing to question the underlying assumptions that were holding you back. For puzzle 2, for example, you may have assumed that surgeons are usually male, not female, and been temporarily stumped by the question. (Answers are upside down at the bottom of this page.)

People reveal their underlying assumptions in what they say. If you listen carefully, you can uncover them. "Go on for a graduate degree after I finish college? No way! I'm out of here in four years, no matter what!" This student's underlying assumption is that college itself isn't as important as what comes afterward (like making money). This student may just tolerate her classes without getting engaged in the subject matter, and she checks off requirements as quickly as she can. Too bad. Getting a college education can be a wonderfully exciting experience in and of itself!

Considering Claims

Evaluating claims is one of the most basic aspects of reasoning. A claim is a statement that can be true or false, but not both. This is different from a fact, which cannot be disputed. What's the difference between a *fact* and a *claim*? Facts can't be disputed; claims can be true or false, but they must be one or the other, not both.

> FACT: Ronald Reagan, George H. Bush, and Bill Clinton have been presidents of the United States during the last thirty years.
>
> CLAIM: Bill Clinton was the most popular American president in the last thirty years.

The fact is obvious. The claim requires evidence to support it. As a critical thinker, it's important to use your reasoning skills to evaluate evidence. Generally speaking, be wary of claims that

➤ are supported by unidentified sources ("Experts claim …").

Great minds discuss ideas. Average minds discuss events. Small minds discuss people.

Eleanor Roosevelt,
First Lady of the United States (1884–1962)

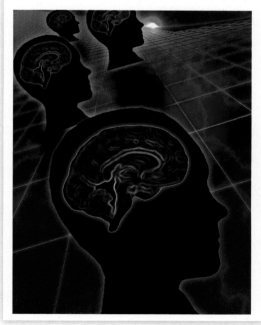

FACT: Half the class failed the first test in Phil 100.

Opinion: Phil 100 is the hardest class I'll ever take!

1. Kerry and Harry and his brother are twins, and they are older than Kerry.
2. The surgeon is the boy's mother.
3. The woman is a justice of the peace.

Box 5.2 Wanted: Liberal Arts Grads

Congratulations, grads! Now begins your so-called real life. But here's a bummer: If you took your parents' well-meaning advice and majored in a seemingly useful discipline you really didn't care about, you may have made a mistake. According to research, most parents believe the point of college is to help their students get a good job right out of school. In fact, in one recent survey, parents viewed getting a liberal arts degree as less valuable than skipping college altogether. Employers feel differently, however. What they actually want are graduates who are critical thinkers, who understand the world, know how to solve problems, and work with others. Most think that having these foundational skills is actually "more important" than a graduate's precise major. Organizations want graduates who can apply their learning to new settings and solve complex problems—broad, underlying skills, rather than specific skills that will be outdated quickly.[15] Even Steve Jobs, tech guru of Apple fame, believed in the value of a well-rounded education. ". . . technology alone is not enough—it's technology married with liberal arts, married with the humanities, that yields us the result that makes our heart sing."[16] So while you're in college, acquire *all* the essential skills you'll need for future success![17]

- are made by interested parties who stand to gain ("Brought to you by the makers of . . .").
- are put forth by a lone individual claiming his experience as the norm ("I tried it and it worked for me!").
- use a bandwagon appeal ("Everybody's doing it.").
- lie with statistics ("over half" when it's really only 50.5 percent).

Sensitive Situation You can almost be certain that someone in your class, right now, is taking their parents' advice about a major and is struggling. Let students know that this is common and maybe it is just because their parents think that it is a good job market. Later in this course, in Chapter 12, they will learn more about careers and majors and can share this with their parents.

On the other hand, we must also keep an open mind and be flexible in our thinking. If you get good evidence to support a view that contradicts yours, be willing to modify your ideas. One way to evaluate the validity of claims is to use the Question Pyramid we discussed earlier. Consider claims by asking these four key questions: "who?" "what?" "why?" and "how?"

Avoiding Faulty Reasoning

? challenge
" reaction

Challenge: List as many reasoning mistakes as you can. Can you provide an example of one or two of them?

Reaction: ______________________________

____

____

Although we can certainly improve our critical-thinking skills, it's impossible to be a perfect critical thinker 100 percent of the time. As thinkers, we make mistakes, and sometimes others try to trick us with false arguments. It's important to cultivate both types of critical thinking skills: your *productive* skills, which you use as a speaker and writer, and your *receptive* skills, which you use as a reader and listener. As responsible communicators, we must understand what a sound argument is and know how to construct one ourselves. We must also understand what a defective argument is in order to avoid getting sucked in when we shouldn't.

Teaching with Technology The Internet is full of examples of faulty logic. Whether from a blogger or a politician, logical fallacies are plentiful on the web. Have students search for examples of faulty logic in advertisements on the Internet. Encourage students to identify what type of fallacy is being used, and how the message is affected.

> **“** There's a world of difference between truth and facts. Facts can obscure the truth. **”**

Maya Angelou,
American author and poet

Here is a top-ten list of logical fallacies, or false logic strategies, we can slip into—or others can use against us—if we're not careful. For each of the ten types, read through the example and then see if you can come up with one of your own.

1. **False cause and effect** (assuming one cause for something when other causes are possible, too)

    I moved into my new dorm room last month. I've failed every exam I've taken since. Living in the residence hall is blowing my GPA!

2. **Personal attack** (reacting to a challenge by attacking the challenger)

    How could anyone believe our professor's views on ethics? We all know he's a very poor teacher.

3. **Unwarranted assumption** (taking too much for granted without evidence)

    You say universities give women equal opportunities. I say they don't. Reply: It's true. I read it on a website.

4. **Emotional appeal** (appealing to someone's feelings in order to gain acceptance of an argument)

    If you care about the institution that made you what you are today, you'll dig deep into your pockets and send a financial contribution now.

5. **False authority** (attributing your argument to someone else in a supposed position of power to get you off the hook)

    I'd really like to be able to change your grade, but my Department Chair frowns upon that.

6. **Hasty conclusion** (jumping to a conclusion when other conclusions are possible)

    I'm sure my roommate stole my textbook. He's too cheap to buy his own.

Great Bluffs Herald

Saturday, September 19, 2014

Cheap Beer + Fraternities = Recipe for Death

Great Bluffs, Colorado It's that time of year again. The fall semester began last month at Rocky Mountain State University, and again this year, a student died of alcohol poisoning within the first three weeks of classes. Clark Cameron of Valdosta, Georgia, a Gamma Beta Gamma pledge, was found dead yesterday morning in the GBG fraternity house on campus. The body of the collapsed student was found in a third-floor bedroom. An anonymous call to 9-1-1 came in at 6:15 A.M.: "We've got a guy here. We can't wake him, and we know he drank way too much last night." Cameron was pronounced dead on arrival at Great Bluffs General Hospital.

The incident represented RMSU's third death from alcohol poisoning in as many years. Roland Bishop, the University's new president, is said to deeply mourn the loss of another RMSU freshman. "No student should die during his first few weeks of college—what should be one of the most exciting times of his life. It's insane and very, very sad."

The national Gamma Beta Gamma office has suspended the RMSU chapter until further notice and banned its 83 members from participating in any Greek events.

Bishop will convene a cross-university panel of faculty, staff, and students to investigate the Greek system on campus and drinking privileges at all campus social functions, including athletic events.

Professor Juan Cordova, Theology Department Chairperson, will head the new committee. A report with specific recommendations to President Bishop is expected by the end of the term.

Alcohol is to blame for the deaths of 1,825 college students per year, according to figures from the National Institute on Alcohol Abuse and Alcoholism. About 599,000 students between the ages of 18 and 24 are injured annually while under the influence of alcohol, more than 690,000 are assaulted by another student who has been drinking, and more than 97,000 students are victims of alcohol-related sexual assault or date rape.

Voted the number two party school in the nation, Rocky Mountain State University is known for its "party-hardy" social life. Away from home for the first time, many freshmen get swept up by the party scene. President Bishop's office indicates that moving "rush" further into the semester is one option under consideration. The president believes that students need more time to adjust to the transition from high school and get their academic careers underway. Being driven to drink, sometimes excessively, is often a "rite of passage" in sororities and fraternities, a spokesman for the President said in a telephone interview. The University will also explore creating several alcohol-free residence halls where students who want to buckle down academically can do so without fearing social pressure to party.

After this article appeared in the *Great Bluffs Herald*, many readers sent letters to the editor on September 20 and 21. Examine the following excerpts.

Trevor Ryan, RMSU Student, Denver, Colorado: "My first few weeks as a freshman at RMSU have been awesome. I knew I wanted to pledge GBG before I ever got here, and I have to say the "rush of rush" was totally cool—one of the highlights of my life so far. I'd do it all over again tomorrow. But I didn't want to join GBG just for the parties. It's an excellent organization with high academic standards. All the members say so."

UNWARRANTED ASSUMPTION!

Mitch Edgars, Father, Englewood, Colorado: "For me, college was a time of awakening. I had plenty of 'good times' and I want my son to do the same. You can't stop college kids from drinking. It's that simple. Sure, all college kids make mistakes. But if they're smart, they'll learn from them. I know my son pretty well, and he makes good decisions most of the time. I don't care what anybody says, experience is still the best teacher."

Carlos Cordova, RMSU Student, Brooklyn, New York: "This whole incident has been very hard on me. Clark was my roommate, and we were getting along great. I still can't believe this happened to him. Yeah, I was at the football game with him where he started drinking and then later at the frat party where he got totally wasted. But I lost him in the crowd, and I went back to the dorm around midnight. I wonder if I could have done something."

Evan Riley, RMSU Senior, Aspen, Colorado: "As president of the Interfraternity Council on campus, I feel fraternities and sororities across the country are being demonized by the press. We're not like that. We are service organizations and we participate in lots of community activities, like the Holiday Fundraiser in Great Bluffs. Last year GBG raised more money for the homeless than any other organization on campus. At a time like this, though, everybody forgets that. We become the bad guys. The University just wants someone to take the fall, and I know it's going to be us. It's unfortunate that a few irresponsible students ruin it for everyone. Ask anyone who's a member: overall, sororities and fraternities do much more good than bad. It's really not fair!" ← OVERSIMPLIFICATION

Professor Ruby Pinnell, Biology Department, RMSU: "As a biologist, I see all the physiological damage today's college students are doing to themselves. The national study I spearheaded last year found that 31 percent of college students meet the clinical criteria for alcohol abuse, and 6 percent could be diagnosed as being alcohol-dependent. Young people don't realize that binge drinking could be risking serious damage to their brains now and actually cause increased memory loss later in adulthood. Many college males consume as many as 24 drinks in a row. These are very sad statistics."

Rufus Unser, Great Bluffs, Colorado, Citizen, Neighbor, and Voter: "I'm sick of my tax dollars going to fund institutions made up of immature college students who make bad decisions. A *Great Bluffs Herald* article published last year reported that neighbors living within one mile of college campuses are 135 percent more likely to suffer from public disturbances—also called "secondhand effects." My house is down the block from the GBG fraternity house, and sometimes the noise is so loud that I have to call the cops! Worse than that, I'm getting ready to sell my house and move into a retirement home next year. I'll bet my property values have dropped because of all the bad press! Higher education? That's a misnomer. 'Lower education' is more like it these days!" ← EITHER-OR THINKING

Jim McArthur, Director, RMSU Residence Life: September is National Alcohol and Drug Addiction Recovery Month, and we're doing everything we can to help educate students about the risks of alcohol poisoning. The binge drinking problem at RMSU isn't unique, and it's not going to go away by itself. We offer weekly classes on drinking responsibly, but no one signs up for them. We put up posters about the dangers of alcohol all over campus, and we also train all of our RAs on alcohol abuse as part of their preparation for the job. They try to keep tabs on their freshmen, but to tell you the truth, I think some of the RAs drink a bit too much, too. This is society's problem, not just RMSU's."

Sergeant Rick Fuller, Great Bluffs Police Department: "I've worked in the Great Bluffs Police Department for 15 years now, and I've seen a dramatic rise in the number of arrests for alcohol possession by minors, arrests for selling alcohol to minors, and alcohol-related admissions to Great Bluffs General Hospital's ER. It's an epidemic, I'm afraid. I also know from my police work that alcohol abuse is a factor in 40 percent of violent crimes committed in the U.S."[18]

Now that you've read the story from the *Great Bluffs Herald* and the excerpts from letters to the editor, answer the following questions:

1. What are the facts relating to the alcohol problem at RMSU? How do you know they're *facts* and not *claims*?

2. Do you see logical fallacies in any of the eight letters to the editor of the *Great Bluffs Herald*? If so, which can you identify? What assumptions do the letter writers hold?

3. Identify an issue that has been generating debate on your campus, in your residence hall, or in a class. Make a list of the claims made on each side of the debate and consider each claim. Then, make a list of the arguments and evaluate each argument, looking at *relevancy* and *adequacy*. Next, list the assumptions that the arguments are based on. Finally, be creative and come up with a new approach to the issue. Is there another way to frame the debate? How can you look at the issue in an entirely different way?

VARK It!

Complete the recommended activity for your preferred VARK learning modality. If you are multimodal, select more than one activity. Your instructor may ask you to (a) give an oral report on your results in class, (b) send your results to him or her via e-mail, or (c) post them online.

 Visual: Create a collage or find an image that represents each letter writer's point of view. Be certain to highlight the faulty reasoning.

 Aural: As a group, talk through the case. Focus on questions like these: Does the incident sound realistic? If you ran the university, how would you handle the situation?

 Read/Write: Write a press release sent from the university to local media outlets. How would you present this difficult situation to readers in the general public?

Kinesthetic: Assume you are a member of President Bishop's new task force on alcohol policy. Role play members of the task force at their first meeting.

Activity Option Alcohol on college campuses is a hot topic. Use this opportunity to talk about this issue and how it pertains to your campus. Brainstorm a list of questions that students would want to know about alcohol use and abuse on campus. Divide students into groups of two to three and give them a specific question from the list they just generated. Tell them to find the answer and bring it to class next week. Make sure that they tell you the source, and why they thought it was credible.

Activity Option You may wish to have students do the VARK exercise on critical and creative thinking individually instead.
V: Look over the letters to the editor. Make notes in the margins about as many faulty arguments as you can identify.
A: Discuss this simulation in class or with a friend. List three points you hadn't really thought about that your partner helped you see.
R: Summarize the case into a single paragraph. Summarizing is a great critical thinking tool!
K: (Use the same K activity.) Would actually serving on a task force help you or other kinesthetic learners become engaged and learn more? Why and how?

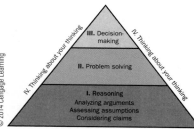

IV. Thinking about your thinking

1. DEFINE:
MY PHILOSOPHY CLASS IS
KILLING ME!

---

7. **Straw man** (attempting to "prove" an argument by overstating, exaggerating, or oversimplifying the arguments of the opposing side)

   We should relax the entrance requirements to help attract more students. Reply: You actually want the quality of students here to take a nose dive? Oh, right, why don't we all just teach high school instead?

8. **Shifting the burden of proof** (shifting the responsibility of proving an assertion to someone else because you have no evidence for what you assert)

   The zero-tolerance policy on alcohol in the residence halls is working. Reply: No, it's not. Reply back: Oh yeah? Prove it.

9. **Oversimplification/overgeneralization** (reducing a complex issue to something very simple or stereotyping)

   College professors have it made. They teach a couple classes a week for a few hours, and then they have free time the rest of the week. That's the kind of job I want!

10. **Either/or thinking** (taking only an extreme position on an issue when other positions are possible)

    Either we ban alcohol on campus or we'll go bankrupt from lawsuits.

II. Problem Solving: The Basic How-To's

When you have to solve a problem, your critical thinking skills should move front and center. Perhaps you need to find a way to earn more money. You run short each month, and the last few days before payday are nerve-racking. What should you do? Use a gunshot approach and try many different strategies at once or devise a more precise way to get the best results? See if the following steps make sense to you and seem like something you might actually do.

STEP 1: Define the problem. What is the exact nature of the problem you face? You must define the problem if you hope to solve it. For example:

> Is it that you don't monitor your spending and run out of money long before the next paycheck?

> Is it that you've never created a budget and you spend money randomly?

STEP 2: Brainstorm possible options. List all of the possible solutions you can come up with. For example:

➤ Eat all your meals in the residence hall instead of hitting the fast-food joints so often.

➤ Stop ordering in pizza four nights a week when you get the munchies at midnight.

➤ Ask your parents for more money. They told you to let them know when you need more.

➤ Look for a job that pays more. Tips at the Pancake House where you work don't really amount to much.

➤ Capitalize on your particular skills to earn extra money. If you're a whiz at math, you could sign on as a tutor at the Math Learning Center on campus.

STEP 3: Set criteria to evaluate each option. For example:

➤ *Distance* is important. Your car isn't very reliable, so it would be good to find a job you can walk or ride your bike to.

➤ *Good pay* is important. In the past, you've always had low-paying jobs. You need whatever solution you arrive at to be worth your while.

➤ *Time* is important. You're taking a challenging load of classes, and you need to keep up your grades to keep your scholarship.

STEP 4: Evaluate each option you've proposed. For example:

➤ Eat all your meals in the residence hall. (This is a good idea because you've already paid for those meals, regardless of which solution you choose.)

➤ Stop ordering in pizza four nights a week. (This is also a good option because impromptu expenses like this can mount exponentially.)

➤ Ask your parents for more money. (You'd really like to avoid this option. You know they're already making sacrifices to help you through school.)

➤ Get a job that pays more. (Unfortunately, your campus is half an hour from the center of town where all the posh restaurants are.)

➤ Capitalize on your particular skills to earn extra money. (Tutors are paid more than minimum wage, and the Math Learning Center is across from your residence hall.)

STEP 5: Choose the best solution. In this case, it looks like the Math Learning Center fits the bill!

STEP 6: Plan how to achieve the best solution. When you call the Math Learning Center to find out how to apply, you discover that you need a letter of recommendation from a math professor. You e-mail your calculus professor and set up a meeting for later in the week. When the letter is ready, you call the Math Learning Center again to make an appointment to schedule an interview, and so forth.

2. BRAINSTORM:
- DROP THE CLASS
- STUDY HARDER
- GET ADVICE FROM MY ADVISOR
- FORM A STUDY GROUP
- GO SEE PROF COURTNEY

3. SET CRITERIA:
A) TIME
B) EFFECTIVENESS
C) CONVENIENCE

4. EVALUATE:
- DROP THE CLASS (LOSING MY FINANCIAL AID WOULD BE VERY INCONVENIENT!)
- STUDY HARDER (I ALREADY AM!)
- GET ADVICE FROM MY ADVISOR (COULD TAKE SOME TIME TO GET IN TO SEE HER)
- FORM A STUDY GROUP (WHEN COULD WE ALL MEET?)
- GO SEE PROF (COULD WORK, BUT HE MIGHT BE HARD TO TALK TO)

5. CHOOSE: GOING TO SEE PROF COURTNEY WOULD BE BEST.

6. PLAN: E-MAIL HIM TONIGHT TO MAKE AN APPOINTMENT. ENTER THE DAY AND TIME ON GOOGLE CALENDAR.

7. IMPLEMENT: WE'LL SEE, BUT AT LEAST I HAVE A PLAN.

STEP 7: Implement the solution and evaluate the results. A month or two after you take on the tutoring job, you evaluate if this solution is really the best one. You may need to request more hours or different days. Or you may find that this job leads to a better one as a Teaching Assistant for the math department. At any rate, you've used your critical thinking skills to solve a problem, systematically, logically, and effectively. College students who successfully solve everyday problems have higher self-esteem and life satisfaction. As it turns out, improving your problem solving skills has big payoffs![19]

IV. Thinking about your thinking

III. Decision Making: What's Your Style?

Arguments lead to decisions, and it's important to make good ones! After you've evaluated the arguments put forth, you must often do something about them. Before you know it, you'll be deciding on a major if you haven't already, a career field, a place to live, a romantic partner—you name it.

When you have an important decision to make, your critical thinking skills should kick into action. The more important the decision, chances are the more thoughtful the process of deciding should be. But people make decisions in their own way. To some extent, decision making is individualistic. Take a look at the Decision Style Inventory in Exercise 5.3 to learn more about your decision-making style.

INTERESTING! I'D LIKE TO KNOW THIS ABOUT MYSELF...

The results of this Decision Style Inventory have been collected from over 2,000 people and provide the basis for the book entitled *Managing with Style* by Alan J. Rowe and Richard O. Mason. After you complete your rankings, total your answers for each letter. Although the Decision Style Inventory is typically used with managers and you may not be one now, it is also a useful way to preview what your style may be when you do have a position of responsibility.

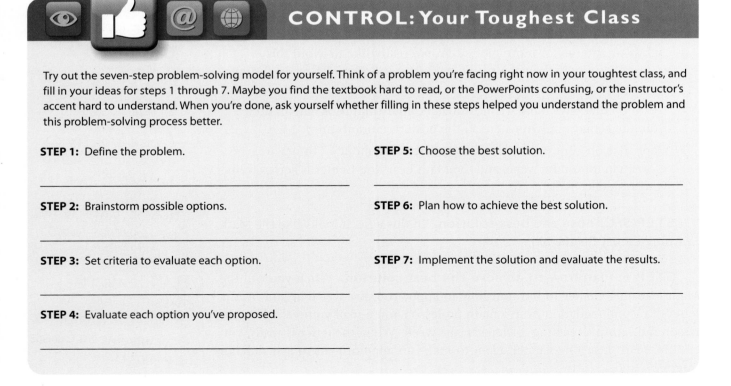

CONTROL: Your Toughest Class

Try out the seven-step problem-solving model for yourself. Think of a problem you're facing right now in your toughest class, and fill in your ideas for steps 1 through 7. Maybe you find the textbook hard to read, or the PowerPoints confusing, or the instructor's accent hard to understand. When you're done, ask yourself whether filling in these steps helped you understand the problem and this problem-solving process better.

STEP 1: Define the problem.

_____

STEP 2: Brainstorm possible options.

_____

STEP 3: Set criteria to evaluate each option.

_____

STEP 4: Evaluate each option you've proposed.

_____

STEP 5: Choose the best solution.

_____

STEP 6: Plan how to achieve the best solution.

_____

STEP 7: Implement the solution and evaluate the results.

_____

Respond to each of the following twenty statements by marking your response according to the rules that follow. There are no right or wrong answers. Generally, the first impression that comes to mind is the best one to put down. Respond to each statement by assigning an 8 to the answer that is most appropriate (for you), a 4 next to the next most appropriate, then a 2, and finally a 1 for the least appropriate answer. In the following example, an individual prefers blue, brown, gray, and red in that order:

When picking clothes, I prefer   Blue __8__   Red __1__   Brown __4__   Gray __2__

Each number may only be assigned once for each statement, and each of the four numbers must be used for each statement.

1. In my career, my prime objective will be to:
   ____ (a) have a position with status.
   ____ (b) be the best in my field.
   ____ (c) achieve recognition for my work.
   ____ (d) feel secure in my job.

2. I enjoy jobs that:
   ____ (a) are technical and well defined.
   ____ (b) have considerable variety.
   ____ (c) allow independent action.
   ____ (d) involve people.

3. If I were a boss, I'd expect people working for me to be:
   ____ (a) productive and fast.
   ____ (b) highly capable.
   ____ (c) committed and responsive.
   ____ (d) receptive to suggestions.

4. In my job, I'll look for:
   ____ (a) practical results.
   ____ (b) the best solutions.
   ____ (c) new approaches or ideas.
   ____ (d) a good working environment.

5. I communicate best with others:
   ____ (a) on a direct one-to-one basis.
   ____ (b) in writing.
   ____ (c) by having a discussion.
   ____ (d) in a group meeting.

6. As I plan on the job, I'll emphasize:
   ____ (a) current problems.
   ____ (b) meeting objectives.
   ____ (c) future goals.
   ____ (d) developing the careers of people working for me.

7. When faced with solving a problem, I:
   ____ (a) rely on proven approaches.
   ____ (b) apply careful analysis.
   ____ (c) look for creative approaches.
   ____ (d) rely on my feelings.

8. When using information, I prefer:
   ____ (a) specific facts.
   ____ (b) accurate and complete information.
   ____ (c) broad coverage of many options.
   ____ (d) limited information that is easily understood.

9. When I am not sure about what to do, I:
   ____ (a) rely on my intuition.
   ____ (b) search for the facts.
   ____ (c) look for a possible compromise.
   ____ (d) wait before making a decision.

10. Whenever possible, I avoid:
    ____ (a) long debates.
    ____ (b) incomplete work.
    ____ (c) using numbers or formulas.
    ____ (d) conflict with others.

11. I am especially good at:
    ____ (a) remembering dates and facts.
    ____ (b) solving difficult problems.
    ____ (c) seeing many possibilities.
    ____ (d) interacting with others.

12. When time is important, I:
    ____ (a) decide and act quickly.
    ____ (b) follow plans and priorities.
    ____ (c) refuse to be pressured.
    ____ (d) seek guidance or support.

13. In social settings, I generally:
    ____ (a) speak with others.
    ____ (b) think about what is being said.
    ____ (c) observe what is going on.
    ____ (d) listen to the conversation.

14. I am good at remembering:
    ____ (a) people's names.
    ____ (b) places we met.
    ____ (c) people's faces.
    ____ (d) people's personalities.

(continued on next page)

15. The work I do will provide me:
    ____ (a) the power to influence others.
    ____ (b) challenging assignments.
    ____ (c) opportunities to achieve my personal goals.
    ____ (d) acceptance by the people I work with.

16. I work well with people who are:
    ____ (a) energetic and ambitious.
    ____ (b) self-confident.
    ____ (c) open-minded.
    ____ (d) positive and trusting.

17. When under stress, I:
    ____ (a) become anxious.
    ____ (b) concentrate on the problem.
    ____ (c) become frustrated.
    ____ (d) am forgetful.

18. Others consider me:
    ____ (a) aggressive.
    ____ (b) disciplined.
    ____ (c) imaginative.
    ____ (d) supportive.

19. My decisions typically are:
    ____ (a) realistic and direct.
    ____ (b) systematic and abstract.
    ____ (c) broad and flexible.
    ____ (d) sensitive to the needs of others.

20. I dislike:
    ____ (a) losing control.
    ____ (b) doing boring work.
    ____ (c) following rules.
    ____ (d) being rejected.

Totals: (a) ____ 1 (b) ____ 1 (c) ____ 1 (d) ____ 5 300

(Note: The sum total for (a) 1 (b) 1 (c) 1 (d) should equal 300.)

Source: Adapted from *Managing with Style: A Guide to Understanding, Assessing, and Improving Decision Making* by A.J. Rowe and R.O. Mason, by permission from Dr. Alan J. Rowe.

The (a) answers represent a *directive* style, the (b) answers represent an *analytical* style, the (c) answers represent a *conceptual* style, and the (d) answers represent a *behavioral* style. What is your decision making style? Which of the four letters (a, b, c, or d) do you have *the most* of?

Hemera Technologies/PhotoObjects.
net/Jupiter Images

> **Directive (a).** This decision-making style emphasizes the here and now. Directives prefer structure and using practical data to make decisions. They look for speed, efficiency, and results, and focus on short-term fixes. Directive decision makers base their decisions on experience, facts, procedures, and rules, and they have energy and drive to get things done. On the down side, because they work quickly, they are sometimes satisfied with simplistic solutions.

© Ian Scott,/Shutterstock.com

> **Analytical (b).** This decision-making style emphasizes a logical approach. Analyticals search carefully for the best decision, and they sometimes get hung up with overanalyzing things and take too long to finally make a decision. They are sometimes considered to be impersonal because they may be more interested in the problem than in the people who have it. But they are good at working with data and doing careful analysis.

Your TYPE is Showing

Researchers have found a relationship between the Decision Style Inventory and the Myers-Briggs Type Inventory style. Is that true for you? It makes sense that your personality and your decision-making style are related, doesn't it?

Locate the two middle letters of your type in Figure 5.3 and see how your type correlates to a decision-making style. This is particularly helpful if you have completed the full MBTI.

Directive decision makers, for example, like well-defined goals, well-developed plans, and detailed calculations. People with those characteristics are typically ST's on the MBTI.

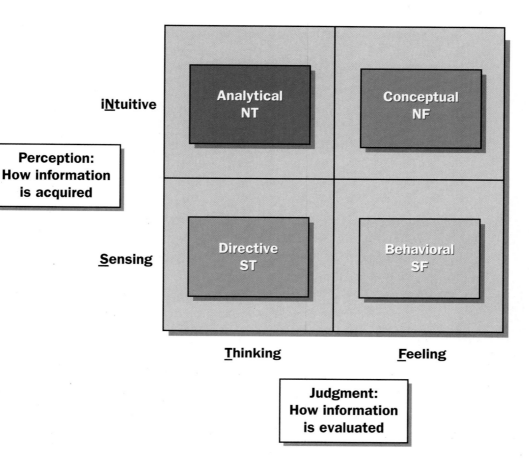

FIGURE 5.3

Relationship between the Decision Style Inventory and the MBTI

Source: From p. 140 of *Managing with Style: A Guide to Understanding, Assessing, and Improving Decision Making* by A.J. Rowe and R.O. Mason. © 1987 by Jossey-Bass. Reprinted by permission from Dr. Alan J. Rowe.

Hemera Technologies/PhotoObjects.net/Jupiter Images

> **Conceptual (c).** This decision-making style emphasizes the big picture. Conceptuals are adaptable, insightful, and flexible, and they look for innovative solutions. They are sometimes too idealistic, but they take risks and are very creative.

© lofoto/Shutterstock.com

> **Behavioral (d).** This decision-making style emphasizes people. Behaviorals enjoy people and the social aspects of work. They use their feelings to assess situations, communicate well, and are supportive of others. On the other hand, they are sometimes seen as wishy-washy or are criticized because they can't make hard decisions or can't say no.

Teachable Moment Remind students that even if they wear the "badge" of an organized personality type (J, for example) or a detailed person (an S), this alone does not make them a good decision maker. It's the big-picture portrait of a person—not only who they are, but what they do and how they do it! So the more they learn about themselves, and the more they reflect on what they do, the better they are able to succeed.

MY SCORE SAYS BEHAVIORAL, AND IT FITS.

Activity Option Have the class fill in their names on a rough chart you draw on the board or create a PowerPoint slide or transparency of Figure 5.3 to indicate where they fit. You should do it first to model how you make decisions based on your personality type and decision-making style. Discuss your commonalities and differences as decision-makers and give some real examples to make the concepts more concrete to students.

Teachable Moment Have students reflect on what they do when faced with learning something new. Ask them why they go about things as they do, and if they had the chance to do it again, ask if they would do it differently. Get students to reflect whenever you can (in writing, in discussions, etc.).

IV. Thinking about Your Thinking

One of the most important aspects of critical thinking is that it evaluates itself. As you're solving problems, for example, you're thinking about how you're thinking. You're assessing your progress as you go, analyzing the strengths and weaknesses in your thinking, and perhaps even coming up with better ways to do it. We call that metacognition, and that's one reason this book contains "Insight → Action" exercises—to give you opportunities to think about how you're thinking and make note of those thoughts. Whenever you're faced with learning something new, metacognition involves three elements. Ultimately, these elements should become the foundation of all your learning experiences so that you improve your metacognitive skills as you go.

> **Develop a plan of action.** Ask yourself what you already know that can help you learn something new. What direction do you want to go in your thinking? What should be your first task? How much time should you give yourself? Talk through your plan with someone else.

> **Monitor your plan.** While you're working, ask yourself how you're doing. Are you staying on track? Are you moving in the right direction? Should you slow down or speed up? What should you do if you don't understand what you're doing? Keep track of what works for you and what doesn't.

> **Evaluate the plan.** How well did you do? Did you do better than expected or not as well as you expected? What could you have done differently? Can you apply what you just did here to future tasks? Give yourself some feedback.[20]

> Education is nothing more, nor less, than learning to think!
>
> *Peter Facione, professor, administrator, author, consultant, and critical thinking expert*

Becoming a Better Critical Thinker

Sharpening your critical thinking skills is vital because these skills underlie all the others in your academic repertoire. If you think well, you will be a better writer, a better presenter, a better listener, and a better reader. You will be more likely to engage more fully in your academic tasks because you will question, probe, analyze, and monitor yourself as you learn. Here are some suggestions for improving your skills. As you read them, think about how they pertain to you.

> **"**And how is education supposed to make me feel smarter?**"**
>
> *Homer Simpson, television cartoon character, The Simpsons*

Akom Production Company/Starstock/Photoshot

1. **Admit when you don't know.** If you don't know enough to think critically about something, admit it, and then find out more. With the volume of information available in today's world, we can't possibly know everything about anything. But the good news is that information is readily available. All you need to do is read, listen, point, and click to be well informed on many issues.

2. **Realize you have buttons that can be pushed.** We all have issues we're emotional about. That's normal. It's natural to feel strongly about some things, but it's also important to understand the reasons why so that you can explain your views to someone else. And of course, realize that you're not the only one with buttons. Your teacher, roommate, significant other, boss, everyone else has them, too.

<aside>
Sensitive Situation We all have buttons that can be pushed, but some more so than others. Bring this to the attention of the class and give some examples such as derogatory words, generalizations (students from broken homes have "issues"), and so on. Remind students that most often, comments like these are simply born of a lack of knowledge, but they still can hurt.
</aside>

3. **Learn more about the opposition.** Many times, it's more comfortable to avoid what we don't agree with and selectively validate what we already believe. But part of being a well-educated person means learning about the history, backgrounds, values, and techniques of people you disagree with so that you can anticipate and deal with their arguments more effectively.

4. **Trust and verify.** During the cold war, President Ronald Reagan liked to quote an old Russian saying to his Soviet counterpart, Mikhail Gorbachev: "Doveryay, no proveryay," or "Trust, but verify." Being a good critical thinker means achieving a balance between blind faith and healthy skepticism.

5. **Remember that critical thinking is the cornerstone of all academic achievement.** There's nothing more important than learning to think critically. In college and in life, the skills discussed in this chapter will make you a better college student, a better citizen, a better employee, a savvier consumer, a better relational partner, and a better lifelong learner.

66 *Optimism is the faith that leads to achievement. Nothing can be done without hope and confidence.* 99

Helen Keller (1880–1968),
American author and educator

Consider a job that you've held in the past. If someone asked you to come up with five adjectives that describe the most memorable boss you've ever had, what words would come to you? Words like *encouraging, smart, visionary, responsive,* or *supportive*—or words like *hasty, unfair, mean, hypocritical,* or *irrational*? What do all the words you think of have in common? Were they mainly *positive* or *negative*?

When asked this question, most people go in one direction: either entirely positive or negative. No one ever says, "What I really love about my boss is his critical nature. He doesn't miss a single mistake I make." Or "My boss has a temper you wouldn't believe. When she nails you on something, you know exactly where you stand."[21] It's natural to lean one way or the other. Critical thinking skills are a useful tool in the workplace. They can help you adjust your thinking appropriately and keep you from getting locked into particular patterns, especially negative ones.

Unfortunately, sometimes negativity is effortless to generate. Imagine a scenario like this. You're desperately looking for a part-time job and meet someone at a party who could be an important resource for you. He says, "E-mail me your résumé, and I'll take a look and get back to you tomorrow." So, you rush home, send off your résumé, and check your e-mail a hundred times the next day, expecting a response. Then you check your e-mail periodically the following day and the day after that. Finally, you give up in disgust, assuming your contact just had a big ego. A month later, while checking your spam folder, you find his message, sent shortly after you met. "I hope this reaches you," the e-mail says. "My e-mail crashed, and I had to set up a new account. Here's my new e-mail address." Like many of us, you assumed the worst and created a derogatory story which you chose to believe. That's normal, too, but the negativity you've generated wasn't necessarily in your best interest: "We can't change the facts, but we do have a choice about what to make of them."[22]

While negativity is generally a downer, sometimes it can propel you toward productive action. If you're overly optimistic and assume that you'll ace every exam without preparing adequately, you may be in for some bad news. Being pessimistic about your performance could actually cause you to prepare more thoroughly—and produce better results. Experts say that it's important to be strategic about your thinking, be aware of your own thinking patterns, and know when to change them. Honestly, the proverbial glass is both half empty and half full at the same time. While too much optimism can hurt us, too much pessimism can destroy us in the long run: our immune systems degenerate, our relationships dissolve, and our careers get derailed.[23]

Remember the words of the environmentalist and founder of Patagonia, the well-known outdoor gear company: "There's no difference between a pessimist who says, 'Oh, it's hopeless, so don't bother doing anything,' and an optimist who says, 'Don't bother doing anything, it's going to turn out fine anyway.' Either way, nothing happens." It's your thinking and your career, and you're in the driver's seat. You want to do things, go places, and make things happen. That's what it's all about.

Think Ahead You're in the process of preparing for your future; examine your thinking *now*. Are you a "glass half full" person or a "glass half empty person"—or both? Reflect on some of your patterns of thinking and how they could affect your about-to-be career.

NEVER THOUGHT ABOUT IT EXACTLY THIS WAY BEFORE...

Cast on Careers

© Larry Harwood Photography.
Property of Cengage Learning

FOCUS: As a brand new student, were you optimistic or pessimistic?

DARIO: I'd say I was optimistic—maybe overly optimistic. For example, I never asked questions in class. I just assumed I'd find the answer in the textbook later. But "later" never quite arrived because I'd forget about it. Then when I was preparing for an exam, I'd check my notes from class and find gaps in what I had written down. I just always assumed I'd do fine and everything would be manageable. For the most part, that was true, eventually. But sometimes I wish I had been a little more realistic as a first-year student and saved myself some major stress!

FOCUS: What are your career plans? How will your thinking patterns play a role?

DARIO: I've decided to be a Student Affairs Professional, like a Director of Residence Life or Campus Activities. I loved college so much that I want it to continue! How I think about students, how I deal with student issues, how I can help them mature, have a good time, and do well academically by being more realistic than I was—all those things will be important!

Who me? Creative? Talented? Gifted? Nah! Some people say: "I'm not creative. I have no talent. I'm just an ordinary guy." Other people settle for good instead of reaching for great: "I'm pretty good. I'm good enough. I have enough to get by." What does it take to be come a truly great thinker, a great creator, a great athlete, a great musician, a great anything?

According to Daniel Coyle, best-selling author of the acclaimed book, *The Talent Code*, talent is something you grow into, not something you're born with. Coyle traveled the world to visit "talent hotbeds," little places that produce great talent: a tennis camp in Russia, a music academy in upstate New York, and an inner city school in California, for example. As he examined these origins of greatness, he discovered that talent is grown by a combination of three principles:

Stockbyte/Photos.com

Deep Practice: Deep practice isn't just practicing regularly or even practicing a great deal, it's practicing a certain way: very slowly and deliberately. That's how your brain gains mastery. At a music academy Coyle visited, young cellists are told that if anyone walking by can recognize the song they're practicing, they're playing too fast. Deep practice is also based on stops and starts, on mistakes, on analyzing what went wrong, and trying over and over again until you can do it perfectly. The trick, Coyle says, is to reach just beyond your grasp.

Ignition: Any kind of practice, let alone deep practice, would be torture unless you really cared. Something or somebody must light a spark in you and ignite the fire that fuels your learning. You must be motivated from within to be great. Only then, with this burst of magnetic attraction to a skill, are you willing to work toward greatness.

Master Coaching: To become truly great, it takes an older, wiser, and more experienced teacher, someone who can show you things you don't see in yourself and help you reach your potential. Olympic athletes need coaches, just as great minds need teachers. To become truly excellent, someone must show you precisely how.

So the next time someone asks you if you're creative, talented, or gifted, you may want to explore what it would take before immediately answering. Talent, according to Daniel Coyle, is something that can be grown depending on how much you want it and hard you're willing to work to get it.

Unleash Your Creativity!

Whether you're eighteen or eighty-one, it's safe to say that your life has been changed by an unending stream of new inventions. Which of the following have come into existence during your lifetime? iPods? GPS systems in cars? The Xbox? DVDs? Microwavable mac and cheese? IMAX movies? Side-impact air bags? Wordsmith, Yogi Berra, once said, "The future ain't what it used to be." Perhaps that's never been more true. According to creativity expert and best-selling author Daniel Pink, the past was built by logical, left-brained people. But the future belongs to right-brained "artists, inventors, designers, storytellers, caregivers, consolers, big picture thinkers." A "seismic shift" is underway, he tells us, and what we will need most in the future is creativity.[24]

Creativity affects us all. It's true that some of these items haven't made a big impact. But other inventions affect you every single day. In his bestselling book, *The Rise of the Creative Class*, Richard Florida discusses the accelerating role of creativity in our lives today: "We live in a time of great promise. We have evolved economic and social systems that tap human creativity and make

Teaching with Technology Assign your students Web 2.0 creative tasks. Students enjoy contributing to a class blog, creating a PowerPoint, Prezi, Visual.ly, SlideRocket, Tiki-Toki, FlipSnack, etc. presentation, or producing a movie, for example. Today's students don't just want to be information "consumers," they want to be information "producers." Technology-based projects (in their own "language") allow them to show off their creativity.

Teaching with Technology Take (or send) your students to *The New York Times* interactive website on the best ideas from the last decade. The 2010 version contains some fascinating "inventions." Each idea can be highlighted, and students can watch or read about it.

> I can't understand why people are frightened by new ideas. I'm frightened by the old ones.

John Cage,
American composer (1912–1992)

use of it as never before. This in turn creates an unparalleled opportunity to raise our living standards, build a more humane and sustainable economy, and make our lives more complete."[25]

Florida notes that in 1900, less than 10 percent of American workers were doing creative work. Farms and factories were most people's work sites. Eighty years later, the figure had only risen to 20 percent. But today, a full third of our working population engages in employment that gets their creative juices flowing, whether they're artists, designers, writers, analysts, musicians, or entrepreneurs. The creative sector of our economy accounts for nearly half of all wage and salary income—$1.7 trillion per year. Today's "no collar" workplace is fueled by creativity. And Florida says, we've barely scratched the surface. Human creativity is virtually limitless. In many ways, it's a choice you make; you decide to be creative.[26]

In fact, in today's world, creativity within organizations can mean the difference between prosperity and survival. Companies must reinvent themselves periodically, and the new ideas they need must come from their own employees.[27] That's why organizations help people fuel their creative intelligence by allowing specific, but related perks, like these:[28]

1. *Thought time*—giving employees opportunities to think creatively. Experts suggest that one way to promote creativity is to engage in *associational thinking*, or putting together two very different fields or ideas to create something new. Ben Silbermann, for example, co-designer of Pinterest, modeled the site's layout on his bug collection as a kid. The daily grind can cause employees' brains to get stuck in a rut, but encouraging creativity by relating two radically different thoughts or ideas—or old products to potentially new ones—is exciting.

2. *Play time*—giving employees opportunities to have fun on the job. Studies have shown that relaxants like humor allow the brain's natural creativity to break through. Too much pressure, too many deadlines, and major stressors on the job, on the other hand, can suppress creativity. At Patagonia, the emphasis is on results, not schedules, even allowing employees freedom under their "Let my people go surfing time" policy. Patagonia believes that many of the ideas for its best-selling products came to employees when they were outdoors.

3. *Flex time*—allowing employees' brains to reenergize by making their own choices. Google allows employees to use up to 20 percent of their time to work on projects they're personally interested in. Additionally, many organizations allow employees to work from home or telecommute, which technology now makes much easier by using Google Drive, Skype, Dropbox, or a host of other e-tools. Changing your work setting can help your brain "reboot."

4. *Networking time*—encouraging employees to interact with others with diverse backgrounds and work styles. Diversity in our surroundings is one thing that increases the potential for creativity. Creativity comes in all sizes, ethnicities, preferences, and genders. If employees are around other open-minded, flexible, tolerant, forward-looking, innovative people, they're more likely to live up to their own creative potential.

What does all this have to do with you as an entering college student? College is a time to sort through your values and determine what you really want from this life of yours. It's about finding out who you are, what you want, why you want it, and how you can get it. Unleash your creativity now and begin building the future you'd like to live. Remember the warning of thinking expert Edward de Bono, "If you take no part in the design of your future, it will be designed for you by others."

> " As competition intensifies, the need for creative thinking increases. It is no longer enough to do the same thing better . . . no longer enough to be efficient and solve problems. "
>
> *Edward de Bono*

I JUST DON'T KNOW IF I SEE MYSELF AS CREATIVE . . .

Creativity: "Thinking Outside the . . . Book"

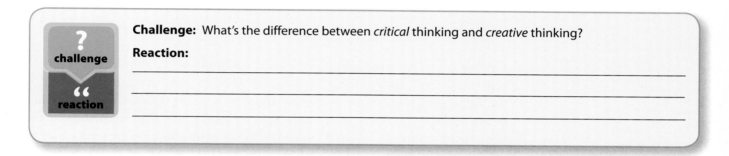

Challenge: What's the difference between *critical* thinking and *creative* thinking?

Reaction:

_____

_____

_____

Do you believe this statement? *Everyone has creative potential.*[29] It's true. Most of us deny it, however. "Me, creative? Nah!" We're often unaware of the untapped ability we have to think creatively. Try this experiment. Look at the following list of words, and divide the list into two (and only two) different categories, using any criteria you devise. Take a few moments and see what you come up with.

dog, salad, book, grasshopper, kettle, paper, garbage, candle

Whenever this experiment is tried, people always come up with very creative categories. They may divide the words into things that you buy at a store (dog, salad, kettle, paper, candle), things that move on their own (dog, grasshopper), things that have a distinct smell (dog, candle, garbage), words that have two consonants, and so forth. People never say it can't be done; they always *invent* categories. Interesting, isn't it? Our minds are hungry for the stimulation of a creative challenge.

Some people might assert that what the experiment demonstrates is intelligence, not creativity. People with average or above average IQs can come up with distinctive categories easily. Smart people, they'd say, are good at tasks like this, and people who come up with the best ideas must be geniuses.

The fact is that intelligence has more to do with coming up with the right answer, and creative thinking has more to do with coming up with many right answers. Often we get so focused on the *right* answer that we rush to find it instead of exploring all the possibilities. Creative thinking is thinking outside

Activity Option Consider asking your students to VARK the course syllabus, as described in the Instructor's Manual. Provide each student with a plain white "jewelry box," purchased from a paper supply store. Students must use all four learning styles as they translate the ordinary paper syllabus: V (a drawing or photo, for example), A (a CD of music to listen to as they study), R (a summary of the course description in their own words), and K (something to manipulate, like a miniature flip chart with assignments). You will amazed at what they produce when given creative license!

Teaching with Technology Blogging is a great way for students to express themselves online. Blogs are like interactive Internet journals, and they allow students to unleash their creativity by making ideas visible and more dynamic with the inclusion of pictures and video. Have students start a blog, and then react to this chapter in their blog. Encourage students to use blogs as a way of thinking both reproductively and productively about the material they've encountered in class, and as an outlet for their thoughts, feelings, and personal creativity. Try Blogger.com or WordPress.org.

> A mind that is stretched to a new idea never returns to its original dimensions.

Oliver Wendell Holmes,
American poet (1809–1894)

> If you have an apple and I have an apple and we exchange these apples, then you and I will still each have one apple. But if you have an idea and I have an idea and we exchange these ideas, then each of us will have two ideas.

George Bernard Shaw, Irish literary critic, playwright, and
essayist, 1925 Nobel Prize for Literature (1856–1950)

the box, or in terms of getting an education, perhaps we should call it thinking outside the book. Going beyond the obvious and exploring possibilities are important parts of becoming an educated person. Employers report that many college graduates today have specific skills, but that what they rarely see "is the ability to use the right-hand side of the brain—creativity, working in a team."[30] Here's one way to explain it. You see, there's a difference between thinking *reproductively* and thinking *productively*. *Reproductive* thinking asks: "What have I learned or experienced in the past that will help me solve this problem?" But when you're thinking *productively*, you generate as many approaches as possible.

In Figure 5.1 we looked at the Question Pyramid. Creative thinking is at the top of the pyramid. It goes beyond critical thinking, is predictive, and multidimensional. It asks "What if …?" questions. Here are some interesting ones: "What if everyone was allowed to tell one lie per day?" "What if no one could perceive colors?" "What if universities didn't exist?" "If you looked up a word like *squallizmotex* in the dictionary, what might it mean?"[31]

According to creativity expert Alan Rowe, also an author of the Decision Style Inventory in Exercise 5.3, our creative intelligence demonstrates itself in four major styles. Look at your totals and see if the description for your lowest score (meaning your most preferred category) makes sense to you. Each of us has aspects of all four styles, but your raw scores may also tell you something about your creative potential. Which of the four letters (a, b, c, or d) do you have *the lowest number* in? That category best describes you.

Teaching with Technology Ask your students to help build a "Human Wiki." Assign a different topic related to items in this chapter (or the entire book) and ask each student to find four things: 1) the best print resource, 2) the best website, 3) the best technology tool (like a YouTube), and 4) the best activity. Students can present their findings in class or make handouts so that every student can build a folder.

Exercise 5.4   Creative Potential Profile

All of us have the potential to think creatively, but interestingly, we do so in different ways. Complete the Creative Potential Profile to explore your creative thinking potential by marking your responses on these twenty-five items. Place a 1 next to the item MOST like you, a 2 for the item MODERATELY like you, a 3 for the item that's a LITTLE like you, and a 4 for the item that's LEAST like you. Don't use a number more than once for an item, and use all four numbers each time.

1. I often wonder how to
   - _____ (a) introduce change.
   - _____ (b) discover new solutions.
   - _____ (c) make ideas exciting.
   - _____ (d) work best with people.

2. My strength is being
   - _____ (a) decisive.
   - _____ (b) thorough.
   - _____ (c) imaginative.
   - _____ (d) understanding.

3. Successful people are
   - _____ (a) ambitious.
   - _____ (b) disciplined.
   - _____ (c) willing to take risks.
   - _____ (d) self-confident.

4. I get my best results by
   - _____ (a) focusing on current problems.
   - _____ (b) applying careful analysis.
   - _____ (c) trying new approaches.
   - _____ (d) gaining the support of others.

5. I see the future as
   - _____ (a) unknown.
   - _____ (c) a challenge.
   - _____ (b) providing many opportunities.
   - _____ (d) facilitating change.

6. I appreciate teachers who
   - _____ (a) explain ideas clearly.
   - _____ (b) make learning interesting.
   - _____ (c) recognize original ideas.
   - _____ (d) involve others in learning.

7. People see me as
   - _____ (a) energetic.
   - _____ (b) persistent.
   - _____ (c) a perfectionist.
   - _____ (d) committed.

8. People who make things happen
   - _____ (a) are highly motivated.
   - _____ (b) enjoy experimenting.
   - _____ (c) have the courage of their convictions.
   - _____ (d) challenge the status quo.

9. Discoveries depend on
   - _____ (a) being committed.
   - _____ (b) being curious.
   - _____ (c) being open-minded.
   - _____ (d) having a broad perspective.

10. A good writer
    - _____ (a) is convincing.
    - _____ (b) presents new ideas.
    - _____ (c) provides a unique perspective.
    - _____ (d) has a compelling vision.

11. Breakthrough thinking
    - _____ (a) makes progress possible.
    - _____ (b) helps to solve difficult problems.
    - _____ (c) explores new frontiers.
    - _____ (d) encourages teamwork.

12. I dislike
    - _____ (a) losing control.
    - _____ (b) doing boring work.
    - _____ (c) following rules.
    - _____ (d) being rejected.

13. I communicate best by being
    - _____ (a) direct.
    - _____ (b) informative.
    - _____ (c) interesting.
    - _____ (d) open.

14. I am committed to
    - _____ (a) achieving results.
    - _____ (b) being the best at what I do.
    - _____ (c) exploring new ideas.
    - _____ (d) contributing to society.

15. Creative organizations
    - _____ (a) look for good answers.
    - _____ (b) encourage experimentation.
    - _____ (c) allow freedom of expression.
    - _____ (d) support new ideas.

16. Achieving results depends on being
_____ (a) responsive.
_____ (b) systematic.
_____ (c) original.
_____ (d) cooperative.

17. I prefer situations where I
_____ (a) am in charge.
_____ (b) have challenging assignments.
_____ (c) can use my own ideas.
_____ (d) can introduce change.

18. Change depends on
_____ (a) gaining support.
_____ (b) exploring options.
_____ (c) independent thinking.
_____ (d) inspiring others.

19. My goal is to
_____ (a) accomplish my objectives.
_____ (b) discover new approaches.
_____ (c) have my ideas recognized.
_____ (d) achieve progress.

20. Leaders
_____ (a) assume responsibility.
_____ (b) deal with complexity.
_____ (c) visualize opportunities.
_____ (d) empower others.

21. Ethical behavior
_____ (a) is expected.
_____ (b) requires honesty.
_____ (c) emphasizes integrity.
_____ (d) enhances society.

22. The arts
_____ (a) help to improve designs.
_____ (b) contribute new perspectives.
_____ (c) broaden education.
_____ (d) enrich people's lives.

23. Creative thinkers
_____ (a) accomplish important goals.
_____ (b) make significant discoveries.
_____ (c) have leaps of imagination.
_____ (d) turn their dreams into reality.

24. Breaking with tradition
_____ (a) is seldom desirable.
_____ (b) needs to be done carefully.
_____ (b) provides new opportunities.
_____ (d) helps to accomplish goals.

25. When under pressure, I
_____ (a) trust my instincts.
_____ (b) rely on known approaches.
_____ (c) carefully explore my options.
_____ (d) avoid conflict.

Totals: (a) _____ (b) _____ (c) _____ (d) _____

Source: Adapted from *Creative Intelligence: Discovering the Innovative Potential in Ourselves and Others* by A. J. Rowe. © 2004 by Pearson Education, Inc., by permission from Dr. Alan J. Rowe.

THIS IS SO ME!

> **Intuitive (a).** This creative style is best described as *resourceful*. If you are an Intuitive, you achieve goals, use common sense, and work to solve problems. You focus on results and rely on past experience to guide your actions. Managers, actors, and politicians are commonly Intuitives.

> **Innovative (b).** This creative style is best described as *curious*. Innovatives concentrate on problem solving, are systematic, and rely on data. They use original approaches, are willing to experiment, and focus on systematic inquiry. Scientists, engineers, and inventors typically demonstrate the Innovative creative style.

> **Imaginative (c).** This creative style is best described as *insightful*. Imaginatives are willing to take risks, have leaps of imagination, and are independent thinkers. They are able to visualize opportunities, are artistic,

enjoy writing, and think outside the box. Artists, musicians, writers, and charismatic leaders are often Imaginatives.

> **Inspirational (d).** This creative style is best described as *visionary*. Inspirationals respond to societal needs, willingly give of themselves, and have the courage of their convictions. They focus on social change and the giving of themselves toward achieving it. They are often educators, motivational leaders, and writers.[32]

According to the Creative Potential Profile, which is your predominant style? Do your results seem accurate for you? Think about how you can make the best use of your natural style. How will your creativity affect the major or career you choose? Most people have more than one creative style. Remember that motivation, not general intelligence, is the key to creativity. You must be willing to tap your creative potential and challenge yourself to show it.[33]

Ten Ways to Become a More Creative Thinker

Becoming a more creative thinker may mean you need to accept your creativity and cultivate it. Consider these suggestions on how to think more creatively.

1. **Find new eyes.** Find a new perspective on old issues. Here's an interesting example. Years ago, a group of Japanese schoolchildren devised a new way to solve conflicts and build empathy for others' positions, called the Pillow Method. Figure 5.4 is an adaptation of it, based on the fact that a pillow has four sides and a middle, just like most problems.

   The middle or *mu* is the Zen expression for "it doesn't really matter." There is truth in all four positions. Try it: take a conflict you're having difficulty with at the moment, and write down all four sides and a middle.[34]

2. **Accept your creativity.** Many mindsets block creative thinking: "It can't be done!" "I'm just not the creative type." "I might look stupid!" Many people don't see themselves as creative. This perception can become a major stumbling block. If creativity isn't part of your self-image, you may need to revamp your image. Everyone has creative potential. You may just have to learn how to tap into yours.

> " At the start of an exam, a student openly wondered, 'But Professor Einstein, this is the same exam question as last year!' To which the great man supposedly replied, 'Correct, young man, but we need to find new answers.' "
>
> *Werner Reinartz, HBR Blog Network*

1. I'M A STUDENT PAYING TUITION FOR PHIL 100.
2. PROFESSOR COURTNEY IS AN EXPERT IN PHILOSOPHY.
3. 1 AND 2 ARE TRUE.
4. 1 AND 2 ARE FALSE. JUST BECAUSE I PAY DOESN'T MEAN I CAN BUY KNOWLEDGE. BEING AN EXPERT DOESN'T ALWAYS MAKE THE PROFESSOR A GREAT TEACHER.
MU = IT REALLY DOESN'T MATTER. HE'S HERE TO TEACH, AND I'M HERE TO LEARN.

FIGURE 5.4

The Pillow Method

Position 1—I'm right and you're wrong.
Position 2—You're right and I'm wrong.
Position 3—We're both right.
Position 4—We're both wrong.

3. **Make your thoughts visible.** For many of us, things become clear when we can see them, either in our mind's eye or displayed for us. Even Einstein, a scientist and mathematician, had a very visual mind. Sometimes if we write something down or sketch something out, we generate a new approach without really trying.

4. **Generate lots of ideas.** Thomas Edison held 1,093 patents, until recently, still the record. He gave himself idea quotients. The rule he set for himself was that he had to come up with a major invention every six months and a minor invention every ten days. Bach wrote a cantata every week, even if he was ill. According to two-time Nobel Prize winner Linus Pauling, "The best way to get a good idea is to get lots of ideas."

5. **Don't overcomplexify.** In hindsight, many of the most ingenious discoveries are embarrassingly simple. Biologist Thomas Huxley said, after reading Darwin's explanation of evolution: "How extremely stupid not to have thought of that!" It's common to bemoan our problems and allow anxiety to make them worse. But sometimes the most simple solution is the best one.[35]

6. **Capitalize on your mistakes.** Remember that Thomas Edison tried anything he could think of for a filament for the incandescent lamp, including a whisker from his best friend's beard. All in all, he tried about 1,800 things before finding the right one. Afterwards he said, "I've gained a lot of knowledge—I now know a thousand things that won't work."[36]

7. **Let it flow.** Mihaly Csikszentmihalyi, the author of *Flow: The Psychology of Optimal Experience* and many other books on creativity, discovered something interesting. For his doctoral thesis, he studied artists by taking pictures of them painting every three minutes. He was struck by how engaged they were in their work, so engaged that they seemed to forget everything around them. He began studying other "experts": rock climbers, chess players, dancers, musicians, surgeons. Regardless of the activity, these people forgot the time, themselves, and their problems. What did the activities have in common? Clear, high goals and immediate feedback. Athletes call it being in the zone. Csikszentmihalyi's suggestions for achieving flow are these: Pick an enjoyable activity that is at or slightly above your ability level, screen out distractions, focus all your senses and emotions, and look for regular feedback on how you're doing.[37]

8. **Bounce ideas off others.** One good way to become more creative is to use your family or friends as sounding boards. Sometimes just verbalizing something helps you understand more about it. Each person who provides a critique will give you a new perspective, possibly worth considering.

9. **Stop searching for the "right" answer.** This advice doesn't pertain to your upcoming math exam. But it does to apply to situations in which there are many ways to solve a problem. There may be more than one acceptable solution. Fear of mistakes can be debilitating.

" A hunch is creativity trying to tell you something. "

Frank Capra, Italian American film director (1897–1991)

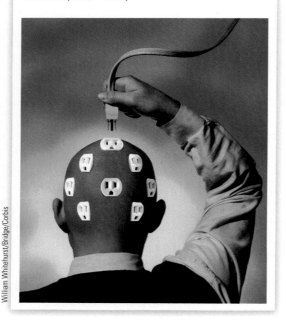

William Whitehurst/Bridge/Corbis

Exercise 5.5 Generating Creative Captions

Einstein once said, "Creativity is intelligence having fun." Look at the following cartoon, and generate as many funny captions as you can. Some websites or Web-based magazines run competitions like this, and one entry sent in by online readers is selected as the winning caption. Often, creativity is about generating many possible answers, rather than a single correct one. Compare your captions with those of your classmates, and see much creativity you come up with, collectively.

1.

2.

3.

4.

5.

10. **Detach your self-concept.** For most of us, creativity is often linked to self-concept. An idea is your brainchild, and you want it to win approval. You've invested part of yourself in giving birth to it. But there's nothing like self-imposed judgment to shut down your creative juices. Your idea may not succeed on its own, but it may feed into someone else's idea and improve it. Or an idea you have about this problem may inform the next problem that challenges you. In the end, in addition to finding a workable solution, what's important is engaging in the creative process with others.

THESE ARE ALL GREAT IDEAS!

> Every day is an opportunity to be creative—the canvas is your mind, the brushes and colours are your thoughts and feelings, the panorama is your story, the complete picture is a work of art called, 'my life.' Be careful what you put on the canvas of your mind today—it matters.

—*Innerspace*

❶ At the beginning of this chapter, Annie Miller, a frustrated student, faced a challenge. Now after reading this chapter, would you respond differently to any of the questions you answered about the "FOCUS Challenge Case"? Knowing what you know now, how would you advise her? Write a paragraph ending to the story, incorporating your best advice.

❷ Identify a time, subject, or event in which you used your critical thinking skills for your own benefit. Perhaps you investigated the salary range for a new job or read blogs on a particular subject to gain new perspectives. Explain what you did, how you went about it, and why. What did you learn about yourself?

❸ Provide real examples of critical thinking from any of your current classes. Are you being asked on exams to compare and contrast? To sort through evidence and make decisions? In class discussions are you encouraged to disagree with your instructor or classmates for the sake of a healthy, vigorous debate? How do you handle these situations? Do you think they help you learn? If so, how?

❹ Do you see yourself as a creative person? Instead of thinking about whether you're creative or not, ask yourself this question, "*How* am I creative?" Describe the ways.

❺ Think of a problem you're facing right now. Use the Pillow Method described in Figure 5.4 to analyze the problem. Why could this approach be helpful?

What did you LEARN?

Reality Check

Activity Option Have students develop a three- to five-slide PowerPoint presentation for the class describing a technique in this chapter for analyzing arguments, becoming more creative, exploring different decision-making styles, applying the Pillow Method (with examples), or any activity in the chapter that helped them reach a new understanding. (Students can work in teams and you can assign topics if you wish.)

On a scale of 1 to 10, answer the following questions now that you've completed the chapter.

    1 2 3 4 5 6 7 8 9 10

In hindsight, how much did you already know about this subject before reading the chapter?

Can you answer these questions about critical and creative thinking more fully now that you've read the chapter?

❶ What's the difference between thinking and critical thinking?

❷ Identify three specific types of faulty reasoning.

❸ What's the difference between critical thinking and creative thinking?

How useful might the information in this chapter be to you? How much do you think this information might affect your success in college? _____

How much energy did you put into reading this chapter? _____

How long did it actually take you to complete this chapter (both the reading and writing tasks)? _____ Hour(s) _____ Minutes

Did you finish reading this chapter? _____

Did you intend to when you started? _____

If you meant to but didn't, what stopped you? _____

Take a minute to compare these answers to your answers from the "Readiness Check" at the beginning of this chapter. What gaps exist between the similar questions? How might these gaps between what you thought before starting the chapter and what you now think after completing the chapter affect how you approach the next chapter in this book?

6 Learning Online

How this chapter relates to YOU

1. When it comes to online learning, using technology, and doing research for your college classes, what are you most concerned about, if anything?

Having the right technology skills

Having enough self-discipline

Missing face-to-face classroom interaction

Knowing how to conduct research

Understanding exactly what plagiarism is

2. What is most likely to be your response? Circle it.

I'll be open to learning more about using technology for schoolwork.	I'll wait and see how much of this chapter I understand.	I'll ask my online or classroom instructor for clarification.	Eventually, I'll just figure it out.

3. What would you have to do to increase your likelihood of success? Will you do it this quarter or semester?

_____

_____

_____

How YOU will relate to this chapter

What are you most interested in learning about? Put check marks by those topics.

☐ How to develop useful strategies for online classes

☐ How to use technology to become more academically successful

☐ How to cultivate your research skills

☐ What information literacy skills are and why they're important

☐ What plagiarism is and how to avoid it

● How motivated are you to learn more about learning online, using technology, and doing research in college? (5 = high, 1 = low) ____

● How ready are you to read now? ____ (If something is in your way, take care of it if you can, zero in and focus.)

● How long do you think it will take you to complete this chapter? If you start and stop, keep track of your overall time. ____ Hour(s) ____ Minutes

175

Dario Jones

© Robert Kyllo/Shutterstock.com

© Ben Mitchell/Shutterstock.com

© Jack Haefner/Shutterstock.com

© CLM/Shutterstock.com

Ever since grade school, Dario Jones had been called a geek. It was a label he hated, but, honestly, most people probably thought of him that way. As a kid, Dario lived for computer games. He played them nearly every waking hour. In high school, he'd shower in record time, throw on whatever clean clothes he could find, and use any spare minutes for computer games. When he got home, he'd log right back on again. His Dad tried threatening him: "You'll lose your eyesight and flunk out of school." Once when he was younger, he faked a sore throat and played World of Warcraft at home for a week while his parents were at work. As he got older, his Dad warned: "You'll never get a date." But Dario wasn't worried. Online relationships were enough. Real-life relationships were too much trouble. After high school, he joined the Army, and now that he was finally back from 12 months in Afghanistan, his cyber life was much more exciting than ever. Dario spent more time surfing the Internet, envisioning how he could improve websites, and grooming his Facebook page than he spent talking to any living being.

© Larry Harwood Photography.
Property of Cengage Learning.

Then one day the obvious truth dawned on him. Now that he was a civilian, he was going to have to get a job—plain and simple. He had joined the Army because he really didn't know what he wanted to do next, and he figured he'd gain some skills there. But now that he was home, he wondered how those skills would translate into a different career—and whether he had the right skills.

Eventually, Dario made a decision. He would use his G.I. benefits and go to college. Because he was such a technology fan, maybe computer science would be a good field

Mike Margol/PhotoEdit

for him. And as he Googled opportunities, he found that he could get an entire degree online! What could be more perfect than that? Sitting in real classrooms with all those young kids didn't appeal to him much at all. Besides, he had survived some pretty intense experiences while deployed, and fighting for parking spots and being in crowded classrooms would just add to his stress. The images of the past twelve months were still very much alive in his memory. Besides, online courses had to be easier than real classes, and that one thing sealed the deal.

But Dario quickly discovered that his considerable tech skills might not be enough. Besides that, all three classes had major assignments that would require a serious time commitment. The first week, he stayed up late, listening to online lectures, downloading handouts, and posting responses on the discussion board. Then before he knew it, he got an e-mail from the instructor in his toughest class, "Fundamentals of Internet Business," reminding him that he needed to post two of his own responses to her questions and respond to two classmates' comments each week. "Your comments need to be substantive, Dario, not just quick entries like, 'I really liked the online lecture for Chapter 6' or 'Good point, Keisha.' And you need to keep up," she wrote. "I didn't hear from you for two weeks." *That kind of criticism is a definite turn-off,* Dario thought to himself. If he had been able to get his tuition back, he would have been tempted to drop out of the course entirely.

The worst part was that his toughest class required a research paper. The assigned topic was Globalization and Internet Commerce. Even though he had always considered himself to be a technology expert, frankly, he didn't know where to start. *Step one*, Dario thought to himself, *is to Google*. He always Googled everything: the directions to a new Mexican restaurant—his favorite food—or some little-known fact that he wondered about, like how many Chihuahuas were sold in the United States last year. (He had just bought one.) But when he Googled "Internet Commerce," he got 196 billion hits. *Better regroup*, he advised himself.

But how? Should he go to a real library or try to do his research online in the comfort of his own apartment? Physically going to a library seemed unnecessary when so much information was available online. Then he had a flash of inspiration: Wikipedia. He found a page on "Electronic Commerce." At least that was a start—that is, until he looked at his instructor's handout on the assignment. Students were discouraged from using Wikipedia as a primary research source. The handout said, "Information literacy is required." He got another idea: He'd close Wikipedia and go back to Googling. This time he'd try "Electronic Commerce." *Ah, only 62 billion hits this time*. He was on a roll. He plugged in "E-Commerce," "E-Business," and "Globalization." He tried "Global Issues," but before he knew it, he found himself knee-deep in articles about "Global Warming." He was so far afield now that he couldn't find his way back to his topic. Should he shut everything down and start over or just give up?

At the last minute, Dario panicked. He found a few useful things online, and cut and pasted from the Internet until he'd filled five pages. At least he had something to turn in. He wondered if this was the way to do research and whether he'd broken any rules. *Well, I can always go back into the military*, he thought to himself. But to be honest, he really wanted to make an entirely new life for himself as a civilian.

Fundamentals of Internet Business
CS 112

Research Paper Guidelines

TOPIC: Globalization and Internet Commerce

For this assignment you will write a 10 page research paper investigating the relationship between globalization and Internet commerce. You should not only focus on how globalization has affected Internet commerce, but how the relationship was a two-way street. In other words, look at how Internet commerce has changed the pace of globalization in the 21st century.

POTENTIAL AREAS OF RESEARCH FOCUS:

- What is Globalization?
- Free Trade
- Transnational Corporations
- Social Equity
- Equality of Access
- Opinion Shaping
- Homogenization of Cultures
- Internet Commerce in the 21st Century
- Intercultural Factors
- Communication Factors
- The Concept of a Global Village

RESEARCH SOURCES: The sole use of research tools such as Wikipedia and/or Google are discouraged. You may use any one of the major styles of citations for this paper. However, once you have chosen your particular style (APA, MLA, Chicago, etc.) you must stick to that style! Please don't use APA in-text citations and an MLA reference page.

DUE DATE: This paper will be due three weeks from today. Please contact me if you have any questions or concerns.

challenge

" reaction

❶ In your view, is Dario addicted to technology? Can being too dependent on technology be a problem? Why?

❷ Do you have anything in common with Dario? For example, do you think (or have you found) that online classes are easier or harder than face-to-face courses? Why?

❸ The instructor's assignment required "information literacy." What is information literacy? Dario was tech-savvy, but did he have the right skills? Why or why not?

❹ Did Dario plagiarize his paper—or did he simply find the sources he needed and use them? Give the reasons behind your answer.

VARK It!

Complete the recommended activity for your preferred VARK learning modality. If you are multimodal, select more than one activity. Your instructor may ask you to (a) give an oral report on your results in class, (b) send your results to him or her via e-mail, or (c) post them online.

Visual: As you read, highlight things you'll do for a research project you're working on right now. If you don't have a current research assignment, propose one you'd expect in a course you might take next term, and do the same.

Aural: At some point while you're reading this chapter, interview a reference librarian on campus to get his or her take on the most common mistakes first-year students make while conducting research. See if your librarian's items match those listed by the reference librarian cited in this chapter.

Read/Write: As you read, watch for an information-rich paragraph that you relate to in this chapter, and practice closing your book and paraphrasing the paragraph in your own words. Paraphrasing is an important skill to cultivate as you learn to do academic research.

Kinesthetic: Before you read further, find a "TED Talk" (at www.ted.com) that fascinates you by clicking on the subject of technology on the ted.com website. E-mail the link to your instructor or show it in class with permission. In your view, how effective are online tools like these for student learning? Why?

Taking Online Classes: E-Learning versus C-Learning

challenge

" reaction

Challenge: Identify three differences in the way students should approach e-learning (electronic) compared to c-learning (classroom) courses.

Reaction:

_____

_____

_____

Teachable Moment Ask students if they have ever been faced with Dario's problem. Have them explain their problem and how they solved it. Encourage students not to struggle and wait until the last minute like Dario. Advise them to e-mail the instructor, go to the writing center, or even ask a friend in the class. The secret is to not wait until the last minute.

What do an American soldier just back from Afghanistan, a single mother of twin toddlers in California, and a victim of cerebral palsy in New York have in common? All three are taking the same online course in psychology. Instead of c-learning (traditionally, in the classroom), they're engaging in *distance education* or e-learning (**e**lectronically, online). E-learning is one kind of technology you may well run into during your time in college.

Of course, most of your college courses are hybrids or blended courses: they each have an online component and a classroom component. You e-mail your professor, use software to track your progress, upload assignments and download handouts, but you still go to a physical classroom with classmates once or twice a term, or perhaps even every week. That's why they're called hybrid (like cars: part electricity and part gasoline) or blended (when mediated and face-to-face learning are meshed) classes. If you haven't already, chances are you'll be engaged in distance learning in a totally online environment for at least one of your college classes. Enrollment in online college classes has climbed for the last ten years with 6.7 million students taking an online course in fall 2011.[1] And because of exciting, new learning technologies, many experts predict that online classes and tools represent an important part of the future of higher education.[2] It's important for college students like you to stay abreast of changes to come.

What are the differences between e-learning and c-learning? E-learning is sometimes defined as structured learning that takes place without a teacher at the front of the room. If you're an independent, self-motivated student, e-learning can be a great way to learn, because *you* are in control.

➤ *You control when you learn.* Instead of that dreaded 8:00 A.M. class— the only section that's open when you register—you can schedule your e-learning when it's convenient for you. If you want to do your course-work at midnight in your pajamas, who's to know?

➤ *You control how you learn.* If you are an introvert, e-learning may work well for you. You can work thoughtfully online and take all the time you need to reflect. If you are an extravert, however, you may become frustrated by the lack of warm bodies around. Jumping into online discussions may satisfy some of those needs, but you may miss real people sitting next to you. If you're a kinesthetic learner, the keyboard action may suit you well. Because you're working independently, you can do whatever you need to do to accommodate your own learning style.

These are good points, but they're not why I decided to take online courses. I just thought they'd be easier.

66

It was not so very long ago that people thought that semiconductors were part-time orchestra leaders and microchips were very small snack foods. 99

Geraldine Ferraro, Democratic politician, 1935–2011

Stockbyte/Getty Images

Teachable Moment Your students may have heard the term MOOC (Massive, Open, Online Course) since these opportunities are becoming more common (although whether courses are accredited and count toward degree completion are important considerations). Discuss the fact that while MOOCs are free, they typically have a completion rate of ten percent or less. They may be more appropriate experiments for more advanced students.

Work harder?? I hadn't thought about any of this, really.

➤ **You control how fast you learn.** You know for a fact that students learn at different rates. With e-learning, you don't have to feel you're slowing down the class if you continue a line of questioning or worry about getting left in the dust if everyone else is way ahead of you.

E-learning can be a very effective way to learn, but it does require some adjustments. Here are some suggestions for making the best of your online learning opportunities:

1. **Work harder.** Many students think that fully online courses will be easier than going to class. After all, you won't have to shower, get dressed, drive through traffic, and cruise the campus for 15 minutes to find a parking spot (or walk from your residence hall). These factors, in and of themselves, should be big time savers. It's true that online classes are convenient, but generally speaking, they take *more* time. Think about it this way: in an online course, you will have to do many of the things that your instructor would normally do for you. In a classroom, she may simply walk around and pass out handouts. Online, you'll have to locate them on the course website, download them, and print them out yourself. You'll need to read everything carefully, both the items posted on the course management shell itself (like the course calendar, syllabus, reminder messages, instructions for each assignment) and every document you download. Instead of taking a seat in the classroom to listen to your professor lecture at the front of the room, you will have to get the information yourself by downloading lecture notes, PowerPoint slides, or videos of your instructors' lectures. The belief that online courses are easier is a myth.

2. **Keep up.** Even though you may be "invisible" in online courses, you can't "hide." Unless your class requires a webcam (to record yourself for an online public speaking class, for example), you're virtually invisible. You'll likely have to keep up by posting regularly to the class blog or online discussion board and comment on your classmates' posts every week. If you decide to "take a vacation" in the middle of your online course, your instructor may inquire about your whereabouts. Just as you'd do for a face-to-face class, consider setting aside a specific time each week for your online course, like Tuesday and Thursday afternoons, and commit to reserving that time for online coursework.

3. **Get advice from other online students.** The first time you take an online course, ask a friend or classmate who has experience with this type of course for advice. That person may save you hours of online wandering with a few simple tips. Besides finding out how to navigate your online course, ask what student services are available online, like advising, tutoring, financial aid, enrollment, and tuition payments.

4. **Communicate your needs to your instructor.** If this is your first online course, ask your instructor for a general assessment of how much time he expects you to set aside each week. Think about the three or more hours or so you usually spend per week sitting in and preparing for a face-to-face class or lab, and use that as a rule of thumb. (Of course, specifics depend on what else you have going on and your individual learning style preferences. And when you begin to see the grades you earn

Can't some of these apply to my regular courses, too? They sound like good ideas . . .

on the assignments you turn in, you may decide to invest more time on your own.) Remember, too, that your instructor won't be able to see your "huh?" looks when you don't understand something. Take direct action by e-mailing her, for example, instead of hiding behind your computer screen and hoping for the best. "The best" usually doesn't come to you; you'll have to work for it. On the other hand, before you fire off a quick question, re-read the assignment. It may be that you just missed something simple, and your question is actually unnecessary.

5. **Stay in touch with other students in the course.** Rather than isolating yourself, which is a mistake, use e-mail to communicate with your cyber classmates to build an online learning community. They may be able to clarify an assignment or coach you through a tough spot.

6. **Take notes.** When you're sitting through an in-class lecture, you handwrite notes to review later. Likewise, if you're reading lecture notes online, open a Word document and switch back and forth for your own note-taking purposes. Or open an e-tool, like evernote.com, which can work well for note taking.

7. **Keep your antivirus program up to date.** When you upload assignment files, you run the risk of infecting your instructor's computer with whatever viruses your computer may have. Make sure your antivirus software is up to date!

8. **Control your learning environment.** Because you'll most likely do your e-learning at home or in your residence hall room, make sure the environment is right for learning. If you're working on your laptop in front of the TV or your roommate keeps wanting to chat, move to another location that's calm, properly lit, and quiet, like the library.

9. **Use each login session as an opportunity to review.** Begin each online session by reviewing what you did or how much progress you made last time. Physically logging on can become a signal to take stock before moving forward with new course material.

10. **Organize, organize, organize!** In your face-to-face classes, you can keep courses separate in your mind by remembering where the different classrooms are located, for example, and who your classmates and teachers are. By contrast, in online courses you may never even meet your classmates or teacher. You'll have to find ways to separate and organize materials for each class either physically by using hard copy files or electronically by using folders on your computer or thumb drive.

11. **Call on your time management skills.** Create a "Term-on-a-Page" master calendar, mark the due dates for each class, and review it at the beginning of every

I need to do this ASAP!

> **Any occurrence requiring undivided attention will be accompanied by a compelling distraction.**

Robert Bloch, American fiction writer, (1917–1994)

week. If your e-course is self-paced, you'll need to plan ahead, schedule due dates, and above all discipline yourself to make continual progress. For many students, this very thing is the biggest challenge of online courses. The instructor isn't there with you, insisting that you turn in assignments. If you're sharing a computer with other family members, or notice that the computer labs on campus are always maxed out at certain time, plan around that. Remember that you may need to be online at particular times to engage in class chats or discussions.

12. **Have a back-up plan.** Technology crashes from time to time, and system platforms go down, sometimes just when you need them. Get to know your campus tech support staff, and don't hesitate to contact them in an emergency. Work ahead, so that you don't fall behind if the dreaded "blue screen" suddenly appears, signaling a tech failure. Watch for campus e-mails about system down time for scheduled upgrades, and work around it. In other words, take responsibility. If your paper is late because you left your thumb drive in the car, and your car is at your sister's house, expect to have points deducted. Most online instructors abide by syllabus rules, and they expect you to do the same.[3]

Teachable Moment Exercise 6.1 can be used to generate a productive in-class or online discussion. These are realistic issues students face regularly when doing online work, and the scenarios can introduce how important motivation, intentionality, and problem solving are to success.

Exercise 6.1   A Day in the Life of an Online Student

You wake up and look out the window. It's a beautiful day, and—lucky you—you don't have any classes. The first thing you decide to do is check your phone. You see a few new posts on your Facebook wall and some new pictures from last weekend. You find a funny new YouTube, a few texts from friends, and an e-mail from the instructor of your online class. *Oh no,* you think. *I haven't done anything for my online class in a while, and there's a big assignment due tomorrow!* With a sigh you glance out the window one more time. It looks like you won't be able to spend the day relaxing outside like you thought.

Assume this is what your day looks like. For each entry in your hypothetical "day timer," look at the obstacles that may get in your way, and describe how you'll address them.

8:00 A.M.

You sit down to work on your online course, but you start to wander, electronically. Maybe you do need to use that $50 iTunes card your Mom gave you for your birthday. Before you know it, an hour and a half has gone by and you get up to get a snack.

SOLUTION:

_____

_____

10:00 A.M.

You successfully get yourself back on task, but you hit a snag. You have the syllabus somewhere, and you have lots of questions about the assignment. Your instructor gave you her contact info, but you can't afford to wait very long for a response.

SOLUTION:

_____

_____

10:30 A.M.

Now that you have clarification on the assignment, you dig into your work. You need to find ten different sources for your research, but you're not having much luck. You try one Google search after another, but the websites don't seem to have what you're looking for.

SOLUTION:

_____

_____

11:00 A.M.

You've finally located some reliable and useful resources for your assignment. As you continue to work, you find yourself copying and pasting a useful word here and there into your paper. Pretty soon, you're clicking and dragging phrases, then sentences into your assignment. *Am I plagiarizing?* you wonder.

SOLUTION:

_____

_____

12:00 P.M.

You're working hard, finding good resources, and using them ethically. Your phone rings. It's one of your friends, inviting you to grab some lunch at your favorite off-campus restaurant and maybe hit the mall afterwards. You glance at your watch. You've been working on this project for a couple of hours now; haven't you earned a little break?

SOLUTION:

_____

_____

7:00 P.M.

Looking back on the day, you've accomplished a lot. You've coped with understanding the assignment clearly, finding good resources and using them well, and managing your time. You're pretty happy with your work, but you wish there was a way to get some feedback on the assignment before you submit it.

SOLUTION:

_____

_____

11:00 P.M.

Turn in for the night. Tomorrow is a new "Day in the Life of an Online Student."

Technology Skills: Wireless, Windowed, Webbed, and Wikied

Ah, technology . . . Does it make our lives simpler or more complicated? Like nearly half of college students, do you sometimes skip studying to play online computer games?[4] Are you tempted by online streaming movies or TV shows, just because they're so convenient? Do you live to text? Do you run, not walk, to any nearby computer to check your Facebook account? Or, on the other hand, do you ever get annoyed because your cell phone is going off continuously—sometimes at the most inopportune moments, like when you can't get to it? Did you find yourself answering "yes" to any of these questions—or maybe answering "yes" to all of them?

Many of us have a love-hate relationship with technology: We love the convenience but hate the dependence. But in college, information literacy and technology skills will be keys to your academic success. You'll need to know things like how to use Microsoft Word with agility to produce a polished essay, how to design an information-rich and visually compelling PowerPoint presentation, and how to use one or more of the many course management systems available, like Blackboard. You don't have to be a technology guru, but you will need to call upon your technology skills to conduct research for your college classes. Many college students are tech savvy, but their skills are more about entertainment than education. In fact, a recent study suggests that many students actually overestimate their technology skills when it comes to using software that is often related to class assignments.[5]

Hmmm... are mine?

Use Technology to Your Academic Advantage

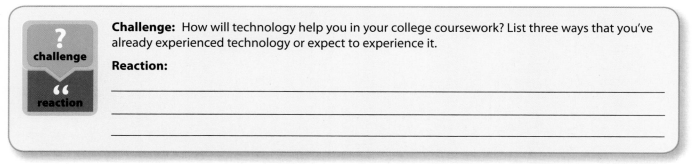

challenge

? reaction

Challenge: How will technology help you in your college coursework? List three ways that you've already experienced technology or expect to experience it.

Reaction:

_____

_____

_____

When you first arrive on campus or even before, you'll see evidence of technology everywhere. Your school may send out regular updates about campus events on Twitter. You may be asked to respond to an on-screen quiz in class by using your cell phone. You'll get an e-mail account and be sent official college documents, like your tuition bill and weather alerts. You will take entire courses or parts of courses online so that you can learn on your own time at your own pace. Many of your instructors will use course management systems, streaming video, and websites in the classroom to increase your learning. Soon, experts say—maybe even now—you will be able to access your course materials via your mobile device from anywhere, direct your computer's operations using hand gestures, and read books *with* other people as a social activity.[6] In fact, these trends are already emerging, and undoubtedly technology will become an even more highly integrated part of learning in the future. What academic benefits does technology provide?[7] Let's look at some examples of the advantages technology will offer you in college. Technology will help you:

> **Manage your courses.** Many of your college classes will be conducted partially or wholly online, using technology shells, like Blackboard, Moodle,

and Desire2Learn. Course management systems help you easily track your grades, access syllabi, and upload assignments, for example, all from one place. About two-thirds of college students use them in their classes.[8]

> **Interact with course content, classmates, and your instructor.** You may have heard the term "Web 2.0." It's not a new version of the Internet. It refers to creative uses of it, like Facebook, Wikis, and blogs, where instead of just reading passively, users help create the content. For example, your instructor may post a question or comment and ask you to post your responses online and to respond to those of your classmates. Everyone can get to know you by your online personality, and some students say they become better writers by reading other students' responses to their blogs (Web logs). You may watch a YouTube clip in class, insert one into a presentation you create as a class assignment, or post one yourself related to your life as a student. Or you may be asked to contribute to a Wiki, today's online, editable encyclopedia. Anyone can add information or change content (currently there are more than 30 million articles in more than two hundred and eighty-seven languages on the most extensive of these sites).[9] In addition to these Web 2.0 possibilities, you will undoubtedly use e-mail, check your classmates' Facebook pages, and listen to podcasts, if your professor posts an audio version of her lecture. Typically, aural learners enjoy podcasts and kinesthetic learners enjoy the interactivity of Web 2.0.

> **Complete assignments.** Your college classes will ask you to use at least three types of software in your academic work:

> > Microsoft Word allows you to type, edit, alphabetize, index, footnote, and do many other things to prepare papers for your classes.

> > Microsoft PowerPoint, used as an electronic visual aid for oral presentations, allows you to create an on-screen guide for your listeners (and you, if you glance periodically and subtly for clues).

> > Microsoft Excel spreadsheets are good for tabulating, record keeping, and organizing.

The industry standard for these applications is generally the Microsoft products listed here, although other possibilities exist. If you need help learning any of these applications, your campus techies, instructors, or online tutorials (which can easily be found by Googling) can help. If you're a techie yourself, you can venture into other software applications like Flash, Camtasia, iMovie, or Adobe Acrobat to make your academic work look even more professional.

> **Increase your learning.** You may also find yourself using textbook websites, like the one you're using for *FOCUS on College Success*. Often these websites are tied closely to the textbook you're using in class, and they contain information and activities to enrich your learning experience, like videos, quizzes, and iAudio chapter summaries. Use these resources to help you master course material.

One final point: While our focus here has been on using technology to your academic *advantage*, it can also put you at a *disadvantage*, if you let it. If

Many college students spend hours on the Internet downloading their favorite tunes and uploading their favorite photos. They think they know technology. But do they? Here's an important question: What kinds of computer skills will help you excel in college and what kind of skills are employers looking for? Look at the lists below. Which of the following tasks can you perform *right now* (without clicking on "help" or Googling)? These software applications are considered to be the "industry standard" used in most organizations.

	Basic	Moderate	Advanced
MS Word	____ open a document ____ bold text ____ cut and paste ____ undo and redo ____ change the page orientation	____ count words ____ highlight text ____ insert page numbers ____ justify a paragraph ____ add bullets	____ alphabetize lists ____ create footnotes ____ use Autocorrect ____ record/run macros ____ merge documents
MS PowerPoint	____ create slides ____ delete slides ____ insert images ____ choose a design template ____ add new slides	____ animate slides ____ change background colors ____ add transitions between slides ____ create and run a slide show ____ print slides, handouts, and outlines	____ merge slides from another slideshow ____ insert hyperlinks ____ edit hyperlinks ____ change animation timing ____ change animation order
MS Excel	____ create spreadsheets ____ move data around ____ make calculations ____ create a chart ____ copy/merge cells	____ use the SUM function to create formulas ____ use the fill handle to copy a cell ____ use a VBA macro ____ freeze panes ____ format cells, rows, and columns	____ create formulas using the IF function ____ use absolute references ____ use Excel as a database ____ use VLOOKUP ____ use PivotTables

In one recent study, college students overestimated their software skill levels, particularly on Word and Excel. Although they perceived their skills as average or high, when tested, their performance didn't measure up. Computer literacy is a critical job requirement. If you're surprised by how few checkmarks you were able to make above, now is the right time to gear up! Take an online tutorial, sign up for a workshop on campus, or enroll in a computer literacy class. Not only will you be able to apply your skills to all your classes, but you'll be ramping up for the job waiting for you in the world of work.[10]

I thought I'd have more checkmarks on this.
I'm going to actually try doing some of these.

you bring your laptop to class to take notes, but actually spend your time surfing online instead, you'll miss out on what's going on. If you don't finish your assignments because Facebook takes up all your free time, your grades will show it. A word to the wise: Excess technology or "misplaced" technology can lead to academic self-sabotage. New research indicates that excessive amounts of time spent on media, texting, chatting on cell phones, and posting to Facebook accounts take a serious academic toll.[11]

It's noon. You decide to check your online life while you chow down a giant burrito. Five new requests from potential Facebook friends. *Who are these people?* you wonder. After a bit of browsing, you decide to update your photo albums by uploading several shots from your weekend adventures. Then you notice an amazing item on eBay that you've been looking for, and a bidding war is underway. You decide to join in, and you cast the winning bid. *Man, how am I going to pay for that?* you wonder. The clock ticks away. You order a new pair of shoes from your favorite website, and then check your watch. It's already 4:30. Four and a half hours have just gone by, and your chem class has already started!

Does this scenario sound uncomfortably familiar? A few minutes start a chain reaction that stretches out for several hours. You hate to admit it, but you're caught in the Net, spending so much time on the Internet that you're neglecting other areas of your life. Just why is the Internet so addicting? Is it the novelty of things like Facebook or eBay? Is it because it allows us to do so much without moving from one spot? Is it because our real lives seem less interesting than the online potential? One addict confessed, "Sometimes I'll sign-off Facebook and just stare at the login screen like a cocaine addict looking at the edge of his coffee table, thinking to myself, 'Well, I've really got nothing better to do right now,' and then I sign right back on. That's when you know you're really addicted."[12]

Are *you* addicted? Ask yourself these questions: Do you obsess about your online life and get nervous if you can't find your phone because it's how you accomplish almost everything? Do you spend more time with your online friends than your real friends? Do you interrupt yourself constantly to check your e-mail or update your online profile while doing Internet research for your class projects? If the answers to the questions in this paragraph are yes, are *you* ready to consider that you may be overly dependent on the Internet?[13]

Don't get caught in the Net. Think about the impact it could have on your college success. Try these suggestions:

1. **Monitor your time online.** Estimate right now how much time you spend online per week. Then actually time yourself. Is your estimate accurate? Or are you way off base? Give yourself a hard-and-fast time limit, and stick to it. Being online tends to distort time. You may think you've only been on for an hour, when three hours have actually gone by. Set an old-fashioned timer or your cell phone alarm, and when it goes off, get up and do something else.

2. **Separate work and play online.** It's easy to find yourself on a fun-seeking detour when you're supposed to be working on a research paper. When work and play are combined, it's easy to lose track of what's what. You end up wasting time because it feels as if you're doing something productive when you really aren't. Facebook, for example, can be a big temptation. Although it's not a clear case of cause and effect, a pilot study found that students who spend more time on Facebook spend less time studying and earn lower grades. However, 79 percent of these same students didn't believe that Facebook impacted their studies.[14]

3. **Take a tech vacation.** Without getting freaked out, think about this option: Turn off your computer, cell phone, or other mobile device for a day, and then extend the time to a week or more. Use a computer lab on campus to do your assignments, rather than tempting yourself to spend hours online at home. Train yourself to withdraw, little by little. Being tied to a electronic device can easily overtake your life. Why disengage from face to face communication to interface with the cyberworld when real-life friends or family members are sitting right beside you or across the table?[15]

4. **Get a life.** Take up yoga, chess, or swimming. Make some new friends, start a relationship, or join a club on campus. Your real life might actually become more interesting.

5. **Talk to people who care about you—a family member or a counselor on campus.** Recognizing the problem and admitting it are the first steps. Being one-sided isn't healthy. There are experts and support groups available to help you deal with your problem and make your real life more fulfilling.[16]

James Cotier/Stone/Getty Images

The Internet: The Good, the Bad, and the Ugly

> **? challenge** / **" reaction**
>
> **Challenge:** In what ways does technology improve our lives, and in what ways does it complicate it? See if you can identify three of each.
>
> **Reaction:**
>
> _____
>
> _____
>
> _____

The Good

Students who enter college right after high school are the leading consumers of digital technology in the United States.[17] In one study, 79 per cent of college students reported that the Internet has had a positive impact on their college academic experience.[18] For many of us, the Internet is how we get our news, our research, our entertainment, and our communication. When it comes to all the potential benefits of the Internet, think about advantages like these:

Teachable Moment Ask students which learning style preference would most likely find computer technology helpful. Most kinesthetic learners prefer using a computer to learn. Have these students share their experiences.

> **Currency.** While some of the information posted on the Internet isn't up to date, much of it is current. This is especially important during a crisis or a national emergency, for example, when it's important to get news fast. Reports, articles, and studies that might take months to publish in books or articles are available on the web as soon as they're written.

> **Availability.** The Internet never sleeps. If you can't sleep at 2:00 A.M., the Internet can keep you company. It can be a good friend to have. Unlike your real instructor, who teaches other classes besides yours and attends marathon meetings, Professor Google is always in. For the most part, you can check your e-mail or log onto the Internet from anywhere, any time.

Hadn't thought about these specific features.

> **Scope.** You can find out virtually anything you want to know on the Internet, from the recipe for the world's best chocolate chip cookie to medical advice on everything from Athlete's Foot to Zits. (Of course, real human beings are usually a better option for serious questions.)

> " Technology is nothing. What's important is that you have a faith in people, that they're basically good and smart, and if you give them tools, they'll do wonderful things with them. "
>
> *Steve Jobs, founder of Apple Computer (1955–2011)*

© arek_malang/Shutterstock.com

> **Interactivity.** Unlike other media, the Internet lets you talk back. You can write a letter to the head of a news organization and wait for a reply, or you can push buttons on your phone in response to an endless list of menu questions ("If you want directions in English, press 1 . . .") and finally get to a real-live human being. But the Internet lets you communicate instantly and constantly. You can Snapchat to your heart's content, if you want to; add to your Facebook page daily; or edit a Wikipedia entry whenever you like.

> **Affordability.** The number of Internet users worldwide is now nearly 2.5 billion; over 245 million Americans are on the Net today.[19] For most of us, when it comes to the Internet, the price is right. After you buy a computer and pay a monthly access fee, you get a great deal for your money.

The Bad

Too much of a good thing—anything—can be bad. When something becomes that central to our lives, it carries risks. Here are some Internet dangers worth thinking about:

> **Inaccuracy.** Often we take information presented to us at face value, without questioning it. But on many Internet sites, the responsibility for checking the accuracy of the information presented there is yours. Bob's Statistics Home Page and the U.S. Census Bureau's website are not equally valid. Not everything published online is true or right, and beyond simple questions of accuracy, many things need interpretation or explanation.

> **Laziness.** It's easy to allow the convenience of the Internet to make us lazy. Why go through the hassle of cooking dinner when you can just stop for a burger on the way home? The same thing applies to the Internet. Why bother doing hours of library research on the topic of your paper when others have already been there, done that, and published it on the Internet? And today's global online "paper mills" make it easy to plug in your credit card number and buy your paper online, perhaps one even authored by someone on the other side of the globe![20] For one thing, if you don't give the rightful author credit, that's plagiarism, which can give you a zero on an assignment, or even cause you to fail a course. But another thing worth considering is that the how of learning is as important as the what. If all you ever did was cut, paste, and download, you wouldn't learn how to do research yourself. You may never have to give your boss a five-page paper on the poetry of Wordsworth—but you may need to write a five-page report on your customers' buying trends over the last six months. No one's researched that particular topic before. Your job now is to develop your skills so that you can do it then.

> **Overdependence.** A related problem with anything that's easy and convenient is that we can start depending on it too much. National studies report that many of us lack basic knowledge. We can't name the chief justices of the Supreme Court or the president of Pakistan. Are we so dependent on the Internet that we're relying on it for information we should learn or know?[21] Using the Internet as your sole source of information can lure you into surface, rather than deep, learning. When information is reduced to screen shots, soundbites, and video clips, it's easy to

Teaching with Technology/Diversity Discussion Consider showing your class the Ted Talk by Sugata Mitra about his "Hole in the Wall" project in which children in remote areas were given computers. These children taught themselves how to use the computers and proceeded to learn by themselves. Show the video or a portion of it, and generate a discussion about access and geographic/diversity issues. To bring the issue into the higher education realm, explore research showing that learning technologies have a greater impact on lower socioeconomic or first-generation college students.

Sensitive Situation Keep in mind that technology has opened up unlimited possibilities for cheating—everything from writing physics formulas on the inside paper label of a plastic soda bottle to creating fake Word documents that look like gibberish when opened, seem like a technology glitch to the instructor, and buy more time to complete an assignment. For an eye-opening sampling of creative cheating techniques, look at the YouTube, "10 Clever Ways to Cheat on Tests!"

Oops! This is about me.

Box 6.1 Are Bullets, Bits, and Bytes Enough?

In today's world, it's tempting to grab information on the run. You run into a friend in the hallway, and she says, "Hey, did you see that...?" (fill in the blank) and quotes a news update from a Facebook post or a *New York Times* breaking news bullet that appeared on her phone's e-mail, for example. Often, we don't take the time to dig deeper on the spot, and then we may forget to do it later. The problem with this approach is that you may end up filling in the blank with your own assumptions, which may or may not be correct.

Consider these two news bullets, received about a major, front-page cheating scandal, and note that each media outlet has chosen slightly different information to report. Even though both are correct, if you read one and not the other, you might jump to a particular conclusion. In the age of e-information, remember that bullets, bits, and bytes don't give you the full story. You must dig deeper to "get to the bottom" of things yourself.

New York Times

Harvard has forced dozens of students to leave in its largest cheating scandal in memory, the university made clear in summing up the affair on Friday.

Maksim Kabakou/Photos.com; text on phone from http://www.nytimes.com/2013/02/02/education/harvard-forced-dozens-to-leave-in-cheating-scandal.html

Wall Street Journal

Dozens of Harvard University students have been disciplined, with many forced to temporarily withdraw, as a result of the cheating scandal that shook the Ivy League institution in late August.

Maksim Kabakou/Photos.com; text on phone from http://online.wsj.com/article/SB10001424127887323926104578273893986039374.html

Teaching with Technology Learning to interpret information from the Internet can go beyond standard websites. Have students look at blogs, videos, podcasts, or even social networking pages. How are these sources different from traditional text-based websites? How might the entertainment value of a source affect credibility? Have students think about the pros and cons of these different types of Internet media.

become an information "nibbler," someone who takes nothing but quick "bytes." Many questions don't have quick answers, and many problems don't have simple solutions.[22]

The Ugly

The Internet can be used in foul ways. Spam, viruses, spyware, and phishing cost American consumers 4.5 billion dollars in damage and affecting 40 percent of U.S. households.[23] Take a look at one student's social networking page in Figure 6.1 to see whether you can guess where things are headed.

Like the hypothetical Victoria Tymmyns (or her online name, VicTym) featured in Figure 6.1, some students publish inappropriate, confidential, and

Teo Lannie/PhotoAlto Agency RF Collections/Getty Images

> **"** For a list of all the ways technology has failed to improve the quality of life, please press three. **"**
>
> *Alice Kahn, technology author*

potentially dangerous information on their social media pages. Victoria has posted her address, phone numbers, and moment-by-moment location. Look at the final entries on her page to find out what potential threat she may be facing. Aside from the risk of serious harm, other types of "danger" can result from bad judgment, too. What some students post just for fun can later cost them a job opportunity. If your webpage has provocative photos of you or descriptions of rowdy weekend activities that you wouldn't want your grandmother to see, remove them! (Employers regularly check these sources for insider information on applicants.) "Living out loud," as social networking is sometimes called, requires constant vigilance so that the details of your life aren't on display. To avoid "social insecurity," keep these five useful suggestions in mind:

1. Use a password with at least eight letters and numbers, like FO34$&CuS.

2. Don't include your full birth date. Identity thieves can use this information.

3. Take advantage of privacy controls. Use the options provided to you, like choosing the "Friends Only" option. Be sure not to check the box for "Public Search Results." Search engines can find your Facebook profile on and off Facebook if you do.

4. You wouldn't put a "No One's Home" sign on your door, so don't post it as your status.

5. Don't post your child's name in a caption. If someone else does, remove it.[24]

Sexting Another example with counterproductive results is sexting—sending sexually explicit messages or posting nude photos (and having nude photos of friends or romantic partners on your computer or cell phone). Sexting is sometimes considered to be a status symbol—an "electronic hickey" that means that you're desirable and sexually active. Advocates argue that it's safe sex: there's no risk of pregnancy or STIs. But when and if sexts go viral, the results can be life-altering![25]

Sensitive Situation Emerging research on "digital natives" suggests that students who have grown up with the Internet and spent large amounts of time using it may be lacking in interpersonal skills and the ability to read nonverbal cues and, in fact, may not be developing the brain circuitry for these skills. You may wish to allude to these early findings, particularly if you are teaching younger students who are digital natives. Some research also suggests that this generation of students is satisfied with doing less and spending more time at home online. Finding a balance is key.

Teachable Moment Conduct a poll on how much time students spend online and what they spend their time doing. Share the results with the class. Have students evaluate whether they are using their time wisely or wasting time on the Internet. Refer any students who do have problems to their advisors.

Activity Option. In small groups, have students examine the fictional ISpy.com web page and decide what parts of the profile should be eliminated to protect this student's identity. Have groups share in class what was left on the profile. Could anything still identify her? Remind students of the benefits of setting their profiles to private on sites like Facebook.com.

ISpy.com

RMSU

View More Photos of Me

Status   **edit**

Doin' shots at Annie Oakley's!

RMSU Friends

425   friends at RMSU   See All

Seymore Bonz   **N.O. Body**

Friends in Other Networks

Cal (12)
UF (40)
CMU (6)
KSU (7)
RMSU (425)

Basic Info

Name: Victoria Tymmyns
Looking For: A Good Time
Residence: Pine Valley 456
Birthday: June 12, 1995

Contact Info

Email: VicTym@rmsu.edu
AIM Screenname   VicTym
Mobile: 719.111.1112
Current Address: 123 Fake St.
              Great Bluffs, CO 80900

Personal Info

Activities: Drinkin' at "Annie Oakley's" every Fri. night
              Karaoke at "All That Jazz" every Sat. night.

Favorite Artists: Adele, Mariah Carey, Bruno Mars
Favorite Shows: Walking Dead, Big Bang Theory, New Girl

Work Info

Company: Common Grounds on Corner Mountview
Schedule: Work M – F 7AM –2PM

The Wall

 N.O. Body wrote: at 11:00am August 1, 2014
Saw u dancing at Annie Oakley's!! Whatta hottie! We should meet.

 N.O. Body wrote: at 1:00pm August 1, 2014
Aw come on! U know u want to meet me!

 N.O. Body wrote: at 3:02pm August 1, 2014
Still no response? What's up? Do u wanna play or not?

 Seymore Bonz wrote: at 4:27pm August 1, 2014
R we still hookin up w/the gang at Annie Oakley's tonight?
Meet you guys at the front door at 10.

 N.O. Body wrote: at 5:20pm August 1, 2014
Sounds fun. Maybe I'll see u there.

 Bay-Bee Face wrote: at 10:17pm August 2, 2014
Can you believe how we much we rocked last night? What was the deal with that guy
who kept staring at us? He gave me the creeps!! You switched shifts w/Mary right?
Working at 4?

 N.O. Body wrote: at 12:39pm August 2, 2014
Gee, BTW u were dressed, I just assumed u liked being stared at... U looked really
amazing at work.

 N.O. Body wrote: at 2:21pm August 3, 2014
What's the matter sweetheart? U looked unhappy to see me at work today. Why
didn't u talk to me? BTW, nice house u got. Who knew you lived in such a nice neighborhood.

 N.O. Body wrote: at 12:57pm August 5, 2014
Nice dog u have. Ur parents must be outta town—no one's been home all night.

 N.O. Body wrote: at 7:26pm August 5, 2014
U never showed up for ur shift today. I waited all day for u. Saw your friends.
They said somebody poisoned your dog. That's a shame—such a yappy
little thing. I hate stuck-up women. Guess I'll just have to find u in person...

Whoa! Maybe I shouldn't post what I'm doing all the time.

FIGURE 6.1

Fictional Ispy.com page

Companion, M. (2006). Victoria Tymmyns Ispy.com. Used with permission.

Cyberbullying. Using the Internet or a cell phone to hurt, humiliate, or harass can leave lasting scars on people, from severe intimidation to emotional distress. In some extreme, newsworthy cases involving children or teenagers, cyberbullying has led to depression or even suicide. If you're the victim, tell someone and get help. Individual states have cyberbullying policies or laws, and these hurtful behaviors are crass at the very least and perhaps even against the law.[26]

What does all of this have to do with you? Everything! It's important to remember that the Internet itself is neutral. It can be used constructively or destructively, based on the choices you make. It can be an exciting, invigorating, essential part of your college experience. Use it wisely!

> "Our attraction to a world of infinite possibility, information and complexity is here to stay. The challenge is how to participate productively in this new and turbulent world, and not be paralyzed by it."
>
> *David Allen, productivity expert*

Writing Effective Online Messages

Being a professional student doesn't just apply to how you act in class, like asking questions if you're unclear or turning in your assignments on time. Online communication has particular rules you must follow. For example, when you're writing discussion board posts in a hybrid or online course, it's important to be civil. "How could anyone ever possibly think that?" as a post to a classmate's entry may be honest, but it's hardly collegial. Instead, why not say, "That's something I hadn't thought of. Can you explain more about it?" Think about the Golden Rule of online posts: How would you feel if a classmate shot down a good idea of yours? Be respectful. When classmates post an idea, they're putting their egos on the line—or so it feels. Remember that you can disagree with a classmate online, but never disrespect him or her personally. "I thought we were always supposed to use good grammar on this discussion board. Jerome's posts are full of mistakes." There's no need to put Jerome on the spot. On the other hand, using good grammar and correct spelling will be important to your instructor, so be conscientious in that regard.

Another thing your instructor will insist on is that your posts are sufficiently informative. When you are in a hurry, it's tempting to write as little as possible, like "Alicia is right on target!" as your entire entry. Tell why. Mention parts of her argument you agree with, and explain your endorsement. A discussion board is a place for online, back-and-forth dialogue, not Tweet-like comments for other people to decipher. And remember to follow the posting assignment's instructions. If you're being asked to reflect on the short story, don't just summarize it. Chances are your instructor has read it, too. He wants to know your thoughts about it, not the plot summary.

Of course IMs and text messages are used more often in social contexts than academic ones, but some of the same rules apply. "Breaking up" with your romantic partner by sending a text message would probably be perceived as a cowardly "low blow." Simply put: Certain situations call for certain types of messages.

E-mail that you send your instructor has netiquette (online etiquette) standards you should follow, too. Take a look at these widely accepted rules for academic settings:

1. **Don't send a message you don't want to risk being forwarded to someone else.** Doing so has caused many a fretful night. ("Aaaaakkk! What have I done?")

Note to self: Keep these pointers in mind for my online courses.

Teachable Moment Many colleges offer students an e-mail address that will give them Internet access for free. Make sure all students know how to access the Internet and school e-mail.

Technology skills: wireless, windowed, webbed, and wikied **193**

2. **Don't hit the "send" key until you've given yourself time to cool off, if you're upset.** Reread it later with fresh eyes; then see how you feel about sending it. You may want to edit what you've written.

3. **Don't forward chain e-mails.** At the very least, they're a nuisance, and sometimes they're illegal.

4. **Don't do business over your school e-mail account.** Sending all 500 new students an invitation to your family's restaurant grand opening is off-limits. Besides, sending messages to lots of people at once is called "spam," and it can really gum up the works.

5. **Don't spread hoaxes about viruses or false threats.** You can get into big trouble for that.

6. **Don't type in all CAPS.** That's called SHOUTING, and it makes you look angry.

Exercise 6.3 — How *Not* to Win Friends and Influence People Online

All four of these e-mail messages from students violate the rules of netiquette. See whether you can identify the rule number above that's been violated in each case.

From Matt   Rule:_____

Professor X,

I just looked at the online syllabus for Academic Success 101. Why didn't you tell us that our first paper is due on Monday? I will be very busy moving into a new apartment this weekend. Writing an essay for your class is the last thing I want to have to think about.

From Tiffany   Rule:_____

Prof X,

i didn't know u were makin us write a paper over the weekend. i won't be able to do it. i hop you don't mind.

Ugh... my e-mails look just like hers...

From Xavier   Rule:_____

PROFESSOR X,

I CAN'T GET MY PAPER DONE BY MONDAY. LET ME KNOW WHAT I SHOULD DO.

From Dameon   Rule:_____

Hey, Section 3

Can you believe our instructor? She gives us a big writing assignment after only one day of class! Who in their right mind would be remotely interested in sitting in their crummy little room writing a bunch of meaningless junk, when we haven't even learned anything yet? What kind of teacher are we stuck with here? Somebody out there respond to me, OK? I'm totally hacked off!

As a class, discuss your responses. Do you all agree on which rules were broken in the four examples provided? See whether you can create some new ones that violate other rules.

7. **Don't be too casual.** Use good grammar and correct spelling. Your instructors consider e-mails to be academic writing, and they'll expect professionalism from you. "Hey Prof, this is a heckuva of a cool class!" may sound enthusiastic, but it's not professional. Language that you use for texts and IMs is not appropriate for academic correspondence.

8. **Don't forget important details.** Include everything the reader needs to know. For example, if you're writing to an instructor, give your full name and the name of the course you're writing about. Professors teach more than one class and have many students.

9. **Don't hit the "Reply to All" key, when you mean to hit the "Reply" key.** Many e-mail message writers have been horrified upon learning that hundreds or thousands of people have read something personal or cranky that was meant for just one reader.

10. **Don't forget to fill in the subject line.** That gives readers a chance to preview your message and decide how soon they need to get to it.

Exercise 6.4 Channel Chooser

Today's wide array of technology options requires that we choose how to communicate on a minute-by-minute basis. Your grandparents used to make long-distance calls (which were expensive) or write snail-mail letters. Besides talking face-to-face, those were the primary options. Today, you can call someone, fire off a text, send an e-mail or Tweet, or post on a Facebook wall, for example. The particular choices you make send a message about you and whether you are a competent communicator. The bottom-line question is this: Is one channel more appropriate than another for a specific message? Look at the following scenarios, decide which particular communication channel you'd choose for each situation, and then explain why. Here's an example:

A student employee who has worked with you for two years wins a prestigious college award. You want to congratulate her. Which channel would you choose, and why?

a. Phone call	e. Written note	*I usually just text or FB everything. Maybe that's not always the best choice.*
b. Text message	f. Face-to-face conversation	
c. E-mail	g. Tweet	
d. Facebook post	h. Other	

E. I'd send her a handwritten note because that's more personal, lasting, and special.

Now try some on your own. Be prepared to defend your choices during a class discussion.

1. You need your instructor's approval on the thesis statement you've written for your first essay in English class. You're having trouble coming up with something. _____

2. You want to break up with your romantic partner of six months. You just found out something disappointing that makes you feel hurt and angry. _____

3. You want to let other students know about an exciting campus event this weekend. It is free and open to everyone. _____

4. Your last college tuition bill contained a major error. It's a big mess. _____

5. The low grade you earned on your history paper counted for a large portion of your overall grade and may put you on academic probation. You need to ask your instructor to reconsider. _____

6. You want to tell your boss you're not coming in to work today because something came up. _____

7. You want to thank your favorite professor for a great learning experience this term. _____

Research Skills and Your College Success

Many of your class assignments in college will require you to conduct research by using technology or by spending time in the real library on campus. Why? Aren't you in college to learn from your instructors? Why do they ask you to do research on your own?

There are unanswered questions all around us in everyday life. Some questions are simple; others are complex. How much time will it take to get across town to a doctor's appointment during rush hour? What can you expect college tuition to cost by the time your kids are old enough to go? What are the chances that someone you know who has cancer will survive for five years? Research isn't necessarily a mysterious thing that scientists in white coats do in laboratories. Research is simply finding answers to questions, either real questions you encounter every day or questions that are assigned to you in your classes. Doing research on your own can be a powerful way to learn, sometimes even more so than hearing answers from someone else, even if those people are your instructors. While going off to a research expedition in the actual, physical library on campus may sound like frustrating busywork, the skills you stand to gain are well worth the effort. And knowing how to do research online in today's world of Internet-based resources is vital!

Conducting research teaches you some important things about how to formulate a question and then find answers. And it's not just finding answers so that you can scratch a particular assignment off your to-do list. It's about learning an important process. When you get into the world of work, your instructors won't be there to supply answers, so knowing how to figure things out on your own will be key to your success. So, exactly what is college-level research?

Never thought about this . . .

What Research Is *Not*	What Research Is
Research isn't just going on a "search and employ" mission. It's not just seeing what all you can find and then using it to get an assignment out of the way.	**Research starts with a question.** If an assignment is broad, you must come up with a specific question to research yourself. More about that later.
Research isn't just moving things from Point A (the library) to Point B (your paper).	**Research is a process with a plan.** A plan is something many students lack. They jump in without a question—or a plan.
Research isn't random rummaging through real or virtual files to find out something.	**Research is goal-oriented.** You've formulated a question, developed a plan, and now you begin to find answers by using both online sources and ones that sit on your library's shelves.
Research isn't doing a quick Internet search. The cutting and pasting some students do to fill a paper's page requirements is actually plagiarism!	**Research often involves breaking a big question into several smaller ones.**[27]

Teachable Moment To help students complete their research papers, explain that another effective site is scholar.google. com. This site searches scholarly works across many disciplines and includes books, abstracts theses, and articles.

Box 6.2   There's an App for That

As baseball "philosopher" and wordsmith Yogi Berra once said, "The future ain't what it used to be." From all appearances, his prediction was right. Tech experts tell us that in a few years, we'll be wearing e-devices as jewelry and embedding them in tattoos. We already have access to Internet-connected glasses with a camera, microphone, GPS, and sound—all controlled by voice.[28] In fact, right now, if you wanted to, you could enroll in a MOOC (Massive Open Online Course) for free with thousands of other students around the world (although the quality, completion rates, and sustainability of these free courses are currently subjects of debate). "The future <u>ain't</u> what it used to be"!

The hottest tech items with the greatest educational potential allow you to work, read, or communicate online from your smartphone or other portable electronic device. In today's world, college students are busy and don't necessarily stay in one spot for long. They want portable learning—to work, read, listen, and study from anywhere, anytime. You may, too, so BYOD! Many applications for your iPhone or Droid or your iPad or similar tablet device offer a world of conveniences. For example, if you're an iPhone user, Siri may easily become your new BFF. You can ask her any question, and she'll search the web to find an answer. Or ask her to remind you when an upcoming assignment is due, and she'll come through for you with an audible and visible alert.

Have you ever used any of these top apps for college students—or do you know of other apps that could help you better organize your life and improve the quality of your academic work?[29]

1. **Dropbox** lets you store your files on the Internet, access them from anywhere, and share them with anyone. You can store the paper or presentation you started at school on Dropbox and finish it at home over the weekend. It's also great for file-sharing so that each group member can access it, and you and your teammates can all work on a project concurrently. How convenient is that?
2. **Evernote** helps you organize your life. According to its website, it helps you remember everything, capture anything, and access it all anywhere. And its feature Evernote Peek helps you convert what it's stored into study materials.
3. **NoRedInk** is an interactive site that uses your own sports, music, TV, and movie preferences to help you improve your grammar by creating personalized exercises and quizzes and graphing your results. It makes learning grammar fun!
4. **iProcrastinate** helps you make lists, check off items as you do them (to note your progress), and break big tasks into manageable chunks.
5. **MyHomework** is an online planner that helps you focus on assignments and their due dates for each of your classes and lower your anxiety levels. Trying to keep everything in your head just doesn't work.

The key (to almost anything, technology included) is finding balance. Technology has a downside, it's true. If you let it, it can waste valuable time, become a bad habit to break, and send your college career into a nosedive. But it also offers you ways to do your best, academically, if you simply realize: there's an app for that. Many apps, in fact.

Navigating the Library

Being "exiled" to the library to do research for a paper may seem like torture that can ruin a perfectly good weekend. But if you look at things differently, it can be a mind-expanding trip into places unknown. Beyond navigating the web to find research for your assignments, it's important to learn your way around the actual, physical space of the library on your campus. The library has many useful resources, including real, very knowledgeable librarians who are there to help you.

Let's say, for example, that you are assigned a research paper for your English Composition class. The field is wide open; you may select any topic you wish. How should you proceed? Here are some of the resources your library offers and how you should use them when you're assigned a research project like this one:

> **Card catalog.** Explore your library's online catalog that lists all of the books available to you. Go to your college's website, and from there, you can find your way to your college library's home page. Click on the

Teachable Moment Arrange for your class to have a library tour. If possible, have the librarian discuss writing research papers and using a variety of sources for documentation.

I should get to know a librarian on campus so I can get help with my paper!

Box 6.3 The Top Five Research Mistakes First-Year Students Make: Advice from a Reference Librarian

Are you guilty of any of these common mistakes first-year students make?

1. **Selecting a topic that is too broad.** Students often start out with a very general topic, and sometimes have a hard time narrowing the focus. Trying to write a paper on "fossil fuels" sets you up for an impossible task. Entire books have been written on that subject. But if you begin to zero in on "the advantages (or disadvantages) of offshore drilling," you're going in the right direction. Figuring out which words to use in the search process can be tricky, too. If you're writing about sustainability, and you enter "green," you'll get everything from "lime, mint, olive, and avocado" (meaning shades of green, not foods) to "Kermit, the frog." Brainstorming different search words and noting the usable results is half the battle.

2. **Taking short cuts.** Major search engines are a great place to start, but don't stop there. Just using Google or Foxfire is the equivalent of academic "wimping out," like just grabbing something quick from a vending machine when there's so much more nutritious and satisfying food out there. Libraries purchase many different electronic databases that have a wealth of information: articles, books, and book chapters, for example. Learn how to use these specialized library databases and really mine them for information. Finding useful information takes time and patience!

3. **Devoting too little time.** Students frequently underestimate how long the research process will take. There are multiple steps required to doing thorough research. It's not a last-minute process, and procrastination isn't the answer. Even if you write like a pro, you can't complete a research paper in an hour or two. Just getting in materials you've ordered from another library can take several weeks.

4. **Not evaluating sources.** Many students don't look closely enough at the sources they find, and then they end up making poor choices or using the first items that come up in search results. Instead, as you scan your results, look for hints about authenticity and accuracy. Compare your findings with other authoritative sites. Note the domain extension (like .gov, for example). One hit may lead you to another, which leads you to yet another. Evaluate your search results and be selective about what you use. Not all sources are created equal; make sure your sources are credible ones that support your argument.

5. **Copying and pasting.** Students sometimes use someone else's work without correct and thorough documentation of the source, especially when time is running out. You can end up plagiarizing unintentionally just because you don't understand how to cite your sources. Or you may intentionally cut and paste to save yourself time and effort. But either way, you're putting your academic success at high risk.

The biggest mistake students make is not asking the reference librarian for help at the beginning of the research process! That's why librarians are there—to provide guidance and help with all of the above. Continue reading this chapter for more strategies on making the most of your research time.[30]

---

library's catalog button. You'll come up with a list of books. Let's say the first one has a call number of HF5415.1265W43, based on the Library of Congress classification system, which most college libraries use. (Some libraries, like your community's public library, may use the Dewey Decimal system. One advantage of the Library of Congress system is that books usually have the same number, no matter which library you find them in. That's not always true for the Dewey Decimal system.) The Library of Congress number identifies subject matter the book is about. Now, after identifying other possible useful books, you need to make your way to campus and find the actual book on the shelf.

> **Databases.** If you go to your library's home page, you can link to the list of online databases it subscribes to. Databases identify articles from academic journals and sometimes contain entire articles online. Generally, different databases exist for different disciplines, for example:

Education	**ERIC** (Educational Resources Information Center)
Psychology	**PsycInfo**
Business	**Business Source Premier**

But more general databases also exist. You might want to search through: Academic Search Premier, WilsonWeb OmniFile Full Text Mega, and Academic OneFile.

> **66**
> I find that a great part of the information I have was acquired by looking up something and finding something else on the way. **99**
>
> *Franklin P. Adams, American journalist and radio personality (1881–1960)*

> **Stacks.** Physically walk through the stacks or collections of books and periodicals (journals, magazines, newspapers, and audiovisual resources, for example). Get to know the stacks in your library, and figure out how to find what you need. Look for the Library of Congress numbers posted on signs at the end of each row of books. When you find the book you're looking for, you're likely to find other books in that section that would also be useful to you. That's why even though doing online research is convenient, there's no substitute for "being there."

Information Literacy and Your College Success

Much of the research you do for your college assignments will take place online. Information literacy is defined as knowing *when* you need information, *where* to find it, *what* it means, *whether* it's accurate, and *how* to use it. Simply put, it's "the ability to use technology to solve information problems." Information literacy includes five components, as seen in Figure 6.2. Think about them as a step-by-step process as we work through a hypothetical assignment.[31]

Activity Option As an assignment for the next class, encourage students to research a career that is of interest to them. Have them find three Internet sources and three articles or books that they can use as research references. They do not need to write a paper. They only need to bring in a list of references.

Step 1. Define

Define what the assignment requires of you. Imagine you were assigned a *research* paper. You aren't being asked to *summarize* or *evaluate* a topic. You are being asked to *find out about it*. Let's say that since you're thinking of majoring in marketing and since you enjoy Facebook and Twitter, you decide your research topic will be social media marketing tools. But using social media as a marketing tool is a huge topic. You must narrow it down and decide which specific research question (or questions) you want to focus on.

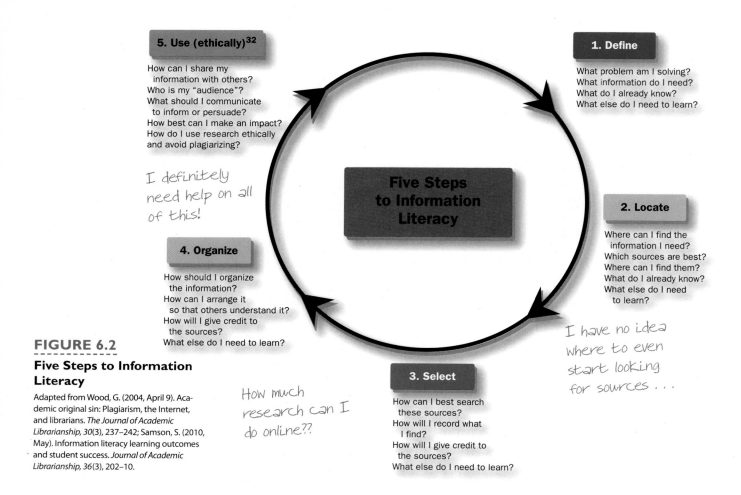

FIGURE 6.2

Five Steps to Information Literacy

Adapted from Wood, G. (2004, April 9). Academic original sin: Plagiarism, the Internet, and librarians. *The Journal of Academic Librarianship, 30*(3), 237–242; Samson, S. (2010, May). Information literacy learning outcomes and student success. *Journal of Academic Librarianship, 36*(3), 202–10.

Teaching with Technology The incredible scope of information available on the Internet can be a blessing and a curse. As the FOCUS Challenge Case illustrates, sometimes it's hard to know where to start when you receive millions of hits for a single Google search. Coach students on a few simple search strategies for more effective Internet research. Remember to keep it simple, use as few words as possible, but also use descriptive terms. Use synonyms for keywords that might yield different results. Search words are often the key to finding the right information.

If you knew very little about marketing and social media, you might start by Googling your topic to help you define it. But the Internet is huge and unstructured. There's really no way to organize that much information into simple, neat categories.[33] And how do you whittle down millions of hits? According to a recent study, 81 percent of college students consider themselves highly skilled at searching the Internet, yet another study reports that less than 1 percent of Google users actually look further than the first page of their Google results, regardless of how many hits they get![34]

If you don't know anything about the topic you need to research—absolutely nothing at all—the Internet is a great place to start. You can type in "marketing social media" using a search engine and information appears instantly. The problem is that you now have too much information, and the challenge is knowing what to do next. Your college instructors will insist you go beyond the Internet and avoid relying too much on encyclopedias and Wikipedia. Even Jimmy Wales, the founder of Wikipedia, sees it as a preliminary resource for academic research, not a final authority: "If you are reading a novel that mentions the Battle of the Bulge, for instance, you could use Wikipedia to get a quick basic overview of the historical event to understand the context. But students writing a paper about the battle should hit the history books."[35] One idea is to "triangulate" a source like Wikipedia, that is compare it against two other authoritative academic sources.[36] College requires you to do more research than you've probably done before, and to do it differently. Instead of being overwhelmed by the number of hits, use your Google search to help you see your topic from different angles and narrow it to specific research questions, like these:

1. **Avoiding Social Media Marketing Mistakes** (What are the challenges?)
2. **Why Business as Usual No Longer Works** (Why are the old "tried and true" methods sometimes less effective than new online tools?)
3. <u>Three</u> **Advantages of Social Media Marketing: Visibility, Speed, and Cost** (What are the reasons why it works?)

Good idea! I could write about Internet Commerce and these <u>three challenges:</u>
- *language*
- *shipping*
- *money*

Let's take that last focused topic and run with it. Suppose you have a new business that you're trying to get off the ground. It's a good idea, but you have to build your customer base fast in a cost-effective way before your start-up money runs out. So the three keys to your success are visibility, speed, and cost. Now we've taken a big, broad topic (marketing and social media) and broken it down into three specific questions or subtopics to research. Your preliminary Google and Wikipedia searches can help you identify what the smaller chunks of your topic could be. But they can't do *all* the work for you, and you can't stop there. You have to know what to do next. (If you think this process is challenging, you're not alone. In one study, only 35 percent of college students knew how to narrow a Google search!)[37]

Step 2. Locate

If you've identified electronic sources, bookmark them in a file labeled with the name of your project. If they're print resources, physically find them in the library. If they're not available in your own campus library, see if it participates in an interlibrary loan agreement among libraries. Your own library may be able to borrow the resource from another library.

> " Plans are only good intentions unless they immediately degenerate into hard work. "
>
> *Peter Drucker, management expert (1909–2005)*

Step 3. Select

With so much information available, how do we know what to believe? Whether or not it's true, we tend to think that if something is on television or in a book or online, it must be important. Exercise your critical thinking skills and turn them into critical searching skills. Just because information is published doesn't automatically make it right or true. In particular, some of the so-called research you encounter online may be bogus, containing inaccuracies or bias. You must read, interpret, and evaluate research to decide whether to use it. Use these five criteria to evaluate any website you come across:

1. **Currency.** How up to date is the information? Some websites don't list a date at the bottom of the screen (where copyright information is often found). If you don't see one, try using other hints on the site to get at how old the information is ("According to a study published in 1995 . . ."). You may find that you need to search for something more up to date.

2. **Accuracy.** How accurate is the information presented? If a website makes an unbelievable claim ("Lose up to 10 pounds a week and still eat everything you want!") or presents shaky statistics to make a case, it's important to be skeptical. Take responsibility to validate the information elsewhere.

3. **Authority.** Does the sponsor of the website have the credentials to post the information you see? Chances are "Steve's Picks" is a collection of one person's opinions. Compare that to a film reviewer's site with information compiled by a professional film critic for a major newspaper. Which one would you trust more? You may not agree with Steve or the professional film critic, but one has credentials, and the other doesn't. Note that domains are often a good indicator for all five of these criteria.

4. **Objectivity.** Does the website sponsor have a reason to convince you of something, or is it presenting unbiased information? If the site wants you to order something online because it claims to have better products than those you can buy at a store, for example, you should be suspicious.

Exercise 6.5 · Critical Searching on the Internet

One place where critical thinking is extremely important today is on the Internet. The Information Age surrounds us with huge amounts of data made readily available through technology. However, you must cultivate your critical searching skills to weed out websites with inaccuracies and bias. Internet research is convenient, but it definitely has its pros and cons. Choose one of the following two assignments to complete. Each one asks you to use your critical searching skills.

Assignment 1: Create a list of ten websites that pertain to your intended major. (If you're not sure of your major right now, choose one to explore anyway.) Evaluate the websites to see which ones seem most useful to you as a student. Checking the sites' domain extensions is a good place to start:

.gov = U.S. government (such as www.irs.gov, the Internal Revenue Service or IRS)

.edu = education (such as www.rmsu.edu, Rocky Mountain State University)

.org = organizations or businesses (such as www.democratic.org, the Democratic Party, or nonprofit organizations, like www.americanheart.org, American Heart Association)

.mil = military (such as www.defenselink.mil, U.S. Department of Defense)

.com = commercial, buying and selling (such as www.realtor.com, National Association of Realtors)

.net = network or Internet provider (such as www.earthlink.net)

.int = international organizations (such as Interpol, Council of Europe, or NATO)[38]

Assignment 2: Compare websites with contradictory information. Choose a controversial subject such as abortion, the death penalty, cohabitation, religion, politics, holistic healing, euthanasia, or some other subject of interest. Find four websites on your topic and compare them on these characteristics: (1) currency, (2) accuracy, (3) authority, (4) objectivity, and (5) coverage. Which of the four websites gets the highest marks? Why? Use your preferred search engine, but remember that different search engines work best for different purposes. These three are popular recommendations:[39]

Google (www.google.com) has a well-deserved reputation as the best search engine you can use. Its size is not disclosed anywhere, but it's generally thought to have the largest assets to search.

Yahoo (www.yahoo.com) can also help you get excellent search results, or allow you to use any of the other specialized search features.

Ask (www.ask.com) became popular because it allows you to ask virtually any question and get an answer.

5. **Coverage.** If a website just presents one side of an issue or a very small piece of a larger picture, check to make sure you're getting all the information you need. If you're left wondering, *but what about . . . ?* you're probably having the right reaction.

Step 4. Organize

Now that you have located the information you need, using a variety of sources, and selected those that will be most useful to you in your research project, it's time to organize. Your paper will be easier to write now that you have created three subtopics: visibility, speed, and cost. Now is the time to begin taking notes on index cards or highlighting pieces of information you want to quote word-for-word (giving credit to the author) or paraphrase (putting information into your own words). You can literally put the index cards, printed articles, and photocopied pages from books you find during your research into three piles and work from those. Organization is the key to an excellent research paper. To help you keep track of the sources you find, consider these suggestions:

> **Pay attention to details.** Write the name of the book or article, author, place of publication, publisher, date, or URL at the top of an index card with your notes or on a photocopied page of information you plan to use. This hint is important. Forgetting to write down the name of a book, title of an article, or page number of a reference has resulted in many a late-night trip to the library or frantic searching through an online database. Here's an example of what two index cards (of the same paragraph) would look like:

Teachable Moment Get a discussion going about domains. What are the basic differences between a ".org" and a ".edu?" Between a ".com" and a ".gov"? Which would be more credible sources and why?

Activity Option For a shorter homework assignment than Exercise 6.5, ask students to find two websites on the same topic, one really credible website and one that is suspect. Students can choose their own topic or you can assign one. For example, if a student is interested in anorexia, she might find the National Institute of Mental Health has a good site, and someone with a personal homepage does not. The important part is that students have to defend their reasoning.

> "
> Work is either fun or drudgery.
> It depends on your attitude.
> I like fun.
> "
>
> *Colleen C. Barrett, President Emeritus and Corporate Secretary, Southwest Airlines*

[Weber. L. (2009). *Marketing to the Social Web: How Digital Customer Communities Build Your Business.* New York: Wiley.]

Direct Quote

Social networks are places where people with a common interest or concern come together to meet people with similar interests, express themselves, and vent. . . . Some sites are devoted specifically to image-sharing, open to the wide world or restricted to a select few through password protection. YouTube (now owned by Google) serves up 10 billion videos a month to U.S. viewers alone; photos and videos posted on Flickr (now owned by Yahoo!) attract more than 40 million visitors monthly. Marketing to the Social Web, p. 5.

[Weber. L. (2009). *Marketing to the Social Web: How Digital Customer Communities Build Your Business.* New York: Wiley.]

Paraphrase

Social networks are online places where people come together to communicate about things they care about. Some sites are especially for image-sharing. YouTube videos are watched by 10 billion Americans per month and Flickr is visited by 40 million visitors per month. Marketing to the Social Web, p. 5.

If you have ideas of your own that don't come from any book, write them on cards or pages, too, and label them, "My Own Ideas."

> **Decide on an organizational format.** Once you have your note cards in stacks, decide on the organizational format that would be most effective. Your research focuses on three different things—visibility, speed, and cost—which lends itself to what's called a *topical* format. Your research will fall into one of those three topics. If you were comparing social media effects in Europe, Asia, and North America, you might use a *compare and contrast* format. If you were going to present *solutions* to the three opportunities (or challenges) you're exploring (visibility, speed, and cost), you'd use a *problem-solution* format. Decide how best to present your information, and then follow the format you choose.

Step 5. Use (ethically)

Although all five steps of the Information Literacy model are important, Step 5 is especially so. Think about how far you've come. The research is done. It's time to do something with it. Why did you do the research in the first place? For a paper or presentation, right? The bottom-line question is: How will you *use* your research, and will you use it ethically?

Many students just sit down at their computers and start typing at 11 P.M. the night before the paper or speech outline is due—hoping for a flash of inspiration—and thereby end up sabotaging themselves. They avoid the up-front work and rationalize that they work better under pressure or they enjoy the adrenaline rush of a tight deadline. But ask yourself this: Would you invite your girlfriend out for dinner before the prom and then just drive around with her until you find a restaurant that looks inviting? Would you start your vacation by going to the airport and wandering around until you see an alluring destination at one of the gates? Of course not! Why then would you sit down at your computer at the eleventh hour and just start typing? Sure, eventually you will have filled enough pages to meet the assignment's required length, but it's not just about *quantity*; it's about *quality*. It's about making good use of the research you've invested in. Quality writing requires patience, focus, and attention to detail. Crafting an outline for an excellent speech does, too.

Writing and critical thinking are inextricably linked. When you write, you're thinking on paper. Doing it well will help you become a better critical thinker and learner in all your courses.[40]

Would compare and contrast work for my paper? Before and after of how Internet commerce changed things?

Teaching with Technology If students need extra writing help, have them turn to an OWL. Online Writing Labs are sources of information about citations, grammar, mechanics, and style. Purdue University launched one of the first OWLs at Owl. English.Purdue.edu, and their website contains free resources for the general public. Many universities also have writing centers on campus. Encourage students to visit OWLs or on-campus writing labs for valuable writing assistance. Using University OWLs may be safer than using other online assistance (which may sell submissions to "paper mills").

I hope we're given THIS assignment!

Exercise 6.6 Technology Project: Group Ad

Working with two or three classmates and using PowerPoint, Flash, or iMovie, create a television ad (as professional-looking as possible) for the course for which you're using this book. Use text, images, and music. The advertisement shouldn't be long—two or three minutes, or the length of the song you use—but it should describe what the course is about and why other students should take it. Be as creative as you like! Play your ad for the class.

Your TYPE is Showing

So how does your MBTI type relate to your social media use as a college student? Are Extraverted students more likely to reach out to others on Facebook? Are Feelers more interested in broadcasting their feelings on Twitter? Take a look at these infographics and check out what's reported about your type. Is type related to social media use? How do *you* interpret these results?

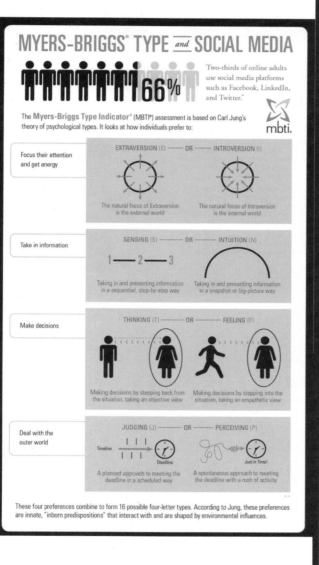

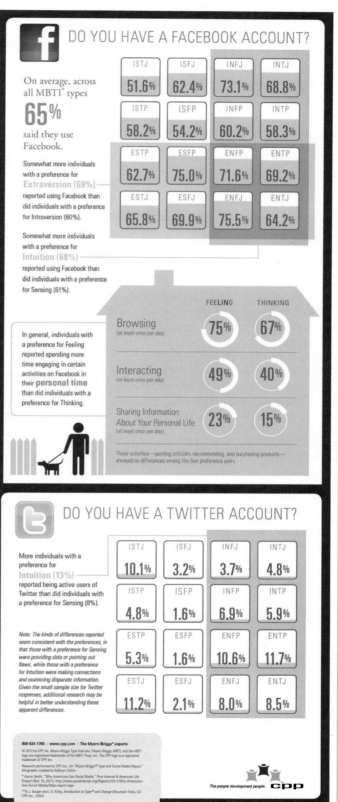

Identify your most challenging assignment this term, one that will require you to use your research and information literacy skills. What is the specific assignment? For example, it could be "write a five-page paper in which you take a position on a controversial theme relating to our course topic." On a scale of 1 to 10 (with 10 being extremely difficult), how challenging do you expect this assignment to be? What would make it easier? Describe your research assignment here.

_____

_____

Now take a look at the website to the right and answer the following questions (without Googling):

1. Does this website appear to be authentic? Why or why not?
2. Would this service be useful to a student like you with a challenging research assignment?
3. In your opinion, is this website acceptable for college students to use? Why or why not?
4. Are there differences between the three available options and their degree of acceptability?
5. What's the difference between using these professional services and using the professional services of a campus reference librarian?
6. Do you know students who use "professional" research services? What are their views on the acceptability of these services?
7. If you were a college instructor, what would you tell your students about these services?

Researchadvisors.com

All the help you need with time-consuming writing assignments! Need a rush job? Call our hurry hotline @ 1-888-555-5555

Top topics | Top grades | Top staff

You have a paper to write for your history class, a midterm to prepare for in your calculus class, and a presentation due in your psychology class. Where do you put your time and effort? There's only so much of you to go around! Consider our affordable options and earn the grade you need!

There's no way I can get all this done—and still have a life! Help!

Option 1: Let our staff of qualified researchers put together an impressive bibliography on your topic. You'll be emailed a list of premium sources—each with a usable summary—and immediately, you're ready to write! No needless trips to the library, no hours of online searching. Let us do it for you! Prices start at just $39.95. Learn more…

Option 2: Upload your assignment and allow one of our talented writers to send you a first draft; then put on the finishing touches yourself to make the paper your own. A professional writer can give you the head start you need! Prices start at just $69.95. Learn more…

Option 3: Eliminate all the worry and stress, and let us handle everything for you. Give us specifics and a timeline, and we'll do the rest. Prices start at just $99.95. Learn more…

researchadvisors.com
Copyright © 2007-2009
researchadvisors.com is affiliated with the Alliance of Southwestern Colleges and Universities

© iStockphoto.com/Antonio Nunes

After you answer these questions on your own, your instructor may wish to generate a discussion among all the members of your class.

Downloading Your Workload: The Easy Way Out?

challenge

reaction

Challenge: In your opinion, is the following passage plagiarized? Compare these two examples:

Original passage: The emotional importance of a spoken message is conveyed by its semantic content ("what" is said) and by the affective prosody used by the speaker ("how" it is said). The listener has to pay attention to both types of information in order to comprehend the emotional message as a whole.

Source: Vingerhoets, G., Berckmoes, C., & Stroobant, N. (2003). Cerebral hemodynamics during discrimination of prosodic and semantic emotion in speech studied by transcranial doppler ultrasonography. *Neuropsychology, 17(1)*, 93–99. The emotional importance of a spoken message is conveyed by its semantic content ("what" is said) and by the affective prosody used by the speaker ("how" it is said). The listener has to pay attention to both types of information in order to comprehend the emotional message as a whole.

Student paper: The emotional importance of a spoken message is conveyed by its semantic content ("what" is said) and by the affective prosody used by the speaker ("how" it is said). The listener has to pay attention to both types of information in order to comprehend the emotional message as a whole.

Reaction: Has this student committed plagiarism? Why or why not?

_____

One of the trickiest aspects of writing papers for your college courses can be expressed in these three words: *What is plagiarism?* First, you should understand the difference between *intentional* and *unintentional* plagiarism. Intentional plagiarism is deliberately downloading a paper from an online source or cutting and pasting text from a website or book, for example. However, you run the risk of committing unintentional plagiarism if you don't understand what plagiarism is or you forget which book you used so you don't cite the words you've borrowed from someone else. Technology today makes plagiarism all too convenient and easy, but by the same token, finding plagiarism in students' papers has become easy for instructors, too.[41] The bottom line? Follow the guidelines you get from your instructors, or ask your instructor questions if you're not sure. Both intentional and unintentional plagiarism can hurt you academically. These FAQs will help.

Q1: If I just list all the sources I used in writing a paper in the bibliography, won't that cover everything? List all your sources in the bibliography at the end of your paper, but also mention that they are other's ideas as you present them. Generally, it's a good idea to cite the original author soon after you present that idea in your paper or speech. In a research paper, it's also useful to name the author(s) ("According to Staley, college success skills are critical in the first year of college.") Each discipline uses a particular format to cite references. These are called *style sheets,* such as

> The first principle is that you must not fool yourself, but you are the easiest person to fool.
>
> *Richard P. Feynman (1918–1988), Nobel Prize Winner, Physics, 1965*

- ➤ *MLA* (Modern Language Association) is often used in the humanities (English, art, and philosophy, for example).

- ➤ *APA* (American Psychological Association) is often used in the social sciences (psychology, communication, and sociology).

- ➤ *Chicago Manual of Style* is used in history.

Check with your instructor if you're not certain which one to use, and Google these terms to find the specifics of formatting.

Q2: Must I cite all my sources if I just put ideas into my own words? Yes, you must cite all your sources, even though you may think that your paper looks cluttered. In academic writing, you must cite all the information you use, whether you paraphrase it, quote it, or summarize it. Some students are even taught bad habits in high school, for example, "It's not plagiarism if you change every fifth word," so they write papers with a thesaurus close by. Unfortunately, that's not the way it works. Try reading what you'd like to paraphrase, and then cover the text with your hand and write what you remember. In this case, you'd still need to cite the reference, but because you're paraphrasing, you wouldn't use quotation marks.

Q3: But I didn't know anything at all about this subject before I started this assignment. Does that mean I should cite everything? Some ideas are common knowledge that need not be cited. For example, it's a well-known fact that the Civil War lasted from 1861 to 1865. If you cited this piece of common knowledge, who would you cite? Generally, however, your motto

Activity Option Make sure students have a copy of your institution's policy on plagiarism. Have them highlight the consequences and discuss them. If students are dismissed from the college, can they return? Does the policy vary by instructor? Make sure students understand the policy.

Teaching with Technology There are several tools available on the Internet that will help you guide students through the sometimes confusing subject of plagiarism. TurnItIn.com is a website that checks student papers for originality based on an up-to-date database of other college papers, as well as books, magazines, websites, and journals. The tool also offers suggestions for proper citations, and can help students see what plagiarism is and what it isn't. Instructors can incorporate TurnItIn.com as an official means of accepting assignments from students, or they can use it as a teaching tool.

Activity Option Remind students that different disciplines use different style sheets. When writing a paper, it is best to check with the instructor to determine which style sheet to follow. Many effective websites can be used to provide guidelines and examples for the various style sheets.

These are ALL questions I've wondered about...

CAREER OUTLOOK: "Write" Your Reputation

> " Writing is making a comeback all over our society. Look at how much people e-mail and text-message now rather than talk on the phone. Look at how much communication happens via instant messaging and blogging. Writing is today's currency for good ideas. "
>
> *Wow! This Is true!*

Jason Fried and David Heinemeier Hansson, Rework, 2010, p. 222.

You've just graduated from college and landed a great job. All that hard work paid off. But now what? How will people in—for example—a large company begin to form an impression of you? The simple answer is that they will *listen* to you—in meetings, during presentations, and while hanging around the proverbial water cooler. But how else will they judge you and your work? One way you may not have thought about yet provides great opportunity, but also significant risk. It can do you in

quickly. At times it's ever so subtle; at other times it's totally in your face.

Imagine this example. Your new boss asks, "Can you get an email out about that new policy?" As the eager company newbie, you reply, "Sure." You quickly compose an email message to send out to everyone in the organization: **The new company policy will go into effect soon.** *Short and sweet,* you think and hit the "send" key. But immediately, you get back a barrage of e-mails from other employees, "What company policy?" "There's a new company policy?" "What new shenanigans is the corporate office up to now?" The request from your boss sounded simple enough. But in your short, sweet message, you've just communicated something relatively meaningless: some new policy from somewhere is about to start sometime. Will your new colleagues assume you're uninformed, unthinking, or unconscious? Think about how composing that one message could start to shape your company reputation right out of the gate.

Instead, you could have sent out an e-mail message like this: **The new software system to report travel expenditures, which has been mandated by the corporate office in response to violations of company travel policy, will go into effect on November 1, 2014, upon the recommendation of the general manager's task force appointed to examine ways to streamline operations and cut company waste.** This message certainly isn't guilty of leaving out all the good stuff like the first one. In fact, you've overloaded your sentence with "TMI"—so much extraneous verbiage that most people will have to read it twice, if they read it at all. Your colleagues may assume you're as boring and stuffy as your message. Even people who haven't met you yet are forming an impression of you through your writing. Are you getting the idea? Pressure? Yes. Overstatement? No. Your writing broadcasts all kinds of information about you.[42]

To make sure that people form the right impression of you, your writing must be clear, powerful, and bold. And actually, if you put some thought into it, the texting and tweeting you do now can help you develop the clear and concise business writing skills you'll need later.[43] (Our second bolded example above wouldn't fly as a tweet, would it? Too many characters.) Writing short, eye-catching, lively messages that people actually *will* read speaks volumes about your potential on the job. If you rock, make sure your writing rocks, too. That kind of writing tells people how effective you will be and "writes" your reputation for ongoing career success. *Oh, I rock! :)*

Think Ahead Look back at the last three texts or tweets you composed. Are they clear, powerful, and bold? Since you're not actually around when the message is read, does the way you communicated reflect the person that you are? What are you saying about *yourself* behind the actual words? Think of an example of a message you sent recently and how you could have communicated a more positive message about yourself.

Cast on Careers

© Larry Harwood Photography. Property of Cengage Learning

FOCUS: Do you think writing skills are really all that important after you graduate from college?

CARSON: To be honest, writing isn't my forté. In fact, making myself write research papers and journals as a first-year student was sheer torture. I'm what you'd call a casual person. I'd rather just talk things over. But that's not the way it works. However, as difficult as writing is for me, I do know it's important. It's not just teachers telling you that to get you to write. Everyone I know who has a career as a professional tells me that, too.

FOCUS: What are your career plans?

CARSON: I'm planning to be a high school history teacher. History is a fascinating collection of stories, and I want to share my passion for them with my students. I plan to ask them to write the same kinds of research papers and journals that I was asked to write in school so that they develop these skills *before* they get to college. I also plan to text and tweet them, and as a teacher, I want to use that kind of writing as potential examples of how to write concise messages with impact.

> 66 Borrowed thoughts, like borrowed money, only show the poverty of the borrower. 99

Lady Marguerite Blessington, English socialite and writer (1789–1849)

should be, "Better safe than sorry." As a rule, you must cite quotations, para-phrases, or summaries. If you use the exact words of someone else, put quotation marks around them, or if they're longer than four lines, indent them in a block. (And generally, only use long quotes if something has been said in a remarkable way.) Also cite specific facts you're using as support and distinctive ideas belonging to others, even if you don't agree with them.

Q4: I've been doing a lot of reading for this paper. Now I'm not really sure which ideas came from others and which are my own. How do I avoid plagiarism? The best solution here is to take careful notes as you do your research and document where you found each piece of information. Avoid cutting and pasting text. That practice can backfire later when you can't remember what you've extracted and what represents your own thoughts and wording. And remember this: Plagiarism applies to speaking as well as writing!

Now look back at your answer to the Challenge → Reaction at the beginning of this section and see if you would change anything.

Sensitive Situation Teaching your students about plagiarism in your first-year seminar is one of the biggest favors you can do them at the beginning of their college careers. Many students have no idea what plagiarism actually is and consider the Internet to be one, giant "library."

Now What Do You Think?

insight
action

❶ At the beginning of this chapter, Dario Jones, a confused college student, faced a challenge. Now after reading this chapter, would you respond differently to any of the questions you answered about the "FOCUS Challenge Case"? Knowing what you know now, how would you advise him? Write a paragraph ending to the story, incorporating your best advice.

❷ If you've taken an online (or even a hybrid class), what's the most challenging aspect of learning in that environment for you? Why?

❸ Is it possible you're addicted to technology? If you received an assignment asking you to give up your cell phone for a day, could you do it? What would be most challenging about the assignment for you?

❹ Which of the Five Steps to Information Literacy is the most difficult for you? Which ones do you resist and which ones do you delve into with eagerness? Explain why.

❺ List three specific actions you will take to avoid plagiarism at all costs. For example, you may decide to begin taking notes on index cards and list a reference at the top of every card when you do research.

What did you LEARN?

On a scale of 1 to 10, answer the following questions now that you've completed the chapter.

low   1   2   3   4   5   6   7   8   9   10   high

In hindsight, how much did you already know about this subject before reading the chapter?

Can you answer these questions about learning online, using technology, and doing research more fully now that you've read the chapter? _____

❶ How would you define research? What steps are involved?

❷ What is information literacy?

❸ How do you know if you're plagiarizing?

How useful might the information in this chapter be to you? How much do you think this information might affect your success in college? _____

How much energy did you put into reading this chapter? _____

How long did it actually take you to complete this chapter (both the reading and writing tasks)? _____ Hour(s) _____ Minutes

Did you finish reading this chapter? _____

Did you intend to when you started? _____

If you meant to but didn't, what stopped you? _____

Take a minute to compare these answers to your answers from the "Readiness Check" at the beginning of this chapter. What gaps exist between the similar questions? How might these gaps between what you thought before starting the chapter and what you now think after completing the chapter affect how you approach the next chapter in this book?

7 Engaging, Listening, and Note-Taking in Class

How this chapter relates to YOU

1. When it comes to engaging, listening, and note-taking in your college classes, what do you find most challenging, if anything?

Focusing during lectures

Having confidence in my note-taking methods

Adjusting how I take notes in different classes

Asking questions in class

Using my class notes to study

2. What is most likely to be your response? Circle it.

| I'll be open to learning more about this subject. | I'll wait and see how much of this chapter I understand. | I'll ask my instructor for clarification. | Eventually, I'll just figure it out. |

3. What would you have to do to increase your likelihood of success? Will you do it this quarter or semester?

_____

_____

_____

How YOU will relate to this chapter

What are you most interested in learning about? Put check marks by those topics.

☐ How to get engaged in class

☐ How to listen with focus to different kinds of lecture styles

☐ How to take good notes

☐ How to adjust your note-taking system and why

☐ How to ask questions in class

☐ How to use your notes to achieve the best results

- How motivated are you to learn more about listening and taking notes in college? (5 = high, 1 = low) ____

- How ready are you to read now? ____ (If something is in your way, take care of it if you can, so you can zero in and focus.)

- How long do you think it will take you to complete this chapter? If you start and stop, keep track of your overall time. ____ Hour(s) ____ Minutes

? challenge

Lindsey Collier

It was Lindsey Collier's first trip home since classes started. Thanksgiving! In addition to the family's traditional feast, she was eager to see her six-year-old sister, her brother who was a sophomore in high school, and her parents. After she left home, she began to appreciate her family more than ever. What great people they are, she kept thinking. Still, she wondered: Will they be glad to see me? Will I fit back into the family? Will Mom have converted my bedroom into a guest room? Will Dad still want to watch our favorite TV shows together? A million questions were running through her mind. Even though they talked on the phone and sent e-mails and text messages nearly every day, actually seeing her family for the first time in three months was going to seem strange. And she hadn't even seen Honey and Nougat yet, the two brand new labrador retriever puppies, except in pictures on her cell phone! How much fun would they be?

© Larry Harwood Photography. Property of Cengage Learning

She knew one thing for sure: Her parents would ask questions about how her classes were going. *Pretty well*, she thought. She'd gotten a B on her English paper, a B on her first math exam,

an A on her College Success "Write Your Own Case Study" assignment, and an A– on her philosophy paper. But then there was Information Systems 102, her computer literacy course. That was a different story.

Her computer literacy instructor was a graduate teaching assistant. This was his first experience teaching a college course, he had announced on the first day of class, and English was his second language. His lectures were jam-packed with information that went

right over Lindsey's head. Take last Wednesday's lecture, for example:

> The real beginning of modern computers goes back to the seventeenth

© Jomar Aplaon/Shutterstock.com;
© Johan Swanepoel/Shutterstock.com

century and intellectual giants such as Descartes, Pascal, Leibnitz, and Napier. In mathematics, particularly, tremendous progress was made in revolutionizing how people saw the world, and their calculations became so laborious that they needed a more sophisticated computing machine.

The development of logarithms by the Scottish mathematician John Napier in 1614 stimulated the invention of the various devices that substituted the addition of logarithms for multiplication. Napier published his great work of logarithms in the book called Rabdologia. This was a remarkable invention since it enabled people to transform multiplication and division into simple addition and subtraction. His logarithm tables soon came into widespread use. Napier is often remembered more by another invention of his, nicknamed "Napier's Bones." This was a small instrument constructed of 10 rods, on which were engraved the multiplication tables. They are referred to as bones because the first set was made from ivory and resembled a set of bones. This simple device enabled people to carry out multiplication quickly if one of the numbers was only one digit (i.e., $6 \times 6,742$).[1]

© Johan Swanepoel/ Shutterstock.com

Lindsey tried to pay attention to his words and copy down the writing scribbled all over the white board, but no matter how hard she tried, her mind seemed to drift to the new guy she'd just met. Frankly, she just wasn't interested in all this stuff. Information seemed to fly out of her instructor's mouth at mach speed, and she used his accent as an excuse. Taking notes that quickly was just plain impossible. She tried giving him quizzical looks to communicate "Slow down, please," but he probably couldn't see her face in the back row.

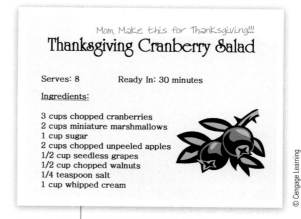

© Juriah Mosin/Shutterstock.com

Because nothing the professor said caught her interest, she knew that asking questions in class would only prove that she wasn't paying attention. Trying to read and take notes from the textbook chapters *before* class took more discipline than she could muster. Once she even tried bringing her laptop to class to take notes, but she couldn't type fast enough, and none of it made much sense. So she drifted to her Facebook page and passed the time in class that way, even though she knew that wasn't a good idea.

Lindsey had thought about trying to stop in during the instructor's office hours some morning, but she worked off-campus as a breakfast server at a local restaurant. She could try making an appointment with him, she thought, but was he really willing to meet with every single student who had a scheduling conflict? *That's why he has office hours*, she told herself. And after all, he was working hard at the same time to earn an advanced degree himself. Besides, did she really want to discuss how poorly she was doing? It was too

Mom, Make this for Thanksgiving!!!

Thanksgiving Cranberry Salad

Serves: 8   Ready In: 30 minutes

Ingredients:

3 cups chopped cranberries
2 cups miniature marshmallows
1 cup sugar
2 cups chopped unpeeled apples
1/2 cup seedless grapes
1/2 cup chopped walnuts
1/4 teaspoon salt
1 cup whipped cream

© Cengage Learning

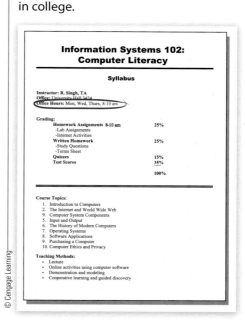

Courtesy of Facebook; © Larry Harwood Photography; Property of Cengage Learning

late in the term to drop the class, and she needed the credits for financial aid. Still, she had to figure something out or computer literacy was going to blow her GPA and her parents' impression that she was doing great in college.

Information Systems 102: Computer Literacy

Syllabus

Instructor: R. Singh, TA
Office: University Hall 3434
Office Hours: Mon, Wed, Thurs, 8-10 am

Grading:

Homework Assignments 8-10 am	25%
-Lab Assignments	
-Internet Activities	
Written Homework	25%
-Study Questions	
-Terms Sheet	
Quizzes	15%
Test Scores	35%
	100%

Course Topics:
1. Introduction to Computers
2. The Internet and World Wide Web
5. Computer System Components
6. Input and Output
6. The History of Modern Computers
7. Operating Systems
8. Software Applications
9. Purchasing a Computer
10. Computer Ethics and Privacy

Teaching Methods:
• Lecture
• Online activities using computer software
• Demonstration and modeling
• Cooperative learning and guided discovery

© Cengage Learning

Activity Option Use a "think-pair-share" approach to this activity. First, have students answer the "What Do *You* Think?" on their own, and then pair up with the student next to them. Pairs of students must agree on the top two mistakes that Lindsey is making, as well as the top two things that she must immediately do. Each pair of students reports to the class and a master list is made. Finally, ask students if there is something that they think is really critical that is not on the list. It is possible that one or two students may key in to some really important underlying issues that Lindsey needs to address.

What Do *You* Think?

❶ List five mistakes Lindsey is making.

❷ Now list five things that Lindsey should do immediately to improve her computer literacy classroom experience.

❸ Do you have any classes this term in which it's challenging to take notes? Have you identified the problem and tried to fix it? How would you need to change your note-taking practices to get the best results?

VARK It!

Complete the recommended activity for your preferred VARK learning modality. If you are multimodal, select more than one activity. Your instructor may ask you to (a) give an oral report on your results in class, (b) send your results to him or her via e-mail, or (c) post them online.

Visual: Color-code the notes you take as you read this chapter to mark important themes (blue highlighter for main points, yellow highlighter for examples, etc.).

Aural: As you tackle this chapter, read the most important sections (that apply to you) aloud, as if you were a TV anchorperson with breaking news. ("This just in . . .")

Read/Write: As you read this chapter, outline it using the major headings as your guide.

Kinesthetic: As you read, decide which of the featured quotes in this chapter is most motivating to you. To keep reminding yourself, make a poster of it to tape on a wall or start a favorite quote file on one of your electronic devices.

Get Engaged in Class

Challenge: What is *engagement*? Exactly what does it take to become engaged in class?

Reaction:

_____

_____

_____

Teachable Moment As you begin this chapter along with your students, make sure they know that you are in this together. As they learn about themselves, you will, too, and sharing *your* learning is one way to engage your students in theirs. Who knows, you may even learn more about yourself!

No, this chapter isn't about buying a ring and getting down on one knee. It's about your willingness to focus, listen, discuss, ask questions, take notes, and generally dive into your classes. It's about being a full participant in what you're learning, not just a spectator sitting on the sidelines. It's about not just memorizing information for exams and then forgetting it. You see, the secret to college success hinges on this one word: *engagement*.

Think about this analogy. How did you learn to swim? Did you read books about swimming? Did you Google the word and check out all the hits? Did you get advice from your friends about swimming? Did you sit on the edge of the pool and watch other people swim? No, you probably jumped in and got wet, right? The same thing is true with your college classes. The more willing you are to jump in and get wet, the more engaged you'll be in the learning process. It's your education, after all, so take the plunge!

Whether online or face-to-face, getting the most out of class means reading, listening, asking questions, participating, and taking good notes. Perhaps you think you've already learned all of these skills, but the truth is they are so important to your college success that it's worth the effort to find out for sure.

Dare to Prepare

If you want to get a head start on developing good academic habits in class, then start before you get there. Preparation separates students into two categories: those who excel at learning and those who don't. Although not all students see the value of preparation, do more than your classmates do—dare to prepare! Follow these suggestions and you'll find that it's easier to get engaged in class because you're ready.

1. **Look ahead.** By checking your course syllabus before class, you'll be prepared for the upcoming topic. You'll also avoid the "oops" factor of sitting down, looking around, and noticing that everyone else knows something you don't about what's supposed to happen today.

2. **Do the pre-work.** If you have a reading assignment due, do it, and take notes as you read. The same goes for PowerPoint slides to preview or a recorded lecture to listen to before class. Write in the margins of your textbook or on sticky notes. Question what you're reading and enter into a mental dialogue with the author. Having some background on the topic will do you a world of good in class. You will be able to listen more actively and participate more intelligently during any discussion: *Yes, I remember the chapter covering that topic*, you'll think when the instructor begins talking about something you recognize. Instead of hearing it for the first time, you'll *reinforce* what you've already read. According to one study, as few as one-third of your classmates will have done the assigned reading prior to class. That factoid isn't a reason to excuse yourself from reading; instead it gives you insider information on how *you* can shine in class by comparison.[2]

3. **Show up physically.** Not only is attending class important for your overall understanding of the material, but it may move your grade up a few notches. There's evidence that your class attendance is a better predictor of how well you'll do in college than your entering ACT, SAT, or GPA scores are![3] Even if attendance isn't required by your instructor, require it of yourself. Research says that missing classes is definitely related to your academic performance.[4] And once you give yourself permission to skip one single, solitary class, it becomes easier to do it the next time, and the time after that, and so on. Studies indicate that on any given day, approximately one-third of your classmates will miss class, that most students think that several absences during a term is "the standard," and that among students who miss class often, only one-quarter do the reading to catch up.[5] Exercise good judgment, even if your classmates don't!

What actually correlates with success are not grades, but 'engagement'—genuine involvement in courses and campus activities. Engagement leads to 'deep learning,' or learning for understanding. That's very different from just memorizing stuff for an exam, then forgetting it.

John Merrow, reporter, USA Today

READ CHAPTER 6 FOR IS 102 tonight!!!!

Teachable Moment Generate a list of reasons why students might miss class, either on your own to bring to class, or with your students in class. Ask them for their opinions on whether or not these are reasons or excuses and which are acceptable in their opinions—and then share your opinion. Examples might include:
—going to a doctor's appointment
—going home for a family emergency (define some)
—making a trip to the airport to pick up a family member
—taking care of your sister after she has her wisdom teeth removed
—giving your boyfriend/girlfriend a ride
—watching your aunt's kids
—extending a break (Labor Day, Thanksgiving)
—going on a family vacation
—letting the dog out

Increasingly, some faculty are concerned that in the views of many of today's students, all reasons for missing class are "created equal." It's much easier to deal with absences during the term if you've discussed the subject thoroughly in class.

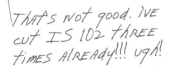
That's not good. I've cut IS 102 three times already!!! ugh!

> Every person in this life has something to teach me—and as soon as I accept that, I open myself to truly listening.

John Lahr, drama critic

No more Facebook in class either!

I'll sit in the "t zone" next class and see if it helps.

Sensitive Situation There may be reasons why students don't want to sit in the T zone. Perhaps they want to be anonymous because they are afraid they will be called on. Remind students that if they have this kind of fear—to the point of almost panicking—it is good to talk with their advisor about what to do. Some individuals actually do have panic attacks when they have to present or are called upon. Think about raising the question about why someone might not want to sit in the T zone with your students and suggesting ways to cope or get help.

4. **Show up mentally.** Showing up means more than just occupying a seat in the classroom. It means assessing what you bring to the class as a learner on any particular day. Just as each chapter of this book asks you to do a "Readiness Check" before you begin reading, it's a good idea to do a mental "Readiness Check" when you arrive in class. Are you *physically*, *intellectually*, and *emotionally* ready to give it your best shot? If not, what can you do to rally for the cause?

5. **Choose your seat strategically.** Imagine paying $150 for a concert ticket, just like everyone else, and then electing to sit in the nosebleed section as high up and far away from the action as you could get. Sitting in the back means you're more likely to let your mind wander and less likely to hear clearly. Sitting in the front means you'll keep yourself accountable by being in full view of the instructor and the rest of the class. Studies show that there is a definite connection between students' academic performance and their seat location. What's the best spot for great concentration? Front and center, literally—the "T zone"! In one study, students who sat at the back of a large auditorium were six times more likely to fail the course, even though the instructor had assigned seats randomly![6] Not only will sitting in the T zone keep you alert throughout the class, but instructors tend to have higher opinions of the students who sit there.

6. **Bring your tools.** Bring a writing utensil and notebook with you to every class. Your instructor may also ask you to bring your textbook, calculator, a blue book for an exam, or other necessary items. If so, do it. Question: how seriously would you take a carpenter who showed up to work without a hammer, nails, and screwdriver? Get the point?

7. **Don't sit by your best friend.** Resist the temptation to sit next to your best buddy in order to catch up on all the latest campus news during

> ## Politeness is the art of choosing among one's real thoughts.

Adlai Stevenson II,
U.S. Presidential candidate (1900–1965)

[handwritten] Not my issue. I'm good here.

class. Of course, it's important to have friends, but class is hardly the best time to devote yourself to helping your friendship blossom. You're there for a reason; now capitalize on it!

8. **Posture counts!** Your parents may have told you more than once as a kid: "Sit up straight!" Sitting up straight in class will help you develop a healthy mind. It's hard to focus when you're slouched into a position that screams, "I could really use a power nap about now!" When your body says, "I'm ready to learn," your mind follows suit.

9. **Maintain your health.** Being sick can wreak havoc on your ability to concentrate, listen well, and participate. Take the preventative approach by getting enough sleep, eating well, and exercising. Remember, *energy management* is key to your ability to focus. Depleted energy can lead to serious *disengagement.*

10. **Focus.** After sitting down in class each day, take a moment to clear your head of all daydreams, to-do's, and worries. Take a deep breath and remind yourself of the opportunity to learn that lies ahead. Promise yourself you'll get the most from this class. Think of yourself as a reporter at a press conference, listening intently because you'll be writing a story about what's going on. You *will* be writing a "story"—often in response to an essay question on an exam!

Follow the Rules of Engagement

Just as is the case with most places you can think of, college classrooms have rules about how to behave. You don't find people yelling in church or staring at other people in elevators or telling jokes at funerals. There are rules about how to behave in a variety of contexts, and college classrooms are no exception. Here are a few rules of engagement that you should know about up front:

1. **Be aware that gab is not a gift.** In class, talking while others are speaking is inappropriate. And it's certainly not a gift—especially to your instructor. In fact, side conversations while your professor is lecturing or your classmates are contributing to the discussion are downright rude. If you're seated next to a gabber, don't get sucked in. Use body language to communicate that you're there to learn, not to gab. If that's not enough to set the gabber straight, politely say something like, "I really need to pay

Activity Option In addition to being cheated out of learning, the issue with interrupting class is really about a student's right to learn. When one student disrupts the class, they have robbed others of their right to learn and in a sense stolen their money. Sometimes students won't speak up about others who are unruly, but you can be sure that you have students in class who are upset if their learning is frequently disrupted. You might even ask students how they would feel if someone was constantly talking to his neighbor. To test this out, before class, ask two students to stage talking in class and then debrief. How did classmates feel about the disruption?

attention right now. Let's talk more later, okay?" Don't let other students cheat you out of learning.

2. **Control your hunger pangs.** If your class meets through a meal hour, get in the habit of eating before or after class. Crunching and munching in the classroom may get in the way of others' learning, not to mention the distraction caused by enticing smells. Instructors differ on their preferences here. It's a good idea to find out what your instructors' preferences are, and then abide by them.

3. **Turn off your cell phone, please!** There's a reason why people are asked to turn off their cell phones before concerts, athletic events, or movies. Imagine being in a jam-packed theater trying to follow the film's plot with cell phones going off every few seconds. You've paid good money to see a film. The same thing goes for your college classes. In one study, a "planted" ringing cell phone caused students to score 25 percent worse on a course quiz, even though the information had just been presented by the instructor before the distraction and was projected up front on a screen during the 30 second ringing.[7] As a general rule, your instructor's presentation deserves the same focus you'd give a feature film, so turn your cell phone off and put it away. (We can hear it when it's set on vibrate, too.) And texting in class shows everyone where your mind *really* is. The bottom line is that you're in school to learn, so give class your undivided attention.

4. **Better late than never?** Not to some instructors. Students arriving late and leaving early are annoying, not only to your instructor but to your classmates. To them, it looks like you don't value the other students or the class content. How would you like dinner guests to arrive an hour late, after you'd slaved over a hot stove all day? Your instructors have prepared for class, and they feel the same way. Build in time to find a parking place, hike to the building where class is held, or stop for a coffee. Do everything you can to avoid coming late and leaving early. And don't schedule a lube job for your car during class or volunteer to watch your aunt's kids. Many things in your life are important—it's true—but while you're in school, coming to class and doing your coursework should be at the top of your list. Preserve class time as a priority.

5. **Actively choose to engage, not disengage.** Engagement isn't something that just happens to you while you're not looking. You're sitting there, minding your own business, and zap—you suddenly realize that you've become engaged in learning. It's a choice you make, and sometimes it's a difficult choice because the material isn't naturally appealing to you, or the course is a required one you didn't choose, or you're just plain out of sorts. Choose to engage, anyway. Instead of actively choosing to *disengage* in class by sleeping through lectures, surfing the Internet, or texting friends, choose to engage by leaning forward, processing information, finding your own ways to connect to the material, and formulating questions to ask. According to one study conducted in the business world, employees addicted to e-mail and text messages showed the equivalent of a ten-point drop in IQ—another piece of evidence that multitasking costs![8]

Teaching with Technology What are your rules on cell phones in class? Some faculty think that cell phones should be banned. Others create community-building penalties for a ringing phone, like requiring the owner to bring small treats for everyone to the next class. Still others recommend that students use their cell phones to a) take pictures of elaborate "concept maps" that have been generated during lively discussion on the white board in front, b) ask students to correlate their cell phone stop watches and use them for timed group activities, c) Google tough questions that no one can answer without doing research, or d) engage students in on-screen quizzes or encourage a Twitter back-channel conversation about the course content during class. Google "using Twitter in the classroom" and you'll find many examples if this is something you would like to consider using in your course as an experiment--even just to demonstrate the challenges of multitasking!

Teachable Moment A controversial debate over smart phone use has erupted not only in higher education, but in the business world, too. (See "Mind Your BlackBerry or Mind Your Manners," *NYT.*) Does a timely e-mail to a customer during a business meeting (about something that's just come up) outweigh paying attention to who's talking and what's going on? You may wish to bring this article or a similar one to class to discuss with your students. Get their input, which may reveal their honest attitudes toward this topic in general.

Teachable Moment Suggest students check with professors about what to do if they are late. There are times when something is unavoidable (i.e., an accident). Also, keep in mind that if we expect students to be on time, then we, as instructors, have to adhere to the same rules.

If you're investing in a college education, then play by the rules of engagement. They're in place for your benefit.

Listening with Focus

> **?** **challenge**
>
> **" reaction**
>
> **Challenge:** What is *focused listening*? How can you achieve it?
>
> **Reaction:**
>
> _____
>
> _____
>
> _____

Listening with focus is more than just physically hearing words as they stream by. It's actually a complicated process that's hard work.

"Easy Listening" Is a "No-Brainer"— Focused Listening Requires Smarts *and* Skills

Stores, restaurants, and elevators are known for their programmed, background "easy listening" music. Chances are you hardly notice it's there. Listening in class, however, requires actual skill, and you'll be doing a great deal of it as a college student. Experts estimate that the average student spends 80 percent of class time listening to lectures.[9]

Many of us naively believe that listening is easy to do. If you happen to be around when there's something to listen to, you can't help but listen. Not so! Did you know that when you're listening at your best, your respiration rate, heartbeat, and body temperature all increase? Just as with aerobic exercise, your body works harder when you're engaging in focused listening. When all is said and done, listening is really about energy management. You can't listen well when your energy is zapped, when you've pulled the mother of all all-nighters, or when your stomach is growling with a vengeance. Focused listening means that you've cleared the deck for class, and you're focusing on engagement.

I did not know that!

Here are some techniques for improving your listening skills in the classroom. Read through the list, then go back and check off the ones you're willing to try harder to do in class this week. It's not always easy to be a good listener, but the investment you make in improving your listening skills will pay off in countless ways.

☐ **Calm yourself.** Take a few deep breaths with your eyes closed to help you put all those nagging distractions on the back burner during class time.

☐ **Be open.** As you listen in class, you may wonder how you'll ever use this information in your career. But keep an open mind and view your class as yet another opportunity to strengthen your intellect and learn something new. Wisdom comes from a broad understanding of many things, rather than from a consistently limited focus on practical information.

Teaching with Technology Wikis are an interactive source of information on the Internet. These knowledge-pools allow users to create, view, and share information on a particular topic. Wikipedia is perhaps the most famous wiki, but there are many other websites that contain user-created content on more specific subjects. Curriki.com is an interactive website that allows educators to share info on curriculum for primarily K-12 classroom teaching. But you may find some useful ideas there for your first-year seminar classroom there.

✓
LiKE IS 102!!

Lucidio Studio Inc/Spirit/Corbis

> ❝ Listening looks easy, but it's not simple. Every head is a world. ❞
>
> **Cuban proverb**

☐ **Don't make snap judgments.** Remember, you don't have to like your instructor's wardrobe to respect his knowledge. Focus on the content he's offering you. You may not even agree with what he's saying, but he may be leading up to a point you can't predict and turn the argument around. Don't jump to conclusions about content or style.

☐ **Assume responsibility.** Speak up! Ask questions! Even if you have a professor with an accent who's difficult to understand, an instructor who talks too fast (or too slow), or a professor who seems not to notice that students are in the room, the burden of clarification rests with you. You will interact with people with all sorts of accents, voices, and speech patterns throughout your life. It's up to you to improve the situation.

☐ **Watch for gestures and speech patterns that communicate "Here comes something important!"** Some typical examples include raising an index finger, turning to face the class, leaning forward from behind the podium, walking up the aisle, or using specific facial expressions or gestures. Listen, too, for changes in the rate, volume, or tone of speech, longer than usual pauses, or repeated information.

☐ **Appreciate your instructor's prep time.** For every hour of lecture time, your teacher has worked for hours to prepare. Although she may make it look easy, her lecture has involved researching, organizing, creating a PowerPoint presentation, overheads, or a podcast, and preparing notes and handouts.

☐ **Trick yourself into focused listening.** Some students are very good actors. They know how to look like they're listening. In class, they sit down, get out their notebooks, find a pen, assume a listening posture, and then mentally go somewhere else. While these students aren't fooling

Activity Option Assign students to listen to the same lecture. You may have some on campus that you can download for the class in podcast format, or ask students to attend the same lecture. Have students watch for gestures and speech patterns to figure out what were the most important points. They can report in class about what they thought was most important. As an alternative, you can give a lecture or videotape someone to do this as an in-class activity.

Teachable Moment Ask students to identify the theme of the lecture in their last two classes. For students that get it right, ask them how they remembered. While they were in class, did they associate what was being discussed with something they knew or experienced (connected knowledge)? Were they prepared for class?

themselves, it *is* possible to trick yourself into focused listening. You may find many of your classes to be naturally fascinating learning experiences. But for others, you will need to be convinced. Even if you don't find Intro to Whatever to be the most engaging subject in the world, you may find yourself intrigued by your instructor. Most people are interested in other people. What makes him tick? Why was she drawn to this field? If you find it hard to get interested in the material, trick yourself by paying attention to the person delivering the message. While tricking yourself isn't always a good idea, it can work if you know what you're doing and why.

I wonder what does make my instructor tick?!

Listening Is More Than Hearing

Perhaps you've never thought about it, but, actually, listening and hearing aren't the same thing. Hearing—the physiological part—is only the first stage of a four-stage process. Listening is a much more complex process—especially *focused listening*, or listening at your best. The four stages of focused listening are as follows and are shown in Figure 7.1:

Box 7.1   Listening Tips If English Is Your Second Language

It's normal to feel overwhelmed in the classroom as a new student, but especially if your first language isn't English. The academic environment in higher education can be stressful and competitive. It's even more stressful if you're also dealing with a new and different culture. You will need to give yourself time to adapt to all of these changes. In the meantime, here are some suggestions for improving your ability to listen well in class:

- Talk to your instructor before the course begins. Let her know that English is not your native language, but that you're very interested in learning. Ask for any suggestions on how you can increase your chances of success in the class. Your instructor will most likely be willing to provide you with extra help, knowing you're willing to do your part to overcome the language barrier.

- Try to get the main points of your professor's lecture. You don't have to understand every word.

- Write down words to look up in the dictionary later. Keep a running list and check them all after class. Missing out on one important term can hurt your chances of understanding something else down the line.

- Don't be afraid to ask questions. If you're too uncomfortable to ask during class, make use of your professor's office hours or e-mail address to get your questions answered. Also, teaching assistants and peer tutors may be available to help you.

- Use all support materials available for the class. Find out if your instructor posts his notes on the course website or if they are available as handouts. Some professors offer guided notes or skeleton outlines for students

to fill in throughout the lecture. Some large lectures are videotaped for viewing by students at a later time. Make full use of podcasts of lectures, if they're available, so that you can listen more than once to portions you found confusing in class. Use any tools available to help reinforce lecture content.

- Team up with a classmate whose native language is English. Clarify your notes and fill in gaps.

- Form a study group with other classmates. Meet on a regular basis so that you can help one another. Remember: just because your native language isn't English doesn't mean you don't have something to offer the other members of your study group.

- Be patient. It will take some time to adjust to the accents of your various instructors. After a few weeks of class, you'll find it easier to understand what is being said.

- Practice your English comprehension by listening to talk radio or watching television or movies. You'll hear a variety of regional accents, for example, and broaden your understanding of American culture.

- Take an "English as a Second Language" course if you think it would help. It's important to keep up with the academic demands of college, and further development of your English skills may improve your comprehension and boost your confidence.

- If you continue to feel overwhelmed and unable to cope after several weeks in school, find out if your campus has an International Students Office, and enlist support from people who are trained to help.[10]

FIGURE 7.1

Four Stages of Focused Learning

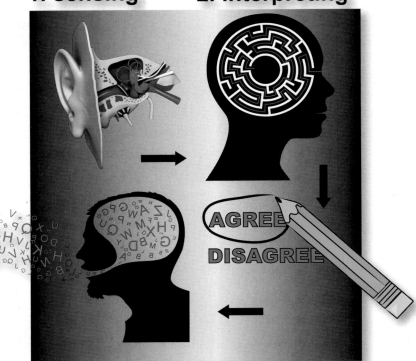

1. sensing   2. interpreting

4. responding   3. evaluating

Activity Option Take students through an example of these four steps by having two students converse in front of the group and identify how the listening process works, step by step.

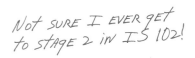

Not sure I ever get to stage 2 in IS 102!

Teachable Moment Ask your students to all talk aloud at once; then continue your lecture. Discuss how to zero in and listen to one thing, truly listen, despite the many noises of life—some external and some internal. Students may share some important insights that relate not only to class, but to other aspects of their lives, like work and relationships.

Teachable Moment Have you ever come back from a meeting or conference where you took notes and then read them later only to find you weren't sure what they meant? Remind students that something as simple as writing legibly, having enough paper, and taking just a few minutes afterwards to clean up the notes helps you remember the important points.

1. **Sensing:** receiving the sounds through your auditory system. As you sit in class, sound waves enter your ears and register in your brain.

2. **Interpreting:** understanding the message. Sounds themselves don't mean anything until you assign meaning to them. Instead of just random noise, the instructor's message must mean something to you.

3. **Evaluating:** weighing evidence. You decide if something is true or important by sorting fact from opinion. Both interpretation and evaluation in class may involve asking questions to clarify things.

4. **Responding:** providing feedback or taking action. You respond by participating in the discussion, asking significant questions, and taking down clear, meaningful notes to study later.[11]

As you're listening in class, you must cycle through all four of these stages. You must *sense* the sound waves coming from your instructor, a classmate, or a guest speaker, *interpret* them, *evaluate* them, and *respond* by jumping into the discussion yourself, asking questions, and taking the best notes you can. If you're not focused, it's possible to skip a step or "listen out of order." You may take notes without really *interpreting* what you're hearing. You're operating on autopilot—you skip the interpretation step completely, and write down things you don't really understand. (And consequently, you can't interpret your notes later.) Or you may try to write down every word you hear without *evaluating* its importance, getting bogged down in insignificant detail. If you want to get the most from your time spent in the classroom, it will help to pay attention to all four stages of focused listening.

Have you ever noticed there's a play-by-play commentary going on inside your head, just like an NFL announcer during a big game: "On third down with no timeouts left. And here's the snap . . . rookie Davis Jones busts off tackle for an eight-yard gain! It's close to a first down. . . ." Compare that to your own play-by-play observations: "And here he comes . . . Matt's walking straight toward me. He's getting closer. Maybe this is my big chance."

It's normal to comment internally about what's going on around you, and it's perfectly human to think that your own internal dialogue is the most important thing on the planet. The question isn't whether or not you're engaged in constant conversation with yourself; it's whether that conversation is productive and useful, and if not, how to make it so.

Sometimes this incessant, internal chatter makes it's hard to be fully present in class because of three P's: **p**ressure, **p**reoccupation, and **p**riorities. While you're sitting there, you feel a rush of stress about your assignments; you worry about a sick relative; and you obsess about whether you should tackle your calculus homework or start on your philosophy research paper tonight. You feel overwhelmed. Productivity expert Kerry Gleeson believes, "This constant, unproductive preoccupation with all the things we have to do is the single largest consumer of time and energy."

Do the three P's highjack your attention? It's true; we all have important things to think about, but let's be honest: Unproductive worry can shut you down. According to time management guru David Allen, "There is usually an inverse proportion between how much something is on your mind and how much it's getting done."[12]

In his book *Quiet Your Mind*, author John Selby reports that we can learn better control over our thoughts, and that the psychological and physiological benefits are well worth it. Being in a permanent state of flight or fight, the body's normal reaction to stress, is hazardous to your health.[13] Here are some tips to coach yourself to quiet your mind:

- **Choose where to focus your attention.** Instead of allowing your mind to run you, make a conscious decision to run it. Horace may have lived many centuries ago, but his quotation below is timeless.

- **Spend your free time; don't squander it.** Do you watch television, exercise, or surf the Net to avoid what you see as unpleasant but necessary tasks, rather than to *revitalize*? Consider whether your free time is about something or about nothing. Short bouts of nothing can be liberating, but long bouts of nothing can be opportunities for negative thoughts to move in and take over.

- **Worry less; do more.** Worry is counterproductive; it drains us of the energy we need to get things done and keeps us from enjoying the present. Write down what's worrying you most, identify the worst that could possibly happen, and ask yourself if your fear is realistic. If it's not, let go of it and do something productive.

- **Forgive and forget.** Some people obsess over the past. They should have done X; if only Y had happened instead. Life is full of ups and downs, but it's important to keep moving. Actress and comedian Lily Tomlin once said, "Forgiveness means giving up all hope for a better past." Focus on the present tense.

- **Be present.** Remember grade school? Your teachers would call the roll every morning, and you'd answer "present" or "I'm here." Life coach Mark van Doren says, "There is one thing we can do, and the happiest people are those who can do it to the limit of their ability. We can be completely present. We can be all here. We can . . . give all our attention to the opportunity before us."

Rule your mind or it will rule you.

Horace (Roman poet, 65–8 B.C.)

Listen Hard!

It's estimated that college students spend ten hours per week listening to lectures.[14] Professors can speak 2,500–5,000 words during a fifty-minute lecture. That's a lot of words flying by at breakneck speed, so it's important to listen correctly. But what does *that* mean?

Think about the various situations in which you find yourself listening. You often listen to empty chit-chat on your way to class. "Hey, how's it going?" when you spot your best friend in the hallway is an example, right? Listening in this type of situation doesn't require a lot of brainpower. Although you wouldn't want to spend too much time on chit-chat, if you refused to engage in any at all, you'd probably be seen by others as odd, withdrawn, shy, or arrogant. You also listen in challenging situations, some that are emotionally charged; for example, a friend needs to vent or relieve stress. Most people who are blowing off steam aren't looking for you to fix their problems. They just want to be heard and to hear something from you like "I understand." Listening to chit-chat and listening in emotionally charged situations require what are called soft listening skills. You must be accepting, sensitive, and nonjudgmental. You don't have to assess, analyze, or conclude. You just have to be there for someone else.

But these two types of listening situations don't describe all the kinds of listening you do. Sometimes instead of soft listening skills, you need something altogether different. When you're listening to someone trying to persuade you of something, you have to pay close attention, think critically, and ultimately make decisions about what you're hearing. Is something true or false? How do you know? When you're listening to a person trying to inform or persuade you, you need hard listening skills instead of soft ones. In situations like these you must be discerning, analytical, and decisive.

What's important about all of this? One mistake many students make in class is listening the wrong way. They should be using their hard listening skills, rather than sitting back and letting information waft over them. Soft listening skills don't help you in class. You must listen intently, think critically, and analyze carefully what you're hearing. It's important to note that neither listening mode is better than the other. They are each simply better suited to different situations. But soft listening won't get you the results you want in your classes. You don't need to be there for your instructor; you need to be there for yourself.[15]

Get Wired for Sound

Aural learners of the world unite! Increasingly professors are providing podcasts (and videocasts) of their lectures so that you can *preview* the lecture in advance or *review* it after class. Some textbooks (like this one) offer chapter summaries you can listen to on the subway, in the gym, or in bed while recovering from the flu via your computer or digital-audio player.

Regardless of your learning style, recorded lectures allow you to re-listen to difficult concepts as many times as needed. You can take part in the live action in class and take notes later while re-listening to the podcast. In one study, students who re-listened to a lecture one, two, or three times increased their lecture notes substantially each time and students who re-listen to a lecture and take notes can increase their test scores.[16] Of course, recorded lectures aren't meant to excuse you from attending class, and in order to take advantage of them, you actually have to find time to listen to them. They're supplemental tools to *reinforce* learning for busy students on the go, which is virtually *everyone* these days.[17]

GREAT PODCAST ONLINE AT WWW.CENGAGEBRAIN. COM FOR THIS CHAPTER! I SHOULD CHECK OUT PODCASTS FOR IS 102. MAYBE LISTENING TO LECTURES MORE THAN ONCE WOULD HELP ME UNDERSTAND MY INSTRUCTOR'S ACCENT!

One way to learn more about note-taking is by using a real-life example. Imagine that you're sitting in an introductory psychology course, listening to a lecture on the Five Factor Trait Theory as you or some of your friends may well be doing this term. Your instructor will read this lecture aloud to you, or have someone else read it aloud to you. Don't take notes; just listen carefully. Afterwards, write down all the main points of the lecture.

The Five Factor Trait Theory

Currently, the most widely accepted trait theory derived from factor analysis is Paul Costa and Robert McCrae's (1992) five factor theory. This theory proposes five core dimensions that can be measured along a continuum in all people.

- *Extraversion:* the degree to which energy is directed inward or outward. People high in extraversion are talkative, sociable, and prefer to be around others. At the other end of the continuum are people low in extraversion (introverts), who are quiet, reserved, and comfortable on their own.
- *Neuroticism:* the degree to which one is emotionally stable or unstable. People high in neuroticism are temperamental, worrisome, and pessimistic. People who score low on this factor tend to be more even-tempered and calm.
- *Openness:* the degree to which one is thoughtful and rational in considering new ideas. People who score high in openness tend to be imaginative, creative, and curious and to prefer variety; those who score low in openness prefer routine and are more narrow-minded in their ideas and experiences.
- *Agreeableness:* the degree to which one gets along well with others. Being easygoing and trusting are traits characteristic of one high in agreeableness. At the other end of the spectrum are people who are unfriendly, antagonistic, and suspicious (low agreeableness).
- *Conscientiousness:* the degree to which one is aware of and attentive to other people and/or the details of a task. People who are high in conscientiousness tend to be hardworking, ambitious, reliable, and self-controlled, whereas individuals low in this dimension are more often described as unreliable, lazy, and spontaneous.

These five dimensions appear in all cultures, suggesting that these five factors may represent universal personality components (Katigbak, Church, Guanzon-Lapeña, Carlota, & del Pilar, 2002; McCrae & Costa, 1998; Yamagata et al., 2006). An easy way to remember the five factors is with the acronym OCEAN. Each letter in OCEAN stands for one of the five factors: O = openness, C = conscientiousness, E = extraversion, A = agreeableness, and N = neuroticism.

(Adapted from Pastorino, E. & Doyle-Portillo, S. (2012). *What Is Psychology? Essentials.* Belmont, CA: Cengage Learning, pp. 548–549.)

1. _____
2. _____
3. _____
4. _____
5. _____

Would taking notes have helped you remember more? Think about how you "naturally" take notes (on your own, without reading the suggestions that follow). Do you simply try to catch phrases that go by? Do you make up abbreviations? Do you have a system? If not, read on!

Identify Lecture Styles So You Can Modify Listening Styles

Regardless of how challenging it is to listen with focus, being successful in college will require you to do just that—focus—no matter what class or which professor. Sometimes your instructors are *facilitators*, who help you discover

> The most basic and powerful way to connect to another person is to listen. Just listen. Perhaps the most important thing we ever give each other is our attention.
>
> **Rachel Naomi Remen, physician and author**

information on your own in new ways. Other times they are *orators*, who lecture as their primary means of delivering information. If you're not an aural learner, listening with focus to lectures will be a challenge for you.

Chances are you won't be able to change your professors' lecturing styles. And even if you could, different students react differently to different lecture styles. But what you can do is expand your own skills as a listener—no matter what class or which instructor. Take a look at the lecture styles coming up and see if you recognize them.

> ➤ **The Rapid-Fire Lecturer:** Have you ever found yourself in a class with an instructor who lectures at breakneck speed? Listening and taking notes in a class like that isn't easy. By the end of class your hand aches from gripping your pen and writing furiously. Because there'll be no time to relax, you'll need to make certain you're ready for this class. Read ahead so that you recognize points the instructor makes. Also take advantage of whatever supplementary materials this teacher provides in the way of audio support, online lecture notes, or PowerPoint handouts.

> ➤ **The Slow-Go Lecturer:** Instead of rushing, some lecturers move very slowly. They contemplate, ruminate, and chew on every word before uttering it. This lecturer speaks so slowly that there are pauses—seconds long—between phrases, while he paces back and forth, pontificating. Your attention tends to drift because you become impatient. Discipline yourself to use the extra time to your advantage by predicting what's coming next or by clarifying what's just been said in your own mind.

> ➤ **The All-Over-the-Map Lecturer:** Organization is not this lecturer's strong suit. While the lecture may be organized in the lecturer's mind, what comes out is difficult to follow. In this case, it will be up to you to organize the lecture content yourself.

> ➤ **The Content-Intensive Lecturer:** This lecturer is hardly aware that anyone else is in the room, intent on covering a certain amount of material in a particular amount of time. This teacher may use extensive discipline-specific jargon that you will need to learn rapidly to keep abreast.

This is him! Note to self: Ask questions in class.

Think about the courses you're taking this term. Use the following form to analyze your various professors' lecture styles. Be discrete as you listen and analyze their styles, of course, but after your chart is completed, decide what *you* can do as a listener to make adjustments in your toughest class. Filling out this chart for all your classes may give you some insights about why one particular class is your toughest and help you develop a plan to become more successful.

LECTURE STYLE ANALYSIS WORKSHEET

COURSES	Information Systems 102				
EMPHASIS Content, students, or both?	Definitely on content. He doesn't seem to notice that students are in the room!				
ORGANIZATION Structured or unstructured?	Lectures seem unstructured with notes written all over the board.				
PACE Fast, slow, or medium?	Very fast. Instructor doesn't seem to notice when students are lost.				
VISUAL AIDS Used? Useful?	Board hard to see from the back of the room.				
EXAMPLES Used? Useful?	Few real examples are given that students can relate to.				
LANGUAGE Terms defined? Vocabulary understandable?	What is a logarithm, exactly? No, not defined.				
DELIVERY Animated via body language?	Although the teacher is trying to communicate, his delivery style isn't lively and interesting.				
QUESTIONS Encouraged?	He rarely pauses to take questions.				
My proposed adjustments in my toughest class:	Make special arrangements to meet with the instructor during his office hours. Must do right away!				

Your **TYPE** is Showing

Just as instructors have lecturing styles, you and your classmates have listening preferences, based on your personality types. See if these research generalizations fit you.

> Extraverts prefer teachers who encourage lively discussion in class, while introverts prefer instructors who give clear lectures.

> Sensors care about teachers who give structured assignments, while intuitives want the freedom to think independently.

> Thinkers expect logical presentations from teachers; feelers want teachers who build rapport with their students.

> Judgers "demand" organization, while perceivers prefer to be entertained and inspired.[18]

When you find yourself in a classroom situation in which your listening preferences and your instructor's lecturing style are mismatched, it's up to you to find a pathway to bridge the two. Believe it or not, according to experts, the responsibility for effective communication lies with the listener, not the speaker!

Teaching with Technology As an instructor, can you identify your own lecture style? Think of ways you can use technology to help students get the most out of your method of lecturing. If you're a Rapid-Fire or Content-Intensive lecturer, you may want to e-mail your PowerPoint lectures to students, or create a blog with the content of the lecture. If you're an Active-Learning or Beyond-the-Text lecturer, you may want to create online videos, podcasts, or web-resources for students to explore.

Activity Option For homework, have students observe their other classes for a week and come to class briefly describing the type of lecturers they have. As a class compare the types and strategize about how students can successfully adapt to the style.

Prepare yourself for a potentially rich learning environment, but be sure to ask questions right away if you find yourself confused.

> **The Review-the-Text Lecturer:** This lecturer will follow the textbook closely, summarizing and highlighting important points. You may assume it's not important to attend class, but watch out for this trap! Receiving the same information in more than one format can be a great way to learn.

> **The Go-Beyond-the-Text Lecturer:** This lecturer will use class time to provide examples, tell stories, and bring in outside materials. Keeping up with reading in the text will be important so that you understand the additional information that you receive in class.

> **The Active-Learning Lecturer:** This lecturer may choose not to lecture at all or to intersperse short lectures with activities and role plays. While you may find it easier to get engaged in class, and you'll most likely appreciate the teacher's creativity, remember that you are still responsible for connecting what happens in class to the course material itself. You will need to read, digest, and process the information on your own outside of class.

Ask and You Shall Receive

challenge

reaction

Challenge: Can you identify different kinds of questions to ask during lectures and in-class discussions?

Reaction:

_____

_____

_____

Even if you listen carefully to every word your instructor utters, it's likely you won't understand them all. After all, your instructor is an expert in the subject you're studying, and you're a novice. At some point or other, you'll need clarification or elaboration, and the best way to get it will be to ask. Even though that makes sense, not all students ask questions in class. Why? See if you've excused yourself from asking questions for any of these reasons:[19]

> I don't want to look stupid.
> I must be slow. Everyone else seems to be understanding.
> I'm too shy.
> I'll get the answer later from the textbook.
> I don't think my question is important enough.
> I don't want to derail the lecture. The instructor's on a roll.
> I don't want to draw attention to myself.
> I'm just not into it.

If any of these reasons for not asking questions in class applies to you, the good news is . . . you're not alone. Unfortunately many students think this way. The bad news, of course, is that your question remains unasked, and therefore, unanswered.

The next time you find yourself in a situation where you don't understand something, consider these points.

1. **Become the class spokesperson.** If you do ask a question that's on your mind, not only will you be doing yourself a favor by asking, but you'll also be helping someone else who's too shy to speak up. When it comes to the discipline at hand—whether it's philosophy, psychology, or chemistry—remember that you and your classmates are novices and the instructor is an expert. Asking questions is a natural part of that equation.

2. **Ask academically relevant questions when the time is right.** As opposed to "Why do we need to know this?" or "Why did you make the test so hard?" ask questions to clarify information. Don't ask questions designed to take your instructor off on a tangent (to delay the impending quiz, for example). If you're really interested in something that's not directly related to the material being covered, bring it up during your instructor's office hours. Otherwise, ask questions when the need to know is there. (Of course, personally relevant questions that apply only to you—for example, about making up work you missed while you were ill—should be asked via e-mail or during office hours).

3. **Build on others' questions.** Listen to the questions other students ask. Use their questions to spark your own. Perhaps another student has a unique way of looking at the issue being discussed that will spark an idea for a follow-up question from you. Remember, to your instructor, good questions indicate *interest*, not *idiocy*.

4. **Consider that questions are a way to s-t-r-e-t-c-h your learning.** Of course, many of the questions you ask in class will be simple questions to clarify information. But be aware of this opportunity: You can ask questions that increasingly move you up the scale toward higher-order thinking. What does that mean? In 1956, learning expert Benjamin Bloom developed a classification system for ways of thinking—from simple to complex. His system, called "Bloom's Taxonomy," shows that thinking occurs on a progression of levels, from low (simple) to high (complex) as shown in Table 7.1. Imagine listening to the lecture in Exercise 7.1, and think

Teachable Moment Students should be beginning to think informally about personality type and how it fits with professors' (hypothesized) types. Get discussions going about how students can deal with professors who are different than they are. For example, ask students to think about professors who are intuitives and how students might respond if they are strong sensors. How would they handle really highly theoretical lectures in class?

yup!

> "
He who is ashamed of asking is ashamed of learning.
"

Danish Proverb

Teaching with Technology Encourage students to ask questions by keeping channels of communication open. Communication technologies such as phones, e-mail, SMS, instant messaging, and even social networking sites like Facebook and Twitter, provide countless opportunities for students to interact with you as their instructor. As a teacher, you must find a balance between privacy and accessibility, but students are certainly using these technologies to communicate with each other. Why not let them communicate with you about course content, too?

Teachable Moment Have you ever heard "there is no such thing as a bad question" or "if you have the question, someone else may, too"? Structure this in class by using a variation of the Cross and Angelo One-Minute Paper: In the middle or at the end of a class, stop for one minute, and ask your students, "What is the most important thing you've learned?" and "What do you still have a question about?" Or ask, "What is the 'muddiest point' from class today?" Have them write their responses on index cards to turn in to you, so that you can address these items at the beginning of the next class.

Teachable Moment It's really important to drive home the point to students about asking for clarification. Ask students why they might not ask questions in a class, even if they know it will help. Some students rely on friends, which is not always an accurate way to get information.

Activity Option Figure 1 and Figure 2 for Exercise 7.2 appear in the Instructor's Resource Manual for *FOCUS* and in FOCUSPoints. If you decide to do this activity in class (and that is highly recommended), and you're not using technology, make a copy of each figure and bring it to class.

Table 7.1 • Bloom's Taxonomy

Level	Explanation	Example
Remembering	recall information and facts	*What are the five traits?*
Understanding	explain ideas	*How is each trait defined?*
Applying	use the information	*If a patient describes sleep disturbances and a general disinterest in life, which trait or traits may be involved?*
Analyzing	examine critically, separate into parts	*Patient X is reserved, temperamental, narrow-minded, antagonistic, and lazy. Based on this information, how would you analyze this person's personality using the five traits?*
Evaluating	assess the relative value	*Which traits (high and low) might be most important in making relationships work productively?*
Creating	design or see from a new point of view	*If you were a college teacher, how would you coach your students about the role of the five traits in achieving academic success?*

Exercise 7.2 — Does Asking Questions Help?

To demonstrate the value of asking questions, try this in-class exercise. A student volunteer, or class "lecturer," will briefly replace the instructor to describe to the rest of the class two different, simple figures she draws herself. Each figure should take up a full piece of paper. The rest of the class must then replicate the drawings as accurately as possible on their own paper as the class "lecturer" describes each figure during two rounds. The point of the exercise is to replicate the two figures the class "lecturer" has drawn as accurately as possible from her description alone.

Round 1: The volunteer should turn her back to the group (to eliminate nonverbal cues), hiding her paper from view, and give the class instructions for drawing Figure 1. *No questions from the group are allowed.* Note the exact amount of time it takes for the rest of the class to listen to the instructions and complete the drawing.

Round 2: Next, the volunteer should now turn around and face the class, giving instructions for drawing Figure 2. *Students may ask questions of the "lecturer" to clarify and elaborate as much as is necessary to get the drawing right (without showing the figure).* Again, note the exact amount of time taken.

After both rounds of the exercise are done, the "lecturer" should ask class members whether they think their drawings closely resemble the two originals and count the number of students who think they drew Figure 1 correctly and the number of students who think they drew Figure 2 correctly. Then the "lecturer" should show the two original figures as drawn, and count the number of students who actually drew Figure 1 and Figure 2 correctly. Finally, as a group, discuss the two rounds and the value of asking questions in lecture classes. Even though questions take more time, the results are usually much better.

Elapsed Time	# Think Correct	# Actually Correct
Round 1		
Round 2		

of questions you could ask to move yourself up this progressive ladder.[20] Remember, your college education is an expensive investment. You've paid to learn, and asking questions is a natural part of that learning experience. Don't be shy—put that hand in the air!

Taking Notes: How Do You Know What's Important?

So, information streams from your instructor's mouth at mach speed, right? What do you do about it? How do you decide what to write down and what to skip? You listen for key words, watch for nonverbal cues, and after a time, you begin to learn what your instructor, as a subject matter expert, values. At least that's the way it works for most students.

Remember that note-taking is paradoxical. The more you write, the less you're free to listen, take part, and become truly engaged. On the other hand, the more time you spend engaged in focused listening, the less you may be free to write down information. Find a happy medium for yourself for each of your classes, and use methods that work best for you to further enhance your learning.

Unfortunately, professors don't speak in *italics,* or **bolded** font, or <u>underlined</u> script. While you can use cues such as these when you're recording notes as you read from a textbook, spoken language doesn't work that way. Try these suggestions:

1. **Listen for an organizing pattern.** Has the instructor been covering the subject of **personality research** by major chronological periods? Has she been listing contributors to the field by specific discoveries? What's her *system*?

2. **Note whether a handout accompanies lecture materials.** If so, chances are that the information is considered to be important. If the instructor interrupts the lecture to give more detailed examples from a handout, he must consider doing so important enough to take up class time. Keep all handouts, and assume they'll be worth reviewing at exam time.

3. **Recognize verbal cues.** If portions of the lecture are highlighted verbally, these portions are probably important. Listen for signal words and phrases such as "There are three reasons . . ." "On the other hand . . ." "For example . . ." "In summary . . ." If your instructor begins, "Today we'll look at the Five Factor Trait Theory in human psychology," you've just received a clue about how many main ideas there will be and what to listen for.

   This is a good suggestion I should think more about.

4. **When in doubt, write it down.** If you're not sure whether to write something down, use the motto, "Better safe than sorry." If you don't know a word the instructor is using, leave a blank to show you omitted something, or sound it out as you're writing and come back to it later. Put the lecture in your own words for the most part, but write down formulas, definitions, charts, diagrams, and specific facts verbatim.

5. **Consider your learning style preferences.** If you're a visual learner, a note-taking system that works well for

When you write down your ideas you automatically focus your full attention on them. Few if any of us can write one thought and think another at the same time. Thus a pencil and paper make excellent concentration tools.

Michael Leboeuf, American business author

you may not work particularly well for a classmate who has a different learning style. Drawing all over your paper may help you see connections, while a classmate next to you is writing the same information down in a structured outline format. If a note-taking system seems awkward to you even after you've tried it for awhile, you may be better off trying a different one.

6. **Create a shorthand system that works.** When you're taking notes quickly, as you often do in class, you won't have time to write out every word your instructor utters. Use abbreviations or a shorthand system that you create for yourself, like this:

Symbol	Meaning	Example
→	leads to, produces, causes, makes	Practice → perfect.
←	comes from, is the result of	Tsunamis ← earthquakes
↑	increased, increasing, goes up, rises	Taxes ↑ 100% last year.
↓	decreased, decreasing, lowering	Salaries ↓ 10% this year.
#	number	Retry problem #3.
@	at	Due @ 4:00 P.M.
/	per	25 miles/gallon
p	page	Read p 99.
pp	pages	Study pp 99–105.
¶	paragraph	Revise ¶ #4.
w/o	without	They revised w/o reading carefully.
?	question	Answer ? 1.
w/i	within	There are problems w/i the tax laws.
i.e.	that is	The SAT, i.e., a college entrance exam, is challenging.
e.g.	for example	Professionals, e.g., doctors and lawyers, have advanced degrees.
etc.	et cetera, so forth	Clinton, Reagan, etc. were popular presidents.
b/c	because	We pay taxes b/c it's the law.
b/4	before	Incidents b/4 the attack.
esp.	especially	Tobacco, esp. cigarettes, causes cancer.
min.	minimum	The min. wage may go up.
max.	maximum	The max. number of people in an elevator is 8.
gov't.	government	The gov't. helped the people.
ASAP	as soon as possible	Complete your certificate program ASAP.
wrt	write	wrt #3 (write number 3)
yr/yrs	year, years	She's 18 yrs old.

Adapted from http://www.english-zone.com with permission from Kaye Mallory.

See which of the following statements describe you. Check the box that most applies to what you usually do in the classroom to assess your current level of note-taking skills. Use this self-assessment to develop a plan for improvement.

	Always True of Me	Sometimes True of Me	Never True of Me
1. I have a system for taking notes that works well.	☐	☐	☐
2. I compare my notes with those of a classmate.	☐	☐	☐
3. I review my notes as soon after class as possible to make sure I understand what I wrote.	☐	☐	☐
4. I read my notes out loud.	☐	☐	☐
5. I try to summarize the information in my notes.	☐	☐	☐
6. I look for organizational patterns within my notes (*e.g.*, causes and effects, lists of items).	☐	☐	☐
7. I take notes while reading an assignment for class.	☐	☐	☐
8. I don't daydream during class and miss out on notes I should be taking.	☐	☐	☐
9. I search for ways to reinforce the notes I take in class (podcasts, instructor's posted lecture notes, etc.).	☐	☐	☐
10. I take notes regularly in all my classes.	☐	☐	☐
11. I use abbreviations to help me keep up with the lecturer.	☐	☐	☐
12. I talk my notes through with someone else.	☐	☐	☐
13. I revise my notes when I consult the textbook and find out that I've left out important material.	☐	☐	☐
14. I organize my notes into a chart or graph, if appropriate.	☐	☐	☐
15. I copy down items from the board or screen.	☐	☐	☐
Total check marks for each column:	_____	_____	_____

Add up the check marks in each column to learn the results of your analysis. Pay particular attention to the total in the "Always True of Me" column.

13–15 "Always True of Me": You're probably an excellent note-taker. Keep up the good work.
10–12 "Always True of Me": You are a good note-taker, but you need to fine-tune a few of your note-taking skills.

7–9 "Always True of Me": You need to change some behaviors so that you get more out of your classes.

6 or less "Always True of Me" or 7 or more "Never True of Me": You need to learn better note-taking skills if you want to achieve academic success in college.

Different Strokes for Different Folks: Note-Taking by the System and Subject

Challenge: Does taking notes help students learn? Why or why not?

Reaction:

_____

_____

_____

This chapter has been leading up to something. Yes, getting engaged and listening in class are essential. But you must have a way to take what's transpired in class with you when you leave. That's where your note-taking skills come in. It's true that you must be a good listener to take good notes, but being a good listener alone doesn't automatically make you a good note-taker. Taking notes in class is actually a very complicated process; there's much more to it than jotting down a grocery list so you won't forget something. After listening carefully (without taking notes) during Exercise 7.1, how many main points did you remember well enough to write down? How many details? How much more of that lecture would you remember later if you had taken notes? Note-taking is a crucial and complex skill, and doing well on tests isn't based on luck. It's based on combining preparation and opportunity, in other words, knowing how to take useful notes in class that work for you.

Actually, one reason that note-taking is so important in the learning process is that it uses all four VARK categories: *visual* (you see your professor and the

Marc Romanelli/The Image Bank /Getty Images

> 66
> Luck is what happens when preparation meets opportunity.
> 99
>
> *Darrell Royal, football coach*

screen, if overheads or PowerPoint slides are being used), *aural* (you listen to the lecture), *read/write* (you write what you see and hear so that you can read it later to review), and *kinesthetic* (the physical act of writing opens up a pathway to the brain). As it turns out your transcription fluency—how quickly you can write clear, complete notes to review later—is a critical skill.[21]

According to one study, 99 percent of college students take notes during lectures, and 94 percent of students believe that note-taking is important.[22] These are good signs, but are these students taking notes correctly, as a result of focused listening? If 99 percent of college students are taking notes, why isn't nearly everyone getting straight A's? Here are some reasons:

> Students typically only record less than 40 percent of the lecture's main content ideas in their notes.[23]

> Only 47 percent of students actually review their notes later to see what they've written.

> Only 29 percent edit their notes later by adding, deleting, or reorganizing material.

> A full 12 percent do nothing other than recopy them verbatim.

> Some students never do anything with their notes once they leave class![24]

> In a recent study, students taking notes on laptops ended up with 5 percent lower GPAs than their counterparts using the old-fashioned paper-and-pencil method. Why? Perhaps these results were due to techies' inability to stay focused on task, or the interference of the clicking sounds, or because the physical act of typing is quicker, giving note-takers less time to process information.[25]

OOPS! BETTER TRY hARdER to STAy focuSEd.

Does note-taking make a difference? Absolutely. During lectures, it serves two fundamental purposes: it helps you understand what you're learning at the time and it helps you preserve information to study later. In other words, both the *process* of note-taking (as you record information) and the *product* (your notes themselves) are important to learning. There is strong evidence that taking notes during a lecture leads to higher achievement than not taking notes, and working with your notes later increases your chances for academic achievement even more. The more notes you take (up to a point—it's possible to get too bogged down in trying to capture every detail), the higher still are your chances of succeeding, and vice versa. Studies show that if you take notes, you have a 50 percent chance of recalling that information at test time versus a 15 percent chance of remembering the same information if you didn't take notes.[26]

But when it comes to note-taking, "different strokes for different folks" is literally true. Many different note-taking systems can work, and different systems work best for different learning styles. Find a system that works well for you. Try taking notes on a stack of index cards in front of you. You can sort them and use them as flashcards later, for example. If your mind works in an orderly fashion, work from an outline—or try one of the four major methods presented in this chapter. Increasingly, professors are providing online lecture notes, miniatures of PowerPoint lecture slides, lecture outlines as handouts, audio support, or some other form of note-taking assistance. There's no doubt these tools may help, but the most helpful learning aids are those you create yourself.

Teachable Moment Note that two students in the same class, listening to the same lecture, can have very different notes. Students who are detail-oriented sensors will have many pages and points. Intuitives will have brief notes, often scrawled on one page. Aural students may be so engrossed in listening to the lecture that they actually write very little and are at a loss when it comes time to study. Pointing out these tendencies based on learning style or personality-based preferences can provide students with self-insight.

Teaching with Technology For more information on note-taking systems, visit EnglishCompanion.com/Tools/notemaking .html. This website offers detailed explanations and examples of various note-taking methods, printable PDF note-taking templates, as well as excerpts from note-takers such as Leonardo da Vinci. Note-taking is clearly an important skill, and allowing students to see the various methods and approaches to note-taking will help them find their most comfortable style.

Whichever strategy you choose to use, an important question to ask is: What constitutes *good* notes? The answer is: Writing down an *accurate, complete, organized* account of what you hear in class (or read in your textbook, which is discussed elsewhere in this book). The last thing you want is a "What in the world did I mean by this?" reaction later. How will you know if your notes are good? Show them to your instructor and get input, or assess your strategy after you see your results on the first exam. Your note-taking skills should steadily improve as you evolve as a student.[27]

So what are the various note-taking methods? What are the steps involved in using each one? Knowing your options, developing your skills, and learning flexibility as a note-taker are keys to your success.

Outlining

Outlining is probably the oldest, and perhaps the most trusted form of taking notes. The problem, of course, is that not all instructors speak from an outline. But if yours does, listen for key points, like the five traits, and list examples beneath each one, like in Figure 7.2.

At the end of the lecture, include a summary of your notes. Summarizing is an excellent way to make sure you've understood the gist of all the information you've written down in Figure 7.3.

Of course, if your instructor's lecture is less organized, you can elect to use an informal variation of outlining, like listing bullets, and perhaps even color-coding them and drawing a picture so they're easier to remember, as shown in Figure 7.4.

FIGURE 7.2
Outlining

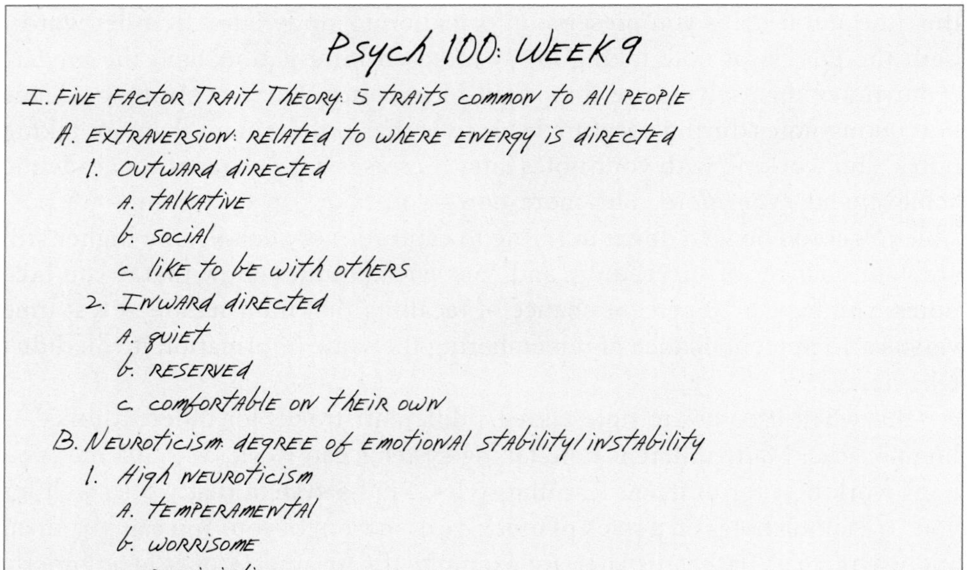

Psych 100: Week 9

I. Five Factor Trait Theory: 5 traits common to all people
    A. Extraversion: related to where energy is directed
        1. Outward directed
            a. talkative
            b. social
            c. like to be with others
        2. Inward directed
            a. quiet
            b. reserved
            c. comfortable on their own
    B. Neuroticism: degree of emotional stability/instability
        1. High neuroticism
            a. temperamental
            b. worrisome
            c. pessimistic
        2. Low neuroticism
            a. even-tempered
            b. calm
    C. Openness: degree to which individuals thoughtfully consider new ideas

FIGURE 7.3

Summarizing

SUMMARY:
The most widely accepted trait theory in psychology is the five factor theory, which consists of scaled (high to low) traits common to all people: EXTRAVERSION, NEUROTICISM, OPENNESS, AGREEABLENESS, AND CONSCIENTIOUSNESS.

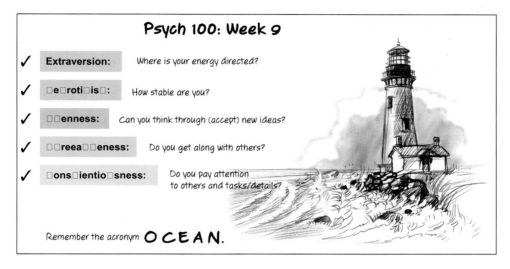

FIGURE 7.4

Informal Outlining (with Bullets)

The Cornell System

The Cornell system of note-taking, devised by educator Walter Pauk, suggests this. On each page of your notebook, draw a line from top to bottom about one and a half inches from the left edge of your paper. (Some notebook paper already has a red line there.) Take notes on the right side of the line. Your notes should include main ideas, examples, short phrases, and definitions, for example—almost like an outline.

Leave the left side blank to fill in later with key words or questions you'd like answered, as shown in Figure 7.5. After class as you review your notes, put your hand or a sheet of paper over the right side and use the words or questions you've written on the left side as prompts to see if you can remember what's on the right side.[28] By doing this to recall the lecture, you can get a good idea of how much of the information you've really understood.

Mind Maps

An alternative to the Cornell system, or a way to expand on it, is to create mind maps. Mind maps use both sides of your brain: the logical, orderly left side and the visual, creative right side. What they're particularly good for is showing the relationship between ideas. Mind maps are also generally a good note-taking method for visual learners, and even the physical act of drawing one may help you remember the information, particularly if you're

KEY WORDS and QUESTIONS	SHORT PHRASES, EXAMPLES, DEFINITIONS
Five Factor Trait Theory	— most commonly accepted trait theory.
Original source:	— Paul Costa and Robert McCrae
What year was their work published? Check!	— 1992?
Five Factors	A. Extraversion: related to where energy is directed
	1. Outward directed
	a. talkative
	b. social
	c. like to be with others
	2. Inward directed
	a. quiet
	b. reserved
	c. comfortable on their own
	B. Neuroticism: degree of emotional stability/instability
	1. High neuroticism
	a. temperamental
	b. worrisome
	c. pessimistic
	2. Low neuroticism
	a. even-tempered
	b. calm
	C. Openness: willingness to consider and accept new ideas

FIGURE 7.5

**Five Factor Trait Theory:
Cornell System Example**

a kinesthetic learner. See Figure 7.6. To give mind mapping a try, here are some useful suggestions:

1. **Use extra wide paper (11 x 17 or legal size).** You won't want to write vertically (which is hard to read) if you can help it.

2. **Write the main concept of the lecture in the center of the page.** Draw related concepts coming from the center.

3. **Limit your labels to key words so that your mind map is visually clear.**

4. **Use colors, symbols, and images to make your mind map livelier and more memorable.**

5. **Consider using software such as MindManager, MindManuals, MindPlugs, MindMapper, or MindGenius, which are all powerful brainstorming and organizing tools.** As you type, these programs will anticipate relationships and help you draw a mind map on screen.

Teachable Moment Ask students to share which technique, the Cornell system or mind maps, worked better in these examples and why. Does each method have pros and cons? Suggest to students that one system, used exactly how it has been presented, may not be the best one for them. Encourage students to experiment with different parts of the Cornell system and mind mapping, and use parts of both. Maybe mind mapping can be used to summarize, after taking notes using the Cornell system.

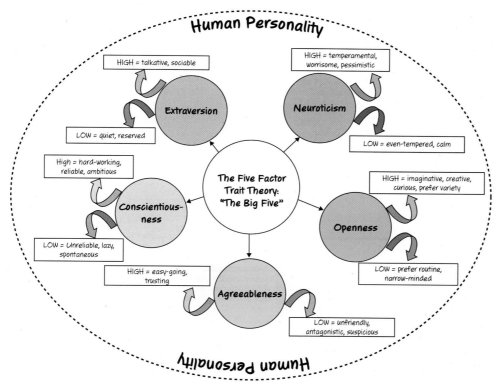

FIGURE 7.6

Five Factor Trait Theory: Mind Map Example

I think I could take notes like this, or at least turn my class notes into something like this to help me study! I love using different colored markers to help me remember!

Note-Taking on Instructor-Provided Handouts

PowerPoint Miniatures

Some instructors provide full-text lecture notes online or copies of their PowerPoint slides (three or six miniatures on a page). Instructors may hand out PowerPoint miniatures in class before the lecture, so you can follow along, hand them out after the lecture so that you still have to take your own notes but have the print outs of the miniatures as back-up, or e-mail them as attachments (see Figure 7.7). If you have copies of the Power-Point slides to use during class, write in specifics on the lines provided next to each slide miniature, more or less as you would if you were using the Cornell System. Put down examples that are discussed in class but don't appear on the slide, or a story that will help

FIGURE 7.7

Five Factor Trait Theory: PowerPoint Miniatures Example

I love it when teachers hand out PP miniatures!

Box 7.2   BYOD: Taking Notes Using e-Tools

Times have changed. Today's college classroom is BYOD ("bring your own device"). Surf the Internet, and you'll see hundreds of articles and YouTube videos with titles like "How My Tablet Saved My…!" or "10 e-Tools I Couldn't Survive Without," written by student e-enthusiasts. It's true that electronic devices can make you more academically productive. You can record lectures (with your instructor's permission), peruse a textbook chapter on your e-reader, or take photos of your professor's PowerPoint slides with your cell phone or tablet device. (Beware, however; being able to snap a quick pic is no guarantee that you'll learn the material any better.) Electronic devices can also help you take notes, organize them, and even convert them into study tools.

Although there are many apps for note-taking, many of them free, Evernote is a popular choice, especially for

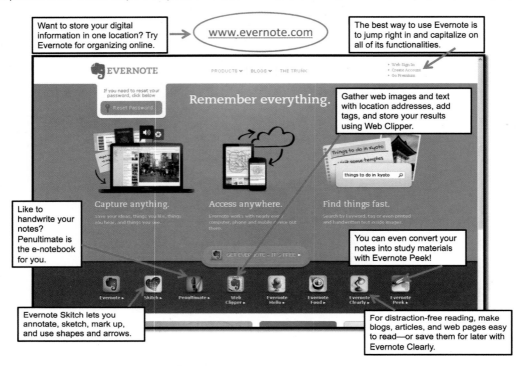

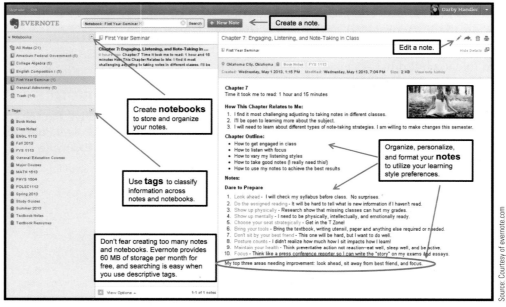

Johnsen, D. (2013). Engaging, Listening, and Note-Taking Annotated Evernote Example for Student Readers. Used with permission.

Source: Courtesy of evernote.com

reorganizing your notes after class or taking notes while you're reading or listening to an online lecture. Check out the following endorsement from one faithful user, and if you haven't used an e-tool for note-taking, consider doing so. One caveat: for in-class lectures, not everyone agrees that taking notes electronically is better than taking good, old-fashioned handwritten notes.[29] For many students, typing is a robotic action; you just go through the motions and tap, tap, tap away, taking down every word the instructor says. Handwriting is slower, allowing for time to select only what's important, and there's some evidence that the hand-brain writing connection promotes better learning. (Of course, it may just be that using your tablet *and* a stylus allows for both.) Another argument against e-tools is that they come with great temptation. Should you send a quick e-mail or check out a Zappos special before you forget—even if it's in the middle of a lecture? If you're taking in-class notes on a laptop or tablet, muster up your willpower, and try using an app like "Anti-Social" or "Cold Turkey" to lock yourself out of the Internet during class time. And one last warning: "pretending" to take notes electronically but actually playing games or communicating with friends who aren't in class also causes you to run the risk of bugging your classmates, big-time. In one study, classmates who wandered electronically were cited as other students' biggest pet peeve.[30]

you remember a main point on a slide. If they're handed out after class, transfer your own notes to the PowerPoint fill-in lines. If they're e-mailed to you before or after class, make sure you use them. They're "insurance" that you have access to what appeared in class on the screen. Tools such as these can be a valuable resource, if you remember to use them. Don't rely on PowerPoints your instructors provide to the extent that you skip taking notes yourself in class altogether. Although it's helpful to have them available as a tool, you still need to take notes on your own to help you process the information you're listening to in class.

Guided Notes

Your instructor may actually help you to pay attention in class by providing what are called "Guided Notes," or copies of lecture outlines or PowerPoint miniatures with key words missing, so that you must listen closely to "fill in the blanks." In one study, students in a college algebra class who used guided notes with problem sets they worked on together in groups liked their math class and did much better than comparable students who weren't using guided notes.[31]

Parallel Note-Taking

Because many instructors today provide e-support for lectures, either through web notes, hard copies of onscreen slides, lecture outlines, or a full transcript, parallel note-taking may be particularly useful, if you go about it in the right way.[32] Here's how it works, ideally.

If they're available, print out lecture notes before class and bring them with you, preferably in a ring binder. As your instructor lectures, use the back (blank) side of each page to record your own notes as the notes from the ongoing, real-time lecture face you. You can parallel what you're hearing from your instructor with your own on-the-spot, self-recorded notes, using a Cornell format on each blank page. It's the best of both worlds! You're reading, writing, and listening at the same time, fully immersing yourself in immediate and longer-lasting learning. Figure 7.8 illustrates how parallel note-taking might look for the psychology 100 lecture.

FIGURE 7.8

**Five Factor Trait Theory:
Parallel Note-Taking
Example**

[Fill in the blank page during actual lecture.]
My In-Class Lecture Notes

The best known and accepted trait theory (Costa & McCrae, 1992) says that there are five factors common to all people. These five factors are scales that can be used to describe everyone:

1) EXTRAVERSION (get energy from outside or inside; outside = sociable, talkative; inside = quiet, reserved).

2) NEUROTICISM (stability, high = pessimistic; low = calm).

3) OPENNESS (accepting of new ideas, high = imaginative, creative; low = narrow-minded).

[Print out instructor's notes and place in binder.]
Instructor's Lecture Notes

The Five Factor Trait Theory
Currently, the most widely accepted trait theory derived from factor analysis is Paul Costa and Robert McCrae's (1992) Ïve factor theory. This theory proposes Ïve core dimensions that can be measured along a continuum in all people.

- *Extraversion:* the degree to which energy is directed inward or outward. People high in extraversion are talkative, sociable, and prefer to be around others. At the other end of the continuum are people low in extraversion (introverts), who are quiet, reserved, and comfortable on their own.

- *Neuroticism:* the degree to which one is emotionally stable or unstable. People high in neuroticism are temperamental, worrisome, and pessimistic. People who score low on this factor tend to be more even-tempered and calm.

- *Openness:* the degree to which one is thoughtful and rational in considering new ideas. People who score high in openness tend to be imaginative, creative, and curious and to prefer variety; those who score low in openness prefer routine and are more narrow-minded in their ideas and experiences.

Note-Taking in Online Courses

So far this chapter has discussed taking notes in class. But what if there's no teacher around? Then how do you take notes? In online courses, you may find that your instructor puts lecture podcasts on the course site, uploads Power-Point slides with a voice-over lecture, or simply expects you to take notes from your textbook. Or since you'll already be online, you may instead want to open an e-tool for note-taking (like evernote.com) and use that to take notes, or print out class materials and highlight. Set up folders for course materials on your computer, and bookmark links by chapter to streamline note-taking. Whichever note-taking methods you prefer to use in your online classes, take what you can and apply it from this chapter, too.

Note-Taking by the Book

What about taking notes as you read from a textbook? Is that important, too? The answer: absolutely! It's easy to go on auto-pilot as you read and have no idea what you read afterwards! Instead, take notes in the margins, on sticky notes, or better yet, keep a spiral-bound notebook next to you, and fill it with your own words as you read. Jot down questions, summarize main points, or use the Cornell System. Actually, the best thing to do is to read a section, close the book, and write down what you remember. You'll prove to yourself what you absorbed and what you didn't. Then you can dive back into the textbook again and clarify concepts that are still fuzzy.[33]

Note-Taking by the Subject

Beyond figuring out which note-taking style seems to "fit" you best, think about times when the subject dictates that you vary your note-taking style. In your

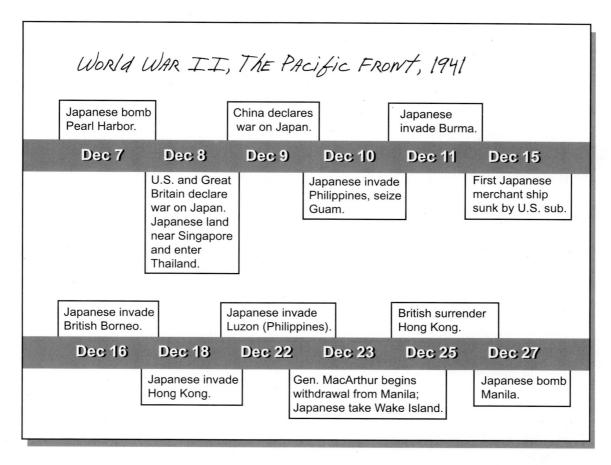

FIGURE 7.9

Timeline Example

Based on http://www.historyplace.com
/unitedstates/pacificwar/timeline.htm

American History class, it may make sense to take your notes along a timeline of the beginning of World War II, for example (see Figure 7.9). Since your instructor and your textbook report key events that took place during World War II chronologically, along a time line, you might want your notes to reflect that.

However, in your college algebra class, you may want to take notes very differently. Let's say, for example, that your instructor lectures by working problems on a white board or by projecting them on the screen. Then you are asked to work a problem and talk it over with a classmate next to you. You may want to divide up your notes into columns by proposing a solution and then showing how you arrived at your answer. Having a record of how you worked a problem can be a valuable aid later when you're studying for a test that will probably contain algebra problems very much like the ones you solve regularly in class. Write everything down, and skip a few lines if there's something you want to fill in later (see Figure 7.10).

Mind mapping, on the other hand, is particularly useful in geology, physiology, biology, psychology, and education courses, where relationships between concepts are important.[34] Some students may make the mistake of thinking that mind maps are "scribbling," but the process of making connections on paper helps you make those same connections in your brain. Successful note-taking does mean "different strokes for different folks"—and different subjects. Be sure to make the right choices about which note-taking system makes the most sense for the course material being presented.

Notes, College Algebra 100, Friday, oct 5

Determine which of the x values are solutions to the equation

$$x^4 + x^3 - 5x^2 + x - 6 = 0$$

a) $x = -3$,   b) $x = -2$,   c) $x = 1$,   d) $x = 2$

STEPS TO SOLUTION	CALCULATIONS	RESULTS
1) Try answer a Substitute -3 into the equation for x and see if the equation is satisfied.	$(-3)^4 + (-3)^3 - 5(-3)^2 + (-3) - 6 \overset{?}{=} 0$ $81 \quad - 27 \quad - 45 \quad - 3 - 6 = 0$ $0 = 0$	YES since both sides are 0.
2) Try answer b Substitute -2 into the equation for x and see if the equation is satisfied.	$(-2)^4 + (-2)^3 - 5(-2)^2 + (-2) - 6 \overset{?}{=} 0$ $16 \quad - 8 \quad - 20 \quad - 2 - 6 = 0$ $-20 \neq 0$	NO since the two sides are unequal.
3) Try answer c Substitute 1 into the equation for x and see if the equation is satisfied.	$(1)^4 + (1)^3 - 5(1)^2 + 1 - 6 \overset{?}{=} 0$ $1 \quad + 1 \quad - 5 \quad + 1 - 6 = 0$ $-8 \neq 0$	NO since the two sides are unequal.
4) Try answer d Substitute 2 into the equation for x and see if the equation is satisfied.	$(2)^4 + (2)^3 - 5(2)^2 + 2 - 6 \overset{?}{=} 0$ $16 \quad + 8 \quad - 20 \quad + 2 - 6 = 0$ $0 = 0$	YES since both sides are 0.

FIGURE 7.10

Math Note-Taking Example

From http://www.math.armstrong.edu /MathTutorial/exerciseSoln/ LinearEqSoln/LinearEq1Soln/ 13LinearEq1.html

Exercise 7.4   "Focused" Multitasking

One reason it's hard to focus in class is because of distractions. You may be tempted to check your Facebook account or text someone about something that pops into your mind. Being pulled in different directions at once is what happens when you multitask. It breaks your concentration and disrupts your learning. Try this experiment instead. Let's call it "Focused Multitasking," meaning that all your attention is directed at one thing. Before you listen to an in-class lecture, divide into groups with each group trying out a different note-taking strategy presented in this chapter. For example, Group 1 members should use outlines. Group 2 should use the Cornell System, Group 3 should create mind maps, etc. Then begin the lecture. The lecture could be your instructor lecturing about this chapter of FOCUS. Or it could be something different, like listening to an NPR podcast that the instructor or the whole class chooses. You are intentionally using all of your VARK preferences at once to focus on a single topic. After the lecture, take a quiz provided by your instructor and see which note-taking group's method earns the highest score!

Using Lecture Notes

Taking good notes is only part of the equation. To get the most value from your notes, you must actually *use* them. As soon as possible after class, take a few minutes to review your notes. If you find sections that are unclear, take time to fill in the gaps while things are still fresh in your mind. One professor found that students who filled in any missing points right after class were able to increase the amount of lecture points they recorded by as much as 50 percent. And students who worked with another student to reconstruct the lecture immediately after class were able to increase their number of noted lecture points even more![35]

This part of the note-taking process is often overlooked, yet it is one of the most helpful steps for learning and recall. If you don't review your notes within twenty-four hours, there's good evidence that you'll end up re*learning* rather than re*viewing*. Reviewing helps you go beyond just writing to actually making sure you understand what you wrote. These three techniques help you get the best use of your notes: manipulating, paraphrasing, and summarizing.

> **Manipulating** involves working with your notes by typing them out later, for example. Some research indicates that it's not writing down information that's most important. Manipulating information is what counts. Work with your notes. Fill in charts, draw diagrams, create a matrix, underline, highlight, organize. Cut a copy of the professor's lecture notes up into paragraphs, mix them up, and then put the lecture back together. Copy your notes onto flash cards. Manipulating information helps develop your reasoning skills, reduces your stress level, and can produce a more complete set of notes to study later.[36] And one other point worth noting: Research indicates that graphically organized notes may help you learn better than notes that are in a traditional linear form.[37]

> **Paraphrasing** is a process of putting your notes into your own words. Recopy your notes or your professor's prepared lecture notes, translating them into words you understand and examples that are meaningful to you. Paraphrasing is also a good way to self-test or to study with a classmate. If you can't find words of your own, perhaps you don't really understand the original notes. Sometimes students think they understand course material until the test proves otherwise, and then it's too late! Advance practice testing helps. Practice paraphrasing key concepts with a friend to see how well you both understand the material. Or ask yourself, if I had to explain this to someone who missed class, what words would I use?

> **Summarizing** is a process of writing a brief overview of all of your notes from one lecture. Imagine trying to take all your lecture notes from one class session and putting them on an index card. If you can do that, you've just written a summary. Why is it so important to rewrite your notes in this extremely condensed version? Research shows that students

I never thought to look at my notes right after class, but that makes sense—when everything is still fresh in my mind...

Teaching with Technology If you're planning on giving students hard-copy PowerPoint mini's as handouts in class, you could also consider e-mailing them a smaller version of your actual PowerPoint slideshow (assuming there are no copyright issues with images you've included). Giving students access to the file will allow them to cut, copy, paste, and manipulate the information in ways that are useful to them. This will not only make it easy for students to rearrange the material into helpful study aids, but it will make it easier to adapt lecture content into their individual learning style.

> ❝ I make progress by having people around me who are smarter than I am and listening to them. And I assume that everyone is smarter about something than I am. ❞
>
> *Henry J. Kaiser, American industrialist (1882–1967)*

Teachable Moment If you can give students one tip, it's to summarize, summarize, summarize their notes. Then, if they are open to a second tip, it's review, review, review. Those two techniques alone are guaranteed to help students succeed.

CAREER OUTLOOK: Increase your SPQ

> ❝ When all is said and done, a lot more is said than done. ❞

Lou Holtz

Do you know people like this? When you start a story, they one-up you: "Oh, you think *that's* something? You should hear what *I* did...." They spend their time (and yours) bragging about what they've done and how good they are at things. They "dot" every sentence with an "I." Let's face it: They're just plain annoying. *Everything* is about them.

Other people are humble. When it comes up in conversation that they won a full scholarship to your school, and you say, "Wow! That's incredible!" they say, "Oh, it was just good luck." When they get the top grade on the economics test that everyone else failed, they say, "I don't know. I just remembered stuff and wrote it down." You stand amazed.

But once you're settled into that new job after college, you have to show your stuff. No one will know exactly what you're capable of, nor can they read your mind (or your growing résumé) on a day-to-day basis. Regardless, you will be evaluated formally by your boss at least annually and informally by your colleagues daily. In order for your career to survive—and to thrive—you need high SPQ. In *FOCUS*, you're reading about IQ, EQ, and CQ, but what is SPQ? It's a fairly new fun, pop concept: Self-Promotion Intelligence (Quotient). It's vital to your career, and getting good at it can be a challenge.[38]

Peggy Klaus, Fortune 500 consultant and author of *Brag: The Art of Tooting Your Own Horn Without Blowing It* says "Today, bragging is a necessity, not a choice. Staying quiet about your achievements only leads to being underappreciated and overlooked.... You don't have to be an over-the-top cheerleader. Just realize how much you have to offer" and let others know through true-life, engaging stories you pull from your "brag bag." No hype; "Just the facts, ma'am."

Here are some other ideas: Note what makes you unique, and be prepared to talk about it, as if you were creating your own personal "brand." If you have a particular area of expertise, become known as the go-to person for it. Like an athlete, "play back" incidents in your head and remember what you did well (or not). Don't be afraid to speak up, even if you're an introvert (although self-promotion is generally better received if you answer questions about your accomplishments, rather than always bring them up yourself.[39] Conversely, ask questions of others and listen carefully to what they have to say about themselves.). Volunteer for visibility by offering to write, speak, or run a meeting. Connect other people so that you become known as a networker. Use the pronoun "we" more than you use its complement, "I." (Rarely is anything accomplished by a single individual in isolation.) And finally, be generous in your praise of others; it *will* come back to you.[40]

Think Ahead What particular strengths will you bring to the organization you join? How can you let others know about them? As you consider your SPQ and how important it is to your future career, think about it from your current vantage point. Which suggestions above do you follow now? Which ones will you try to incorporate into your repertoire of career skills?

SPQ—a very interesting idea I've never even thought about...

Cast on Careers

© Larry Harwood Photography. Property of Cengage Learning

FOCUS: Have you ever thought about SPQ? In your opinion, is it important in a career?

SYLVIA: I've never really thought about it before, but it makes perfect sense to me. I have friends now who accomplish great things, but I only find out about it through a mutual friend or read about it on someone else's Facebook page. One friend of mine was invited to join the freshman national honor society because she had a 3.9 her first semester. I didn't even know about this invitation until much later, but I would have enjoyed going to the induction ceremony with her to celebrate. She was always taught that bragging was "wrong," so she kept it to herself. Really, it depends on how you do it. It's possible to talk about your accomplishments and have other people listen without sounding egotistical.

FOCUS: What are your career plans?

SYLVIA: I'm planning to be a nurse. My grandmother was a nurse, and my mother is a nurse. It's not just a tradition in my family; it's genuine interest in helping others. Nursing is a competitive field right now, and in order to get the job I want, I'll have to be able to talk about my college achievements during interviews. I've worked hard and been very active on campus. I'll need some good examples to share with interviewers. I plan to start paying more attention to my SPQ now so that I can do that!

who use the summarizing technique have far greater recall of the material than those who don't. In one study, students were given a multiple-choice quiz immediately following a lecture. One group in the study had written summaries; the other had not. There was no noticeable difference in the students' performance immediately following the lecture; however, when the same quiz was given twelve days later, the students who had used the summarizing technique did much better on the quiz than those who had not.[41]

Some students think that simply going over their notes is the best way to practice. Research shows that simply reading over your notes is a weak form of practice that does not transfer information into long-term memory.[42] You must actually *work with* the material, rearrange or reword it, or condense it to get the most academic bang for your buck. Active strategies always work better than more passive ones.

Teachable Moment Encourage a mental One-Minute Paper. As students are working with their notes, ask them to ask themselves, "What is the main point?" and "Is there anything else I need to know?"

Manipulating, paraphrasing, and summarizing are more effective learning techniques. Even if your instructor provides you with verbatim notes online or hands you hard copies of her PowerPoint slides, you will still need to work with the information in order to learn it. Think of it this way. If you came to class with a friend you'd "hired" to take notes for you, who do you think would do better on the exam—him or you? Even if someone else hands you a set of notes, the truth is your ability to focus, listen, discuss, ask questions, take notes yourself, and get engaged in class are the things that help you learn best.

Now What Do You Think?

insight
↓
! action

❶ At the beginning of this chapter, Lindsey Collier, a frustrated college student, faced a challenge. Now after reading this chapter, would you respond differently to any of the questions you answered about the "FOCUS Challenge Case"? Knowing what you know now, how would you advise her? Write a paragraph ending to the story, incorporating your best advice.

❷ Look over the ten "Dare to Prepare" suggestions at the beginning of this chapter.
  • Look ahead.
  • Do the pre-work.
  • Show up physically.
  • Show up mentally.
  • Choose your seat strategically.
  • Bring your tools.
  • Don't sit by your best friend.
  • Posture counts!
  • Maintain your health.
  • Focus.
  Which of the suggestions do you find most difficult to do? For which of your classes? What can you do to help you prepare better for these classes?

❸ How well do you take notes? Which behaviors will you target in order to become a better note-taker? Select three of the items in Exercise 7.3 to focus on. Start with any item that you marked as "Never True of Me" and practice doing that behavior in class for several days. Then practice with an additional behavior from that column, and so on. Put the insights you've gained about yourself from reading about note-taking into action in class and describe your results.

❹ Do you understand Bloom's Taxonomy? Can you provide examples of questions for each level you'd ask that relate to the information in this chapter?

- Remembering _____
- Understanding _____
- Applying _____
- Analyzing _____
- Evaluating _____
- Creating _____

❺ What are your strengths and weaknesses as a note-taker? Are you a good listener? Can you write quickly and legibly? Do you ask questions easily? Use this opportunity to critique yourself and identify some areas for improvement.

What did you LEARN?

Reality Check

On a scale of 1 to 10, answer the following questions now that you've completed the chapter.

 low   1   2   3   4   5   6   7   8   9   10   high

In hindsight, how much did you already know about this subject before reading the chapter?

Can you answer these questions about engaging, listening, and note-taking in class more fully now that you've read the chapter?

❶ What does in mean to sit in the "T zone" in class and why is it important?

❷ This chapter discusses "hard" and "soft" listening skills. What's the difference between the two and which one is the right one to use in class?

❸ Identify three possible formats for taking notes in class.

How useful might the information in this chapter be to you? How much do you think this information might affect your success in college? _____

How much energy did you put into reading this chapter?

How long did it actually take you to complete this chapter (both the reading and writing tasks)? _____ Hour(s) _____ Minutes

Did you finish reading this chapter? _____
Did you intend to when you started? _____
If you meant to but didn't, what stopped you? _____

Take a minute to compare these answers to your answers from the "Readiness Check" at the beginning of this chapter. What gaps exist between the similar questions? How might these gaps between what you thought before starting the chapter and what you now think after completing the chapter affect how you approach the next chapter in this book?

8 Reading, Writing, and Presenting

How this chapter relates to **YOU**

1. When it comes to reading, writing, and presenting in college, what do you find most challenging, if anything?

| Understanding what I read | Struggling with writing assignments | Getting nervous speaking in front of others | Procrastinating on these types of assignments | Always completing and turning in assignments |

Readiness Check

2. What is most likely to be your response? Circle it.

| I'll be open to learning how to improve my skills. | I'll wait and see how much of this chapter I understand. | I'll get help from a support center on campus. | Eventually, I'll just figure it out on my own. |

3. What would you have to do to increase your likelihood of success?

_____

_____

_____

How **YOU** will relate to this chapter

What are you most interested in learning about? Put check marks by those topics.

☐ Why reading is important
☐ How to build reading skills
☐ How to read right
☐ How the writing process works
☐ What the seven C's (writing) and seven P's (presenting) are
☐ How to make your PowerPoint pop

● How motivated are you to learn more about reading, writing, and presenting in college? (5 = high, 1 = low) ____

● How ready are you to read now? ____ (If something is in your way, take care of it if you can, zero in and focus.)

● How long do you think it will take you to complete this chapter? If you start and stop, keep track of your overall time.
____ Hour(s) ____ Minutes

Katie Alexander

© Larry Harwood Photography. Property of Cengage Learning

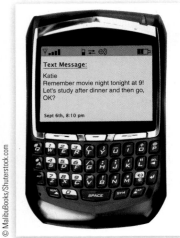

© MalibuBooks/Shutterstock.com

College would be a lot more fun if it weren't for the stress that all the reading and studying caused. That was Katie Alexander's take on things. She wasn't much of a reader; she much preferred playing softball or volleyball with her friends to sitting in one spot with a book propped open in front of her. Reading for fun wasn't something she'd ever even consider doing—at least not reading books. To Katie, reading 75 text messages a day was necessary; reading books was boring. *Anyway, why read the book when you can just watch the movie?* she always asked. Katie was an energetic, active, outgoing person, and "doing" and "socializing" were her things. Reading, writing papers, and studying definitely weren't.

The stress began before school even started when Katie Facebooked her future roommate. Amanda was her name, and she was from the Midwest, too. But here was the challenge. As active and physically fit as Katie was, she was shocked to find out that Amanda was handicapped. She'd been in a wheelchair since an automobile accident in third grade. *Can I handle that?* Katie wondered. *She seems nice, but how can I possibly take care of someone else? I can hardly take care of myself!* But as they communicated on Facebook over the summer, they became great friends before school ever started. And as things turned out, Amanda was the one who took care of Katie, not the other way around. When it came to academics, Amanda wanted to become Katie's personal trainer!

For Katie, reading and writing papers were hard work. She was smart enough to make it in college—she was sure of that—and she was motivated, especially with Amanda as a roommate. But reading was a labor-intensive activity that tried her patience, and after she'd read something, she was hard-pressed to summarize what it had been about. Before she knew it, she was off in some other

Hemera Technologies/Photos.com

© Waxen/Shutterstock.com

1027

9-13-2014

PAY TO THE ORDER OF University Bursar's Office $ 3059 00

Three thousand fifty nine and 00/00 DOLLARS

FOR

Katie Alexander

⑆22222222⑆ ⑇ 000 111 555⑈ 1027

© Johanna Goodyear/Shutterstock.com

ST# 34 OP#   TE#   TR#
005749801035   3.38
007065200750   2.97
007065200750   2.97
006025835503   14.96
06811316369   4.97
002340035457   0.93
005963148202   3.87
002340035458   0.93
005920000731   0.93
        SUBTOTAL   35.91
        HST 15%   4.88
            TOTAL   40.79
        DEBIT TEND   40.79
        CHANGE DUE   0.00
GST/HST   RT

Metro Sports Equipment
PURCHASE TRANSACTION RECORD
          40.79
CHEQUING
RRN #   ************
AUTH #
00 APPROVED-THANK YOU
TERMINAL ID:

 # ITEMS SOLD 9
TC#

world, thinking about her friends, or her schedule at work, or everything else she had to do, which resulted in more stress. Writing papers was just as hard, if not harder. And the mere thought of giving presentations for a class was enough to totally freak her out!

Amanda, on the other hand, was an English major who loved to read. In fact, that's all she ever seemed to do. Her other best friend, Brittney, however, had a different strategy. "There's so much required reading in all my classes that I don't even know where to start," Brittney admitted, "so I just don't do it. I go to class, listen to the lectures, and write down what the instructor has said on the essay tests. Learn to play the game!"

But Brittney's strategy definitely wasn't going to work for Katie in Professor Harris-Black's Introduction to Ethnic Studies class. She'd assigned a shocking number of articles to read. The

professor didn't even go over the readings in class, and her lectures didn't even relate to the reading. Whenever she sat down to read an assignment, Katie found what to her were unfamiliar words and unnatural phrasing. The professor had suggested that students read with a dictionary at their sides, but who'd ever want to keep stopping to look up words? You'd never finish!

With a midterm exam coming up in her Ethnic Studies class next week, Katie's stress level was starting to skyrocket. She'd only read one of the nine articles assigned. In fact, she hadn't made it through the first article when she got discouraged and gave up. She knew the midterm essay test would be challenging. Winging it wouldn't work, and choosing to "watch the movie" instead of reading the book wasn't an option. Exactly what did Ethnic Studies have to do with anything, she puzzled, and why had her advisor suggested the course in the first place?

The night before the test, Katie decided to get serious. Amanda was already asleep, so she sat down at her desk, armed with her yellow highlighter. As she began reading, however, she realized she didn't know exactly what to highlight since she didn't really understand what she was reading. Looking back at the page she had just finished, she saw that she had basically highlighted everything. Exasperated, Katie told herself that she

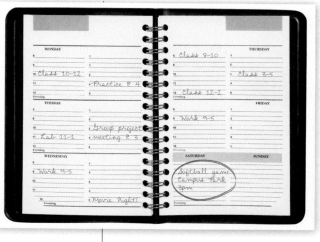

couldn't go to bed until she'd finished reading everything, no matter when that was. She started with the second article, since she'd read the first one, and by morning, she'd be as ready as possible. Anyway, it wasn't up to her—it was up to Professor Harris-Black; she was the one making up the test.

Getting an A on her Introduction to Ethnic Studies midterm exam was probably out of the question. But if she could just manage to pass, Katie knew she would have to settle for that. On the other hand, she secretly hoped that maybe she'd just luck out.

Ethnic Studies Reading List

Caste, Class and Race
    Cox, Oliver C.
Race: History of an Idea
    Gossett, Thomas F.
Ethnic Groups and Boundaries
    Barth, Frederick
The Predicament of Culture
    Clifford, James
Varieties of Ethnic Experience
    Di Leonardo, Micaela
In Search of Cultural History
    Gombrich, Ernst
Ethnic Enterprise in America
    Light, Ivan
Strangers From a Different Shore
    Takai, Ronald

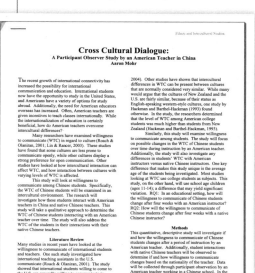

Cross Cultural Dialogue:
A Participant Observer Study by an American Teacher in China
Aaron Mohr

The recent growth of international connectivity has increased the possibility for international communication and education. International students now have the opportunity to study in the United States, and Americans have a variety of options for study abroad. Additionally, the need for American educators overseas has increased. Often, American teachers are given incentives to teach classes internationally. While the internationalization of education is certainly beneficial, how do American teachers overcome intercultural differences?

Many researchers have examined willingness to communicate (WTC) in regard to culture (Roach & Olaniran, 2001; Lin & Rancer, 2003). These studies have found that some cultures are less prone to communicate openly, while other cultures display a strong preference for open communication. Other studies have looked at how intercultural interaction can affect WTC, and how interaction between cultures with varying levels of WTC is affected.

This study will look at willingness to communicate among Chinese students. Specifically, the WTC of Chinese students will be examined in an intercultural environment. The research will investigate how these students interact with American teachers in China and native Chinese teachers. This study will take a qualitative approach to determine the WTC of Chinese students interacting with an American teacher over time. The study will also address the WTC of the students in their interactions with their native Chinese teachers.

Literature Review
Many studies in recent years have looked at the willingness to communicate of international students and teachers. One such study investigated how international teaching assistants in the U.S. communicate (Roach & Olaniran, 2001). The study showed that international students willing to come to the U.S. are generally willing to communicate in intercultural settings. Another study looked at the willingness to communicate of Japanese students learning English (Yashima, Zenuk-Nishide & Shimizu,

2004). Other studies have shown that intercultural differences in WTC can be present between cultures that are normally considered very similar. While many would argue that the cultures of New Zealand and the U.S. are fairly similar, because of their status as English-speaking western-style cultures, one study by Hackman and Barthel-Hackman (1993) found otherwise. In the study, the researchers determined that the level of WTC among American college students was much higher than students from New Zealand (Hackman and Barthel-Hackman, 1993).

Similarly, this study will examine willingness to communicate among students. The study will focus on possible changes in the WTC of Chinese students over time during instruction by an American teacher. Additionally, the study will also investigate any differences in students' WTC with American instructors versus native Chinese instructors. One key difference that makes this study unique is the average age of the students being investigated. Most studies looking at WTC use college students as subjects. This study, on the other hand, will use school age children (ages 11-14); a difference that may yield significant variation. RQ1: In an educational setting, how will the willingness to communicate of Chinese students change after four weeks with an American instructor? RQ2: How will the willingness to communicate of Chinese students change after four weeks with a native Chinese instructor?

Methods
This quantitative, descriptive study will investigate if and how the willingness to communicate of Chinese students changes after a period of instruction by an American teacher. Additionally, student interactions with native Chinese teachers will be observed to determine if and how willingness to communicate changes based on the nationality of the teacher. Data will be collected through participant observation by an American teacher working in a Chinese school. In the case of this study, the researcher, participant observer and American teacher are one and the same. Since I as a researcher and teacher

© Cengage Learning

What Do *You* Think?

challenge

reaction

❶ How would you characterize Katie as a student? Identify five specific problems described in this case study that could interfere with her college success.

❷ Katie is probably an intelligent student, but she has decided that she dislikes schoolwork, so she avoids it. How important will her reading, writing, and presenting skills be as she continues to pursue a college degree? Is she likely to succeed her second time around?

❸ Is Katie like students you know? If so, in what ways?

❹ Identify three specific things Katie should do to get her college career on track.

VARK It!

Complete the recommended activity for your preferred VARK learning modality. If you are multimodal, select more than one activity. Your instructor may ask you to (a) give an oral report on your results in class, (b) send your results to him or her via e-mail, or (c) post them online.

Visual: As you begin reading this chapter, start constructing a chart or graph comparing how much time you spend on three things this week: talking or texting on your cell phone, using social media, and completing assignments for your classes. Which activity has the longest line?

Aural: Choose a classmate as a discussion partner for this chapter. IM, text, or talk through main points and how they relate to both of you as you read. (These are all aural strategies, according to VARK.)

Read/Write: Start reading this chapter with a stack of blank index cards next to you. On each card, write a word you couldn't define in this chapter. When you're done reading, look them up in the dictionary and write out the definitions. Then compare your stack with the ones of other classmates.

Kinesthetic: Find a YouTube or other online resource on reading, writing, or presenting that adds to this chapter. Show your resource or "compete" with other "K" students to show the best one in class as you begin discussing this chapter.

Who Needs to Read?

Teachable Moment Many students feel that reading is "hard work." They often lose interest because it takes them so long to complete a reading assignment, and then they often do not remember what they have read. Encourage students to time themselves as they read the chapter, and if they seem to be losing interest, have them stop and take a five- to ten-minute break and then start again. Keeping track of their time can be a motivator. With each new chapter, encourage them to try to keep on task a little longer, which will build their reading stamina and their concentration power.

Diversity Discussion Consider asking your students to research literacy as a global issue. Are other cultures more (or less) literate than the U.S. culture? "Approximately 20 percent to 30 percent of adults in the United States lack the literacy skills needed to meet the reading and computation demands associated with daily life and work." (Lasater & Elliott, 2005; National Institute for Literacy, 2009).

What's so important about reading? Teachers seem to think it's important, and parents consider it to be an admirable pastime, but times have changed, haven't they? Now you can just skim predigested information on websites, get a summary of the day's news from television, and watch movies for entertainment. Who needs to read? Look around the next time you're in a doctor or dentist's waiting room. You'll see some people staring at the TV screen mounted on the wall and others on their smartphones. A few may be skimming through magazines, but does anyone ever pick up a book to actually read it cover to cover anymore? Does it matter?

The answer, according to many experts, is a resounding yes, it does![1] Reading helped create civilization as we know it and taught us particular ways of thinking. "We are losing a sort of psychic habit, a logic, a sense of complexity, an ability to spot contradictions and even falsity," says Neil Postman, author of *Amusing Ourselves to Death*.[2] Eventually, he predicts, our culture will see the effects. What kinds of changes might experts like Postman predict?

> **Reading skills will deteriorate.** One fairly predictable result of doing anything less is that eventually you may not do it as well. Practice keeps your skills sharp. Even an Olympic athlete who doesn't stick with training

gets rusty after a while. According to the National Survey of Adult Literacy, "The average American college graduate's literacy in English [has] declined significantly. . . . In 1992, 40 percent of the nation's college graduates scored at the proficient level . . . on the 2003 test, only 31 percent of the graduates demonstrated those high-level skills." Why? "Literacy of college graduates had dropped because a rising number of young Americans in recent years had spent their free time watching television and surfing the Internet."[3]

As students read less, their reading skills deteriorate and they don't enjoy doing it. Conversely, the better you get at reading, the more you may enjoy it. Falling down every ten minutes the first time you get on skis isn't all that much fun, but once you can zip down the mountain like a pro, you begin to appreciate the sport.

➤ **Reading will become less popular.** Some might say that reading was much more essential to previous generations because they didn't have all the choices we have today.[4] Words like *lazy* and *bookworm* were used to describe Abraham Lincoln as a child because reading was all he ever wanted to do. Today, you'd be unlikely to hear those two particular insults combined. A hundred years ago, books took us places we could not easily go otherwise. Now there are much easier ways of getting there. Thomas Jefferson once told John Adams, "I cannot live without books." Evidently, today many people can.[5] According to experts, when we do read in today's fast-paced world, we often do so while doing something else—quickly and with less focus.

Perhaps reading isn't your favorite pastime. You may feel about reading like many people do about eating cauliflower. You know it's good for you, but you'd prefer to avoid it. However, this chapter wouldn't be worth its weight in trees if it didn't try to convince you otherwise. One aspect of reading some people particularly dislike is that reading is not a social or physical activity. You can read with someone else in the room, of course, or talk about what

Handwritten note: Wow! I did not know this!

Teachable Moment Students will probably admit to not knowing as much as they should about this chapter's topic. Many students begin college with weak reading and study skills. Encourage them to really invest time and effort in this chapter. They are bound to learn some key skills and tips that they did not know before.

Sensitive Situation You can be guaranteed that you have more than one student in your class who has not read many books cover to cover. The reasons may vary, so try and present these statistics in a way that does not make them feel like reading in college will be an impossible task, rather that it will be manageable with the right support and tools.

Teachable Moment Ask students if they believe it is true that today you would not hear the words *lazy* and *bookworm* combined. What is the first word that comes into their heads when they know a student is doing all of the assigned readings for a class? They may not want to tell you!

Teachable Moment As convinced as we are about the value of reading, students may still not be convinced that watching a movie or getting information from the Internet is a less valuable way of learning to think. Point out the simple reality that in Katie's class, there is no movie, no *Spark or Cliffs Notes* to help her prepare for this exam. She needs to learn some strategies for reading.

❝ No matter how busy you may think you are, you must find time for reading, or surrender yourself to self-chosen ignorance. ❞

Confucius, Chinese philospher, 551–479 b.c.e.

Tomasz Trojanowski/Fotolia LLC

Activity Option Although it's not a good idea to publicize individual reading rates and comprehension scores from Exercise 8.1, students may still be curious about what constitutes fast or slow reading. Ask them to write down their times and the number of questions they answered correctly and submit them anonymously. Ask them to identify which question(s) they answered incorrectly. Collect these items and report back to the class. Students can make their own comparisons. Remind students to send you an e-mail or see you if they have some questions about their own reading.

you read afterward with friends, but basically, reading is something you do alone. It's a solitary activity that involves you, words on a page, an invisible author, and your brain. You need to do it with a minimum of physical movement. Reading while playing a game of volleyball would be tough to pull off.

If you enjoy reading, congratulations! When you settle in with an exciting novel, you can travel to the far corners of the Earth, turn back the clock to previous centuries, or fast-forward to a future that extends beyond your lifetime. You can inject yourself into the story and be someone else for a while. Novelist Scott Corbett once said: "I often feel sorry for people who don't read good books; they are missing a chance to lead an extra life."

Exercise 8.1 What Is Your Reading Rate?

Before continuing, you'll need a stopwatch or a watch with a second hand. Keep track of how long it takes you to read the following article about pushing yourself. The object of the exercise isn't to race through; it's to read at your normal speed. After you read the article, you'll be asked to record your reading time and answer some questions to check your comprehension.

How Hard Are You Willing to Push Yourself? by Tony Schwartz

From author's blog, July 2, 2012. (http://blogs.hbr.org/schwartz/2012/07/how-hard-are-you-willing-to-pu.html). Reprinted with permission from Harvard Business Publishing.

Tony Schwartz is a best-selling author, speaker, performance expert, and CEO of "The Energy Project," a company that helps people and organizations perform better and more sustainably.

What do all people who achieve true excellence and consistently high performance have in common?

The answer isn't great genes, although they're nice to have. It's the willingness to push themselves beyond their current limits day in and day out, despite the discomfort that creates, the sacrifice of more immediate gratification, and the uncertainty they'll be rewarded for their efforts.

The first way I've seen this is physically, through my body. I work out regularly with weights. I do push myself to discomfort, and I've grown considerably stronger over the years. At 60, I'm stronger than I was at 30.

But in truth, I rarely push myself to exhaustion. If I did, the evidence suggests I would get significantly stronger than I already am. The key here is intensity, not duration. If I was willing to push hard, I could do fewer repetitions, and derive more benefit in way less time than I invest now.

So why don't I do it? The answer, I'm slightly embarrassed to admit, is that I'm not prepared to endure more discomfort than I already do. The mind tricks us into thinking we've hit our limits long before we actually have.

Human beings have two powerful primal instincts. One is to avoid pain, an instinct that helped us to survive when we were vulnerable to predators in the savanna. The other is to move towards pleasure, an instinct that once kept us foraging for food, which was scarce, and still helps to ensure that we pass on our genes.

Unfortunately, neither of these instincts prompt us to delay gratification in the service of longer-term gain. For that, we need to enlist the more advanced, reflective part of our brain — prefrontal cortex — to consciously resist the primitive cravings that originate in the lower part of our brain.

The other place I've seen this play out is in my writing. I'd love to stop working right now and check my email, or visit my refrigerator, not just because either one would provide a hit of pleasure, but also to get away from the discomfiting challenge of trying to wrestle the jumble of ideas in my head into clear, evocative sentences.

Over the course of my life, I've taught myself to stay focused in front of my computer. But even after four decades as a writer, it's never easy. The Pavlovian pull of email has only made it harder to focus in recent years — and nearly impossible for many people I know.

The unavoidable truth is that the willingness to endure discomfort and sacrifice instant gratification is the only way to get better at anything, and to achieve true excellence.

There are three keys to strengthening this counterintuitive capacity:

1. Minimize temptation, which operates the same way the house does in a casino. It will always defeat you if you expose yourself to it for too long. Think about cake or cookies at an office party. If they sit there in front of you, you're eventually going to succumb. The same is true of incoming email. If you don't turn it off entirely at times, the ongoing pings will inevitably prove irresistible.

2. Push yourself to discomfort only for relatively short and specific periods of time. Interval training is built on short bursts of high intensity exercise offset by rest and recovery. It's harder than aerobic training, but it's also a more efficient, less time-consuming way to increase fitness.

3. Build energy rituals — specific behaviors done at precise times — for your most difficult challenges. Try beginning the day by focusing without interruption on the most important challenge in front of you, for no more than 90 minutes, and then take a real renewal break. It's much easier to tolerate discomfort in short doses.

Choose one area of your life and push yourself just a little harder than you think is possible every day. You'll feel better about yourself, and over time, you'll get better at whatever it is you're doing.

Now let's see how you did.

Yikes! Took me 4 min. 30 sec. I'm slower than average :(

Reading Speed: Stop! Look at your watch. Mark down how long it took you to read the article: _____ Minutes _____ Seconds. If it took you roughly two or three minutes, your reading rate is average for a college student. (Note: Article contains 663 words. According to one recent study, college students read 350–450 words per minute, on average.)[6] If you read faster or slower than that, what does that mean? If it took longer than two or three minutes, but you answer the three questions in the "Reading Comprehension" that follows correctly, reading slowly may not be as much of a problem for you as you may think it is. Right about now, however, you may be thinking, *Hey, I don't have time to spare! I'm juggling several different courses, a job, family responsibilities—a dozen things.* That's the point! Read with focus so that you can record, retain, and retrieve information. If you don't understand what you read, it's difficult, if not impossible, to learn it. Reading without comprehension is just going through the motions.

Reading Comprehension: Answer the following questions without going back and rereading the article.

1. What was this article's main point? _____

2. Tony Schwartz says human beings have two powerful primal instincts. One is to avoid pain. What is the other? _____

3. Identify one of the author's three key points about pushing yourself harder to achieve excellence. _____

Now go back and check the accuracy of your answers. Are you "reading right"?

➤ **Academic skills will be affected.** Whether or not you enjoy reading, it will be one of the primary skills you need to cultivate in college. According to one study, 85 percent of the learning you'll do in college requires careful reading.[7] First-year students often need to read and comprehend 150–200 pages per week in order to complete their academic assignments.[8]

What's more, reading skills go hand in hand with writing skills, which makes them even more important. The better you get at reading, the more you raise your probability of academic success. Believe it or not, some students choose to skip the reading. But this is a dangerous, self-sabotaging strategy. Many of your classes will require intensive reading of complex material, including primary sources by original authors and scholarly research. Sometimes reading in college is just plain difficult. It takes focus, even if you do find the material to be highly engaging and truly fascinating! However, if you complete reading assignments, and your classmates don't, think about how much ahead of the nonreaders *you* will be! Now is the time to begin enhancing these skills. But how do you become a better reader?

Read Right!

Challenge: Are there right ways to read? What have you learned about reading in college thus far? Provide as many suggestions about reading right as you can.

Reaction:

_____

_____

_____

What do we know about reading? How *should* you tackle your many reading assignments in college? Consider these twelve essential points:[9]

1. **Understand what being a good reader is all about.** Reading isn't a race. Remember the old children's story about the tortoise and the hare? The turtle actually won the race because he plodded along, slowly and steadily, while the rabbit zipped all over the place and lost focus. The moral of that story applies to reading, too. Reading is a process; understanding is the goal. The point isn't simply to make it through the reading assignment by turning pages every few minutes so that you can finish the chapter in a certain amount of time. When your instructors read difficult material, which they do regularly in their profession, they don't rush. They chew on the tough parts, reread sections, and make notes to themselves in the margins. Reading requires you to back up occasionally, just like when you back up a DVD to catch something you missed: "What did he say to her? I didn't get that." Students sometimes mistakenly think that good readers are speed-readers.[10] But reading actually has two

components: speed and comprehension. Often, comprehension is sacrificed when speed is increased because most speed-readers actually just skim. Yes, you can improve your reading speed with focused effort, but more importantly, you can improve your comprehension skills by managing your attention. Science fiction writer Isaac Asimov once wrote, "I am not a speed reader. I am a speed understander."

2. **Take stock of your own reading challenges.** Which of the following are reading issues for you? Put a check mark next to any that apply to you.[11]

___ boredom	___ vision	___ speed	___ comprehension	___ time
___ amount	___ interest	___ motivation	___ surroundings	___ fear
___ fluency	___ fatigue	___ level	___ retention	___ laziness

✓ boredom
✓ amount
✓ interest
✓ speed
✓ motivation

Many people find reading challenging. You may have worked with an impatient teacher as a youngster, or you may have been taught using a method that didn't work well for you—factors that still cause you problems today. Reading involves visually recognizing symbols, transferring those visual cues to your brain, translating them into meaningful signals—recording, retaining and retrieving information (here's where your memory kicks in)—and finally using these meanings to think, write, or speak. Reading challenges can be caused by *physical factors* (your vision, for example) and *psychological factors* (your attitude). If you want to become a better reader in the future, it's a good idea to assess honestly what's most challenging about the process for you right now.[12]

66
Outside of a dog, a book is man's best friend. Inside of a dog, it's too dark to read. 99

Groucho Marx, American comedian, actor, and singer (1890–1977)

Andersen Ross/Brand X Pictures/Jupiter Images

"

It matters, if individuals are to retain any capacity to form their own judgments and opinions, that they continue to read for themselves.

"

Harold Bloom, literary critic (1930–)

Teaching with Technology Aural learners may prefer to hear a piece of text rather than read it from the page or screen. Although students with different learning styles must learn to adapt to all learning environments, some learners may want to experiment with adapting the material to their style. If you have aural learners, first encourage them to read the text normally. Then, for better clarity, they can try using free Text-to-Speech converters available on the web. These Web sites allow users to copy and paste large chunks of text, which are then read aloud by a computerized voice.

Teachable Moment Although we don't want to encourage students to multitask by using the computer while reading, remind them that there are excellent online dictionaries where they can simply type in the word for the definition. This would also be a useful resource when students are typing a paper or taking notes on their computer.

Teaching with Technology Consider Skype or Google Hangout as a way to do Exercise 8.2 in real time and "in person," with your class. Contact your Cengage representative for details about setting up a Skype session or Google Hangout with the author. She can also send a personalized video message to your class as an Eyejot e-mail attachment.

3. **Adjust your reading style.** Reading requires versatility. Contrast these two situations: reading the menu on the wall at your local fast-food joint and poring over the menu at a fancy, high-end restaurant. You'd just scan the fast-food menu in a few seconds, wouldn't you? You wouldn't read word by word and ask: "Is the beef in that burger from grass-fed cattle?" "What, exactly, is in the 'special sauce'?" If you did, the exasperated attendant would probably blurt out, "Look, are you going to order something or not?" That kind of situation requires quick skimming. But you'd take some time to study the menu at a pricy restaurant you might go to with friends and family to celebrate your college graduation. It's an entirely different situation, and the information is more complicated. And if it's a fancy French restaurant, you might even need to ask the definitions of some terms like *canard* (duck) or *cassoulet* (a rich, hearty stew). That kind of situation requires slow, considered study, word by word. You're going to pay for what you choose, and you want the best results on your investment. That's true about college, too. You're investing in your college degree, so reading right is important!

You don't read a textbook or a novel in the same way you skip around when you read a magazine, only choosing articles that interest you: "How to Totally Redecorate Your Apartment on Fifty Bucks" or "Does Your Love Life Have a Pulse?" Books require starting at the beginning and reading straight through. The plot of most novels would be very different if readers just picked certain sections to read! You'll face an enormous amount of reading in your combined college classes. The question is, what's fast food (to carry through with the analogy) and what's fine dining? According to research on reading, good readers know the difference and adjust their reading styles.[13]

It's important to devote more time to reading and studying than you think you'll actually need. If you don't understand difficult material, go back and reread it, instead of assuming it will be explained by your instructor in class. Keep a dictionary at your side, and check unusual new terms. You'll be able to digest what you're reading much better.

4. **Converse with the author.** In every book you read, the author is trying to convince you of something. Take this book, for example. We have been engaged in a conversation all the way through. What do you know about

Exercise 8.2 **A Press Conference with the Author**

If you could interview the author of this text, what would you ask her? What would you like to know about her? What would you argue with her about? Play devil's advocate and come up with a list of challenging questions and the responses you think she'd provide. Then role-play this activity with one student playing the role of the author in a press conference on television and the rest of the class playing reporters from major newspapers and magazines of their choosing or as assigned by your instructor.

CURIOSITY: Reading When English Is Your Second Language

Hints on Pronunciation for Foreigners

I take it you already know
Of laugh and bough and cough and dough?
Others may stumble but not you,
On hiccough, thorough, laugh and through.
Well done! And now you wish, perhaps,
To learn of less familiar traps?

Beware of heard, a dreadful word
That looks like beard and sounds like bird,
And dead: It's said like bed, not bead—
For goodness' sake don't call it "deed"!
Watch out for meat and great and threat
(They rhyme with suite and straight and debt.)

A moth is not a moth in mother
Nor both in bother, broth in brother
And here is not a match for there
Nor dear and fear for bear and pear,
And then there's dose and rose and lose—
Just look them up—and goose and choose,
And cork and work and card and ward,
And font and front and word and sword,

And do and go and thwart and cart—
Come, come, I've hardly made a start!
A dreadful language? Man alive.
I'd mastered it when I was five.

—T.S.W. (only initials of writer known) or possibly written by George Bernard Shaw

Go ahead. Try reading the preceding poem aloud. Even if English is your first language, you probably had to pause and think about how to say a word occasionally. Most anyone would. English isn't exactly the easiest language in the world to learn, non-native English speakers say. It's filled with perplexing irregularities. Think about the raw courage it would take to pursue a college degree by reading and writing in a language other than your native tongue. If English is your first language, could *you* do it in German or Arabic or Hindi? That being acknowledged, what strategies can ESL (English as a Second Language) students use to help with challenging reading assignments?

1. Remember that spoken English differs from the written English you'll find in textbooks and academic articles. In casual conversation, you'll hear, "And she's . . . like, 'wow!' and I'm . . . like, 'really?'" If you read that in a book, you'd have no idea what the speakers were communicating about. But if you're standing next to the conversationalists in the hallway, you have a chance of figuring it out. Learning to speak informally in conversation is very different from learning to read scholarly discourse. When you read, there's no body language to rely on or real-live author around to whom you can address questions. Address these questions to your instructor or study-group mates instead.

2. Ask your English-speaking friends and instructors to coach you. For example, ESL speakers sometimes struggle with the hundreds of idioms found in English. Idioms are groups of words with a particular, nonliteral meaning. For example, "I have a frog in my throat" means your voice is hoarse, not that you literally have swallowed a green amphibian. Idioms must be learned as a set of words in order to communicate their intended meaning. If you change one word ("I have a *toad* in my throat"), the idiom doesn't work. Considering how many idioms English has and how freely English speakers use them without consciously thinking about it, non-native speakers may find learning them all to be a challenge. You'll more likely hear idioms spoken, rather than read them; however, you may come across them frequently in fiction or poetry assigned in a literature class. If you're an international student, ask about unique phrases that don't make sense to you.

3. Use the Internet or an online course to improve your language skills. According to one study, international students in an online course made significant gains in their language skills, compared with a control group of students who sat through the same course in a classroom. Online courses provide good exposure and practice in your reading and writing skills via e-mail, web searching, threaded discussions, and online postings.[14]

4. Try explaining what you're reading to someone else. Talking something through while you're reading, especially with a native English speaker, can help you clarify meanings on the spot—and may help the other student achieve better comprehension, too.

5. Mark up the textbook so that you can pursue difficult passages in greater detail later. Insert question marks in the margin. Read with your English–native tongue dictionary in front of you. If you get completely stuck, find another book that may explain the concepts differently.

me? What am I trying to persuade you to think about or do? Even though I'm not right in front of you in person on every page, you are forming impressions of me as you read, and I'm either convincing you to try the suggestions in this book or I'm not. As you read any book, argue with the author ("That's not how I see it!"), question her ("What makes you say that?"), agree with her ("Yes, right on!"), relate something she said earlier to something she's saying now ("But what about …?"). Instead of just coloring with your yellow highlighter, scribble comments in the margins, or keep a running commentary in a notebook. Make small ticks in the margins to mark words you'll look up in your dictionary at a good breaking point. Reading is an active process, not a passive one in which the words just float by you. In fact, mark up this page right now! How do you decide what's really important? One thing you can do is ask your instructor in this course to show you his or her mark-ups in this book, and see if the two of you agree on what's important.

5. **Dissect the text.** Whether you did it virtually online or physically in a real lab, cutting up those little critters in your biology class helped you figure out what was what. The ability to dissect text is important in reading. As you read and make notes in the margins, write what and why statements. Try it: beside each paragraph on this page, write a one-sentence summary statement: a *what* statement. Put the author's words into your own words. Then write another sentence that focuses on *why* the paragraph is included. Does it contain *evidence* to make a point? Is it an *example* of something? If you can tackle this recommendation, you'll do wonders for yourself when exam time rolls around. Think of an essay question on a test that asks, "Discuss three reasons why it's important to read right." You'd remember the why statements you've written in the margins of this section, and be ready with your answer!

6. **Make detailed notes.** Knowing how to use a highlighter while you read is most students' idea of good study skills. Highlighting skills are important, but there's more to it. Choose headings, phrases, and individual words that relate to main points, rather than just highlighting everything that could possibly be important. But even if you highlight selectively, you'll be much more likely to actually master a challenging reading assignment if you keep a notebook beside you and take full-blown notes as you read. Go back and forth, detailing main points and supporting evidence, so that you have a set of notes using the Cornell note-taking system, for example, by the time you've finished reading. If you're reading onscreen, open a new document and annotate there. The physical act of writing or typing can consolidate what you're reading and act as a form of rehearsal that helps you remember it later.

7. **Put things into context.** Reading requires a certain level of what's called cultural literacy, core knowledge that puts things into context and gives them meaning. Authors assume their readers have a common background. They refer to other books or current events, or historical milestones, and

OK, authors, you're persuading me!

Teachable Moment Ask students to discuss times when they really do pay attention to what they are reading. To get everyone involved, go around the room and ask students to fill in the blank: "I really pay attention when I read ___." Most often students pay attention to something they think is important, but how do they decide what is important and what isn't? College is the ticket to many aspects of a quality life, so paying attention to learning and doing well is critical.

Activity Option This activity can be assigned for homework or done in class. Give students a two- or three-page article or current newspaper story to read. Tell them to read the article only once, writing their comments, questions, and reactions as suggested in this chapter. Have students pair up and show each other what they highlighted and what kinds of notes they put in the margins. Was their approach different from their partner's? If so, what differed and why? Have them share their responses with the class.

Teaching with Technology If students can resist the temptation of Facebook or other online favorites, free applications like Evernote, OneNote, Simplenotes, or Springpad can work extremely well for taking notes while reading. You might ask students to research the top 10 free online notetaking sites and select one they'd like to try.

Activity Option Go back through the section of this chapter on reading with your students. Ask them to make notes to themselves in the margins (or on another sheet of paper) about why they underlined or highlighted a word, phrase, or section. Why did they consider that part to be important? Knowing the answers to these questions is more important than the act of "coloring," which students sometimes do with a highlighter.

unless you know what they're referring to, what you're reading may not make sense to you. An example you might be familiar with is how the television show *Seinfeld* made real words that everyone now knows and uses out of fake ones: *yada yada yada*, for example. Those words are now part of our cultural literacy that have meaning for you and everyone you know, probably, but may not for people from another culture. They know the literacy of their own culture instead.

Imagine the "Far Side" cartoon in which a caveman and cave-woman (Mom and Dad) are reviewing the report card that Junior (who is slouched in the foreground) brought home to the cave. Dad says, "Oh look…this get better. 'F' in history! You even flunk something not happen yet." Getting the joke requires an amazing amount of cultural literacy:

> That American Moms and Dads typically review report cards with their children.

> That report cards are important to American parents.

> That students worry when their grades are poor.

> That cavemen and women spoke a rudimentary form of human language.

> That history is a subject taught in school.

> That history is a cumulative record of events over time.

These examples of cultural literacy are fairly easy to figure out, but what about this less familiar historical reference? You might think, for example, that Walt Whitman's 1888 poem "O Captain! My Captain!" is something a sailor wrote when his skipper died. Instead, it's a poem about Abraham Lincoln, who was assassinated as the Civil War drew to an end.

> O captain! my captain! our fearful trip is done;
> The ship has weathered every rack, the prize we sought is won;
> The port is near, the bells I hear, the people all exulting,
> While follow eyes the steady keel, the vessel grim and daring.
>
> But O heart! heart! heart!
> O the bleeding drops of red!
> Where on the deck my captain lies,
> Fallen cold and dead.

Lincoln was the captain, the ship was the United States, the storm was the Civil War, and the prize was keeping the union together, surviving the war, and abolishing slavery. At the time, the poem held a highly prominent place in American cultural literacy. Whitman said he was asked to recite it so often that he was almost sorry he had ever written it.[15] Today, far fewer people in our culture know this once familiar reference. Did you? If you come across it in a book now, you are culturally literate and understand the reference. You're an insider, which is an important aspect of reading. Keep your eyes and ears open, read and listen, or buy a cultural literacy dictionary so that, as a reader, you're "in the know."[16]

> "Perhaps the most valuable result of all education is the ability to make yourself do the thing you have to do, when it ought to be done, whether you like it or not."
>
> *Thomas Henry Huxley, British biologist (1825–1895)*

I had to learn this in school! It never made sense until now!

Diversity Discussion You may wish to discuss subcultures within our own as you discuss cultural literacy. Variations in slang, for example, can identify subcultures and their members.

Activity Option Even simple, everyday reading requires cultural literacy. Ask students to bring a cartoon or joke to class that requires cultural literacy to understand. The amount of information out there increases exponentially every day, especially with the advent of the Internet, so one can't know everything. But the more one reads, the more likely one is to be culturally literate.

> Reading is to the mind what exercise is to the body.
>
> *Joseph Addison, British politician and writer (1672–1719)*

Hill Street Studios/Blend Images/Corbis

Paul Burns/ Flame/Corbis

8. **Read to learn with the SQ6R method.** Much of the reading you'll do in college includes complicated sentences that are difficult to navigate. When you try reading complex passages aloud, you may stumble because you don't immediately recognize how the words are linked into phrases. But practicing reading aloud is one way you can become more familiar with difficult language. Many instructors teach their first-year students a common approach to reading and studying called SQ3R:

   Survey—Skim to get the lay of the land quickly.

   Question—Ask yourself what, why, and how questions. What is this article or chapter about? Why is it included? How might I use this information?

   Read (1)—Go ahead now and read the entire assignment. Make notes in the margins or even create a study guide for yourself.

FIGURE 8.1

Read to Learn

Photo credits: (clockwise, starting at top left): © Avera/Shutterstock.com; © mm_design/Shutterstock.com; © Avera/Shutterstock.com; © Avera/Shutterstock.com; © Arek_Malang/Shutterstock.com; © Arek_Malang/Shutterstock.com; © Marin/Shutterstock.com; © Arek_Malang/Shutterstock.com; © Henryk Sadura/Shutterstock.com; © Beboy/Shutterstock.com

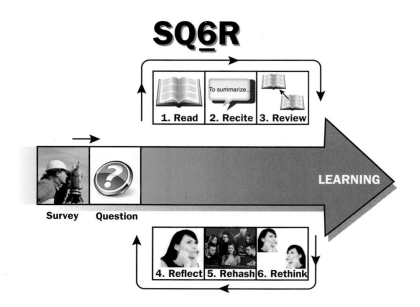

✓ **Recite** (2)—Stop every now and then and talk to yourself. See if you can put what you're reading into your own words.

✓ **Review** (3)—When you've finished, go back and summarize what you've learned.

One expert suggests, however, that for scholarly articles, original published research, and complicated academic prose, you may need to add a few R's to make a new formula, SQ6R:

✓ **Reflect** (4)—You may need time to truly understand what you've read. Put it down and come back to it later—but definitely come back. ← *must try this out! I'll take any help!*

✓ **Rehash** (5)—Communicate your views to your study partners. They may be having trouble with the language, too, and multiple heads may be better than one. You may gain some insights from them, and vice versa.

✓ **Rethink** (6)—Evaluate whether or not you understood the article on your own. Do you understand it better after rehashing it with other students? And finally, how will you use put the information you read to good use?[17]

9. **Learn the language.** Every discipline has its own perspective and its own vocabulary. In many of the introductory classes you take, you'll spend a good deal of time and effort learning terms to be used in classes you'll take later. In order to study *advanced* biology, everyone has to learn the same language in *introductory* biology. You can't be calling things whatever you want to call them. You call it a respiratory system, but your classmate calls it a reproductive system. Imagine the medical problems that might bring on! Here's a fun challenge—read these three passages written by authors representing three different disciplines. All three authors (two of whom are my daughters) were asked to translate the same passage as a parody, using the language of their own discipline. See if you can guess what the original passage was and which disciplines these authors are representing.

Passage 1: Our human experience suggests that the light that radiates from a star actually shimmers, but we are forced to examine not only whether such a visual phenomenon is an accurate representation of reality, but also whether it truly constitutes empirical evidence of a star's fundamental existence. Such questioning could lead us to explore further the nature of the human condition and our very existence as inhabitants of the universe.
—Shannon (Staley) Rothenberg

Passage 2: The pinpoints of light we see in the night sky are the imprints left on our retinas by photons that have traveled hundreds of millions of light years across the near-vacuum of interstellar space. Experts theorize that stars are actually super-heated balls of hydrogen gas, so massive that the force of their own gravity triggers atomic fusion in their cores. This process produces electromagnetic energy, as well as subatomic particles and increasingly complex elements. By studying the stars, we gain valuable insights into the nature of matter, energy, and the space-time continuum. *What?? I don't think I get this...*
—Stephanie Staley

Passage 3: As we look out into the heavens late at night, we wonder what it all means. According to a recent survey, only one-third of Americans

Teachable Moment Rehashing with a partner or group is a great technique, especially for aural learners and extraverts. Teaching someone something is an especially powerful tool for remembering and understanding.

are "very happy" with their lives.[18] The pace and stress of modern-day life, the drive to succeed, the pressure to accumulate material wealth and have it all are evident in our society. Ironically, is happiness sacrificed in the pursuit? Can balance be achieved? What are the roles of spirituality, wellness, counseling, and drug therapies in coping with our complex lives? —Constance Staley

Can you guess the original passage? If you guessed "Twinkle, twinkle, twinkle little star; how I wonder what you are," you're right! These three authors were asked to use the language of their disciplines in a humorous way to make a point. The writer of Passage 1, a philosophy major, uses the poem to question the nature of reality. Passage 2's writer, an astrophysics major, translates it into a scientific treatise on stars. In Passage 3, your author, posing as a psychology major, is prompted to discuss mental health. All three interpreted the original children's verse in different ways based on the "languages" spoken by their disciplines. In college you will learn about the humanities (philosophy, for example), the natural sciences (astrophysics, for example), and the social sciences (psychology, for example) as you take what are often called general education or core courses. It's important to get to know a discipline. Pay attention to its perspective, priorities, and practices as you read, study, and learn.

10. **Bring your reading to class.** Some of your instructors will build the outside course readings into their lectures. They may justify the readings in their course syllabus, preview the readings in class, talk about their importance, or create reading worksheets for use in small groups. If they don't, however, it's up to you to integrate them. Bring up the reading in class, ask questions about it, and find out how it relates to particular points in the lecture. Doing so is an important part of being responsible for your own learning.

11. **Be inventive!** Students who are the best readers invent strategies that work for them. Perhaps you're an auditory learner. Reading assignments aloud might drive your roommate or another family member to distraction (so find a place where you can be alone), but it might be the perfect way for you to learn. If you're a kinesthetic learner, you might make copies of particular passages from your textbook, and build your own scrapbook for a course. Or cut up the professor's lecture notes into small chunks and reassemble them. Using what you know about yourself as a learner is a big part of college success, so don't just do what everyone else does or even follow your instructor's advice verbatim, if it doesn't work for you. Figure out what does, and then do it!

12. **Make friends with your dictionary.** Okay, so it's annoying to stop every few minutes to look up a word. It's absolutely necessary, however. From the preceding "Twinkle, Twinkle" examples, which terms would you need to look up? What does the term *empirical evidence* mean? What, exactly is the *space-time continuum*? Yes, sometimes it's important to break your stride, stop, and look up a word or phrase because what follows in the

ah-ha! Now I do!

Teachable Moment If any of the students guessed what the passage was about, ask them what hints they used to figure it out.

Sensitive Situation Entering students learn quickly that some professors ask students to purchase and read books but don't address the readings in class or test students on them. Advise students that if this is the case, it is their responsibility to ask how the readings and lectures should be integrated. Some students learn not to "waste time" on the reading. They are taking their chances, and at some point, their strategy won't work. On the other hand, it's our responsibility to help students see the value of what we're asking them to read!

Teachable Moment Students can also be encouraged to keep their own online course-specific glossaries. They can set up folders for separate classes by simply cutting and pasting from an online dictionary and refer back to it whenever they need to.

I like dictionary.com, but then I wind up surfing the web... maybe a paper copy would be better...

CONTROL: Your Toughest Class

Look back over the section of this chapter on reading and honestly assess the extent to which reading is part of what you find challenging about your toughest class.

	Yes	No
1. Do you understand what being a good reader in this discipline is all about?	___	___
2. Do you understand, accept, and work to improve your reading skills in this course?	___	___
3. Do you adjust your reading style? If the reading required in this course is challenging, do you read more carefully and with more focus?	___	___
4. Do you converse with the author of the textbook for this course as you read?	___	___
5. Do you dissect the text, writing what and why statements in the margins of the textbook?	___	___
6. Do you make detailed notes?	___	___
7. Do you put things you read for this course into context? Is cultural literacy a part of the challenge you face?	___	___
8. Do you tackle the reading with gusto, even if it's tough stuff?	___	___
9. Are you learning the language of this discipline?	___	___
10. Do you bring up questions about the reading in class?	___	___
11. Do you invent your own reading strategies to help you?	___	___
12. Do you make regular use of your dictionary to help you understand what you're reading for this class?	___	___

If you put more checkmarks under No than Yes in the above assessment, it's time to make an action plan. Cite which recommendations you'll put into effect immediately and how you'll do it. If it's appropriate, e-mail your plan to your instructor in this class.

reading is based on that particular definition. Other times, these strategies might be appropriate:

➤ Keep a stack of blank index cards next to you and write down the unknown word or phrase, the sentence it appears in, and the page number. Then when you have a stack, or when you have a chunk of time, look them all up.

➤ Try to guess the word's meaning from its context. Remember Lewis Carroll's "Jabberwocky" poem from Through the Looking-Glass? Even though the poem contains made-up words, when you read it, you infer that something was moving around sometime, somewhere, right?

'Twas brillig ⬅ ['twas usually indicates a time, as in 'twas daybreak],

and the slithy toves ⬅ [we don't know what *toves* are, but *slithy* sounds like a combination of slimy and slithering]

Did **gyre** and **gimble** in the **wabe** ⬅ [the meaning of *wabe* is unclear, but *gyre* sounds like gyroscope, suggesting movement, and so forth]

Often you can infer a word's meaning from how it's used or from other words around it, but not always. Many of your courses will require you to learn precise meanings for new terms. If you can't detect the meaning from the context, use your dictionary—and see it as a friend, rather than an enemy.

Teaching with Technology There are also many free online dictionaries that allow users to search multiple databases of English words, including jargon and slang. Dictionary.com is one of the largest free online dictionaries. Not only can students find definitions for tough words, but the Web site also allows users to hear most words spoken aloud, which could be particularly helpful with unfamiliar words or especially useful to international students.

Teachable Moment You may discover some students in your class who love to read. Ask them why they enjoy reading and to name some of their favorite books. Consider adopting a local elementary school and engage your students in a service learning project by reading to younger students or tutoring them in their reading skills.

> ❝ Chains of habit are too light to be felt until they are too heavy to be broken. ❞
>
> *Warren Buffett*

Wow! I've always wondered about habits. This is good stuff!

What do you do first when you get up in the morning? Pour yourself a cup of coffee? Hop in the shower? Wrestle with your dog? Reach for your smartphone? What's your routine? As it turns out, much of what we do each day isn't based on minute-by-minute decision making. You don't wake up wondering *what should I do now? I just can't figure out what to do.* You just do it, and you do it pretty much the same way most days.

Much of what we do is based on habits—perhaps up to 40 percent, experts say.[19] Small habits streamline our lives and free our minds for big, important decisions, like where to go to college, which career to prepare for, and whether to choose life partner A, B, or C. Imagine how little you'd get done if you labored over every little detail of your life; you'd be so bogged down, you couldn't function. Habits may feel like decisions, but they're routines you follow without much thought.

The subject of habits, however, raises some interesting questions. How do they develop? How do you stop one if you want to? And, most importantly for our purposes, how do you cultivate one you want but don't currently have? Once you figure out the answer to that last question, you're likely well on your way to launching a positive college experience and a successful career.

Let's say, for example, that every afternoon around four o'clock, you get the urge to whip out a dollar for a "vending machine special," the biggest candy bar you see through the glass. There's one down the hallway from your class. You put your money in the machine, hit "A1" or

"E4," wait for it to drop, and "inhale" it. After eating the chocolate bar, you feel satisfied, energized, and happy, but then you begin to feel guilty about this new habit that's somehow shrinking your jeans, not to mention your cash stash. It needs to end. You try various techniques, like putting a "NO MORE CANDY!" note on your mirror (you ignore it), not bringing any money to school (you borrow it), or taking a solemn vow to swear off chocolate forever (you know you're lying to yourself). Whatever you try doesn't seem to work, and despite your best promises and whatever willpower you can muster, you can't find a way out of the habit loop. Tomorrow will look very much like today.

As it turns out, habits are more complicated than they seem. A "habit loop" has three parts: a cue or trigger, a routine or behavior (the actual habit itself), and a reward, the reason your brain turns a particular behavior into a habit.[20] The habit loop looks like this.

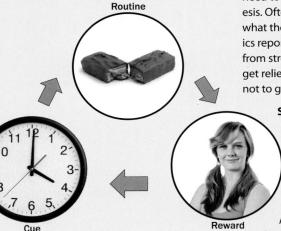

THE HABIT LOOP

The way to change a habit is to analyze the three-part "anatomy" of your habit loop. Most people only think of the behavior itself when they think of habits, but the cue and the reward are essential to the formula, and getting out of one is actually a complicated, four-step proposition that involves some soul-searching.[21]

Step 1: Describe the routine. This is the easiest step because it's the aspect you

want to change, in this case, eating a chocolate bar every afternoon. But what's the real cue that triggers the routine? Is it hunger pangs? The clock? Boredom? What's the reward? A sugar high? A burst of energy? To totally figure out the answers to these questions, you need to move on to Step 2.

Step 2: Try different rewards. What are you really craving? If it's a sugar high, try eating a cookie instead of a candy bar and see if you get the same results. You may think you're craving a sugar high when what you really want is a detour that lets you hit the "pause button" in the middle of a busy day. If what you're really after is energy, try a cup of coffee instead, and see if that fills the bill. During Step 2, just remember that you're experimenting to understand the loop fully. Try a different reward, and then let 15 minutes go by. If the craving is still there, you may need to move on to another hypothesis. Often habits aren't really about what they seem to be about. Alcoholics report that they drink to escape from stress, forget bad memories, or get relief from worrisome problems, not to get drunk.

Step 3: Pinpoint the cue. This is the most challenging part of exploring a habit loop. What's really driving your habit? Is it truly the clock? Are you really hungry (or would a stick of gum do)? Are you bored and craving a distraction? Most habits are triggered by one of several things: time, place, person (people), or a particular emotion.[22] Figure out where you are when the cue kicks in, what you're doing, how you feel, and what you were doing right before the urge. After all this analysis, you may figure out that what you really want is a way to stall while walking back to your dorm room to start working on your reading, writing, or presenting assignment.

Cast on Careers

© Larry Harwood Photography. Property of Cengage Learning

FOCUS: Were there times during your first year of college that it seemed like <u>all</u> your assignments involved reading, writing, and presenting? How solid were your study habits?

ANTHONY: Actually, I really didn't know how to study. I did well in high school and expected to do well in college. But I wouldn't say I had even developed any study habits other than avoiding it. I failed two courses with heavy reading and writing assignments as a new college student—English and history. I remember my father began to doubt whether I was "college material." But I realized that I wasn't the only student who had ever gotten overwhelmed, and I believed that I'd get better at writing and overcome my fear of public speaking. I also talked with a mentor who told me that he had been in the same situation but had perservered and eventually earned a master's degree. With that kind of personal encouragement from someone I admired, I knew I could succeed, too.

FOCUS: What are your career plans?

ANTHONY: I majored in Spanish. Eventually, I'd like to teach Spanish to high school students. People tell me I'd be good at it, and since I've overcome obstacles in my own life, I believe I could serve as a positive role model for them.

Step 4: Make a plan. If boredom is the issue, walk with a friend. Make a point of meeting up with a buddy or roommate on the way. Fill the void with a fun distraction. But definitely create a plan and stick to it. "When I get out of class and start walking back to my residence hall, I'll find someone along the way to talk to. I'll do this every day, even if I have to talk to a stranger." If you stick to your plan, after three or four weeks you won't even be aware that it's a plan. It will have become a new habit.

Think Ahead Think about the various habits you've developed that interfere with your ability to focus on your class assignments. They may need to be examined using the four-step model described here so that you can become more productive. As you look ahead to your eventual career, can these lessons apply to the world of working professionals, too? How?

Exercise 8.3   Getting Started

The mystery writer Agatha Christie once said, "The secret of getting ahead is getting started." Look at the topics below, and choose one of them. Write the first paragraph for an essay on the topic. If you do this exercise in class, your instructor may only give you one minute, for example, to get something down on paper. When it comes to getting started, one of the biggest challenges is commitment. You have an idea that could go in a dozen different directions, but in order to get started, you have to settle on one direction and run with it. If you do this exercise on your own, set a timer so that you're forced to commit to something. Give it your best effort, and use correct grammar and spelling. The point of the exercise is to practice getting started, which is sometimes the most difficult part of a writing assignment.

A. Why I will (won't) be quitting Facebook

B. Why I love to read (or don't)

C. Why writing is good therapy (or why writing stresses me out)

D. Why public speaking is (or isn't) my strong suit

Now look back at what you have written. Give your paragraph a grade (based on your own standards), or trade with a classmate who chose the same option (A, B, C, or D), and explain the grade you've assigned to him or her. What is the grade based on? Does the writing have a topic sentence that can be identified? Is there a clear thesis statement? If your instructor thinks there is time, try another option. Practicing the art of getting started (when the threat is low because no real grade will be assigned) can be a helpful exercise.

Write Right!

Challenge: Reading and writing are two sides of the same coin; in one case you're taking in information, and in the other, you're producing it. Would any of this chapter's suggestions on how to "Read Right" also help you "Write Right"?

Reaction:

_____

_____

_____

Although your reading skills will be critical, they are only one of the several types of communication skills you will need in college. Good writing skills will be essential, too. The question we'll explore next is how to build the writing skills you'll need. If you can do that, you're well on your way to successful outcomes.

An old Doonesbury cartoon may very well hang on the wall in the Writing Center on your campus. It shows two college students. One is tapping away at a typewriter and mutters, "Man, have I got a lot of papers due!" as he types the paper's opening: "Most problems, like answers, have finite resolutions. The basis for these resolutions contain many of the ambiguities which conditional man daily struggles with. Accordingly, most problematic solutions are fallible. Mercifully, all else fails; conversely hope lies in a myriad of polemics. …" The other student is looking over his shoulder and asks, "Which paper is this?" to which the writer replies, "Dunno, I haven't decided yet." Obviously, cranking out college papers just for the sake of getting them done isn't the best idea. But, unfortunately, it happens.

Why do some students put off writing assignments? Is it because they worked with a cranky writing teacher in the past? Are they afraid of producing something less than perfect? Have they been unsuccessful at previous writing projects? Or do they simply dislike writing? As shown in the cartoon dialogue above, it's tempting to start with something so general that it could work for literally any paper. Or you may fall into a boring habit, like starting every paper with the dictionary definition for whatever you're writing about. Or perhaps you don't even get that far. You may simply stare at the blank screen until it's time to do something else and move on. Writing is hard work. That's why having discrete steps to follow produces optimal results.

Teaching with Technology If students need extra writing help, have them turn to an OWL. Online Writing Labs are sources of information about citations, grammar, mechanics, and style. Purdue University launched one of the first OWLs at Owl. English.Purdue.edu, and their website contains free resources for the general public. Many universities also have writing centers on campus. Encourage students to visit OWLs or on-campus writing labs for valuable writing assistance. Using University OWLs may be safer than using other online assistance (which may sell submissions to "paper mills").

> " I do not like to write—I like to have written. "
>
> *Gloria Steinem, journalist and political activist (1934–)*

Writing as a Process

How should the writing process work, ideally? It should involve three basic stages: prewriting, writing, and rewriting.

Prewriting

Think of this analogy: When you speak, you may not know exactly which words will come out, but you have some idea of what you want to say before you open your mouth, right? Just as you prethink what you're going to say, you must prewrite what you're going to put down on paper. This is the stage of writing many students skip. They just sit down and start writing whatever comes into their heads. But devoting some time to prewriting can actually save you time later—and improve your results. During the prewriting state, you must ask yourself questions like these:

1. **What is the assignment asking me to do?** Let's say one assignment asks you to summarize interviews with three marketing professors on campus to find out what makes them effective teachers. And another assignment asks you to compare and contrast social media marketing with traditional marketing. You'd go about these two writing papers differently. Zero in on the verbs in the assignment—*summarize* versus *compare* and *contrast,* in this case. The specifics of the assignment must be crystal clear to you, and if you're given a choice of topic, pick something that really interests you.

2. **Who is my audience, and what do I want them to know or do?** You write differently for different audiences—for your composition class or for the school newspaper, for example. If you're writing for the school newspaper, you may aim for catchy phrasing, short sentences, and an intriguing title. Once you know who you're writing to or for, then you can ask: What do I want them to know? Am I trying to inform, persuade, or entertain

66
Finis origine pendet (The end depends on the beginning.)
99

Manlius, first century Roman poet

Marvy!/Corbis

them? You'll use your research differently, depending on your specific purpose.

3. **Have I done enough research?** If you've followed the guidelines provided so far in this chapter about research, it's now time to ask: Do I have enough support for my thesis? Have I gathered sufficient statistics, expert testimony, and examples to persuade my reader?

4. **Can I compose a strong thesis statement?** Your paper's thesis statement should be the specific argument you're making, summarized into one sentence, ideally. For example, for the scenario we've been using, your thesis may be something like: "In today's world, social media marketing works better than conventional methods for three reasons: visibility, speed, and cost." Formulating a strong thesis is half the battle.

5. **Set in-between target dates for the three stages of writing, even if your instructor doesn't.** Some instructors will ask to see your work at each stage of the writing project. If you try to print your paper at 9:50 a.m. for your 10 a.m. class, you can count on something going wrong, like your printer cartridge shriveling up or your hard drive plummeting to an untimely death. To beat the odds, schedule in-between deadlines for yourself for prewriting, writing, and rewriting to keep the project moving along.

Writing

Have you ever experienced writer's block, or nowadays, the "tyranny of the blank screen"? You sit down to write and suddenly go blank? Whatever you call it, you'll be relieved to know there are ways around it.

Some professional writers resort to strange, almost ritualistic strategies to get themselves going. Victor Hugo supposedly wrote in his study at the same time every day—naked! His valet was ordered to lock away all Hugo's clothes until he had finished each day's writing.[23] Apparently, the method worked—witness *Les Misérables*. But this technique may not be well received by your roommate or your family. Just write freely about whatever comes into your head, whether it's on target or not. But, how do you start? Take a look at these techniques for starting the writing process.

1. **Begin by writing what's on your mind.**

   I'm having trouble starting this paper because there's so much to talk about in terms of social media and marketing. All businesses want to grow, but there are different ways to do it. Why not just go with tried true marketing methods like making cold calls, sending flyers through bulk mail, or creating radio and TV ads? Today, thanks to social media, there are better ways. When visibility, speed, and cost are factors—and they usually are—you need to update your marketing strategies.

   Now stop and look at what you've written. Based on your "stream of consciousness," you now have the beginnings of a paper. You can talk about how new social media marketing techniques can work better for the three reasons you've identified, and you're on your way.

2. **Begin with the words, "The purpose of this paper is...."** and finish the sentence. You may be surprised by what comes out of your fingertips.

Activity Option Often, students need help writing a good, clear thesis statement and need opportunities to practice. Give students a scenario about some controversial, current topic. Ask them to take a stand and bring a thesis statement to class. Encourage students to look online or in a writer's handbook for suggestions on how to write a good thesis. Have students bring their thesis statements to the next class and they can critique each other's.

Teachable Moment First-year seminar courses often include journal assignments. One purpose of assigning journals is to increase the amount and fluency of students' writing. Journals are a great way to accomplish this since they sometimes cover everyday things and events and issues that are on students' minds. Or "Insight → Action" prompts make great journal topics for self-reflection and change.

Activity Option Show your students some online examples of visual organizers for writing or provide handouts that explain visual techniques to help them become better writers. There are many visual organizing tools online or your writing center will have examples such as outlining, mapping, and brainstorming activities. Use one of the visual organizers to help students, as a class, structure an essay about why it's important to go to class.

3. **Work with a tutor in your campus Writing Center.** Sometimes talking through the assignment with someone else can help, particularly if that person is a writing expert. Or talk it through with your roommate or a family member.

4. **Change the audience.** If it helps, assume you're writing your paper to someone who sharply disagrees with you or to a middle school student who just asked you a question. Sometimes thinking about your audience—instead of the topic in the abstract—helps you zero in on the writing task.

5. **Play a role.** Imagine yourself as a nationally-known tech guru or a network newscaster deciding what to include on the evening news. Separate yourself from the task, and see it from another perspective.

Rewriting

Rewriting is often called "revision," and that's a powerful term. It means not merely changing, but literally re-seeing, re-en*vision*ing your work. Sometimes students think they're revising when they're actually just editing: tinkering with words and phrases, checking spelling, changing punctuation. But the word revision actually means more than that. It means making major organizational overhauls, if necessary. According to many writing experts, that's what you must be willing to do. You're on a search and destroy mission, if that's what it takes.[24] Try these suggestions for rewriting to see if they work for you:

1. **Leave it alone.** To help you see your paper as others will see it, set it aside for a while. If you can wait an hour, a day, or a weekend before revising, you'll have distanced yourself long enough to see your writing for what it is, and then improve it. Of course, this suggestion isn't meant to serve as an excuse for a late paper ("I couldn't turn my paper in today because I need to wait before I rewrite."). That won't fly. But coming back later is usually illuminating. ("What? I wrote that? What was I thinking?")

2. **Ask for feedback.** One way of discovering how your writing will affect others is simply to ask them. Share your writing before it becomes final.

3. **Edit ruthlessly!** Cutting a favorite phrase or section may feel like lopping off an arm or a leg. But sometimes it must be done. The goal here is to produce the best paper possible, even if it's painful!

4. **Proofread, proofread, proofread!** You may think you have just written an unbelievable essay, but if it's littered with errors, your instructor may pay more attention to those than to your paper's brilliant ideas. Sometimes it also helps to proofread out loud. Somehow hearing the words, especially if you're an aural learner, makes errors more apparent. Be proud of the document's final appearance—paper clean, type dark and crisp, margins consistent, headings useful, names and references correct, no spelling

> I must write it all out, at any cost. Writing is thinking. It is more than living, for it is being conscious of living.

Anne Morrow Lindbergh, American writer and aviation pioneer (1906–2001)

Myron Jay Dorf/Cusp/CORBIS

I wish I'd read this sooner!

Sensitive Situation While it is a good idea to have students in class read each other's papers, keep in mind that you might have a student who is very embarrassed about his writing. Since you probably already are familiar with your students' work, if you have a student who is really struggling, you might want him to read a sample of your work, and you his, especially if this is an in-class activity.

errors. And remember that spellcheck, for all its convenience, can let you down. If the word you use is an actual one, but not the right on, it will give its approval, regardless. (Did you catch the spelling error in that last sentence? Spellcheck didn't.)

One more tip. Throughout these three stages be prepared to move fluidly from one to the other at the slightest provocation. If you're rewriting and you come across some <u>prewriting</u> information (as in *new research*) copy it down and fit it in. If in the <u>prewriting</u> stage you think of <u>writing</u> that strikes you as powerful—a good argument or a well-constructed phrase—write it down.[26]

> "
> A C essay is an A essay turned in too soon.
> "

John C. Bean, Professor of English, Seattle University

Steve Cole/Photodisc/Getty Images

Build a Better Paper: The Seven C's

Challenge: Without looking ahead, can you identify seven traits of good writing (all beginning with the letter C) that college students should aim for? Finish this sentence with seven adjectives beginning with C: Good writing should be 1) <u>c</u>lear, etc.

Reaction:

1. _____   5. _____
2. _____   6. _____
3. _____   7. _____
4. _____

In many ways, writing is like building. But instead of using nails, planks, and sheetrock to construct our communication, we use words, sentences, and paragraphs. Here are seven suggestions—all of which begin with C to help you remember them.[27]

1. Be <u>C</u>lear. Unfortunately, the English language gives you endless opportunities to write something quite different from what you mean. You can flip

Teachable Moment As a class, come up with the top five most common writing weaknesses and the top five that are most difficult for class members themselves to overcome. It is good for students to see that they are not alone in the struggle to become an effective writer.

Teachable Moment You might be able to use this opportunity to see who has been reading the book. Give students five minutes to write down, the seven C's without looking in their books.

Exercise 8.4   What's in an "A"?

Take a look at this first-year student's essay and offer the writer advice.

Assignment: Describe a problem you have faced as a first-year student and identify a possible solution.

Last summer, I worked for a bank in my hometown to earn money for college. I was told to show up for the interview at 8:30 a.m. I usually don't get up that early, so on Thursday night, I set my alarm clock, my cell phone alarm, and my clock radio to make sure I didn't miss it. Afterward, I thought that I had really hit it off with the interviewer. When I first got the job on a Friday, I was thrilled. Imagine me working for a bank! I thought that sounded like a prestigious job. When I told my Dad about getting the job, he said that he thought banks really shouldn't hire young people because they don't know the value of money. I decided he was probably kidding around.

But after my first week at Citizen's National Bank, I found myself bored stiff. Counting bills and tallying numbers really aren't that interesting. I did meet this girl named Nicole, and she was kind of cool, but everyone else at the bank was a little standoffish, including my supervisor, Ned. I didn't want to have a strained relationship with my supervisor, so I was friendly with him and serious about getting my work done. But by the following Wednesday, I was ready to quit. I heard about an opening at the coffee shop close to my house that included free food. So that's where I ended up. The moral of this story is to only take a job if you are really interested in the work. And I've definitely decided not to major in accounting.

What's the main problem with this essay? The writer has written about a problem she faced as a first-year student. The essay contains no grammatical errors. But is it likely to earn an "A"? Actually, the assignment calls for a problem-solution organizational pattern. Instead, it follows a chronological pattern (and then this happened, and then this . . .). What is the writer's thesis statement? Is it the next-to-the last sentence? *Only take a job if you are really interested in the work*. Instead of telling a story from start to finish, how would the essay change if the writer had asked a question like this: What mistakes do students make when looking for a job to help them pay for college? Then the writer could have organized the essay around the thesis statement (only take a job if you are really interested in the work) and found evidence, including her own experience, to back up the claim. Meeting the specific requirements of an assignment is the first step in earning a good grade.

through your thesaurus and use a word that sounds good, but isn't recognizable (as in profundity, below), or you can write a convoluted sentence that can't be understood. Compare the problems in these two sentences, both of which are unclear:

> *The profundity of the quotation overtook its author's intended meaning.*

> *The writing was profound, but on closer examination, not only was it devoid of content, but it was also characterized by a preponderance of flatulent words.*

Yes, many of us will be able to figure out what these sentences mean, though perhaps we'll need to check the dictionary. Sometimes beginning college students decide they must write to *impress* rather than to *express*. They assume instructors like this kind of convoluted writing. They think it sounds more academic. Instructors see through that guise. Mean what you say, and say what you mean.

2. **Be Complete.** Ask yourself what your reader needs to know. Sometimes we're so close to what we're writing that we leave out important information, or we fail to provide the background the reader needs to get our meaning. Put yourself in your reader's shoes.

3. **Be Correct.** If your writing is littered with grammatical, spelling, and punctuation errors, readers may generalize that you also don't know what you're writing about either. If grammar, punctuation, and usage aren't your strong points, ask someone you know who's a crackerjack writer to look over your first draft.

Don't agonize.
Organize.

Florynce Kennedy, American lawyer and African American activist

Hans Neleman/Comet/Corbis

4. **Be Concise.** In the past, you may have used tricks like enlarging the font or increasing the margins to fill an assigned number of pages. But college students sometimes face the opposite problem: they find that writing less is more challenging than writing more. Think of this formula: A given idea expressed in many words has relatively little impact. But that same idea expressed in few well-chosen and well-combined words can be penetrating. You could say:

> *"Whether or not a penny, or any amount of money, is earned or saved, it has the same or at least a similar value, fiscally speaking, in the long run."*

Compare that weak, wordy blather with this concise expression of Ben Franklin's:

> *"A penny saved is a penny earned."*

5. **Be Compelling.** Your writing should be interesting, active, and vivid, so that people want to read what you have to say. Compare these two headlines. Which article would you want to read?

> ➤ *Protests against tuition increases have been led by student government.*

> ➤ *SGA leaders urge campus-wide protests over tuition hikes.*

The sentences create different images, don't they? The first sentence makes the situation sound like something that happens every day. The second sentence uses the active voice (*leaders urge campus-wide protests*) instead of the passive voice (*protests have been led*), and the second sentence uses a more descriptive verb (*urge* versus *lead*) and noun (*hikes* versus *increases*). Of course, you can go too far (*SGA leaders spearhead crushing student fury over radical tuition upsurge*). But this principle is a good one to remember.

6. **Be Courteous.** Courtesy is important in any kind of writing. E-mail is often one place where people are discourteous to one another in writing—perhaps because distance gives them courage or they're out of sorts. Having a meltdown on paper or your computer screen is rarely the right choice.

7. **Be Convincing.** You'll be a more successful writer if you support your views with solid evidence and credible testimonials. Give specific examples to illustrate your point—anecdotes, testimonials from experts, experiences, analogies, facts, statistics—and your writing will be more credible.

Keep these seven C's in mind. The secret to learning to think in college is to become a better writer. And as you're learning critical thinking skills, you'll also become a more clear, complete, correct, concise, compelling, courteous, and convincing writer.

> ❝ What's another word for Thesaurus? ❞
>
> *—Steven Wright, American comedian*

> ❝ I am returning this otherwise good typing paper to you because someone has printed gibberish all over it and put your name at the top. ❞
>
> **English Professor, Ohio University**

In a Manner of Speaking . . .

Sensitive Situation Most likely you will have at least one or two students who have very high anxiety about giving speeches in class. You may even have a student who stutters for whom the thought of having to stand up in front of class is unbearable. Make sure you tell students to let you know if they have high anxiety. Work with them outside of class, or bring them to the oral communication center, if one exists on your campus.

Teachable Moment If individual students are really nervous about presenting, ask others in the class to encourage those who are fearful. Make sure everyone is supportive of one another. Tell them not to worry, and that it is okay if they make a mistake. Let students who are nervous go first, so that their anxiety doesn't build.

Instead of using your research for a paper, your assignment may ask you to use it for a presentation. Your public speaking skills will be on the line. You may be thinking something like this: *I'm not going to be a public speaker. I'm going to be a surgeon. I'll spend all my time hunched over an unconscious person lying on an operating table. All I'll need to know how to do is hold a scalpel with a steady hand.* But is that really true? What about the communicating you'll need to do with totally conscious hospital administrators, other physicians, and patients before and after surgery?

Most people think of public speaking as an episode, a one-time event. You stand up to give a speech, and when you're finished, you sit down. But actually, there's a sense in which all the speaking we do is public. By contrast, what would *private* speaking be? Thinking? On the job, you'll communicate with others every day. Unless you join a profession that requires you to take a vow of silence, you'll be speaking publicly all the time!

Box 8.1   Ten Ways to Oust Speaking Anxiety

High anxiety. It's the bane of many a speaker. Although doing your best on a writing assignment can certainly generate stress, giving a presentation is an even more personal, more immediate representation of you and your work. There you are, up front, doing your thing. If you can harness your anxiety and actually look forward to opportunities to speak, you'll build more confidence and get better at doing it. See if you think the items on this checklist of fear-suppressing suggestions might work for you.

1. **Ready, set, go.** Being unprepared will cause your anxiety to skyrocket, and winging it won't help your presentation fly! The best antidote to anxiety is to prepare, prepare, prepare!

2. **Dress for success.** Confidence in your physical appearance can increase your confidence overall. Looking good isn't everything, but it helps.

3. **Ease the tension with humor.** Humor can ease tensions, both for your audience and for you. Say something funny that occurs to you at the moment, rather than repeating a joke you read on the Internet.

4. **Don't be a mannequin.** Move around. Use gestures. Look at your audience. Talk as if you were conversing with each individual in the room alone. Be real,

be yourself, and you'll feel more confident. Let your personality shine through.

5. **Practice in your presentation room.** Doing so can help put you at ease during your actual speech.

6. **Find some guinea pigs.** When you practice your presentation, do it in front of a live audience to prepare yourself for natural distractions, like people coughing or sneezing. Practice in front of your roommate or your family. Research indicates your grade is likely to go up.[28]

7. **Channel your energy.** Harness your fear, and turn it into positive energy that increases your dynamism.

8. **Visualize success.** When you see yourself giving your presentation in your mind's eye, visualize success, not failure.

9. **Remember that mistakes are made to be corrected.** If disaster strikes, remember that how you handle it is what's important. Perhaps you fear making a "tip of the slung." Don't worry; instead, make the most of a few moments of lightheartedness!

10. **If you can't shake it, fake it.** If your nerves get the better of you, fake it. Pretend you're confident. You assume the role, and before you know it, your confidence begins to rise.

Craft a Winning Presentation: The Seven P's

Challenge: Without looking further in this section, can you identify seven useful key points, all beginning with P, that relate to presentations? When preparing a presentation, it's important to think about 1) purpose, etc.

Reaction:

1. _____
2. _____
3. _____
4. _____

5. _____
6. _____
7. _____

When you prepare for a presentation in one of your classes, what is your primary goal? To impress your instructor? To amaze your classmates? To get your presentation over with?

Many of the suggestions about using your research in this chapter apply to both writing and speaking. As both a writer and a speaker, you should be clear, complete, correct, concise, compelling, courteous, and convincing. You should choose an organizational pattern and use it to help your audience understand what you're saying. (Unlike reading a written paper, they only have one chance to hear your words go by.) You must have a strong thesis in a speech, just as you must in a paper. But let's examine some other advice that relates primarily to speaking. Use these suggestions to create winning presentations that set you apart in all your courses.[29]

1. **Purpose.** What is the purpose of your presentation? Often the purpose is given to you directly by your instructor: Prepare a five-minute speech *to inform*. . . . But other assignments will allow you to select your own purpose: "The Trials and Tribulations of a Commuting Student" (to inform), "Sustainability in an Age of Materialism" (to persuade), "Five Sure-Fire Ways to Flunk Out of College . . . Not!" (to entertain), "How Being President of the Student Body Can Change Your Life" (to inspire). Knowing exactly what you're trying to accomplish helps!

2. **People.** Who will be your listeners? Generally, you'll be speaking to an audience of students in your classes, right? But what are their specific characteristics as they relate to your purpose? For example, if you're addressing parents and friends at commencement, you might create a different speech than the one you'd present to your co-members of a student club on campus.

3. **Place.** Where will you deliver your presentation? The location of your presentation may affect its tone and style. A presentation you might give to a group of tourists at a national park would allow for informality, and your visual aid would be the scenery around you. But if you gave the same presentation as a geography major to high school seniors, you'd be more formal and scholarly, using a PowerPoint presentation or maps in the classroom.

Sensitive Situation In today's world of business and education, being able to make effective presentations is a key component of success. Giving students opportunities to make presentations in the classroom is preparing them for the future. Many students have presentation anxiety. Explain to students how important the assigned activity is and how this class is a safe place to practice. Also explain the importance of critiquing the presentation both from the viewpoint of the listener and the presenter. Remind students that the evaluations are used to help the presenter improve. Listeners should use tact when they evaluate, and presenters should read the evaluations with the idea of using all of the positive and negative comments to improve their presentation abilities.

Activity Option Have students watch a presentation on television or provide a speech for students to watch and ask them to identify the seven P's.

> " The trouble with talking too fast is you may say something you haven't thought of yet. "
>
> *Ann Landers, syndicated advice columnist (1918–2002)*

Now the 7 "P's" of presentations I like it!

Preparation will help lower my anxiety!

© iStockphoto.com/Baran Özdemir

Good advice. That's what I had planned to do . . .

4. **Preparation.** How should you prepare your speech? Developing the content of a speech is often similar to writing a paper. You'll need to develop a thesis statement and find support for each point by researching examples, statistics, and expert testimonies. Depending on the assignment, you may be asked to write an outline or create a set of PowerPoint slides with talking points. You may also find it helpful to create a storyboard, a map, or flowchart of your slides on paper before moving to the screen (see Figure 8.2). Then, after you know your basic format, you'll need to come up with an attention-grabbing introduction and a memorable conclusion. Keep this acronym in mind: make sure your presentation is SHARP. SHARP stands for stories, humor, analogies ("this" is like "that"), references (or quotes), and pictures/visuals.[30] SHARP is a good formula for a successful presentation, one that your audience will remember. Imagine that you decided to give a presentation about "exiting from college and finding a job." You might start with a horrendous story (S) about a plane trip you just took, where you ran through three airports but missed all three connections (H); compare a plane trip to the journey in college toward a "career destination" (A); include the quote "Map out your future, but do it in pencil. The road ahead is as long as you make it. Make it worth the trip," Jon Bon Jovi (R); and include this photo you took with your cell phone camera on the plane (P).[31] You'd have the makings of a very SHARP presentation.

5. **Planning.** What planning should you do? For example, are visual aids available, or do you need to bring your own? Is there a plug in the room, if you need one? Should you bring a backup of your presentation on a flash drive? Should you test the LCD projector to make any necessary adjustments? Many a speaker has been unnerved at the last minute by some overlooked detail.

6. **Personality.** How can you connect with the audience? How can you demonstrate your competence, charisma, and character to your listeners? Eye contact is important. Look at each person individually, if possible. Inspire trust by telling a story or relating your topic to some aspect of your own experience. Rather than playing a role, act natural and be yourself.

7. **Performance.** This last P relates to delivering your presentation. Rehearsal is important (although too much rehearsal can make your presentation sound singsongy and memorized). Beware of bringing a full written draft to the podium. If you do, you may be tempted to read it, which is the last thing you want to do. Aim for a dynamic delivery, both verbally and nonverbally, that helps keep your listeners listening.

One final thing: After you've finished a paper or presentation, you're not really done. It's time to sit back and think about what you've accomplished. Are you pleased with your work? What have you learned? What will you do differently next time? If you do this every time you finish a writing or speaking assignment, you'll build your skills over time and take them with you to your other college classes, graduate school, or the world of work.

Storyboard a PowerPoint? This is a great idea!

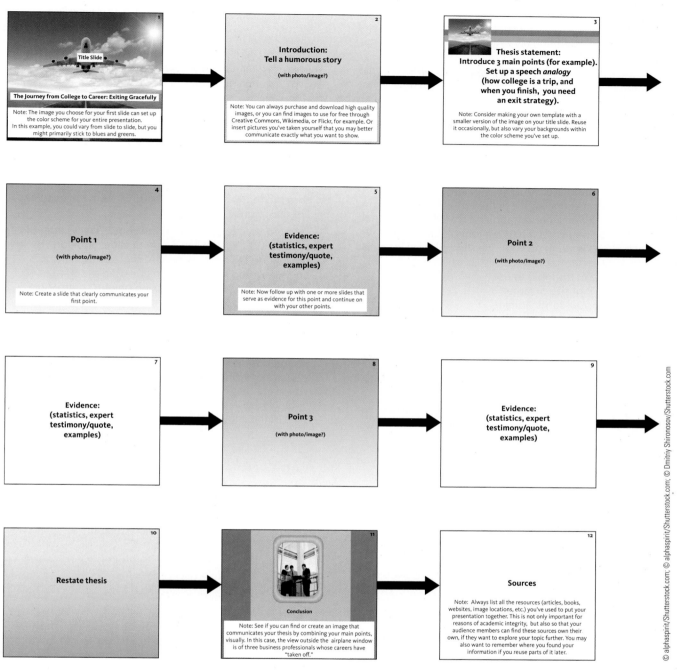

FIGURE 8.2
- - - - - - - - - - - -
Storyboarding a PowerPoint

Instead of (or in addition to) writing a research paper, your instructor may require you to present your findings in an oral presentation using PowerPoint. While PowerPoint has the potential to be a powerful visual aid, it can also be PowerPointless if some simple rules are ignored. Keep these five suggestions in mind to turn presentations you create for class assignments into powerful ones:

1. **DO use your whole brain.** When it comes to designing PowerPoint presentations, the challenge is to combine useful information with attractive design. Think of it as using both sides of your brain—your logical left hemisphere and your creative right hemisphere. For example, if you're giving a presentation on teaching young children, you might want to use a font that looks like this (children's writing) on your title slide. (Just make sure it's legible from a distance. A good rule of thumb is to use 24-point font size or larger and keep your fonts simple unless you have a particular reason to change them.) You also might want to include a high-quality graphic like this one here.

2. **DO use color to your advantage.** Choose an attractive color scheme and stick to it. That doesn't mean that every background on every slide must be the same. In fact, if you do that, your listeners may die of boredom. But if your title slide is blue, orange, and white, then use one, two, or all three of these colors in some hue or shade on every slide. Some speakers create PowerPoint presentations that seem fragmented and messy because the individual slides aren't connected visually.

3. **DON'T crowd your slides with text.** Your listeners won't pay attention to you if they're spending all of their time reading. Be kind, and spare them the trouble by limiting the text on your slides. Some of the most deadly PowerPoint presentations are those in which the speaker turns around, faces the screen, and flies through slide after slide. The only way your listeners can live through that is if oxygen masks drop from the overhead compartments!

4. **DON'T let your slides steal the show.** Always remember that YOU are the speaker. Your slides shouldn't be so fascinating that your audience ignores you. Gunshots and screaming sirens shouldn't be used as sound effects unless, of course, you're speaking on gun control or ambulance response times. Any special effects should be used sparingly to make a point, rather than to shock your listeners.

5. **DO include a bibliography slide, both for words and images.** Some students assume that plagiarism only pertains to writing papers. Not so! Always give credit where credit is due. List your references, either on individual slides (if you use a direct quote, cite it) or on one slide at the end.

© Ardni/Shutterstock.com

Great info! I just found out about prezi.com, and that's a great presentation tool, too!

Box 8.3 **Can You Read the Future?**

Imagine you're a college student ten years from now. Will all the reading and studying you're doing now be different then? Although no one has a crystal ball, experts are already busy describing today's students: "Generation C" which stands for **c**onnected, **c**ommunicating, **c**ontent-centric, **c**omputerized, **c**ommunity-oriented, and always **c**licking. Here's what the prognosticators are saying about students and reading, now and in the future.[32]

Since everyone will be connected virtually all the time, reading will become a more *social* activity. Readers will be able to see additional "layers" of information: comments written by others (alongside what they're reading), the results of debates and polls on whatever they're reading about, extra facts that verify the reliability of the sources, ongoing discussions in the popular media from various perspectives, and others' recommended booklists. They'll be able to touch the screen to drag a book recommendation to a contact's profile or even contribute themselves by performing certain on-screen actions, unlocking secret chapters, and adding their own content.[33]

In the future, college students' lives will be organized around PDDs (primary digital devices) that will keep them connected at home, in transit, and at school. They'll be able to read textbooks, attend lectures, do research, take exams, pay bills, shop online, watch videos, listen to music, and communicate with friends instantly, 24/7, from one portable device. Much of this you do now, but when it comes to academic success, FOCUSING will be just as important, and just as challenging, if not more so.

> **A sign on the door
> of Opportunity
> reads Push.**
>
> *Unknown*

Now What Do You Think?

insight

action

❶ At the beginning of this chapter, Katie Alexander, a frustrated and disgruntled college student, faced a challenge. Now after reading this chapter, would you respond differently to any of the questions you answered about the "FOCUS Challenge Case"? Knowing what you know now, how would you advise her? Write a paragraph ending to the story, incorporating your best advice.

❷ How would you characterize your reading skills, based on all your years of schooling and feedback you have received from teachers? Are you an above average, average, or below average reader? Why?

❸ Considering how important reading will be to your college success, what can you do to improve? For example, would it be worthwhile to try reading for pleasure to see if you can become better at it? Can you set a timer to give yourself reading goals, or create practice quizzes to assess your comprehension?

❹ Which of the three stages of writing do you find most challenging, personally? Why?

❺ Of the "10 Ways to Oust Speaking Anxiety," which ones work best for you? Why?

Reality Check

On a scale of 1 to 10, answer the following questions now that you've completed the chapter.

 low   1   2   3   4   5   6   7   8   9   10   high

In hindsight, how much did you already know about this subject before reading the chapter?

Can you answer these questions about reading, writing, and presenting more fully now that you've read the chapter?

❶ How many words per minute does the average college student read?

❷ What does SQ6R stand for?

❸ Can you identify one of the seven C's of writing and the seven P's of speaking?

How useful might the information in this chapter be to you? How much do you think this information might affect your success overall? _____

How much energy did you put into reading this chapter? _____

How long did it actually take you to complete this chapter (both the reading and writing tasks)? _____ Hour(s) _____ Minutes

Did you finish reading this chapter? _____

Did you intend to when you started? _____

If you meant to but didn't, what stopped you? _____

Activity Option This is a good opportunity for reflection. Ask students to summarize their responses to the "Reality Check" and send it to you via e-mail. Tell students that they must also include references to both their VARK and MBTI types. Ask them to give at least two examples of when they were aware of how their types either helped or hindered their reading and studying.

Take a minute to compare these answers to your answers from the "Readiness Check" at the beginning of this chapter. What gaps exist between the similar questions? How might these gaps between what you thought before starting the chapter and what you now think after completing the chapter affect how you approach the next chapter in this book?

© Larry Harwood Photography. Property of Cengage Learning

9 Developing Memory, Taking Tests

How this chapter relates to YOU

1. When it comes to memorizing material for tests and taking exams in college, what do you find most challenging, if anything?

Focusing on test material

Developing good memorization strategies

Going completely blank when I see the test

Not showing what I really know on tests

Getting nervous about exams

2. What is most likely to be your response? Circle it.

| I'll be open to learning how to improve my skills. | I'll wait and see if this chapter helps me. | I'll get help from a support center on campus. | Eventually, I'll just figure it out on my own. |

3. What would you have to do to increase your likelihood of success? Will you do it this quarter or semester?

_____

_____

_____

How YOU will relate to this chapter

What are you most interested in learning about? Put check marks by those topics.

☐ How your memory works like a digital camera

☐ How to improve your memory, using 20 different techniques

☐ Why you should change your thinking about tests

☐ What to do before, during, and after a test

☐ What text anxiety is and what to do about it

☐ How to take different kinds of tests differently

☐ How cheating can hurt your chances for success

- How motivated are you to learn more about developing your memory and taking tests in college?
  (5 = high, 1 = low)? ____

- How ready are you to read now? ____
  (If something is in your way, take care of it if you can, zero in and focus.)

- How long do you think it will take you to complete this chapter? If you start and stop, keep track of your overall time.
  ____ Hour(s) ____ Minutes

Rudyanto Wijaya/Photos.com; RuthSoh/Photos.com; © Ross Aaron Everhard/Shutterstock.com; malija/Photos.com; © Bevan Goldswain/Shutterstock.com

Darnell Williams

Quite honestly, Darnell Williams hadn't found high school all that challenging. Playing football his last two years had made it bearable. But at his school, if you showed up and had a pulse, you could pass your courses. There wasn't anything in particular he really wanted to do after high school, but he'd decided to go to the college in his hometown anyway. Maybe something there would appeal to him. So he increased his hours at the chain store where he worked to 40 hours per week to help pay for tuition and enrolled as a full-time student.

But after two weeks, Darnell admitted that he didn't find his classes all that engaging. Although he was strong physically from working out for football, he knew he was out of shape academically. In high school, he never cracked a book or did any homework, but just how well would that work here? Now he wished he'd buckled down more in high school instead of blowing it off.

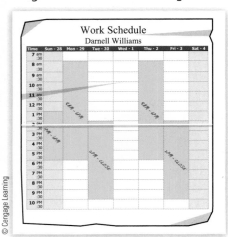

What Darnell really liked to do could be summarized in three words: sports, movies, and photography. Armed with a couple of burgers, fries, and a shake, he spent most weekends watching movies half the night; cheering on his favorite football teams; or uploading his pictures to Instagram, Twitter, and Facebook. He now had many friends and followers,

but truthfully he spent far too much time online.

Since Darnell had no idea which college classes to take, he figured he'd just get some basic requirements out of the way during his first term: Introduction to Physics, Introduction to Psychology, Public Speaking, and English Composition. *Might as well start at square one,* he thought. But after his first few classes, Darnell had already decided that college might not be for him. His writing instructor assigned weekly papers, and his public speaking instructor required outlines for every speech.

By mid-semester, Darnell was really starting to stress out, especially about his two hardest classes. His psychology professor blasted through several chapters of the textbook every week, and his physics professor acted as if the entire class was made up of

budding scientists. *Not quite,* Darnell privately objected. He had no idea college consisted of such challenging coursework, and he was clueless about how to memorize all the information he needed to know for midterms. The psychology exam would cover the first twelve chapters of the book, and he knew his entire final grade in that class would be based on a midterm exam and a final exam, each worth 50 percent. Twelve chapters—at once? His Introduction to Psychology textbook had a twenty-five-page glossary at the end of the book.

CINEMA
Good Only Date Sold
ADMIT ONE
04810 7

Twenty-five pages of new terms to memorize! Impossible!

The physics midterm would require him to have memorized all kinds of mathematical formulas. The syllabus said: "The laws of nature can often be stated in words or written as a mathematical formula. In this course, you will learn to use mathematics and the rules of algebra to make predictions.... Students

sometimes try to memorize the formula as just symbols and don't understand the meaning of the symbols."[1] *No kidding,* Darnell thought, cynically. He saw the words and symbols on the page of his physics book, but what did they mean?

$$X = \frac{1}{2}\, at^2 + vt + x$$
X = distance traveled,
a = acceleration,
t = time,
v = starting velocity,
x = starting position
if X is what?

When it came time to study for his two midterm exams, Darnell stared at his open textbooks for a while, trying to memorize complicated formulas or psych terms that made no sense to him. He'd think he had a handle on a term, and then the next thing he knew, it had flown out of his head. *How does anyone memorize all this stuff?* Darnell wondered. *Isn't there a class that teaches you how to memorize, since that's what college is all about?* Darnell could sense his anxiety level starting to rise. He even started to break out in a cold

sweat. Was pulling an all-nighter the solution? He could stay up all night when he was on a movie marathon jag, but it was hard to focus on physics when he was this tired. Watching a movie when you're tired and studying physics when you're tired are two different things. So he just gave up. Besides, posting his photos was much more fun.

Glossary

A

A-B-A design Experimental design in which participants first experience the baseline condition (A), then experience the experimental treatment (B), and then return to the baseline (A).

Abnormal psychology The area of psychological investigation concerned with understanding the nature of individual pathologies of mind, mood, and behavior.

Acquisition The stage in a classical conditioning experiment during which the conditioned response is first elicited by the conditioned stimulus.

Acute stress A transient state of arousal with typically clear onset and offset patterns.

Addiction A condition in which the body requires a drug in order to function without physical and psychological reactions to its absence; often the outcome of tolerance and dependence.

Aggression Behaviors that cause psychological or physical harm to another individual.

Agoraphobia An extreme fear of being in public places or open spaces from which escape may be difficult or embarrassing.

Altruism Prosocial behaviors a person carries out without considering his or her own safety or interests.

Alzheimer's disease A chronic organic brain syndrome characterized by gradual loss of memory, decline in intellectual ability, and deterioration of personality.

Ambiguity A perceptual object that may have more than "one interpretation".

Amnesia A failure of memory caused by physical injury, disease, drug use, or psychological trauma.

Amygdala The part of the limbic system that controls emotion, aggression, and the formation of emotional memory.

Analytic psychology A branch of psychology that views the person as a constellation of compensatory internal forces in a dynamic balance.

Anticipatory coping Efforts made in advance of a potentially stressful event to overcome, reduce, or tolerate the imbalance between perceived demands and available resources.

Anxiety An intense emotional response caused by the preconscious recognition that a repressed conflict is about to emerge into consciousness.

Archetype A universal, inherited, primitive, and symbolic representation of a particular experience or object.

Assimilation According to Piaget, the process whereby new cognitive elements are fitted in with old elements or modified to fit more easily; this process works in tandem with accommodation.

Attachment Emotional relationship between a child and the "regular caregiver".

Attention A state of focused awareness on a subset of the available perceptual information.

Attitude The learned, relatively stable tendency to respond to people, concepts, and events in an evaluative way.

Attribution theory A social-cognitive approach to describing the ways the social perceiver uses information to generate causal explanations.

Automatic processes Processes that do not require attention; they can often be performed along with other tasks without interference.

Axon The extended fiber of a neuron through which nerve impulses travel from the soma to the terminal buttons.

B

Basic level The level of categorization that can be retrieved from memory most quickly and used most efficiently.

Basilar membrane A membrane in the cochlea that, when set into motion, stimulates hair cells that produce the neural effects of auditory stimulation.

Behavior The actions by which an organism adjusts to its environment.

Behavior analysis The area of psychology that focuses on the environmental determinants of learning and behavior.

EAST HIGH SCHOOL
OFFICIAL TRANSCRIPT

STUDENT INFORMATION

FULL NAME: Darnell Williams
PARENTS/GUARDIAN: Michael and Joan Williams

ACADEMIC RECORD

SCHOOL YEAR: 2009–2010	GRADE LEVEL: 9th		SCHOOL YEAR: 2011–2012	GRADE LEVEL: 10th	
Course Title	Credit Earned	Final Grade	Course Title	Credit Earned	Final Grade
English I	1.0	B	English II	1.0	B
Mathematics I	1.0	C	Mathematics II	1.0	B
Biology w/lab	1.0	C	Chemistry w/lab	1.0	C
Geography	1.0	B	Computer Lab	1.0	A

❶ Why is Darnell having problems remembering course content in his classes? List five reasons you identify from the case study.

❷ Is Darnell overreacting? Is his situation common to first-year students? To you? Why or why not?

❸ Identify three memory techniques that Darnell should use to help him memorize all the formulas and terms he needs to know.

❹ Some college students have test anxiety. Does Darnell? How would you know?

VARK It!

Complete the recommended activity for your preferred VARK learning modality. If you are multimodal, select more than one activity. Your instructor may ask you to (a) give an oral report on your results in class, (b) send your results to him or her via e-mail, or (c) post them online.

Visual: Create a mind map of the twenty ways to master your memory presented in this chapter. As you read, think about which ones you've used and which ones would work best if you were trying to memorize the twenty ways.

Aural: As you read, create an auditory mnemonic device to help you remember the five major ways to master your memory. Announce it during an in-class discussion. (It may help other students!)

Read/Write: Which one of the suggestions for before, during, and after a test do you find most useful, potentially? Close the book and summarize it in a tweet or text to a classmate or your instructor. Then check to see how well you summarized the point you were trying to make.

Kinesthetic: As you read, think of real examples of times when you were disappointed in your test results and a time you were pleasantly surprised by how well you did. What were the differences in how you prepared? Bring these examples up in a class discussion.

Memory: The *Long* and *Short* of It

Challenge: List something you memorized as a child: perhaps a poem, a song, or lines from a school play. Why do you remember this passage verbatim after all these years?

Reaction:

_____

_____

_____

Activity Option Students should take a few minutes to share their responses to "What Do *You* Think" questions. Ask students to work in small groups and assign one or two questions to each group, then have them report to the class.

Teaching with Technology Send your students to Luminosity.com for personalized exercises in memory training.

Your grandparents used to dance to a popular song called "Memories Are Made of This." Of what, exactly? What are your earliest memories and how old were you? Most of us have "childhood amnesia," as Sigmund Freud called it, until we're three and a half or so. You may remember playing in the sand on the beach during a family vacation, dressing up to attend your cousin's wedding, or riding on an airplane for the first time. Before that age, you may not remember things because you weren't paying attention, because you didn't have the language skills to encode the memories, or because you hadn't yet formed the web of interconnections in your brain that you have now.[2]

Whenever it was that those first memories became available to you, and no matter what they are, think about how chock full your memory is now with both significant and seemingly insignificant memories, going all the way back to that poem your teacher asked you to memorize in fourth grade, the one you still remember ten or more years later, oddly enough. Through the years, your memories will continue to accumulate, and interestingly, you'll never run out of room! It's a good thing, too. Imagine what life without memory would be like. We'd have the same conversations with the same people over and over again, and we'd need to relearn how to drive each time we got behind the wheel of a car. Fortunately, our memories do

Teachable Moment As you begin this chapter, get a feel for the number of students in the class who want to improve their ability to memorize information for exams. Most likely you will find just about everybody is interested. Have the class commit to each other that as a group, by the end of the chapter, they all will be better at knowing how to develop their memories. However, make sure you stress that memorization without understanding is short-lived and pointless. It is much easier to master what they comprehend.

Exercise 9.1	Subjective Memory Test

How would you rate your memory overall?

	Excellent		Good		Poor
	1	2	3	4	5

A. How often do the following general memory tasks present a problem for you?

	Never		Sometimes		Always
1. Names	1	2	3	4	5
2. Where I've put things	1	2	3	4	5
3. Phone numbers I've just checked	1	2	3	4	5
4. Words	1	2	3	4	5
5. Knowing whether I've already told someone something	1	2	3	4	5
6. Forgetting things people tell me	1	2	3	4	5
7. Faces	1	2	3	4	5
8. Directions	1	2	3	4	5
9. Forgetting what I started to do	1	2	3	4	5
10. Forgetting what I was saying	1	2	3	4	5
11. Remembering what I've done (lock the door, etc.)	1	2	3	4	5

I don't remember phone numbers at all anymore thanks to cell phones.

B. How often do the following academic memory tasks present a problem for you?

	Never		Sometimes		Always
12. What I've just been reading	1	2	3	4	5
13. What I read an hour ago	1	2	3	4	5
14. What I read last week	1	2	3	4	5
15. Assignment/exam due dates	1	2	3	4	5
16. Appointments with instructors	1	2	3	4	5
17. Assignment details	1	2	3	4	5
18. Factual information for exams	1	2	3	4	5
19. Theoretical information for exams	1	2	3	4	5
20. Information from readings for exams	1	2	3	4	5
21. Information from in-class lectures for exams	1	2	3	4	5
22. Including everything I should study for exams	1	2	3	4	5

My score's definitely worse in Part B—I'm a kinesthetic learner. Part A #2 is a problem for me tho.

> ❝ The existence of forgetting has never been proved: We only know that some things don't come to mind when we want them. ❞
>
> *Friedrich Nietzsche, German philosopher (1844–1900)*

Activity Option Exercise 7.1 is a wonderful opportunity to get students in groups to disclose their different responses to Parts A and Part B. In small groups, have them determine two to three reasons why they did better on one part (most likely it will be Part A). Have students stay in groups to look at Part B and decide which top three things they have trouble with. You can teach this chapter with the class working in teams to make sure that all students learn effective strategies for developing their memories and using these strategies when they take tests.

Teaching with Technology For more information on human memory, visit "How Stuff Works" on human memory. This website contains more information on how memories are encoded, retrieved, and sometimes lost. The site also includes a short video which describes aspects of human memory that students might find interesting.

an amazing job of streamlining life for us. But how much do we really understand about how our memories work—and why they sometimes don't?

These informal assessments may help you understand your own perception of how well your memory works. The lower your score on each portion, the better you perceive your memory to be. Do your scores for Part A and Part B differ? The general tasks in Part A are presented in the order of concern reported by older adults cited in one study (with the top items perceived as most problematic).[3] Are your priorities similar? Did your numbers drop as you went down the list?

In one recent study in which college students were asked which aspects of memory they most wanted to improve among general and academic tasks, the top three items were improving schoolwork or study skills, remembering what was read, and remembering specific facts and details.[4] Understandably, the academic aspects of memory were those most personally valued. Is that true for you, too? Are the items in Part B generally higher priorities for you now as a college student?

Most of us may not even realize just how important memory is. We talk about our memories as if they were something we own. We say we have good memories or bad memories, just like we have a crooked smile or a nice one. But no one would ever say, "Hey, that's one nice-looking memory you've got there!" in the same way they'd say, "Wow, you have a really nice smile!" Memory isn't a thing; it's a process. You can't see it or touch it or hold it. Even one specific memory has many different features: You can remember something by what you saw, smelled, heard, or felt. And even within one of these categories, individuals may differ in what they recall. You may be able to hum the movie's theme song, but your friend may remember conversations between the main characters almost word for word.

Don't believe it when someone claims to have a one-size-fits-all, magic formula to help you unlock the secrets of your memory. It isn't that easy. Still, there are techniques that can help you do your best academically. We can only begin to grasp the rich complexities of memory by understanding it as a process. However, it's important to recognize first that mastering memory depends on the answers to several questions like these:[5]

For a more objective assessment of your memory, try this test. Study the following list of words for up to one minute. Then cover them with your hand and see how many you can remember and list them in the right-hand column.

theory   _____

rehearsal   _____

student   _____

bone   _____

frostbite   _____

camera   _____

rose   _____

calculus   _____

lecture   _____

Man! I only got 5 right the first time!

How many words were you able to remember? Which words did you forget? Unfamiliar words? Words that had no meaning in your life? What memory techniques did you use to help you remember? Specific strategies to help you master your memory are worth learning.

1. **Who is learning?** An algebra instructor and a beginning algebra student would approach memorizing the main points of an article on math differently.

2. **What needs to be learned?** How you learn your lines for a play would differ from how you learn to recognize paintings for your art appreciation test.

3. **How will learning be tested?** Learning information to *recall* uses different memory techniques than learning information to *recognize*. Recognition requires that you select from several possibilities; recall requires that you come up with memorized information on your own.

4. **How long must the information be remembered?** Learning your multiplication tables as a child is something that must remain with you throughout your life. You use it on a daily basis to do routine things like figure how much it will cost you to fill up your gas tank.

Teachable Moment This is an opportunity to remind students that mastering memory depends not only on the who, what, how, and how long but also on how they best learn. Ask students how they think their learning styles impact the way they can best memorize something.

Teachable Moment Point out to students the difference between recall and recognition. Explain that recognition is used for true and false and multiple choice questions and that recall is used for short answer, fill in, and essay questions. Knowing which type of memory they will use can help them know how to prepare for the exam.

Teachable Moment Ask students if they are having any trouble memorizing information for tests in other classes. Make a list of the type of information on the board. Ask others to suggest how to learn this type of information. Can you think back to a time when you were confused while studying something and share this with the students?

The Three R's of Remembering: Record, Retain, Retrieve

Challenge: Think of three ways in which using your memory is like taking pictures with a digital camera.

Reaction:

_____

_____

_____

© chris brignell/Alamy

> 66
>
> I have a photographic memory but once in a while I forget to take off the lens cap.
>
> *Milton Berle, comedian (1908–2002)*
>
> 99

Improving your memory is easier if you understand how it works. Memory consists of three parts:

> ➤ Your sensory memory
> ➤ Your working memory (called short-term memory by some psychologists)
> ➤ Your long-term memory

These three parts of the memorization process are connected to these three memory tasks, the "Three R's of Remembering"[6]:

> ➤ Recording
> ➤ Retaining
> ➤ Retrieving

We'll compare the three R's of remembering to the process involved when taking pictures with a digital camera: record, retain, retrieve.

Your Working Memory: Record

To understand the way your memory works, it may be helpful to use a digital camera as a metaphor (Figure 9.1). The first thing you have to do is focus on whatever you want to take a picture of. That's obvious, but it requires that you slow down, clear your mental "deck," and focus. After you've focused your camera on your subject, you're ready to take a picture, right? But with a digital camera, you don't just click and walk away. You actually click and then review the picture on the small viewing screen to decide whether you want to save it or delete it.

Similarly, *recording* sensory impressions involves an evaluation process that takes place in your short-term or *working memory*. Your working memory is

FIGURE 9.1
- - - - - - - - - - - - -
Your Memory as a Digital Camera

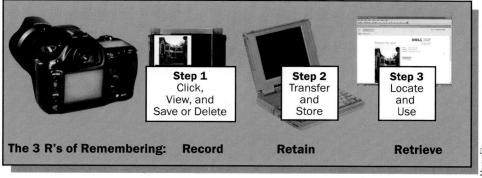

Step 1
Click, View, and Save or Delete

Step 2
Transfer and Store

Step 3
Locate and Use

The 3 R's of Remembering: Record   Retain   Retrieve

MorgueFile

CURIOSITY: Act On Your Memory

Have you ever watched a movie, wondering how *do* actors learn all those lines? Do they have superhuman memory powers? The average movie-goer assumes that actors simply repeat their lines over and over until they learn them. However, actors themselves say that's not all there is to it.[7]

Actually, what actors are most concerned with is convincing you that they're not playing a role. British actor Michael Caine once commented, "You must be able to stand there *not* thinking of that line. You take it off the other actor's face. Otherwise, for your next line, you're not listening and not free to respond naturally, to act spontaneously."[8] But actors' contracts require them to be absolutely precise in conforming to the script, so how do

AbleStock/Index Open/Photos6Go

they do it? Studying how actors learn their parts with precision has confirmed what learning experts know about memory.

Most actors aren't memory experts, but they do use the memory techniques described in this chapter. They manipulate the lines, elaborate on them to themselves, relate the lines to experiences or feelings of their own, or try writing or saying the lines themselves, rather than just reading them. Four of the techniques used by actors may also be useful to you as you try to commit course material to memory. Maybe you've even tried some of these techniques.

Chunking: Actors chunk their material into beats. For example, an actor might divide a half page of dialogue into three beats: to flirt, to sweet-talk, and to convince. In other words, the character would first flirt with the other actor, then sweet-talk him to lower his guard, and then convince him to do something he might not want to do. The results? Three chunks to remember instead of twelve lines of double-spaced text.

Goal Setting: Notice that the chunks are based on goals, a strategy that also works well while you're studying. Actors ask themselves goal-oriented questions such as: "Should I be flirting with him here?" "Am I trying to sweet-talk him?" "Should I be trying to convince him to do something he doesn't really want to do?" In the same way, you can ask yourself, "Am I trying to learn the underlying formula so that I can work other problem sets?" or "Should I be coming up with my own reasons for why the play is considered to be

Shakespeare's best comedy?" When you ask yourself goal-oriented questions while you study, you steer your actions, as actors do, toward learning. Eventually, actors know their lines; they're "off book" in acting jargon. Being off book is where you'll be during an exam, so asking goal-oriented questions while you study is a good idea.

Moving: Going through the motions while rehearsing their lines helps actors memorize them. Imagine the hypothetical actor whose goals were to flirt, to sweet-talk, and to convince, glancing toward the other actor from across the room, moving closer and smiling, and then touching his arm while making the persuasive case. The actor must know the meanings behind the movements to give meaning to the lines. (She could be glancing across the room to give a dirty look instead of to flirt, for example.) The meanings are tied to the movements, which are tied to the lines, and the lines become committed to memory. In one study, actors who were moving when they first spoke their lines had better recall than actors who didn't, even though they weren't moving during the test itself.[9] Likewise, when you study, moving around may help you learn. Even if you're not primarily a kinesthetic learner, pieces of information become tied to motions in ways that help you recall information. Some learning experts believe that mental actions—memory and understanding—are actually grounded in physical actions.[10]

Meaning: "Say what you mean" and "mean what you say" was Lewis Carroll's advice in *Alice's Adventures in Wonderland*. When actors concentrate on truly meaning what they're saying, they learn their lines more easily than they do when they simply try to memorize them.[11] Researchers use the term *active experiencing* to refer to what actors do when they use all their physical, mental, and emotional channels to communicate the meaning of their lines to someone else, real or imagined. As you study course material, do the same thing. Imagine you need to communicate the information to someone you know who needs it. Put emotion into it. Mean it! Use *all* your channels—physical, mental, and emotional—to communicate the meaning of what you're learning. In a sense, when you do this, *you* become an actor, and as a result, you "learn your lines."

> # "
> The true art of memory is the art of attention.
> "

Samuel Johnson, British poet, essayist, and biographer (1709–1784)

© Larry Harwood Photography. Property of Cengage Learning

like a review screen, where you review recently acquired sensory impressions. In fact, your working memory is often involved in the focus process.

The problem with working memory is that the length of time it can hold information is limited. You probably don't remember what you ate for dinner last Monday, do you? You'd have to reconstruct the memory based on other clues. Where was I? What was I doing? Who was I with?

The other problem with working memory is that it has limited capacity. It fills up quickly and then dumps what it doesn't need. If you look up a number in the campus directory, you can usually remember it long enough to walk over to the phone, right? A few minutes after you've dialed, however, the number is gone. Current estimates are that you can keep something in working memory for one to two minutes, giving your brain a chance to do a quick review, selecting what to save and what to delete.[12] Look at these letters and then close your eyes and try to repeat them back in order.

SAJANISMOELIHHEGNR

Can't do it? This task is virtually impossible because the string contains eighteen letters. Researchers believe that working memory can recall only seven pieces of information, plus or minus two.[13] (There's a reason why telephone numbers are prechunked for us.) Chunking these eighteen letters into five units helps considerably. Now look at the letters again and try to recall all eighteen.

SAJA NISM OELI HHEG NR

If we rearrange the letters into recognizable units, it becomes even easier, right?

AN IS MAJOR ENGLISH HE

And if the words are rearranged to make perfect sense, the task becomes simple.

HE IS AN ENGLISH MAJOR

The principle of chunking is also used to move information from your working memory to your long-term memory bank, and it's used in memorization techniques described later in this chapter.

Your Long-Term Memory: Retain and Retrieve

Once your camera's memory card gets full, you probably transfer the photos to your computer, or you print them out and put them in photo albums or picture frames. However, before you do that, you generally review the photos, decide how to arrange them, where to put them, whether to print them, and so forth. In other words, you make the photos memorable by putting them into some kind of order or context.

Just as you must transfer photos from your camera's memory stick to a more permanent location with more storage room, you must transfer information from short-term, or working, memory to long-term memory. You retain the information by transferring it, and this transfer takes place if you review and use information in a way that makes it memorable. It is this review process that we use when we study for a test. You transfer information to long-term memory by putting the information into a context that has meaning for you, linking new information to old information, creating stories or using particular memory techniques, or organizing material so that it makes sense. You can frame material you're learning by putting a mental border around it, just as you put pictures into frames.

> We all have our time machines. Some take us back, they're called memories. Some take us forward, they're called dreams.
>
> *Jeremy Irons, actor*

Your long-term memory is the computer in which you store new knowledge until you need to use it. However, although the memories in long-term memory aren't easily disturbed, they can be challenging to retrieve.[14] Ideally, you'd like your memories to be readily available when you want to retrieve them, just like the pictures or digital images that you have transferred to your computer, posted online, or put in a photo album. You can click on them to view them again, arrange them into a slideshow, put them on Facebook, Instagram, or Snapchat, or send them to your friends as attachments. If you just dump your photos onto your hard drive or print them out and then put them into a box, with no organization or labeling system, how easy will it be to find a specific photo? Difficult, right? Retrieving information from your long-term memory can be equally challenging if you haven't organized your information or created mental labels that will help you retrieve them later. Good recall often depends on having a good storage system. The remainder of this chapter will be about how to *retain* information by transferring it from working memory into long-term memory and how to *retrieve* information when you need to.

Activity Option Present this scenario to your students. Explain to them that they have three hours to learn a chapter. Have them write down what they would do to master the material. Make a list of the approaches on the board. Have students identify which approaches would be active, effective approaches and why. Would there be any that would be just a waste of time?

Teaching with Technology Manipulating information to enhance memorization is where VARK learning styles can make a big difference. You may want to split up your class into work groups based on learning styles, and then have each group brainstorm ways to choose memorization strategies that fit their learning styles. Students can also incorporate technology into their learning groups. For example, kinesthetic learners may want to create a PowerPoint quiz game, and visual learners may want to use drawing software to create a virtual mind map or poster.

Twenty Ways to Master Your Memory

Some students think memorization is old-fashioned. If you need a piece of information, just Google it. But having that perspective can give you a sense of false assurance. Google isn't always available, and there will be information that you actually have to remember on your own in school and throughout your life. What can you do to sharpen your memory for the test taking you'll do in college? Try the following twenty techniques, grouped into five major categories (to help you remember them). As you consider each one, think about what you know about your own learning style. Of course, memorizing means more than simply being able to "regurgitate" back what you've learned. Most exams will supply you with a new problem and ask you to analyze it

> Whenever I think of the past, it brings back so many memories.
>
> *Stephen Wright, comedian*

Totally! What a cool comparison.

I should space out and separate my studying for these two midterms.

This category is much easier for psych than for physics.

OCEAN is a good acronym for the five factor trait theory I need to know for psych.

Since I'm a kinesthetic learner, this is the category I need to use most.

Make it stick[15] **Rehearse and practice.**	**1. Rehearse.** Practice makes better. Repeat or re-read things over and over again. It helped you learn your multiplication tables as a child, but re-reading a chapter over and over, for example, especially when you don't understand parts of it, isn't the best strategy. But rehearsal and repetition can help in some instances. **2. Overlearn.** If you practice something so much that it becomes almost second-nature, then you get to the point where you can do it on "auto pilot." The more you over-practice, the better at it you may become.[16] **3. Space it out.** Instead of studying algebra for six straight hours, break it up. For a week before the exam, study an hour a day instead.[17] **4. Separate it.** If you're taking two social science courses and notice some overlap in the content, study psychology on Mondays and sociology on Wednesdays. Or find another way to distinguish and separate, like making your own compare and contrast chart.[18] **5. Mind the middle.** People tend to remember what they're introduced to *first* and what they heard *last*. Information in the middle can get lost unless you pay particular attention to it.[19]
Make it meaningful **Ask: How does this relate to me?**	**6. Feel.** Emotions are powerful motivators. If reading a novel for your English class makes you cry or laugh or actually feel fear, your memory can light up.[20] But be advised: Generating feelings may take some effort. You may be used to reacting neutrally to what you're learning in school. **7. Connect.** As you study, connect the dots. "Oh, we talked about this in another class this week. I remember." Connecting one thing to something you already know helps you know where to "file" it in your brain. **8. Personalize.** What does what you're trying to learn have to do with you? Remember *Pride and Prejudice*? You may think of it as a 1813 Jane Austin book, which it is, but does any of it remind you of you and your family? You may be surprised at similarities you begin to notice between the Bennet family described in the novel and your own, especially in terms of human relationships.
Make it mnemonic **Use a proven system.**	**9. Spell.** Acronyms work. If someone asks you how much RAM your new computer has, they're talking about <u>R</u>andom <u>A</u>ccess <u>M</u>emory. The word RADAR, which everyone knows, stands for <u>Ra</u>dio <u>D</u>etecting <u>and</u> <u>R</u>anging. Shortcuts like these can help us lock in information. **10. Locate.** Sometimes "placing" things can help us remember. If your classmates always sit in the same seats every week, you may learn their names by connecting them with their locations. **11. Narrate.** World Memory Championship Masterminds remember by creating a story and then connecting parts of the story to specific things they're trying to memorize. Make up a story, for example, about "theory," "rehearsal," "student," etc. to remember the list of words in Exercise 9.2. **12. Peg.** In the Peg System, you learn a list of rhyming words (used as "pegs") to hang items on in your memory.[21] Create mental stories to go along with them. For example, the most common "pegs" are: One—bun six—sticks Two—shoe seven—heaven Three—tree eight—gate Four—door nine—wine Five—hive ten—hen If you're trying to memorize, the first ten American presidents for your American History class, you might imagine George Washington standing in line at a fast food restaurant ordering a cheeseburger on a <u>bun</u>. Then think of John Adams with big, old-fashioned buckles on his <u>shoes</u> and Thomas Jefferson dressed as a lumberjack sawing down a <u>tree</u>, etc. Once you learn the rhyming pegs, you can memorize any kind of list by making up mental images to remember the items. Try it with the words in Exercise 9.2.
Manipulate it **Work with the material.**	**13. Mark it up.** As you read this book (or any other one, for that matter), mark all over it. Write your reactions in the margins, highlight things, circle and underline. Actually putting things on paper tells you what you think and feel, instead of ignoring a vague impression.[22] **14. Mark it down.** Sometimes trying to remember something isn't really all that important at all. In that case, write it down, and then go about your business doing other things until you need it. Save your memory for something more important. **15. Organize.** Another way to manipulate information is by moving it around. Create a chart that clearly defines the three major branches of government for your political science class, for example. Organizing information can help you "own" and hold onto it. **16. Picture.** Draw a mind map or create an elaborate picture that includes all the things on your memorization list. Visual learners do well with this option. **17. Act.** Put motions to your memorizing. Deliver Martin Luther King's "I Have Dream" speech in front of the mirror, as if you were him. Chances are you'll be much more likely to remember the main points if you learn them kinesthetically by putting them into motion. **18. Produce.** Put things into your own words.[23] Redeliver the instructor's lecture. Stop while you're reading and explain aloud what you've just read. When you take ownership of information, it becomes incorporated into your learning. **19. ☐est.** Make a practice test for yourself or a classmate. When you do this, you must ask yourself what's important enough to be included. You may just get a preview of the actual test!

Make it funny **Be silly and creative.**	**20. Mock it.** Think about how easy it is to remember your favorite comedy scenes. Create a David Letterman-like top ten list of why Shakespeare's tragedies are tragic. To remember that Romeo was a Montague and Juliet was a Capulet, and not the other way around, write a silly limerick: *There once was a girl named Cap* *Who fell for a guy and was hap* *But her family and his* *Wouldn't stand for the biz* *So they both ended up playing taps.* Set it to music. Be imaginative. We tend to remember what's bizarre, funny, or even obscene![24]

I've never thought about this, but I have a ton of lines memorized from my favorite funny movies!

FIGURE 9.2

Twenty Ways to Master Your Memory

or apply information you've learned to a new situation. But developing your memory will underlie these tasks, too, so expanding your repertoire of memorization strategies is a major key to doing your best on tests. You can't analyze a new problem, if you don't remember how you solved the one you studied.

> ❝ A memory is anything that happens and does not completely unhappen. ❞
>
> *Edward de Bono, creative thinking expert and author of* Lateral Thinking: Creativity Step by Step

Testing 1, 2, 3 . . . *Show* What You *Know*

All the memorizing you do in college leads to one thing—or so it seems—tests. And often tests feel like nothing more than a big hassle. Are they worth it? Exactly what do they prove?

Let's face it, life would be very different without grades in college, time clocks on the job, or performance reviews throughout your career, wouldn't it? You wouldn't have to show up at work if you didn't feel like it, and you'd get a paycheck anyway. You wouldn't have to do a good job because no one would care. And you wouldn't have to write papers, give presentations, or take tests in college. What a wonderful world that would be—or would it? Realistically, it would probably bring total chaos.

Life's not like that. Results count. Accountability is the bottom line. Achievement is taken seriously. You may be thinking, "I'll never have to take another test once I get out of here," but exams are actually realistic representations of life's requirements. The experience of taking a test is similar to running a critical meeting or giving a high-stakes presentation on the job. You'll need to walk into the room, ready to show what you know, and answer unanticipated questions. Tests are inevitable; so rather than complain about them, perhaps we should change the way we think about them.

Teachable Moment Effective test-taking strategies are critical to college success, and students will be most successful if they see tests as a challenge rather than as something to fear. Remind students that identifying their learning style preferences can help them relieve test anxiety. Are test anxiety workshops available on campus to help them? Don't forget to share your experiences, too, particularly obstacles you've overcome.

Teachable Moment Explain to students that effective test-taking strategies are essential life skills. Many degree programs require specific pretest scores for admittance or posttest scores for the degree. Explain to students that in the workplace, most employers today require applicants to take several types of tests before they are considered for employment.

Good point!

The first step of test taking, of course, is to make sure you're prepared. All of the information in this chapter is worthless if you haven't gone to class or read the textbook or taken good notes during lectures. Miracles, by their very definition, are in very short supply. Nothing can substitute for being conscientious about your work. Think about preparing for an exam as you would for running the 26-mile New York City Marathon. You'd have to work for months to develop the stamina you would need to finish successfully. You wouldn't want to just show up for kicks and wing it. If you did, at the very least, you'd probably pull a muscle. At the very worst, they'd carry you away on a stretcher.

The same principle holds true for exams in college. In order to have the stamina required and avoid the "injury" of not doing well, tests require this same kind of step-by-step, long-term preparation. Using specific test-taking strategies, like the ones discussed in this chapter, improve your test scores, change your attitude about tests, and boost your self-confidence.[25]

Think about taking tests as a three-stage project with a beginning, middle, and end. What do you do *before* the test to get ready? What do you do *during* the test to do your best? What do you do *after* the test to ensure a productive learning experience you can use for future exams?

Before the Test: Prepare Carefully

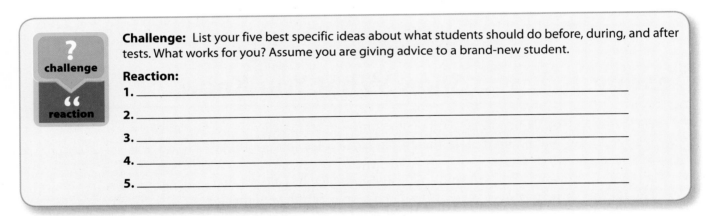

Challenge: List your five best specific ideas about what students should do before, during, and after tests. What works for you? Assume you are giving advice to a brand-new student.

Reaction:

1. _____

2. _____

3. _____

4. _____

5. _____

As you read the upcoming sections about *before, during,* and *after* a test, evaluate how many of these suggestions apply to you. Put a plus sign (+) in front of each item you already do regularly and a check mark (✓) in front of items you could start doing more regularly to improve your test-taking skills.

1. _____ **Begin preparing for an exam on the first day of class.** Nothing can replace consistent, regular study before and after each class. If you work along the way, then when it comes time for the exam, you will be much more ready and much less in need of last-minute heroics. Keep up with the reading, even if there are things you'd rather be doing, and make a study schedule for yourself leading up to each exam.

2. _____ **Identify the days and times of all your exams for the whole term up front.** At the beginning of the term, record the days and

times of all the exams in all your courses—even finals, which will seem very far off—in your planner, cell phone, or online calendar. You'll thank yourself many times over for completing this essential task.

3. _____ **Find out exactly what the test will cover.** There's nothing more terrifying than having a classmate next to you say something like this before the exam begins, "I can't believe this test covers the entire first six chapters," when you thought it only covered the first four chapters. Clarify whether handouts will be included, previous quiz questions—anything you're not sure of. Phone, text, or e-mail other students, or better yet, ask your instructor questions like these: How long will the test be? What material will it cover? Which topics are most important? It's also a good idea to ask about criteria that will be used in grading. Do punctuation and grammar count? Will you be asked to turn in your notes or draft so that the instructor can see your work? Will there be an in-class review? All these questions are usually fair game.

Tatyana McFadden won a victory at the 2010 New York City Marathon.

4. _____ **Understand that specific types of preparation are required for specific types of tests.** Different subjects require different kinds of preparation. What will the test ask you to do: write an essay or work problem sets, for example? And as described in later sections in this chapter, objective and subjective tests should be approached differently, and online tests require that you know the answers to important questions up front. For example, will the test time out? Must you complete the exam once you start, or can you save your answers and come back to finish later? Should you compose essay answers elsewhere and paste them into the online exam so that you don't lose all your work in case of a technology hiccup?

I should have thought about this. Psych tests and physics tests need different kinds of prep.

5. _____ **Begin serious reviewing several days before the test.** The best strategy is paying regular attention to class material, just as you take care of other things you care about, like your car or your dog. After each lecture, work with your notes, revising, organizing, or summarizing them. Then several days before the exam, step up your effort. Divide up the work by days or study blocks. Begin putting your lecture notes and reading notes together. Make flashcards, outlines, charts, summaries, tables, diagrams—whatever works for your learning style and fits the material.

6. _____ **Maximize your memory.** Research indicates that specific techniques, like the ones discussed in this chapter, help transfer information from short-term to long-term memory. Remember to "Make It Stick" (rehearse, overlearn, space it out, separate it, and mind the middle), "Make It Meaningful" (feel, connect, and personalize), "Make It Mnemonic" (spell, locate, link or narrate, and peg), "Manipulate It" (mark it up, mark it down, organize, picture, act, produce, and test), and "Make It Funny" (mock it). Go back to Exercise 9.2 and try using several of the

Activity Option Ask students to briefly write down how they prepare for tests. Then type out the following questions and pass them out. Have students answer them honestly. Are you a last-minute person? Do you always show up a little bit late? Do you cram too many things into a day? Do you prepare ahead of time for anything? Or do you just show up and take your chances in most areas of life? Have students think about their responses and write a short paragraph about how they respond to tasks in general.

Teaching with Technology You can help students prepare for tests by periodically checking their comprehension during class. You can use clickers; however, they are often reserved for larger classes. PollEvery-where.com is a website that allows audience members to send instant feedback to a presenter via text message. Instructors can use this tool to give informal quizzes or pre-tests to check what students already know and posttests to see what they've learned, for example, with immediate results. Additionally, this tool can be used as a way of creating connections to students with high communication apprehension. Students can submit questions or comments to the instructor in real time via text message.

twenty memory techniques to master the list. Do some techniques work better than others for you?

7. _____ **Manage your energy so that you're ready to focus and work quickly.** You've heard it before, but if you're exhausted or feverish, you're not as likely to "show what you know" as you will if you're healthy and rested. "All-nighters" are something students brag about, but they catch up with you, and they're a bad habit to get into. According to one expert, "For every hour of sleep we lose, we drop one IQ point."[26] A series of all-nighters during midterms or final exams can seriously impair your intellectual performance. It's also a good idea to get everything ready the night before so that you remove as much hassle as you can from test day, and arrive early, but not too early. Find a good seat and get situated, but don't allow your anxiety to skyrocket while you're waiting.

8. _____ **Don't give in to a nonproductive, negative attitude.** Emotions are contagious. Stay away from other students who are freaked out or pessimistic about the exam. Think—and feel—for yourself. Make sure your self-coaching is productive ("I've studied this section for an hour; if it's on the exam, I'll nail it."), rather than punishing ("I'm so stupid. Why didn't I keep up with the reading?").

9. _____ **Study with other students.** When you teach something to someone else, you must first learn it thoroughly yourself. Why not study with other students? You can take turns teaching one another, comparing class notes, and making practice exams for each other. For most of us, talking things through helps us figure them out as we go. But don't wait to be invited; take responsibility and start a study group yourself. And if you're concerned that a study group of several students may degenerate into a social club, study with just one other person—find a study buddy and commit to doing the work.

10. _____ **Don't pop pills to stay awake.** You may know students who use Ritalin, Adderall, Vicodin, and OxyContin as study aids. This is a bad idea. When these drugs are used for the wrong reasons, they can help you stay awake for hours and enter a dreamy state. The potential side effects include insomnia, nausea or vomiting, dizziness, palpitations, headaches, tremors, and muscle twitching—even seizures. With such horrible potential health risks staring you in the face, not to mention possible legal sanctions if you obtain these drugs without a prescription, why not make things simple? Just study.[27]

11. _____ **Don't let open-book or take-home tests lull you into a false sense of security.** What could be easier than an open-book test? What could be better than taking a test in the comfort of your own home? Actually, these two types of tests require more preparation than you'd expect. Time is the

I think I do this a lot.

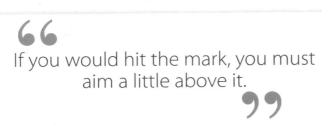

> "If you would hit the mark, you must aim a little above it."

Henry Wadsworth Longfellow, American poet (1807–1882)

Comstock/Jupiter Images

Your TYPE is Showing

How would you answer the following yes or no questions about your test-taking strategies as they may relate to your type?

1. I usually end up changing answers to some questions on exams, and usually lose points in the process. _____ *yes*
2. Essay questions are much harder for me than true-false or multiple-choice questions. _____ *sometimes*
3. If I had a choice, I'd take an exam in a room all by myself so that I could really concentrate. _____ *No, I'd rather be in a group.*
4. I prefer open-ended questions that allow me to include everything I know. _____ *no*
5. Organizing my response to an essay question is difficult for me. I prefer to just start writing and see where the answer goes. _____ *yup*
6. I sometimes read more into a question than is really there. _____ *no*
7. I usually end up making careless mistakes on exams. _____ *yes*
8. I feel most comfortable answering questions that have a specific, concrete clue about the answer. _____ *yes*
9. I take my time on tests, reading and rereading questions. _____ *sometimes*
10. I understand my strengths and weaknesses as a test-taker, and I'm consciously working to improve. _____ *maybe I will now*

Does personality type impact test-taking strategies? If so, how? You'd probably assume that an *introvert* would say yes to item 3, or that a *perceiver* would agree with item 4. Look at your responses and see how they relate to what you know about your type. According to one study, *judgers* are less likely than *perceivers* to change answers, and *introverts* who change their answers—as opposed to *extraverts*—are more likely to gain, rather than lose, points by doing so.[28]

Actually, the MBTI scale that shows the biggest differences on test-taking is the Sensing-iNuition scale. *Sensors* are less likely than *iNtuitives* to trust their hunches when answering text questions. They may read a question over and over, searching for some kind of concrete clue, so much so that they read into the question. They may miss the big picture, answer theoretical questions based on their own practical experience, and lose points by changing answers. People who are *iNtuitives* tend to jump to conclusions when they read test questions. They may fill in a missing word with their mind's eye, or make an inference upon which they base another inference until they are far afield from the answer the question is seeking.[29]

Do these research results apply to you? *I'm an ESFP*

issue here. If you're unfamiliar with the material, flipping through pages of notes or skipping around in the textbook won't help. Create a reference guide or page tabs for yourself so that you can find various topics in your notes or textbook and use your time efficiently.

12. _____ **Remind yourself of your long-term goals.** Why are you going to college? All this hard work is worth something, or you wouldn't be doing it. Keep your sights on the finish line! Enjoy the feeling of accomplishing something now that contributes to your goal-oriented success later.

13. _____ **Don't mess with success.** If you're doing well and earning the grades you deserve, don't discard what is working for you. Honestly assess the efficiency and effectiveness of your current practices, and then decide what ideas from this chapter you should add to your test-taking preparation routine.

Cramming: Does "All or Nothing" Really Work?

Imagine yourself as the actor in the following scenarios. Compare these situations to cramming for tests.

➤ You haven't called your significant other since last year. Suddenly you appear at her door with candy, flowers, concert tickets, and dinner

Teachable Moment Have students take a few moments to write down three long-term goals. Beneath each goal, list several steps they will take to achieve that goal.

Activity Option VARK the test. Let students' learning styles work for them by creating a test that includes all four learning style options. For example, include a section in which students create a diagram from text material (visual), a portion in which questions are given aloud (aural), a traditional true-false, multiple choice, and short-answer section (read/write), and a case study (kinesthetic).

reservations at the most exclusive restaurant in town. You can't understand why she isn't happier to see you.

➤ You don't feed your dog for several months. When you finally bring him
a plate loaded with ten T-bone steaks to make up for your neglect, you
notice he's up and died on you. Oops!

Of course, these situations are ridiculous, aren't they? How could anyone ever
neglect such basic necessities of life? There's an important point to be made
here. Many things in life require continuous tending. If you ignore them for a
time, catching up is next to impossible. Your college courses should be added
to the list.

Believe it or not, some students give themselves permission to follow this all-
or-nothing principle of cramming in their academic work. They sail along without
investing much time or energy in their studies, and then they try to make up for
lost time right before an exam by cramming. The word *cram* provokes a distinct
visual image, and rightly so. Picture yourself packing for a vacation in a warm,

Exercise 9.3 — Test Anxiety Survey

*What is test anxiety? What are the symptoms? Do you have it? Fill out the following informal survey to
determine whether you may have test anxiety. For each of the twelve statements, rate your degree of agreement or disagreement.*

1	2	3	4	5
Disagree	Disagree	Unsure	Agree	Agree
Completely	Somewhat		Somewhat	Completely

1. I cringe when I suddenly realize on the day of an exam that a test is coming up. _____

2. I obsess about the possibility of failing an upcoming exam. _____

3. I often experience disappointment, anger, embarrassment, or some other emotional reaction during an
exam. _____

4. I think that instructors secretly get enjoyment from watching students squirm over exams. _____

5. I experience physical symptoms such as an upset stomach, faintness, hyperventilation, or nausea before an
exam. _____

6. I tend to zone out during exams; my mind goes blank. _____

7. I feel extreme pressure to please others by doing well on exams. _____

8. If I'm honest, I'd have to admit that I really don't know how to study for tests. _____

9. I'd much rather write a paper or give a presentation than take an exam. _____

10. I usually fear that my exam grade will be lower than that of other students. _____

11. After taking an exam, I obsess on my performance, going over and over questions that I think I may have
missed. _____

12. I convince myself that I'm not good at taking exams even though I often do fairly well on them. _____

TOTAL (add up your score) _____

*If your score equals 49–60, you are a likely candidate for test anxiety. For suggestions on how to manage your
anxiety, read on.*

*If you scored between 37 and 48, you have some signs of anxiety and may need help in managing your stress
level.*

*If you scored 36 or below, you most likely experience a normal amount of anxiety and have already devel-
oped coping skills to help you.*

sunny place and hardly being able to close your suitcase because it's crammed full. You can't decide what to bring so you bring everything you can think of.

The same holds for cramming for a test. You try to stuff your brain full of information, including things you won't need. Because you haven't taken the time to keep up with learning as you go, you try to learn everything at the last minute. Cramming is an attempt to overload information into your unreliable working memory. It's only available for a very short time. However, there are other reasons why cramming is a bad idea:

> Your anxiety level will rise quickly.

True for me!

> Your sleep will suffer.

> Your immune system may go haywire.

> You may oversleep and miss the exam altogether.

Despite the warnings here, most students cram at some time or other while taking college courses, and doing so may even give them a temporary high and make them feel like they're suffering for a cause.[30] But generally, slow and steady wins the race.[31]

Test Taking: High Anxiety?

Test anxiety—what is it? And more importantly, does it affect you? Although most people think of test anxiety as a negative, the truth is, it's natural to be anxious before, during, and even after an exam. Most everyone is. In fact, some anxiety is useful. The adrenaline rush that accompanies anxiety can keep you alert and focused.

But for some students, test anxiety takes over and sabotages their efforts. They may say, "I knew it all before the test, but when I saw the questions, everything I knew vanished before my very eyes." These students experience fainting spells or even gastric distress that requires them to make a quick exit from the room. Some of them may be reacting to prior bad experiences with exams. Others may put intense pressure on themselves because they're perfectionists. Clearly, there's evidence from medical science that too much anxiety can work against you. Corticosterone, a hormone released during times of extreme stress, can actually hurt your ability to retrieve information from long-term memory.[32] Regardless of the reason, the first part of the solution is understanding exactly what test anxiety is. It has four different, but related, components in terms of what you think, feel, and do, as well as how your body reacts:[33]

> **cognitive aspects**—nonproductive thoughts that run through your head before, during, and after an exam ("I have to get an A on this test. If I don't, I'll flunk out of school.")

> **emotional aspects**—negative feelings you experience related to the exam (disappointment, frustration, sadness, and so on)

> **behavioral aspects**—observable indications of stress (fidgeting, drumming your fingers on the desk, and so on)

> **physiological aspects**—unhelpful physiological reactions (dry mouth, butterflies in your stomach, your heart pounding in your chest, and so on)

Sensitive Situation Keep in mind that test anxiety or panic attacks are not all that uncommon. If students are willing, have them share their symptoms and how they deal with this anxiety.

Positive thinking will let you do everything better than negative thinking will.

Zig Ziglar, motivational speaker and author

Chase Jarvis/Photodisc/Getty Images

Because you can't expect the tests you take in college to change for your sake—to reduce your anxiety—the possibility for change must come from within *you*. Consider these suggestions as they relate to the four indicators of test anxiety.

Cognitive

> **Understand your testing strengths and challenges, based on your learning style.** Although research indicates that most students prefer multiple-choice tests over essay tests, you have your own strengths and preferences.[34]

> **Don't catastrophize!** Stop yourself from engaging in negative, unproductive self-talk. It's easy to imagine worst-case scenarios: "If I fail this exam, I'll probably fail the exams in all my courses and flunk out of college, and if I don't go to college, I'll probably end up as a homeless person, begging for change on the street." Negative thinking can easily spiral downward, and before you know it, you're thinking about major life catastrophes and the end of the world. Although some exams do have crucial outcomes, it's important to put things in perspective.

Emotional

> **Monitor your moods.** Your emotions change based on many factors; they vary by type, intensity, and timing.[35] If you eat well and get enough sleep before an exam, your moods are more likely to be stable than if you skip meals, give in to sugar highs and lows, and pull all-nighters. An eight-hour sleep debt will cause your mood to take a nosedive.[36]

> **"Park" your problems if you can.** When you go into a store, you leave your car outside in the parking lot and come back to it when you're finished shopping. Think about how that example can relate to taking a test. Park your problems for a while. Focus on your work, and challenge yourself to do your best.

Behavioral

> **Relieve some stress with physical activity.** Expend some of that extra, pent-up energy before the exam. Sprint to class or take a walk to clear your head in the hour before the test begins.

> **"Step out of your life" by spending time outdoors.** Being in the outdoors is liberating. It's easy to forget that when you're spending large amounts of time in classrooms or at work.

Physiological

> **Teach yourself how to relax.** Relaxation training can be used to overcome test anxiety. As simple as it sounds, that may involve learning how to breathe. Watch a new baby sleep, and you'll see instinctive, deep, even breathing in which only the baby's stomach moves up and down. As adults, when we're anxious, we breathe rapidly and shallowly, which doesn't sufficiently oxygenate our brains.

> **Seek help from a professional.** An expert who works with anxiety-ridden college students can diagnose your problem and help you visualize success or take steps to overcome your fears.

Activity Option Divide students into four groups and ask each group to focus on the cognitive, emotional, behavioral, or physiological aspect of test anxiety. Ask the groups to come up with five suggestions on how to deal with this area of anxiety. Share the suggestions with the group.

catastrophize—good word!

Teachable Moment Ask students how the cognitive, emotional, behavioral, and physiological aspects of stress are connected. Which might come first and impact the others?

Activity Option Divide students into groups. Have students make a list of positive self-talk they can refer to when negative, unproductive self-talk sets in. Have students share their lists with the class.

Teachable Moment As a class, have students generate a list of things that they might "park" while studying for or taking a test. For example, they could park why their best friend seems a bit upset with them. They might park the fact that their money is running low and payday is not for a few more days. Parking thoughts that interfere with a task can help students focus.

Reduce Math Anxiety and *Increase* Your Test Scores

Let's zero in on a particular type of test anxiety that plagues many college students. Honestly, most people feel some twinge of anxiety about working a complex set of math problems on an exam. But if your level of anxiety interferes with your test success, you may suffer from math anxiety. One expert estimates that roughly 20 to 25 percent of college students are in that category.[37] And some estimates are that as many as 85 percent of college students in introductory math classes experience some degree of math anxiety.[38]

If you're one of them, admitting the problem is the first step. Next, it's important to understand how math anxiety can work against you during exams so that you can do something about it. The most effective strategies to cope are direct and uncomplicated.[39]

Think back; perhaps you can pinpoint where your fears began. It may have been a teacher or a class or a particular test. Experts believe math anxiety is *learned* and that it's up to you to "unlearn" it.

Why and how does math anxiety affect people? Try this experiment: multiply 86 ×7. To arrive at the answer, you must first multiply 6 × 7, make note of the 2, and carry the 4. Then you must multiply 7 × 8 and add the 4 to arrive at 602. Notice the steps involved in this simple math problem. You have to keep certain numbers in your head while you continue to work through it, which is often the case with math. Your working memory allows you to pull it off.

Working memory is your short-term, temporary-storage, limited-space memory. It's the memory you use to hold certain pieces of information—your brain's scratchpad—keeping them available for you to work with and update.[40] A task like multiplying 639 × 924 would be too much for most people's working memories, but some people have more capacity than others. Here's the kicker: math anxiety actually eats up your working memory.

Why? Managing anxiety takes up working memory space that could be used to solve math problems. When you reduce your anxiety, you have more room to use your working memory productively. Math anxiety also causes people to take longer to do math and to make more mistakes.[41] It's not the case that you use up your working memory because you think and think and think about how to work the problem and get the right answer. Instead, your working memory is hijacked by negative thoughts, causing you to choke.[42]

The solution? Practice for stressful exams under pressure. Set a timer, and tell yourself you must finish before it goes off. Make a game of it: for every question you miss on a practice exam, you must put a quarter in the kitty and pay off your friend, romantic partner, or mom. In other words, practicing in an equally stressful environment (or nearly so) can help during the actual test.[43] Because math anxiety is a learned fear, it can be unlearned.

As you study for math tests, keep these five suggestions in mind.[44]

1. **Get to know your calculator (like it's your best friend).** If your instructor allows you to use a calculator in class, learn its functions inside and out. Even though today's calculator can do amazing things, it won't help you much during an exam if you don't know how to use it. Your graphic calculator can plot graphs, solve several equations at once, and you can even program it to run customized applications. But it can't do those

Activity Option Many college students have math anxiety. Invite a math instructor to class to discuss math anxiety and some ways to deal with it.

Teachable Moment Math anxiety is a learned fear that can be unlearned. Steven Stein and Howard Book tell us that there are three aspects to tolerating stress: plan a course of positive action to limit and contain stress, maintain an optimistic attitude in the face of sudden change and negative experiences, and feel that you have control or at least influence over stress-inducing events.

things on its own; it requires you to run it. So part of your study strategy should be to learn what your calculator can do and become so familiar with it that using it is almost second-nature.

2. **Concentrate on *comprehension, not memorization.*** Memorizing formulas or rules is fine, but it won't help you if you don't know how to apply them. This formula, $a^2 + 2ab + b^2 = (a + b)^2$, is a good thing to know about factoring in algebra, but on a test it wouldn't help you factor $w^2 + 8w + 16$ unless you knew exactly how to apply the formula, step by step. Here's a sample practice problem, showing the steps you should learn to feel comfortable with:

Problem:
Simplify: $5(a - 4) + 3 = 8$

Solution:

<table>
<tr><td>

Step 1: Remove the brackets
$5a - 20 + 3 = 8$

</td><td>

Step 2: Isolate variable a
$5a = 8 - 3 + 20$
$5a = 25$
$a = 25/5$
$a = 5$
Answer: $a = 5$

</td></tr>
</table>

Teaching with Technology Give students a list of helpful web sites that supply practice tests online—they're everywhere. Just search the web for "practice math tests for college students."

3. **Maximize opportunities to practice.** Homework isn't just busywork; it's practice so that you can succeed. Besides homework, you can find countless web sites with practice tests online. Here's an example of a question you might encounter on a test:

Question: There are 2,000 liters of water in a swimming pool. Water is filling the pool at the rate of 100 liters per minute. How much water, in liters, would be in the swimming pool after m minutes?

Answer: The amount of water added to the pool after m minutes will be 100 liters per minute times m, or $100 \times m$. Because we started with 2,000 liters of water in the pool, we add this to the amount of water added to the pool to get the expression $2,000 + (100 \times m)$.

Having experience reformulating problems like this means that you know how to extract the math from the words used to describe the math. If you can translate a word problem into a mathematical expression, then you can easily plug in any value to get an answer, given a specific value for m. But in order to do that, you need to understand what you're doing. "Practice makes perfect" may be hard to actually accomplish, but it's important to keep practicing in small chunks. Most experts recommend that you take math classes that meet more than once a week, just for the regular practice.

4. **Make flash cards.** The simple act of creating the flashcards will help commit the information to your memory. And if no one is available to help you go through the flash cards, go through them yourself, and write down the answers as you go.
$$\frac{a/c}{b/c} = \frac{a}{b}$$

The act of writing this fact on a flashcard reminds you to look for commonalities in the denominator and numerator.

5. **Hit the "redo" button.** Mistakes are invitations to "do it right" the next time. For example, if you get a homework problem wrong, figure out why, rework the problem, write down a sentence about the right way to solve it, and then work a similar problem to prove to yourself that you understand now. Don't just skip it or convince yourself that you'll probably get it right next time. It's called "self-regulated learning," and it works.[45]

During the Test: Focus and Work Hard

During an exam, the heat is on! Do you use these strategies? If not, which ones can you incorporate to improve your performance? Put a plus sign (+) in front of each item you already do regularly and a check mark (✓) in front of items you could start doing more regularly to improve your test-taking skills.

1. _____ **Jot down what you don't want to forget right away.** When you first receive your exam, turn it over and jot down everything you want to make sure you remember—mnemonic devices, charts you've created—assuming, of course, that writing on the test is allowed. Some students treat the exam itself as if it were a sacred document, but marking up your exam is usually allowed. Circle key words and strike through answers you eliminate.

2. _____ **Preview the exam.** Just going through all the questions may help you review terms you know. And you'll notice which questions are easier and which are harder right away. It's also likely that reading sample questions will trigger your memory and help you come up with information you need. After the first few minutes, you may relax a bit, and answers will come to you more easily.

3. _____ **Start with what you know.** Make sure you get credit for answers you know; don't waste time early on struggling with the more difficult questions. This strategy will also boost your confidence and help you relax. Studies show that running up against extremely difficult test questions at the beginning of a test can actually hurt your ability to answer simpler questions later on.[46]

4. _____ **Weigh your answers.** Allocate your time based on the relative weight of the questions. Don't wrestle with one question for ten minutes when it's only worth one point. Go on to one that's worth more.

We all have ability. The difference is how we use it.

Stevie Wonder, singer and composer

5. _____ **Read directions thoroughly.** Misreading or skipping the directions altogether can be a lethal mistake. Remember that your instructor can't read your mind. ("But that's not what I meant!") Slow down and make sure you understand what you're being asked to do.

6. _____ **Read questions carefully.** Sometimes skipping over a word in the sentence (or filling one in where there isn't one) will cause you to jump to a false conclusion. Don't let your eyes (or your brain) play tricks on you!

7. _____ **If the test has a mixed format, complete the multiple-choice questions first.** Often instructors create exams using both *objective* (multiple-choice, true-false) questions and *subjective* questions (fill in the blank, essay). Generally, objective questions ask you to *recognize* answers from several alternatives, and subjective questions ask you to *recall* answers from memory. A multiple-choice question may remind you of something you want to include in an essay. Keep a pad of paper nearby during the exam. Jot down ideas as you answer multiple-choice questions. You'll feel more confident and do a better job if you keep a running list of ideas that occur to you as you go.

8. _____ **Explain your answer to a confusing question in the margin of your test.** You may point out a problem your instructor wasn't aware of or get partial credit.

9. _____ **Change your answers if you're convinced you're wrong.** Despite advice you've probably always received from teachers and classmates alike, changing answers when you're sure you've made a mistake is usually a good idea, not a bad one. In one study, less than 10 percent of students made changes that decreased their scores, whereas 74 percent made changes that increased their scores.[47]

10. _____ **Ask your instructor for clarification.** If the exam appears to have a typo or something seems strange, ask your instructor to clarify for you. Of course, if you ask for the definition of a word that is a clue, you probably won't get an answer, but if you have a legitimate question, don't be afraid to ask.

11. _____ **Pay attention to "aha" moments.** Don't let your "aha" moments turn into "oh, no" moments. If you remember something you couldn't think of earlier, go back to that question and finish it right away.

12. _____ **Don't give in to peer pressure.** If, while you're working away, you look around and see that many students are leaving because they're already finished, don't panic. Take as much of the allowed time as you need. Everyone works at a different rate.

13. _____ **Save time for review.** When you're finished, go back over all your answers. Make sure you've circled the right letter or filled in the correct bubble. Be certain you've made all the points you intended to make in your essay. Look at your work critically, as if you were the instructor. Careless errors can be costly!

14. _____ **Be strategic about taking online tests.** Often tests posted online are timed. If you're taking a distance education course or a classroom course with an online test component, watch for e-mail announcements that tests have been posted, and note particular instructions. When

Activity Option Make a test that starts out with "Read the entire test before you begin." Then list fifteen simple questions. Make Question 14 read "After reading this question, just write your name on the paper. Do not answer any other questions." Pass the papers out. Give students about five minutes. Ask students what was the trick to the test. Explain to students that it is vital to read over the entire test before beginning. Instructors expect students to read, understand, and carefully follow directions when taking a test.

Whoa!

will the test expire and disappear? Can you reenter the test site and redo answers before you hit the submit button? Can you take tests together with other students? With online tests, of course, the other recommendations in this chapter for true-false or multiple-choice tests apply as well.

Taking Objective Tests

Many of the exams you'll take in college will be objective, rather than subjective, tests. Let's examine the best strategies for taking objective tests.

True-False: Truly a 50–50 Chance of Getting It Right?

> Exam questions that test your ability to remember are always more challenging than questions that test your ability to recognize the right answer. T or F?

Activity Option Have students review the five strategies for taking true–false tests. Create a true-false test that includes absolutes, qualifiers, and negatives. Ask students to use a highlighter to highlight key words that they can use as clues when answering questions. After students complete the test, share the results.

True-false tests may seem straightforward, but they can be tricky. You assume you have a 50–50 chance of answering correctly. But don't forget, you also have a 50–50 chance of answering incorrectly. Sometimes the wording of the statements makes the *process* of taking true-false tests more challenging than their *content*. Consider these helpful guidelines:

> ➤ **Watch for parts of statements that make the entire statement false.** The statement must be all true to be "true," and a few words may make an otherwise true statement "false." Here's an example:

> Derek Bok, who was president of Harvard University for thirty years, once said, "If you think education is expensive, try ignorance." T or F

The main part of the statement is true; the quotation does belong to Derek Bok. But Bok wasn't president of Harvard for a full thirty years, making the entire statement false.

> ➤ **Assume statements are true until you can prove them false.** Statistically, exams usually contain more true answers than false ones. You have a better than 50 percent chance of being right if you guess "true." But teachers vary; yours may not follow the norm.

> ➤ **Watch for *absolutes*; they often make a statement false.** Words like *always, never,* and *entirely* often make otherwise true statements become false. "You can *always* get an A on an exam if you study for it." Unfortunately, no.

> ➤ **Look for *qualifiers*; they often make a statement true.** On the other hand, words like *sometimes, often,* and

I am easily satisfied with the very best.

Winston Churchill, Prime Minister of England (1874–1965)

Image Source(RF)/Corbis

ordinarily often make statements true. "You can *sometimes* get an A on an exam if you study for it." Fortunately, yes.

> **Remember that negatives can be confusing.** Is this statement true or false? "Students who don't lack motivation are likely to excel." "Don't lack" really means "have," right?

Multiple *Choice* or Multiple *Guess?* Taking the Guesswork Out

e
Nope.

Which of the following statements is (are) true?

a. Richard Greener, who became Harvard's first African American graduate in 1870, later became a lawyer, educator, and distinguished U.S. consul and diplomat.

b. Elizabeth Blackwell, who graduated from Geneva Medical College in New York, was the first woman in the United States to earn a medical degree.

c. Oberlin College was the first U.S. college to admit women and the last to admit African American students on an equal footing with Caucasians.

d. a and b

e. a, b, and c

Are multiple-choice tests difficult for you? Often what's difficult about multiple-choice tests has more to do with the structure of the test than the content. Studying for these tests requires a particular approach, and if you master the approach, you'll find taking multiple-choice tests to be much easier. You can actually think of them as similar to true-false tests. [The correct answer to the question, by the way, is (d).]

> **Think of answers on your own before reading your choices.** You may get hung up on the wording of an answer. Answer it on your own so that you can recognize it, no matter how it's worded. You may want to do this by covering up the alternatives first and then going ahead after you know what you're looking for. Sometimes the alternatives will differ by only one or two words. It's easy to become confused.

> **Line up your test and answer sheet.** This sounds like a simple suggestion, but getting off a line can be very disruptive when you have to erase like crazy and start over!

> **Determine the TPI (time per item).** Divide the number of questions by the allotted time. If there are seventy-five questions to answer in an hour, you know that you'll need to work faster than one question per minute. Remember to save some time for review and revision at the end, too.

> **Don't decide answers based on the law of averages.** If you flip a coin three times, and it comes up "heads," most of us assume it's probably time for "tails" to come up next. Likewise, on exams, if you've answered (d) for three questions in a row, you may think it's time for an (a), (b), or (c). It may not be.

66
Failure is a comma, not a period.
99

Bonnie McElveen-Hunter, Founder and CEO, Pace Communications

> **Use a process of elimination and guess if there's no penalty.** Some instructors subtract points for wrong answers, but if you do guess, guess wisely. And don't skip questions. Always mark something unless you're penalized for doing so. Take a look at this example:

Before you write an answer on an essay test, you should do all but the following:

a. Read all the questions.

b. Begin with the hardest question.

c. Look at what the questions are asking you to do, specifically.

d. Underline key words in the question.

You know that you should do (a). Reading all the questions before you start is a must. You know that option (d) makes sense, and so does (c). But you're not quite sure about option (b). You can eliminate (a), (c), and (d), so (b) must be the right answer based on a process of elimination. As you work, eliminate answers that you know are incorrect by marking through them ~~like this~~.

> **Look for highly similar pairs.** Sometimes two options will differ by a single word or the order of words. Often one of these is the right choice.

> **Look for contradictory answers.** If two statements are complete opposites, one of them is often the right choice.

> **Watch out for tricks intended to separate the prepared from the unprepared!** For example, avoid answers that are true in and of themselves, but not true when attached to the first part of the question being asked. For example, imagine this question option on a multiple-choice exam:

Global warming is considered to be a serious issue among some scientists because:

a. Former President Bill Clinton describes global warming as a greater threat to the world than terrorism.

Sounds right...

While Clinton did say this in a 2006 speech, it is not the reason for scientists' concern, so (a) isn't the correct answer.[48] Two other tips: generally, when numbers are in each alternative, choose numbers in the middle range. Choosing answers that are longer and more descriptive usually pays off, too.

> **Consider each answer as an individual true-false question.** Examine each option carefully, as if you had to decide whether it is true or false, and use that process to decide which answer is correct.

> **Be careful about "all of the above" or "none of the above" options.** Although instructors sometimes make these options the correct ones, it's also possible they resort to these options because making up enough possible answers is challenging.

Knowing is not enough; we must apply. Willing is not enough; we must do.

Johann Wolfgang von Goethe, German writer and scholar (1749–1832)

Answer the following multiple-choice questions. Beneath each question, identify which of the principles of test taking from this chapter you are using to identify the correct answer.

1. "I know of no more encouraging fact than the unquestionable ability of man to elevate his life by conscious endeavor." These words were said by:
   a. Bill Clinton
   b. Abraham Maslow
   c. Ronald Reagan
   d. Henry David Thoreau

Got two out of three right!

2. Which of the following statements about the ACT test is not true?
   a. The ACT includes 215 multiple-choice questions.
   b. ACT results are accepted by virtually all U.S. colleges and universities.
   c. Students may take the ACT test as many times as they like.
   d. None of the above.

3. Which of the following suggestions about preparing for college is (are) true?
   a. Get involved in co-curricular activities in high school.
   b. Always take challenging courses that show your effort and ability.
   c. Involve your family in your decisions and preparation for college.
   d. Find a mentor, a teacher, or a counselor who can give you good advice.
   e. All of the above.

[Answer key: (d), (d), (e)]

> **Watch for terms that have been emphasized.** Look for key terms that appeared in your lecture notes and in chapters of the text. These words may provide links to the correct answer. Remember when taking multiple-choice tests that you are looking for the *best* answer, not simply the *right* one.[49]

Short-Answer, Fill-in-the-Blank, and Matching Tests

Short-answer tests are like essay tests, which we'll discuss shortly, in many ways. You're required to come up with an organized, thoughtful answer on your own. But instead of a long essay, you only need to write a paragraph or two. Is that easier? It may be, but sometimes it's just as hard or harder to say what you need to say in fewer words. Generally, however, the suggestions for essay tests hold.

For fill-in-the-blank tests, first think the statement through. What does it mean? Try inserting different words. Which one sounds best? Which one was used during lectures or appeared in the textbook? If one word looks awkward, try another one. Although it's not a completely reliable hint, look at the number of words, placement of spaces, and length of the space. If you don't know the exact terminology the question is looking for, insert your own words. You may at least earn partial credit.

Matching tests require particular strategies, too. First of all, you must determine whether items should be used only once or if they can be reused. If it's not clear from the test directions, ask for clarification. Match the items you're certain about first and cross them out if once only is the rule. If you mismatch an item early on, all your subsequent choices will be wrong, too.

Taking Subjective Essay Tests

Essay Question: Please discuss the value of brain research in relation to our current knowledge of how learning takes place.

Essay questions are difficult for some students because details are required. Rather than being able to *recognize* the correct answer, you must be able to *recall* it totally from your own memory. Here are some recommendations you should consider:

> **Save enough time for essays.** If the test has a mixed format with different types of questions, it's important to save enough time to write well-thought-through essays. Often objective questions such as multiple-choice or true-false only count a point or two, but essay questions often count into the double digits.

> **Read all the questions before you start.** To sharpen your focus and avoid overlap, give yourself an overview of all the questions before you start writing.

> **Make brief notes.** Somewhere on the exam or on scratch paper, write a brief plan for your responses to essay questions. A few minutes of planning may be time well spent. As you plan your answer, keep basic questions in mind—*who, what, when, where,* and *why*—as an organizing framework.

> **State your thesis up front.** How will you handle this question? What's your plan of attack? Your first paragraph should include your basic argument in a thesis statement.

> **Provide support for your thesis.** Writing an answer to an essay question requires you to make assertions. However, it's not enough that you assert things; you must try to prove that they are true. If your thesis asserts that college students cheat more today than they did when your parents went to college, you must present evidence—statistics, examples, or expert testimony—to demonstrate that what you're asserting is true.

> **Zero in on the verb.** The heart of an essay question is its verb. Take a look at this list and think about how each verb dictates what is required:

> **Analyze**—break into separate parts, and examine or discuss each part

> **Compare**—examine two or more things, and find the similarities and differences (usually you emphasize the similarities)

Sensitive Situation Although some students have trouble with reading, just as many students have trouble with writing. Essay exams require students to be able to think, organize, and communicate thoughtfully and thoroughly. If your campus has a writing center, send students who need help there for coaching on how to construct essay exam answers.

Teachable Moment Anytime you can bring in some real tests and go through the strategies, it will become more meaningful for students. Consider using the test bank provided for this book, and use actual chapter examples.

Contrast—find the differences between two or more things

Critique, criticize, or evaluate—make a judgment, describe the worth of something

Define—provide the meaning (usually requires a short answer)

Describe—give a detailed account, listing characteristics or qualities

Discuss—describe a cause/effect relationship, the significance of something, the pros and cons, or the role played by someone or something

Illustrate—give concrete examples

Interpret—comment on, give examples, provide an explanation for, discuss

Outline—describe the plot, main ideas, or organization of something

Prove—support an argument with evidence from the text or class notes

Relate—show the relationship or connection between two things

State—explain in precise terms

Summarize—give a condensed account of key points, reduce to the essential components

Trace—describe a process or the development of something

This is something I've never even thought about. It's like a hint about how to respond to the question!

Activity Option Create a list of essay questions. Have students highlight the key verb in each question and explain how they would answer the question. They are not asked to answer the questions—just to explain how they would answer them.

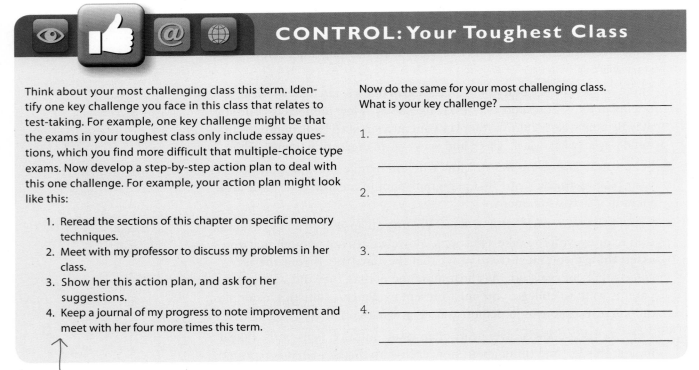

CONTROL: Your Toughest Class

Think about your most challenging class this term. Identify one key challenge you face in this class that relates to test-taking. For example, one key challenge might be that the exams in your toughest class only include essay questions, which you find more difficult that multiple-choice type exams. Now develop a step-by-step action plan to deal with this one challenge. For example, your action plan might look like this:

1. Reread the sections of this chapter on specific memory techniques.
2. Meet with my professor to discuss my problems in her class.
3. Show her this action plan, and ask for her suggestions.
4. Keep a journal of my progress to note improvement and meet with her four more times this term.

Now do the same for your most challenging class. What is your key challenge? _____

1. _____
   _____
2. _____
   _____
3. _____
   _____
4. _____
   _____

This is what the list for my physics class should be, I think.

> **Use terms from the course.** Perhaps more than any other type of exam, an essay test allows you room to truly display your knowledge. Use the opportunity! Reflect new terms you have learned, and tie your answer directly to course content.

> **Rifle your answer, don't shotgun.** Here's an analogy: A shotgun fires many small metal pellets. A rifle fires a single bullet. When writing an essay answer, some students write down everything they know, hoping that something will be correct. You may actually lose points by doing this. It's better to target your answer and be precise.

Good analogy!

> **Generalize if you're unsure of small, exact details.** You can't quite remember, was it 1884 or 1894? The best idea is to write, "Toward the end of the nineteenth century" instead of choosing one of the two and being wrong.

> **Follow all the rules.** When answering an essay question, it's important to be as concise yet thorough as possible. Number your ideas ("There are *three* major . . . "). Avoid slang ("Wordsworth elaborated . . . " not "Wordsworth *jazzed up* the poem."). Refer to researchers or authors or noteworthy people by their last names ("Jung wrote . . . " not "Dr. Carl Jung wrote . . . ").

> **Watch your grammar.** The reason why its important, to do this, is because many student's dont and there answers are marked wrong. They wish they would of done better afterwards. (You get the point.)

> **Write an answer that corresponds to how much the question is worth.** It's important to be concise, but generally, if one essay answer is worth 10 points and another is worth 25 points, your instructor will expect you to write more for the question that's worth more. A more detailed, thorough response is what is called for, but make sure you're adding content, not just padding your answer.

> **Put down what you do know.** If you see a question you didn't predict, don't panic. If you've studied, you know *something* that might help give you partial credit even if you don't know the answer in full.

> **Proofread and make sure your handwriting can be read.** Although most instructors will count the number of points you covered and use specific standards, grading essays requires instructors to use their own judgment. A good essay answer is taken less seriously if it's littered with mistakes or a real mess to read. This is the real world; neatness counts. Anything you can do to create a positive impression may work in your favor.

> **If you run out of time, jot down any remaining points in the time that's left.** You may not get full credit, but partial credit is better than none.

> **Include a summary statement at the end.** Your essay answer should read like a real essay with an introduction, a body, and a conclusion. Don't just stop mid-sentence without wrapping things up.[50]

> ❝ Professor Marlin's (tongue-in-cheek) Rule: If you have an open-book test, you will forget your book. If you have a take-home test, you will forget where you live. ❞
>
> *Anonymous*

Don't Cheat Yourself!

What if you were in one of these situations? How would you respond?

> ➤ Many students in your math class get through the homework by sharing answers on their Facebook pages. The instructor doesn't know, and the course isn't all that interesting anyway.

> ➤ A friend of yours stores all the names and dates she'll need to know for her history exams on her cell phone. With just one click she can call up whatever information she needs. "Try it," she says. "Everyone else does it, and you'll feel cheated if you don't cheat. If you don't do what other students do, you'll graduate with so-so grades, and you'll never be able to compete for the jobs you've always wanted. Besides, getting away with it here just helps prepare you for the business world where things are *really* cutthroat!"

I've heard of people doing this kind of stuff for some of my classes.

> ➤ You hear about an entrepreneurial student who operates an underground paper-writing service. For $20 a page, he will guarantee you the grade you want (based on the grade you already have going in the course so that your paper won't raise the instructor's suspicions), and he "doctors" each sentence so that the source can't be found on the Internet. You have four papers, a presentation, and an exam all due the same week, and one or two papers would only run you around $150 to $200. That's not all that much considering the tips you make as a server. Hmm....

How did you respond to these three scenarios? Are you aware of cheating schemes at your school? Could students you know be the ones these scenarios were written about? Notice that these students have practical-sounding reasons for what they are doing. If you want to cheat, it's not hard, and you can always blame someone else. What's the harm? You get better grades, your teachers think they're doing a good job, your school brags about the fine academic

> 66
> For nothing can seem foul to those that win.
> 99
> *William Shakespeare, British poet and playwright (1564–1616)*

record of its students, and you pat yourself on your back for skillfully managing a very busy, demanding life. Everyone wins, right? Wrong.

According to some studies done fifty years ago, one in five college students admitted to cheating. Today's figures range from 75 to 90 percent or even higher. Here's some straight talk about cheating:[51]

Teachable Moment Many schools have a Code of Conduct or Academic Integrity Policy. If these are available at your college, distribute hard copies and discuss these documents.

1. **Remember that cheating snowballs.** What started as secretly pocketing some kid's toy or glancing at your neighbor's reading test in grade school turns into writing a math formula between your fingers or hiding the names of the constellations under your shirt cuff in middle school. Then these violations as a kid turn into full-fledged, sophisticated rule-breaking as students "download their workload" in high school and knowingly violate their school's Academic Integrity Policy in college. Where does it stop?

2. **Instead of saving time, cheating can take time.** Everyone is busy. Most students are working at jobs for pay in addition to taking classes. How can anyone get everything done that needs to get done? But instead of devising elaborate cheating schemes, which take time to design, why not just use that time to study?

3. **If you cheat now, you'll pay later.** Sooner or later, cheating will catch up with you. You may get past your math instructor this time, and you may even get good grades on others' work you turn in as your own. But someday your boss will ask you to write something, do some research, or use a skill a student is expected to have mastered in college, and you won't know where to start.

4. **If you do get caught, cheating may do you in.** Some students cheat because they know other students have gotten away with it. Cheating for them is a thrill, and not getting caught is like winning or beating the system. Roll the dice and see what happens, they say. But you should know that instructors are in the know these days. Academic hallways are abuzz with faculty talk about cheating. If you do get caught, your academic career may come to an abrupt halt. Take it upon yourself to become totally clear about what constitutes cheating, and follow the rules explicitly.

Teachable Moment Cheating is a serious offense in college. First-year students are often not fully aware of just how serious it is. To some, the Internet is like a giant "library." However, a first-year seminar course is an excellent place to introduce them to the consequences of cheating. If possible, relate some experiences you or your colleagues have had with students who have been caught.

5. **Cheating is just plain wrong.** You may or may not agree with this point, but it deserves some serious consideration. How would you like to be cheated out of money that's owed you or days off that are due you? The Golden Rule may sound old-fashioned, but the fact that it's been around for a long time with roots in a wide range of world cultures tells you something. "Intellectual Property" and "Academic Integrity" may not be as tangible as money you deserve or eight hours of free time, but they are things that are increasingly protected by every college.

cheating is too easy — I'm a better person than that . . .

What are your personal ethical standards? Are you willing to cut corners? Would you cheat to achieve top grades in college? What kind of "devil's bargain" would you be willing to strike?

Some students today believe that technology is a tool, and using technology to avoid work isn't cheating, it's just plain smart. Some experts call it the "technological detachment phenomenon." These students think: schoolwork is just busywork, so if you download homework answers, buy a paper online, or collaborate with other students over the Internet when the assignment calls for your own work, you're just saving valuable time. They think the pervasiveness of technology somehow justifies cheating. But cheating, no matter how you do it, is still cheating—and the person you're cheating most is yourself. One student went to a campus computer lab and happened to find another student's homework saved there. So he changed the name to his own name, and turned the assignment in as his own. But he mistakenly forgot to change the name on one page. Busted.[52]

If you're tempted, remember this. Learning is about *doing,* not figuring out ways *not to do,* and sooner or later, cheating costs you—big time! Don't cheat yourself out of learning what you need to learn in college. Learning is not all about *product*—the exams, papers, grades, and diplomas themselves—it's about *process,* too. The process involves gaining skills that will prepare you for life after college. That's a goal worth working toward.

You can't go through life devising elaborate schemes, hiring someone else to do your work for you, or rationalizing about finding a way to beat the system because you're too busy to do your own work. Cheating in your college classes now just makes it that much easier to risk cheating your employer—and yourself—later on the job. Look at online news stories or watch the evening news to see who's been caught lately. It's a competitive world out there, but more and more companies find that having a good reputation, which comes from being honest, is good business. Integrity starts now: *earn what you learn.*[53]

After the Test: Continue to Learn

After you finish an exam and get your results, you may be thrilled or discouraged. Regardless, exams can be excellent learning experiences if you take these steps. Put a plus sign (+) in front of each item you already do regularly and a check mark (✓) in front of items you could start doing more regularly to improve your test-taking skills.

1. _____ **Analyze your results.** Conduct a thorough analysis of your test results. For example, an analysis like this one might tell you what kinds of questions are most problematic for you.

Type of Question	Points Earned/Right	Points Deducted/Wrong	Total
Multiple-Choice	32	3	35
Fill-in-the-Blank	15	2	17
True-False	20	8	28
Essay	10	10	20
Total	77	23	100

> ❝ *Non scholae sed vitae discrimus.*
> *(We do not learn for school,*
> *but for life.)* ❞
>
> —*Lucius Annaeus Seneca, Roman philosopher and statesman (4 B.C.–A.D. 65)*

Or analyze your results by comparing how many lecture questions there were versus textbook questions to find out where to concentrate your efforts on future tests. Or do an analysis by chapter to tell you where to focus your time when studying for the final exam.

2. _____ **Read your instructor's comments and take them to heart.** After an exam, ask yourself: What was the instructor looking for? Was my writing ability part of the issue? Does the test make more sense now than it did while I was taking it? Are there instructor's comments written on the test that I can learn from? What do the results of this exam teach me about preparing differently, perhaps, for the next test?

3. _____ **Explain your grade to yourself.** Where did you go wrong? Did you misread questions? Run out of time? Organize essay answers poorly? Does the grade reflect how much time you studied? If not, why not? Did test anxiety get the better of you? On the other hand, if you studied hard and your grade reflects it, that's an explanation, too!

4. _____ **Be honest.** It's easy to get caught up in the blame game: "I would have gotten a better grade if the exam had been fairer, if the test had been shorter, if the material hadn't been so difficult, if I'd had more time to study...." Your instructors have heard every excuse in the book: "My dog ate my notes," "A relative died," "A family emergency made it impossible to study," "My hard drive crashed"—you name it. Of course, sometimes crises do overtake events. But rather than pointing fingers elsewhere if you're disappointed with your results, take a close look at what you can do differently next time.

5. _____ **Make a specific plan for the next test.** Most courses have more than one exam. You'll probably have an opportunity to apply what you've learned and do better next time.

6. _____ **Approach your instructor politely if you believe your exam has been mismarked.** Sometimes teachers make mistakes. Sometimes they're interrupted while grading and forget to finish reading an essay answer, or the answer key is wrong, or they make a mistake adding up points. Even if the scoring is correct, it may be a good idea to approach your instructor for help about how to improve your next test score.

7. _____ **Reward yourself for good (study) behavior.** After you've worked hard to prepare and the exam is over, reward yourself—take in a movie, go out with friends, do something to celebrate your hard work.

Deepen Your Learning

The final point this chapter will make about memory and tests is this: in a classic study conducted in the mid-1970s, two Swedish scholars decided to find out the difference between effective and ineffective learners. They gave students this task: read an essay, summarize it, and solve a problem. Then they interviewed the students to find out how they had approached the task.

The interviews revealed two types of learners. One group of students said things like, "I just tried to remember as much as I could" or "I just memorized what I read." Other students said, "I tried to look for the main idea" or "I looked for the point of the article." The professors who conducted the study then characterized the difference between *surface-level processing,* looking at words and numbers alone, and *deep-level processing,* searching beneath the surface for underlying meaning.[54] To become a truly focused learner, you must process information as you go. Dig deep for increased learning, better test results, and greater success!

FIGURE 9.5

Memory Processing: Skipping a Stone versus Deep Sea Diving

I'll remember this image—skipping a stone across the water is much different than deep sea diving!

This chapter will really help me!

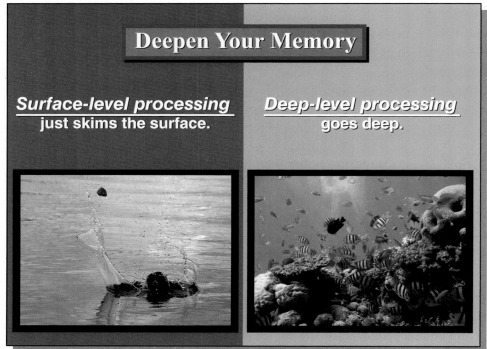

> 66 The way we communicate with others and with ourselves ultimately determines the quality of our lives. 99

Anthony Robbins,
American author and success coach

Imagine this: You're appealing to your professor to change an exam grade: *"Why did you give me a D? Now I'm going to lose my scholarship."* "Open mouth, insert foot." Often during challenging conversations, you know intuitively that your communication choices are crucial. You also know intuitively (by that sinking feeling in the pit of your stomach) when you've said the wrong thing. Unfortunately, by implying that your poor grade is your professor's fault, you've probably "failed the test." You're unlikely to get the results you were seeking. There are ways in which crucial conversations are tests of our communication skills, and it's clear that most of us don't always know how to get the "grade" we want.

In this example, like many others in your life—with teachers, friends, family, bosses, colleagues, romantic partners, you name it—you're smack dab in the middle of a *crucial conversation*. When is a conversation crucial instead of just plain important? Crucial conversations are said to be those with results that could potentially change the quality of your life. It may be true that whether or not you get your grade changed actually *will* affect your scholarship and impact your ability to stay in school. According to experts, crucial conversations have three components: high stakes, strong emotions, and differing opinions—a potentially toxic triangle. Not to add pressure to the discussion, but it's safe to say that they're the most important conversations of our lives.[55]

At times like these, results are on the line, and sometimes our communication skills don't rise to the occasion. We under-react with silence, overreact with a meltdown, or choose a safe, but inappropriate medium (like sending a text message that says, "The wedding is off," for

example). Other times, we somehow get it right. The question is: How do we develop the communication skills we need for these inevitable crucial conversations? When we're at our best, we demonstrate a willingness to speak up when we disagree, deal with issues head-on rather than resorting to the "silent treatment," and dive into dreaded conversations with bravery and resolve, rather than fear. Underneath it all is this advice—"engage brain before opening mouth." Intentionality and planning make a crucial conversation work.[56]

On down the road, "Could the ability to master crucial conversations help your career? Absolutely. Twenty-five years of research with twenty thousand people and hundreds of organizations has taught us that individuals who are the most influential—who can get things done, and at the same time build on relationships—are those who master their crucial conversations…. As it turns out, you don't have to choose between being honest and being effective. You don't have to choose between candor and your career. People who routinely hold crucial conversations and hold them well are able to express controversial and even risky opinions in a way that gets heard."[57]

In your coming career, crucial conversations will be nothing short of crucial. When you're seeking an opportunity, responding to criticism, giving your boss feedback, asking a difficult teammate to cooperate, or requesting help, your career may be on the line. How well you communicate will make all the difference. *I need to improve my communication skills.*

Think Ahead Think about a recent crucial conversation you've had. If you could hit the "redo" button, what would you do or say differently? Can the lesson you just identified be applied to your future career in the workplace? If so, how?

Cast on Careers

© Larry Harwood Photography.
Property of Cengage Learning

FOCUS: Looking back, what crucial conversations did you have as a first-year student?

SERENA: I had some awkward conversations with my roommate, friends, and boyfriends, like most college students. But my biggest problems as a first-year student were the result of crucial conversations I should have had, but didn't. Looking back, I wish I had taken advantage of my professors' offers to help, especially in biology, which I struggled with. It was my first college lecture class, and I wasn't used to learning that way. In my major, biology is an important class, so the stakes were high, my emotions were strong (as in fear), and I argued with myself about whether or not I needed any help. Part of me said, "Reach out—stop struggling!" and part of me said, "Just try harder!" Now that I'm further along in my college career, I have those crucial conversations with professors if I need to!

FOCUS: What are your career plans?

SERENA: I'm going to be a nurse. It's a demanding major, but I think it will be a rewarding career. When I think about helping people battle serious illnesses, or saving the life of a child who's really sick, I know I'm headed toward a career that's right for me.

insight

action

❶ At the beginning of this chapter, Darnell Williams, a frustrated and discouraged college student, faced a challenge. Now after reading this chapter, would you respond differently to any of the questions you answered about the "FOCUS Challenge Case"? Knowing what you know now, how would you advise him? Write a paragraph ending to the story, incorporating your best advice.

❷ Of the Twenty Ways to Master Your Memory you read about in this chapter, which ones do you plan to use in your toughest class this term? Select particular ways that are new to you.

❸ Reflect on your own situation and answer the following questions. As you assessed your own test-taking strategies in this chapter, how many checkmarks did you make for the suggestions on *before*, *during*, and *after* tests, indicating potential areas for improvement? Which of the suggestions from all three sections will you try to focus on in the future? What test-taking problems have you had in the past, and how will this information help you?

What did you LEARN?

Reality Check

Activity Option For the final activity in the chapter, have students design a one-page tip sheet that contains suggestions for taking different types of tests that have personal relevance for them and e-mail it to you. Put all the tip sheets into one document and send it to the entire class.

On a scale of 1 to 10, answer the following questions now that you've completed the chapter.

low   1   2   3   4   5   6   7   8   9   10   high

In hindsight, how much did you already know about this subject before reading the chapter? _____

Can you answer these questions about developing your memory and taking tests more fully now that you've read the chapter?

❶ Can you identify three of the five major categories that help memorization?

❷ Identify three hints to managing your time during tests.

❸ Why are subjective (essay) tests often perceived to be more challenging than objective (true-false, multiple-choice) tests?

How useful might the information in this chapter be to you? How much do you think this information might affect your success overall? _____

How much energy did you put into reading this chapter? _____

How long did it actually take you to complete this chapter (both the reading and writing tasks)? _____ Hour(s) _____ Minutes

Did you finish reading this chapter? _____

Did you intend to when you started? _____

If you meant to but didn't, what stopped you? _____

Take a minute to compare these answers to your answers from the "Readiness Check" at the beginning of this chapter. What gaps exist between the similar questions? How might these gaps between what you thought before starting the chapter and what you now think after completing the chapter affect how you approach the next chapter in this book?

10 Communicating in Groups, Valuing Diversity

How this chapter relates to YOU

1. When it comes to communicating in groups and valuing diversity in college, what do you find most challenging, if anything?

Developing emotional intelligence

Communicating productively in groups

Appreciating the varied aspects of diversity

Developing cultural intelligence

Understanding the impact of globalization

2. What is most likely to be your response? Circle it.

I'll be open to learning how to improve my skills.	I'll see whether this chapter helps me.	I'll pay particular attention to these issues in my classes.	Eventually, I'll just figure it out on my own.

3. What would you have to do to increase your likelihood of success? Will you do it this quarter or semester?

_____

_____

_____

How YOU will relate to this chapter

What are you most interested in learning about? Put check marks by those topics.

☐ Whether your emotional intelligence can be improved

☐ How to improve communication in groups and with people you care about or work with

☐ Why diversity enriches our lives

☐ What cultural intelligence is and why it's important

☐ How globalization changes our world

- How motivated are you to learn more about communicating in groups and valuing diversity in college? (5 = high, 1 = low) ____

- How ready are you to read now? ____ (If something is in your way, take care of it if you can, zero in and focus.)

- How long do you think it will take you to complete this chapter? If you start and stop, keep track of your overall time. ____ Hour(s) ____ Minutes

Serena Jackson

© Larry Harwood Photography. Property of Cengage Learning

As Professor Arnold read the group members' names aloud for the assigned presentations in "Introduction to Mass Media" on Monday, it was all Serena could do to keep her cool. She listened intently: "Group 1: Jessica Andrews," "Jordan Nelson," "Cassie Phillips," and "Serena Jackson." Even as the names were coming out of Professor Arnold's mouth, Serena could see how it would all play out. Jessica would want to run the group, Cassie wouldn't come through on her part, and Jordan would totally blow off the assignment. *Great,* Serena thought. *A random group of students I don't even know very well will earn 35 percent of* my *grade.* It just didn't seem fair.

They had the last fifteen minutes of class to exchange cell phone numbers and e-mail addresses, which everyone did. There was even some excitement in the room. At least the group presentations would break the repetitive cycle of weekly lectures. But the very thought of speaking in front of the class made Serena's heart race, and now with questionable teammates, things were looking grim. She had only earned a B on the first exam, and she desperately needed an A in this class to balance out her likely disappointing calculus grade.

Serena sent off an e-mail to the group on Wednesday, suggesting they meet at the library on Friday morning to decide on a topic and divide up the work. Jessica wrote back immediately, "I work off campus on Friday mornings." Cassie took her time but finally replied on Sunday, "I'm out of town this weekend. Let's wait until next week." Jordan didn't write back at all. "You e-mailed me?" he said, with a puzzled look on his face in class on Monday. "Oh, I never check my e-mail. I only respond to texts." Serena planned to catch everyone's attention to set a new meeting time as class let out, but Cassie wasn't there, and the other two had bolted by the time she zipped up her backpack.

MEDIA NOW
Understanding Media, Culture, and Technology
EIGHTH EDITION

Straubhaar | LaRose | Davenport

© Cengage Learning 2013

© f9photos/ShutterStock.com

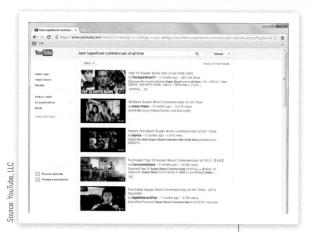

On Tuesday morning, it was Jessica who texted everyone: "Meeting in UC 213 tomorrow at 2. I know that works for three of us." *Three of us?* Serena asked herself. No one had even checked with her. Were they working around her? Her calc class met from 1:15 to 3:30, and she couldn't afford to skip it. She texted back, "I have class then." "No worries," Jessica replied. "We three will get started. Then we can just circulate a PowerPoint, and talk through it for the actual presentation." Serena replied, "I could meet at 4. Can you?" "No, Cassie has a doctor's appointment, and I have a student government meeting." What was the group's topic? Who was doing what? Were they trying to exclude her, or did it just seem that way? Sometimes Serena felt isolated as the only minority student in this class, and at her school, that happened fairly often. Although she was seething inside, the last thing she wanted to do was rock the boat.

Intro to Mass Communication
Professor Karen Arnold

Although she didn't want to bother Professor Arnold, Serena finally decided to alert her to the group's issues. But when she dropped by during office hours, Professor Arnold defended the assignment. "I know group projects can be challenging," she said. "But you'll be working through team issues like these in the workplace in a few years—and you'll be 'graded' on the team's results. I could step in and try to fix things, but you four should work through it yourselves. It's good practice for '*the real world*.'" Although Serena knew Professor Arnold was right in the long run, her wisdom didn't help right now.

At least the group had updated her after they met. Jessica's e-mail read, "We only had time for a half-hour meeting, but we decided our presentation would be about the best Super Bowl commercials of all time. Cassie and I will research the communication and marketing databases, Jordan will find examples of commercials on the Internet, and your job will be doing the PowerPoint slides."

A week before their presentation was due, the group finally managed to agree on a time that everyone could meet—a waste of time, as it turned out. No one was prepared. Jessica spent the meeting time texting her boyfriend. Jordan was on his phone with somebody, and Cassie sat there scarfing down a huge burrito. Somehow they managed to get nothing done in an hour and twenty minutes. The presentation was next Monday, and no one else seemed to be the least bit interested in doing a good job. "Group projects are a pain," Jessica tweeted

after class. "Let's just get through it." What Serena's mother had always told her appeared to be true: "If you want to get something done *right*, do it yourself." But "doing it herself" wasn't an option for Serena's group project, and, most likely, neither was getting an A.

Tweet

Jessica
@twitter

Group projects are a pain. Let's just get through it.

27 seconds ago

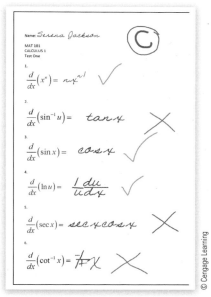

Name: Serena Jackson
MAT 181
CALCULUS 1
Test One

C

1.
$$\frac{d}{dx}(x^n) = nx^{n-1}$$ ✓

2.
$$\frac{d}{dx}(\sin^{-1}u) = \tan x$$ ✗

3.
$$\frac{d}{dx}(\sin x) = \cos x$$ ✓

4.
$$\frac{d}{dx}(\ln u) = \frac{1}{u}\frac{du}{dx}$$ ✓

5.
$$\frac{d}{dx}(\sec x) = \sec x \cos x$$ ✗

6.
$$\frac{d}{dx}(\cot^{-1}x) = \frac{1}{x}$$ ✗

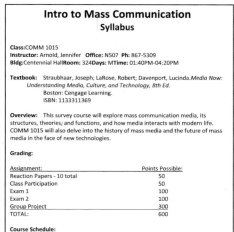

Intro to Mass Communication
Syllabus

Class: COMM 1015
Instructor: Arnold, Jennifer **Office:** N507 **Ph:** 867-5309
Bldg: Centennial Hall **Room:** 324 **Days:** MTime: 01:40PM-04:20PM

Textbook: Straubhaar, Joseph; LaRose, Robert; Davenport, Lucinda. *Media Now: Understanding Media, Culture, and Technology, 8th Ed.*
Boston: Cengage Learning.
ISBN: 1133311369

Overview: This survey course will explore mass communication media, its structures, theories, and functions, and how media interacts with modern life. COMM 1015 will also delve into the history of mass media and the future of mass media in the face of new technologies.

Grading:

Assignment:	Points Possible:
Reaction Papers - 10 total	50
Class Participation	50
Exam 1	100
Exam 2	100
Group Project	300
TOTAL:	600

Course Schedule:

❶ How would you characterize Serena's group project experience? Have you ever been in a similar position? What, if anything, should she be doing differently?

❷ There's a difference between intelligence quotient (IQ) and emotional quotient (EQ). What EQ skills would Serena need in order to improve this situation? Describe them as best you can.

❸ Serena's relationships with her group members are important to her. After all, she may end up in other classes with them in the future. What advice would you give her?

❹ Describe Serena's conflict management style. What clues does the case study provide you?

❺ Identify three things Serena should do to try for a better group experience and grade.

VARK It!

Complete the recommended activity for your preferred VARK learning modality. If you are multimodal, select more than one activity. Your instructor may ask you to (a) give an oral report on your results in class, (b) send your results to him or her via e-mail, or (c) post them online.

Visual: As you read about emotional intelligence in this chapter, think about your own strenths. Make a chart of the five scales of emotional intelligence and select representative artwork or graphics for each scale to help you remember its meaning and importance.

Aural: As you start this chapter, write an e-mail to an "e-mail partner" in class about a good or bad relationship with a friend, roommate, boss, sibling, or classmate, for example, and what you think made it that way. (Your instructor may assign "e-mail partners" or let you choose your own.) While you read the chapter, find things that relate to your partner's story.

Read/Write: Before you start reading this chapter, write a paragraph about a peer relationship gone wrong. After you finish the chapter, look back at your paragraph to see how information from the chapter could have helped to improve the relationship.   *Maybe I'll write about myself . . .*

Kinesthetic: Before reading, interview an international student on your campus about college life on your campus and what would be different at colleges in his or her home country. When you get to class, relate what you found out to your classmates.

© iStockphoto.com/Marcela Barsse; Joanna Goodyear/Dreamstime.com; © iStockphoto.com/Nadezda Firsova; © iStockphoto.com/Pascal Genest

The Heart of College Success

Sensitive Situation Just as in other chapters, take advantage of this "FOCUS Challenge Case" to discuss students' behaviors and attitudes in a safe situation. You are highly likely to have a student who has had a similar experience in your class. It's important not to come across as judging Serena or her groupmates, but to simply approach this case as a common real-life situation.

Hadn't thought of it this way . . .

Every day, in many ways, you make choices about how you react to situations and other people. College is no exception. As a new college student, you're on your own, continually adapting to new situations, adjusting your past relationships with friends and family, and forming new ones rapidly.[1]

College is a time of transition; it can be an emotionally turbulent time that will require you to make some major adjustments in your life.

Here's a fundamental truth you may not have thought about: College isn't just about your head. Yes, academics are the reason you're in college, but your heart plays a critical role in your success, too. From friends to classmates and teachers, how you handle relationships can make or break you academically. Emotional reactions to troubling circumstances have the raw potential to stop you dead in your tracks. Some students, for example, have the *academic* skills

Exercise 10.1 How Would You Respond?

Read these five scenarios and identify your most likely reactions.[6]

Hmm, let me try this ...

1. a

2. b

3. d

4. b

5. b

Whoa! This seems strangely familiar!

1. You peer over a classmate's shoulder and notice she has copied your online response from a class chat and submitted it as her paper in the course, hoping the professor won't notice. What do you do?

   a. Tell the student off to set the record straight, right then and there.

   b. Tell the professor that someone has cheated.

   c. Ask the student where the research for the paper came from.

   d. Forget it. It's not worth the trouble. Cheaters lose in the end.

2. You're riding on a plane that hits a patch of extreme turbulence. What do you do?

   a. Grab hold of the person in the next seat and hold on for dear life.

   b. Close your eyes and wait it out.

   c. Read something or watch the movie to calm yourself until things improve.

   d. Panic and lose your composure.

3. You receive a paper back in your toughest course and decide that your grade is unacceptable. What do you do?

   a. Challenge the professor immediately after class to argue for a better grade.

   b. Question whether or not you're really college material.

   c. Reread the paper to honestly assess its quality and make a plan for improvement.

   d. Deemphasize this course and focus on others in which you are more successful.

4. While kidding around with your friends, you hear one of them tell an offensive, blatantly racial joke. What do you do?

   a. Decide to ignore the problem and thereby avoid being perceived as overly touchy.

   b. Report the behavior to your residence hall advisor or an instructor.

   c. Stop the group's conversation. Make the point that racial jokes can hurt and that it's important to be sensitive to others' reactions.

   d. Tell your joke-telling friend later that racial jokes offend you.

5. You are working on a group project, and one member is a total slacker. What do you do?

   a. Pick up the ball and do that person's work. That's easier than getting the member to come through for the group.

   b. Call or text the person and express your displeasure. You're busy, too, and it's not fair to the rest of the group.

   c. Generate some strategies with the rest of the group and approach the wayward member with the group's suggestions.

   d. Contact the instructor as soon as possible and ask to be placed in a different group.

required for success, but *nonacademic* issues can interfere. There's no doubt about it: How you manage your emotions and respond to stressful situations will impact your college success.

In college and in life, your EQ (emotional quotient), or *emotional intelligence,* can be just as important as your IQ (intelligence quotient). Studies show that first-year students often feel overwhelmed, lonely, homesick, or friendsick. Friendsickness can interfere with your adjustment to college.[2] In one study,

Teachable Moment Students who are most successful in college are those who make both academic progress and connect to you, other students, and the institution. Although students may not see the direct link initially, stress the fact that healthy relationships as well as understanding and appreciating diversity are critical to college success.

freshmen who felt the loneliest and most socially isolated had weaker immune systems than their counterparts who didn't report these feelings.[3] According to a former university administrator at a large, prestigious school, "More students leave college because of disillusionment, discouragement, or reduced motivation than because of lack of ability."[4] *That's* how important emotional intelligence is to college success! According to emotional intelligence expert, Daniel Goleman, "Even the most academically brilliant among us are vulnerable to being undone by unruly emotions."[5]

Perhaps you've found yourself in settings such as those described in Exercise 10.1. You might need more actual details to make the best choice in these five scenarios, but according to some experts, choice (c) is the most emotionally intelligent one in each case. Do you agree? How do *you* make decisions such as these? What constitutes an emotionally intelligent response?

What Is Emotional Intelligence?

> **?** challenge
>
> " reaction
>
> **Challenge:** Have you ever heard the term emotional intelligence? How would you define it?
>
> **Reaction:**
> _____
> _____
> _____

Many experts believe that intelligence is multifaceted. Rather than a narrow definition of intelligence, they believe in Multiple Intelligences: Linguistic, Logical-Mathematical, Spatial, Kinesthetic, Musical, Interpersonal, Intrapersonal, and Naturalistic.[7] Emotional intelligence may well be a combination, at least in part, of *intrapersonal* and *interpersonal* intelligences.

Emotional intelligence is a set of skills that determines how well you cope with the demands and pressures you face every day. How well do you understand yourself, empathize with others, draw on your inner resources, and encourage the same qualities in people you care about? Emotional intelligence involves having people skills, a positive outlook, and the capacity to adapt to change.

Lack of emotional intelligence has the potential to derail you.

Emotional intelligence can propel you through difficult situations. Take the case of the window washer during the September 11, 2001, World Trade Center terrorist attack. Six men—five of whom were executives—were trapped in an elevator after the first tower was hit. The sixth man, Jan Demezur, was a window washer who showed the others that the end of his squeegee could be used to pry open the elevator door. When the group finally forced the door open only to find the number 50 painted on the wall of the elevator shaft, they realized that their express elevator didn't stop at floor 50. There was no way out. Demezur began using the

> " Our emotions are the driving powers of our lives. "
>
> *Earl Riney, American clergyman (1885–1955)*

sharp edge of his squeegee to poke a hole in the wall. The six men took turns, scratching through three layers of drywall to safety. Under extreme pressure and the threat of imminent death, the window washer demonstrated ingenuity, confidence, optimism, teamwork, leadership, and emotional intelligence.[8]

In that elevator, the most effective individual wasn't the one who earned the most money, dressed the best, or had the highest status. It was the person who could rally others to extraordinary effort—the person who could connect with other people.

Research describes the powerful effects of emotional intelligence. For example, in a forty-year study of 450 boys who grew up in Somerville, Massachusetts, two-thirds came from poor families and one-third had below average IQs. Later in life, however, intelligence as traditionally defined had little to do with their success. What was more important was how well they handled frustration, controlled their emotions, and got along with others.[9] In another study looking back over the careers of scientists now in their seventies, social and emotional abilities were four times as important as IQ in determining professional success.[10] Of course, there's no doubt that IQ is important. You must be smart to become a scientist, or any type of professional, for that matter. But assuming you're qualified and prepared, how your career unfolds and how successful you actually are may have more to do with your EQ than it does your IQ.[11]

Research demonstrates that your emotions and your thought processes are closely connected.[12] There's also evidence that being in a happy mood can help you generate more creative solutions to problems.[13] The bottom line? New research links emotional intelligence to college success, and learning about the impact of EI in the first year of college helps students stay in school.[14]

As you read about the five scales of emotional intelligence, begin assessing your own competence in these areas. We'll discuss how to gain a better understanding of your actual capabilities later in this chapter. As each scale is introduced, ask yourself whether you agree or disagree with the sample statement presented as it pertains to you.[15]

Intrapersonal Skills (Self-Awareness)

"It's hard for me to understand the way I feel." Agree or disagree?

To what extent are you in tune with your emotions? Do you fully realize when you're anxious, depressed, or elated? Or do you just generally feel up or down? Are you aware of layers of emotions? Sometimes we show *anger*, for instance, when what we really feel is *fear*. (For example, you might scream at your brother in anger when you're actually really afraid he'll embarrass you in front of your friends.) Are you emotionally self-reliant, rather than emotionally dependent on others? Do you realize that no one else can truly make you happy, that you are responsible for creating your own emotional states? Do you set goals that relate to things *you* value and work toward achieving them? How well do you understand yourself and what makes you tick?

Teachable Moment The ability to listen to yourself and understand how you are feeling is an intrapersonal emotional intelligence skill. Developing the habit of getting to the "why" you are feeling the way you do will enhance not only intrapersonal skills but also interpersonal skills used in personal and professional relationships.

Managing your emotions is an inside job.

Doc Childre and Howard Martin, performance experts

I'm sensitive to the feelings of others, but sometimes I don't pay enough attention to my own . . .

Look up these words!

Interpersonal Skills (Relating to Others)

"I'm sensitive to the feelings of others." Agree or disagree?

Are you aware of others' emotions and needs? Do you communicate with sensitivity and work to build positive relationships? Are you a good listener? Are you comfortable with others, and do you have confidence in your relationships with them?

Stress Management Skills

"I feel that it's hard for me to control my anxiety." Agree or disagree?

Can you productively manage your emotions so that they work *for* you and not *against* you? Can you control destructive emotions? Can you work well under pressure? Are you in control, even when things get tense and difficult?

Adaptability Skills

"When trying to solve a problem, I look at each possibility and then decide on the best way." Agree or disagree?

Are you flexible? Do you cope well when things *don't* go according to plan? Can you switch to a new plan when you need to? Do you manage change effectively? Can you anticipate problems and solve them as they come up? Do you rely on yourself and adapt well?

General Mood

"I generally expect things will turn out all right, despite setbacks from time to time." Agree or disagree?

Are you optimistic and positive most of the time? Do you feel happy and content with yourself, others, and your life in general? Are you energetic and self-motivated? Do people tell you you're pleasant to be around?

From EQ-i: HEd version. Reprinted by permission.

Emotional intelligence and its effects reverberate throughout our lives. For example, researchers study related concepts: "hardiness," "resilience," and "learned optimism."[16] Some people are more resistant to stress and illness. Hardy, resilient, optimistic people are confident, committed to what they're doing, feel greater control over their lives, and see hurdles as challenges. Emotional intelligence is part of the reason why.

Emotional intelligence and its five scales are important in all aspects of life, including your future career.[17] When *Harvard Business Review* first published an article on the topic in 1998, it attracted more readers than any article in the journal's previous forty years. When the CEO of Johnson & Johnson read it, he ordered copies for the company's 400 top executives worldwide.[18]

> 66
> If you want to build a ship, don't drum up people together to collect wood and don't assign them tasks and work, but rather teach them to long for the endless immensity of the sea. 99

Antoine de Saint-Exupery
French writer, poet,
and aviator (1900–1944)

Why? Emotional intelligence is a characteristic of true leaders. Immediately after the first shock of the September 11, 2001, tragedy, the world tuned in to a press conference with New York's Mayor Rudy Giuliani. He was asked to estimate the number of people who had lost their lives in the World Trade Center collapse that day, and his reply was this: "We don't know the exact number yet, but whatever the number, it will be more than we can bear." In that one sentence, Giuliani demonstrated one of the most important principles of true leadership. Leaders inspire by touching the feelings of others.[19]

Teachable Moment Ask students to describe the characteristics of the best leaders they've known. Help them make connections between these characteristics and general scales of emotional intelligence, intrapersonal and interpersonal skills, stress management, adaptability, and general mood.

Can Emotional Intelligence Be Improved?

Everyone wants well-developed emotional intelligence, but how do you get it? Can EI be learned? While researchers admit that genes definitely play a role, most experts believe that emotional intelligence can be increased. One of the most convincing pieces of evidence is from a study that followed a cohort of students over seven years. Students assessed their emotional intelligence, selected particular competencies to strengthen, and then each created an individual plan to develop them. Seven years later, their competencies remained high.[20]

Recent physiological research, indicating that the human brain's hippocampus is more "plastic" than originally thought, also endorses the notion that EI can be improved. New "mindfulness" training to help people regulate their own emotions actually alters parts of the brain. A group of scientists who received mindfulness training an hour a week for eight weeks had measurable changes in their brains and reported more positive emotions than their non-trained counterparts at the end of the eight weeks, and again four months later.[21] Researchers continue to study emotional intelligence to fully grasp its implications in many different areas of life, but its central role in college success is increasingly understood. So what can you do to improve your EI skills?[22]

Seek Honest Input from Others

It's hard to be objective about yourself. But it is possible to tap some of that necessary objectivity from those who interact with you regularly. How do they see you? Use other people as coaches to help you see which aspects of your emotional intelligence need strengthening.

Find an EI Mentor

A mentor on the job is someone who's older and more experienced than you are and can help you navigate your way through tough problems and manage your career. Mentors help, and an EI mentor—someone with finely honed EI skills you admire—can provide you with invaluable advice about handling challenging emotional situations.

Complete an Assessment Tool

Other than just feeling generally up or down, is there a way to know more about your own level of emotional intelligence? The oldest and most widely used instrument to measure emotional intelligence is the Emotional Quotient Inventory, the EQ-i, from which the sample statements for the five scales we have been discussing come. It was the first instrument of its kind to be published and the first to be validated by psychologists in the well-respected *Mental Measurement Yearbook* (1999).[23] The results provide you with a self-assessment of your emotional intelligence on each of the five major scales and further subscales.

As a part of the course for which you're using this textbook, you may have an opportunity to complete the EQ-i or an equivalent instrument. (But be careful of fully trusting the results of online "pop" instruments.)

Work with a Counselor to Learn More

Some areas of emotional intelligence may be too challenging to develop on your own. You may need some in-depth, one-on-one counseling to work on areas that need enrichment. Recognize that doing so isn't a stigma. Instead, you are taking advantage of the resources available on your campus and maximizing the potential for growth that can come during your college years.

Be Patient with Yourself

Learning to become more empathetic or more attuned to a friend or family member's emotions in a close relationship aren't skills you can enhance overnight using cookbook techniques. Building emotional skills is a gradual process that involves awakening insights, acting on them, and noting the results over time.

Keep at it: It's safe to say that EI is something all of us can strengthen, if we're willing to work at it. Relationships that are important to us require the best of our emotional intelligence skills. In fact, studies show that the way in which we provide emotional support is strongly related to relationship satisfaction.[24]

Robert Recker/zefa/Corbis

"What's going on in the inside shows on the outside.

Earl Nightingale, success consultant

Teachable Moment If possible, have students take the EQ-i in class and refer back to it throughout the term. Students can look at their results and set goals to work on. It takes a minimum of about fifteen weeks (a semester) to see real changes in emotional intelligence.

Teaching with Technology There are many EI assessments available on the Internet. Although these tests may not be as comprehensive or valid as the EQ-i, which is discussed in *FOCUS*, they may provide students with revealing insights into their emotional intelligence. Try DiscoveryHealth.com and Psychology.About.com for a free EI assessment, but let students know that these instruments are not scientifically valid; they are intended to generate discussion.

Sensitive Situation Accepting honest feedback without becoming defensive isn't easy. However, emphasize that emotional intelligence can be developed with feedback and support.

This is making me think ...

> ❝ When something is missing in your life, it usually turns out to be someone. ❞
>
> *Robert Brault*

Have you ever been accused of taking things personally? Your Mom looks askance at your new, multi-tone hair color or your ever-so-stylish "runway" outfit, or your roommate makes an ambiguous, off-handed comment about something that's dear to your heart. *How dare she?* you think to yourself! When you relay the story to your best friend, she provides a reality check, "Oh, lighten up. You don't have to take it personally."

People count. We care about what they think of us. But what about the often overlooked reverse point of view? They care, too. People prop us up, validate us (or not), and meet our personal needs—and we do the same for them. Even though we know it, we don't always show it. It explains why some very intelligent, highly capable people fail and why misunderstandings are common. It's not so much that people always take things personally; it's that they sometimes forget to *make* things personal.

Take a look at these post-college examples: imagine that your co-worker is just about out the door to pick up a sub for lunch, and you yell out, "Hey, can you get me a six-inch combo with a diet drink?" He looks miffed. *What's the big deal?*, you wonder. *It's just a sandwich; he's always so cranky!* But maybe your regular, last-minute orders are starting to get to him and he resents serving as your "errand boy." Maybe he was hoping you'd stop what you're doing and come along for once, but you're so into your work that the thought never occurs to you. Maybe he's dealing with big challenges outside the office. "Maybe you need to cut him some slack. Give him the benefit of the doubt. 'Be kind,' a common saying goes, 'for everyone you meet is fighting a hard battle.'"[25]

Or consider this scenario: You're on a team with a colleague who's a bear to work with. She may be the hardest worker in the company, have the best ideas, and sport a sales record that no one can touch. But ultimately she fails miserably in your organization and moves to another one … again. She moves from job to job, and she just can't figure out why she's not seen as successful. But to her, the job is all about the work. The people she works with are invisible to her. She doesn't realize that the people are *how* the work gets done. According to one career expert, "There's a simple reason for it: we rarely take the time to pause, breathe, and think about what's working and what's not. There's

just too much to do and no time to reflect." Making things personal is about listening carefully to the layers of communication and remembering that people count. Actually, it's less about time and more about mindset. Appreciate your differences, explore your commonalities, and above all, remember that work, like the rest of life, is about building productive relationships.[26]

Here's a recommendation: At the end of every workday, take five minutes to reflect, not only about the work, but also about your *co-workers*. Ask yourself these three questions:

1. What went well today and what didn't?
2. What lessons from today will help me do a better job tomorrow?
3. Who contributed to my success? Is there someone I should update or thank? If so, do it.[27]

Doing so will not only help you do your best, but it will do the same for others. Remembering to "make it personal" will affect your career more positively than you can possibly imagine now.

Think Ahead Think about a time that you were involved in a college project (a group presentation, for example) when things either did or didn't work well. Which principles you've just read about were (or would have been) important?

This is advice I should remember . . .

Cast on Careers

© Larry Harwood Photography. Property of Cengage Learning

FOCUS: How important are people to you—and how do you show it?

ANNIE: I'm one of those people who collects friends— and not just Facebook ones! I genuinely like people. Everyone tells me that I'm a good friend, and that's part of it. I'm very close to my family, too, and we're in constant communication. It's not uncommon for me to get emails, calls, and texts from various family members all day long.

FOCUS: What are your career plans?

ANNIE: I'm majoring in nursing, so people will be my job! My goal is to be competent and caring. Often in medicine, kindness can boost a patient's spirits even more than medicine can. That's why I'm drawn to the field.

	Yes	No
Are you involved in a group project in the class for which you're using this book or another class this term? If so, which of these ten statements describe your opinions about how groups should operate? Put a checkmark in the "yes" or "no" column for each one.		

1. Groups have emotional intelligence, just like individuals do. _____ _____
2. Teams should discuss the group process up front, before the work begins. _____ _____
3. Teams should always work to reach consensus. _____ _____
4. Teams are generally more productive working face-to-face, as opposed to working online. _____ _____
5. A team is only as strong as its weakest link. _____ _____
6. Having team members all talk at once shows great energy for the project. _____ _____
7. Group conflict should be avoided whenever possible. _____ _____
8. The best teams are the ones in which all the members are friends. _____ _____
9. Teams should only meet when all members can be present. _____ _____
10. Roles for team members should evolve, not be assigned. _____ _____

Now continue reading to find out more about productive teamwork.

Communicating in Groups: Soft Skills Are Hard!

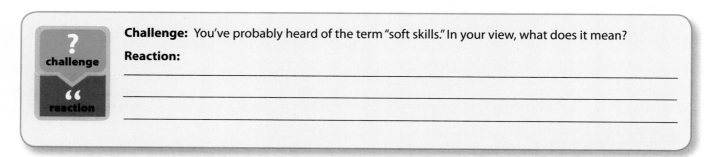

Challenge: You've probably heard of the term "soft skills." In your view, what does it mean?

Reaction:

_____

_____

_____

Emotional intelligence isn't just important for individuals; it plays a role in teamwork. "It unlocks productivity and creativity in a way that nothing else does. Specifically, an effective team must know how to play the EI equivalent of three dimensional chess. It must be mindful of the emotions of its members, its own group emotions or moods, and the emotions of other groups and individuals outside its boundaries."[28] That's a challenge, and in all truthfulness, not all groups reach that level of self- and other awareness.

Think of it this way: A group's IQ isn't the sum total of the IQ of each of its members (Tom = 110 + Katie = 125 + Jillian = 115 + Brent = 130 for a grand total of 480). High group intelligence—or "collaborative intelligence"—brings an entirely new level of rational thinking and creative ideas. In the same way, a group's emotional intelligence is more than just the sum total of the EI of all

Box 10.1   How Well Do *You* "Play with Others"?

When you were a grade schooler, you probably got As, Bs, and Cs on your report card and comments from your teacher about your behavior in school: "John is a good student, but he doesn't play well with others." What does that kind of comment mean, exactly? Was it from whispering too much in class or duking it out with a classmate on the playground? Hopefully, your comments from the teacher were positive. But if you ever did get a negative comment about "playing well with others," you may not have known what your teacher meant for sure, but whatever it was, it didn't play well at home.

As an adult, the ability to "play well with others" translates into what is often referred to as "people skills," a necessity in the professional world. You can be a whiz at numbers as a CPA, have amazing design talent as an architect, or display exacting precision as a top surgeon. But if your people skills aren't honed, your career is likely to self-destruct or at least stall out. That's always been true, but now the importance of people skills has resurfaced with a new slant.

For digital natives, those for whom technology has always been a part of life, new research suggests that "people skills" can be impacted by many years of spending long hours spent in front of a computer. In fact, there is evidence that computers actually rewire our brains. "Research on the brain's response to electronic media is fascinating, and not a little disturbing. On the plus side, it suggests that digital natives have higher baseline activity in the part of the brain governing short-term memory, the sorting of complex information, and the integration of sensations and thoughts—so, in certain respects, computers make you smarter."[29]

But on the down side, computers don't require you to figure out what they're thinking or interpret their nonverbal cues. Less interaction with people and more interaction with computers can lead to lower empathy, a reduced ability to read nonverbal cues, a reluctance to interact socially or maintain eye contact with others, and less evolved overall interpersonal skills. Some researchers also fear that neural networks in the brain for these types of skills may not be developing as they should. Naturally, the more time you spend online, the less time there is available for honest-to-goodness human interaction. These characteristics of digital natives, especially if you are one, may be so subtle that you've never even thought about or even noticed them.

Okay, so all this is interesting, you say, but what does it have to do with me? Potentially, a great deal, if you're a digital native. Here's an example. During the 2008 financial collapse, some bright young workers lost their jobs because they didn't empathize with distraught clients who lost everything. Instead of listening to them, the young employees simply sent e-mails saying, "Sorry, we can't help you." So they were let go and replaced with older employees who were willing to meet face-to-face and listen to clients' personal stories of disastrous financial loss.[30]

Although these characteristics may not apply to every digital native, the most immediate test of your people skills may be during job interviews when you graduate from college. Your people skills will be on the line. Because interviewers know that interpersonal skills like these are crucial to career success, they may keep an eye on your eye contact during the interview or watch for clues about your willingness to interact socially. Interviewers may ask you hypothetical questions about how you'd deal with difficult interpersonal situations and note whether you'd simply gravitate toward sending a simple e-mail to "fix" the situation or suggest a face-to-face meeting to find a solution. When that time comes, you'll want to think through your responses and what they communicate about you.

Awareness is always the first step to getting better at anything. You've left the playground you frequented as a youngster, but "playing well with others" is even more important in the adult world of professional relationships, teamwork, and the productive communication required in today's organizations.

I'm going to dogear this page...

66

At the extreme, we are so enmeshed in our connections that we neglect each other.

99

Sherry Turkle, **Alone Together: Why We Expect More from Technology and Less from Each Other**

its members. It's a new level of productivity that results from uniting sensitive, tactful people who trust one another, believe in their task, capitalize on their strengths, and realize that they need one another to do their best.[31]

Sometimes emotional intelligence is referred to as "soft skills." These skills aren't based in hard science, facts, or numbers. Instead, they involve values, judgment, and sensitivity. As a matter of fact, however, soft skills are hard! It's hard to work with a "difficult" teammate and get good results. It's hard to work under a tyrant of a boss and perform at your best, or rebuild a working relationship after a colleague has "backstabbed" you during a meeting. Anyone can learn new "hard skills," but those who rise to the top of their careers are those with the best soft skills. Interestingly, a survey of Microsoft business leaders rated soft skills as more valuable than academic qualifications![32] Ask anyone who has had a long career: "What are the most difficult issues you have faced over your years on the job?" It's unlikely the answer will have anything to do with the actual job itself ("I just couldn't seem to learn Excel. It totally stumped me!" or "I'll tell you, those cavities in the back molars are really hard to reach!"). Instead, you're likely to hear a story about a coworker who made life difficult until one person or the other eventually moved on. Soft skills are tested day in and day out, so learning more about them now, while you're in college, is excellent preparation for upcoming challenges.

Why Groups in College?

In school, the word "group" is used most commonly, meaning a collection of people who share a purpose. A random assortment of students walking down the hallway of a classroom building on campus isn't defined as a group for our purposes. But students in your history class would qualify as a group because they identify as a group, interact among themselves, and all have the same goal—to succeed in your history class. "Teams," on the other hand, usually exist on the playing field or in the workplace. They have assigned roles (pitcher versus shortstop), have fewer members than groups, and share a distinct purpose—to design the most fuel-efficient car of the future, for example. However, in this chapter, we'll use the terms interchangeably to gain an understanding that will help you engage in group projects for your classes productively.[33]

You may have entered college thinking you would need to write papers, submit homework, take tests, and give presentations—by yourself. True enough. But actually, in many ways, "college is a team sport." In addition to the effort you invest in classes, forming relationships and getting involved in campus groups will play a major role in your success. Besides papers, presentations, and exams, which are typically your individual responsibility, another common course requirement is for professors to assign group projects—with classmates. You may wonder why. Here's one explanation. When you write a paper, you learn about your paper's topic, naturally. But you also learn about writing as a practical skill that you can take with you to graduate school or the workforce. The same thing is true when it comes to group projects. You'll learn about the project's topic. But you'll also learn invaluable skills about working with people, and if you actually make that part of the project a personal goal, you'll leave college with well-developed people skills, which will give you a definite advantage later. As one student in favor of group work said in a recent interview, "It really

My Mom talks about an assistant like this she once had...

enhances learning of the material, and it's also more interesting than individualized learning. You get to practice the things you're learning about. I've also had a lot of employers when I'm interviewing for internships harp on the fact that we do a lot of team-focused things here, and they seem to like that." There's evidence that students working in group settings retain information better.[34]

How important are groups and teams in general? If you're under the knife in the OR, you'd better hope that the medical team functions well together. Or if you're on a transatlantic flight, you'd likely have similar hopes for the crew. And for that matter, it helps if they've worked together before. "The National Transportation Safety Board found that 73% of the incidents in its database occurred on a crew's first day of flying together, before people had the chance to learn through experience how best to operate as a team—and 44% of those took place on a crew's very first flight."[35]

Wow! I didn't know this!

Experience does count, but there's a common misperception that a team of friends works together best; they produce more harmonious results. Actually, however, in a study of symphony orchestras, groups of cranky musicians actually played slightly better than groups of happy ones. Emotions at the end of the concert were more telling of how well the musicians played than emotions beforehand.[36]

Or perhaps you have the perception that all groups are democratic, which can't always be true. ("Okay, let's vote. How many of us think the appendix is above the belly button, and how many of us think it's below?") Sometimes, in some types of groups, someone has to be in charge. A leader may emerge naturally, one may be appointed, or one may be the obvious choice (like the surgeon herself), depending on the situation. Or maybe you've heard that bigger is better when it comes to teams. Actually, that's not quite true, either. Many experts agree that five or seven (no ties when members vote) or six is the magic number for class-based groups, and groups of ten work well in organizational settings; beyond that, groups may lose interest, find it impossible to coordinate schedules for meetings, and form cliques without even realizing it.

Or finally, consider this "truism." Some students think that online groups are impersonal and boring. There's no doubt that the lack of warm bodies can downplay some members' commitment and that it may take more work to build rapport. But virtual groups have some advantages, like overriding conflicting schedules or capitalizing on the convenience of e-tools like storing the work in Dropbox, building a shared Google Doc, or using a Google Hangout to talk together even though some members are commuters and some live in residence halls.

Why Groups at All?

Although groups can certainly have their challenges, it's common knowledge that often they can be more effective than a single contributor. People commonly say things like "the more, the merrier," "two heads are better than one," or "many hands make light work." But besides these remarks we've all heard, think about other specific advantages:

> **Groups have a bigger "knowledge pool" to draw from.** Often, the collective knowledge of the group amounts to more than any one individual knows. If an in-class group is tasked with creating the ideal fuel-efficient car of the future, unless there happens to be an automotive

> Talent wins games, but teamwork and intelligence win championships.
>
> **Michael Jordan, American NBA Basketball Player, widely considered to be the greatest player in the history of the game**

AP Images/Beth A. Keiser

I need to keep these positive factors in mind.

engineer in the mix, it's likely a group can do better with the assignment than any one member can. When the situation calls for it, a team can be a better option than an MVP.

> **Groups give individuals a chance to learn from one another.**
> Chances are that someone in the group knows more about some aspect of the project than you do, and vice versa. Use the opportunity to teach and learn from one another.

> **Groups allow everyone to participate.** If you're an introvert, you may find it easier to talk in a small group than you do in the larger class. If the entire class is split into groups, everyone plays a role during discussions, not just the dominant personalities.

> **Groups can have more influence.** If you're the CEO, this generalization may not be true. But if you're a first-year student asked to convene a student group to give the faculty input on how to become better teachers, and you invite members from six different departments on campus—chemistry, English, communication, nursing, engineering, and criminal justice—there's better representation, and the results may be taken more seriously than if you came up with a set of recommendations yourself.

> **Interdependence among members can lead to better results.** If you're dining out, and the kitchen staff doesn't have its act together, the servers' tips may reflect customers' displeasure. Everyone has a stake in the team's results. Although knowing this fact doesn't always fix things, it could help everyone want to do a better job.

> **Temporary teams or pairs—collaborative learning—can be powerful.** Rather than or in addition to lecturing, some instructors will engage you through what's called collaborative learning. Imagine coming to class in an auditorium with 500 seats and listening to a fifty-minute

lecture on physics. (Good time to catch a nap?) Many such classes have been replaced on college campuses with smaller classes with whiteboards and display screens on the walls. After the instructor gives a "micro-lecture" on the topic of the day, groups of students work at computers, write formulas on the white boards, and argue about how to solve problems. Although there was initial resistance by students when these changes were first instituted at some schools (it's hard to take a nap with all that noise), attendance increased and failure rates decreased.[37] Even in large lecture classes, instructors can stop, ask pairs to discuss, and give a clicker quiz or present a "*ConcepTest*" (i.e., "Work the problem individually for two to three minutes, and then I'll give you three minutes to discuss with three or four students right around you to reach consensus on the right answer.").[38] Actively communicating in small groups can make a big difference in how much students learn.

➤ **Groups generate more and better ideas through diversity.** On your campus, student government may be made up of representatives from the various clubs and organizations on campus. Diverse membership will ensure that ideas from all populations have representation—the Fellowship of Christian Athletes, the rugby team, the Black Student Alliance, Phi Beta Kappa, "Humans vs. Zombies"—you name it. Look around in the Student Union or search on Facebook to find out just how many student clubs exist on your campus. But the point is that variety guarantees that good ideas can surface from many diverse sectors of your college or university.

The Top 10 Rules of Responsible Group Membership

> **?** challenge
> **"** reaction
>
> **Challenge:** What makes groups work at their best? Generate three rules on your own.
> **Reaction:**
> _Everyone takes responsibility!_
> _____
> _____
> _____

Like everything else, groups have pros and cons. What can you do to ensure a positive group experience in class? Think about this top ten list as it relates to your classes this term:

1. **Make sure every member is clear on the assignment.** A group can waste a great deal of start-up time by arguing about what the actual "deliverables" are. What is to be delivered on the due date? "Does she want each of us to give an individual speech, or can we come up with a more creative format?" "What kinds of outside resources can we use, or

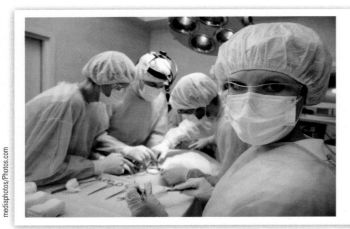

66

Contrary to popular belief, there most certainly is an 'I' in 'team'. It is the same 'I' that appears three times in 'responsibility.

Amber Harding

99

can we use outside resources at all?" Clarifying answers to questions like these before you start your work can save a great deal of time later.

2. **Talk about ground rules up front.** If you think it will be helpful, design a group "pre-nup." Just as an actual pre-nup is an agreement two romantic partners enter into before formalizing their relationship, a group agreement before the work relationships begin may be a good idea. Discuss or even write down how the group will proceed: "We will each attend all meetings and let everyone know if last-minute emergencies interfere." "We will contribute our own ideas, and not take credit for the ideas of other members." "We will each complete our assigned tasks on time and with our best effort." "If conflict erupts, as it usually does in groups, we'll try to set aside our egos for the sake of the project's quality."

3. **Remember that teamwork is an individual skill.** Discourage "social loafing" in advance, and call out "slackers" if they appear. A hundred years ago, a researcher conducted a famous experiment in which he learned that individuals pulled on a rope less hard when they were members of a group than they did when they pulled by themselves. He called this behavior "social loafing," and "free riders" are a common problem in groups. "Oh, someone else will do it" can become one or more members' prevailing mindset. "We're getting a group grade, anyway."[39] Talk about this issue in advance, so that everyone can recall the initial discussion if slackers emerge, and you can return to it later if need be.

Aha!

Sensitive Situation One way to discourage social loafing is to include peer review as a part of the grading process. Or take this idea a step further and triangulate grades with one-third *group* grade, one-third *individual* grade, and one-third *peer review* grade. An isolated instance of one student giving another student a low grade may be a personality conflict. But if you see a trend (i.e., several students have given the same team member a low grade), that member may not have contributed his or her share.

4. **Let roles emerge.** It's a known fact that particular types of communicators often emerge in groups. Some members tend to concentrate more on the task ("Okay, we've got a solid introduction; let's move on."), while others focus more on the members themselves ("Is everyone okay with the introduction? Let's make sure we all agree.") Both are needed. A group of all taskmasters can make you feel breathless, like you're running a marathon. At the extreme, a group of all relational types can feel like social skills training. Destructive roles, of course ("I've tried all of these ideas before, and they've all flopped!" or "Let's just get this over with! It's a silly assignment, anyway!") should be checked at the door, and it may be someone's role (perhaps yours) to suggest that.

5. **Coordinate the work.** Groups that work well are like a well-oiled machine. When person A finishes, the project continues on sequentially to person B, and so forth. Or work can be cut up like pieces of a pie and

all take place at once, concurrently. Either way, cooperation and coordination are key. ("If you work on the PowerPoint, and Josh does the research, I'll put the bibliography together.")

6. **Appoint a "Yoda."**[40] Remember Yoda? He was the *Star Wars* wise Jedi master, and every group needs one. It's Yoda's job to notice whose voice hasn't been heard, who is tromping on another member's ideas ("That's a really dumb idea! I can't believe you actually suggested that." or "Why do we always have to listen to Carrie? Who died and made her leader?"), or what has gone unsaid that needs to be said.

7. **Cultivate "caring criticism."**[41] Groups aren't very productive if everyone is always "walking on eggshells." "That's a really good idea, Mike, and I don't want to stifle your creativity or suggest that you're wrong in any way whatsoever, but don't you think that maybe…" Yes, it's important to be sensitive ("Good idea, Mike, but what if we explored this angle, too?"), but it's also important to be honest. Caring criticism is a balanced approach that breeds openness, not defensiveness.

8. **Remember that on-going groups typically go through stages.** When groups first begin, they are in a *forming* stage. Everyone is getting to know everyone else, and the members are building rapport. Then groups tend to go through a *norming* stage, where members establish spoken or unspoken rules about how to behave. Most groups then progress through a *storming* stage, during which conflict erupts. (Stages two and three can also occur in reverse order.) And finally, the group emerges into the *performing* stage—the goal is reached, the work is done, and the final product is ready to display. Tuckman, the original researcher who described these stages many years ago, added a final stage called *adjourning* (although more recently, psychologists have used a word that rhymes better, *mourning*, meaning the group comes to an end).[42] The theory asserts that all these stages must be experienced, although the duration of each stage can differ among groups. Does your experience match the theory? ("Oops, here we go into the *storming* stage. I just knew that would happen next!")

> 66 Remember upon the conduct of each depends the fate of all. 99
>
> *Alexander the Great*

9. **Create ways to get unstuck.** Sometimes groups get stuck. Everyone is busy with other obligations, and group conversations seem to be going nowhere because distractions intervene. At times like these, it's everyone's job to kick in and shake things up. Ask some tough questions. Introduce a crazy idea that may lead to something productive. Passivity kills groups; challenge the status quo. Do something to get things moving again.

10. **Use your strengths and help others find theirs.** You may think you don't have particular strengths when it comes to participating in a group. ("What do I know? They don't need me to do this assignment.") Everyone has something to contribute—either a piece of the content (your expertise about the topic or your ability to find expertise via research) or a piece of the process (like positivity, for example). Your particular strength may be helping other people find theirs. Use your best talents, and remember the words of Babe Ruth: "It's hard to beat a person who never gives up."

After the Korean War, the U.S. Army's chief psychiatrist studied the psychological warfare used against 1,000 American prisoners of war who had been kept at a North Korean camp. He made a startling discovery: negativity kills.[43]

The prisoners had not been treated cruelly. They were given food, water, and shelter. They hadn't been tortured, yet many American soldiers died in the camp. They weren't surrounded by barbed wire and armed guards, yet no one ever tried to escape. Instead, many of them turned against each other, formed relationships with their North Korean guards, and when they were finally freed, many didn't even bother to call home when given the opportunity to let their loved ones know they were alive.

Many of these men died of extreme hopelessness caused by a total removal of emotional support. Soldiers were rewarded for informing on one another and required to stand up in groups of their peers and tell all the bad things they had ever done, as well as the good things they should have done. All positive letters from home were withheld, but negative ones telling of relatives passing away or wives divorcing their husbands were delivered right away. Even notices of overdue bills from collection agencies were passed along. Eventually, many of these American prisoners simply gave up. They died of "give up-itis," as they called it, raising the overall death rate in the camp to 38 percent—the highest American POW death rate in U.S. history.

The record of what happened raised this fundamental question, described in the *New York Times* and *Wall Street Journal* bestseller *How Full Is Your Bucket?* If negativity can have such a devastating impact, what can positivity do? That's where the analogy of buckets and dippers begins. Most of us will never endure the kind of psychological warfare these soldiers did, but all of us can examine the negativity we inflict on others, and by contrast, the positivity we can bring to others' lives.

How Full Is Your Bucket? by Tom Rath and Donald Clifton claims that each of us has an invisible bucket; we function at our best when our buckets are full. We each also have an invisible dipper. In every interaction, we use our dipper to fill others' buckets or to dip from them. The principle of the book is simple; following its advice, however, is challenging. *How Full Is Your Bucket?* makes these five recommendations:

1. **Dip less.** Get in the habit of listening to yourself. Are your words cynical, insensitive, or critical? If so, push the pause button and rephrase what you're trying to communicate. Keep track by scoring your interactions as positive or negative, and set a goal of five positive exchanges for every negative one.

2. **Bring out the best.** By filling others' buckets, we set off a chain reaction that comes back to us. Imagine a scenario in which something really annoys you about your romantic partner, and you find yourself being critical much more often than you should be. If you make a conscious decision to focus instead on all the good things instead of the one bad thing, you'll have a positive impact on the relationship, and your partner will begin responding more positively to you. Watch and see!

3. **Make more than one best friend.** Who ever said people are only allowed one best friend? High-quality relationships improve the quality of your life. Bucket filling from the start is the way to begin a new best friendship, and regular bucket filling is how to keep it.

4. **Fill a drop at a time.** Giving a small unexpected gift is a great way to fill someone else's bucket. It needn't be much: a token, a trinket, a compliment, or a thank you. Put your positive comments in an e-mail or a note to make them last. Make a habit of giving "drops."

5. **Apply the Golden Rule backwards.** Rather than "Do unto others as you would have them do unto you," try this: "Do unto others as *they would have you do unto them*."

How full is your bucket? In your interactions, are you filling or dipping? Building a relationship is a process that occurs one drop at a time.

This section makes me realize just how important positive communication is...

Communicating in Important Relationships

Teachable Moment Ask students what it means to be a good communicator. What are the characteristics of communication competence? Do the requirements for competence change across types of relationships—those with peers, instructors, roommates, etc.? Why is understanding the answers to these questions important? Ask them to give examples.

Think of all the kinds of communicating you do—and with whom. And think of all the ways you communicate—by texting, talking face-to-face, or posting a photo of yourself with a few descriptive words online. Not only do you work in groups with classmates, as we've just discussed, but you also have friends you care about. You may think the primary thing friends help you do is fill up your spare time. But new research shows that friends can actually help you fight illness

> ❝
> Eighty percent of life's satisfaction comes from meaningful relationships. ❞

Brian Tracy, personal and career success author

and depression, boost your cognitive functioning, and even prolong your life. In one study, student participants were taken to the bottom of a steep hill while wearing a heavy backpack. They were asked to estimate the steepness of the hill. Participants standing next to friends, rather than by themselves, thought the hill looked much less steep, and friends who had know each other longer gave increasingly less steep estimates. Researchers summarized that "People with stronger friendship networks feel like there is someone they can turn to. Friendship is an undervalued resource. The consistent message of these studies is that friends make your life better." If that's true, then how you communicate with them is more important than you may even realize.[44]

Or consider family members. These people make up the core of who you really are. Your kid brother may drive you crazy at times, and a parent may seem to smother you, but generally, these people care about you most. Often we "let it all hang out" with family members, perhaps because we know they'll overlook our flaws. When we're tired or stressed, this is often where we "veg" or vent. But because of the central, enduring role they play in our lives, they deserve more quality communication than we sometimes give them.

Classmates and instructors, too, deserve your best communication, even when you disagree with the perspective they're voicing in class. You may see your instructors as intimidating or helpful, but you'll need to make the first move to get to know them, rather than the other way around. Take the initiative to meet them during their office hours and bring up points from class that you'd like to know more about. It's unlikely a professor will single you out ("John, you looked puzzled when I got to the part of the chapter on pages 160–170. Did you understand what I was talking about?"). You have many classmates, and your instructor may not be able to pay attention to each individual student. It'll be your job to go to your professor to get the clarification you need. Do some of your best communicating with instructors and classmates, and remember that face-to-face communication often works best.

Sensitive Situation It's very possible that you have a few students in your class who have some serious communication issues going on in their lives. Be sensitive to the fact that relationships gone awry can cause wounds that are raw and deep, and conversations about relationships can be very emotionally upsetting to these students.

Managing Conflict: Life Is Not a Sitcom

Research documents the far-reaching effects of bad relationships in many different contexts. They can hurt your job performance, your finances, your physical and mental health—even your life span.[45] Conflict with anyone you're in close proximity to—friends and roommates, for example—can bring on major stress that affects your academic performance, not to mention your overall happiness.[46]

Unfortunately, movies and television often communicate—subtly or not so subtly—that conflict can be resolved by the end of the show. Just lighten up or settle down and you can resolve almost any problem. And if you can't, just swallow, take a deep breath, and move on. But life isn't like that, nor should it be. Managing the conflict in your life takes time, energy, and persistence. It requires understanding your natural tendencies, considering why you communicate as you do, and making productive choices as a communicator.

If you've ever monitored yourself during a particularly heated conflict, you may remember doing something like this: yelling in anger at someone at the top of your lungs, being interrupted by a phone call and suddenly communicating calmly and quietly to the caller, and then returning to the original shouting match after you hang up.

Why? We make *choices* as communicators. Sometimes our choices are productive ones, and sometimes they aren't. And that goes for electronic communication, too. You can pump yourself full of e-courage and send a text or email you'd never actually say to someone face-to-face—and regret it later! As a child, you may have heard the phrase: "Sticks and stones can break my bones, but words will never hurt me!" Actually, words *can* be used as weapons, and lethal ones at that! It's important to remember that we *do* choose what we say and how we behave. Our choices affect both the *process*—how things go during the conflict—and the *product*—how it turns out

Interesting . . . I usually don't think about choices. I just think about winners and losers.

Exercise 10.3 What's Your Conflict Style?

For each of the following statements, please rate your response on a scale of 1 to 5, with 1 representing "strongly agree" and 5 representing "strongly disagree."

1. _____ I usually end up compromising in conflict situations. (CO)
1 2. _____ Someone always loses in a conflict. (CP)
3. _____ I usually let other people "win" in conflicts because I often feel less strongly about the outcome than they do. (AC)
4. _____ When I really care about a relationship, I devote unusual amounts of time and energy into coming up with creative solutions so that each of us can get what we want. (CL)
1 5. _____ "Don't rock the boat" is a good philosophy. (AV)
6. _____ "Winning" in conflict situations gives me a real "high." (CP)
7. _____ Sacrificing what I want so that someone else can achieve a goal is often worth it. (AC)
? 8. _____ It's possible for both parties to "win" in conflict situations. (CL)
9. _____ Sometimes you have to settle for "part of the pie." (CO)
1 10. _____ I try to avoid conflict at all costs. It's not worth it. (AV)

Now find a partner in class and compare your responses. Circle the items on which the two of you differed most, for example, where one of you marked a "1" and the other a "5." See if you can explain your own choice and also come to understand your partner's thinking. On how many items did you differ? If the answer is "several" or "many," you might experience substantial conflict as roommates or members of the same group.

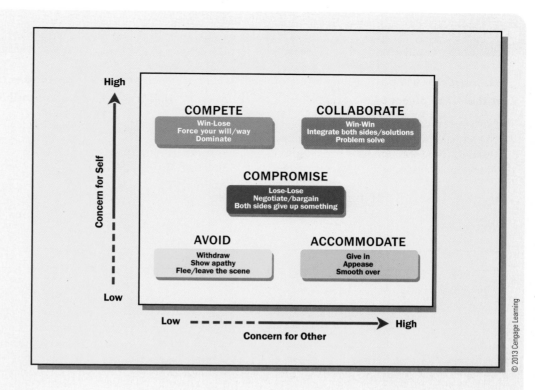

FIGURE 10.1
Conflict Management Styles

I think I avoid too much...

People often come at conflicts using differing styles. Not only do you disagree on the topic at hand—whatever it is—but you approach conflict itself differently. This quick quiz is based on a well-known, five-part model of conflict styles (see Figure 10.1). In our version of the model, the horizontal axis is labeled "Concern for Other" (or cooperativeness) and the vertical axis is labeled "Concern for Self" (or assertiveness).[47]

Where are your highest scores? Notice the letters at the end of the ten statements.
If you like to win and care most about your own goals, you *compete* (CP).
If you care more about the other person's goals, and give in or sacrifice your own, you *accommodate* (AC).

If you don't care about (or are wiling to neglect) your goals or your conflict partner's, you *avoid* (AV).

If you care somewhat about both and are willing to settle for "part of the pie," you *compromise* (CO). Strictly speaking, when you compromise, neither of you gets exactly what you want.

If you care about your own goals and your conflict partner's, and you're willing to devote the time and energy required to reach a win-win solution, you *collaborate* (CL).

What's your style? Do you have a conflict style you're most comfortable with? Do you fall into the habit of using one style, even if it's not productive in particular situations? Flexibility is the key to managing conflicts productively, and if the relationship really counts, collaboration is the ideal.

in the end. Sometimes our choices are negative ones that produce destructive conflict—personal attacks, name calling, an unwillingness to listen, or devious strategies that erode trust. Positive choices are much more likely to bring productive conflict that helps us learn more about ourselves, our partners in conflict, and our relationships.

Your instructor will pass around a bag of M&M®s and ask each person in class to take three M&Ms, but not to eat them. The object of the exercise is to collect as many M&Ms of one color as possible. Here are the rules:

1. Don't start until the instructor says "go."
2. Use any strategies you like (except for physical force) to win.
3. Use only the M&Ms that have been distributed. (You may not use any M&Ms still in the bag.)
4. At the end of five minutes, your instructor will call "time" at which point the exercise is over.

After the exercise, all students should retake their seats and answer these questions:

1. Who won? How did he or she do it?

_____

_____

2. What other strategies could have been used to win?

_____

_____

3. What did this game teach you about your conflict management style?

_____

_____

(Based on Miller, G. V. "The M&M® Conflict Game," pp. 247-255 in Beich, E. (2008). *The Pfeiffer book of successful team-building tools: Best of the annuals.* San Francisco: John Wiley & Sons.)

Teachable Moment   Several key points about conflict management should be made during the debrief. First, students most likely will assume that the word "you" is singular, rather than plural. Generally speaking, competition between individuals will lead to conflict and resentment of the tactics that are used to win. Discuss this assumption, based on the emphasis on competition within our society. Second, the instructions are "to collect as many M&M®s of the same color as possible." If only four blue M&M®s were taken from the bag, originally, and an individual or group collects all four, that constitutes winning. Brown is the most common color in a bag of M&Ms, so an individual or group with many browns may assume they have won, based on sheer numbers. This may not be true. Third, if class members had formed teams, they could have collaborated to win. If the entire class had collaborated, all groups could have won by dividing into as many teams as the number of M&M colors originally removed from the bag and doling out a single color of available M&Ms to each group. Fourth, note negotiation strategies that are used; negotiation becomes difficult because after a few minutes, individuals may be left with nothing of value to trade.. Finally, make the point that the only strategy that leads to a long-term positive solution is collaboration. After the debrief, pass around the bag again and enjoy!

AP Photo/Al Behrman

> " Gettin' good players is easy. Gettin' 'em to play together is the hard part. "
>
> —*Casey Stengel, major league baseball player and manager (1890–1975)*

Your TYPE is Showing

So how does your psychological type play into group communication? Good question! Besides the obvious expectations (introverts are less likely to speak up, extraverts may all be competing for "air time," and so forth), what role does type play? Here's what the research says; see how these suggestions compare with your past experiences as you think back on them.

☐ The more similar the psychological types of group members, the more easily they understand each other. That makes sense. If all members of a high school reunion committee are iNuitives, they may operate as a group of impractical "dreamers" who enjoy exploring "what if…" questions. ["Hey, what if we rented an enormous tent for the dance? That would be great fun!" Without sensors in the group, no one may be around to ask how much renting a huge tent might cost.]

☐ The more unlike the types of group members, the more time (and communicating) it may take to see everyone's point of view. ["Hey, what if we rented an enormous tent for the dance? That would be great fun!" (N) "Yes, it would be fun, but it would break the bank. We have a tight budget." (S) "Well, let's just take a vote. I have other things to do, and I'd like to get this resolved." (J) "No, I think we should slow down and explore other options." (P) You can see how the discussion could go on for a very long time.]

☐ Groups with similar types may reach decisions quickly, but their decisions may be flawed. ["A tent it is then! See you guys next week!" (all J's)] Groups with dissimilar types may take longer to make a decision, but it may be a better decision in the end because all viewpoints are expressed.

☐ A group member who is different from everyone else (the only introvert in an extraverted group) is seen as different from everyone else. ["What do the rest of you think Caitlin had on her mind? She didn't say a word. She seemed totally out of it."]

☐ Group members who differ on all four preferences may have particular difficulty understanding each other. ["Tom (an INTJ) and Sam (an ESFP) are really bogging down the group! Why can't they just see eye to eye?"]

☐ Leadership roles within the group may shift, based on which preferences are needed for particular tasks. ["What do you say we put Emma (an S) in charge of the budget, Grace (an E) in charge of making phone calls, Jason (a J) in charge of the agenda, and Bruce (a P) in charge of exploring venues."]

☐ Groups that are most successful take realities (S), new possibilities (N), rational decision-making (T), and individual and group values (F) into account—in other words groups that use psychological type to their advantage, rather than letting differences hold them back or cloud their collective judgment.[48]

Diversity Makes a Difference

Exercise 10.5 What Are Your Views on Diversity?

Look at the following ten statements and indicate the extent to which you agree or disagree.

Strongly Agree	Agree	Not sure	Disagree	Strongly Disagree
1	2	3	4	5

1. Race is still a factor in hiring decisions today.
2. Multiculturalism implies that all cultures have equally valid viewpoints.
3. Workforce diversity improves the quality of work.
4. The number of male versus female corporate CEOs is nearing the halfway mark in the United States.
5. In some situations, sexual orientation is a justifiable basis for discrimination.
6. All cultures tend to see the rest of the world through their own cultural lens.
7. Feminism is a set of beliefs held by females.
8. A global perspective ensures objectivity.
9. Religious persecution is a thing of the past.
10. There is less racism in the United States today than there was ten years ago.

As you continue reading this section of the chapter, search for points relating to these topics. Also, your instructor may wish to use these ten items to begin a discussion in class.

One of the best things about groups is that they are made up of diverse people. Each member of a group has her own past experiences, his own present reality, and along with all of that, a different set of perceptions about the world. Diversity makes the group process potentially rich in terms of process—how members communicate—and product—the decision they eventually reach or project they create. The ten statements above are intentionally provocative to stimulate your thinking. They relate to diversity broadly: the differences between human beings based on gender, race, ethnicity, age, culture, physical features and abilities, mental capability, socioeconomic status, religion, politics, sexuality, gender identity, and points of view. Diversity is a fact of life.

But consider this: you may think people of your age, religion, race, ethnicity, or gender with characteristics like yours are somehow more "normal" or "better" without even realizing it. But others unlike you may think the same thing about their particular "group," and see you very differently. If you're from a well-to-do family, for example, you may see yourself as "fortunate," but others may see you as "privileged." Perceptions are important in discussions about diversity. They influence our interactions with others, and sometimes perceptions can lead to bias. Let's take a closer look:

Each of us is a unique human being. Some of us are taller, some are shorter, some are older, some are younger. Some aspects of our uniqueness are visible. It's not hard to tell the difference between someone who's five feet tall and someone who's seven feet tall or someone who's twenty versus someone who's eighty. But other

> ## " You must look into people, as well as at them. "
>
> *Lord Chesterfield, British statesman (1694–1773)*

Type of Diversity	Possible Perceptions	Things to Consider
Age Diversity	"Those youngsters with all the tattoos and piercings! What do they know?"	Trends change, and outward expressions vary from one generation to the next.
	"Older drivers! They're so slow!"	Reaction times slow down, and vision can worsen.
Gender Diversity	"I'm all for women's rights, but a female President? I'm not sure we're ready for that!"	Actually, in the last Presidential race several women rose to prominent roles at the top of their parties.
	"Why would a guy want to be a nurse? That's a woman's job."	Nursing is a top career field for men or women, now and in the future.
Geographic Diversity	"The South is so backwards."	Southerners are proud of their traditions.
	"Northerners are such snobs."	Regional accents can carry particular stereotypes.
Physical Diversity	"Boy, if I only had a handicapped sticker, I could park anywhere on campus."	Physical challenges warrant access capability.
	"That professional signer in class is really distracting!"	In-class signers help deaf students follow lectures and discussions—like a language translator.
Sexual Orientation Diversity	"Call me homophobic, but all my friends are straight."	Homophobia can be a highly negative hidden bias.
	"Bisexual? How can somebody be attracted to both sexes? That's just not normal!"	College will be a time to become aware of differences, including things you may never have been exposed to.
Religious Diversity	"Religious people are unthinking."	Religious beliefs are highly personal, and spirituality in some form can bring balance and meaning.
	"I'm glad I was raised believing in the right religion."	While it can be natural to see your family traditions as "right," realize that others may feel equally strong about theirs.

aspects of our uniqueness aren't as obvious. Would people necessarily know your religion, your sexual orientation, or even your race, just by looking at you? If you had a stack of photos—a headshot of every student who attends your school—could you sort them by race into the same stacks they'd sort themselves into? Anyone can tell an Asian-American from an African-American, just by looking. Or so they may think.

Race is often the first thing people think of when they hear the word diversity. But some experts say race is a relatively modern idea. Centuries ago people tended to classify other people by status, religion, or language, for example, not by race. Actually, diversity is about much more than physical appearance. It's becoming more and more impossible to draw clear lines between what separates us physically. Keanu Reeves is Hawaiian, Chinese, and Caucasian; Mariah Carey is Black, Venezuelan, and Caucasian; and Johnny Depp is Cherokee and Caucasian.[49] Most of us are a blend of ethnicities, and how we perceive ourselves may be different from the way others see us. People may assume that a Pacific Islander with light brown skin, dark hair, and dark eyes, for example, is Hispanic. And a classmate you may assume is White may think of himself as Black. Or consider this: If you have a Chinese mother and a White father, you may not know which "race box" to check on standard forms. Should you choose Mom or Dad?[50] Biologists tell us that there's more variation within a race than there is between races. Race isn't biological, they say, but *racism* is real.[51]

Teaching with Technology Try an onscreen activity like Exercise 10.5 in class or send students to the PBS website called "Sorting People." Ask them to try the sorting people activity and report their results. The activity demonstrates that sorting accurately, according to how the subjects self-report their race, is nearly impossible. Self-identity is an important key that students—and instructors—shouldn't overlook!

Teaching with Technology For interesting statistics about world demographics, go to http://www.100people.org/.

Exercise 10.6   Facing the Race Issue

Take a look at the faces below. Can you categorize them into common racial types: White, Black, Hispanic/Latino, Native American, or Asian? After you've identified each one, check the answers below. How accurate were you? Does this activity confirm the point above that although race is used as a common identifier, it isn't an easy or accurate way to classify people?[52]

Answers: (top row): B, H, NA, A, H and (bottom row): B, H, H, W, W.

From top lieft: © iStockphoto.com/Andresr; © iStockphoto.com/Bill Noll; © iStockphoto.com/Thomas Gordon; © iStockphoto.com/Goldmund Lukic; © iStockphoto.com/Jacom Stephens; © iStockphoto.com/Lisa Marzano; © iStockphoto.com/Jason Lugo; © iStockphoto.com/Roberto A Sanchez; © iStockphoto.com/TriggerPhoto; © iStockphoto.com/erel photography

And Exactly Why Should Diversity Be Valued?

Challenge: Identify three advantages diversity brings to any society.

Reaction:

_____

_____

_____

Although some of you may have grown up in a fairly homogeneous community with less racial, ethnic, or cultural diversity than others, no doubt you have experienced the multicultural nature of our society in many different ways, even in terms of food, music, and clothing, for example. The media have introduced you to aspects of diversity vicariously, and perhaps you've even traveled to other parts of the United States or the world yourself.

But here's the challenge: Have your experiences with diversity and your learning about it in school truly made a difference in the way you think and act? Do you choose to diversify your awareness, your relationships, and yourself as a person? Do you think that the fact that we live in a multicultural society in which we've all been taught to respect and appreciate diversity means that discrimination no longer exists?

> I take as my guide the hope of a saint: In crucial things, unity; in important things, diversity; in all things, generosity.

George H. W. Bush, forty-first president of the United States

Many college students today do believe that racial discrimination is no longer a problem. Been there; done that, they've concluded. According to a recent survey, "helping to promote racial understanding" was considered "essential" or "very important" by only slightly more than one-third of incoming first-year students.[53] In another study, students were asked to identify the five most critical and two least critical outcomes of a college education from a list of sixteen possibilities. Tolerance and respect for people of other races, ethnicities, and lifestyles were identified as among the least important goals for college learning.[54] Why do you think they responded that way? Do they think they've already achieved these goals, or do they devalue them for other reasons?

Teachable Moment Pose these questions to the class: Why might students think that tolerance and respect for people of other races, ethnicities, and lifestyles are among the least important goals for college learning?

If you conducted a survey on your campus to find out if discrimination exists, you might be surprised at the results. Research continues to show that minority students experience discrimination at higher rates than majority students. Many of us downplay the prejudice all human beings harbor to one extent or another. Our brains are "programmed" to group like entities and standardize our views about these groups, resulting in stereotypes. We feel safe around others like us and fear those unlike us.

Refraining from stereotyping groups of people and appreciating individuals for what they are could drastically alter the way we think and act. Perhaps you've always assumed that all nerds are A, all athletes are B, and all sorority women are C. What if you switched the labels around? Are the results ludicrous? When labels come to us easily, they are probably negative, and it's likely they apply to groups *other than* the ones *we* belong to. However, when you liberate yourself to think differently, you're not bogged down by tired, old labels. If you open up your thinking to new possibilities, all kinds of new options present themselves. Imagine a band made up of only trombones, a meal with nothing but potatoes, a song played on one note, or a world where everyone looks exactly like you. Diversity enriches our lives.

A University of Michigan study demonstrated that students who had more positive interactions with diverse peers, and in particular took a college course on diversity, were more likely to have more academic self-confidence, be more personally proactive, and be more disposed to developing better critical thinking skills.[55] Research also shows that having a roommate of a different race can not only reduce prejudice but it can also diversify your friendships. Although it can be a challenge to communicate through your differences, having a roommate of a different race can also teach you what it's like to be someone other than yourself.[56] Learning to deal effectively with diversity can actually change you as a college student!

College is a perfect time to immerse yourself in diversity—in the classroom and beyond it. Classrooms are becoming more diversely populated; it's true. By the standard definition, a minority of today's college students are "traditional" (meaning a high school graduate who immediately goes on to college, depends on parents fully for financial support, and doesn't work or works only part-time). And most traditional students today don't fit the traditional definition of "traditional."[57] Adult nontraditional learners have varied backgrounds, interests, and approaches to getting an education. Often they try to work their way through systems that are designed around the needs of younger students.[58] In 2011, Hispanic enrollments in college reached an all-time high, representing 16.4 percent of all enrollments in higher education.[59] Of African American high school graduates in 2011, 67.5 percent were enrolled in college by October 2011. Diversity in higher education gives you an opportunity to expand your world view and develop empathy for others who have vastly different experiences.

Aside from meeting students of other races and ethnicities in college, taking advantage of diversity can help you become a more sophisticated thinker, one who can see problems from multiple perspectives, and a better-prepared employee, ready to hit the ground running in today's highly diverse workplace. Appreciating diversity also helps us become better citizens. Diversity is what our society is based on. In a democratic society such as ours, citizens must be able to recognize and endorse creative solutions to complex problems. A former Chief Justice of the U.S. Supreme Court, Charles Evans Hughes, once said, "When we lose the right to be different, we lose the privilege to be free."

One mistake many college students make is not taking advantage of what diversity offers them. Because like attracts like, they join groups of people just

Teaching with Technology DiversityWeb .org is a Web site developed by the Association of American Colleges and Universities to foster civic engagement and global awareness among college students. The site provides information on current projects, research, and programs related to diversity, as well as curriculum choices and learning outcomes. Visit this site for more ideas on how to encourage students to become involved in diversity awareness both on and off campus.

> 66
> We have become not a melting pot, but a beautiful mosaic. Different people, different beliefs, different yearnings, different hopes, different dreams.
> 99
>
> *Jimmy Carter, thirty-ninth president of the United States*

Activity Option If you are comfortable with this activity, create a "Human Continuum" (Staley, 2003) as a way to launch a discussion about diversity in class. Create an imaginary line along the front of the room, for example, and label each opposite pole. You can use descriptors such as majority/minority, 100 percent American/foreign, and so on. Then ask students to place themselves along the line. You may be surprised at how students place themselves on this continuum. For example, students who are light-skinned may place themselves closer to a label for students of color than someone who has darker skin. Often, how we identify ourselves is by using internal, rather than external, indicators. Defining the meanings the two poles held for students can lead to a rich discussion.

Exercise 10.7   What's the Difference?

Find a partner to work with on this exercise. Individually, list all the various ways in which you differ: age, height, gender, eye color, hometown, and so on. When your instructor calls "time," read your lists aloud. The point of the exercise is to begin a discussion on the meaning of diversity, to explore its many different facets—beyond just external appearance—and to appreciate the fact that each individual is unique.[60]

Exercise 10.8   25 Things We Have in Common

Conflict is based on differences. Two people each want different things—or two people want the same thing, but only one can have it. But when you think about it, we have many things in common as human beings. Try this experiment: work with three classmates (in a group of four), and when your instructor announces "go," begin listing things that all four of you have in common. The first group to reach 25 items wins! After the exercise, discuss the kinds of things you listed and how easy or hard it was to create a list of 25 different items.[61]

Teachable Moment It's a good idea to debrief Exercise 10.6. Ask students to indicate one or two things that they learned or were surprised about when doing this activity. Doing Exercises 10.6 and 10.7 as a set can work well since both differences and commonalities are important.

Teachable Moment You might want to ask the class if anyone would like to reveal a unique background. As an instructor do you have a "blend" in your background that you would be willing to tell them about?

Teaching with Technology Encourage students to participate in service learning, and provide the resources and research to make their involvement even easier. Most cities have catalogs of the non-profit organizations that accept volunteer help. Look online for resources or lists of organizations students could serve. VolunteerMatch.org allows users to search for volunteer opportunities by city and region. Give students a list of local resources and volunteer organizations, and they can search for a cause they're passionate about serving.

like themselves based on religion, sexual orientation, or majors, for example. You can choose to belong to the Young Republicans; the Gay, Lesbian, Bisexual, Transgender (GLBT) student group; or the Chemistry Honor Society. Joining a group of like students assures you a place where people accept you for who you are and you feel comfortable. Think about the groups you belong to and what they say about you.

Of course, being comfortable and feeling accepted are important. But instead, imagine choosing to join groups composed of very different types of people. Consider what philosopher and educator John Dewey once said, "Conflict . . . shocks us out of sheep-like passivity," or political philosopher Edmund Burke's words, "Our antagonist is our helper. He that wrestles with us strengthens our nerves, and sharpens our skill." A famous American lawyer, Louis Nizer, once put it like this: "Where there is no difference, there is only indifference." Valuing diversity relates directly to your empathy skills and your emotional intelligence. What about stretching ourselves to learn fully what diversity has the potential to teach us?[62]

Imagine you were engaged in a service-learning project for a class, working in your local soup kitchen. It's easy to look at a homeless person with a critical eye and think, "Why doesn't he just get a job?" But when you actually sit down and share a bowl of soup across the table, you might see things differently. You might hear stories of personal illness, family tragedy, unbelievable trauma—a string of coinciding misfortunes, the likes of which you've never contemplated. Rather than assigning all homeless people to a group with a negative label, learn more about the individuals that make up that group. You might change your views.

One professor says this: "I tell my students to keep in mind that everything they see is a snapshot. That guy drinking from a bottle in a paper bag, he's a photograph. How did he get to where he is? From there, we can share some of the rage at the inherent injustice that awaits so many of our poor children as they grow up. As we examine people, the snapshots become a motion picture that links the past, present, and future—what was, what is, what can be."[63]

Choose a stereotype you recognize, one you suspect you subscribe to if you're honest, and decide what you can do to test it. Ask yourself whether it affects your thinking and actions. For example, are you aware of these facts attesting to the persistence of stereotypes in our culture?

wow ➤ **Sexism is still an issue in corporate America.** In 2012, eighteen of America's top 500 companies[64] were run by a woman, up from one out of forty in 1995. Then, only one of those companies had a female CEO; by 2003, seven did. Experts predict that by 2020, it could be one in five; however, the numbers remain grossly lopsided with women currently holding four percent of Fortune 500 CEO positions.[65]

➤ **Racism is still an issue in hiring decisions.** A Gallup poll asked: "Do you feel that racial minorities in this country have job opportunities equal to whites, or not?" Among Caucasians, the answer was 55 percent yes and 43 percent no. (The rest were undecided.) Among African Americans, the answer was 17 percent yes and 81 percent no. You might also be shocked to read about an experiment conducted by University of Chicago and MIT economists in which fabricated applicants of one race were 50 percent more likely to be called for interviews than applicants of another race, based solely on racially based fictitious names! As one *Wall Street Journal* reporter noted, "Someday Americans will be able to speak of racial discrimination in hiring in the past tense. Not yet."[66]

If you help others, you will be helped, perhaps tomorrow, perhaps in one hundred years, but you will be helped. Nature must pay off the debt. . . . It is a mathematical law and all life is mathematics.

G. I. Gurdjieff, philosopher (1872–1949)

Teachable Moment Some colleges have Common Reading Programs where all entering students read the same novel. If this is the case on your campus, ask students if they felt this book provided a springboard for conversation about diversity. If your campus does not have such a program, ask students what books they have recently read that provides diverse perspectives about groups or individuals,

---

Box 10.2   Service-Learning: Learning by Serving

One of the best ways to learn about diversity in college is by serving others. Instead of spending all your time in a classroom, imagine a class on aging in which you team up with an elder in your community and work together on a term project. You might help a senior write her memoirs, for example, or help an elderly man create a family tree for the next generation. You might be wondering, *How would that work? What could we possibly have in common—an 18-year-old teamed up with an 88-year-old?* You might be surprised.

What might you learn in a college reading course in which you tutor first graders at an inner-city elementary school, or a college success course in which you teach middle school students how to apply what you're learning right now about academic achievement? Centuries ago, a French philosopher wrote, "To teach is to learn twice." You need to know your stuff in order to teach it to someone else effectively, and you learn twice as much if you serve others who differ from you in important ways.

(continued on next page)

(continued from previous page)

Campus Compact, a national organization with more than 1100 member colleges and universities estimates that college student volunteering was worth $9.7 billion to the communities they served in 2012. They report that 44 percent of students in member colleges regularly do community service.[67]

Beyond the dollars calculated, college students' community service provides invaluable support. Literally thousands of college students volunteered to help with Hurricane Katrina and Rita relief efforts in 2005, for example, to help displaced victims of one of the country's worst natural disasters ever.

However, here's an important point: *community service* and *service-learning* aren't quite the same thing.[68] Service-learning is specifically about the learning. It's a learning experience in which you connect what you're learning for credit in the classroom with what you're learning in the community. You're applying what you're learning, which in turn solidifies—and modifies—your perspective. "Service, combined with learning, adds value to each and transforms both."[69] While you're engaged in a service-learning experience, you'll also be engaged in critical reflection. Critical reflection is like critical thinking, recalling or looking back at the service experience and writing about what you're learning in a continuous, connected, challenging, and contextualized way.[70] That's not the same thing as donating your time for a good cause, as important as that is, in terms of you and your own personal development and the lives of the people you help.

Years ago, learning expert John Dewey wrote that the best learning experiences:

- Generate interest
- Are intrinsically worthwhile
- Present problems that evoke new curiosity and require new information
- Cover a considerable time span so that your learning evolves as you go.[71]

Think about it: Might a service-learning project like helping an eighty eight-year-old person, someone who's lived through nearly a century of triumphs and tragedies, record her life's story meet these four requirements?

The average number of college professors who include service-learning in their courses nearly tripled between 2000 and 2005. Search out these opportunities to enhance your own learning and your appreciation for diversity by serving other people.[72]

Sounds interesting—maybe I'll look for a service learning course for next semester . . .

© Larry Harwood Photography. Property of Cengage Learning

VOTER REGISTRATION TODAY!

VOTER REGISTRATION HERE LAST NAME A–M

VOTER REGISTRATION HERE LAST NAME N–Z

> ❝ We make a living by what we get, but we make a life by what we give. ❞
>
> *Winston Churchill, Prime Minister of England (1874–1965)*

Great quote!

> **Discrimination and stereotypes persist.** Students with disabilities report a "chilly classroom climate" for students with disabilities in higher education.[73] According to one college president, "With all [the change in racial demographics], diversity has become the largest issue behind unrest on campus, accounting for 39 percent of student protests."[74] A recent study of closeted and out gay and lesbian college students reported that these students perceived unfair treatment and a need to hide their identity from most other students. Both groups reported experiencing a similar amount of antigay attacks.[75] In 2011, 7,254 hate crime offences were reported in the U.S., according to the Federal Bureau of Investigation. Racially motivated crimes accounted for approximately 46.9 percent, religious bias accounted for 19.8 percent, bias against sexual orientation for 20.8 percent, bias against disabilities for .9 percent, and bias against ethnicity or national origin accounted for 11.6 percent.[76] People still harm one another out of hatred for differences they may not understand.

Diversity makes a difference, and as educator Adela A. Allen once wrote, "We should acknowledge differences, we should greet differences, until difference makes no difference anymore." What can we do about it? Some campuses have launched programs in Sustained Dialogue, used in the past to deal with international tensions. This structured approach brings together students with different backgrounds for a year of deep conversation in small groups. Other colleges have developed similar programs to allow students to dialogue about deeply rooted prejudices—sometimes buried to an extent that they are not even realized—to discuss commonalities, and to recognize the potential for conflict—and change.[77] Raising awareness is a first step on the road to recognizing the reality and the richness of diversity.

Exercise 10.9   Circles of Awareness

Write your name in the center of the drawing, then label each of the surrounding circles with a word that represents a group with whom you identify. You may use categories such as age, gender, ethnicity, social, political, and so forth. After your drawing is labeled, your instructor will ask you to circulate around the room and find three classmates who have listed at least three of the same subgroups. Following that, you will be asked to find three students who listed at least three categories that you did not. In the second group you formed, based on differences, use the activity to discuss diversity, differences between individuals and groups, and how awareness can change behavior. Look over everyone's list, and to diversify your thinking, select one group on someone else's list, but not on yours. Find out more about that group, or decide to attend a group meeting to raise your awareness of differences between yourself and the group or between your preconceptions of what the group would be like, and what it's actually like.[78]

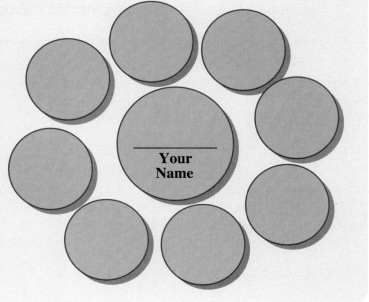

Your Name

What's Your CQ?

Exercise 10.10 **Diagnosing Your Cultural Intelligence**[79]

These statements reflect different aspects of cultural intelligence. For each set, add up your scores and divide by four to arrive at an average. As you answer, think about your answers in each category as they compare to the other two categories.

Rate how much you agree with each statement, using this scale:

1 =	2 =	3 =	4 =	5 =
Strongly Agree	disagree	neutral	agree	strongly agree

_____ Before I interact with people from a new culture, I think about what I'm going to communicate.

_____ If I come up against something unexpected in a new culture, I use the experience to think about how I should respond in other cultures in the future.

_____ I plan how I'm going to relate to people from a different culture before I even meet them.

_____ When I'm communicating in a new culture, I have a clear sense of whether things are going well or not.

_____ **Total divided by 4 =** _____ **COGNITIVE CQ**

_____ It's easy for me to change my body language (eye contact or posture, for example) to match that used by people from a different culture.

_____ I can change my expression when I need to interact with people from another culture.

_____ I can modify my speech (for example, accent or tone) when interacting with people from another culture.

_____ I can easily change the way I act when a cross-cultural situation seems to require it.

_____ **Total divided by 4 =** _____ **PHYSICAL CQ**

_____ I have confidence that I can deal well with people from another culture.

_____ I am certain that I can make friends with people from a culture that's different from mine.

_____ I can adapt to the lifestyle of another culture when I need to fairly easily.

_____ I am confident that I can deal with a cultural situation, even if it's unfamiliar.

_____ **Total divided by 4 =** _____ **EMOTIONAL/MOTIVATIONAL CQ**

Generally, an average lower than three identifies an opportunity for improvement, and an average greater than 4.5 identifies a true CQ strength.

From "Cultural Intelligence" by P. Christopher Earley and Elaine Mosakowski. *Harvard Business Review*, October 2004, pp. 139–146. Reprinted with permission.

Teachable moment If you have students in your class who are "world travelers," have them share their cross-cultural experiences—perhaps the ones that surprised them the most, like the three views of grasshoppers in the chart below.

An advertisement for an international bank gets the point across well. It shows a picture of a grasshopper. Below the grasshopper are these three sentences that describe three different cultural views of grasshoppers: USA—Pest, China—Pet, Northern Thailand—Appetizer.[80] One insect, three cultural perspectives. Americans tend to shoo away pesky grasshoppers. But if you travel

America	China	Northern Thailand

to China, be careful of stepping on one that may be someone else's beloved pet. And if you travel to Northern Thailand, try not to look disgusted when you see fried grasshoppers on the appetizer plate.

Just as individuals have emotional intelligence, they also have cultural intelligence. Some of us are more naturally sensitive to cultural differences, and we know how to handle ourselves. But all of us can grow our cultural intelligence with training and preparation. EQ relates to self-awareness and relationship skills; CQ relates to awareness and responses to other cultures (and subcultures of our own culture). EQ and CQ are linked.

Here's a definition: Cultural intelligence is an outsider's seemingly natural ability to interpret someone's unfamiliar and ambiguous gestures the way other people of that culture would.[81] CQ has three components that involve your head, your body, and your heart. All three work together to help you interact in a foreign culture—or a subculture that's new to you within your own larger culture. Think, for example, about taking a job in a new culture, either by transferring overseas or by entering an organization with different rules: "Casual Fridays," "Bring Your Dog to Work Day," "Follow Strict Communication Rules and Always Go Through Your Boss," or "Choose Your Own Project to Work on One Day a Week" (if you work for Google). These rules might be different for you, and you'd need good CQ skills to adapt. Or think about entering a subculture you're unfamiliar with: like being "straight" and having a gay best friend, or marrying someone of another ethnicity. CQ can be broken down into three parts, all of which work together:

1. **Cognitive quotient (head):** Do you understand the differences between another culture and your own? Before entering a new culture, do you think before you act? Do you learn about the culture in advance of interacting with its members so that you don't make embarrassing mistakes?

2. **Physical quotient (body):** Do you watch for behaviors that are different in other cultures? Do you mimic the gestures and customs of the people? Do you shake hands correctly? Do you notice if the culture is "high-touch" or "low-touch? Do you adopt their habits so that you earn their trust?

Teachable moment Have students research, act out, and compare simple gestures across cultures to explore the physical quotient aspect of cultural intelligence.

3. **Emotional/motivational quotient (heart):** Do you empathize with people from this culture? Can you imagine what it's like to be a member of this culture? Do you want to connect despite your differences? This aspect of CQ is thought to be most like EQ.

To have good CQ skills, you must be more than a "mimic," simply repeating what you see and hear in another culture. You must be a "chameleon," taking on what it's like to be a member of that culture. You must—through your head, your body, and your heart—prove to others that you have entered their world. Not only are CQ skills important within the American culture, they're also important in today's global society. How culturally intelligent are you? CQ is a natural extension of EQ, and the suggestions for how to improve your EQ apply to strengthening your CQ. If your cognitive quotient is low, read up about other cultures. If your physical quotient is low, watch for differences in gestures or movements and find out what they mean. If your emotional/motivational quotient is low, ask others for input, for example, or find a CQ mentor.

Think Globally; Act Locally

Hey! My Dad used to have this bumper sticker on his car!

The 1972 United Nations international conference on the human environment in Stockholm was the origin of the phrase "Think Globally, Act Locally." Perhaps you've heard it. Simply put, it originally meant "Do what you can to 'save the environment.'"

Today the phrase takes on added meaning. True, recycling is commonplace and *sustainability* is the watchword of modern corporations. Beyond environmental concerns, the world is characterized by networks of connections that span continents and distances. As citizens of the world, we are interdependent; small, seemingly insignificant actions can have monumental effects. Realize that we are all connected, if not geographically, then economically, militarily, socially, and technologically. Google offers an interface in 123 languages.[82] By 2003, 66 percent of all e-commerce spending originated outside of the United States, and as of June 31, 2012, now only 11.4 percent of all Internet users reside in North America.[83] A famous song title once made the claim: "We are the world."

Many universities now have Centers for the Study of Globalization, a major in Global Studies, or a general education requirement in Global Learning.[84] In today's world, a college education should enable you to:

> Understand the world's peoples and problems;

> Explore the historical roots of the dynamics and tensions in today's world;

> Develop competencies across cultures so that you can navigate boundaries and see the world from multiple perspectives;

> We have not inherited the world from our forefathers—we have borrowed it from our children.
>
> *Kashmiri proverb*

➤ Investigate difficult, sometimes emotionally charged issues we face across and among cultures;

➤ Engage in practical work with issues facing communities and societies.

The education you get now must prepare you to solve the problems of the future. It will require you to look beyond the walls of your classrooms, refine your critical and creative thinking skills, and expand your worldview. The course for which you're using this textbook is a good place to start.

Now What Do You Think?

1. At the beginning of this chapter, Serena Jackson faced a series of challenges as a new college student. Now after reading this chapter, would you respond differently to any of the questions you answered about the "FOCUS Challenge Case"? Knowing what you know now, how would you advise her? Write a paragraph ending to the story, incorporating your best advice.

2. Of the five EI scales, which do you experience as most challenging? Why? What can you do to improve your emotional intelligence in this area?

3. Do you agree with the suggestions for effective group communication in this chapter? Which one do you think is most important? Why? Give an example of its importance from your own experience.

4. Do you think most college students value diversity? Why or why not?

5. Are there particular groups on campus you'd like to learn more about to develop and diversify your awareness? What might you learn by doing so?

6. Have you traveled outside the United States? If so, have those experiences broadened your worldview? How? If not, how might you do so even without the opportunity to travel and see differences firsthand?

What did you LEARN?

On a scale of 1 to 10, answer the following questions now that you've completed the chapter.

 low   1   2   3   4   5   6   7   8   9   10   high

In hindsight, how much did you already know about this subject before reading the chapter?

Can you answer these questions about communicating in groups and valuing diversity more fully now that you've read the chapter?

❶ What is emotional intelligence and how does it relate to college success?

❷ Identify one of five basic conflict styles.

❸ Describe three benefits of valuing diversity.

How useful might the information in this chapter be to you? How much do you think this information might affect your success overall? _____

How much energy did you put into reading this chapter? _____

How long did it actually take you to complete this chapter (both the reading and writing tasks)? _____ Hour(s) _____ Minutes

Did you finish reading this chapter? _____

Did you intend to when you started? _____

If you meant to but didn't, what stopped you? _____

Take a minute to compare these answers to your answers from the "Readiness Check" at the beginning of this chapter. What gaps exist between the similar questions? How might these gaps between what you thought before starting the chapter and what you now think after completing the chapter affect how you approach the next chapter in this book?

©Larry Harwood Photography. Property of Cengage Learning.

11 Working Toward Wellness

How this chapter relates to YOU

1. When it comes to working toward wellness in college, what do you find most challenging, if anything?

Controlling my stress levels

Eating a healthy diet

Getting enough exercise

Getting enough sleep

Not giving in to unwanted alcohol/drugs/sex

2. What is most likely to be your response? Circle it.

I'll be open to learning how to make the best choices.

I'll see whether this chapter helps me.

I'll pay particular attention to my own challenges.

Eventually, I'll just figure it out on my own.

3. What would you have to do to increase your likelihood of success? Will you do it this quarter or semester?

_____

_____

_____

How YOU will relate to this chapter

What are you most interested in learning about? Put check marks by those topics.

☐ How wellness is defined

☐ The importance of physical, mental, and spiritual health

☐ How to assess your own wellness choices

☐ How to deal with six areas of wellness that affect first-year students: stress, nutrition, exercise, sleep, alcohol and drugs, and sex

☐ How to create a wellness plan for yourself that will impact your college success

● How motivated are you to learn more about working toward wellness in college? (5 = high, 1 = low) ____

● How ready are you to read now? ____ (If something is in your way, take care of it if you can, zero in and focus).

● How long do you think it will take you to complete this chapter? If you start and stop, keep track of your overall time. ____ Hour(s) ____ Minutes

gofugui/Photos.com; Jupiterimages/Photos.com; Edward Lam/Photos.com; Comstock Images/Photos.com; © iStockphoto/Thinkstock.com

challenge

Anthony Lopez

© Larry Harwood Photography. Property of Cengage Learning

Anthony Lopez was average in nearly every sense of the word. He wasn't a record-breaking athlete, nor was he the top student in his high school class. He was even sandwiched between two older brothers and two younger sisters. His brothers had excelled in college—one was an attorney and the other a computer engineer. Anthony knew that measuring up would be difficult for him. He wasn't exactly sure why he was in college or what career he might aim for, but he knew his parents expected him to be successful. They never had the opportunity to go to college, so they wanted to make sure their children did.

Somos/Veer/Getty Images

the time of his life! He'd already made loads of friends, and even the ladies, who regularly snubbed him in high school, thought he was worth getting to know here.

In the first weeks of school, Anthony did his part to help Huntington Hall live up to its reputation. Partying was especially heavy on Tuesday ("Booze-day") and Thursday ("Thirstday"), not to mention the weekends. Besides, drinking helped him forget his academic worries, which were beginning to mount, and bolstered his confidence with the opposite sex.

Weekends were supercharged with partying before and after football games and going online

to find out where the action was or hitting the local bars. Fake IDs weren't hard to get, and no one ever questioned him anyway. Most students got a buzz on before even leaving Huntington for a night of drinking so that they could get a head start. The freedom he had in college was overwhelming. No one seemed to care if he cut class, turned in his assignments, or drank too much.

After he didn't call home for a week and ignored several texts, Anthony's Mom called him as he walked from his

© Cengage Learning

HUNTINGTON HALL
UNOFFICIAL SCHEDULE OF EVENTS

MONDAY	STRIP POKER
TUESDAY	BOOZEDAY
	CHIP IN IF YOU WANT PIZZA
WEDNESDAY	BEER PONG
THURSDAY	THIRSTDAY DRINKING GAMES
FRIDAY	STUDY NIGHT (NOT)

Now that he was here at the university, Anthony was going to make his mark. He was away from home for the first time ever, and he was having

FLORIDA DRIVER LICENSE
License No. P99999999 Expires 07-10-15
Anthony Lopez
3424 East First Avenue
Ft. Lesterville, FL
Sex: M Hair: Black
Ht: 6-0 Eyes: Brown
Wt: 200 DOB: 07-10-87
DONOR

© Patrimonio designs limited/Shutterstock.com

Messages

Tony, Call me when you get back... —Eric

555—2313

IT's TUESDAY BOOZE—DAY!!!

Bryan was here!

© Cengage Learning

history class back to Huntington Hall for one of the regular Thursday night gatherings—this time in his room. He'd already decided to skip math because it was a huge lecture course, and he figured he was invisible among so many students anyway.

"Anthony, what's going on?" his Mom asked. "We haven't heard from you!" Suddenly Anthony realized she was right. "I've been really busy," he replied. "You know, college is hard work, Mom." He tried to sound convincing. "I'm sure you're working hard, Anthony, but I want to know about you. How are *you* doing?"

Then she started in with the usual list of parental questions: "Are you eating well?" "Sure, Mom," was his answer, although he knew his diet had changed radically since he left home—and not for the better. He hadn't gotten up in time for breakfast once, and his fast-food cravings were particularly hard to ignore. He'd been on the track team in high school, but even running had fallen by the wayside. "Are you getting enough rest?" "Yeah, Mom," he replied, although he and his buddies regularly played "Grand Theft Auto" online late into the night. "Are you feeling okay? You sound like you have a cold." "It's nothing, Mom," he said, although his throat was awfully sore. "Are you making some friends?" "Am I ever!" he answered a little too enthusiastically. "How about girls? Have you met anyone worth mentioning?" "I'm a popular guy in college, Mom. You'd be surprised! I'm making my mark!" At the moment, he was juggling three

different relationships, and although it was his least favorite of the three, one had recently become intimate, and without much warning, too. That reminded him: he really should go on one of those medical websites to find out more about STIs. He was beginning to worry. Why hadn't anyone told him that college could be so stressful?

When the questions came around to academics, Anthony's answers weren't so well rehearsed. "Have you had any exams in your math course yet? How did you do?" Anthony faltered, "Not too well, but I'll bring my grade up next time." Anthony didn't like the way the conversation was going. "Let me call you back later, Mom," he interrupted. Academics were down on his list of priorities, and his Mom's barrage of questions was making him very uncomfortable. What *was* foremost on

his mind was the huge off-campus party coming up on Friday night.

However, Friday night was when Anthony's social life came to a screeching halt. The party was so big and noisy that neighbors called the campus police. Anthony and a few other students were issued an MIP, "Minor in Possession" ticket, a misdemeanor that came with a $500 fine and possible jail time. According to state law, Anthony would lose his driver's license and insurance for six months to one year, too. He'd had far too much to drink that night, and it showed.

Nicole

Lisa

Kara

Now what? An MIP was something that would definitely require a phone call home, and he'd have to face the consequences. He knew how disappointed his parents and older brothers would be. *I'm making my mark all right,* he thought to himself, *but this wasn't exactly what I had in mind.*

What Do *You* Think?

challenge

reaction

❶ Is Anthony representative of students on your campus? In your opinion, why do these types of wellness problems arise among college students?
❷ Do you predict that Anthony will be successful in college? Why or why not?
❸ What would be required to reverse Anthony's rocky start to college?
❹ Anthony says his new freedom in college is overwhelming. Do you see evidence of that feeling among your classmates? If so, how is it expressed?

VARK It!

Complete the recommended activity for your preferred VARK learning modality. If you are multimodal, select more than one activity. Your instructor may ask you to (a) give an oral report on your results in class, (b) send your results to him or her via e-mail, or (c) post them online.

Visual: Start this chapter by drawing a circle to represent a Wellness Wheel. As you read each section, redraw the Wellness Wheel in pie chart fashion by giving each of the six sectors different sized slices, based on how important they are to you and your personal college success.

Aural: Before you start reading this chapter, write an e-mail to a friend who has wellness issues (not getting enough sleep, not exercising, stressing out, etc.). As you read, add specifics to your e-mail.

Read/Write: As you read, compile a list of issues about your own personal wellness issues. What do you need to work on? Bring a list to class (if you're willing to discuss it) or submit it to your instructor via e-mail, if asked.

Kinesthetic: Find a YouTube with some good ideas about working toward wellness to share with the class. E-mail the link to your instructor.

Vertical credit text (left margin): © iStockphoto.com/Marcela Barsse; Joanna Goodyear/Dreamstime.com; © iStockphoto.com/Nadezda Firsova; © iStockphoto.com/Pascal Genest

Exercise 11.1 Wellness Survey

This chapter will focus on the relationship between wellness and college success. Six specific aspects of wellness are impacted by regular choices you make. Before you begin reading the chapter, complete this wellness survey. For each statement, rate yourself on a scale of 5 to 1.

	Yes!	Yes	Not Sure	No	No!
	5	4	3	2	1

1. STRESS

_____ 1. I control my stress level.

_____ 2. I find ways to relax and let off steam that are healthy and productive.

_____ 3. I'm aware of my limits and don't take on too much.

_____ 4. I make time for social activities that are reenergizing.

_____ 5. I learn from poor wellness choices I make and change my behavior.

_____ 6. I don't pattern my own wellness choices on those of my friends, particularly if they may cause problems for me.

_____ 7. I think before I act when it comes to choosing wellness.

_____ 8. I plan ahead to achieve a healthy lifestyle.

_____ 9. I understand the relationship between wellness and academic success and act accordingly.

_____ 10. I know that working toward wellness is key to the future I want for myself.

_____ TOTAL SCORE for STRESS

2. NUTRITION

_____ 1. I am knowledgeable about what constitutes a well-balanced, nutritious diet.

_____ 2. I eat frequently throughout the day to keep up my energy, as opposed to overeating at mealtimes.

_____ 3. I eat at least five servings of fruits and vegetables per day.

_____ 4. I eat breakfast most or all mornings.

_____ 5. I use food for nourishment, rather than to comfort myself or relieve boredom.

_____ 6. I eat when I'm experiencing stomach hunger, rather than simply mouth hunger.

_____ 7. I avoid skipping meals to lose weight.

_____ 8. I avoid unhealthy foods, such as fast food or foods high in sugar, fat, or sodium.

_____ 9. I read food labels to learn the nutritional value of foods.

_____ 10. I pay attention to my body's signals about which foods make me feel fit and healthy.

_____ TOTAL SCORE for NUTRITION

3. EXERCISE

_____ 1. I recognize when I need to get some exercise.

_____ 2. I take advantage of natural opportunities to exercise, like climbing stairs instead of using elevators.

_____ 3. I am satisfied with the amount of exercise I get.

_____ 4. I enjoy exercising.

_____ 5. I try to get some exercise, even if in small amounts, every day.

_____ 6. I exercise moderately without overdoing it, which can be unhealthy.

_____ 7. I walk or ride my bike instead of driving whenever I can.

_____ 8. I have a regular exercise routine that I follow.

_____ 9. I exercise to help elevate my mood when I feel anxious or depressed.

_____ 10. I use physical exercise to relieve stress.

_____ TOTAL SCORE for EXERCISE

4. SLEEP

_____ 1. I go to bed when I'm tired.

_____ 2. If I nap during the day, I make sure it's a short one in the early afternoon.

_____ 3. I get seven or more hours of sleep per night.

_____ 4. I don't vary the times I go to sleep and wake up by more than two hours during the week.

_____ 5. I don't study or read assignments in bed.

_____ 6. I am able to fall asleep on my own without resorting to pills.

_____ 7. I don't use alcohol to help me fall asleep.

_____ 8. I exercise regularly to help my sleeping habits.

_____ 9. I avoid caffeine late in the day.

_____ 10. I understand the importance of sleep to my academic success.

_____ TOTAL SCORE for SLEEP

(continued on next page)

5. ALCOHOL and DRUGS

_____ 1. I drink responsibly or not at all.

_____ 2. I don't need alcohol or drugs to have fun.

_____ 3. I don't drink with the intention of getting drunk.

_____ 4. I intervene when my friends are intoxicated or high and help them.

_____ 5. I limit my drinking episodes per week.

_____ 6. I associate with others who drink responsibly or not at all.

_____ 7. I think while I'm drinking and don't lose my good judgment.

_____ 8. I plan ahead when I'm out with friends and choose a designated driver beforehand.

_____ 9. I don't use alcohol or drugs to escape from my problems.

_____ 10. I don't let alcohol and parties affect my academic performance.

_____ **TOTAL SCORE for ALCOHOL**

6. SEX

_____ 1. I am sexually responsible and practice safe sex or abstain from sex.

_____ 2. I am considerate and appropriate in the ways I talk about sex.

_____ 3. I explore my own sexuality in ways that are both positive and pleasurable.

_____ 4. I feel good about my body.

_____ 5. I am comfortable with my sexual orientation.

_____ 6. I understand birth control options and exercise them, if appropriate.

_____ 7. I communicate clearly what I want or don't want from a partner, if appropriate.

_____ 8. I avoid unplanned sex.

_____ 9. I am content with the amount of sexual activity I engage in.

_____ 10. I allow others to express their sexual orientation, even if it is different from mine.

_____ **TOTAL SCORE for SEX**

You will use your scores on this survey later in the chapter to better understand yourself and your wellness choices and how they may be affecting you.

I hope we don't have to discuss this in class! Some of my scores don't look so good!

Health, Education, and Welfare

Sensitive Situation Students probably won't want to share their results from this survey. Prior to having students fill in their personal data, you might make up a fictitious survey and share it with the class for discussion. Remind students that this activity is solely for their benefit. Students must assess their own behavior and decide what to do about it. Your job is to make them fully aware of the consequences.

Teachable Moment It's easy to discuss someone else's issues rather than one's own. The case study about Anthony Lopez gives students an opportunity to talk about someone else while really talking about themselves. Ask students if alcohol, drugs, and sex can impact college success. What underlying issues are putting Anthony on a self-destructive path? What should he do?

From 1953 to 1979, the United States government had a Department of Health, Education, and Welfare, and the secretary of HEW was a member of the president's cabinet. The history isn't important here, but the point that those three things—health, education, and welfare—are connected is. Although you may not have thought much about it, your health and well-being significantly impact your college success.

Without good health, education is at risk. Your physical, mental, and spiritual health affect your ability to learn. In a letter to John Garland Jefferson in 1790, Thomas Jefferson encouraged his studious young cousin to remember that "Exercise and recreation ... are as necessary as reading. I will rather say more necessary because health is worth more than learning." What did Jefferson mean? Is his advice centuries ago still pertinent today?

Think about this: College is about learning and understanding, cultivating the "life of the mind," as it's sometimes called. However, the life of the mind is related to the state of the body. Your brain is obviously connected to the rest of

> When health is absent, wisdom cannot reveal itself; Art cannot become manifest; Strength cannot be exerted; Wealth is useless; and Reason is powerless.

Herophilus, Greek physician, called the father of scientific anatomy

you. Wellness—or a lack of it—can get in the way of an otherwise productive academic career. Wellness isn't merely the absence of illness. It's a process that moves you toward optimal health, based on smart choices. This chapter is about six specific areas of wellness that you can influence to improve your college success.

Physical health is only part of the picture. Mental health issues—depression or anxiety, for example—can also affect your efforts. Spiritual health that comes through searching and self-understanding provide the motivation to make the right wellness choices in the first place.

Here's a sobering wake-up call about wellness and first-year college students. First-year students represent 40 percent of undergraduate deaths from natural causes; 40 percent of all undergraduate suicides; 50 percent of all undergraduate deaths from falls from windows, balconies, and rooftops; and 47 percent of the undergraduates who die on campus.[1] Unfortunately, some first-year students seek thrills, ignore danger, or seriously overextend themselves and become one of these statistics. One reason is because the brains of young college students are still developing the circuitry that acts as an "early warning system" in the brains of older adults.[2]

Whoa! Those are scary numbers.

Teachable Moment Take this opportunity to discuss some of the public figures who have struggled with wellness issues. Do students feel that reckless behavior is glamorized in movies, on television, and in magazines?

These statistics are alarming, to be sure, but at the same time, knowing the risks and making wise choices can keep you safe. This chapter's intention isn't to alarm you, however; it's to equip you with the information you need to be at your best physically, psychologically, and academically. Unwise decisions may make adjusting to college more difficult than it needs to be; wise ones bolster your academic efforts. As one headline puts it boldly, "Grades in College Directly Linked to Health-related Behaviors."[3]

Wellness is about making *informed* choices: knowing the range of choices you have, understanding why making productive choices is important, and then doing it. Wellness requires you to slow down, think, listen to your inner voice or your gut, and plan ahead.

It's easy to observe other people and pinpoint all the wellness mistakes they're making. As you watch them, you may think, *That's not a good idea!* or *You're going to regret doing that!* It's not so easy, however, to be objective about

I think this chapter is going to make me uncomfortable . . . :(

your own wellness choices. What's easy is going with the flow and zipping right along without stopping to think. That's where this chapter comes in. Its goal is to change some *counterproductive* choices you may be making—and to validate *productive* ones. As you read, you will explore your physical, mental, and spiritual health; and you'll learn more about where to go if you need help. Later, you'll use the wellness survey you filled out in Exercise 11.1 to create your own Wellness Wheel to identify areas for improvement.

Thomas Jefferson said that health is worth more than learning. Fortunately, you don't have to choose between the two in college. You can achieve both. But you do have to make choices—positive, productive ones—in order to achieve wellness. Much of the responsibility for a healthy lifestyle rests squarely on your own shoulders, and if tough problems do surface, getting the help you need is vital. Find out the kinds of wellness resources available on your campus, where they're located, how to contact them, and what kind of help you can expect if you go.

In many ways, your degree of wellness is up to you. After all, who decides when you'll tuck yourself in at night, go back for seconds or thirds, or skip meals so that your jeans fit better? Who monitors your visits to the doctor, your stress levels, and your alcohol consumption? Who requires you to take the necessary precautions for safe sex or suggests you exercise to stay fit? Who does all these things? None other than you! Responsibility for wellness is the place to start this discussion. If you don't agree with this principle, you'll be in denial throughout much of the rest of the chapter.

> "
> To keep the body in good health is a duty … otherwise we shall not be able to keep our mind strong and clear.
> "
>
> *Buddha (c. 563–483 B.C.)*

Did my mom write this???

Physical Health: In Sickness and in Health

? challenge

" reaction

Challenge: Fill in the blanks for the following statement.

Reaction: I would seek the help of a physician if I had:

1. a fever above _____ degrees.
2. a headache accompanied by _____.
3. a mole that _____.
4. digestive problems that included alternating _____ and _____.
5. a persistent symptom of _____ that won't go away.

Of course, everyone loses at "germ warfare" from time to time. A virus may assault you, seemingly out of nowhere, or an infection may attack when you least expect it. What kinds of physical health problems do college students generally face?[4]

Acute Medical Problems

(Urgent—and important.) You need help fast! Appendicitis or toxic shock syndrome, for example, require immediate, life-or-death medical attention. Unfortunately, sometimes serious health problems occur among college students because they delay treatment by waiting for a convenient time between assignment due dates. Acute complications can set in.

Chronic Medical Problems

(Somewhat less urgent, but very important.) Approximately one-third of asthma sufferers and one-fourth of diabetics are diagnosed by the time they're in their thirties. While most college students are a relatively healthy group, cancer is the fifth leading cause of death among people between the ages of fifteen and twenty-four, following AIDS, accidents, homicide, and suicide.

Infectious Diseases

(An ounce of prevention …) In many developing countries, infectious diseases such as mononucleosis (known to many as the kissing disease) occur in early childhood when they can be fought off fairly easily. In the United States, however, these infections are often contracted later, during your college years. Complications can sometimes occur, and illnesses in this category can be major reasons for medical withdrawals from college. Life-threatening infectious diseases, such as meningitis, have the capability to spread rapidly on a college campus where students are in close proximity. Or take another kind of infectious disease: sexually transmitted infections. Two-thirds of STIs occur in people under age twenty-five, and many of these diseases can have long-term consequences such as infertility or even cancer. Contagious illnesses are hard to avoid when you're surrounded by classmates or roommates who have them, so anything in this category is worth paying attention to.

> ❝ Take care of your body. It's the only place you have to live. ❞

Jim Rohn, business philosopher and author

You're likely to have your share of aches and pains, colds, and flu symptoms during your first year of college, but you should seek medical attention if you have any of these symptoms:

➤ Fever of 102.5 degrees or higher

➤ Headache accompanied by a stiff neck

➤ Unexplained, significant weight loss

➤ A mole that bleeds, itches, or changes shape, color, or size

➤ Sudden vomiting

➤ Difficulty swallowing

➤ Blood that is vomited or coughed up

➤ Alternating diarrhea and constipation

➤ Pain or blood with urination

➤ A lump or thickening in the breast

➤ Unusual discharge from your genitals

➤ Change in your menstrual cycle

➤ Pain in your abdomen that won't go away

➤ Persistent cough, chest pain, or trouble breathing

➤ *Any* symptom that doesn't seem to go away and worries you

Hmmm … I do worry about a couple of these …

Mental Health: Up or Down

Challenge: Fill in the blanks for the following statement.

Reaction: I would seek the help of a counselor if I:

1. had negative feelings such as _____, _____, or _____.
2. experienced changes in habits such as _____.
3. had trouble doing academic tasks requiring _____.
4. lost interest in _____.
5. experienced troublesome symptoms of depression for longer than _____.

Activity Option Break up the class into three or four groups and have them respond to the five questions in the "Challenge ⊠ Reaction." Ask students to come up with a number of responses to each question. Some students may not want to reveal their real responses, but hearing members of the group discuss the issues might encourage those who need help to get it.

I was really psyched for college, but now...

Activity Option Get students up and out of their chairs by doing a "human continuum" related to several of the Wellness Wheel scales (the more general, less personal ones). For example, ask students to place themselves on the imaginary continuum with one end representing "I have increased my exercise since I have come to college" and the other end representing those who have decreased their exercise. Ask students to report how changes in exercise make them feel. For those who are exercising, ask them to share their strategies with the class.

People who are mentally healthy have particular characteristics. They see things realistically, make and keep close relationships, do what's required of them, accept their own strengths and weaknesses, value themselves, and get fulfillment from life.[5] They may feel down on occasion, but they pop right back up again. According to the Centers for Disease Control and Prevention (CDC), the average American adult feels depressed or unhappy approximately three days per month. In their research, college-aged people (ages 18–24), smokers (a pack or more per day), and women reported more down days; people with good jobs and those who exercised regularly reported fewer days.[6]

College can be a particularly vulnerable time for ups and downs because of your new environment, new freedom, new pressures, and new temptations. One place to start examining your own ups and downs is to look at the wellness choices you're making. If you are engaging in excessive casual sex, running on no sleep, experimenting with drugs, or drinking too much alcohol too often, these unproductive choices could be contributing to feelings of unhappiness. But these behaviors can also be symptomatic of deeper problems, so it's important to pay attention: "A 2012 study by the American College Counseling Association found that 37.4 percent of college students seeking help have severe psychological problems, up from 16 percent in 2000."[7]

Mental illness is "a diagnosable mental, behavioral, or emotional disorder that interferes with one or more major activities in life, like dressing, eating, or working."[8] Mental health problems include *anxiety* disorders (such as generalized anxiety disorder or obsessive-compulsive disorder), *mood* disorders (such as depression or bipolar disorder), and, more rarely, *psychotic* disorders (such as schizophrenia).

What causes mental illness? There's no germ we know of for depression or anxiety, and there's no easy answer to that question. However, several factors come into play. You can have a genetic predisposition to a particular mental illness, such as schizophrenia. Although rare in the general population, if you have a relative with schizophrenia, your odds of developing it go up.[9] However, startling research reports that marijuana use has the potential to trigger schizophrenia.[10] Research also reveals that former chronic ecstasy users report higher levels of depression than their counterparts who don't use the drug.[11] Genetics are outside your control, but the choice to use drugs that may worsen an underlying predisposition is yours to make.

What types of mental health issues do college students sometimes face? Two key problems are worth examining in more detail.

Depression

Your psychological makeup may also be a key factor in developing some mental health problems. Some of us are highly sensitive, pessimistic, or have low self-esteem. These characteristics may make us more vulnerable to mental illness such as depression. Some students feel more down than up; for them, depression can become a serious health issue. They may feel isolated, even among so many hundreds of other students.

Clinical depression is a serious problem. It isn't a passing mood, and you can't simply pull yourself together and get over it. According to the National Institute of Mental Health (NIMH), approximately 9.5 percent of American adults, or 20.9 million people, suffer from some form of depression.[12] And recent research shows that college students with particular types of depression are twice as likely to drop out of school as their classmates.[13] But depression can be treated, and 80 percent of those who ask for help get better.[14] Read the accounts from these college students to see if they sound like statements you've heard recently from anyone you know.

Catherine: "I haven't stopped crying since I got here weeks ago. I don't know what's wrong with me, but I feel empty and sad all the time, and no one seems to understand."

Alex: "I sleep all weekend, every weekend, and I'm still tired. I have trouble concentrating on my schoolwork, and nothing is as much fun as I thought it would be. Why can't I just buckle down and get on with it?"

John: "When I finally got to college, I wanted to 'come out' about being gay, but some of my buddies are always making jokes about homosexuals, so I've kept my mouth shut. Sometimes the stress is overwhelming, and I'm feeling pretty hopeless."

Are these students depressed? How would you know? The symptoms of major depression include:

➤ Sadness, anxiety, or feelings of emptiness

➤ Low energy and fatigue

➤ Loss of interest in enjoyable activities

➤ Changes in sleep patterns (insomnia, early waking, oversleeping)

➤ Appetite and weight changes (loss or gain)

➤ Feeling worthless or guilty or hopeless

➤ Suicidal thoughts (or attempts)

➤ Trouble concentrating, remembering, or making decisions

Every adversity, every failure, every heartache carries with it the seed of an equal or greater benefit.

Napoleon Hill (1883–1970), author, Keys to Success: The 17 Principles of Personal Achievement

Teachable Moment Consider sending your students to see the TedTalk, "Why 30 Is Not the New 20." In this presentation, Meg Jay, therapist and author of *The Defining Decade*, gives three suggestions about how twentysomethings can best use this critical decade of their lives.

I'm upset with myself for being arrested, but I don't think I'm actually depressed ...

Activity Option Have students create new entries with hypothetical names and examples they're heard from other students who may be experirencing depresseion.

> Excessive crying or irritability

> Aches and pains that come and go without explanation[15]

If five or more of these symptoms last for several weeks without letting up, and they interfere with your normal functioning, visit your campus counseling center to find out if depression is your problem. But depression is only one type of mood disorder. Bipolar disorder can be a confusing malady because periods of deep, dark depression alternate with periods of excitability, racing thoughts, and distractibility. Just when you decide depression may be your problem, you enter a hyperactive period in which you can't sleep for days.

If you suspect a mental health problem, and if you don't have the energy or courage to visit your campus counseling center alone, ask your best friend to go with you. Medication and counseling can help.[16] For example, drugs such as Zoloft, Paxil, or Lexapro help many people who suffer from depression, and lithium carbonate helps sufferers of bipolar disorder. Left untreated, depression can push people to the edge.

According to recent data, every year about 1,300 college students commit suicide and another 31,469 attempt to.[17] Always take suicidal thoughts, impulses, or attempts—your own or someone else's—seriously and get help right away. Tell your residence hall advisor, a teacher, a coach, a staff member— someone you know and trust—that you need professional help immediately. If you suspect a friend is contemplating hurting herself, ask her. Show your concern and persuade her to get help, rather than risking her decision to become a statistic. Call 911 or a suicide hotline. Experts say that talking about suicide to someone who is considering it doesn't push him over the edge. The most important factor is getting help, and you may play a role in saving his life.

The long list of public figures—historical and contemporary—who have suffered from depression might surprise you.[18] Abraham Lincoln (1809–1865), now considered one of the greatest American presidents, suffered from "melancholy" much of his life, and after he broke off his engagement to Mary Todd in 1841, his friends feared he would commit suicide and watched him around the clock. Eventually, he harnessed his depression by pouring all his energies into his political career. Sigmund Freud (1856–1939), the revolutionary psychoanalyst, was also a patient. He was fixated on his sex life and wrote 900 love letters to the woman he loved. He suffered from depression and despair and was, in fact, susceptible to many of the same problems he diagnosed in his patients. Marilyn Monroe (1926–1962), actress and "silver screen siren," couldn't beat depression and overdosed, it's believed, on barbiturates. She was under the constant care of a psychiatrist, even during the height of her career. Greg Louganis (b. 1960), winner of five Olympic medals and perhaps the best diver in history, had attempted suicide three times by the time he was eighteen. Louganis experienced severe inner turmoil about being gay, and he learned in 1987 that he was HIV-positive. He now speaks across the country about his life experiences as a role model for young people.

Today many modern-day celebrities are open about their battles with depression—Jim Carrey, Sheryl Crow, and Drew Barrymore, for example.[19] Historically, effective medications weren't available, and often people chose to suffer in silence. Today depression has come out of the closet. Public awareness is the goal, and getting help is the path to wellness.

I had no idea about these famous people!

Anxiety

For some students, anxiety skyrockets out of control, and some develop full-fledged anxiety disorders. Anxiety disorders are real, common, often linked to depression, and treatable. They include:

> *Generalized Anxiety Disorder (GAD):* six months or more of extreme worry about things that aren't true immediate concerns, like health, loved ones, money, or jobs—or a generalized anxiety about everything

> *Obsessive-Compulsive Disorder (OCD):* uncontrollable urges to perform repeated actions (like hand washing); making yourself follow specific, unrealistic rules (like forcing yourself to always do X before you do Y and Z) and becoming upset when you can't; and checking and rechecking something over and over even though you've already made sure

> *Panic Disorder:* an attack in which your heart pounds, your chest hurts, you tremble, sweat, feel out of breath, and are overcome by dread; the attacks occur out of the blue, repeatedly, and without a recognizable physical cause

> *Phobias:* deep fears that are irrational yet guide your behavior. Everyone has certain fears, but phobias are extreme. Some people have phobias related to heights (acrophobia) or confined spaces (claustrophobia), for example, and these fears are debilitating.

Help is available on your campus at the Counseling Center or Student Health Center. Check these online sources for further information, too:[20]

Mental Health America: http://www.mentalhealthamerica.net/

Anxiety and Depression Association of America: www.adaa.org

Anxiety Panic Attack Resource: www.anxietypanic.com

National Anxiety Foundation: http://lexington-on-line.com/naf.html

National Institute of Mental Health: www.nimh.nih.gov

Check these out next time I'm online...

According to a recent study, nearly one-third of students have had counseling at some point in the past.[21] And experts say about 10 percent of the student body on most campuses visits the campus counseling center each year, and many more could be helped by doing so.[22] The percentage of students seeking counseling increases from freshman to senior year.[23] But why wait? If you think you could be helped, take action now!

Spiritual Health: Department of the Interior

Challenge: How can college help you examine your values, find direction, and ponder the meaning of life?

Reaction:

_____

_____

_____

Who are you? What do you want? For most students, college is a time of personal exploration and growth.[24] Many students are searching for meaning in their lives. For some, it can be a time of struggle as they try to envision what appears to be a distant future. "What am I going to do with my life?" is a pervasive question. Nearly three-quarters of college freshmen report having discussions with friends about the meaning and purpose of life.[25]

According to a national study of 112,232 college students, four out of five first-year students are interested in spirituality, and nearly three-fourths report feeling a sense of connection with a higher power. Eighty-one percent say they attend religious services occasionally or frequently. Most college freshmen consider it "essential" or "very important" that college help increase their self-understanding (69 percent), help prepare them to be responsible citizens (67 percent), develop their personal values (67 percent), and assist in their emotional development (63 percent). Nearly half believe that college should help encourage their expression of spirituality.

Many college students are on a spiritual quest. Over half of first-year students report questioning their religious beliefs (57 percent) and nearly as many (52 percent) disagree with their families on religious matters. They also report a high level of religious tolerance and concern for others who are in difficulty.[26] Eighty-two percent report doing volunteer work while in high school. However, by the end of the first year of college, students report spending less time volunteering their time or attending religious services.[27]

Teachable Moment It's important to point out that spirituality is not necessarily synonymous with religion. Also, students need to know that college is a good time to explore beliefs about spirituality in a thoughtful and meaningful way.

Sensitive Situation Responding to questions about spirituality may be a very private matter for some students, perhaps it's a better topic for journaling than for a full-class discussion. Don't put anyone on the spot.

Can college help you examine your values, find inner direction, and ponder the meaning of life? Think about the courses you're taking this term. Are questions that relate to spiritual health explored, directly or indirectly? A course in philosophy might be a natural place to begin thinking about them, or a course in psychology, or many others, actually. How about the course for which you're using this textbook? Are you being asked to explore your values and your aspirations? In the end, where any course takes you is determined partly by you, and many issues related to spirituality can be examined on your own while you're in college, not necessarily during any particular class. There are also many ways to work on "your interior," such as yoga, meditation, prayer, or exercise. The point is to free up your mind and slow down long enough to search on your own.

Eric Robert/CORBIS SYGMA

66

It is not what we get but who we become, what we contribute . . . that gives meaning to our lives.

99

Anthony Robbins, motivational speaker and author

> " The reinvention of daily life means marching off the edge of our maps. "

Bob Black

You're a winner. You're working hard as a highly motivated, ultra competent employee. Your boss is impressed—so much so that you get promoted. Your new position requires you to work harder, and before you know it, you're promoted again. This cycle keeps repeating itself, and over time, you have success written all over you. You're well on your way to mapping out a great future.

There's an underlying question worth exploring, however. Why are you working so hard? Is it because you're passionate about your work? Perhaps it fuels you, gives you purpose, direction, and fulfillment. You love it.

But what if your success isn't about fulfillment at all? What if it's about moving up, making more money, reveling in the prestige? What if you actually dislike your work? You're tethered to your computer, your weekends have disappeared, your weeknights are filled with "homework," and your family has forgotten your name. It can happen gradually, sometimes so gradually that you hardly notice that someone is cranking up the heat. Suddenly, it hits you like a ton of bricks: you've become a classic "workaholic." The company owns you, and you've lost your balance. One work-life balance expert asks, why do people "work long hard hours doing things they hate to enable them to buy things they don't need to impress people they don't like"?[28] Good question. The why of success is fundamentally important.

If you ever lose your professional balance, "march off the edge of your map," and take charge of your own future. Your company is unlikely to say, "You know what? You've been working far too hard. You need to chill for a few weeks." Corporations won't fix things *for* you. They'll usually use as much of you as you let them. You have to do it yourself. You must take control and assume responsibility for living the type of life you want to live. For example, make a rule for yourself that evenings are for family or your romantic partner, and stick to it. Or make a pact that you'll only check your email once a day on weekends so that you can let your mind "idle" for a while. "If you don't design your life, someone else will design it for you. And you may just not like their idea of balance."[29]

A recent study asked dying people to identify their biggest regrets. "Their most common regret? 'I wish I'd had the courage to live a life true to myself, not the life others expected of me.' Their second most common regret? 'I wish I didn't work so hard.' There are two ways to address these regrets. One, work less hard and spend your time living a life true to yourself, whatever that means. Or two, work just as hard— harder even—on things you consider to be important and meaningful. If you put those two regrets together, you realize that what people really regret isn't simply working so hard, it's working so hard on things that don't matter to them. If our work matters to us, if it represents *a life true to us* . . . . then we will have lived more fully."[30]

What does a balanced life look like? It's a life that *you* create, based on who you are and what you want. It's about making your career work for you, not the other way around.

Think Ahead Think about the idea of balance. What does it mean to you as a college student? What will it mean in your anticipated profession?

Cast on Careers

© Larry Harwood Photography. Property of Cengage Learning

FOCUS: Is finding balance important to college students?

LINDSEY: Absolutely! And it's one of the things that was very hard for me. I wanted to do it all: dance team, campus involvement, a high GPA. But in the end, I had to make choices. I learned the hard way that I had to prioritize and find the right balance for me.

FOCUS: What are your career plans?

LINDSEY: I'm majoring in nursing. I will have to find balance between helping people and practicing medicine. I think I can do it, but finding balance will always be a challenge. Not letting the bureaucracy of a hospital and the potential burnout of the job get in the way of the human element will be important. My goal will be to always remember that!

I know my brothers probably work too hard, and I probably don't work hard enough. But I've never even thought about the idea of <u>balance</u>...

Activity Option In preparation for the following section, ask students to make a copy of their Wellness Wheel and bring it to class, without their name on it. Collect the wheels and redistribute to the class. As a group, develop a class Wellness Wheel. What are the areas of strength in the class, and where are the areas that many students feel they need to focus on? Alternatively, you may draw a blank wellness wheel on the board and invite students to put tick marks, representing their own scores (anonymously). Then you can all get a visual profile of the strengths and challenges of the class.

According to one recent study, college students who integrate spiritual components that help them make choices and assess risks into their lives report better health.[31]

If these values are important to you, make a conscious decision to pursue your personal search for meaning and purpose, despite the many conflicting demands of college life. Your college experience is as much about these vital questions as it is about preparing for a particular career.

You Take the Wheel!

We've already established that some aspects of wellness, like genetic predispositions, are outside your control. But other aspects are mostly or entirely up to you. The remainder of this chapter examines six areas of wellness that impact your college success. The bottom line? Your decisions in these six areas will greatly affect how quickly and how well you adjust to college.

Now return to your completed wellness survey at the beginning of this chapter, and enter your scores for each of the six sectors on the Wellness Wheel in Figure 11.1 by placing a dot on or near the appropriate concentric circle (10, 20, 30, 40, or 50). Then connect the dots. While the survey isn't truly scientific, you will get a clear visual sense of where you are now and where to concentrate your future wellness efforts. For which of the six sectors did you score the lowest total? Were you surprised by your scores, or could you have predicted them?

How is your wheel shaped? Is it dented? Does the figure you get when you connect the dots fill up most of the wheel (representing healthy decisions), or

FIGURE 11.1
The Wellness Wheel

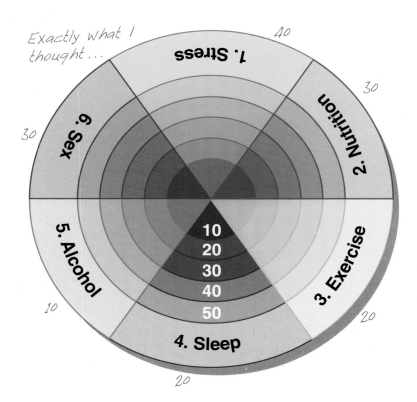

is it smaller, closer to the hub (representing less healthy decisions)? Dots closer to the center represent areas for improvement. Visualize how well your wheel will "roll" in its current shape (and how well *you* will function), and then decide what to do about it. Where do *you* need to focus?

Stress: Fast and Furious

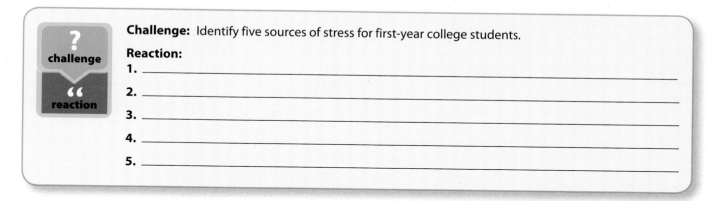

Challenge: Identify five sources of stress for first-year college students.

Reaction:

1. _____
2. _____
3. _____
4. _____
5. _____

Stress—isn't some stress good for you? Don't Olympic athletes, who train for years and perform on the world's stage, subject themselves to unbelievable stress, and isn't that stress part of what helps them achieve excellence? It's true that stress can produce results. Short-term stress—giving a speech or doing a tough math problem in your head—can actually bring out the best in you. However, long-term stress such as living through a natural disaster or caring for a disabled relative can take its toll. Stress can also come from distant trauma, such as child abuse in your past that continues to haunt you. Short-term stress "revs up" your immune system and protects you, but long-term or chronic stress tears it down, making you more vulnerable to illness.[32]

In some ways, stress is in the eye of the beholder. What's stressful to you may not be stressful to your best friend. There's a difference between stressors (the actual events or circumstances) and *perceived* stressors (how you react to them). Some experts say stress results from being both anxious and fatigued. Anxiety spikes your energy level, but if you're in a state of exhaustion at the same time, your body interprets the cross signals as stress.[33]

Ahhh, I see—when I make bad choices, my stress goes up. I get it—makes sense.

How do you know when you're reacting adversely to stress? Pay attention if you are depressed, irritable, anxious, fearful, lethargic, if you can't sleep (or sleep too much and still feel tired), wake up frequently, experience stomach-aches, headaches, shakiness, excessive sweating, heartburn, nausea, rapid and shallow breathing, or frequent colds. Not coping well with stress can show up in your health, your relationships, your job, and your academic work.

So what's so stressful about college? Aside from the adjustment factor, basically, everything! Try these common factors on for size, and see if they produce stress in you, perhaps even in just reading about them.[34]

Goodbyes. For many students, homesickness and friendsickness generate stress. Perhaps you left an ill family member behind or a favorite pet that rarely left your side.

Hellos. Meeting so many new people, while exciting, can feel like pressure. Will you make friends quickly and easily? Will you be accepted for who you are? Nevertheless, forging connections helps provide you with the support system you need in a new situation.

Grades. Perhaps you're attending college on a scholarship, and keeping your grades up is a top priority for you, or test anxiety gets the better of you. If you're a perfectionist, you may put unrealistic expectations on yourself, too, and that can seriously up your stress.

Peaks and valleys. Terms in college—quarters or semesters—have a rhythm to them. Your energy requirements are continuous, but they spike for midterm and final exams. Peak times can bring stress that affects your immune system. Just listen to the hacking and coughing during exams; it's a fairly common soundtrack.

Academic load. College brings a relentless lineup of assignments. As soon as you turn in one assignment, another one is waiting right behind it. Each class by itself would require a substantial investment of time, let alone the entire lot.

Academic challenge. At the beginning of the term you may be reviewing material from high school in some of your courses, and your confidence may climb. You may even become overconfident. But soon your instructor will be moving into uncharted territory, and the learning curve will take off, perhaps bringing your stress level right along with it.

Finances. Are you working more hours than you should? Everyone has legitimate bills, but are lifestyle choices adding to your financial burden? If you can afford luxuries like tanning sessions or a gas-guzzling truck, that's one thing. But if you can't and they compound your stress, that's another.

Eating and sleeping habits. Now that you're in college, you may be running from one thing to the next, grabbing the wrong food (or no food at all), and not getting the sleep you need in order to cope. Stress begets stress, you could say, and the results can be unhealthy.

What can you do about stress that seems to be spiraling out of control in your life? Here are five suggestions that may help.

1. **Change the situation.** If you're living with an impossible roommate who stays up all night making a racket while you're trying to get some decent shut-eye, consider moving. Do what you can to take control of the situation that's generating the stress.

2. **Change your reaction.** If you can't change the situation, try to change the way you react to it. Rather than letting the anxiety continue to build up, bunk with a friend and get the sleep you need until the situation is resolved.

3. **Keep up.** Keep up with your academic work in all your classes. Letting assignments slip in even one class is a guaranteed stress inducer.

4. **Improve your problem-solving skills.** If you can figure out what to do about what's stressing you, and you have confidence in your problem-solving skills, you'll be better off.[35] Take a class in problem solving or read up on increasing your skills on your own.

Teaching with Technology The University of Maryland Medical System has developed a series of brief and informal health calculators on their free website HealthCalculators.org. This site has wellness tests that calculate everything from stress levels, to the cost of a smoking addiction, to body mass index. These calculators can be a great resource for students who want to get a general idea of their overall health and potential risk factors.

Teachable Moment Remind students that they do have control over many things in their lives—maybe more than they know. If they truly have no control over a situation (for example, their parents' divorce), the thing they can control is how they respond to it.

> 66
> For fast-acting relief, try slowing down.
> 99

Lily Tomlin, Comedian

© Larry Harwood Photography. Property of Cengage Learning

Exercise 11.2 | Workplace Stress Survey

If you work for pay in addition to going to school, describe the organization for which you work. How many employees work there? What kind of work does the organization do? Describe your job. How long have you worked for this organization? What is your role?

Check the items that you consider to be workplace stressors in your current position. Each item includes several examples for clarification.

_____ 1. Economic uncertainty: the possibility of layoffs, mergers, acquisitions, closings

_____ 2. Superiors: a boss or bosses who are difficult to work for or who micro-manage

_____ 3. Coworkers: peers who don't pull their share, take credit for your work, or engage in destructive behavior

_____ 4. Subordinates: people you manage who are unmotivated or challenging to lead

_____ 5. Workload: too much work, too little work, not enough variety in the work

_____ 6. Pace: constant pressure, unrealistic deadlines

_____ 7. Communication: being kept in the dark about decisions, an overactive grapevine, gossiping about other employees

_____ 8. Role: unclear expectations, conflicting job demands

_____ 9. Physical environment: noise, air quality, working conditions

_____ 10. Safety: threats, fears, harassment

Elaborate on your stress management techniques for one of the items you checked.

5. **Work with an expert.** If none of these techniques helps, you may benefit from working with a physician or a counselor on campus. Stress has the potential to adversely affect your college experience. Research shows a relationship between stress, low self-esteem, poor health habits, and reduced perceptions of health status.[36] You needn't continue to struggle with unmanageable stress when help is readily available close by. Take action to change things.

Nutrition: Feast or Famine

Challenge: What do you think the heading of this section refers to, specifically? Can you identify the two ends of the nutrition continuum as they refer to college students?

Reaction:

_____

_____

_____

Many first-year students change their eating habits in college; specifically, they eat too much or too little. Some students pack on double-digit pounds, resulting in what is commonly known as the "freshman 15." If you're paying for a meal plan that includes all you can eat, you may unknowingly

Nutrition Facts

Serving size 1 container, individual (64.0 g)

Amount Per Serving

Calories 296   Calories from Fat 127

	% Daily Value*
Total Fat 14.1g	22 %
Saturated Fat 6.3g	31%
Cholesterol 0mg	0%
Sodium 1434mg	60%
Total Carbohydrates 36.8g	12%
Protein 5.6g	

Vitamin A 8%	•	Vitamin C 0%
Calcium 0%	•	Iron 12%

*Based on a 2000 calorie diet

http://www.calorie-count.com/calories/item/6582.html

FIGURE 11.2

Nutritional Label for Ramen Noodles

Diversity Discussion You may wish to ask your students if they think cultural differences exist when it comes to the general dietary or snacking patterns of college students. Has anyone traveled, for example, or has anyone befriended an international student? If students have stories to share, generate a diversity discussion.

I have no clue what my weight is—I'm sure I've put on weight with Huntington Hall's all-you-can-eat food plan.

(or knowingly) max out your diet and your time to socialize with friends while you eat. College students are at particular risk of packing on the pounds and keeping them into adulthood.[37] Current estimates by the American College Heath Association are that 3 of every 10 college students are overweight or obese.[38] Or perhaps you dislike the food at your school, or are trying to save money by eating tons of Ramen Noodles on your own. Did you know that Ramen Noodles are high in carbohydrates, low in vitamins and minerals, and high in sodium and fat (see Figure 11.2)?

In fact, many college favorites are loaded with calories. If you chow down on a cheeseburger and fries for lunch (600 + 600 = 1,200 calories) and four pieces of pizza with "the works" (2,400 calories), a side of garlic bread (400 calories), and a large soda (300 calories) for dinner, you've just weighed in with a grand total of 4,300 calories for the day, not including breakfast. (By the way, skipping breakfast in order to sleep in or cut down on calories is one of the biggest mistakes you can make. Breakfast *breaks* your overnight *fast,* replenishes the glucose in your body, and keeps your metabolism going all day.) To burn up 4,300 calories, you'd need to walk briskly for nearly six hours! Think of it this way, "If you eat 100 more food calories a day than you burn, you'll gain about one pound in a month. That's about 10 pounds in a year. The bottom line is that to lose weight, it's important to reduce calories and increase activity."[39]

In one study, 764 college students (53 percent women, 47 percent men) had their height and weight measured and completed questionnaires about their exercise and dietary patterns. At the beginning of their first year, 29 percent reported that they didn't exercise, 70 percent didn't eat the recommended five servings of fruits and vegetables per day, and over 50 percent reported eating high-fat fast food at least three times during the previous week. Two hundred and ninety students were reassessed at the end of their second year, and 70 percent had gained weight.[40] Although researchers didn't find major changes in students' behaviors over that time, their incoming unhealthy behaviors may have caught up with them.

Does that mean you should totally avoid foods you love? In our culture, food is a social activity. We don't eat to live, some would say; we live to eat. However, if you begin to notice that your jeans are shrinking, and you just can't understand why, you may find the answer on the end of your fork! The United States has the highest obesity rate of any developed country, and obesity in America has become a leading national health concern with 69.2 percent of adults either overweight or obese today.[41] Grocery store shelves are stocked with a huge selection of tempting treats and prepackaged foods, and fast foods are readily available. Portion sizes have increased over time, too, and a less active lifestyle is part of the problem. Choosing taste and convenience over good nutrition has become far too common.

Think of yourself as an athlete in training. Eat sensibly—and pay attention to nutrition. Here are some key recommendations from the U.S. Department of Agriculture:[42]

1. Take a look at what your dinner plate looks like and then compare it with the image on the right. Overall, aim for fewer calories and make half your plate fruits and vegetables, and make at least half your grains whole grains.[43]

2. Limit less healthy foods. Saturated and trans fats, cholesterol, added sugars, and salt make food taste good, but they don't do your health any favors.

3. Balance the calories you take in with the energy you expend. If you're physically active, you need more fuel for your body. If you're not, eat moderately. Spending three hours on your Facebook page, for example, may do wonders for your social life, but it doesn't require much physical exertion.

4. Replace solid fats with oils when you can. The average American diet is fat-rich, but be aware! Many fat-free or low-fat food items contain more calories than their fat-laden counterparts. Become a faithful label reader, and pay particular attention to ingredients if you have food allergies.[44]

5. Choose fruits and vegetables, and vary your selections. Grab an apple instead of a bag of chips.

6. Consume fat-free or low-fat milk or milk products (like cheese or yogurt).

7. Choose lean meats or poultry—bake, broil, or grill it, and vary your selections with fish, beans, nuts, seeds, and peas.

8. Consume less than one teaspoon of salt (or sodium) per day.

9. Choose foods that are rich in calcium, vitamin D, dietary fiber, and potassium. The average American doesn't get enough of these important nutrients.

10. When in doubt, toss it out! Many foods spoil within two hours or less.[45]

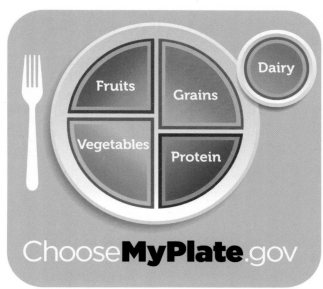

USDA

 Fear less, hope more, eat less, chew more, whine less, breathe more, talk less, say more, love more, and all good things will be yours.

Swedish proverb

Stephen Welstead/Corbis

Teaching with Technology If students have particular wellness goals, such as losing weight, quitting smoking, or exercising, encourage them to engage in journaling or blogging. Externalizing goals, successes and failures, especially with the support of others, is a great way to stay motivated on the path to an objective. You could even offer extra credit to students who are willing to share their wellness blog with the rest of the class.

Exercise 11.3 "How Do I Love Thee? Let Me Count the Ways"

What are your favorite foods? Are you a chocoholic? Do you crave salty snacks with a vengeance? Do you scarf down pizza like there's no tomorrow? Do you have any idea how many calories you devote to your food passions in one sitting? Next time you indulge, take note. Measure the volume of food (six slices of pizza, half a bag of chocolate kisses), and then tabulate the results via an online calorie calculator or by reading the label and doing the math. Fill in the number of calories here: _____. Are you surprised by the grand total? If the average adult needs roughly 2,000 calories per day, how much of your daily intake did you just consume? Remember, there's no need to abstain; just refrain from eating too much of your "love object" at one sitting.

I'm a Reese's Pieces junkie, but I had no idea how many calories are in a bag!

Teaching with Technology As Exercise 11.3 suggests, online calculators can give you a rough estimate of how many calories you consume each day. CaloriesPerHour.com is particularly effective because it contains a large database of nutritional info from packaged foods, as well as a catalog of the average calorie content of many common meat and vegetable servings. Have students use this website to complete Exercise 11.3, or use it as an in-class demonstration of how small food choices can make a big impact on daily calorie intake.

Teachable Moment See if students can share with each other some healthy snacks that they enjoy. Sometimes stocking one's room with a few healthy snacks can cut down on trips to the vending machines.

While general guidelines are good, in the daily rush of campus life, it's even better to have a more specific plan for managing your weight. Many Body Mass Index (BMI) calculators are available online, which is a good place to start as you "weigh" these issues. Online BMI calculators give you an immediate assessment of whether you're underweight, normal, overweight, or obese by simply entering your height and weight.

For some students, college isn't one long feast, it's the origin of famine. The most common age for the onset of an eating disorder is eighteen, and a majority of American college women exhibit at least a few symptoms. According to the National Institute of Mental Health, 25 percent of college students have eating disorders.[46] Over 90 percent of the 5 million Americans with eating disorders are female. One percent of adolescent girls develop anorexia and 2 to 3 percent develop bulimia.[47]

Anorexics see themselves as fat or flabby, even when others don't. They may literally starve themselves, induce vomiting, or exercise obsessively. Bulimics

Exercise 11.4 Which Dinner Would You Order?

Consider these three dining options and decide which one would be the healthiest choice. Think in terms of fats, calories, and the various nutritional recommendations made in this chapter. Assume that you had cereal and a banana for breakfast and a slice of cheese pizza and a soda for lunch.

1. Vegetable Lasagna
   Caesar Salad
   Wheat roll with Butter
   Neapolitan Ice Cream
2. Roast Pork with Gravy
   Garlic Mashed Potatoes
   Corn on the Cob with Butter
   Chocolate Cake
3. Taco Salad
   Apple Pie a la Mode

I'd guess number 1. Vegetables are healthy.

Once you've made your choice, go to an online calorie and nutrient calculator to see how your selection measured up. Were you on target or surprised by the nutritional analysis you found online? The answers are upside down at the bottom of this page.

(Answers to Exercise 11.4: Meal 1: 1,059 cal, 67 g fat, 1,400 mg sodium; Meal 2: 770 cal, 29 g fat, 1,111 mg sodium; Meal 3: 1,993 cal, 95 g fat, 2,786 mg sodium. Note: Calorie count varies by portion size, preparation method, and restaurant/brand. Nutritional information sources: http://www.calorie-count.com/; http://www.benjerry.com/.)

Activity Option Have students go online and calculate the number of calories they burned for the week using an online calculator.

So happiness is an advantage? *Tell me something I don't know*, you're thinking. Of course, happiness is an advantage. Who wouldn't want to be happy? But according to some experts, happiness may be on the decline. Research shows that only 45 percent of American employees are happy in their jobs today[48], and depression rates are ten times higher than they were fifty years ago.[49] Were the classic rockers the Rolling Stones right all along: we just "can't get no satisfaction"? Or has something changed? Inquiring minds (as in, researchers) want to know.

One of these inquiring minds belongs to happiness expert Shawn Achor. The author of *The Happiness Advantage*, he might start by saying that we have things backwards. As a society, we've always been told that if we work hard, we'll be successful, and when we're successful, then we will be happy. Actually, it works the other way around. Studies in neuroscience and positive psychology show that when we're happy, we're more successful. Happy salespeople outsell pessimistic ones. Happy physicians make faster, more accurate diagnoses, and happy students outperform unhappy or even neutral ones.[50] The happiness advantage can be summed up as being realistic about the present but working toward the best future possible. It's a mindset, and more than that, it can actually become part of your work ethic.

You may be saying, "But wait! I'm just not a naturally happy person" or "You have no idea how hard my life is." That's true. We all have obstacles, hardships, and challenges, and sometimes life just doesn't seem fair. Sometimes we assume that a "happiness quotient" is inherited: "My mother is on antidepressants and always has been. It's a brain chemistry thing." Achor isn't recommending that we just put a smile on our faces, a four-leaf clover in our pockets, or cross our fingers. He's certainly not suggesting that if we put on rose-colored glasses, suddenly everything will be "sunshine, lollipops, and rainbows." Not at all. "Happiness," says Achor, "is not the belief that we don't need to change; it is the realization that we can." What does that mean?

Here's what the happiness advantage is all about. See if these recommendations might be worth trying:[51]

1. **Prime your mind.** Right before you dig into your schoolwork, take a few minutes to think about something positive. Study after study shows that people who do this accomplish more, increase their accuracy, and finish faster. Students who were told to think about the happiest day of their lives before beginning a standardized math test did much better than students of equal ability who weren't

given those instructions. "In other words," says Achor, "a quick burst of positive emotions doesn't just broaden our cognitive capacity; it also provides a quick and powerful antidote to stress and anxiety, which in turn improves our focus and our ability to function at our best level" (p. 49).

2. **Capitalize on your "signature" strengths.** Everyone has strengths. Maybe one of yours is showing incredible patience with older folks or attracting little kids like a magnet. Maybe you always solve the math problems on the whiteboard before any of your classmates. It's easy to obsess on the negative. "Why, oh, why didn't I proofread? Ugh!" But research shows that whenever you use one of the strengths you're known for—a "signature strength"—your positivity pops. (You can take a free online test to find out your top five character strengths at www.viasurvey.org.) If you need a boost in your happiness, pull out one of your best strengths and use it. In one study, nearly 600 volunteers were asked to use one of their top strengths in a new way each day for a week. Six months later, these same participants remained happier than control groups of nonparticipants.

3. **Shift your mindset.** If you're not quite sure about this whole college thing and coursework seems like drudgery to you, it will be much harder to sit down and get it done than if you think of it as an opportunity to learn something new. Try changing, not only the way you think about it but the way you talk about it to other people. Instead of saying, "I have to finish chapter six before I can do the problem sets. Oh, brother!" try saying, "Wow! I finished chapter six before noon; I never knew half of that stuff!" Not everyone has the chance you have to earn a college degree; that, in and of itself, is worth celebrating.

4. **Focus.** Researcher Matt Killingsworth created an app (Track Your Happiness) to explore what makes people happy. Periodically, on a daily basis, he sent 15,000 people a signal and asked three questions: 1) "How do you feel (from very bad to very good)?" 2) "What are you doing?" (from among 22 options) and 3) "Are you thinking about something other than what you're doing right now—and if so, are your thoughts about this other thing pleasant, neutral, or unpleasant?" After analyzing 650,000 real-time responses, Killingsworth discovered an important truth. People who were focused, who were "in the moment," who were fully engaged in what they were doing were happiest.[52] Focus counts! If *you*, too, want the happiness advantage, the first step is to practice that!

klaikungwon/Photos.com; Yulia Glam/Photos.com

binge on food until they can't eat any more or are interrupted, and then induce vomiting or take large doses of laxatives and diuretics. Both anorexia and bulimia can have serious medical consequences.

In one study of college women attending a large pubic university, 17 percent of the 578 respondents were found to be struggling with a probable eating disorder. They indicated they would prefer to be helped by a friend.[53] "Friends don't let friends drive drunk" can be extended to many areas of wellness. Medication and therapy can be essential, too. Research indicates that body image and self-esteem are related, particularly for women.[54]

Sensitive Situation While friends can be a good resource for individuals struggling with an eating disorder, emphasize that very often professional intervention is needed. When eating disorders are addressed early, the chances of long-term consequences are diminished.

Exercise: Don't Be a Couch Potato!

Research shows that just twenty minutes of exercise can help to calm you for as long as twenty-four hours. Vigorous exercise helps you get rid of excess adrenaline and pumps in endorphins that block pain and anxiety.[55] Research also shows that people who get regular exercise fall asleep more quickly and report fewer sleep difficulties. Pilots, who have bizarre sleep schedules due to long transoceanic flights, follow this advice. Morning walks are a good way to expose yourself to daylight and to get your exercise early in the day. In one study of college freshmen, students who increased their exercise during the first several

© Herbert Kratky/Shutterstock.com

66
Lack of activity destroys the good condition of every human being, while movement and methodical physical exercise save it and preserve it.
99

Plato (c. 428–348 B.C.)

Your TYPE is Showing

Have you ever started a new exercise plan and then up and quit on yourself? If so, have you ever wondered why? Maybe you made a New Year's resolution to slim down or you decided to get buff to try out for the team. Over time you lost interest, however, and your new exercise plan died a slow death. One possible explanation might have been that the type of exercise you chose didn't fit your psychological type. Now there's a thought!

It makes sense that introverts would prefer activities they can pursue alone or with one close friend, like jogging or cycling. Extraverts might go for team sports or coordinated exercise, like volleyball or rowing. Sensors may like practical, results-oriented activities, like lifting weights, whereas iNtuitives may like creative activities such as aerobics set to music. Thinkers may prefer physical activities that require reasoning and logic, like timing your laps across the pool and figuring out ways to beat your own record. Feelers may prefer activities in

which others can be part of an interconnected group effort, like team relay races. Judgers may prefer structured exercise routines, like yoga or aerobics. Perceivers, on the other hand, may enjoy spontaneity while they work out, like dancing or exploring new hiking paths, for example.

According to Canadian researcher Dr. James Gavin of Concordia University in Quebec, exercise regimens should "fit" people's personalities. Today, only one out of five North American adults participates in some type of regular exercise. But Dr. Gavin asks, "Does it fit with who the person is? Will it challenge long-standing habits? You might think of it this way: people have personalities . . . and so do sports and fitness activities. People generally feel better when they do activities within their comfort zones, i.e., that match their styles."[56]

Of course, when it comes to exercise, body type, strength, and endurance count; but think, too, about your exercise preferences and your psychological type. Does your new fitness program fit you? If so, it may be much more likely to become part of your lifestyle.

months of school reported feeling more vigorous, less tired, and less stressed than those who exercised less than they had previously.[57] On the other hand, another study comparing the exercise patterns of college students from Costa Rica, India, South Korea, and the U.S. found that American students watched more television and videos than students from the other three cultures, resulting in less exercise.[58]

Not only does exercise help you burn off cheeseburgers, recent brain-imaging and neurochemical studies indicate that "sweating makes you smart." Physical exercise helps reinforce existing connections between neurons and forge new ones via a protein called BDNF (brain-derived neurotrophic factor). A dense neural network helps you process and store information: "Learning is taking signals that come in from your senses and embedding them into brain anatomy," according to Dr. Vassilis Koliatsos, a psychiatrist at Johns Hopkins University. BDNF affects memory and mood; it literally helps rewire your brain.[59]

Sleep: Are You a Night Owl?

Does this describe you? You're running on no sleep . . . <u>no sleep</u>! You have bags under your eyes. You're dizzy, moody, irritable, anxious, or depressed. You can't keep your eyes from closing while reading your assignments, and you have to prop your head up to stay awake in class. You could be starring in a movie called *Sleepless in School*.

Unfortunately, this description fits thousands of first-year college students. When you're running on no sleep, being at your academic best is next to impossible. In fact, you can't really be at your best at anything. Sleep affects your academic performance and—believe it or not—may even adversely affect your decision to stay in college and succeed![60]

Activity Option Ask students to make the connection between their psychological type and the way they have approached exercise in the past. What is their type and what kind of exercise do they do, if any? If they don't exercise, can they figure out why based on their type? Ask students to send you a two-paragraph e-mail about their analysis.

Yes!

Activity Option Ask everyone who went to bed before 10:00 p.m. more than half of the days of the week last week to stand. Have these students move to the front of the room on the left. Then ask in two-hour intervals for students to form groups around the room until everyone is out of their seats. Next ask groups to come up with a number between 1 and 10 that describes how rested and alert they feel. Compare group responses.

> Oh sleep! It is a gentle thing,
> Beloved from pole to pole.

Samuel Taylor Coleridge,
English critic and poet (1772–1834)

Fuse/Jupiter Images

Many college students don't get enough sleep and don't get the right kind of sleep. Researchers believe the average college student needs eight to nine hours of sleep per night; some experts say as much as ten hours! But the actual number of hours college students are sleeping has been decreasing steadily for years.[61] And the results of going without enough sleep are cumulative. The negative impact on your ability to think and learn gets worse as time goes by.[62] Today, many college students average six hours or less per night, or go to bed at 4 a.m. and sleep until noon, upsetting the natural rhythm of their bodies based on nature's cycle of daylight and darkness. A once-in-a-while upset in your equilibrium isn't the end of the world, but if not getting enough sleep is your normal practice, you're building up sleep debt. Think of sleep debt as a buildup of the cumulative amount of sleep you owe yourself to be at your best. If sleep debt were tracked like credit card debt, just how high would your bill be?

Sleep restores us physically and emotionally. It recharges our batteries. College students who don't get enough sleep—particularly REM (rapid eye movement) sleep that takes place most during the last few hours while dreaming occurs—may be hurting their chances at college success. Sleep deprivation causes problems like these:[63]

1. **Learning.** During REM sleep, your brain creates sleep spindles: one- to two-second bursts of brainwaves that help transfer information to long-term memory. Sleeping less than six hours may block the production of sleep spindles and result in less learning.[64] In tests comparing sleep-deprived students' learning with students who get eight hours of sleep, nonsleepers were less able to learn new information. Interestingly, many students rated their cognitive abilities as higher when they were sleep deprived, but all the evidence indicated the reverse was true.[65]

2. **Grade Point Average.** In one study that compared college students who were short sleepers (six hours or less), average sleepers (seven to eight hours), and long sleepers (nine or more hours), average GPAs reported for the three groups were 2.74, 3.01, and 3.24, respectively.[66]

3. **Relationship Strain.** Who wants to interact with a cranky, sleep-deprived person? Sleep deprivation may put your relationships at risk because of increased irritability and decreased interpersonal sensitivity. What's more, getting less sleep may start a chain reaction. In one study of college students' sleep troubles, worrying about relationships was the most often cited reason for not getting enough sleep.[67]

4. **Anxiety, Depression, and Illness.** Sleep deprivation triggers all sorts of emotional, psychological, and physical risks. Students who report getting less sleep appear to be less psychologically healthy and more prone to

Box 11.1 — Some ZZZZZZZs Please

So not getting enough sleep is a bad idea, but what are college students doing instead of sleeping? Many stores and restaurants are open twenty-four hours a day, TV programming is continuous, and the Internet never rests. What *aren't* they doing?

Some students are Internet addicts, regularly choosing a computer over their pillows. For example, in one study, 26 percent of college men reported gambling in online card games like Texas Hold 'Em or Omaha High at least once a month, and 4 percent reported doing so once a week or more. One student admitted playing 17,190 hands of online poker over three months, playing for thirteen to fifteen hours out of every twenty-four.[68] Another student discovered he had logged 1,008 hours—forty-two full days—playing World of Warcraft online over seven months. "He had what addicts call a 'moment of clarity,' and he decided to hang up his armor for good."[69] Still other students are Facebook addicts, checking their accounts twenty or more times around the clock.

How do you know if you're addicted? Ask yourself these questions: Are you able to tolerate increasing amounts of leisure time online? Is your time online hurting your grades, your relationships, and your health? Are you losing sleep over it—literally?

Intentionally depriving prisoners of war of sleep is a controversial subject, considered by some to be a form of torture. There are reasons for that. If Internet addiction is keeping you up at night, do what you can to get some ZZZZZZZs—please!

catching every bug that comes along.[70] Research indicates that sleep deprivation definitely puts a dent in your emotional intelligence and your ability to think constructively.[71]

5. **Car Accidents.** According to the National Highway Traffic Safety Administration, fatigue accounts for approximately 1,550 deaths, 71,000 injuries, and more than 100,000 police-reported automobile crashes on our highways each year. Young drivers (ages sixteen to twenty-nine) are particularly at risk.[72]

6. **Lowered Life Satisfaction.** In the grand scheme of things, getting less sleep seems to throw off everything. One study, for example, examined students' reported average length of sleep and their scores on a well-known life satisfaction scale. Getting less sleep was significantly related to being less satisfied with life in general.[73]

What should you do? Consider these simple, but important suggestions for avoiding sleep deprivation.[74]

> **Set a coffee deadline.** Just one cup of coffee within four to five hours of bedtime can cause you to have trouble falling asleep, reduce overall sleep time, make you waken more frequently, and produce lighter sleep.

> **Avoid using alcohol to help you sleep.** Alcohol may help you fall asleep more quickly, but it causes you to sleep in fragments, rather than continuously.[75]

> **Take an early afternoon nap or none at all.** A short nap after lunch can increase your ability to focus later in the day, but taking a long one too close to bedtime can reduce your overnight sleep quality.

> **Save your bed for sleeping.** Use your bed for sleeping exclusively, so that your mind associates being in that particular location with going to sleep, not reading, watching TV, or doing homework.

> **Stick to a routine.** Sleeping in on the weekends doesn't make up for lost sleep during the week. Try not to vary your sleep schedule by more

I certainly didn't know all these statistics!

Teachable Moment Incompatible sleep schedules between roommates is a real challenge in college. Varying class schedules as well as different sleep habits and needs can cause extreme conflict. Ask students to identify a few common sleep-related roommate challenges they have experienced or heard about. Similar problems can be generated for commuting students when family members' sleep patterns conflict. Discuss ways to resolve these problems.

than two hours in either direction. If you stay up late on Friday night, gradually move closer and closer to your normal bedtime over the weekend. Large variations in your sleep schedule can do almost as much damage as not getting enough sleep.

Teachable Moment Have any of your students had difficulty falling asleep? Sometimes when students stay up late studying or working on the computer, their minds are racing afterwards, and it's difficult to fall asleep. Last-minute cramming or cranking out a paper at midnight may lead to a very restless night's sleep.

Thomas Edison, who believed sleep is a waste of time, invented the electric lightbulb in the late 1800s, hoping to reduce the human propensity to sleep. His invention worked, but he might be disturbed today to see the potential physical, psychological, and sometimes even academic, results.[76]

Alcohol and Drugs: The "Party Hardy" Syndrome

Love those Tuesdays and Thursdays!

challenge

reaction

Challenge: What is the common definition for binge drinking?

Reaction:

_____

_____

_____

During the 1960s in the United States, many college students experimented with marijuana and hallucinogenic drugs like LSD. In recent studies, 30 percent of undergraduates say they have used marijuana in the last year. (Two states—Colorado and Washington—have voted to legalize marijuana; however, it's still illegal on college campuses within those states.[77]) Ecstasy use has more than doubled on college campuses to 7.1 percent of students reporting they have used it in the last year. Opiates (other than heroin) were reportedly used by 7.3 percent, PCP by 4.8 percent, tranquilizers by 4.6 percent, and cocaine by 3.8 percent of college students in the last year.[78] Interestingly, students generally overestimate the number of other students who use drugs.[79]

Chuck Savage/Bridge/Corbis

"
Drunkenness is simply voluntary insanity.
"

Lucius Annaeus Seneca, Roman philosopher and statesman (4 B.C.–A.D. 65)

Alcohol is today's drug of choice on most college campuses. Although 28 percent of college students smoke cigarettes, a habit that brings a well-known set of health risks, 85 percent report they have drunk alcohol in the last year.[80] Not all students drink irresponsibly, but there's no doubt that drinking is identified by many campuses as their top-ranking concern. Binge drinking, the leading cause of preventable death among college students, is typically described as four or more drinks in a row for a woman and five or more for a man.[81] In fact, despite attempts to educate students about the risks, binge drinking is on the rise.[82] High-risk drinking among college students has been linked to academic problems such as missed classes, lower grades, dropping out, failing, and other serious problems such as vandalism, unplanned sex, sexual assaults, fatalities, alcohol poisoning, and attempted suicides. Some students combine drinking alcohol with drinking energy drinks so that they can drink more, resulting in dangerous "jolt and crash" episodes.[83] Alcohol has become the "liquid courage" that fuels "hooking up" on many campuses, and for many college students "hooking up" has replaced traditional dating.[84]

➤ College students spend $5.5 billion on alcohol per year, more than they spend on coffee, tea, juice, soda, milk, and textbooks combined.[85]

➤ Adolescents may be more vulnerable to brain damage from excessive drinking than older adults.[86]

➤ Brief episodes of excessive drinking are damaging to the brain. "There is evidence that repeated, abrupt increases of alcohol levels in the brain, followed by abstinence, induces more damage than the same amount of alcohol taken uninterrupted in the same length of time."[87] Of course, the solution to this problem isn't to drink excessively all the time!

➤ College drinkers drink more, drink more often, and engage in more high-risk drinking than their counterparts the same age who aren't in college, and the beginning of the first year of college is when the most drinking occurs, period.[88]

➤ Approximately 1,825 college students between eighteen and twenty-four years of age die each year from alcohol-related unintentional injuries.[89]

➤ Excessive drinking in college may put students at greater risk of alcohol dependence later in life.[90]

➤ Students tend to drink more if they believe their friends also drink excessively and do not disapprove.[91]

➤ In one study of community college students in which the average age was twenty-six, 25 percent of the sample engaged in high-risk drinking.[92]

➤ College women who are preoccupied with alcohol are more likely to drink more.[93]

➤ College student drinking is lower in states with fewer high-risk adult drinkers and stricter alcohol control laws.[94]

➤ Heavier alcohol use in college may put both males and females at greater risk of heart disease later in life.[95]

➤ Students significantly overestimate how much other students drink.[96]

Activity Option In addition to defining binge drinking, students should be able to describe what binge drinking can lead to. Pair students up and have them think of as many consequences of binge drinking as they can by filling in the blank: If someone binge drinks, he or she might _____. Generate a class list.

Yikes!

Sensitive Situation According to one recent study, college students who drink alcohol spend more time drinking per week than studying. This is a sensitive, but important, topic for a class discussion or, more privately, a journal topic. Or consider creating an impersonal writing assignment that requests an opinion or research, like the pros and cons of having a dry campus.

Sensitive Situation There is a connection between any kind of substance abuse and anxiety or depression. Sometimes the reason for substance abuse is to numb the pain for something that is more deep-seated than partying. Students who self-medicate by abusing drugs or alcohol need to address the causes of their behavior.

Teaching with Technology CollegeDrinking Prevention.gov is an informative Web site developed by the National Advisory Council on Alcohol Abuse and Alcoholism. Here you can find statistics, summaries, and other information related to alcohol abuse on college campuses. This site is a great resource for both students and instructors, and will help spark in-class conversations about the impact of alcohol on college life.

Think about the most challenging course you're taking this term. Are wellness issues affecting your success? Think about these potential reactions from students:

1. **Stress:** "This class is so challenging academically that my stress level soars."
2. **Nutrition:** "I skip breakfast, right before this class. Hunger pangs distract me."
3. **Exercise:** "I feel lethargic and unable to jump into the discussion."
4. **Sleep:** "I stay up far too late, and sleep through this class."
5. **Alcohol and drugs:** "I make a habit of partying the night before this class and feel unwell."
6. **Sex:** "I'm so attracted to a classmate that I can't concentrate on the lecture!"

Contemplate the role wellness plays, and circle any of the six sectors of wellness listed above that are impacting your success in this class. Develop a step-by-step plan, based on the information you've read in this chapter, to help you do your best. If it's appropriate, e-mail your plan to your professor in the course.

If you and your friends do drink, remember this: The only thing that helps a drunken person sober up is time. Black coffee and cold showers are myths. Watch for symptoms of alcohol poisoning—a stupor or coma, vomiting, seizures, more than ten seconds between breaths, and a bluish skin color, indicating a very low body temperature. If you see these signs, call for help immediately. Putting someone to bed to sleep it off can be a lethal mistake.[97]

Know the facts, know the risks, and if you drink, drink responsibly. Pace yourself, keep track of how much alcohol you've had, or ask someone else to let you know when it's time to quit. Alternate alcoholic and nonalcoholic drinks, avoid drinking games—and remember: It *is* possible to have fun without alcohol!

Sex: Better Safe Than Sorry

Sensitive Situation Revealing how a very personal wellness issue is impacting their life may be a sensitive situation that students are not comfortable with. If you have a peer leader, this might be a place where, if appropriate, the peer leader can lead a discussion or respond to e-mails.

Intimacy, STIs, unplanned pregnancies, sexual orientation. Being sexual is part of being human, and for most college students, sex is a fact of life. In one national study, only 18 percent of women and 32 percent of men aged eighteen to twenty-four reported never to have engaged in sex. The average number of partners students reported in the previous year was 1.2, and two-thirds of women and one-third of men said they were in committed relationships.[98] However, today increasing numbers of students are choosing abstinence or delaying sex until they find a partner they have first gotten to know in other ways.[99] Whatever choices you make are personal ones, and responsibility is key.

What do you need to know about sex in college? Here are twelve FAQs first-year students often ask.

1. *I'm a sexually active college woman. How do I know which type of contraception is best for me?* Consider these factors:
   Effectiveness. On the one hand, in order for a contraceptive to work, you must actually use it. "Just this once" can be one time too many. How conscientious are you? On the other hand, it's important to remember that no method of contraception is 100 percent reliable.

Suitability. The pill has risks and side effects. It may not be appropriate for you if you only have sex on rare occasions. On the other hand, if you have multiple partners, you are at higher risk for STIs or HIV. Consider using a condom along with a cervical cap or diaphragm.

Side effects. Discuss your personal health history with your physician, and make sure you understand what side effects may occur, so that you don't worry needlessly if they do.

Cost. Pills, diaphragms, spermicidal foam or jelly, and condoms cost money. The most inexpensive contraceptive is abstinence!

2. *How would I know if I had an STI?* Symptoms vary for men and women, but many STIs bring burning, itching, rash, sores, discharge, warts, blisters, and sometimes fever or flu-like symptoms. Some STIs have no symptoms whatsoever. If you have any concerns, visit your personal physician or Student Health Center for testing. It's also possible to contract more than one, and curing one does not necessarily cure another. More Americans are infected with STIs than at any other time in history, and the number of new infections annually stands at 20 million.[100]

3. *I'm a sexually active college man. Condoms destroy the pleasure. Do I have other options?* Abstinence, "outercourse," and oral sex are always possibilities (although the last two options may not protect you from STIs). Withdrawal, the "rhythm method" (based on the woman's predicted ovulation), and female condoms are unreliable. A vasectomy is a radical decision with long-term consequences! However, college women who want the protection of condoms should use assertive communication strategies, like withholding sex or directly requesting their partners use a condom (as opposed to suggesting or hinting).[101]

4. *Whose responsibility is contraception, anyway? Isn't it usually up to the woman?* For anatomical or societal reasons, or both, historically, contraception was seen more as a woman's responsibility than a man's. However, contraception is actually the responsibility of both partners. "The bottom line is that it takes two people to conceive a baby, and two people should be involved in deciding not to conceive a baby. In the process, they can also enhance their skills in communication, critical thinking, and negotiating."[102]

5. *My partner insists on sex even when I say no. How can I be more convincing?* Technically speaking, when one partner says no, and the other partner proceeds against her or his wishes, the situation could be labeled as rape. Women are more vulnerable than men, and various studies show that 25 to 60 percent of college men have coerced women into sex. Sometimes drugs like Rohypnol or GHB are involved: odorless and tasteless drugs that erase the memory of what happened. Assertive communication at the beginning of the relationship is critical. "When she says no, she really means yes" is a distorted view of reality that can have serious consequences for both partners.

I've thought this exact question before …

6. *I have decided to save sex for marriage, but my friends don't respect my decision. How can I explain my choice?* Decisions about sex are highly personal. What's right for someone else may not be right for you, and reaching the right decision requires self-understanding. Abstinence is free, safe, and reliable. Don't be pushed into sex until you're ready, and be assertive and confident in your decision. Your friends may or may not understand, but they should respect your choice as the right one for you, even if they've decided differently for themselves.

Teaching with Technology In class, you may wish to show the Ellen DeGeneres commencement speech at Tulane University in 2009 in which she describes "coming out of the closet." (The humor is tame, but you may wish to preview it first to make sure it's appropriate for your first-year students. For example, students would enjoy her, but Ellen refers to the graduates' likely hangovers, which is counter to this chapter's message.)

7. *I think (or already know) I'm gay, bisexual, or transgender. Should I "come out"?* The decision to come out is a difficult one for many students. They worry about the reactions of family and friends. Some believe that homosexuality is immoral, based on upbringing and religious beliefs. Each individual is different. If you want to explore these issues, the counseling center on your campus can help. Studies show that most male and female homosexuals are happy and well adjusted, particularly those in long-term, committed relationships, and an estimated 3 to 5 million gay and lesbian couples have become parents through artificial insemination or adoption.[103]

8. *I'm uncomfortable around gay people. What should I do?* In a landmark national study conducted by the University of Chicago, 2.8 percent of men and 1.4 percent of women described themselves as homosexual.[104]

Ha! Clever quote!

" Contraceptives should be used on every conceivable occasion. "

Spike Milligan, The Last Goon Show of All

If these statistics are representative (and they may be conservative for college campuses), of the approximately more than 15 million college students in the United States, that's 420,000 gay men and 210,000 lesbian women. College is about learning, and that includes exposing yourself to diverse viewpoints on a range of academic and nonacademic issues. If you close your mind, think about what you may be refusing to learn. Isolating yourself against others' sexual differences in college or later in the workplace is impossible, just as isolating yourself against people of other faiths, ethnicities, and races will be. College is the right place to embrace empathy and tolerance.

9. *I want to be sexually responsible, but I don't like the idea of planning for sex because it makes me feel promiscuous and takes away the spontaneity. Should I really carry a condom around in my purse or wallet?* "Be prepared": it's the Boy Scout motto. Many aspects of life require planning. If you were embarking on a long airplane flight without food service, you'd bring along a snack, wouldn't you? If you find preparing for a sexual encounter disruptive or unpleasant and you're female, use an alternative, longer-term form of contraception. The old saying "An ounce of prevention is worth a pound of cure" was never truer than it is here. Remember the ABC rule: Abstain, Be faithful, or use a Condom.[105]

10. *My friend had a baby in high school; now I'm terrified that the same thing will happen to me. How can I get over my fear?* Some amount of fear can lead you to make more responsible choices than your friend may have, but if the fear has become irrational and disrupts your life, a counselor may be able to help you work through it.

11. *I'm particularly vulnerable to unplanned sex when I drink alcohol, but all my friends drink. I don't want to be ostracized; how can I say no?* Although it may take courage, know yourself, and follow Shakespeare's advice: "to thine own self be true." Which types of situations are dangerous for you? Which friends tempt you to do things you regret? Drinking games, for example, chugging a drink whenever a certain word is spoken or song is played, are dangerous forms of entertainment because it's hard to keep track of how much alcohol you've downed. If reckless friends are your problem, you might consider finding new ones!

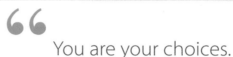

" You are your choices. "

Lucius Annaeus Seneca, Roman philosopher and statesman (4 B.C.–A.D. 65)

12. It may sound strange, but I haven't met anyone at college I'd want to have sex with. Am I abnormal? No, you're not abnormal. Perhaps you've decided not to settle. You may well know what you're looking for in a romantic partner, and perhaps you've not yet met anyone who displays all these characteristics. Someone who shares your basic values but is different enough to make life interesting is worth searching for, and getting to know someone before jumping into a physical relationship is always smart. Be patient.

Now that you've read about the six sectors of the Wellness Wheel, look at your profile once more. Are you satisfied with where you are now? Are you committed to "taking the wheel"? What can you do to maximize your wheel? If you follow through with the actions you've prescribed for yourself in this chapter, you'll most likely see the positive results of working toward wellness in all aspects of your life, including your college success.

Now What Do You Think?

❶ At the beginning of this chapter, Anthony Lopez, a frustrated student, faced a series of challenges. Now after reading this chapter, would you respond differently to any of the questions you answered about the "FOCUS Challenge Case"? Knowing what you know now, how would you advise him? Write a paragraph ending to the story, incorporating your best advice.

❷ What is the relationship between responsibility for wellness and college success? Is it a responsibility you accept, and if so, what will you do to take charge of your own wellness?

❸ Keep a stress diary for a week. Record what causes you stress each day and how strongly you react. What symptoms appeared? How high was your stress level? What did you do about it? After a week, you'll have a substantial amount of data that not only tells you about your stress level but also your coping mechanisms. It's important to stay attuned to sensations and signals: "Hey, I must be really stressed out over this! My heart's racing and I feel panicky." It's also important to pay attention to what helps, like exercise, meditation, yoga, or prayer. Summarize your results, what you learned in doing this, and what actions you can take in the future to better manage the stress in your life.

❹ Keep an exercise log for a week. On a daily basis, record the type of physical activity, the length of time you do it, and the level of workout (mild, medium, or high exertion). Using an online exercise calculator, record the number of calories you burned.

	Sunday	Monday	Tuesday	Wednesday	Thursday	Friday	Saturday
Activity							
Time							
Exertion Level							
Calories Burned							

❺ Do you have any idea how much sleep you're actually getting? According to sleep experts, you should be getting seven or more hours per night, or a minimum of forty-nine hours per week. Keep a sleep log for a week. Every morning, write down the number of hours of sleep you've gotten. Are you surprised to see the actual numbers? Is there much variation from night to night? From weekdays to weekends? Formulate a new strategy to become better rested.

Sunday	Monday	Tuesday	Wednesday	Thursday	Friday	Saturday

❻ Keep a record of your alcohol consumption over an average week. If you don't drink, skip this box. If you do, look at related factors, such as the cost in time, caloric intake, and money. Are you surprised by what your record shows? Are your weekly totals in line with what you expected to see? What steps will you take to improve your wellness in this area, and how will you begin?

	Sunday	Monday	Tuesday	Wednesday	Thursday	Friday	Saturday	TOTAL
Number of Drinks in One Sitting								
Time Spent Drinking								
Calories Consumed								
Money Spent								

❼ Of the six sectors of the Wellness Wheel you've read about in this chapter, choose one on which to focus your improvement efforts. What will you do specifically to change your practices? Who can help you? What results do you predict? How are these changes likely to impact your college success?

What did you LEARN?

Activity Option For a final class activity, have each student come to class with a four-slide PowerPoint presentation. The slides should be titled, in order: "What I thought I would learn in this class," "What I did learn in this class," "The one thing that hit me the most," and "One thing I do now that I didn't before."

Reality Check

On a scale of 1 to 10, answer the following questions now that you've completed the chapter.

 low   1 2 3 4 5 6 7 8 9 10   high

In hindsight, how much did you already know about this subject before reading the chapter?

Can you answer these questions about working toward wellness more fully now that you've read the chapter? _____

❶ Identify three of the fifteen specific symptoms that should signal you to seek medical attention right away.

❷ How would you define wellness? Is it more than just not being sick?

❸ What's the formal definition of binge drinking?

How useful might the information in this chapter be to you? How much do you think this information might affect your success overall? _____

How much energy did you put into reading this chapter? _____

How long did it actually take you to complete this chapter (both the reading and writing tasks)? _____ Hour(s) _____ Minutes

Did you finish reading this chapter? _____
Did you intend to when you started? _____
If you meant to but didn't, what stopped you? _____

Take a minute to compare these answers to your answers from the "Readiness Check" at the beginning of this chapter. What gaps exist between the similar questions? How might these gaps between what you thought before starting the chapter and what you now think after completing the chapter affect how you approach the next chapter in this book?

12 Choosing a College Major and Career

How this chapter relates to YOU

1. When it comes to choosing a college major and career what do you find most challenging, if anything?

Trying to choose the "right" major

Knowing how to assess my strengths

Using social media to create my "personal brand"

Communicating my value to an organization

Building professionalism skills

Readiness Check

2. What is most likely to be your response? Circle it.

I'll be open to learning how to make this decision.	I'll see whether this chapter helps me.	I'll start exploring my options now.	Eventually, I'll just figure it out.

3. What would you have to do to increase your likelihood of success? Will you do it this quarter or semester?

_____

_____

_____

How YOU will relate to this chapter

What are you most interested in learning about? Put check marks by those topics.

☐ How to choose a major and a career

☐ How to LEAP to success

☐ How internships, co-ops, and service-learning can give you experience

☐ How to build your personal brand

☐ How to launch your upcoming career

☐ How to interview at your best

☐ How to build your professionalism skills

• How motivated are you to learn more about choosing a college major and career? (5 = high, 1 = low) ____

• How ready are you to read now? ____ (If something is in your way, take care of it if you can, zero in and focus.)

• How long do you think it will take you to complete this chapter? If you start and stop, keep track of your overall time. ____ Hour(s) ____ Minutes

Ethan Cole

One thing was certain: Ethan Cole was unsure. Unsure of his abilities, unsure of which major to choose, unsure of what he wanted to do with his life, unsure of himself. Unsure of almost everything.

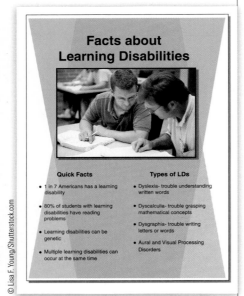

Facts about Learning Disabilities

Quick Facts

- 1 in 7 Americans has a learning disability
- 80% of students with learning disabilities have reading problems
- Learning disabilities can be genetic
- Multiple learning disabilities can occur at the same time

Types of LDs

- Dyslexia- trouble understanding written words
- Dyscalculia- trouble grasping mathematical concepts
- Dysgraphia- trouble writing letters or words
- Aural and Visual Processing Disorders

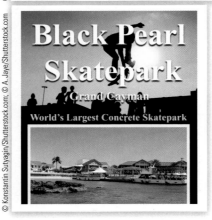

Black Pearl Skatepark

Grand Cayman

World's Largest Concrete Skatepark

Ethan came from a good family, and his parents were actually his best friends. They had been very successful, and they wanted to share the wealth—literally—with their three children. They supported Ethan, no matter what. When he ended up in the principal's office time after time in grade school, they defended him. When he totaled his car in high school, they bought him another one. When he wanted to take a term off to travel and "find himself," they said yes without raising one, single eyebrow.

And now that he was thinking of dropping out of college, they said he could move back home, so long as he agreed to a few ground rules and promised to take back his old chores, like mowing the yard. That seemed only fair to him.

The only thing Ethan was sure of was that skateboarding was his life right now. It's all he wanted to do and all he ever thought about. He'd look at a curve on a window frame or an arc in a picture and imagine what skating on it would feel like. All his friends were skateboarders, too, and he read skateboarder magazines and dreamed of the day he might even go pro. He realized not many

people make a living at it, but a few really talented athletes did, and maybe—just maybe—he'd be one of them. Recently, he'd found out about the largest concrete skatepark on the globe, Black Pearl in the Grand Cayman Islands—62,000 square feet! He'd made a promise to himself to skate there someday. *Life couldn't get much better than that*, he thought.

But school . . . that was a different story. Schoolwork had never captured his attention. In primary school, his physician had diagnosed Attention Deficit Disorder (ADD), and in middle school, a learning specialist had discovered that Ethan was dyslexic. *No wonder I don't like school*, he remembered thinking then. But finally knowing why he couldn't focus didn't

change his attitude. He still hated sitting in a classroom.

Despite these challenges, his parents had always told him he was smart. "You can do anything you want to do," they'd said. "Look at you: you're a good-looking kid with plenty of talents. The world is your oyster!" *What a funny phrase*, he'd always thought when they said that. By the time he finally learned what it meant, he totally believed it. His life would become whatever he chose to make of it.

The problem was there were too many choices. How could anyone decide what he wanted to be when he was only nineteen? Ethan remembered liking geometry, he was good at creative writing, he played the drums like a real jazz musician, and he was an incredible artist. *But what do you do with that combination of skills?* he'd asked himself more than once. What possible college major and career would really fit him? He'd spent plenty of time on career websites to try and figure it out.

He'd managed to pull decent grades his first term—a B average—at the arts college close to home. He'd taken Freshman Composition, Introduction to Communication, Drawing 101, and Study Skills, and while he'd done well, none of the course material really sparked a genuine interest.

His professors didn't take much of an interest in him, either. His Study Skills instructor was friendly and tried to interest him in the course, but Ethan had been hearing that information repeated in school for years now. He claimed he already had all those skills; he just wasn't motivated to apply them. Instead, he skateboarded every minute he could.

The more he thought about it, the more he thought it was a good idea to take a year off from college. He could get a job delivering pizzas, think about his life, and try to figure it all out. He'd have

nobody to tell him what to do, nobody to hold him accountable, nobody to pressure him to study, nobody to force him into making decisions— and plenty of free time to skateboard.

Study Skills (ID 102)
Course Syllabus

INSTRUCTOR: Anna Morgan
OFFICE: 342 University Hall
HOURS: 9 a.m.-12 p.m. Mon-Thurs

TEXT: *FOCUS on College Success* by Constance Staley

COURSE OBJECTIVES: This course is designed to give you the tools to make college easier, more productive, and a more successful learning experience. The goal of this course is to make you a better student by building your study skills and enhancing your learning strategies.

EXPECTATIONS: Students are expected to be respectful of instructors and peers at all times. Assignments should be turned in on time unless you have a valid reason for missing the due date. Please see me if you have any questions. Water bottles are allowed in class, but no food or sugary drinks are permitted. Please turn off your cell phone before you come to class.

GRADING: 100 Possible Points
-Participation: 10 Points.
-Final Presentation: 20 Points.
-Final Exam: 20 Points.
-Assignments (3) and Quizzes (2): 50 Points (10 each)

GRADES: 100-90 = A   89-80 = B   79-70 = C   69-60 = D   59-0 = F

Course Schedule

WEEK 1:   Overview and Pre-Test
WEEK 2:   Managing Time and Stress
WEEK 3:   Reading Skills
WEEK 4:   Test Taking
WEEK 5:   Listening and Memory
WEEK 6:   Diversity
WEEK 7:   Effective Writing

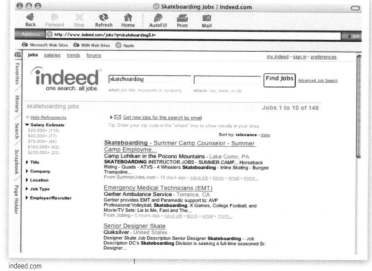

indeed.com

challenge

" reaction

❶ In your view, what will become of Ethan? What are his prospects for the future? Do you think he'll decide on a major and finish college? Why or why not?

❷ Why is Ethan experiencing problems? Are these problems serious? Should they hold him back? List all the problems you can identify.

❸ Which majors and careers might Ethan be well suited for? If you were an academic advisor, what advice would you give him?

❹ Who would you send Ethan to on your campus for help? What are his options? What do you think he should do at this point?

VARK It!

Complete the recommended activity for your preferred VARK learning modality. If you are multimodal, select more than one activity. Your instructor may ask you to (a) give an oral report on your results in class, (b) send your results to him or her via e-mail, or (c) post them online.

Visual: As you scan this chapter, before you actually start reading, find a quotation that fits you. When you finish reading, create a poster about yourself and your career planning, using the quote as a theme.

Aural: When you get to the section of this chapter about conducting a SWOT analysis talk it through aloud to help make sure it takes everything into account. It's a brand new way of thinking about careers that could be right for you.

Read/Write: When you get to the halfway point in this chapter, stop. Find a *Harvard Business Review* blog that extends what you're reading in *FOCUS*. Share the gist of the article in class.

Kinesthetic: Role play some interviewing scenarios with a classmate or friend. Try asking realistic but challenging questions, and brainstorm afterwards to think of the best answer possible to each question.

Who Are You? and What Do You Want?

? challenge

" reaction

Challenge: If you've chosen a major, what factors played a role in your decision? If you're still deciding, what factors are you considering?

Reaction:

_____

_____

_____

Teachable Moment As you begin this chapter, remember that while choosing a major is critical to college success, the old thinking that students should enter college having already decided on their major isn't realistic. Students need to explore their options, learn about themselves, and ultimately choose a major that keeps them engaged and excited throughout college, one that will lead to productive and fulfilling work.

Right now, you're in the thick of it. You're going to classes, completing assignments, studying for exams, and maybe holding down a job (or more than one). Growing up, you may have dreamed of becoming a physician or a teacher or an engineer. At this point, those dreams may still be alive. Or perhaps they've evolved as you've experienced more coursework, found out that a particular subject isn't your forte after all, or discovered that something you hadn't even considered is. But at some point in your college career, you'll need to commit

> ❝ It takes courage to grow up and become who you really are. ❞
>
> *e. e. cummings, American poet (1894–1962)*

to a major, right? In order to do that, the two key questions at the beginning of this book immediately resurface: Who are you, and What do you want? As you've focused on these two questions, you've discovered some answers along the way.

Like many students, you probably put value in how well college prepares you for a profession.[1] Choosing a college major and directing yourself toward a prospective career can be stressful. Many students feel pressure to make the right decision—and make it right now! You might hear conflicting advice from family members that put a high priority on financial success above other important factors. Your Uncle Keith may tell you he just read an article that says that software developers, accountants and auditors, market research analysts, computer systems analysts, and HR training and labor relations specialists are the top five career fields today. If one of those is a top choice of yours, you may feel validated. If it isn't, you may feel overwhelmed by the number of possibilities from which to choose.[2] Perhaps you know what you want to do with the rest of your life right now, but many of your classmates don't, and even if they say they do, they may well change their minds several times. Yes, these decisions are important. But where do you start? The decision-making process should involve these critical steps. If you're still deciding, or even if you think you already have, consider how they apply to you.

Sensitive Situation It would not be at all surprising to have more than one student like Ethan in your class. It's possible that you will also have students who are very judgmental of Ethan. Make sure that you portray Ethan as a normal student who is struggling. How can he help himself, and if he were a member of our class, what could we do to support him?

Pay attention here since I'm clueless!

CONTROL: Your Toughest Class

Think about your most challenging class this semester. In what ways can it be useful in your future career? Make a list of all the ways this course can help you either to further your career or to become a well-educated person. Why is the challenge so great? Do you understand the course content? Do you keep up with readings and assignments? Can you follow your professor's teaching style? If appropriate, send your instructor in this class an e-mail indicating your specific efforts to do your best and detailing your progress.

Jose Luis Pelaez, Inc./Corbis

> You can be just like me. Don't just pussy foot around and sit on your assets. Unleash your ferocity upon an unsuspecting world.
>
> *Bette Midler, singer*

1. Follow Your Bliss

In an ideal world, which major and career would you choose? Don't think about anything except the actual content you'd be studying. Don't consider career opportunities, requirements, difficulty, or anything else that might keep you from making these choices in an ideal world. What are you passionate about? Let's say you have a dream of becoming a famous athlete, for example, a football player, like Peyton Manning or a skateboarder, like Shawn White or a tennis player, like Venus Williams. Can you translate your dream into goals and actually become a pro? Perhaps. Some pro athletes like these people are extremely successful. Peyton Manning is said to have a net worth of $115 million dollars. He signed a five-year $96 million dollar contract with the Denver Broncos, even though he had previously suffered injuries and undergone several surgeries when he was with the Indianapolis Colts.[3] Shawn White is said to be worth 20 million dollars. If it's skateboarding, think about which majors might apply. Majoring in physics would help you understand skateboard ascent versus decent, trajectories, spin, and angles. Majoring in landscape architecture would allow you to design skateparks. You would spend time outdoors, build computer and 3-D models of parks, and perhaps even interview other skateboarders about desirable features. Majoring in journalism would put you in a good position to write for a skateboarding magazine.

Like many students, you may be wondering what to do with your life. Perhaps the *idealist* in you has one potential career in mind and the *realist* in you has another. The $300,000 salary you'd earn as a surgeon may look very compelling until you consider the years of medical school required after college, the time invested in an internship and residency, and the still further years of necessary specialization. It takes long-term diligence, commitment, dedication, and resources—yours or borrowed ones—to make that dream come true. Do these factors lessen the appeal?

Perhaps there's conflict between your *idealism* and your family's *pragmatism*. Comedian Robin Williams once said, "When I told my father I was going to be an actor, he said, 'Fine, but study welding just in case.'"

And perhaps you just don't know yet. If that's the case, don't panic. Despite the increased pressure these days to choose the right major because of rising tuition and a changeable economy, it's hard to have it all figured out from the

Hey! Cool! This is what I would love to do!

> To live is to choose. But to choose well, you must know who you are and what you stand for, where you want to go and why you want to get there.
>
> *Kofi Annan, Ghanaian diplomat, seventh secretary-general of the United Nations*

I love this guy!

start.[4] Some college students rush into something that doesn't suit them, which just increases their stress level later. Other students delay making a decision for many different reasons; they are instead waiters, wonderers, wanderers, or watchers. Many college graduates are still tweaking their plans! While you don't want to leap before you look, there's also a sense in which declaring a major can help you gain focus as you work through all your courses. That's the positive side of choosing wisely.

On the other hand, remember this (but don't let it derail you). According to one recent study, only 27 percent of college graduates work in a job directly related to their college major (excluding professionals like doctors, lawyers, and college professors). While that figure may seem shocking, several points are worth clarifying. If you work in a big city, as opposed to a small town, your odds of working in a career related to your major go up. That makes sense; there are more diverse opportunities in big cities. And beyond the state of the economy, which complicates things, come jobs require a college degree but not a specific major.[5]

Here are some examples: with their refined math skills, physics majors are often sought after by Wall Street. Literature majors prepare themselves for all kinds of careers based on the ability to "read people." Or look at this letter from an upset father to his son: "I am appalled, even horrified, that you have adopted Classics as a major. As a matter of fact, I almost puked on my way home today. . . . I am a practical man, and for the life of me I cannot possibly understand why you should wish to speak Greek. With whom will you communicate in Greeks? . . . I suppose you will feel that you are distinguishing yourself from the herd by becoming a Classical snob." The letter was written to Ted Turner, founder of CNN.[6] It's true that some professions require specific degrees (like nursing or engineering), but aside from those, many experts think that graduate school is a more appropriate place to specialize. An undergraduate degree like the one you're more than likely pursuing now is more about getting a broad, basic education, and following your bliss is the place to start.

One thing is certain: you'll be a happier, more productive person if you do what *you* want to do *and* pursue it vigorously. When it comes to success, ability (*Can* you do it?) and effort (Are you *willing* to invest what it takes?) go hand in hand. Research shows that most first-year college students choose a major based on interest first. However, women base their decisions on aptitude second, while men are more influenced by career advancement opportunities and salary.[7]

I think I'm a wanderer.

Teachable Moment A great book by Mihaly Csikszentmihalyi, *The Evolving Self: The Psychology of Optimal Experience,* stresses the importance of doing what one enjoys to experience peak flow or a psychological high.

" Follow your bliss and be what you want to be. Don't climb the ladder of success only to find it's leaning against the wrong wall. "

Dr. Bernie Siegel, physician and writer

Bryan Allen/Corbis

Teachable Moment Go around the room and ask students to talk about their passions. Other members of the class can help brainstorm what possible majors they should consider as well as what kinds of jobs might connect with their passion.

Whatever your motivation, remember this. It's unusual for people to become truly successful halfheartedly. There are undeniable emotional and psychological components involved in success. Look at what some successful people have had to say, and note their use of emotional words such as *passion, love,* and *heart:*

> ➤ *God gave me a special talent to play the game…maybe he didn't give me a talent, he gave me a passion.* (Wayne Gretzky, called the greatest player in the history of hockey)

> ➤ *To waste time doing something you don't really <u>love</u> is, to me, the ultimate waste of time.* (Peter Jennings, ABC Nightly News, 1938–2005)

Cool quote! Remember this one to put in my room!

> ➤ *My father always told me, "Find a job you <u>love</u> and you'll never have to work a day in your life.* (Jim Fox, former player, LA Kings, NHL Hockey)

> ➤ *I am seeking, I am striving, I am in it with all my <u>heart</u>.* (Vincent van Gogh, Dutch painter, 1853–1890)

> ➤ *When <u>love</u> and skill work together, expect a masterpiece.* (John Ruskin, Oxford University scholar and writer, 1819–1900)

> ➤ *To <u>love</u> what you do and feel that it matters—how could anything be more fun?* (Katherine Graham, publisher, *Washington Post,* 1917–2001)

> ➤ *My <u>heart</u> is in the work.* (Andrew Carnegie, American industrialist, richest man in the world in 1901)

Having said that, what if your "bliss" just isn't feasible? You'd give anything to play for the NBA, but you're five foot two and female. You dream of being a rock star, but you can't carry a tune. Then it may be time to set aside the idealism and resurrect the realism in you. Maybe then it's time to revise your dreams by setting updated goals that <u>are</u> achievable.

Why do students tend to choose particular majors and careers? Research says these factors about you tend to be some of the most important:

1. **Your salary motivation.** While salary is certainly something you should be interested in, too much emphasis can force you to choose a major you're not really suited for, which can then lead you to decide college isn't for you.[8]

2. **Your brain.** Research indicates that students who are left-brained (whose left hemispheres are dominant) most often choose majors such as business, engineering, and science. Students who are right-brained choose majors such as education, nursing, communication, and law.[9]

Sensitive Situation Be alert to the fact that the mothers of some students in the room may no longer be around or were never a major influence in their lives. While this research is valid, you can elaborate that in addition to mothers, there are other individuals in our lives who can influence our career paths. Ask for volunteers to tell who else in their lives influenced their decision to come to college or the career path they will take. How about you?

3. **Your Mom.** While past research has focused on the effect fathers or both parents have on helping their children choose a major, recent studies show that mothers are influential, most readily through emotional channels, for example.[10]

4. **A faculty role model.** You may be attracted to a particular major because a teacher—a female, or a minority—someone like you, serves as a role model.[11]

5. **Your personality.** We'll explore this topic later in the "Your Type Is Showing" feature.

The huge printing presses of a major Chicago newspaper began malfunctioning on the Saturday before Christmas, putting all the revenue for advertising that was to appear in the Sunday paper in jeopardy. None of the technicians could track down the problem. Finally, a frantic call was made to the retired printer who had worked with these presses for over forty years. "We'll pay anything; just come in and fix them," he was told.

When he arrived, he walked around for a few minutes, surveying the presses; then he approached one of the control panels and opened it. He removed a dime from his pocket, turned a screw ¼ of a turn, and said, "The presses will now work correctly." After being profusely thanked, he was told to submit a bill for his work.

The bill arrived a few days later, for $10,000.00! Not wanting to pay such a huge amount for so little work, the printer was told to please itemize his charges, with the hope that he would reduce the amount once he had to identify his services. The revised bill arrived: $1.00 for turning the screw; $9,999.00 for knowing which screw to turn. (Anonymous)

So what does it take? After forty years on the job, the retired printer knew many things, including one elusive but critical piece of knowledge—which screw to turn. But perhaps you're just starting out, and experience is something you don't have yet. How will you achieve life and career success?

Some experts on growing up in our society say it's difficult to transition into adulthood. For many college students today, childhood was where they were given many opportunities: baseball, tennis, soccer, art, music, dance, travel. Their parents—with whom they have close ties—desperately want to help their children become successful. Many parents want to help solve their children's problems for them—with the best of intentions. They may be so eager to help that they try to motivate them with "ladder talk": "If you do well at the local campus, then you can get admitted to the big university, and if you graduate with a high grade point average there, you can get into a really good law school, and if you do well there, you'll be offered a job with a prestigious firm, and if you prove yourself to your superiors there, eventually you'll make partner." See how it goes—up the ladder of success? This type of communication, which is intended to encourage, can actually *discourage* some students. Such a long chain of challenging hurdles looks like an impossible dream.

Mel Levine, author of *Ready or Not, Here Life Comes,* says, "We are in the midst of an epidemic of work-life unreadiness because an alarming number of young adults are unable to find a good fit between their minds and their career directions.... Because they are not finding their way, they may feel as if they are going nowhere and have nowhere to go."[12]

How can anyone have nowhere to go with more than 12,000 different occupations or careers to choose from with 8,000 alternative job titles—for a total of over 20,000 options?[13] Some students start college and become overwhelmed. Sometime during the first year, or possibly later, they take a step back and announce in so many words, "There are too many choices. I refuse to choose at all."[14]

Here's another tough issue many college graduates face when entering the world of work. Many of them have already decided that work is boring because their part-time jobs in high school and college were boring. They don't want to climb the ladder of success. They'd like to skip the bottom and start somewhere closer to the top rung. But every job involves some element of grunt work, even those at the top. No job is round-the-clock fun, and in every new job, eventually the honeymoon is over, and the tough challenges begin. The simple truth is this: building a career takes time, persistence, dedication, and focus. Seemingly overnight successes like J. K. Rowling of Harry Potter fame are rare; steady progress toward a goal is the norm.[15]

So what does it take to launch your career successfully? You'll need to focus your I's on four things: Inner direction, Interpretation, Instrumentation, and Interaction—the four I's of career-life readiness. Here's what they mean.[16]

Inner direction. You've lived with yourself for some time now, but how well do you know yourself? How accurate is your view of yourself? Are you honest about your potential? You must first understand the inner you before you can direct it toward a career that fits.

Interpretation. Many students have memorized their way through countless classes, becoming very good at it, but often not fully understanding what they're learning. Somehow they get by, but they miss the larger principles beneath the specific facts they've memorized. On the job there's more required than repeating back what the boss has told you. You must interpret the information and apply it in your own way, which demonstrates whether you do (or don't) understand what you're doing.

(continued on next page)

Instrumentation. In your career, you'll need a toolkit filled with different kinds of abilities—engaging in high-level thinking, brainstorming, problem solving, making decisions, tapping your creativity, and cultivating both hard (technical) and soft (interpersonal) skills. And not only must you know how to use each of these tools, but you'll need to know when and why.

Interaction. Business (or any profession) isn't just about facts and figures. It's about people, values, and relationships.

People will be what help you build your career. Without people to buy, sell, trade, consume, or produce, there is no business.

The more you focus your I's, the better prepared you'll be for the challenges ahead. Centuries ago, the German poet Johann Wolfgang von Goethe wrote these words—true then and true today: *Whatever you do or dream, you can begin it. Boldness has genius, power and magic in it. Begin it now.*

My I's are NOT focused yet, especially Inner Direction.

Teachable Moment What do students think about the printing press anecdote? Was the repair the retired printer made worth $10,000? Why or why not?

> " Journalists coin silly nicknames for twentysomethings like 'twixters' and 'kidults.' … As a culture, we have trivialized what is actually the defining decade of adulthood. "

Meg Jay, "Why 30 Is Not the New 20," TEDTalk

Activity Option Ask students to interview a person who is very successful in a career. What does the person do, what specific jobs has the person held previously, and for how long? Students can do this as an outside assignment and bring their findings to class. Were there many instant success stories? Probably not.

Becoming a famous athlete can certainly be a valid dream, one you're passionate about. Can you set goals that will help you achieve your dream and become a pro? Perhaps. On the other hand, it's important to be realistic. What about aging and injuries—not to mention real ability? And how many professional athletes are there—especially compared to other professionals such as teachers, architects, and physicians? When the statistics are against you, achieving success isn't impossible, but it might take more than expert skill. It might also take some luck. However, Barbara Bush once wisely said, "You just don't luck into things as much as you'd like to think you do. You build step by step, whether it's friendships or opportunities."

2. Conduct Preliminary Research

Has it ever occurred to you that you may not have all the facts—accurate ones—about your ideal major? Do you know what it *really* takes? Have you gotten your information from qualified sources—or are you basing your opinion on your roommate's reaction to one course he took in the major or on the campus grapevine?

Try an experiment. Choose three majors you're considering, one of which is your ideal major, and send yourself on a fact-finding mission. To find out if you're on target, get the answers to the following ten questions for each of the three possibilities. Go to the physical location (department) where each major is housed, and interview a professor. The experiment requires legwork; don't just let your fingers do the clicking.

1. What is the major?

2. Who is the interviewee?

3. What is the name of the academic department where this major is housed? Where are the department offices physically located on campus?

4. Which introductory courses in this major would inform you about your interests and abilities?

5. Which upper-level courses in this major interest you? (List three.)

6. What are the department's entry requirements to become a major?

7. How many students major in this discipline on your campus?

8. Which required course in the major do students usually find most challenging? Which is most engaging? Which is most valued? Why?

9. How would the interviewee describe the reputation of this department on campus? What is it known for?

10. From the interviewee's perspective, why should a student major in this discipline?

After you complete your interviews, review the facts. Did you change any of your opinions, based on what you learned?[17]

Activity Option The ten questions here can be turned into a project. First, find out which majors most students are interested in. Group students together and have each group interview for one major. Make sure that all majors of interest in the class are covered. In the same groups, have students develop a fact sheet about the major to be presented in class and distributed to all students.

3. Take a Good Look at Yourself

Here's a bottom-line question: Looking back at Dr. Bernie Siegel's quote several pages ago, what *is* the "right wall" to lean your ladder of success on? How do you know? Many first-year college students don't know. They don't have enough experience under their belts to plan for a lifetime. They're in college to *discover*. It all comes down to questions this book has been asking you all along: Who are you? And what do you want? If you're unsure of how to proceed in your decision making, follow these recommendations to see if they help you bring your future into focus.

Activity Option After students complete Exercise 12.2 ask them to fill in the blanks in the following sentence and bring it to the next class: *Based on what I discovered about myself in doing this activity, three career choices for me are* _____, _____, *and* _____, *because* _____

Send in the SWOT Team!

A SWOT analysis is an excellent way to begin taking a good look at yourself in relation to your future. SWOT stands for Strengths, Weaknesses, Opportunities, and Threats. SWOT analyses are typically used in business, but creating one for yourself may be useful when it comes to deciding on a college major

---

Exercise 12.1   How Do You Look?

Take a good look at yourself and answer the following questions about how you prefer to work. Rank each item 1 or 2 based on your general preference. While many careers, if not most, require both, your task is to decide which of the two you prefer.

I prefer to work at a job:

				My answers:
1. Alone	_____	With other people	_____	alone
2. Indoors	_____	Outdoors	_____	outdoors!
3. With people	_____	With equipment or materials	_____	equipment
4. Directing/leading others	_____	Being directed/led by others	_____	??
5. Producing information	_____	Managing information	_____	??
6. In an organized, step-by-step way	_____	In a big-idea, holistic way	_____	big idea way
7. Starting things	_____	Completing things	_____	starting
8. Involving a product	_____	Involving a service	_____	product
9. Solving challenging problems	_____	Generating creative ideas	_____	creative ideas
10. Finding information	_____	Applying information	_____	applying
11. Teaching/training others in groups	_____	Advising/coaching others one-on-one	_____	one-on-one

Now look at your eleven first choices. Identify several career fields that come to mind that would allow you to achieve as many of them as possible.

> Are you fit company for the person you wish to become?

Anonymous

© Larry Harwood Photography, Property of Cengage Learning

Teachable Moment Encourage each student to go the campus career center to find out if there are any résumé writing workshops or sample résumés to compile. Also, encourage students to look online for résumé templates and bring at least one example to share with the class.

and a career. Make a matrix with four quadrants, label each one, and fill them in as objectively as you can.

> **Strengths** are traits that give you a leg up. These are talents you can capitalize on and qualities you can develop.

> **Weaknesses** are traits that currently work against you. You can, however, work to reduce or eliminate them.

> **Opportunities** are conditions or circumstances that work in your favor, like a strong forecast for your prospective career's future.

> **Threats** are conditions that could have adverse effects. Some of these factors are beyond your control; however, sometimes you can successfully lessen their potential effects.

As you create the matrix, begin with two basic questions:

What kinds of forces will impact your potential career?

Internal—forces inside you, such as motivation and skill

External—forces outside you that may affect your success: the job market or economy, for example

What kind of influence can these forces exert?

Positive—some forces will give you a boost toward your goals

Negative—other forces will work against you[18]

Let's complete a SWOT analysis for the earlier example of becoming a professional skateboarder. Of course, you might say that, technically, you don't need an academic degree for that particular career. But if you want to pursue related, more traditional careers—design a new skatepark or write for a skateboard magazine, for example—you would need an array of knowledge and enhanced skills from writing and design to finance and marketing. Besides, college isn't just about jobs, it's about living a fuller life as a well-educated person. Look at the SWOT analysis for a college student who dreams of becoming a professional skateboarder in Figure 12.1.

FIGURE 12.1
SWOT Analysis

Ah-ha! This helps!

Teachable Moment Get the class involved in a discussion about what this hypothetical student should do.

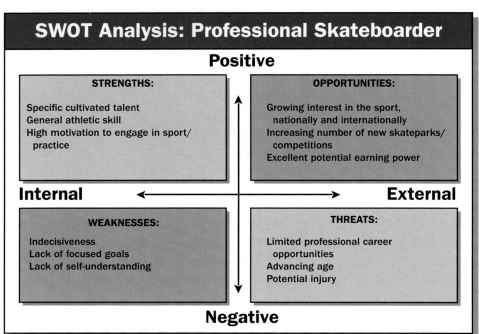

SWOT Analysis: Professional Skateboarder

Positive

STRENGTHS:
Specific cultivated talent
General athletic skill
High motivation to engage in sport/ practice

OPPORTUNITIES:
Growing interest in the sport, nationally and internationally
Increasing number of new skateparks/ competitions
Excellent potential earning power

Internal ←——————→ **External**

WEAKNESSES:
Indecisiveness
Lack of focused goals
Lack of self-understanding

THREATS:
Limited professional career opportunities
Advancing age
Potential injury

Negative

What do you think? Is professional skateboarding a good career option for him? In your view, do the opportunities outweigh the threats? For example, does the potential earning power of a professional skateboarder outweigh the risks associated with possible incapacitating injuries? Do his well-cultivated athletic skills compensate for his lack of focus in other areas? If not, might he gravitate toward other potential careers, perhaps those that also involve skateboarding, like a degree in business to run a sports facility, for example, or a degree in journalism to write for a sports magazine?

Exercise 12.2   SWOT Analysis

Looking at the model in Figure 12.1, try doing a SWOT Analysis of a career you're considering. If you have no idea where to begin, choose the career of someone you know—a friend or family member. Carefully analyze the individual's and career's Strengths, Weaknesses, Opportunities, and Threats as you see them. It may help to Google the career for specifics and check information-rich, accurate sites like OOH (*Occupational Outlook Handbook*), compiled by the U.S. Bureau of Labor Statistics. After you're done, write your conclusions below, and share your results in class, if asked. Is the career you've analyzed worth pursuing in your view?

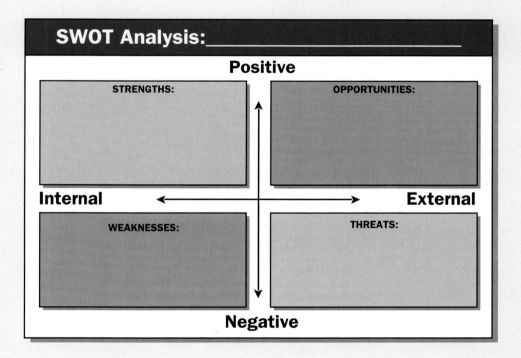

1. _____

2. _____

3. _____

> ❝ The elevator to success is out of order, but the stairs are always open. ❞
>
> *Zig Ziglar*

LEAP to Success[19]

What skills should all college graduates have? That's the question explored by a team of academic experts and leading employers, resulting in a ten-year national initiative (2005–2015)—LEAP. Leap stands for "Liberal Education and America's Promise." (And here liberal has nothing to do with politics. Instead, it's a time-honored approach to college learning that helps students learn to deal with complexity, diversity, and change—no matter which specific major they choose).

We live in a world where change—global, technological, cross-cultural, economic, ecological, you name it—is the only constant. How do you prepare for change? Can you prepare? What will get you ready? According to LEAP, four broad goals addressed in college will help you deal with twenty-first century challenges. As you look over the list below, assess your work-readiness in each area. In the blank that follows the examples, decide whether you'd rate yourself as 1 (making good progress) or 2 (need further development).

1. **Knowledge of Human Cultures and the Physical and Natural World**
   _____broad knowledge in science, math, social sciences, humanities, history, languages, and the arts: *Do you have a multidisciplinary background with fairly extensive cultural and cross-cultural knowledge? If someone mentions a painting like* **American Gothic***, a word like* **octogenarian***, a historical period*

*like the **Peloponnesian Wars**, or **Pi** as the world's most famous number, can you follow? You don't have to know everything, of course, but you do need some basic knowledge about many different kinds of things.*

2. **Intellectual and Practical Skills**

_____Inquiry and analysis: *Do you know how to ask the right questions of the right people? Can you figure out multiple possible solutions to real problems?*

_____Critical and creative thinking: *Can you evaluate ideas other people propose? Can you generate new ideas yourself and judge their feasibility?*

_____Written and oral communication: *Can you speak and write with precision and power?*

_____Quantitative literacy: *Can you understand numerical data, comprehend (and possibly generate) statistics, track a budget over time, or make financial projections about the future?*

_____Information literacy: *Can you use technology to find answers? Are you able to manipulate software, even for advanced purposes? Can you discern between valid and biased online information?*

_____Teamwork and problem solving: *Do you "work well with others?" Can you negotiate your role on a team, such that you're not perceived as either domineering or freeloading? Can you collaborate to generate good solutions to problems?*

3. **Personal and Social Responsibility**

_____Civic knowledge and engagement, both locally and globally: *Are you engaged in your community and willing to stay informed or get involved? Do you have a basic knowledge of the role local, state, and federal governments play? Are you aware of global issues?*

_____Intercultural knowledge and competence: *Are you interested in exploring the similarities, differences, and interrelationships between countries and cultures? Is your CQ strong? Can you interact well with others unlike you?*

_____Ethical reasoning and action: *Do you think about the ethical ramifications of your decisions and take the right actions—ones that are not only best for you, but also others around you?*

_____Foundations and skills for lifelong learning: *Do you want to continue learning beyond what's required of you in college? Are you setting learning goals now that will continue into your future?*

4. **Integrative and Applied Learning**

_____Synthesis and application of what you know to new contexts and complex problems: *Can you connect knowledge from a variety of fields, rather than keeping it isolated in standard "compartments" (math, English, history, etc.)? Can you apply what you've learned, moving beyond memorization into real world usefulness?*

LEAP is broad and comprehensive. As a first-year college student, you wouldn't be expected to have everything mastered now. But notice that even though *FOCUS* is about college success, many of the skills that are addressed throughout the book will help you get ready for your career—and hit the ground running. The skills you need for college and career success are more similar than you might imagine![20]

what are my strengths here???

Test Your Strengths and Interests

If you're not sure which majors or careers might be good ones for you, consider using an assessment instrument to find out. Many such tools are available through your school's Counseling or Career Center, perhaps through your instructor for this course, or through particular career assessment workshops. These assessment tools don't focus on one specific job, but instead they give you general information about which types of work might fit you. And remember that's what you're looking for—general information, hints, suggestions, clues, something to go on. It's also a good idea to try more than one assessment tool. That way you can look for overlap—one test reinforcing the results of another. For the most part, standardized, published, paper-and-pencil assessments such as the Myers-Briggs Type Inventory and the Strong Interest Inventory are most reliable, but others, including popular online tests, can give you some helpful guidance as well. Here are several assessment tools that you may want to try that are available online. Some charge a fee to obtain your results; others are free.

I'll go online soon to look for these!

> Livecareer's Free Career Test
> The Princeton Review Career Quiz
> The Career Key
> The Career Interests Game
> John Holland's Self-Directed Search
> The Princeton Review Career Quiz
> Analyze My Career

4. Consider Your Major versus Your Career

challenge ? **reaction** ''

Challenge: What is the relationship between choosing a major and choosing a career?

Reaction:

_____

_____

_____

Which comes first, the chicken or the egg? The major or the career? Silly question? The obvious answer, of course, is that you must first major in something in college before you can build a career on it. But the question isn't as straightforward as it seems.

Should you choose a major based on an intended career? Perhaps you know you want to be a science teacher, first and foremost. You don't know whether to major in one of the sciences or in education. You like all sciences, but teaching is your real interest. If you major in science, which one should it be (see Figure 12.2)?

Or instead, should you choose a major first, and then decide on a career? Say you made a firm decision to major in chemistry when your favorite science teacher did "mad scientist" experiments for the class in eighth grade. But at

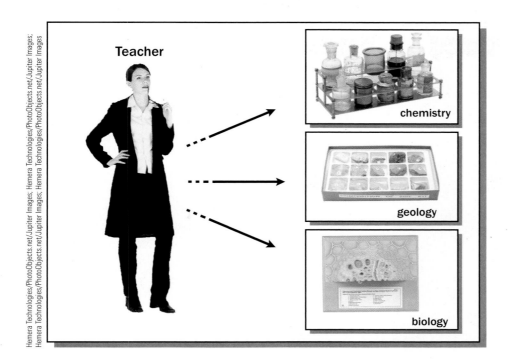

Teacher

chemistry

geology

biology

FIGURE 12.2

Which Science Should a Science Teacher Major In?

egg or chicken for me?

this point, you're not certain of the professional direction you'd like to pursue. Chemistry is your passion, but should you apply your chemistry degree as a forensic scientist, a physician, a researcher, or a teacher (see Figure 12.3)?

A few schools don't actually use the word *major*, preferring the term *concentration*, and some schools encourage *interdisciplinary studies*, a tailor-made system in which you create your own major with guidance from advisors and faculty. Other schools may even encourage double majors, which can make sense, particularly some combinations (international business and Chinese

Teaching with Technology Go to CollegeBoard.com for a list of majors and careers. This tool allows users to select a particular career field, and then see the most logical choices for college major. Alternately, selecting a particular college major displays the best personality type for that major, course spotlights, and potential careers related to the discipline. Allow students to explore this resource if they have an idea about their major or career interests.

FIGURE 12.3

Which Career Should a Chemistry Major Choose

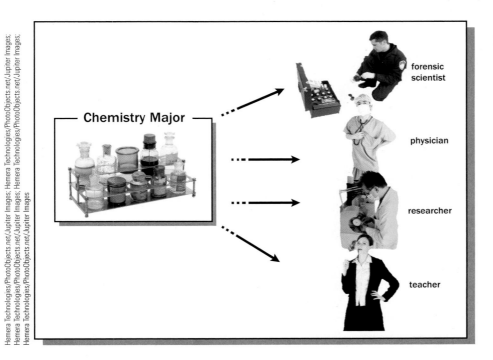

Chemistry Major

forensic scientist

physician

researcher

teacher

> We can never see past the choices we don't understand.

The Oracle, _The Matrix_

language, for example). But by and large, the concept of having a major (and sometimes a minor) in college is the norm.

So which comes first—major or career? It depends.[21] The answer sounds ambivalent, and it's meant to. Although some professional degree programs put you into a particular track right away (nursing or engineering, for example), generally either direction can work well. Doors will open and close for you, and as you gain more knowledge and experience, you'll narrow your focus. As you learn more about your chosen major, you'll also learn about its specific career tracks. But it's important to remember that a major doesn't have to lock you into one specific career. And you can always narrow or refocus your area of emphasis in graduate school after you earn your undergraduate degree.[22]

What's Your Academic Anatomy?

Thinking about your academic anatomy is a simple way to begin to get a handle on what you find fulfilling. If you had to rank order the four parts of you listed in Figure 12.4, what would you put in first place? Second, third, and last? To get yourself thinking, ask these questions:

1. Do you find fulfillment by using your _head_? Do you enjoy solving complex problems or thinking through difficult situations? Do you like to reason things out, weigh evidence, and think critically? A philosophy major who continues on to a career in law might be what students with this preference choose, for example.

FIGURE 12.4

What's Your Academic Anatomy?

Definitely these:
1. whole body
2. hands
3. heart
4. head

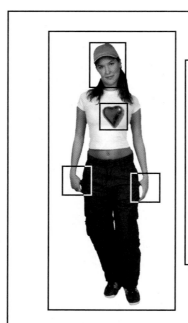

Another way of analyzing your preferences is by considering your "Academic Anatomy." What do you find most satisfying? Working with your

Head?
Heart?
Hands? or
Whole Body?

2. Do you find it satisfying to work with matters of the *heart*? Are you the kind of person others come to with problems because you listen and care? Does trying to make others happy make you happy? A psychology major who pursues a counseling career might be what students with this preference choose, for example.

3. Do you like to create things with your *hands*? Do you enjoy making art? Doing hands-on projects? Building things out of other things? An architecture major who designs and builds models might be what students with this preference choose, for example.

4. Do you excel at physical activities that involve your *whole body*? Are you athletic? Do you like to stay active, no matter what you're doing? A physical therapy major who goes on to work in a rehabilitation facility helping stroke victims relearn to walk might be what students with this preference choose, for example.

Sensitive Situation Sometimes people stereotypically think that jobs that use the hands (manual labor) are not as academic as others. You might point out that jobs that require this kind of labor, a plumber, for example, require high-level skills in other areas such as problem solving, interpersonal, and business skills, especially if plumbers are in business for themselves.

Now look at your academic anatomy rankings. Of course, the truth is that "all of you" is involved in everything you do. And achieving balance is important. But what are your priorities? This type of simple analysis can be one way of informing you about who you are and where you should be headed.

However, no system for choosing a major is perfect. In fact, most are imperfect at best. Here are four things to consider.

1. Sometimes students who don't select a likely major based on their "anatomical preferences" can still be successful. A whole-body person may decide to major in art (using his hands). But he'll have to find other ways to meet his whole-body needs unless he becomes a sculptor involved in creating large constructed projects.

2. You may intentionally choose an unlikely major. Perhaps art (using your hands) comes so naturally to you that you decide to major in

Exercise 12.3 Group Résumé

Your instructor will provide a sheet of newsprint and several markers per team of three to four students. Your job is to work on the floor, desktops, or somewhere with sufficient space to create a group résumé, highlighting all the characteristics you bring with you as a group that can help you succeed in college. Your combined group qualifications may look like this:

Qualifications:

- 27 combined years of work experience
- background in four different industries
- familiarity with Word, PowerPoint, Photoshop, and Excel
- proven research skills
- eagerness to learn
- well-developed time management skills
- interest in networking with others

After each team has completed the task, hang the newsprint sheets on the walls to create a gallery and present your group résumé to the rest of the class.

Sources: Staley, *50 Ways to Leave Your Lecturn*, p. 33. Based on "Group Resume." (1995) in M. Silberman, *101 Ways to Make Training Active*, pp. 49–50. Johannesburg: Pfeiffer.

astrophysics (using your head). You need the challenge to stay fully involved in getting your education. While it may sound unlikely, it's been known to happen.

3. You may choose an unlikely major because one particular course turns you on. You had no idea majoring in this subject was even possible, and you didn't know what it entailed. But you find studying it fascinating—so you shift gears to focus all your attention on it.

4. You may be equally engaged, no matter what. You love subjects that require using your head, hands, heart, and whole body. The anatomy of learning is less important to you than other factors—a teacher whose enthusiasm is contagious, for example.[23]

Think about your rankings. And if "head" is in last place for you, don't assume you're doomed in college. A career as a financial analyst sitting behind a desk might not be your cup of tea, for example. But it may well be someone else's. Whatever major and career you're thinking about, you may want to consider whether it's "anatomically correct."

How to Launch a Career

Exercise 12.4 Career Auction

Assume you have $100,000 to spend on the following items. In a few minutes, your instructor will begin a real-live auction, putting one item at a time up for auction. Before the auction begins, budget your money in the first column. You may select as many items as you wish to bid on, but you may not place all your money on any single item. As the group auction proceeds, fill in the appropriate amounts that are actually spent by members of the class for each item.

	BUDGETED AMOUNT	WINNING BID
1. Becoming the CEO of a leading Fortune 500 company	_____	_____
②. Being a top earner in your career field	_____	_____
3. Being the number one expert in your profession	_____	_____
4. Having good friends on the job	_____	_____
5. Being your own boss	_____	_____
6. Creating a good balance between productive work and a happy family life	_____	_____
⑦. Having opportunities for travel and adventure in your job	_____	_____
8. Doing work you find fully satisfying	_____	_____
⑨. Working in a beautiful setting	_____	_____
10. Being a lifelong learner so that your career can develop and change over time	_____	_____

I'd put most of my money on these.

After you graduate from college, it'll be time to launch your career, right? What do you really want from a career? What's important to you? Even though your views may change over time, it's important to start thinking about them now. Item 7, "Having opportunities for travel and adventure in your job," may be a top priority now, but item 6, "Creating a good balance between productive work and a happy family life," may be more appealing a few years down the road if you have several young children to parent.

Interestingly, according to research, the most important factor in job satisfaction isn't any of these ten items. The number one contributor to job satisfaction, statistically speaking, is the quality of your relationship with your boss.[24]

If all your jobs thus far have been just that—*jobs*—to help you pay the bills, how do you know what you want in a *career*? Your career is something you haven't launched yet. Exactly how do you do that?

Teachable Moment This is a great time to revisit Exercise 12.1 "How Do You Look?" Did students' highest bids match their career preferences there? Are there differences between men and women? Do students vary based on their personality types or learning modalities?

Get Some Experience

challenge / **reaction**

Challenge: What's the best way to get job experience, if you have none?

Reaction:

_____

_____

_____

You have to start somewhere, so perhaps you'd go online or open the newspaper want ads. You'd be likely to read this: *"Opening in… (anything). Experience required."* Isn't that the way it always goes? You have to *have* experience in order to get a job that will *give* you experience. So how do you launch a career?

This problem is one many college graduates face. Sure, they have experience. It's just not the right kind. They've bagged fries, mowed yards, bussed tables, and chauffeured pizzas to help pay for college expenses. If that's not the

> Experience is like a comb that life gives you when you are bald.

Navjot Singh Sidhu, former Indian cricketer and Indian Member of Parliament

© iStockphoto.com/AlbyDeTweede

	Description: What is a …?	What kind of experience do I get?	Why would I want to do it?	How do I get involved?
An Internship	An internship is an opportunity for you to work alongside a professional in a career field of interest to you.	Your supervisor will mentor you, and you'll get a clearer picture of what the career field is like.	Some majors will require you to complete an internship as a part of your program, for licensure or certification, for example.	Internships may be offered through your academic major department, or through a central office on campus, or you can pursue one on your own.
A Co-op Program	Co-op programs allow you to take classes and then apply what you've learned on the job, either after or while you take classes.	You may take classes for a term and then work full-time for a term. You can test a career field.	A potential employer can get a sense of your potential, and you can gain practical experience to put on your résumé.	Your advisor will be able to tell you if your program has co-op opportunities.
Service-Learning	Some classes contain service-learning experiences in which you volunteer your time.	A service-learning component built right into the syllabus can give you valuable, practical experience.	The emphasis is on hands-on learning and connecting what you're learning in class with what you're experiencing out of class.	If you're particularly interested in hands-on learning, ask your advisor to recommend classes with service-learning components that will benefit you.

kind of experience the posted opening is looking for, how do you get the right kind? Try a job on for size.

These experiences help you in two ways. First, they allow you to test a potential career field. The actual day-to-day work may be exactly what you expected, or not. They show you whether or not that particular career field is one you'd really be interested in. *I had no idea this field was so cutthroat, hectic, dull . . . exciting, stimulating, invigorating. . . .* A thumbs-down can be just as informative as a thumbs-up. At least you can eliminate one option from your list. Second, internships, co-ops, and service-learning opportunities give you experience to list on your résumé. That's invaluable!

Sometimes internships are offered through your academic major department, or through a central office on campus, or sometimes you can pursue one on your own through the Internet or personal connections. If you want to major in journalism, for example, you might try contacting your local newspaper, a business magazine that focuses on your city, or some other published outlet to find out if they're willing to sponsor you. *I'm a journalism major at X university, and I'm looking for an internship opportunity. I'm particularly interested in working at the* Daily Planet, *especially on the Education Beat, because I'm trying to learn more about this city and its school system.* If you receive pay, it may be a modest amount. You're in a learning mode, and you don't have experience, after all. If you land the internship through your school, you may receive course credit instead of pay.

The key to successful "trial" experiences such as internships is the relationship between you and your sponsor in the host organization. If you're not being given enough to do, or not allowed to test your competence in a particular area, speak up. The answer may be put in terms of "company policy," your "not quite ready for prime time" skills, or your supervisor's unwillingness to experiment in high-stakes areas. Nevertheless, the two of you must communicate about these kinds of important issues. No one can read your mind!

Teachable Moment Ask students if they know whether or not the major they are thinking of requires either an internship or service-learning that could help them gain helpful insights. If not, encourage students to consider doing this for real-life experience and application of their in-class learning.

Teaching with Technology Have students help each other polish their résumés with Docs.Google.com. This free Google application lets users upload documents, such as résumés, then invite friends to edit the document online. Organize your class into small teams, and then have them use this tool to upload and edit their résumés. This way, the editing process can be a collaborative effort and students can polish their résumés with input from others.

As you work your way toward launching your career, keep up with the latest information. Read up on interviewing (starting with the upcoming section in this chapter), résumé writing (see Box 12.2), cover letters (see Exercise 12.5), networking, hot career fields, and the latest employment trends. As you continue studying in your college courses, apply what you're learning to your future career. You'll be the winner!

Remember: You don't have to have it all figured out right now. Many students become discouraged and give up on college when, if they'd been patient and paid close attention to their preferences and abilities, they would have found their way. If, as in Figure 12.5, "You are here" and "You want to get here" (generally), realize that there are many routes. You can go around the lake or over the mountains. You can go directly there or wander around a bit until you find it. You can even change routes somewhere along the way. The wise thing is to start moving and keep going. Before you know it, you will have reached your original goal or a new and better one.

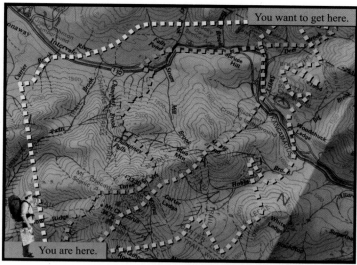

FIGURE 12.5
Finding Your Way

Brand Yourself

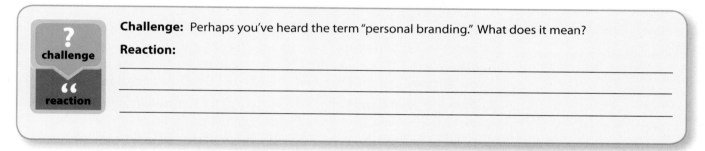

Challenge: Perhaps you've heard the term "personal branding." What does it mean?

Reaction:

_____

_____

_____

As business guru Tom Peters put it, "It's a new brand world."[25] It's not a typo; it's true. The coffee mug you may have in your hand right now has a logo on it. So does the tee shirt you're wearing, the phone in your hand, and the flat screen on your wall. Brands are everywhere; they stand for something—for example, quality, consistency, or status. If you're true to a particular brand of coffee, you know you'll get the exact same double mocha latte with nonfat milk in Detroit, Duluth, or Denver. In today's "new brand world," you can use the Internet to publicize the brand called <u>you</u>. Think about it: instead of posting empty status updates ("I'm sitting in my car in the parking lot and…") or, as some people do, putting up photos you wouldn't want everyone to see on the front page of *The New York Times*, why not use the Internet to launch your career?[26] If you're just getting a start on the power of social media to build your credibility, follow these steps:

1. **Identify your brand.** Think about famous people. What does Oprah Winfrey stand for? Empowerment? Generosity? Business acumen? What do *you* stand for? What are you known for? What's your reputation? (Hint: You already have one.) What's unique about you? What sets you apart from other job applicants? What do you value? What are your passions? Do you speak

Twiggy Van Daele/Photos.com; Ilya Andriyanov/Photos.com

> 66
> It's this simple: You are a brand. You are in charge of your brand. There is no single path to success. And there is no one right way to create the brand called you. Except this: Start today. 99
>
> **Tom Peters, "The Brand Called You,"** *Fast Company*

another language or two? Have you traveled to other cultures? Have you completed projects that won awards? Internships that gave you experience?

2. **Create a personal branding statement.** Most resumes begin with a wordy, vague objective statement like this, "Objective: To get a job in social media and put my skills to good use." What does that mean, exactly? Instead, either write a stronger objective statement or put some thought into your personal brand and sum it up in a pithy, memorable statement: "I'm known for having a head for business and a heart of gold." Then in your resumé, you can describe your entrepreneurial efforts starting "pizza and poli sci" study groups that raised everyone's exam grades (head) and also point out your volunteer work (heart). Or "I see opportunity in every challenge." Then during an interview, you can describe working your way through college by holding down three jobs at once. Or, "I help people plug in and power up their technology skills." Use action verbs; they stand out. People might remember "plug in" and "power up" because you used two verb phrases and created a mental image.

3. **Manage your brand.** Blog passionately about something you care about to increase your visibility, read articles about the career field you'd like to join, or buy a domain that consists solely of your name and build a website that attracts viewers. Update all your brand accounts at least weekly. Use professional sites like LinkedIn, and use the many functions associated with it by building a complete profile, joining groups, following particular companies, and making connections. LinkedIn is a professional social media site, a virtual online rolodex with 225 million members from more than 200 countries.

4. **Design business cards.** "But wait," you say. "I don't even have a job yet." It doesn't matter; everyone should have a business card with a high-quality headshot, personal brand statement, and contact information. After you create your business card, you can share it virtually via your phone using CardMunch.com or the app Bump.com (https://bu.mp), for example.[27] During interviews, give every interviewer your actual card or an e-version, and you'll demonstrate just how serious you are about the job search. And as you think about possible opportunities based on who you know, consider both "strong ties" (like former bosses and professors) and "weak ties" (your neighbor's colleague's boss).[28]

5. **Leverage social media.** Establishing a personal brand takes time and thought, but social media comprise the best advertising anyone could buy—and it's (mostly) free! Use it to publicize your enthusiasm, your skills, and your energy. It's never too soon to start your job search.[29]

Box 12.1 — Did I Really Post That?

When you apply for a job, chances are that many other graduates will be applying for the same one, especially if it's a good job. The first thing many employers will do is Google you.[30] When they do, what will pop up? Of course, if nothing pops up at all, that doesn't say much for how seriously you're taking the job search process, at least in terms of establishing a professional presence online. But what if they see all your social media connections, old blogs, websites, posts, photos, Twitter messages—basically, your total online life from Day One? You may think your privacy settings will protect you, but employers have ways of getting in, and they may even ask you for your Facebook login information (although this practice is illegal in some states). Take a look at these four candidates who lost pending job offers, and see if you can derive "principles to post by" that *you* should adopt, if you haven't already.

Box 12.2   **A Model Résumé**

In today's competitive world, when literally hundreds of people may be applying for one choice position, how should a résumé be written? Can a résumé be appealing, but not flashy? Solid, but not stuffy? Professional, but still personal? Thorough, but brief? Take a look at Jared's and see what you think.

> This résumé uses a skills approach, rather than a chronological approach. A chronological approach works best if you have a career underway and can list various relevant positions that prepared you for this one.

> Center your name, and use a standard résumé format. Many companies now scan résumés so that they can be read conveniently from one source. Skip the neon pink paper. Go for a highly professional look.

JARED DANIELS

Current Address:
Evelyn Edwin Living-Learning Center
Rocky Mountain State University
Great Bluffs, CO 89898
(100) 555–6543 or jdaniels@rmsu.edu

Permanent Address:
1234 Aspen Way
Vail, CO 81657
(101) 555–9128

> Provide both your temporary address, if you're attending college away from home, and your actual home address. The employer may save your résumé and call you later, over the summer, for example, if the current opening is filled by someone else.

Dog ear this page for when I need to write my résumé!

CAREER OBJECTIVE

> Build your career objective according to the position's advertised needs. "One size fits all" doesn't work when it comes to résumés.

To obtain a position as a communications specialist in a large company, designing web pages, creating internal e-newsletters, and planning corporate events.

EDUCATION

> Provide numbers whenever you can. Text can be glossed over, but numbers stand out and make your accomplishments more quantifiable.

Rocky Mountain State University, Great Bluffs, CO
Bachelor of Arts, Communication Major, 2013 (Minor: Spanish)
GPA 3.6/4.0
Personally financed 80% of college tuition through employment and athletic scholarship

HONORS
Vice President, RMSU Freshman Honor Society
Vail "Invest in the Future" League Soccer Scholarship (4 years, chosen from 150 applicants)

SUMMARY OF BEST ACADEMIC COURSEWORK

> Select coursework that applies directly to the advertised position.

Organizational Communication
Business and Professional Communication
Principles of Web Design

Advanced Composition
Emerging Technologies
Event Planning

SKILLS
Technology

> Technology is important in today's workplace. Don't underrate your competence. Many senior employees don't know as much as you do!

Part-time work, web page design
Proficient in Word, PowerPoint, Excel, Access, Macromedia Flash, Adobe Acrobat, and Photoshop
Event Planning
RMSU Freshman Honor Society, planned campus ceremonies for 1,000 guests (2 years)
Student Government, Campus Life Committee Chair (1 year)
Soccer Fundraising Events, Planning Committee Chair (3 years)
1st place winner, campus creative writing competition, 2013

EMPLOYMENT HISTORY

> If you're able, show that you have worked all throughout college to demonstrate your commitment to your goal.

Intern, Peak Industries, Human Resources Department, fall 2013
Student Assistant, Office of the Dean, Arts and Sciences, spring 2011
Residence Life, Floor Supervisor (2 years)
Hostess, Pancake Heaven, summers, 2009–2012

REFERENCES (available on request)

> Always obtain preapproval from your references, even if you don't list their names. You may be asked to provide them on a moment's notice.

> ❝ [It's] like driving at night in the fog. You can only see as far as your headlights, but you can make the whole trip that way. ❞

E. L. Doctorow, in Writers at Work

Perhaps the most common question asked during hiring interviews is this one: "Where do you see yourself in five years?" Undoubtedly, it's a tough question. In today's uncertain economy, the most honest answer is "Are you kidding—who knows? I'm not even sure what I'll have for dinner tonight." Five years seems like forever. While your imaginary answer may be the most truthful one, it's not necessarily smart.[31]

One thing that trips up many first-year college students is thinking that they have to have it all figured out—now. They think there should be a linear path between their major and their career.[32] For example, a student should enter college having declared a business major, earn a business degree, and then land a good job in the business world. "On a clear day," as the old song goes, "you can see forever." It *should* be that easy.

Realistically, clarity typically unfolds as you go. Many students don't have a particular major or a career in mind. When things become increasingly foggy during their "trip" through college, they lose their way or maybe even give up. But as the quotation above indicates: you may only be able to see as far as your headlights shine in the fog, but if you had to, you could make the whole trip that way. Rather than being linear, the path is often non-linear. You may meet someone who knows someone, or one thing will need to another, and somehow you land somewhere else. (Jay Leno, for example, majored in speech

© iStockphoto.com/Mordolff

therapy.) Success is "time-released," not a single-dose, magic pill. You work toward it by keeping two concurrent perspectives in mind: zooming out on your big-picture goals and zooming in on the "up close and personal" details of managing yourself on a daily basis. The ability to zoom in and out is

a great tool to have on your cell phone, digital camera, or computer.[33] Likewise, while you're in college, you must be able to zoom in on your individual courses and zoom out to your overall degree plan. The same principle definitely holds in your career.

So when the time comes and the interviewer asks you the inevitable question, "Where do you see yourself in five years?" take this advice:

1. Reflect on what you will say beforehand.
2. Figure out what the interviewer is trying to learn about you. Does she expect a full-blown answer, or is she just trying to see how you think.
3. Shorten the time-frame so that you *can* answer: "I'm not really sure how many years it will take, but I do know that I want to join an organization just like this one and work on a highly creative team to learn all I can. Challenges are important to me."

On the other hand, don't:

1. Make up something so far-fetched that even *you* don't believe what you're saying.
2. Identify the exact job you want in the future. ("Honestly? I'd like your job. Are you planning to retire in the next five years?")
3. Feel obliged to answer the question literally, even if you don't really know for sure. Turn the question into one you can answer, communicating what you want the interviewer to know about you.[34]

Although you're being asked to zoom out, instead zoom in on who you are and what you want. It's important to keep both perspectives in mind in your journey toward success.

Think Ahead Think about how you would answer the question identified in this section if you were applying for a job you could get today. When you graduate in four or five years, would you expect your answer to be different in some ways? Might it be the same in some ways?

Cast on Careers

© Larry Harwood Photograph. Property of Cengage Learning

FOCUS: What was easiest for you as a college student—zooming in or zooming out?

DEREK: I was pretty foggy in general my first semester of college. It took all the energy I could muster just to focus on getting to all my classes and trying to do my best. To be honest, I didn't really think much about the big picture. But I'm starting to do that now, and I think everything I've learned thus far will help me build that future—but it will be a different future than the one I once would have imagined.

FOCUS: What are your career plans?

DEREK: My real passions are photography and graphic design, and I'd like to put them to good use in the field of advertising. Right now I'm looking into getting a paid internship, and then I'd like to work in South America, maybe Brazil. I know Spanish, and I'm learning Portuguese. Someday I'd like I'd like to start up my own creative/production agency.

Interview at Your Best

Challenge: Can you identify one interviewing tip you've heard or read? What common mistakes do interviewees make?

Reaction:

_____

_____

_____

By now, you've probably already been interviewed several times to get a job. But when you're ready to launch your career, you'll be facing interviews for the new job you really want, the one you prepared for by earning a college degree. Often interviewers aren't particularly skilled at asking questions. They haven't been trained on interviewing techniques, so they just ask whatever questions come to them. And often, interviewees don't quite know what they're doing either. Of course, you should always be honest, but there are various ways to communicate the same information. Telling an interviewer you "like to work alone" sounds antisocial. But if you say you "really like to focus on what you're doing without distractions," you show dedication to your work ethic. You also need to be aware of real pitfalls to avoid. See what you think of these suggestions:

1. **Play up the positive, and downplay the negative.** A trap question interviewers sometimes ask is "What's your worst fault?" Although you may be tempted to say the first thing that comes to mind, that could be a big mistake. "Umm . . . sleeping too much! I really like to sleep in. Sometimes I sleep half the day away." Not good. But some faults you could identify might actually be seen as strengths: "I have a little too much nervous energy. I'm always on the go. I like to stay busy."

2. **Stay focused.** "Tell me about yourself" is a common question interviewers ask. How much time do you have? Most of us like to talk about ourselves, but it's important to stay on track. Think possible questions through in advance, and construct some hypothetical answers. Keep your answers job focused: what your long-term career goals are, how this job can help you prepare, what you liked about your last job. You don't need to go into your family background, or your personal problems, or bash a previous job or former boss. (The interviewer may worry that you'll bring whatever didn't work there with you to this new job.) And whatever you do, don't answer a phone call or respond to a text during an interview. This is your shot at a good job. Stay focused and use it!

3. **Don't just give answers, get some.** A job interview is like a first date. Find out what you need to know. If the job is one you're interested in long term, ask questions such as these three key ones:

    ➤ **What does this company value?** Listen to the answer. Hard work? New ideas? Communication skills? The answer will tell you about the personality of the company.

> **What's a typical day like for you?** Ask the interviewer. An answer such as "I get up at 5:00 a.m., get here at 6:30 a.m., and go home around 7:00 p.m.—and then I do paperwork all evening" tells you something. This may—or may not—be the job or the company for you.

> **What happened to the last person in this job?** If you find out he was promoted, that's one thing. But if you learn he was fired or quit, see whether you can find out why. Maybe he had job performance problems, or maybe this is an impossible job that no one could do well. Listen to the interviewer. She may be looking for an opportunity to tell you things she thinks are important, too.

4. **Watch for questions that seem to come out of left field.** Some companies like to get creative with their interviewing. Microsoft, for example, is known for asking problem-solving questions, such as "If you could remove any of the 50 states, which would it be? Be prepared to give specific reasons why you chose the state you did." There is no right or wrong answer, although some answers are better than others. ("We should just nuke state X. I had a bad experience there once" would probably concern some people, and naming Washington State, where Microsoft is located, might be a bad choice.) The interviewer just wants to hear how you can think critically and give reasons for your answers.[35] Sometimes interviewers even ask candidates to solve brainteasers or unsolvable problems ("How many sticks of gum does the average American chew in one year?"). There's no way to know an exact answer, so stop and figure out the real, underlying question (Do you get ruffled under pressure?), a plausible response ("I chew about five pieces a week, so…"), or ask a follow-on question to buy yourself time to think ("Do you mean regular gum or bubble gum?") Remember: Today's interviewers are looking for more than technical skills; they're looking for critical thinking skills, problem-solving skills, and creativity. They're looking for you to identify the contribution you would make. Why should they should hire you over the next person in line? Can you do this job? Will you love this job? And will they like working with you?[36] Whatever the interviewer's question, always tie your answer back to the job you're applying for and your potential contribution. For example, let's say the interviewer asks, "What's your favorite app?" and the answer that pops out of your mouth immediately is "'LastPass.' It stores all my passwords in one place and is totally secure." Technically, LastPass may have nothing to do with the job you're interested in, but find a link and connect the dots for the interviewer: "Being organized is a top priority for me. I'm always looking for tools that help me get and stay organized—in my personal life and on the job."

5. **Don't start off with salary questions.** Make sure the first question out of your mouth isn't "So tell me about the salary again? Any way to notch that up a bit?" The last thing you want to do is give the interviewer the idea you're in it for the money. Of course, you are, but not just for that. More importantly, in every job you have, you'll gain experience and knowledge that will always better prepare you for every job that will be a part of your long-term career. Don't start negotiating a salary until you've actually been offered a job.

6. **Negotiate wisely.** If the interviewer asks you to name a salary figure, be careful. Saying "I could probably live on $35,000" when the actual figure the

Activity Option Assign students a real or fictitious possible job opportunity (perhaps on campus or in the surrounding area) to research, and ask them to come to class prepared for a mock interview. Time permitting, let as many students participate in the mock interview as possible. The rest of the class should decide who they would hire and why.

interviewer is authorized to start with is $40,000, has just given the employer the option to lower the salary, based on your expectations. A good rule of thumb is: Never name a number. It's always best to ask the interviewer what the salary range for the job is. It's also good to research the salaries of similar jobs, and it's even better to have another job offer you're considering, so you have choices. Otherwise, you're not negotiating; you're begging.[37]

7. **Realize you may be asked to *demonstrate* your skills.** Increasingly, interviews involve "showing what you know" or applying your knowledge as you would on the job. For example, "if you want to be a social media manager, you will have to demonstrate familiarity with Twitter, Facebook, Pinterest, Google+, HTML, On-Page SEO, and Key Word Analysis. Sample question: 'Kanye West just released a new fashion collection. You can see it here. Imagine you had to write a tweet promoting this collection. What would your tweet be?'"

I should practice for this!

8. **Know what you're dealing with.** One of the easiest ways to ruin a job interview is by doing nothing. Candidates who don't do their homework usually don't pass an interview. If the interviewer asks, "So what do you know about the company?" and you reply, "Oh, not much, but I'm a fast learner," you'll be perceived to care very little about the outcome of the interview. Go online to read up about the place you'd like to work. Your knowledge, and therefore your interest, will show. And it goes without saying (although here it is, anyway) that you should arrive early, dress professionally, overprepare, and send a follow-up thank-you note or e-mail.[38]

Exercise 12.5 Cover Letter Critique

In this day and age, do you still need an old-fashioned cover letter? The answer is, yes! When you submit a résumé, either in person, through the mail, or online, you should send a well-written cover letter along with it that briefly outlines your qualifications for the job, expresses your interest, and gives the person who reviews your résumé some idea of who you are (in roughly three paragraphs or less). Cover letters give you chance to make yourself stand out, especially when the average recruiter is said to spend 30 seconds or less on each resume. Take a look at the following cover letter from Jared Daniels and critique it. What has he done right, and what has he done wrong?

15 September

To Whom It May Concern,

I'd like to apply for your opening at BYB Industries. I have heard a lot about your company and it sounds great. A friend of mine works there, and he said his starting salary was unbelieveable. What exactly do you do at your company besides make electronics? He's told me a few things, but I'm eager to learn more!

As you can see from my résumé, I don't have much experience. But I have just earned a degree in communication from Rocky Mountain State University, and I did pretty well. I want to start my career at a great company like yours.

I hope to hear from you soon.

Warmly,

Jared Daniels

After finding the mistakes Jared made, rewrite this letter to bring to class or submit to your instructor.

Your TYPE is Showing

What does your psychological type have to do with your college major and career choices? Actually, a great deal. Your personality is the very core of who you are, so you need to know what possible effects it can have on your choices. Which type are you?

- **"I want to decide and move on."** *EJ Types* (ESTJ, ESFJ, ENFJ, ENTJ) like to make a decision quickly and get it over with. They may talk over the process of deciding and then jump in with both feet. They are organized students, keep track of credits, and work their way through a degree. If their intended major doesn't work out, they'll jump ship quickly and try another. The wiser decision might be to slow down and learn more about other options.

- **"I want to major in everything!"** *EP Types* (ESTP, ESFP, ENFP, ENTP) want to take their time deciding. Closing off options by making a choice provoke anxiety for them, so they'd rather experiment for a while. They may try one major, and then another, and then another until they find a fit—or run out of time or money. They want to plunge into co-curricular activities to experience it all! P students with J parents, however, can be at cross purposes. While the P student experiments, the J parent becomes frustrated. P students can stall out, too. When presented with too many options, they may opt out entirely.

- **"I want to be absolutely sure."** *IJ Types* (ISTJ, ISFJ, INFJ, INTJ) research, think, and reflect before coming to any conclusion. They read books, consult websites, and consider all the information carefully because they tend to stick with a decision once they've made it. Being introverts, they may spring their decisions on people (especially F's) who haven't been aware of what they're thinking.

- **"I wish I knew what I was going be when I grow up!"** *IP Types* (ISTP, ISFP, INFP, INTP) resist coming to a decision, so much so that they may miss important deadlines. Sometimes they need a nudge from someone, "Hey, did you know that you have to declare a major by your fifth semester?" IP's are wanderers. They'd rather believe that no decision is final so that they remain true to their inner values.[39]

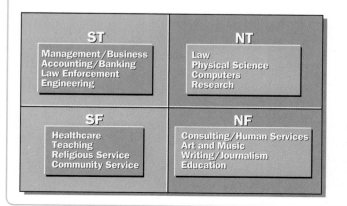

Your Work Style

Each of the four dimensions of your type tells something about your likely work preferences. Here are some examples.

Extraverts (E)

Like activity and variety
Get impatient with long projects
Like to work with other people

Sensors (S)

Like order and work steadily
Like to use skills they already have
Are good at work that requires precision

Thinkers (T)

Like to work in an orderly setting
Can reprimand someone when needed and are firm
Are analytically oriented

Judgers (J)

Like to work according to plan
Like to complete things
May not notice things that should get done
Want only what they need to know to get started

Introverts (I)

Like to concentrate in quiet
Can focus on one project for a long time
Are content to work alone

Intuitives (N)

Dislike routine and work in energy bursts
Like learning new skills
Dislike taking time to be precise

Feelers (F)

Like to work in a harmonious setting
Dislike telling people unpleasant things
Are people-oriented and sympathetic with others

Perceivers (P)

Can adapt to changes
Like to leave things open to change
May put off things they don't like doing
Want to know everything about a new project[40]

Your Career Choice

Some studies show that the two middle letters (ST, SF, NT, or NF) of psychological type are relatively good predictors of what career fields people are attracted to. See if you find a career field you're considering in the four quadrants in Figure 12.6, and if what you're considering "fits" your type. But remember that research reports statistical regularities, not individual destinies.

FIGURE 12.6

Career Choice and Psychological Type: What Do the Two Middle Letters Say?

Source: Based on J.K. DiTiberio & A.L. Hammer (1993). Introduction to Type in College. Palo Alto, CA: Consulting Psychologists Press.

Build Your Professionalism Skills: Ten Things Employers Hope You Will Learn in College

At the end of your college degree, you'll come to a fork in the road. You'll either decide to launch your career or you'll decide to continue your schooling by going to medical school, law school, or graduate school. Regardless of which fork in the road you choose, college teaches many lessons, and they're not all about the subject matter in your classes. If you continue on for an advanced degree, you'll be thankful for the academic professionalism you've developed as an undergraduate student. Graduate studies require even more commitment, and the competition is stiff. However, if you decide to launch your career, much of the *academic professionalism* you've developed in college can easily translate into *career professionalism*, with some thought and application on your part. Thanks to having gone to college, you can begin your career with some ready-to-go professional advantages. Here is a set of ten things employers care about, regardless of exactly which college courses you've taken or degree you've earned.[41] As you read, think about which ones are already in place for you. Employers want you to:

I appreciate this advice. It gives me a leg up.

1. **Exhibit a strong work ethic.** In college, you demonstrated your work ethic. Perhaps you labored over assignments to produce your best work. In the world of work, organizations prefer to hire winners, not slackers. Winners are motivated and reliable. They know how to kick into high gear when necessary. Not only is day-to-day performance important, but so is how you handle yourself at crunch time. Someone once said, "Every job is a self-portrait of the person who did it. Autograph your work with excellence." Your work ethic says a great deal about who you are.

2. **Study up.** In college, you were encouraged to learn deeply, not just memorize facts. Transfer this principle to the workplace. On the job, learn the ins and outs of your industry. If you are an automotive engineer, know more than just the design specs of the cars you work on. Learn

> ❝
> When you come to a fork in the road, take it. ❞
>
> *Yogi Berra, baseball player and manager*

about the automobile maker's history, what the company stands for, its vision and values, and the reputation it has earned from customers. It's easy to get tunnel vision and lose sight of the bigger picture.

3. **Prove you're a problem solver.** While taking your college classes, you learned problem-solving skills. Some of those problems were personal (*My car won't start! Who can I get to drive me to class at the last minute?*), and some were academic (*Why was Edgar Allen Poe so "dark"?*). On the job, everyone values the person who comes up with a workable solution when everyone else is stumped. And your boss will value you more if you come up with solutions yourself. Instead of, *What should I do about X?* say, *We're facing Problem X. Should I do A, B, or C?* You've proven that you've already thought about the problem, generated three possible solutions, and demonstrated that you can think on your own.

4. **Speak and write well.** Your college career may have put more emphasis on these skills than any others. In today's world of abbreviated text messages (AYS = Are you serious?) and empty conversation ("And she's . . . like so . . . you know . . . whatever . . ."), you can become a super star on the job by just speaking and writing well. And in addition to speaking and writing, learn to listen to what's *really* being said and why. With practice, you can listen past the bravado or baloney and get to the *real* message. That's important!

> ❝ I always wanted to be somebody, but I should have been more specific. ❞
>
> *Lily Tomlin, comedian*

5. **Polish your people skills.** Your college instructors may have assigned group projects in your classes to help you learn teamwork skills. Good teamwork skills are key to a successful career in anything! People can be difficult to work with, yet *people* are the way work gets done.

6. **Learn the rules of the game.** In school—and throughout your life—you have learned what's sometimes called "The Hidden Curriculum": things everyone knows, more or less, but never learned formally. For example, most people know that it's not polite to tell off-color jokes to people you've just met or smack your gum while giving a speech. In the same way, on the job, the "grapevine," or informal network, is important to understand. To be successful, you must be tuned in. Understand the culture of the organization you work for. What does it value? Who holds the power? Where do you fit in, and what can you contribute?

> " That would never work in the real world. . . . The real world isn't a place, it's a justification for not trying. "
>
> *Jason Fried and David Heinemeier Hansson,* **Rework**

7. **Know how to gather information and use it.** In college, you're asked to develop your research skills. It's easy to think that each paper for a class is just another assignment to check off the list, when, actually, you're developing skills that will be critical to your success later. You don't just string together pieces of information when you do research for your college classes. You analyze research through the "eyes" of the problem you're trying to address and *your* perspective on it. You weave ideas together to make an argument.

8. **Understand that numbers count.** Unfortunately, math gets a bad rap. Many people approach math classes in college with "fear and loathing," when, actually, math is a key to success in the world of work. If you can understand spreadsheets or figure out the budget, you'll be ahead of the game. Some people deemphasize the importance of financial skills by referring to them as "bean counting" or "number crunching," but people who know how to apply math on the job are highly sought after.

9. **Go for extra credit.** In some of your courses, your instructors may give extra credit. You could be allowed to do something extra, beyond the requirements on the syllabus, to raise your grade. But what's extra credit in terms of your career? On the job, you have "extra credit" when your abilities stand out. You speak German and no one else does, so when something needs translating, you're the go-to person. Or you're so exceptional at PowerPoint that you're affectionately referred to as the "Power-Point King."

10. **Manage your time, your attention, and yourself.** College is about self-responsibility. You're in charge of your education; you call the shots. If you manage your time and money, for example, you can focus as you should on your courses. If you "spend" unwisely—in either area—you lose your focus and your performance slips. In your career, the same will be true. Your ability to manage your time, your attention, and yourself will affect your personal and professional future.

My, How You've Grown! Goodbye and Good Luck!

Remember Aunt Ruth (or whatever her name was)? Every time she visited when you were a kid, she remarked about how much you'd grown. Or when you went to visit her, she'd measure you and mark a notch on the wall to compare your height now to the one from last year's visit. She loved watching you grow, and the fact that she noticed made you feel special. There's no doubt about it. In this first term of college, you have grown. You have gained new perspectives, new insights, and new ways of thinking about things. Like Aunt Ruth, others may notice. If those close to you are threatened

> The self is not something that one finds. It's something one creates.

Thomas Szasz, Professor Emeritus in Psychiatry, State University of New York Health Science Center, Syracuse

by these changes, reassure them that your newfound knowledge hasn't made you think less of them. Remember: "You should have education enough so that you won't have to look up to people; and then more education so that you will be wise enough not to look down on people." If they are proud of you and your accomplishments, and have supported you along the way, thank them!

Here's the bottom line. Morpheus said it well in *The Matrix*, "There is a difference between knowing the path and walking the path." You now know the path to college success, but here's a much more important question: will you walk it? Will you step onto the path and apply the advice you've read in *FOCUS* in all your classes?

The important thing is to keep learning and never stop. Continuing to learn—whether in college or in life—is what will determine who you are and what you will become. This book, and the course for which you're reading it, have begun that process. Now the rest is up to you!

Now What Do You Think?

insight

! action

❶ At the beginning of this chapter, Ethan Cole, a frustrated and discouraged college student, faced a challenge. Now after reading this chapter, would you respond differently to any of the questions you answered about the "FOCUS Challenge Case"? Knowing what you know now, how would you advise him? Write a paragraph ending to the story, incorporating your best advice.

❷ Assess your LEAP skills. Which areas are particular strengths of yours and which seem most challenging?

❸ Have you taken a formal career strength or interest test? If not, locate one online, take it, and discuss the results.

❹ Create your own personal brand statement. What's unique about you, and what could you contribute to an organization?

❺ If you wrote a case study about yourself at the beginning of this course, revisit it. Analyze what you've learned and what you'll apply to achieve academic success.

This chapter really helped me!

Reality Check

Teachable Moment Since this is the last chapter, ask students to take a minute to talk about the book. Is this the most interesting chapter? If not, which one is and why? Did their attitudes about the "Readiness Check" activity change over time? Why or why not? Did it become a productive habit that carried over into reading assignments for other courses?

Teachable Moment Students have probably had some eye-opening moments working through this chapter. Take a moment to go around the room and ask students to report on one key thing they learned. Students cannot repeat what someone else said. They can say "I learned that, too, but I also learned _____."

On a scale of 1 to 10, answer the following questions now that you've completed the chapter.

low   1   2   3   4   5   6   7   8   9   10   high

In hindsight, how much did you already know about this subject before reading the chapter?

Can you answer these questions about choosing a major and a career more fully now that you've read the chapter? _____

❶ What is a SWOT analysis and how might it help you choose a major and career?

❷ How can you try on a career before actually entering it?

❸ What is personal branding, and how can you use social media to promote yourself to potential employers?

How useful might the information in this chapter be to you? How much do you think this information might affect your success overall? _____

How much energy did you put into reading this chapter? _____

How long did it actually take you to complete this chapter (both the reading and writing tasks)? _____ Hour(s) _____ Minutes

Did you finish reading this chapter? _____

Did you intend to when you started? _____

If you meant to but didn't, what stopped you? _____

Take a minute to compare these answers to your answers from the "Readiness Check" at the beginning of this chapter. What gaps exist between the similar questions? How might these gaps between what you thought before starting the chapter and what you now think after completing the chapter affect how you approach your next term of college?

Reality FOCUS
Exit Interview

Although you have not quite completed your first term as a college student, we're interested in your reactions to college so far: how you have spent your time, what challenges you've experienced, and your general views about what college has been like. Please answer thoughtfully.

INFORMATION ABOUT YOU

Name _____

Student Number _____   Course/Section _____

Instructor _____

Gender _____   Age _____

NOTE: Questions 1–10 were asked on the Entrance Interview and need not be repeated here. The numbering below begins with number 11 so that the Entrance and Exit Interview results can be compared, if you or your instructor would like to do that. It may be interesting to see how your original expectations of college compare to your actual experience. Note, too, that the Exit Interview contains several added questions at the end about your future education.

YOUR COLLEGE EXPERIENCE

Your Reactions to College

11. **Which of the following reasons to finish your college degree seem important to you now? (Check all that apply.)**

_____ I want to build a better life for myself.

_____ I want to be well off financially in the future.

_____ My friends are going to college.

_____ It is expected of me.

_____ I want to continue learning.

_____ I am unsure of what I might do instead.

_____ I want to build a better life for my family.

_____ I need a college education to achieve my dreams.

_____ My family is encouraging me to continue.

_____ I want to continue playing the sports for which I was recruited.

_____ The career I am pursuing requires a degree.

_____ other (please explain)

12. **How did you find you learned best in college? (Check all that apply.)**

_____ by looking at charts, maps, graphs

_____ by listening to instructors' lectures

_____ by reading books

_____ by going on field trips

_____ by looking at color-coded information

_____ by listening to other students during in-class discussions

_____ by writing papers

_____ by engaging in activities

_____ by looking at symbols and graphics

_____ by talking about course content with friends or roommates

_____ by taking notes

_____ by actually doing things

13. **The following sets of opposite descriptive phrases are separated by five blank lines. Put an X on the line between the two that best represents your response, like this:** For me, high school was easy _____:___X___:_____:_____:_____ hard

My first term of college:

challenged me academically _____:_____:_____:_____:_____ was easy

was very different from high school	____:____:____:____:____ was a lot like high school
was exciting	____:____:____:____:____ was dull
was interesting	____:____:____:____:____ was uninteresting
motivated me to continue	____:____:____:____:____ discouraged me
was fun	____:____:____:____:____ was boring
helped me feel a part of this campus	____:____:____:____:____ made me feel like an outsider

14. **How many total hours per week did you study outside of class for your college courses?**

____ 0–5   ____ 6–10   ____ 11–15   ____ 16–20   ____ 21–25

____ 26–30   ____ 31–35   ____ 36–40   ____ 40+

15. **Now what do you expect your grade point average to be at the end of your first term of college?**

____ A+   ____ A   ____ A–   ____ B+   ____ B

____ B–   ____ C+   ____ C   ____ C–   ____ D or lower

Your Strengths, Personality, and Interests

16. **Which of these *strengths* or personal characteristics contributed to your college success? (Check all that apply.)**

____ a. I am good at building relationships.

____ b. I can usually convince others to follow my plan.

____ c. I like to win.

____ d. I work toward future goals.

____ e. I like to be productive and get things done.

____ f. I have a positive outlook on life.

____ g. I'm usually the person who gets things going.

____ h. I enjoy the challenge of learning new things.

____ i. I am focused.

____ j. I can usually look at a problem and figure out a plan of action.

____ k. I work to keep everyone happy.

____ l. I'm a take-charge kind of person.

____ m. I help other people develop their talents and skills.

____ n. I'm a very responsible person.

____ o. I can analyze a situation and see various ways things might work out.

____ p. I usually give tasks my best effort.

17. **How confident are you now in yourself in each of the following areas? (1 = very confident, 5 = not at all confident)**

____ overall academic ability

____ mathematical skills

____ leadership ability

____ reading skills

____ public speaking skills

____ study skills

____ technology skills

____ physical well being

____ writing skills

____ social skills

____ emotional well being

____ teamwork skills

18. **For each of the following pairs of descriptors, which set sounds most like you based on what you've learned about yourself this term?**

(Please choose between the two options on each line and place a checkmark by your choice.)

____ Extraverted and outgoing	or	____ Introverted and quiet
____ Detail-oriented and practical	or	____ Big-picture and future-oriented
____ Rational and truthful	or	____ People-oriented and tactful
____ Organized and self-disciplined	or	____ Spontaneous and flexible

19. *FOCUS* is about 12 different aspects of college life. Which did you find to be most interesting as they applied to your academic success? (Check all that apply.)

_____ Starting strong, building resilience

_____ Learning styles and studying

_____ Thinking critically and creatively

_____ Engaging, listening, and note-taking in class

_____ Developing memory, taking tests

_____ Working toward wellness

_____ Setting goals, achieving dreams

_____ Managing your time, energy, and money

_____ Learning online

_____ Reading, writing, and presenting

_____ Working in teams, valuing diversity

_____ Choosing a college major and career

Your Challenges

20. Of the 12 aspects of college life identified in the previous question, which were most challenging to apply to yourself in your academic work? (Check all that apply.)

_____ Starting strong, building resilience

_____ Learning styles and studying

_____ Thinking critically and creatively

_____ Engaging, listening, and note-taking in class

_____ Developing memory, taking tests

_____ Working toward wellness

_____ Setting goals, achieving dreams

_____ Managing your time, energy, and money

_____ Learning online

_____ Reading, writing, and presenting

_____ Working in teams, valuing diversity

_____ Choosing a college major and career

21. Which one of your current classes was most challenging this term and why?

Which class? (course title *or* department and course number) _____

Why? _____

Did you succeed in this course? _____ yes _____ no _____ Somewhat (please explain): _____

22. Please mark your *top three areas of concern* relating to your first term of college by placing 1, 2, and 3 next to the items you choose (with 1 representing your top concern).

_____ I did not fit in.

_____ I was not academically successful.

_____ I had difficulty handling the stress.

_____ I overextended myself and tried to do too much.

_____ I did not reach out for help when I needed it.

_____ I did not put in enough time to be academically successful.

_____ I am now tempted to drop out.

_____ I was not organized enough.

_____ I was distracted by other things, like spending too much time online.

_____ Other (please explain) _____

_____ I had difficulty making friends.

_____ My grades disappointed my family.

_____ I had financial problems.

_____ I cut class frequently.

_____ I procrastinated on assignments.

_____ My professors were hard to communicate with.

_____ I was homesick.

_____ I was bored in my classes.

_____ My job(s) outside of school interfered with my studies.

Your Future

23. How certain are you now of the following (1 = totally sure, 5 = totally unsure)?

_____ Finishing your degree

_____ Choosing your major

_____ Deciding on a career

_____ Completing your degree at this school

_____ Continuing on to work toward an advanced degree after college

> You may gain some personal insights if you compare the questions in this "Your College Experience" section of the Exit Interview with the matching questions from the "Your College Expectations" section in the Entrance Interview at the front of the book. Or your instructor may ask you to write about your Insights and intended Actions. Now continue on to these final questions about "Your Next Steps."

24. What are you most looking forward to after this semester/quarter?

25. Did you achieve the outcomes you were hoping to achieve at the beginning of this first semester/quarter? Why or why not?

YOUR NEXT STEPS

26. Looking ahead, how satisfied do you expect to be with your decision to attend this school?

_____ very satisfied　　　　_____ satisfied

_____ somewhat dissatisfied　　_____ very dissatisfied

_____ not sure

27. Which of the following statements best reflects your educational intentions?

_____ I plan to stay at this school until I complete my degree.

_____ I plan to transfer to another institution (please identify which one _____)

_____ I plan to stop out of college for awhile (to work, for example) and then return to this school.

_____ I plan to drop out of college.

28. If you are thinking about transferring to another institution, why would you do so?

This school does not offer my intended major (which is _____).

This school is too large.

I don't feel I fit in.

I want to go to a school further from home.

I want to be closer to my friends.

I want to transfer from a two-year to a four-year institution.

This school is too small.

This school is too expensive.

I want to go to a school closer to home.

I want to be closer to my boy/girlfriend.

I will change job locations.

I want to transfer from a four-year to a two-year institution.

other (please explain)

29. What was the biggest difference between what you thought college would be like and what it was actually like for you?

30. How have you changed most over this first semester/quarter? In what ways are you different now that you've been in college?

How will this introductory semester/quarter affect or change your future college experience?

Notes

Chapter 1

1. (2012, May 17). College graduation: Weighing the cost . . . and the payoff. *Pew Research Center*. Retrieved from http://pewresearch.org/pubs/2261/college-university-education-costs-student-debt.

2. Pope, J. (2012, August 20). College costs: New research weighs the true value of a college education. *The Huffington Post*. Retrieved from http://www.huffingtonpost.com/2012/08/20/college-costs-new-research-weighs-value-of-college-education_n_1813337.html.

3. Ibid.

4. Leonhardt, D. (2011, June 25). Even for cashiers, college pays off. The *New York Times*. Retrieved from http://www.nytimes.com/2011/06/26/sunday-review/26leonhardt.html?_r=0; Rampell, C. (2011, June 6). Once again: Is college worth it?" *The New YorkTimes*. Retrieved from http://economix.blogs.nytimes.com/2011/05/20/once-again-is-college-worth-it/.

5. (2012). Financial literacy. *Wichita State University*. Retrieved from http://webs.wichita.edu/?u=ofdss&p=/Students/FinancialLiteracy/.

6. Hyman, J. S., & Jacobs, L. F. (2010). 10 reasons to go to a research university. *U.S. News*. Retrieved from http://www.usnews.com/education/blogs/professors-guide/2010/04/28/10-reasons-to-go-to-a-research-university.

7. Community colleges. *The College Board*. Retrieved from http://www.collegeboard.com/student/repository/final_cc_flyer_pdf_8_11_05__49035.pdf.

8. Koebler, J. (2012, April 21). Report: Community college attendance up, but graduation rates remain low. *U.S. News*. Retrieved from http://www.usnews.com/education/best-colleges/articles/2012/04/21/report-community-college-attendance-up-but-graduation-rates-remain-low.

9. (2013). Career and technical colleges: Careers in focus. *NACAC*. Retrieved from http://www.nacacnet.org/studentinfo/articles/Pages/CareerandTech.aspx.

10. Spielberg finally to graduate. (2002, May 15). *BBC News*. Retrieved from http://news.bbc.co.uk/2/hi/entertainment/1988770.stm.

11. Gregory, M. (2003, September 12). A liberal education is not a luxury. *The Chronicle of Higher Education, 50*(3), B16.

12. Staley, R. S., II. (2003). In C. Staley, *50 ways to leave your lectern* (pp. 70–74). Belmont, CA: Wadsworth.

13. Schawbel, D. (2010). *Me 2.0: 4 steps to building your future.* New York: Kaplan Publishing; Driscoll, E. (2012, June 4). What employers want from college grads. *Fox Business*. Retrieved from http://www.foxbusiness.com/personal-finance/2012/06/04/what-are-employers-want-from-college-grads/.

14. College enrollment and work activity of 2012 high school graduates. *Department of Labor Statistics*. Retrieved from http://www.bls.gov/news.release/hsgec.nr0.htm.

15. Leonhardt, D. (2011, June 25). Even for cashiers, college pays off. The *New York Times*. Retrieved from http://www.nytimes.com/2011/06/26/sunday-review/26leonhardt.html?_r=0.

16. Tugend, A. (2012, September 27). That elusive diploma. *National Journal*. Retrieved from http://www.nationaljournal.com/next-economy/finishing-college-is-not-easy-when-you-have-to-work-too-20120927.

17. Ibid.

18. Hyman, J. S., & Jacobs, L. F. (2010, 1 September). The five biggest mistakes college students make. *U.S. News & World Report*. Retrieved from http://www.usnews.com/blogs/professors-guide/2010/09/01/the-5-biggest-mistakes-college-students-make.html.

19. Leonhardt, D. (2011, June 25). Even for cashiers, college pays off. *The New York Times*. Retrieved from http://www.nytimes.com/2011/06/26/sunday-review/26leonhardt.html; http://cew.georgetown.edu/.

20. Data show value of college degree. (2005, April 8). *The Chronicle of Higher Education, 51*(31), A22.

21. (2006, January 10). Parents' unexpected divorce destabilizes new college students. *PENNSTATE Live*. Retrieved from http://news.psu.edu/story/206200/2006/01/10/parents-unexpected-divorce-can-destabilize-new-college-students-life.

22. Brooks, R., & Goldstein, S. (2004). *The power of resilience: Achieving balance, confidence, and personal strength in your life.* Chicago: Contemporary Books, ix.

23. http://dictionary.reference.com/browse/grit.

24. Halvorson, H. G., (2011, February, 25). Nine things successful people do differently. *Harvard Business Review Conversation*. Retrieved from http://blogs.hbr.org/cs/2011/02/nine_things_successful_people.html#.

25. Wise, J. (2010, May 23). Extreme fear: How to thrive under stress. *Psychology Today*. Retrieved from http://www.psychologytoday.com/blog/extreme-fear/201005/how-thrive-under-stress.

26. Grierson, B. (2009, May 1). Weathering the storm. *Psychology Today*. Retrieved from http://www.psychologytoday.com/articles/200904/weathering-the-storm.

27. Adams, S. (2011, April 9). How to get a real education. *The Wall Street Journal*. Retrieved from http://online.wsj.com/article/SB10001424052748704101604576247143383496656.html.

28. Di Meglio, F. (2012, May 10). Stress takes its toll on college students. *BloombergBusinessweek*. Retrieved from http://www.businessweek.com/articles/2012-05-10/stress-takes-its-toll-on-college-students.

29. Goleman, D. (2007). *Social intelligence: The new science of human relationships.* New York: Bantam.

30. Pascarella, E. T., & Terenzini, P. T. (2005). *How college affects students: A third decade of research.* San Francisco: Jossey-Bass, p. 403.

Chapter 2

1. Crenshaw, D. (2011, January 20). Think you're good at multitasking? Take this test. *Dave Crenshaw.com*. Retrieved from http://davecrenshaw.com/tag/multitasking-exercise/.

2. Carr, N. (2011). *The shallows: What the Internet is doing to our brains.* New York: W. W. Norton; Multi-tasking adversely affects brain's learning, UCLA psychologists report. (2006, July 26). *ScienceDaily*. Retrieved from http://www.sciencedaily.com/releases/2006/07/060726083302.htm.

3. Bregman, P. (2010, May 20). How (and why) to stop multitasking. *HBR Blog Network*. Retrieved from http://blogs.hbr.org/2010/05/how-and-why-to-stop-multitaski; 'Infomania' worse than marijuana. Retrieved from *BBC News*. Retrieved from http://news.bbc.co.uk/2/hi/uk_news/4471607.stm.

4. Seven, R. (2004, November 28). Life interrupted. *Pacific Northwest*, seattletimes.com. Retrieved from http://seattletimes.com/pacificnw/2004/1128/cover.html; Richtel, M. (2010,

June 6). Attached to technology and paying a price. *The New York Times*. Retrieved http://www.nytimes.com/2010/06/07/technology/07brain.html?ref=yourbrainon computers; Richtel, M. (2010, August 24). Digital devices deprive brain of needed downtime. *The New York Times*. Retrieved from http://www.nytimes.com/2010/08/25/technology/25brain.html?ref=yourbrainoncomputer.

5. Hamilton, J. (2008, October 9). Multitasking teens may be muddling their brains. *NPR: Your Health*. Retrieved from http://www.npr.org/templates/story/story.php?storyId=95524385; Tierney, J. (2009, May 5). Ear plugs to lasers: The science of concentration. *The New York Times*. Retrieved from http://www.nytimes.com/2009/05/05/science/05tier.html?scp=1&sq=%22ear%20plugs%20to%20lasers:%20the%20science%20of%20concentration%22&st=cse; Tugend, A. (2008, October 25). Multitasking can make you lose . . . um . . . focus. *The New York Times*. Retrieved from http://www.nytimes.com/2008/10/25/business/yourmoney/25shortcuts.html?scp=1&sq=%22multitasking%20can%20make%20you%20lose%22&st=cse; Wallis, C. (2006, March 27). genM: The multitasking generation. *Time*. Retrieved from http://www.time.com/time/magazine/article/0,9171,1174696,00.html

6. Brooks, K. (2009). *You Majored in What?* New York: Viking, based on chapter 2.

7. Cranton, P. (1994). *Understanding and promoting transformative learning: A guide for educators of adults.* San Francisco: Jossey-Bass.

8. Davis, J. R. (1993). *Better teaching, more learning.* Phoenix: Oryx Press.

9. Sei, S. A. (2010, June). Intrinsic and extrinsic motivation: evaluating benefits and drawbacks from college instructors' perspectives. *Journal of Instructional Psychology, 37*(2), 153–160.

10. French, B. F., & Oakes, W. (2003). Measuring academic intrinsic motivation in the first year of college: Reliability and validity evidence for a new instrument. *Journal of the First-Year Experience, 15*(1), 83–102; French, B. F. Executive summary of instruments utilized with systemwide first-year seminars. Policy Center on the First Year of College.; French, B. F., Immerkus, J. C., & Oakes, W. C. (2005). An examination of indicators of engineering students' success and persistence. *Journal of Engineering Education, 94*(4), 419–425.

11. Anderson, S. (2009, May 17). In defense of distraction. *New York* (nymag.com). Retrieved from http://nymag.com/news/features/56793/; Gallagher, W. (2009). *Rapt: Attention and the focused life.* New York: Penguin Press; Hamilton, J. (2008, October 2). Think you're multitasking? Think again. *NPR.* Retrieved from http://www.npr.org/templates/story/story.php?storyId=95256794; Tierney, J. (2009, May 4). Earplugs to lasers: The science of concentration. *The New York Times.* Retrieved from http://www.nytimes.com/2009/05/05/science/05tier.html.

12. Achor, S. (2010). *The happiness advantage.* New York: Crown Business.

13. Rosenbaum, M. (2012, January 20). Facebook: Friends' happy pictures make you sad? *ABCnews.* Retrieved from http://abcnews.go.com/blogs/technology/2012/01/feeling-sad-facebook-could-be-the-cause/.

14. Di Meglio. F. (2012, May 10). Stress takes its toll on college students. *Businessweek.* Retrieved from http://www.businessweek.com/articles/2012-05-10/stress-takes-its-toll-on-college-students.

15. Achor, S. (2012, January-February). Positive intelligence. *Harvard Business Review.* Retrieved from http://hbr.org/2012/01/positive-intelligence/ar/1.

16. Grasgreen, A. (2012, July 6). Here's hoping. *Inside Higher Ed.* Retrieved from http://www.insidehighered.com/news/2012/07/06/researchers-apply-hope-theory-boost-college-student-success#ixzz2Cu8hva6C; Lopez, S. J. (2012, August 31). Ready or not, here they come. *Huffington Post.* Retrieved from http://www.huffingtonpost.com/shane-j-lopez-phd/ready-or-not-here-they-co_b_1845029.html.

17. Based on Harrell, K. (2003). *Attitude is everything: 10 life changing steps to turning attitude into action.* New York: Harper Business.

18. Deci, E. (2012, August 13). Promoting motivation, health, and excellence. *TEDxTalks.* Retrieved from http://www.youtube.com/watch?v=VGrcets0E6I&feature=youtu.be&hd=1&t=22s.

19. Yuhas, D. (2012, November 21]. Three critical elements sustain motivation. *Scientific American.* Retrieved from http://www.scientificamerican.com/article.cfm?id=three-critical-elements-sustain-motivation.

20. Deci, E. (2012, August 13). Promoting motivation, health, and excellence. *TEDxTalks.* Retrieved from http://www.youtube.com/watch?v=VGrcets0E6I&feature=youtu.be&hd=1&t=22s.

21. Bregman, P. (2012, January 4). Your problem isn't motivation. *HBR Blog Network.* Retrieved from http://blogs.hbr.org/bregman/2012/01/your-problem-isnt-motivation.html.

22. Ibid.

23. Dweck, C. S. (2000). *Self-theories: Their role in motivation, personality, and development.* New York: Psychology Press, p. 1.

24. Brooks, D. (2009, May 1). Genius: The modern view. *The New York Times.* Retrieved from http://www.nytimes.com/2009/05/01/opinion/01brooks.html.

25. Berglas, S., & Jones, E. E. (1978). Drug choice as a self-handicapping strategy in response to noncontingent success. *Journal of Personality and Social Psychology, 36,* 405–417; Jones, E. E. & Berglas, S. (1978). Control of attributions about the self through self-handicapping strategies: The appeal of alcohol and the role of underachievement. *Personality and Social Psychology Bulletin, 4,* 200–206; Dweck, C. S. (2006). *Mindset: The new psychology of success.* New York: Random House.

26. McCarron, G. P., & Inkelas, K. K. (2006). The gap between educational aspirations and attainment for first-generation college students and the role of parental involvement. *Journal of College Student Development, 47*(5), 534–549.

27. Martinez, J. A., Sher, K. J., Krull, J. L., & Wood, P. K. (2009). Blue-collar scholars? Mediators and moderators of university attrition in first-generation college students. *Journal of College Student Development, 50*(1), 87–103; Collier, P. J., & Morgan, D. L., (2008). Is that paper really due today? *Higher Education, 55*(4), 425–446.

28. Cox, R. D. (2009). *The college fear factor: How students and professors misunderstand one another.* Cambridge, MA: Harvard University Press.

29. http://www.counselingcenter.illinois.edu/?page_id=142.

30. Dweck, *Mindset,* 7.

31. Ibid., 7.

32. Fischer, M. (2007, March-April). Settling into campus life: Differences by race-ethnicity in college involvement and outcomes. *The Journal of Higher Education, 78*(2), 125–161.

33. Dweck, C. S. (2000). *Self-theories: Their role in motivation, personality, and development.* New York: Psychology Press; Dweck, *Mindset.*

Chapter 3

1. Glenn, D. (2009, May 1). Close the book. Recall. Write it down. *The Chronicle of Higher Education.* Retrieved from http://chronicle.com/article/Close-the-Book-Recall-Write/31819.

2. Chabris, C. F. (2009, April 27). How to wake up slumbering minds. *Wall Street Journal.* Retrieved from http://online.wsj.com/article/SB124079001063757515.html.

3. Hallowell, E. M. (2011). *Shine. Using brain science to get the best from your people.* Boston: Harvard Business Review Press.

4. Brookfield, S. (1995). *Becoming a critically reflective teacher.* San Francisco: Jossey-Bass, p. 62.

5. Cousin, G. (2006), in Meyer, J. H. F., & Land. R. (eds.), *Overcoming barriers to student understanding: Threshold concepts and troublesome knowledge.* London and New York: Routledge. Cousin, G. (2006, December). Section I: Introduction to threshold concepts. *Planet,* 17. Retrieved from http://www.gees.ac.uk/planet/p17/gc.pdf.

6. Leamnson, R. (1999). *Thinking about teaching and learning: Developing habits of learning with first year college and university students.* Sterling, VA: Stylus.

7. Winne, P. H., & Nesbit, J. C. (2010). The psychology of academic achievement. *Annual Review of Psychology, 61,* 653–678.

8. Caine, R. N., & Caine, G. (1994). *Making connections: Teaching and the human brain.* Menlo Park, CA: Addison Wesley.

9. Doidge, N. (2007). *The brain that changes itself: Stories of personal triumph from the frontiers of brain science.* New York: Viking.

10. *Newsweek* writer with Ian Yarett. (2011, January 10 & 17). Can you build a better brain? *Newsweek,* pp. 40–45.

11. Jozefowicz, C. (2004, May 1). Sweating makes you smart. *Psychology Today.* Retrieved from http://www.psychologytoday .com/articles/200405/sweating-makes-you-smart; Wu, A., Ying, Z., & Gomez-Pinilla, F. (2004). Dietary omega-3 fatty acids normalize BDNF levels, reduce oxidative damage, and counteract learning disability after traumatic brain injury in rats. *Journal of Neurotrauma, 21,* 1457–1467; PT Staff. (1998, March–April). Brain Boosters. *Psychology Today*; Alzheimer's Association. (2004). Maintain your brain. Retrieved from http://www.alz.org/we_can_help_brain_ health_maintain_your_brain.asp.

12. Neergaard, L. (2005, June 21). Doctors say mental exercise essential for a healthy brain. *Star-Banner.* Retrieved from http://news.google.com/newspapers?nid=1356&dat =20050621&id=SP1PAAAAIBAJ&sjid=XwkEAAAAIBAJ&pg =6686,2404440.

13. Springer, M. V., McIntosh, A. R., Winocur, G., & Grady, C. L. (2005). The relation between brain activity during memory tasks and years of education in young and older adults. *Neuropsychology, 19*(2), 181–192.

14. Brandt, R. (1998). *Powerful learning.* Alexandria, VA: Association for Supervision and Curriculum Development, p. 29.

15. Campbell, B. (1992). Multiple intelligences in action. *Childhood Education, 68*(4), 197–201; Gardner, H., & Hatch, T. (1989). Multiple intelligences go to school: Educational implications of the theory of multiple intelligences. *Educational Researcher, 18*(8), 4–9; Gardner, H. (1983). *Frames of Mind: The Theory of Multiple Intelligences.* New York: Basic Books.

16. Griggs, L., Barney, S., Brown-Sederberg, J., Collins, E., Keith, S., & Iannacci, L. (2009). Varying pedagogy to address student multiple intelligences. *Human Architecture: Journal of the Sociology of Self Knowledge 7*(1), 55–60.

17. Armstrong, T. (2000). *MI and cognitive skills.* Retrieved from http://www.ascd.org/publications/books/109007/chapters /The-Foundations-of-MI-Theory.aspx.

18. Checkley, K. (1997). The first seven . . . and the eighth: A conversation with Howard Gardner, *Educational Leadership, 55*(1), 8–13.

19. Davis, B. (2009). *Tools for teaching, second edition.* San Francisco: Jossey-Bass, p. 273.

20. Fleming, N. D. (1995). I'm different; not dumb: Modes of presentation (VARK) in the tertiary classroom. In A. Zeimer (Ed.), *Research and Development in Higher Education, Proceedings of the 1995 Annual Conference of the Higher Education and Research Development Society of Australasia (HERDSA),HERDSA, 18,* 308–313; Fleming, N. D., & Mills, C. (1992). Not another inventory, rather a catalyst for reflection. *To Improve the Academy, 11,* 137–149.

21. Fleming, I'm different; not dumb.

22. Neil Fleming, personal communication, November 14, 2006.

23. Fleming, N., & Baume, D. (2006, November). Learning Styles Again: VARKing up the right tree! *Educational Developments, 7.4,* 4–7.

24. Schwartz, T., Gomes, J., & McCarthy, C. *The way we're working isn't working.* New York: Free Press, pp. 178–179.

25. Rock, D. (2009). *Your brain at work: Strategies for overcoming distraction, regaining focus, and working smarter all day long.* New York: HarperCollins Business.

26. Schwartz, T., Gomes, J., & McCarthy, C., pp. 104–105.

27. Chabris, C. F. (2009, April 27). How to wake up slumbering minds. *Wall Street Journal.* Retrieved from http://online.wsj .com/article/SB124079001063757515.html. (2008, May 10). Do the math dance: Mathematicians and choreographers use dance to teach mathematics. *Science Daily.* Retrieved from http://www.sciencedaily.com/videos/2008/0503-do_the _math_dance.htm. Pashler, H., McDaniel, M., Rohrer, D., & Bjork, R. (2008). Learning styles: Concepts and evidence. *Psychological Science in the Public Interest, 9*(3), 105– 119. Retrieved from http://www.psychologicalscience.org /journals/pspi/PSPI_9_3.pdf.

28. Based on DiTiberio, J. K., & Hammer, A. L. (1993). *Introduction to type in college.* Palo Alto, CA: Consulting Psychologists Press.

29. Tessler, L. G. (1997). How college students with learning disabilities can advocate for themselves. *LD OnLine.* Retrieved from http://www.ldonline.org/article/6136.

30. Mangrum, C. T., & Strichart, S. S. (Eds.) (1997). *Peterson's guide to colleges with programs for students with learning disabilities.* Princeton, NJ: Peterson's Guide.

31. Strichart, S. S., & Mangrum, C. T. II. (2002). *Teaching learning strategies and study skills to students with learning disabilities, attention deficit disorder, or special needs,* 3rd ed. Boston: Allyn and Bacon; *Learning Disabilities Online.* Retrieved from http://ldonline.org; Sousa, D. A. (2001). *How the special needs brain learns.* Thousand Oaks, CA: Corwin Press.

32. Soldner, L. B. (1997). Self-assessment and the reflective reader. *Journal of College Reading and Learning, 28*(1), 5–11.

33. VanBlerkom, M.L., & VanBlerkom, D.L. (2004). Self-monitoring strategies used by developmental and non-developmental college students. *Journal of College Reading and Learning, 34*(2), 45–60.

34. Melchenbaum, D., Burland, S., Gruson, L., & Cameron, R. (1985). Metacognitive assessment. In S. Yussen (Ed.), *The growth of reflection in children.* Orlando: Academic Press. p. 5.

35. Hall, C. W. (2001). A measure of executive processing skills in college students. *College Student Journal, 35*(3), 442–450; Taylor, S. (1999). Better learning through better thinking: Developing students' metacognitive abilities. *Journal of College Reading and Learning, 30*(1), 34–45.

36. Learning to learn. *Study Guides and Strategies.* Retrieved from http://www.studygs.net/metacognition.htm.

37. Simpson, M. L. (1994/1995). Talk throughs: A strategy for encouraging active learning across the content areas. *Journal of Reading, 38*(4), 296–304.

38. How Air Traffic Control Works. *How Stuff Works.* Retrieved from http://travel.howstuffworks.com/air-traffic-control.htm.

39. Glenn, D. (2010, February 7). How students can improve by studying themselves. *The Chronicle of Higher Education.* Retrieved from http://chronicle.com/article/Struggling-Students-Can/64004/.

40. Elias, M. (2004, April 5). Frequent TV watching shortens kids' attention spans. *USA Today.* Retrieved from http://www .usatoday.com/news/health/2004-04-05-tv-kids-attention -usat_x.htm.

41. Carey, B. (2010, September 6). Forget what you know about good study habits. *The New York Times.* Retrieved from http:// www.nytimes.com/2010/09/07/health/views/07mind.html? pagewanted=all.

42. Bol, L., Warkentin, R. W., Nunnery, J. A., & O'Connell, A. A. (1999). College students' study activities and their relationship to study context, reference course, and achievement. *College Student Journal, 33*(4), 608–622.

43. When students study makes a difference too. (2005, November). *Recruitment & Retention.*

44. Trainin, G., & Swanson, H. L. (2005). Cognition, meta-cognition, and achievement of college students with learning disabilities. *Learning Disability Quarterly, 28,* 261–272.

45. Guibert, S. (2012, March 23). Learning best when you rest: Sleeping after processing new info most effective. *Science Daily.* Retrieved from http://www.sciencedaily.com/releases/2012 /03/120323205504.htm.

Chapter 4

1. Hallowell, E. M. (2006). *Crazy busy: Overstretched, overbooked, and about to snap! Strategies for coping in a world gone ADD*. New York: Ballantine Books.
2. Khawand, P. (2009). *The accomplishing more with less workbook*. On the Go Technologies, LLC.
3. Marklein, M, B. (2009, April 13). Facebook use linked to less textbook time. *USATODAY.com*. Retrieved from http://www.usatoday.com/news/education/2009-04-13-facebook-grades_N.htm.
4. Achor, S. (2011, August 13). Shawn Achor on happiness. *YouTube*. Retrieved from http://www.youtube.com/watch?v=8IdR76uegDg.
5. Nowell, D. D. (2013, February 9). Boundaries and time management. *Psychology Today: Intrinsic Motivation and Magical Unicorns*. Retrieved from http://www.psychologytoday.com/blog/intrinsic-motivation-and-magical-unicorns/201302/boundaries-and-time-management.
6. Khawand, P. (2009). *The accomplishing more with less workbook*. On the Go Technologies, LLC.
7. Austin, C. (2010). Go with the flow: Fresh ideas for managing time. Prezi.com. Retrieved from http://prezi.com/7gypurup9uke/go-with-the-flow/.
8. Halvorson, H. G. The secret of shrinking your to-do list. *Psychology Today: The Science of Success*. Retrieved from http://www.psychologytoday.com/blog/the-science-success/201212/the-secret-shrinking-your-do-list.
9. Rafter, M. V. (2012, February 23). Siri says it's time to get to work. *Workforce.com*. Retrieved from http://www.workforce.com/articles/siri-says-it-s-time-to-get-to-work.
10. Eade, D. M. (1998). Energy and success: Time management. *Clinician News*, July/August. Retrieved from http://finance.dir.groups.yahoo.com/group/HRinIndia/message/11186?l=1.
11. Loehr, J., & Schwartz, T. (2003). *The power of full engagement: Managing energy, not time, is the key to high performance and personal renewal*. New York: Free Press.
12. Bittel, L. R. (1991). *Right on time! The complete guide for time-pressured managers*. New York: McGraw-Hill, p.16.
13. Ibid.
14. Loehr, *The power of full engagement*; Mokhtari, K., Reichard, C. A., & Gardner, A. (2009). The impact of Internet and television use on the reading habits and practices of college students. *Journal of Adolescent & Adult Literacy, 52*(7), 609–619.
15. Williams, R. L., Verble, J. S., Price, D. E., & Layne, B. H. (1995). Relationships between time management practices and personality indices and types. *Journal of Psychological Type, 34*, 36–42.
16. Demarest, L. (2001). *Out of time: How the sixteen types manage their time and work*. Gainesville, FL: Center for Applications of Psychological Type.
17. Nathan, R. (2005). *My freshman year: What a professor learned by becoming a student*. Ithaca, NY: Cornell University Press.
18. Fried, J., & Hanson, D. (2010). *Rework*. New York: Crown Business, pp. 25–26.
19. Rock, D. (2009). *Your brain at work: Strategies for overcoming distraction, regaining focus, and working smarter all day long*. New York: HarperCollins Business.
20. Pozen, R. C. (2012). *Extreme productivity: Boost your results, reduce your hours*. New York: HarperCollins.
21. Ibid.
22. Based on Covey, S. R., Merrill, A. R., & Merrill, R. R. (1996). *First things first: To live, to love, to learn, to leave a legacy*. New York: Free Press, 37.
23. Fortino, M. (2001). *E-mergency*. Groveland, CA: Omni Publishing.
24. Hobbs, C. R. (1987). *Time power*. New York: Harper & Row, pp. 9–10.
25. Can you really manage time? BusinessTown.com. Retrieved from http://www.businesstown.com/time/time-can.asp.
26. Solomon, L. J., & Rothblum, E. D. (1984). Academic procrastination: Frequency and cognitive-behavioral correlates. *Journal of Counseling Psychology, 31*, 503–509.
27. Hoover, E. (2005, December 9). Tomorrow I love ya! *The Chronicle of Higher Education, 52*(16), A30–32. Retrieved from http://chronicle.com/free/v52/i16/16a03001.htm; Zarick, L. M., & Stonebraker, R. (2009). I'll do it tomorrow: The logic of procrastination. *College Teaching, 57*(4), 211–215.
28. Ferrari, J. R., McCown, W. G., & Johnson, J. (2002). *Procrastination and task avoidance: Theory, research, and treatment*. New York: Springer Publishing.
29. Schouwenburg, H. C., Lay, C. H., Pychyl, T. A., & Ferrari, J. R. (Eds.). (2004). *Counseling the procrastinator in academic settings*. Washington, DC: American Psychological Association.
30. Steel, P. (2007). The nature of procrastination. *Psychological Bulletin, 133*(1), 65–94.
31. Hoover, Tomorrow I love ya!.
32. Felton, S., & Sims, M. (2009). *Organizing your day*. Grand Rapids, MI: Revell.
33. Sandholtz, K., Derr, B., Buckner, K., & Carlson, D. (2002). *Beyond juggling: Rebalancing your busy life*. San Francisco: Berrett-Koehler Publishers.
34. http://en.wikipedia.org/wiki/Juggling_world_records.
35. Adapted from K. Sandholtz, B. Derr, F. Buckner, & D. Carlson (2002). *Beyond Juggling: Rebalancing your busy life*. San Francisco: Berrett-Koehler Publishing.
36. Farrell, E. F. (2005, February 4). More students plan to work to help pay for college. *The Chronicle of Higher Education, 50*(22), AI. Retrieved from http://chronicle.com/weekly/v51/i22/22a00101.htm.
37. Norvilitis, J. M., & Santa Maria, P. (2002). Credit card debt on college campuses: Causes, consequences, and solutions. *College Student Journal, 36*(3), 356–364.
38. Muller, K. New credit card laws (2009) and students. *ezine@rticles.com*. Retrieved from http://ezinearticles.com/?New-Credit-Card-Laws-(2009)-And-Students&id=2410035; Miranda, M. (2009, May 21). Credit CARD Act of 2009: How it affects you. *Personaldividends*.com. Retrieved from http://personaldividends.com/money/miranda/credit-card-act-of-2009-how-it-affects-you.
39. Kantrowitz, M. (2007). FAQs about financial aid. FinAid: The Smart Student Guide to Financial Aid. Retrieved from http://www.finaid.org/questions/faq.html; Jevita Rogers, Director of Financial Aid, University of Colorado, Colorado Springs.
40. Adapted from Sandholtz et al., *Beyond juggling*.

Chapter 5

1. Perry, W. (1970). *Forms of intellectual and ethical development in the college years*. New York: Holt, Rinehart & Winston; Perry, W. G. Jr. (1981). *Cognitive and ethical growth: The making of meaning*. In A. Chickering & Associates (Eds.), *The Modern American College: Responding to the New Realities of Diverse Students and a Changing Society*. San Francisco: Jossey-Bass; Erickson, B. L., Peters, C. B., & Strommer, D. W. (2006). *Teaching first-year college students*. San Francisco: Jossey-Bass; Belenky, M. F., Clinchy, B. M., Goldberger, N. R., & Tarule, J. M. (1986). *Women's ways of knowing*. New York: Basic Books; Pascarella, E. T., & Terenzini, P. T. (1991). *How college affects students*. San Francisco: Jossey-Bass; Magolda, M. B. (1988). *The impact of the freshman year on epistemological development: Gender differences*. Paper presented at the meeting of the American Educational Research Association, New Orleans; Magolda, M. B. B. (2006). Intellectual development in the college years. (2006, May/June). *Change, 38*(3), 50–54; Herbert, B. (2011, March 4). College the easy way. *The New York Times*. Retrieved from http://www.nytimes.com/2011/03/05/opinion/05herbert.html?_r=0.
2. Halx, M. C., & Reybold, E. (2005). A pedagogy of force: Faculty perspective of critical thinking capacity in undergraduate students. *The Journal of General Education, 54*(4), 293–315.

3. Walkner, P., & Finney, N. (1999). Skill development and critical thinking in higher education. *Teaching in Higher Education, 4*(4), 531–548.

4. Diestler, S. (2001). *Becoming a critical thinker: A user friendly-manual.* Upper Saddle River, NJ: Prentice Hall.

5. Halpern, D. F. (1996). *Thought and knowledge: An introduction to critical thinking.* Mahwah, NJ: Lawrence Erlbaum.

6. Barnett, R. (1997). *Higher education: A critical business.* Buckingham: SRHE and Open University Press.

7. Falcione, P. A. (1998). *Critical thinking: What it is and why it counts.* Millbrae, CA: California Academic Press.

8. Stupnisky, R. H., Renaud, R. D., Daniels, L. M., Haynes, T. L., & Perry, R. P. (2008). The interrelation of first-year college students' critical thinking disposition, perceived academic control, and academic achievement. *Research in Higher Education, 49,* 513–530.

9. Twale, D., & Sanders, C. S. (1999). Impact of non-classroom experiences on critical thinking ability. *NASPA Journal, 36*(2), 133–146.

10. Thomas, C., & Smoot, G. (1994, February/March). Critical thinking: A vital work skill. *Trust for Educational Leadership, 23,* 34–38.

11. Kaplan-Leiserson, E. (2004). Workforce of tomorrow: How can we prepare *all* youth for future work success? *Training & Development, 58*(4), 12–14.

12. Wade, C. (1995). Using writing to develop and assess critical thinking. *Teaching of Psychology, 22*(1), 24–28.

13. Schommer-Aikins, M., & Easter, M. (2009). Ways of knowing and willingness to argue. *The Journal of Psychology, 143*(2), 117–132.

14. Van den Brink-Budgen, R. (2000). *Critical thinking for students.* (3rd ed.). Oxford: How to Books; Ruggiero, V. R. (2001). *Becoming a critical thinker.* (4th ed.). Boston: Houghton Mifflin.

15. Budryk, Z. (2013, April 10). More than a major. *Inside Higher Ed.* Retrieved from http://www.insidehighered.com/news/2013/04/10/survey-finds-business-executives-arent-focused-majors-those-they-hire; Jaschik, S. (2013, March 20). Jobs, value and affirmative action: A survey of parents about college. *Inside Higher Ed.* Retrieved from http://www.insidehighered.com/news/survey/jobs-value-and-affirmative-action-survey-parents-about-college.

16. Career counselor: Bill Gates or Steve Jobs? *The New York Times. The Opinion Pages.* Retrieved from http://www.nytimes.com/roomfordebate/2011/03/20/career-counselor-bill-gates-or-steve-jobs.

17. Wanted: Liberal arts grads. *Fortune* (1997, May 12), *135*(9), 151.

18. Buddy, T. (2003, November 20). *About.com: alcoholism.* Crime and alcohol. Retrieved from http://alcoholism.about.com/cs/costs/a/aa980415.htm.

19. Hamarta, E. (2009). A prediction of self-esteem and life satisfaction by social problem solving. *Social Behavior and Personality, 37*(1), 73–82.

20. Blakey, E., & Spence, S. (1990). Developing metacognition. ERIC Clearinghouse on Information Resources, Syracuse NY. Retrieved from http://www.vtaide.com/png/ERIC/Metacognition.htm.

21. Schwartz, T., Gomes, J., & McCarthy, C. (2010). *The Way We're Working Isn't Working: The Four Forgotten Needs That Energize Great Performance.* New York: Free Press. pp. 128–129.

22. Ibid., p. 149.

23. Brokaw, L. (2012, April 29). Why a little pessimism is a good thing. *MIT Sloan Management Review.* Retreived from http://sloanreview.mit.edu/article/why-a-little-pessimism-is-a-good-thing/; Garfinkel, R. (2013, March 14). Up with pessimism! *Psychology Today.* Retrieved from http://www.psychologytoday.com/blog/time-out/201303/pessimism-0.

24. Pink, D. H. (2006). *A whole new mind: Why right-brainers will rule the future.* New York: Riverhead Books.

25. Florida, R. (2002). *The rise of the creative class: And how it's transforming work, leisure, community and everyday life.* New York: Basic Books, xii.

26. Ibid.

27. Nair, K. D., & Gopal, R. (2011, March). Advocating different paradigms: Relevance of workplace creativity. *Journal of Management, 7*(2),142-150

28. Saber, K. (2012, December 13). Three ideas for cultivating creativity at work. *Fast Company.* Retrieved from http://www.fastcompany.com/3003901/3-ideas-cultivating-creativity-work; Kotler, S. (2012, February 3). How to be more creative at work (or what corporations can learn from boozehounds and baby elephants). *Forbes.com.* Retrieved from http://www.forbes.com/sites/stevenkotler/2013/02/03/how-to-be-more-creative-at-work/; Schawbel, D. (2011, June 28). How to harness your creativity at work. *Forbes.com.* Retrieved from http://www.forbes.com/sites/danschawbel/2011/06/28/how-to-harness-your-creativity-at-work/; Lesonsky, R. (2013). Providing employee perks: Flextime and telecommuting. *Success.* Retrieved from http://www.success.com/articles/1187-providing-employee-perks-flextime-and-telecommuting.

29. Livingston, L. (2010). Teaching creativity in higher education. *Arts Education Policy Review, 111,* 59–62.

30. Vance, E. (2007, February 2). College graduates lack key skills, report says. *The Chronicle of Higher Education, 53*(22), A30.

31. Kurtz, J. R. (1998). It's all in your mind! Creative thinking essential in times of change. *Outlook, 66*(3), 5.

32. Rowe, A. J. (2004). *Creative intelligences: discovering the innovative potential in ourselves and others.* Upper Saddle, NJ: Pearson Education, pp. 3–6, 34.

33. Michalko, M. (2001). *Cracking creativity: The secrets of creative genius.* Berkeley, CA: Ten Speed Press.

34. Adapted from Adler, R., & Towne, N. (1987). *Looking out/Looking in.* (5th ed.) New York: Holt, Rinehart, and Winston, pp. 99–100.

35. Douglas, J. H. (1977). The genius of everyman (2): Learning creativity. *Science News, 111*(8), 284–288.

36. Harris, R. (1998). Introduction to creative thinking. *Virtual-Salt.* Retrieved from http://www.virtualsalt.com/crebook1.htm.

37. Eby, D. Creativity and flow psychology. *Talent Development Resources.* Retrieved from http://talentdevelop.com/articles/Page8. html.

Chapter 6

1. Sheehy, K. (2013, January 8). Online course enrollment climbs for 10th straight year. *U.S. News.* Retrieved from http://www.usnews.com/education/online-education/articles/2013/01/08/online-course-enrollment-climbs-for-10th-straight-year.

2. Hardesty, L. (2013, March 6). Higher-ed leaders meet to discuss future of online education. *MIT News.* Retrieved from http://web.mit.edu/newsoffice/2013/edx-summit-0306.html.

3. Bollet, R. M., & Fallon, S. (2002). Personalizing e-learning. *Educational Media International, 39*(1), 39–45; Barber, S., in Shank, P. (Ed.). (2011). *The online learning idea book: Proven ways to enhance technology-based and blended learning, vol 2.* San Francisco: Pfeiffer.

4. Weaver, J. (2013, July 6). College students are avid gamers. *NBCNews.com.* Retrieved from http://www.nbcnews.com/id/3078424/ns/technology_and_science-games/t/college-students-are-avid-gamers/#.UlgwiRbfbFI.

5. Grant, D. M., Malloy, A. D., & Murphy, M. C. (2009). A comparison of student perceptions of their computer skills to their actual abilities. *Journal of Information Technology Education, 8.* Retrieved from http://www.jite.org/documents/Vol8/JITEv8p141-160Grant428.pdf.

6. Johnson, L., Smith, R., Willis, H., Levine, A., & Haywood, K., (2011). The 2011 Horizon Report. *The New Media Consortium.* Retrieved from http://net.educause.edu/ir/library/pdf/HR2011.pdf.

7. Smith, S. D., & Caruso, J. B. (2010). ECAR study of undergraduate students and information technology, 2010. Educause. Retrieved from http://www.educause.edu/Resources/ECARStudyofUndergraduateStuden/217333.

8. Ibid.

9. Wikipedia. In *Wikipedia.* Retrieved from https://en.wikipedia.org/wiki/Wikipedia.

10. Read, B. (2009, July 20). Students may not be as software savvy as they think, study says. *The Wired Campus: The Chronicle of Higher Education.* Retrieved from http://chronicle.com/blogs/wiredcampus/students-may-not-be-as-software-savvy-as-they-think-study-says/7276. Grant, D. M., Malloy, A. D., & Murphy, M. C. (2009). A comparison of student perceptions of their computer skills to their actual abilities. *Journal of Information Technology Education, 8.* Retrieved from http://jite.org/documents/Vol8/JITEv8p141-160Grant428.pdf.

11. Lifespan (2013, April 11). Texting, social networking and other media use linked to poor academic performance. *ScienceDaily.* Retrieved from http://www.sciencedaily.com/releases/2013/04/130411131755.htm.

12. Benner, J. (2005, 15 November). Facebook more than a way of life. *The BG News.*

13. Greene, L. (2006, March 8). You might be a Facebook stalker if. . . *Winonan;* Hollister, L. (2005, October 5). Facebook addiction is needless, yet compelling. *The Volante Online.*

14. (2009, April 12). Study says Facebook can impact studies. *UPI.com.* Retrieved from http://www.upi.com/Entertainment_News/2009/04/12/Study-says-Facebook-can-impact-studies/UPI-84181239555532/.

15. Turkle, S. (2011). *Alone together: Why we expect more from technology and less from each other.* New York: Basic Books; Turkel, S. (2011, March 30). Productivity, multitasking, and the death of the phone. *HBR Ideacast.* Retrieved from http://blogs.hbr.org/ideacast/2011/03/productivity-multitasking-and.html. Parker-Pope, S. (2010, June 6). An ugly toll of technology: Impatience and forgetfulness. *The New York Times.* Retrieved from http://www.nytimes.com/2010/06/07/technology/07brainside.html?ref=taraparkerpope; Latham, T. (2011, July 26). Can you really become addicted to the Internet? *Psychology Today.* Retrieved from http://www.psychologytoday.com/blog/therapy-matters/201107/can-you-really-become-addicted-the-internet.

16. Greenfield, D. N. (1999). *Virtual addiction.* Oakland, CA: New Harbinger Publications; Yair, E., & Hamburger, A. (2005). *The social net.* Oxford: Oxford University Press; Young, K. S. (1998). *Caught in the net.* New York: John Wiley.

17. Roach, R. (2004). Survey unveils high-tech ownership profile of American college students. *Black Issues in Higher Education, 21*(16), 37.

18. Jones, S., & Madden, M. (2002, September 15). The Internet goes to college: How students are living in the future with today's technology. *Pew Internet.* Retrieved from http://www.pewinternet.org/Reports/2002/The-Internet-Goes-to-College.aspx.

19. *Internet World Stats.* Retrieved from http://www.internetworldstats.com/stats.htm.

20. Bartlett, T. (2009, March 20). Cheating goes global as essay mills multiply. *The Chronicle of Higher Education, 55*(28), p. A-1.

21. Billout, G. (2008, July/August). Is Google making us stupid? The Atlantic.com. Retrieved from http://www.theatlantic.com/magazine/archive/2008/07/is-google-making-us-stupid/306868/

22. Wood, G. (2004, 9 April). Academic original sin: Plagiarism, the Internet, and librarians. The Journal of Academic Librarianship, 30(3), 237–242. Carr, N. (2008, July/August). Is Google making us stupid? *The Atlantic.* Retrieved from http://www.theatlantic.com/magazine/archive/2008/07/is-google-making-us-stupid/6868/; Nelson, F. (2009, April 29). Podcast: Is Twitter making us stupider? *Information Week Personal Tech.* Retrieved from http://www.informationweek.com/personal-tech/podcast-is-twitter-making-us-stupider/229206696; Carr, N. (2010). *The Shallows: What the Internet is doing to our brains.* New York: W. W. Norton & Company.

23. (2012, July 11). Computer virus statistics. *Statistic Brain.* Retrieved from http://www.statisticbrain.com/computer-virus-statistics/.

24. (2010, June). Social insecurity. *Consumer Reports: Best and worst computers,* 24–27.

25. (2011, March 26). What they're saying about sexting. *The New York Times.* Retrieved from http://www.nytimes.com/2011/03/27/us/27sextingqanda.html?_r=3&ref=us&; Hoffman, J.(2011, March 26). A girl's nude photo, and altered lives. *The New York Times.* Retrieved from http://www.nytimes.com/2011/03/27/us/27sexting.html?pagewanted.

26. Common Sense Media. (2013). Retrieved from http://www.commonsensemedia.org/cyberbullying; Patchin, J. & Hinduja, S. (2010). Retrieved from http://www.cyberbullying.us/Students_Guide_to_Personal_Publishing.pdf; Hinduja, S. & Patchin, J. (2013, July). Retrieved from http://www.cyberbullying.us/Bullying_and_Cyberbullying_Laws.pdf.

27. What is research? In Leedy, P. (1997). *Practical Research: Planning and Design,* Sixth Edition, Upper Saddle River, NJ: Merrill Prentice Hall.

28. Rivington, J. (2013, April 10). Google glass: What you need to know. *TechRadar.AV.* Retrieved from http://www.techradar.com/us/news/video/google-glass-what-you-need-to-know-1078114; Langmead, S. (2013, April). Prediciting ed tech's future. *E-campus News.* Retrieved from http://www.ecampusnews.com/publications/digital-issue-article/ecampus-news-april-2013/.

29. Lytle, R. (2012, September 12). 5 apps college students should use this school year. *US News Education.* Retrieved from http://www.usnews.com/education/best-colleges/articles/2012/09/21/5-apps-college-students-should-use-this-school-year; La Ruffa, E. (2013). 5 apps that help college students get organized. *New Futuro.* Retrieved from http://www.newfuturo.com/articles/the-top-five-apps-for-college-students.

30. Christina Martinez, Reference Librarian, University of Colorado, Colorado Springs.

31. Fitzgerald, M. A. (2004). Making the leap from high school to college. *Knowledge Quest, 32*(4), 19–24; Ehrmann, S. (2004). Beyond computer literacy: Implications of technology for the content of a college education. *Liberal Education.* Retrieved from http://www.aacu.org/liberaleducation/le-fa04/le-fa04feature1.cfm; Thacker, P. (2006, November 15). Are college students techno idiots? *Inside Higher Ed.* Retrieved from http://www.insidehighered.com/news/2006/11/15/infolit.

32. Samson, S. (2010, May). Information literacy learning outcomes and student success. *Journal of Academic Librarianship, 36*(3), 202–10.

33. Ableson, H., Ledeen, K., & Lewis, H. (2008). *Blown to bits: your life, liberty, and happiness after the digital explosion.* Boston: Pearson Education, Inc.

34. Thacker, P. (2006, November 15). Are college students techno idiots? *Inside Higher Ed.* Retrieved from http://www.insidehighered.com/news/2006/11/15/infolit. Smith, S. D., & Caruso, J. B. (2010). ECAR study of undergraduate students and information technology, 2010. *Educause.* Retrieved from http://www.educause.edu/Resources/ECARStudyofUndergraduateStuden/217333.

35. Young, J. (2006, June 12). Wikipedia founder discourages academic use of his creation. *The Chronicle of Higher Education, Wired Campus.* Retrieved from http://chronicle.com/blogs/wiredcampus/wikipedia-founder-discourages-academic-useof-his-creation/2305.

36. Jaschik, S. (2007, January 26). A stand against Wikipedia. *Inside Higher Education.* Retrieved from http://www.insidehighered.com/news/2007/01/26/wiki.

37. Thacker, P. (2006, November 15). Are college students techno idiots? *Inside Higher Ed.* Retrieved from http://www.insidehighered.com/news/2006/11/15/infolit. Smith,

S. D., & Caruso, J. B. (2010). *ECAR study of undergraduate students and information technology, 2010*. *Educause*. Retrieved from http://www.educause.edu/Resources /ECARStudyofUndergraduateStuden/217333.

38. Mitchell, B. (2013). Internet domain extensions. Retrieved from http://compnetworking.about.com/od/dns_domainnamesystem /a/domain-name-tld.htm; Top 10 domain name extensions. Retrieved from http://lists.econsultant.com/top-10-domain -name-extensions.html; Davies, D. (2013, September 26). Major search engines and directories. *Search Engine Watch.com*. Retrieved from http://searchenginewatch.com/article/2048976 /Major-Search-Engines-and-Directories.

39. Davies, D. (2013, September 26). Major search engines and directories. *SearchEngineWatch.com*. Retrieved from http://search enginewatch.com/article/2048976/Major-Search-Engines-and -Directories. (2008). Recommended search engines. *UC Berkeley Library. Regents of the University of California*. Retrieved from http://www.lib.berkeley.edu/TeachingLib/Guides/Internet /SearchEngines.html; http://www.thesearchenginelist.com/.

40. McCarroll, C. (2001). To learn to think in college, write—a lot. *Christian Science Monitor, 93*(177), 20.

41. Gabriel, T. (2010, August 1). Plagiarism lines blur for students in the digital age. *The New York Times*. Retrieved from http://www.nytimes.com/2010/08/02/education/02cheat .html?_r=2./.

42. Cassagrande, J. (2010). *It was the best of sentences, it was the worst of sentences*. Berkeley, CA: Ten Speed Press.

43. Selberg, A. (2011, March 19). Teaching to the text message. *The New York Times. Opinion Pages*. Retrieved from http://www.nytimes.com/2011/03/20/opinion/20selsberg .html?_r=3&emc=tnt&tntemail1=y&.

Chapter 7

1. Based partially on http://www-sop.inria.fr/acacia/personnel /Fabien.Gandon/lecture/uk1999/history/.

2. Burchfield, C. M., & Sappington, J. (2000). Compliance with required reading assignments. *Teaching of Psychology, 27*(1), 58–60; Hobson, E. H. (2004). *Getting students to read: Fourteen tips*. IDEA Paper No. 40, Manhattan, KS: Kansas State University, Center for Faculty Evaluation and Development; Maleki, R. B., & Heerman, C. E. (1992). *Improving student reading*. IDEA Paper No. 26, Manhattan, KS: Kansas State University, Center for Faculty Evaluation and Development. Most Idea Center papers. Retrieved from http://www.theideacenter.org/.

3. Credé, M.; Roch, S. G.; & Kieszczynka, U. M. (2010). Class attendance in college: A meta-analytic review of the relationship of class attendance with grades and student characteristics. *Review of Educational Research*, 80(2), 272–295.

4. Gump, S. E. (2005). The cost of cutting class: Attendance as a predictor of student success. *College Teaching, 53*(1), 21–25.

5. Marburger, D. R. (2001). Absenteeism and undergraduate exam performance. *Journal of Economic Education, 32*, 99–109.

6. Perkins, K. K., & Wieman, C. E. (2005). The surprising impact of seat location on student performance. *The Physics Teacher, 43*(1), 30–33. Retrieved from http://scitation.aip.org/getpdf /servlet/GetPDFServlet?filetype=pdf&id=PHTEAH0000430 00001000030000001&idtype=cvips&doi=10.1119/1.1845987& prog=normal&bypassSSO=1.

7. Everding, G. (2009, May 28). Cell phone ringtones can pose major distraction, impair recall. *Washington University in St. Louis Record*. Retrieved from http://news.wustl.edu/news /Pages/14225.aspx.

8. "Infomania" worse than marijuana. (2005, April 22). *BBC News*. Retrieved from http://news.bbc.co.uk/2/hi/uk_news/4471607 .stm; Bugeja, M. J. (2007, January 26). Distractions in the wireless classroom. *The Chronicle of Higher Education, 53*(21), C1. Retrieved from http://chronicle.com/article/Distractions -inthe-Wireless/46664/; Young, J. R. (2006, June 2). The fight for classroom attention: Professor vs. laptop. *The Chronicle of Higher Education, 52*(39), A27. Retrieved from http://chronicle

.com/article/The-Fight-for-Classroom/19431; *2008 Campus Computing Project Executive Summary*. Retrieved from http:// www.campuscomputing.net/sites/www.campuscomputing .net/files/CC2008-Executive%20Summary_3.pdf; Cole, D. (2007, April 7). Laptops vs. learning. *Washington Post*. Retrieved from http://www.washingtonpost.com/wp-dyn /content/article/2007/04/06/AR2007040601544.html.

9. Armbruster, B. B. (2000). Taking notes from lectures. In R. F. Flippo & D. C. Caverly (Eds.), *Handbook of college reading and study strategy research* (pp. 175–199). Mahwah, NJ: Erlbaum.

10. Based partially on Mackie, V., & Bair, B. Tips for improving listening skills; *International student and scholar services*. University of Illinois at Urbana-Champaign.

11. Staley, C. C., & Staley, R. S. (1992). *Communicating in business and the professions: The inside word*. Belmont, CA: Wadsworth, p. 223.

12. Allen, D. (2001). *Getting things done: The art of stress-free productivity*. New York: Penguin Books, p. 21.

13. Selby, J. (2004). *Quiet your mind*. Makawao, Maui, HI: Inner Ocean Publishing.

14. Hughes, C. A., & Suritsky, S. K. (1993). Notetaking skills and strategies for students with learning disabilities. *Preventing School Failure, 38*(1).

15. Staley, C. C., & Staley, R. S. (1992). *Communicating in business and the professions*, pp. 229–236.

16. Kiewra, K. A., Mayer, R. E., Christensen, M., Kim, S., & Risch, N. (1991). Effects of repetition on recall and note-taking: Strategies for learning from lectures. *Journal of Educational Psychology, 83*, 120–123. Cheng, J. (2009, February 25). Study: Class podcasts can lead to better grades. *arstechnica*. Retrieved from http://arstechnica.com/science/2009/02 /study-listening-to-podcasts-better-than-going-to-lectures/.

17. Brock, R. (2005, October 28). Lectures on the go. *The Chronicle of Higher Education, 52*(10), A39–42; French, D. P. (2006). iPods: Informative or invasive? *Journal of College Science Teaching, 36*(1), 58–59; Hallett, V. (2005, October 17). Teaching with tech. *U.S. News & World Report, 139*(14), 54–58; *The Horizon Report*. (2006). Stanford, CA: The New Media Consortium.

18. DiTiberio, J. K., & Hammer, A. L. (1993). *Introduction to type in college*. Palo Alto, CA: Consulting Psychologists Press.

19. Van Blerkom, M. L., & Van Blerkom, D. L. (2004). Self-monitoring strategies used by developmental and non-developmental college students. *Journal of College Reading and Learning, 34*(2), 45–60.

20. Bloom, B. S. (Ed.). (1956). *A taxonomy of educational objectives (cognitive domain)*. New York: Longman; http://www.odu.edu /educ/roverbau/Bloom/blooms_taxonomy.htm.

21. Peverly, S. T., Ramaswamy, V., Brown, C., Sumowski, J., Alidoost, M., & Garner, J. (2007). What predicts skill in lecture note taking? *Journal of Educational Psychology, 99*(1), 167–180.

22. Palmatier, R. A., & Bennett, J. M. (1974). Note-taking habits of college students. *Journal of Reading, 18*, 215–218; Dunkel, P., & Davy, S. (1989). The heuristic of lecture notetaking: Perceptions of American and international students regarding the value and practices of notetaking. *English for Specific Purposes, 8*, 33–50.

23. Armbruster, *Handbook of college reading and study strategy research*.

24. Van Meter, P., Yokoi, L., & Pressley, M. (1994). College students' theory of note-taking derived from their perceptions of note-taking. *Journal of Educational Psychology, 86*, 323–338.

25. Read, B. (2007, February 1). Lecture-hall laptops hurt students' grades, study says. *The Chronicle of Higher Education*. Retrieved from http://chronicle.com/blogPost/Lecture-Hall -Laptops-Hurt/2812/; Fischman, J. (2009, March 16). Students stop surfing after being shown how in-class laptop use lowers test scores. *The Wired Campus: Chronicle of Higher Education*. Retrieved from http://chronicle.com/blogPost/Students-Stop -Surfing-After/4576.

26. Davis, M., & Hult, R. (1997). Effects of writing summaries as a generative learning activity during note taking. *Teaching of*

Psychology 24(1), 47–49; Boyle, J. R., & Weishaar, M. (2001). The effects of strategic notetaking on the recall and comprehension of lecture information for high school students with learning disabilities. *Learning Disabilities Research & Practice 16*(3); Kiewra, K. A. (2002). How classroom teachers can help students learn and teach them how to learn. *Theory into Practice 41*(2), 71–81; Aiken, E. G., Thomas, G. S., & Shennum, W. A. (1975). Memory for a lecture: Effects of notes, lecture rate and informational density. *Journal of Educational Psychology, 67*, 439–444; Hughes, C. A., & Suritsky, S. K. (1994). Note-taking skills of university students with and without learning disabilities. *Journal of Learning Disabilities, 27*, 20–24.

27. Bonner, J. M., & Holliday, W. G. (2006). How college science students engage in note-taking strategies. *Journal of Research in Science Teaching, 43*(8), 786–818.

28. Pauk, W. (2000). *How to study in college*. Boston: Houghton Mifflin.

29. Aguilar-Roca N. M., Williams, A. E., & O'Dowd, D. K. (2012). The impact of laptop-free zones on student performance and attitudes in large lectures. *Computers & Education, 59*(4), 1300–1308. Retrieved from http://www.sciencedirect.com /science/article/pii/S0360131512001236; Weisman, S. (2012, March). Five ways to avoid the pitfalls of technology in college. *USA Today College*. Retrieved from http://www .usatodayeducate.com/staging/index.php/campuslife /five-ways-to-avoid-the-pitfalls-of-technology-in-college.

30. Weisman, S. (2012, March 5). Five ways to avoid the pitfalls of technology in college. *USA Today College*. Retrieved from http:// www.usatodayeducate.com/staging/index.php/campuslife /five-ways-to-avoid-the-pitfalls-of-technology-in-college; https://plus.google.com/+evernote/posts/ABvMT7y3fsk#+ evernote/posts/ABvMT7y3fsk; Gordon, W. (2013, March 12). *Lifehacker*. http://lifehacker.com/5989980/ive-been-using-evernote -all-wrong-heres-why-its-actually-amazing; Zweig, B. (2012, September 21). Can you go to school with just an iPad? We tried it. *NYU Local*. Retrieved from http://nyulocal.com /on-campus/2012/09/21/can-you-go-to-school-with-just-an-ipad -we-tried-it/.

31. Montis, K. K. (2007). Guided notes: An interactive method of success in secondary and college mathematics classrooms. *Focus on learning problems in mathematics, 29*(3), 55–68.

32. Pardini, E. A., Domizi, D. P., Forbes, D. A., & Pettis, G. V. (2005). Parallel note-taking: A strategy for effective use of Web-notes. *Journal of College Reading and Learning, 35*(2), 38–55.

33. Glenn, D. (2009, May 1). Close the book. Recall. Write it down. *The Chronicle of Higher Education*. Retrieved from http:// chronicle.com/article/Close-the-book-Recall-Write/31819.

34. De Simone, C. (2007). Applications of concept mapping. *College Teaching, 55*(1), 33–36.

35. Kiewra, K. A. (2002). How classroom teachers can help students learn and teach them how to learn. *Theory into Practice 41*(2), 71–81.

36. Porte, L. K. (2001). Cut and paste 101. *Teaching Exceptional Children, 34*(2), 14–20.

37. Kiewra, K. A., DuBois, N. F., Christian, D., & McShane, A. (1988). Providing study notes: Comparison of three types of notes for review. *Journal of Educational Psychology, 80*, 595–597; Larkin, J. H., & Simon, J. A. (1987). Why a diagram is (sometimes) worth ten thousand words. *Cognitive Science, 11*, 65–99; Robinson, D. H., Katayama, A. D., DuBois, N. F., & DeVaney, T. (1998). Interactive effects of graphic organizers and delayed review in concept acquisition. *The Journal of Experimental Education, 67*, 17–31; Winn, W. (1991). Learning from maps and diagrams. *Educational Psychology Review, 3*, 211–247.

38. Ancowitz, N. (2010, June 24). How to increase your self-promotion intelligence, or SPQ. *Psychology Today*. Retrieved from http://www.psychologytoday.com/blog/self-promotion-introverts /201006/how-increase-your-self-promotion-intelligence-or-spq.

39. Tal-Or, N. (2010). Bragging in the right context: Impressions formed of self-promoters who create a context for their boasts. *Social Influence, 5*(1), 23–39.

40. Hanson, M. (2009, June 17). Is bragging good for your career? *LiveCareer*. Retrieved from http://www.livecareer .com/career-tips/bragging#.UoUdEhrkvt8.

41. Kiewra, K. A. (2002). How classroom teachers can help students learn and teach them how to learn. *Theory into Practice 41*(2), 71–81.

42. Craik, F. I. M., & Watkins, M. J. (1973). The role of rehearsal in short-term memory. *Journal of Verbal Learning and Verbal Behavior, 12*, 599–607.

Chapter 8

1. Rogers, M. (2007, March–April). Is reading obsolete? *The Futurist*, 26–27; Waters, L. (2007, February 9). Time for reading. *The Chronicle of Higher Education, 53*(23), 1B6.

2. Postman, N. (1985). *Amusing ourselves to death*. New York: Penguin Books; Stephens, M. (1991, September 22). The death of reading. *Los Angeles Times Magazine*. Retrieved from http:// www.nyu.edu/classes/stephens/Death%20of%20Reading%20 page.htm.

3. Dillon, S. (2005, December 16). Literacy falls for graduates from college, testing finds. *The New York Times*. Retrieved from http://www.nytimes.com/2005/12/16/education/16literacy .html?_r=1& (2006). A first look at the literacy of America's adults in the 21st century. *National Center for Education Statistics*. Retrieved from http://nces.ed.gov/NAAL/PDF/2006470 .pdf; (2006, January 20). Reports on college literacy levels sobering. *MSNBC*. Retrieved from http://www.nbcnews.com /id/10928755#.UmCMnmSglF8.

4. Mokhtari, K., Reichard, C. A. , & Gardner, A. (2009). The impact of Internet and television use on the reading habits and practices of college students. *Journal of Adolescent & Adult Literacy, 52*(7), 609–619; Clemmitt, M. (2008, Feburary 22). Reading crisis: Do today's youth read less than past generations? *CQ Researcher, 18*(8).

5. Stephens, M. (1991, September 22). The death of reading. Retrieved from http://www.nyu.edu/classes/stephens/Death %20of%20Reading%20page.htm.

6. Nelson, B. (2012, June 4). Do you read fast enough to be successful? *Forbes*. Retrieved from http://www.forbes.com /sites/brettnelson/2012/06/04/do-you-read-fast-enough-to -be-successful/; Thomas, M. (2013). What is the average reading speed and the best rate of reading? *HealthGuidance.org*. Retrieved from http://www.healthguidance.org/entry/13263 /1/What-Is-the-Average-Reading-Speed-and-the-Best-Rate-of -Reading.html.

7. Caverly, D. C., Nicholson, S. A., & Radcliffe, R. (2004). The effectiveness of strategic reading instruction for college developmental readers. *Journal of College Reading and Learning, 35*(1), 25–49; Simpson, M. L., & Nist, S. L. (1997). Perspectives on learning history: A case study. *Journal of Literacy Research, 29*(3), 363–395.

8. Caverly, D. C., Nicholson, S. A., & Radcliffe, R. (2004). The effectiveness of strategic reading instruction for college developmental readers; Burrell, K. I., Tao, L., Simpson, M. L., & Mendez-Berrueta, H. (1997). How do we know what we are preparing students for? A reality check of one university's academic literacy demands. *Research & Teaching in Developmental Education, 13*, 15–70.

9. Bean, J. C. (1996). *Engaging ideas: The professor's guide to integrating writing, critical thinking, and active learning in the classroom*. San Francisco: Jossey-Bass; Wood, N.V. (1997). College reading instruction as reflected by current reading textbooks. *Journal of College Reading and Learning, 27*(3).79–95.

10. Saumell, L., Hughes, M. T., & Lopate, K. (1999). Underprepared college students' perceptions of reading: Are their perceptions different than other students? *Journal of College Reading and Learning, 29*(2), 123–125.

11. Buzan, T. (1983). *Use both sides of your brain*. New York: E. P. Dutton.

12. Ibid.

13. Sternberg, R. J. (1987). Teaching intelligence: The application of cognitive psychology to the improvement of intellectual skills. In J. B. Baron & R. J. Sternberg (Eds.), *Teaching thinking skills: Theory and Practice.* New York: Freeman. pp. 182–218.

14. Al-Jarf, R. S. (2002). Effect of online learning on struggling ESL college writers. San Antonio, TX: National Educational Computing Conference. Retrieved from http://faculty.ksu.edu.sa/aljarf /My%20Press%20Room/al-jarf%20-%20NECC%20paper.pdf.

15. Walt Whitman wrote a letter. Retrieved from http://www.americas library.gov/jb/gilded/jb_gilded_whitman _2.html.

16. Hirsch, Jr., E. D., Kett, J. F., & Trefil, J. (2002). *The new dictionary of cultural literacy: What every American needs to know.* New York: Houghton Mifflin.

17. Based partly on Williams, S. (2005). Guiding students through the jungle of research-based literature. *College Teaching, 53*(4), 137–139.

18. (2013, May 30). Are You Happy? It May Depend on Age, Race/ Ethnicity and Other Factors. *Harris Interactive.* Retrieved from http://www.harrisinteractive.com/NewsRoom/Harris Polls/tabid/447/ctl/ReadCustom%20Default/mid/1508 /ArticleId/1200/Default.aspx.

19. Duhigg, C. (2012). *The power of habit: Why we do what we do in life and business.* New York: Random House.

20. Ibid.

21. Duhigg, C. (2013, January-February). The power of habit. *Experience Life.* Retrieved from http://experiencelife.com /article/the-power-of-habit/.

22. Fox, J. (2012, June 7). Why we do what we do. *HBR Blog Network.* Retrieved from http://blogs.hbr.org/ideacast/2012/06 /habits-why-we-do-what-we-do.html.

23. De Vos, I. (1988, October). Getting started: How expert writers do it. *Training & Development Journal,* 18–19.

24. Bean, J. C. (1996). *Engaging ideas: The professor's guide to integrating writing, critical thinking and active learning in the classroom.* San Francisco: Jossey-Bass.

25. Jensen, G., & DiTiberio, J. K. (1984). Personality and individual writing processes. *College Composition and Communication, 35*(3), 285–300; DiTiberio, J. K., & Hammer, A. L. (1993). *Introduction to type in college.* Palo Alto, CA: Consulting Psychologists Press; Sampson, E. (2003). *Creative business presentations.* London: Kogan Page.

26. Portions of this section are based on Staley, C., & Staley, R. (1992). *Communicating in business and the professions: The inside word.* Belmont, CA: Wadsworth.

27. Portions based on Staley & Staley, *Communicating in business and the professions.*

28. Smith, T. E., & Frymier, A. B. (2006). Get "real": Does practicing speeches before an audience improve performance? *Communication Quarterly, 54*(1), 111–125.

29. Engleberg, I. N. (1994). *The principles of public presentation.* New York: HarperCollins; Daley, K., & Daley-Caravella, L. (2004). *Talk your way to the top.* New York: McGraw-Hill.

30. Decker, K. (9 May, 2012). Airline-inspired analogies. *Decker Blog.* Retrieved from http://decker.com/blog/airline-inspired -analogies/

31. Ibid.

32. Carey, B. (2010, September 8). Forget what you know about good study habits. *The New York Times.* Retrieved from http:// www.nytimes.com/2010/09/07/health/views/07mind.html.

33. Bol, L., Warkentin, R. W., Nunnery, J. A., & O'Connell, A. A. (1999). College students' study activities and their relationship to study context, reference course, and achievement. *College Student Journal, 33*(4).608–622.

Chapter 9

1. (2004). Model secondary school for the deaf: physics syllabus. Retrieved from http://sci.gallaudet.edu/Physics12 /Syllabus04.html.

2. Gordon, B. (1995). *Memory: Remembering and forgetting in everyday life.* New York: Mastermedia Limited.

3. Bolla, K. I., Lindgren, K. N., Bonaccorsy, C., & Bleecker, M. L. (1991). Memory complaints in older adults: Fact or fiction? *Archives of Neurology, 48,* 61–64.

4. Higbee, K. L. (2004). What aspects of their memories do college students most want to improve? *College Student Journal, 38*(4), 552–556.

5. Higbee, K. L. (1988). *Your memory: How it works and how to improve it* (2nd ed.). New York: Prentice Hall.

6. Ibid.

7. Noice, H., & Noice, T. (2006). What studies of actors and acting can tell us about memory and cognitive functioning. *Current Directions in Psychological Science, 15*(1), 14–18.

8. Caine, M. (1990). *Acting in film: An actor's take on moviemaking.* New York: Applause Theatre Books.

9. Noice, T., Noice, H., & Kennedy, C. (2000). The contribution of movement on the recall of complex material. *Memory, 8,* 353–363.

10. Glenberg, A. M., & Kaschak, M. P. (2002). Grounding language in action. *Psychonomic Bulletin & Review, 9,* 558–565.

11. Noice & Noice, What studies of actors and acting can tell us about memory and cognitive functioning.

12. Nairine, J. S. (2006). *Psychology: The adaptive mind.* Belmont, CA: Wadsworth/Thomson Learning.

13. Miller, G. A. (1956). The magical number seven plus or minus two: Some limits on our capacity for processing information. *Psychological Review, 63,* 81–97; Raman, M., McLaughlin, K., Violato, C., Rostom, A., Allard, J. P., & Coderre, S. (2010). Teaching in small portions dispersed over time enhances long-term knowledge retention. *Medical Teacher, 32,* 250–255.

14. Narayanan, K. The neurological scratchpad: Looking into working memory? (2013, February). *Brain Connection.com.* Retrieved from http://brainconnection.positscience.com /the-neurological-scratchpad-looking-into-working-memory/. Kerry, S. (1999–2002). Memory and retention time. *Education Reform.net.* Retrieved from http://www.education -reform.net/memory.htm; Goodhead, J. (1999). The difference between short-term and long-term memory [On-line].

15. Rozakis, L. (2003). *Test-taking strategies and study skills for the utterly confused.* New York: McGraw Hill; Meyers, J. N. (2000). *The secrets of taking any test.* New York: Learning Express; Ehren, B. J. *Mnemonic devices.* Retrieved from http://online academy.org/modules/a304/support/xpages/a304b0_20600 .html; Lloyd, G. (1998–2004). Study skills: Memorize with mnemonics. *Back to College.* Retrieved from http://www .back2college.com/memorize.htm; Raman, M., McLaughlin, K., Violato, C., Rostom, A., Allard, J. P., & Coderre, S. (2010). Teaching in small portions dispersed over time enhances long-term knowledge retention. *Medical Teacher, 32,* 250–255.

16. Willingham, D. T. (2004). Practice makes perfect—but only if you practice beyond the point of perfection. *American Educator.* Retrieved from http://www.aft.org/newspubs/periodicals/ae /spring2004/willingham.cfm.

17. Raman, M., McLaughlin, K., Violato, C., Rostom, A., Allard, J. P., & Coderre, S. (2010). Teaching in small portions dispersed over time enhances longterm knowledge retention. *Medical Teacher,* 32, 250–255.

18. Tigner, R. B. (1999). Putting memory research to good use: Hints from cognitive psychology. *College Teaching, 47*(4), 149–152.

19. Murdock, B. B., Jr. (1960). The distinctiveness of stimuli. *Psychological Reports, 67,* 16–31; Neath, I. (1993). Distinctiveness and serial position effects in recognition. *Memory & Cognition, 21,* 689–698.

20. Cahill, L. (2003). Similar neural mechanisms for emotion–induced memory impairment and enhancement. *Proceedings of the National Academy of Sciences, 100*(23), 13123–13124. Retrieved from http://www.pnas.org/cgi/content/full/100/23/13123.

21. Higbee, K. L. (1988). *Your memory: How it works and how to improve it* (2nd ed.). New York: Prentice Hall.

22. Bean, J. (1996). *Engaging ideas.* San Francisco: Jossey-Bass.

23. Higbee, K. L. (1988). *Your memory: How it works and how to improve it* (2nd ed.). New York: Prentice Hall.

24. Berk, R. A. (2002). *Humor as an instructional defibrillator.* Sterling, VA: Stylus; Berk, R. A. (2003). *Professors are from Mars®, students are from Snickers®.* Sterling, VA: Stylus.

25. Dodeen, H. (2008). Assessing test-taking strategies of university students: developing a scale and estimating its psychometric indices. *Assessment & Evaluation in Higher Education, 33*(4), 409–419.

26. Coren, S. (1996). *Sleep thieves.* New York: Free Press; Cox, K. (2004, October 14).

27. Grant, K. B. (2003, September 4). Popping pills and taking tests. *The Ithacan Online.* Retrieved from http://www.ithaca.edu/rhp/ithacan/articles/0309/04/news/2popping_pill.htm.

28. Frederickson, C. G. (1999). Multiple-choice answer changing: A type connection? *Journal of Psychological Type, 51,* 40–46.

29. Jensen, G. H. (1987). Learning styles. In J. A. Provost & S. Anchors (Eds.), *Applications of the Myers-Briggs type indicator in higher education.* p. 201. Palo Alto, CA: Consulting Psychologists Press.

30. Brinthaupt, T. M., & Shin, C. M. (2001). The relationship of academic cramming to flow experience. *College Student Journal, 35*(3), 457–472.

31. Tigner, R. B. (1999). Putting memory research to good use: Hints from cognitive psychology. *Journal of College Teaching, 47*(4), 149–152.

32. Small, G. (2002). *The memory bible.* New York: Hyperion.

33. (2010). Test anxiety. *University of Oregon Counseling and Testing Center.* Retrieved from http://counseling.uoregon.edu/dnn/SelfhelpResources/StressandAnxiety/TestAnxiety/tabid/337/Default.aspx.

34. Tozoglu, D., Tozoglu, M. D., Gurses, A., & Dogar, C. (2004). The students' perceptions: Essay versus multiple-choice type exams. *Journal of Baltic Science Education, 2*(6), 52–59.

35. Schutz, P. A., & Davis, H. A. (2000). Emotions and self-regulation during test taking. *Educational Psychologist, 35*(4), 243–256.

36. Coren, S. (1996). *Sleep thieves.* New York: Free Press.

37. Perina, K. (2002). Sum of all fears. *Psychology Today.* Retrieved from http://www.psychologytoday.com/articles/pto-20021108-000001.html.

38. Perry, A. B. (2004). Decreasing math anxiety in college students. *College Student Journal, 38*(2), 321–324.

39. Ibid.

40. Jonides, J., Lacey, S. C., & Nee, D. E. (2005). Processes of working memory in mind and brain. *Current Directions in Psychological Science, 14*(1), 2–5.

41. Ashcraft, M. H., & Kirk, E. P. (2001). The relationships among working memory, math anxiety, and performance. *Journal of Experimental Psychology: General. 130*(2), 224–237.

42. Beilock, S. L., Kulp, C. A., Holt, L. E., & Carr, T. H. (2004). More on the fragility of performance: Choking under pressure in mathematical problem solving. *Journal of Experimental Psychology: General, 133*(4), 584–600.

43. Mundell, E. J. (2005, March 9). Test pressure toughest on smartest. *Healingwell.com.* Retrieved from http://news.healingwell.com/index.php?p=news1&id=524405.

44. Based partially on Arem, C. (2003). *Conquering math anxiety,* second edition. Belmont, CA: Brooks/Cole.

45. Glenn, D. (2010, February 7). How students can improve by studying themselves. *The Chronicle of Higher Education.* Retrieved from http://chronicle.com/article/Struggling-Students-Can-Imp/64004/.

46. Firmin, M., Hwang, C., Copella, M., & Clark, S. (2004). Learned helplessness: The effect of failure on test-taking. *Education, 124*(4), 688–693.

47. Heidenberg, A. J., & Layne, B. H. (2000). Answer changing: A conditional argument. *College Student Journal, 34*(3), 440–451.

48. (2006, May 10). Clinton warning on global warming. Retrieved from http://news.bbc.co.uk/2/hi/uk_news/scotland/glasgow_and_west/4755297.stm.

49. Kennedy, R. A. Successful Exam Preparation and Test Taking Strategies (2007). *York University.* Retrieved from http://access.ewu.edu/Documents/Academic%20Support%20Center/Test%20Taking%20Strats/examsYORK.pdf.

50. Taking exams. *Brockport High School.* Retrieved from http://www.frontiernet.net/~jlkeefer/takgexm.html. Based partially on Penn State University; On taking exams. *University of New Mexico.* Retrieved from http://www.unm.edu/~quadl/college_learning/taking_exams.html; Lawrence, J. (2006). Tips for taking examinations. *Lawrence Lab Homepage.* Retrieved from http://cobamide2.bio.pitt.edu/testtips.htm; The multiple choice exam. (2003). *Counselling Services, University of Victoria.* Retrieved from http://www.coun.uvic.ca/learning/exams/multiple-choice.html; Test taking tips: Guidelines for answering multiple-choice questions. *Arizona State University.* Retrieved from http://neuer101.asu.edu/additionaltesting tips.htm; Landsberger, J. (2007). True/false tests. *Study Guides and Strategies.* Retrieved from http://www.studygs.net/tsttak2.htm; Landsberger, J. (2007). Multiple choice tests. *Study Guides and Strategies.* Retrieved from http://www.studygs.net/tsttak3.htm; Landsberger, J. (2007). The essay exam. *Study Guides and Strategies.* Retrieved from http://www.studygs.net/tsttak4.htm; Landsberger, J. (2007). Short answer tests. *Study Guides and Strategies.* Retrieved from http://www.studygs.net/tsttak5.htm; Landsberger, J. (2007). Open book exams. *Study Guides and Strategies.* Retrieved from http://www.studygs.net/tsttak7.htm; Rozakis, L. (2003). *Test-taking strategies and study skills for the utterly confused.* New York: McGraw-Hill; Meyers, J. N. (2000). *The secrets of taking any test.* New York: Learning Express; Robinson, A. (1993). *What smart students know.* New York: Crown Trade Paperbacks.

51. *Plagiarism.org.* Retrieved from http://www.plagiarism.org/resources/facts-and-stats/; A cheating crisis in America's schools. (2007, 29 April). *ABC News.* Retrieved from http://abcnews.go.com/Primetime/story?id=132376. Pérez-Peña, R. (2012, September 7). Studies find more students cheating, with high achievers no exception. *The New York Times.* Retrieved from http://www.nytimes.com/2012/09/08/education/studies-show-more-students-cheat-even-high-achievers.html?_r=1&emc=tnt&tntemail1=y.

52. Young, J. R. (2010, March 28). High tech cheating abounds, and professors bear some blame. *The Chronicle of Higher Education.* Retrieved from http://chronicle.com/article/High-Tech-Cheating-on-Homew/64857/; Gabriel, T. (2010, August 1). Plagiarism lines blur for students in digital age. *The New York Times.* Retrieved from http://www.nytimes.com/2010/08/02/education/02cheat.html?_r=1&src=me&ref=homepage.

53. Caught cheating. (2004, April 29). *Primetime Live,* ABC News Transcript. Interview of college students by Charles Gibson; Zernike, K. (2002, November 2). With student cheating on the rise, more colleges are turning to honor codes. *The New York Times,* p. Q10, column 1, National Desk; Warren, R. (2003, October 20). Cheating: An easy way to cheat yourself. The Voyager via U-Wire. *University Wire (www.uwire.com);* Thomson, S. C. (2004, February 13). Heyboer, K. (2003, August 23). Nearly half of college students say Internet plagiarism isn't cheating. *The Star-Ledger Newark, New Jersey;* Kleiner, C., & Lord, M. (1999).

54. Tagg, J. (2004, March-April). Why learn? What we may really be teaching students. *About Campus,* 2–10; Marton, F., & Säljö, R. On qualitative differences in learning: I-Outcome and process. (1976). *British Journal of Educational Psychology, 46,* 4–11.

55. Patterson, K., Grenny, J., McMillan, R. Switzler, Al, & Covey, S. R. (2012, August 6). *Crucial conversations: Tools for talking when stakes are high.* New York: McGraw-Hill; *Crucial conversations explained in two minutes.* Retrieved from http://www.youtube.com/watch?v=lWNkpecde40.

56. Ibid.

57. Patterson, K., Grenny, J., McMillan, R. & Switzler, A. (2004–2006). Crucial conversations. *DailyOM*. Retrieved from http://www.dailyom.com/cgi-bin/display/printerfriendlylib.cgi?articleid=1687.

Chapter 10

1. Tinto, V. (1975). Dropout from higher education: A theoretical synthesis of recent research. *Review of Educational Research, 45,* 89–125; Tinto, V. (1993). *Leaving college: Rethinking the causes and cures of student attrition* (2nd ed.). Chicago: University of Chicago Press.
2. Paul, E. L., & Brier, S. (2001). Friendsickness in the transition to college: Precollege predictors and college adjustment correlates. *Journal of Counseling & Development, 79*(1), 77–89.
3. Pressman, S. D., Cohen, S., Miller, G. E., Barkin, A., Rabin, B. S., & Treanor, J. J. (2005). Loneliness, social network size, and immune response to influenza vaccination in college freshmen. *Health Psychology, 24*(3), 297–306; Hitti, M. (2005, May 2). Researchers say lonely college freshmen show weaker immune response. *WebMD Medical News.* Retrieved from http://www.webmd.com/balance/news/20050502/loneliness-may-hurt-your-health.
4. Clifton, D. O., & Anderson, E. (2001–2002). *Strengths-quest: Discover and develop your strengths in academics, career, and beyond.* Washington, DC: The Gallup Organization.
5. Goleman, D. (1994). Emotional intelligence, quoted in *Funderstanding.* Retrieved from http://www.funderstanding.com/v2/tag/emotional-intelligence-2/; Goleman, D. (1995). *Emotional intelligence.* New York: Bantam; Lawry, J. D. (2008, July–August). Are you emotionally intelligent? *About Campus,* 27–29.
6. Emotional intelligence: when it comes to emotional intelligence, how savvy are you? Retrieved from http://atrium.haygroup.com/us/quizzes/emotional-intelligence-quiz.aspx.
7. Gardner, H. (1993). *Multiple intelligences: The theory in practice.* New York: Basic Books; Checkley, K. (1997). The first seven . . . and the eighth: A conversation with Howard Gardner. Expanded Academic ASAP (online database). Original Publication: *Education,* 116.
8. Goleman, D. (2002, June 16). Could you be a leader? *Parade Magazine,* pp. 4–6.
9. Snarey, J. R., & Vaillant, G. E. (1985). How lower- and working class youth become middle-class adults: The association between ego defense mechanisms and upward social mobility. *Child Development, 56*(4), 899–910.
10. Feist, G. J., & Barron, F. (1996, June). *Emotional intelligence and academic intelligence in career and life success.* Paper presented at the Annual Convention of the American Psychological Society, San Francisco, CA.
11. Emmerling, R. J., & Goleman, D. (2003). *Emotional intelligence: Issues and common misunderstandings.* Consortium for Research on Emotional Intelligence in Organizations. Retrieved from http://www.eiconsortium.org/pdf/EI_Issues_And_Common_Misunderstandings.pdf.
12. Grewal, D., & Salovey, P. (2005, July–August). Feeling smart: The science of emotional intelligence. *American Scientist, 93*(4), 330. Retrieved from http://www.americanscientist.org/my_amsci/restricted.aspx?act=pdf&id=3621818932653.
13. Isen, A. M, Daubman, K. A., & Nowicki, G. P. (1987). Positive affect facilitates creative problem solving. *Journal of Personality and Social Psychology, 52*(6), 1122–1131; Ciarrochi, J., & Scott, G. (2006). The link between emotional competence and well-being: a longitudinal study. *British Journal of Guidance & Counselling, 34*(2), 231–243.
14. Parker, J. D. A., Duffy, J. M., Wood, L. M., Bond, B. J., & Hogan, M. J. (2005). Academic achievement and emotional intelligence: Predicting the successful transition from high school to university. *Journal of the First Year Experience & Students in Transition 17*(1), 67–78; Schutte, N. S., & Malouff, J. (2002). Incorporating emotional skills content in a college transition course enhances student retention. *Journal of the First Year Experience & Students in Transition 14*(1), 7–21; Di Fabio, A., & Palazzeschi, L. (2009). An in-depth look at scholastic success: Fluid intelligence, personality traits or emotional intelligence? *Personality and Individual Differences 46,* 581–585.
15. EQ-i: HEd, Multi-Health Systems, Inc. North Tonawanda, NY. Retrieved from http://www.mhs.com/eihe.aspx. Used with permission.
16. Turning lemons into lemonade: Hardiness helps people turn stressful circumstances into opportunities. (2003, December 22). *Psychology Matters.* Retrieved from APA Online at http://www.apa.org/research/action/lemon.aspx; Marano, H. E. (2003). The art of resilience. *Psychology Today.* Retrieved from http://www.psychologytoday.com/articles/200305/the-art-resilience; Fischman, J. (1987). Getting tough: Can people learn to have disease-resistant personalities? *Psychology Today, 21,* 26–28; Friborg, O., Barlaug, D., Martinussen, M., Rosenvinge, J. H., & Hjemdal, O. (2005). Resilience in relation to personality and intelligence. *International Journal of Methods in Psychiatric Research, 14*(1), 29–42; Schulman, P. (1995). Explanatory style and achievement in school and work. In G. M. Buchanan & M. E. P. Seligman (Eds.), *Explanatory style* (pp. 159–171). Hillsdale, NJ: Lawrence Erlbaum; American Psychological Association. (1997). Learned optimism yields health benefits. *Discovery fit & health.* Retrieved from http://health.howstuffworks.com/mental-health/coping/learned-optimism-health-benefits.htm.
17. Maher, K. (2004) Emotional intelligence is a factor in promotions. *College Journal from the Wall Street Journal.*
18. Cherniss, C. (2000). *Emotional Intelligence: What it is and why it matters.* Paper presented at the Annual Meeting of the Society for Industrial and Organizational Psychology, New Orleans, LA. Retrieved from http://www.eiconsortium.org/reports/what_is_emotional_intelligence.html.
19. Goleman, Could you be a leader? p. 4.
20. Boyatzis, R. E., Cowan, S. S., & Kolb, D. A. (1995). *Innovations in professional education: Steps on a journey from teaching to learning.* San Francisco: Jossey-Bass.
21. Davidson, R. J., Kabat-Zinn, J., Schumacher, J., Rosenkranz, M., Muller, D., Santorelli, S. F., Urbanowski, F., Harrington, A., Bonus, K., & Sheridan, J. F. (2003). Alterations in brain and immune function produced by mindfulness meditation. *Psychosomatic Medicine, 65,* 564–570. Retrieved from http://www.psychosomaticmedicine.org/content/65/4/564.full.pdf+html; Hughes, D. (2004). Interview with Daniel Goleman. Share Guide. Retrieved from http://www.shareguide.com/Goleman.html.
22. Saxbe, D. (2004, November/December). The socially savvy. *Psychology Today.* Retrieved from http://www.psychologytoday.com/articles/200501/the-socially-savvy.
23. Bar-On, R. (2006). The Bar-On model of emotional-social intelligence (ESI). *Psicothema, 18* (Supl.), 13–25. Consortium for Research on Emotional Intelligence in Organizations. Retrieved from http://www.eiconsortium.org/reprints/bar-on_model_of_emotional-social_intelligence.htm.
24. Knox, D. H. (1970). Conceptions of love at three developmental levels. *The Family Coordinator, 19*(2), 151–157; Fisher, *Why we love;* Cramer, D. (2004). Satisfaction with a romantic relationship, depression, support and conflict. *Psychology and Psychotherapy: Theory, Research and Practice, 77*(4), 449–461.
25. Bregman, P. (2010, July 21). How to avoid (and quickly recover from) misunderstandings. *HBR Blog Network.* Retrieved from http://blogs.hbr.org/bregman/2010/07/how-to-avoid-and-quickly-recov.html.
26. Ibid.
27. Bregman, P. (2011, January 3). The best way to use the last five minutes of your day. *HBR Blog Network.* Retrieved from http://blogs.hbr.org/2011/01/the-best-way-to-use-the-last-f/.
28. (2012, June 12). Boosting team productivity through emotional intelligence. *Agile Project Management Student.* Retrieved from http://agilepmstudent.blogspot.com/2012/06/boosting-team-productivity-through.html; Barth, S. (2001). *3-D chess: Boosting team productivity through emotional intelligence.* Boston:

Harvard Business Publishing; (2004). *Teams that click*. Boston: Harvard Business School Press.

29. Mullen, J. K. (2012, March 16). Digital natives are slow to pick up nonverbal cues. *HBR Blog Network*. Retrieved from http://blogs.hbr.org/2012/03/digital-natives-are-slow-to-pi/.

30. Ibid.

31. (2012, June 12). Boosting team productivity through emotional intelligence. Agile Project Management Student. Retrieved from http://agilepmstudent.blogspot.com/2012/06/boosting -team-productivity-through.html; Barth, S. (2001). *3-D chess: Boosting team productivity through emotional intelligence*. Boston: Harvard Business Publishing; (2004). *Teams that click*. Boston: Harvard Business School Press.

32. Tims, A. (2011, March 4). The secret to understanding soft skills. *The Guardian*. Retrieved from http://www.guardian.co .uk/money/2011/mar/05/secret-to-understanding-soft-skills.

33. Levi, D. (2014). *Group dynamics for teams*. Thousand Oaks, CA: Sage.

34. Waterman, M. (2013, February 6). Students working in groups have greater understanding, study suggests. *The Daily Free Press*. Retrieved from http://dailyfreepress.com/2013/02/06 /students-working-in-groups-have-greater-understanding -study-suggests/.

35. Coutu, D. (2009, May). Why teams don't work: An interview with J. Richard Hackman. *Harvard Business Review*. Retrieved from http://hbr.org/2009/05/why-teams-dont-work/ar/1.

36. Ibid.

37. Rimer, S. (2009, January 12). At M.I.T., Large lectures are going the way of the blackboard. *The New York Times*. Retrieved from http://www.nytimes.com/2009/01/13/us/13physics.html?_r=0 &gwh=3FBCA0C879951CF50F6EF9A7A184772D.

38. (2013). *Mazur Group*. Retrieved from http://mazur.harvard .edu/research/detailspage.php?rowid=8.

39. Perron, B. E. (2011). Reducing social loafing in group-based projects. *College Teaching*. Retrieved from http://www .tandfonline.com/doi/full/10.1080/87567555.2011.568021# .UmqlgWSglF8.

40. Ferrazzi, K. (2012, January-February). Candor, criticism, teamwork. *Harvard Business Review*. Retrieved from http:// hbr.org/2012/01/candor-criticism-teamwork.

41. Ibid.

42. Tuckman, B. (1965). Developmental sequence in small groups. *Psychological Bulletin 63*(6): 384–99.

43. Rath, T., & Clifton, D. O. (2004). *How full is your bucket?* New York: Gallup Press.

44. Parker-Pope , T. (2009, April 20). What are friends for? A longer life. *The New York Times*. Retrieved from http://www.nytimes .com/2009/04/21/health/21well.html; Ybarra, O., Burnstein, E., Winkielman, P., Keller, M. C., Manis, M. Chan, E., & Rodri-guez, J. (2008). Mental exercising through simple socializing: Social interaction promotes general cognitive functioning. *Personality and Social Psychology Bulletin, 34,* 248–259.

45. Dakss, B. (2009, March 5). Study: Bad relationships bad for heart. *CBS News*. Retrieved from http://www.cbsnews.com /stories/2006/03/03/earlyshow/contributors/emilysenay /main1364889.shtml; (2005, December 5) Unhappy marriage: bad for your health. *WebMD*. Retrieved from http://www .webmd.com/sex-relationships/news/20051205/unhappy -marriage-bad-for-your-health. Based on Keicolt-Glaser, J. (2005). *Archives of general psychiatry*, 62, 1377–1384.

46. Dusselier, L., Dunn, B., Wang, Y., Shelley, M. C., & Whalen, D. F. (2005). Personal, health, academic, and environmental predic-tors of stress for residence hall students. *Journal of American College Health, 54*(1), 15–24; Hardigg, V., & Nobile, C. (1995). Living with a stranger. *U.S. News & World Report, 119*(12), 90–91. Retrieved from http://www.usnews.com/usnews /edu/articles/950925/archive_032964.htm; Nankin, J. (2005). Rules for roomies. *Careers & Colleges, 25*(4), 29. Owens, R. A. (2003). Friendship features associated with college students' friendship maintenance and dissolution following problems. University of West Virginia. (Dissertation). Retrieved from http://wvuscholar.wvu.edu:8881//exlibris/dtl/d3_1/apache _media/L2V4bGlicmlzL2R0bC9kM18xL2FwYWNoZV9t ZWRpYS82NTY0.pdf; Valeo, T. (2007, January). Good friends are good for you. *WebMD*. Retrieved from http://www.webmd .com/balance/features/good-friends-are-good-for-you.

47. Thomas, K. (1977). Conflict and conflict management. In M. D. Dunnette (Ed.), *Handbook of industrial and organizational psychology,* 889–935 Chicago: Rand McNally; Kilmann, R., & Thomas, K. W. (1975). Interpersonal conflict-handling behav-ior as reflections of Jungian personality dimensions. *Psycho-logical Reports, 37,* 971–980; Rahim, M., & Magner, N. R. (1995). Confirmatory factor analysis of the styles of handling interpersonal conflict: First-order factor model and its invari-ance across groups. *Journal of Applied Psychology, 80,* 122–132; Wilmot, W. W., & Hocker, J. L. (2001). *Interpersonal* con-flict (6th ed.). New York: McGraw-Hill. Kilmann, R. H., and K. W. Thomas. (1977). Developing a Forced-Choice Measure of Conflict-Handling Behavior: The MODE Instrument," *Educa-tional and psychological measurement, 37*(2), 309–325.

48. McCaulley, M. H. (1975). How individual differences affect health care teams. Health Team News, 1(8), 1-4. In Hirsh, S. K. (1992). MBTI Team Building Program: Team member's guide. Palo Alto, CA: Consulting Psychologists Press.

49. Bucher, R. D. (2004). *Diversity consciousness: Opening our minds to people, cultures, and opportunities* (2nd ed.). Upper Saddle River, NJ: Pearson Education.

50. *Race, the power of an illusion. PBS.* California Newsreel. Retr-ieved from http://www.pbs.org/race/000_General/000_00 -Home.htm.

51. Based on "Sorting People" activity at http://www.pbs.org /race/002_SortingPeople/002_00-home.htm.

52. Fulbeck, K. (2010). *Mixed: Portraits of multiracial kids.* San Francisco: Chronicle Books.

53. Wyer, K. (2007). Today's college freshmen have family income 60% above national average, UCLA survey reveals. *UCLA News.* Retrieved from http://heri.ucla.edu/PDFs/PR _TRENDS_40YR.pdf.

54. Humphreys, D., & Davenport, A. (2004, Summer/Fall). What really matters in college: How students view and value lib-eral education. *Liberal Education.* Excerpt: Diversity and civic engagement outcomes ranked among least important. Retrieved from http://www.diversityweb.org/Digest/vol9no1 /humphreys.cfm.

55. Laird, T. F. (2005). College students' experiences with diver-sity and their effects on academic self-confidence, social agency, and disposition toward critical thinking. *Research in Higher Education, 46*(4), 365–387.

56. Lewin, T. (2009, July 7). Interracial roommates can reduce prejudice. *The New York Times.* Retrieved from http://www .nytimes.com/2009/07/08/us/08roommate.html?adxnnl =1&adxnnlx=1312161887-Q1CKZUXsZ081TbxZkjR5w.

57. Moore, D. G. (2003, November 14). Toward a single defini-tion of college. *The Chronicle of Higher Education, 50*(12), B7; Diversity defines new generation of college students. (2009, June 18). *The Chronicle of Higher Education.* Retrieved from https://www.phoenix.edu/colleges_divisions/office-of-the -president/articles/diversity-defines-new-generation-college -students.html; Bell, S. (2012, March 8). Nontraditional students are the new majority. *Library Journal.* Retrieved from http://lj.libraryjournal.com/2012/03/opinion/nontraditional -students-are-the-new-majority-from-the-bell-tower/#_.

58. Pusser, B., Breneman, D. W., Gansneder, B. M., Kohl, K. J., Levin, J. S., Milam, J. H., & Turner, S. E. (2007). *Return-ing to learning: Adults' success in college is key to America's future.* Lumina Foundation; (2012, April 20). Racial equality in initial college enrollment rates. *Journal of Blacks in Higher Education.* Retrieved from http://www.jbhe.com/2012/04 /racial-equality-in-initial-college-enrollment-rates/.

59. Fry, R., & Lopez, M. H. (2012). Hispanic student enrollments reach new highs in 2011. *Pew Hispanic Center.* Retrieved from http://www.pewhispanic.org/files/2012/08/Hispanic -Student-Enrollments-Reach-New-Highs-in-2011_FINAL.pdf.

60. Staley, C. (2003). *50 ways to leave your lectern.* Belmont, CA: Wadsworth, p. 67. Based on Defining "Diversity." (1995). In B. Pike & C. Busse, *101 games for trainers* (p. 11). Minneapolis: Lakewood Books.

61. Staley, C. (2003). *50 ways to leave your lectern,* Belmont, CA: Wadsworth, p. 32.

62. Carnes, M. C. (2005). Inciting speech. *Change, 37*(2), 6–11.

63. Lyons, P. (2005, April 15). The truth about teaching about racism. *The Chronicle of Higher Education, 51*(32), B5.

64. Bosker, B. (2012, May 7). Fortune 500 list boasts more female CEOs than ever before. *Huffington Post.* Retrieved from http://www.huffingtonpost.com/2012/05/07/fortune-500-female ceos_n_1495734.html.

65. Epstein, G. (2005, June 5) More women advance, but sexism persists. *College Journal from the Wall Street Journal;* 2008 Women CEOs. *CNNMoney.* Retrieved from http://money.cnn.com/magazines/fortune/fortune500/2008/women-ceos/; (2013, May 8). Women CEOs of the Fortune 1000. *Catalyst.* Retrieved from http://www.catalyst.org/knowledge/women-ceos-fortune-1000.

66. Wessel, D. (2003, September 9). Race still a factor in hiring decisions. *CollegeJournal from the Wall Street Journal.*

67. Farrell, E. F. (2005, August 5). Student volunteers are worth billions. *The Chronicle of Higher Education, 51*(48), A33; (2012) Creating a culture of assessment. *Campus Compact.* http://www.compact.org/wp-content/uploads/2013/04/Campus-Compact-2012-Statistics.pdf.

68. Zlotkowski, E. (1999). Pedagogy and engagement. In R. G. Bringle, R. Games, & E. A. Malloy (Eds.). (1999). *Colleges and Universities as Citizens* (pp. 96–120). Needham Heights, MA: Allyn & Bacon.

69. Honnet, E. P., & Poulsen, S. J. (1989). *Principles of good practice for combining service and learning: A Wingspread special report.* Racine, WI: The Johnson Foundation.

70. Eyler, J., Giles, Jr., D. E., & Schmiede, A. (1996). *A practitioner's guide to reflection in service-learning: Student voices and reflections.* Nashville, TN: Vanderbilt University Press.

71. Dewey, J. (1933). *How we think.* Boston: Heath.

72. Farrell, Student volunteers are worth billions.

73. Beilke, J. R., & Yssel, N. (1999). The chilly climate for students with disabilities in higher education. *College Student Journal, 33*(3), 364–372.

74. Parker, P. N. (2006, March–April). Sustained dialogue: How students are changing their own racial climate. *About Campus, 11*(1), 17–23.

75. Gortmaker, V. J., & Brown, R. D. (2006). Out of the college closet: Differences in perceptions and experiences among out and closeted lesbian and gay students. *College Student Journal, 40*(3), 606–619.

76. Incidences and Statistics. (2009). Hate crime statistics 2009. *Department of Justice, Uniform Crime Reporting Program.* Retrieved from http://www2.fbi.gov/ucr/hc2009/index.html; *FBI Hate Crimes Accounting* (2012, December 12). FBI 2011 hate crime statistics. Retrieved from http://www.fbi.gov/news/stories/2012/december/annual-hate-crimes-report-released/annual-hate-crimes-report-released.

77. Parker, P. N. (2006, March–April). Sustained dialogue: How students are changing their own racial climate. *About Campus,* 17–34.

78. Based on Nilsen, L. B. (1998). The circles of [blank]. *Teaching at Its Best.* Bolton, MA: Anker Publishing.

79. Based on Earley, P.C., Mosakowski, E. (2004, October). Cultural intelligence. *Harvard Business Review,* p. 143.

80. Earley, P.C., & Mosakowski, E. (2004, October). Cultural intelligence. *Harvard Business Review,* 139–146; Early, C. P., Ang, S., & Tan, J. (2006). CQ: *Developing Cultural Intelligence at Work.* Stanford, CA: Stanford University Press; Osborn, T. N., (2006). *"CQ" Cultural Intelligence: Another Aspect of Emotional Intelligence.* Retrieved from http://www.teaminternational.net/resources/docs/cultural%20intelligence.pdf.

81. Earley, P. C., & Mosakowski, E. (2004, October). Cultural intelligence. *Harvard Business Review,* 139–146.

82. Wikipedia. *Google Search.* Retrieved from http://en.wikipedia.org/wiki/Google_Search.

83. (2012) World internet users and population stats. *Internet World Stats.* Retrieved from http://www.internetworldstats.com/stats.htm.

84. General Education for global learning. American Association of American Colleges & Universities. Retrieved from http://www.aacu.org/SharedFutures/index.cfm.

Chapter 11

1. Davis, R., & DeBarros, A. (2006, January 25). In college, first year is by far the riskiest. *USA Today.* Retrieved from http://usatoday30.usatoday.com/news/nation/2006-01-24-campus-deaths-cover_x.htm.

2. Monastersky, R. (2007, January 12). Who's minding the teenage brain? *The Chronicle of Higher Education, 53*(19), A14.

3. University of Minnesota (2008, October 22). Grades in college directly linked to health-related behaviors. *Science Daily.* Retrieved from http://www.sciencedaily.com/releases/2008/10/081021120925.htm.

4. Common health problems in college students. (2000). Previously *Medem: Medical Library.* American Academy of Pediatrics. Health problems of college students. *Journal of American College Health, 45*(6), 243–250. (2009); The American College Health Association–National college health assessment spring 2008 reference group data report (abridged). *Journal of American College Health, 57*(5), 477–488.

5. Hales, D. (2006). *An invitation to health, brief.* Belmont, CA: Thomson Wadsworth, p. 32.

6. Kobau, R., Safran, M. A., Zack, M. M., Moriarty, D. G., & Chapman, D. (2004, July 30). Sad, blue, or depressed days, health behaviors and health-related quality of life, behavioral risk factor surveillance system, 1995–2000. *Health Quality of Life Outcomes, 2*(1).

7. Di Meglio, F., (2012, May 10). Stress takes its toll on college students. *Businessweek.* Retrieved from http://www.businessweek.com/articles/2012-05-10/stress-takes-its-toll-on-college-students.

8. Hilts, P. J. (1993, May 22). U.S. defines mental illness as standard for treatment. *The New York Times.* Retrieved from http://www.nytimes.com/1993/05/22/us/us-defines-mental-illness-as-standard-for-treatment.html.

9. Heredity and the Genetics of Schizophrenia. *Schizophrenia.com.* Retrieved from http://www.schizophrenia.com/research/hereditygen.htm.

10. Scientists show how cannabis/marijuana may trigger schizophrenia. (2007, April 30). *Schizophrenia.com.* Retrieved from http://www.schizophrenia.com/sznews/archives/004987.html.

11. MacInnes, N., Handley, S. L., & Harding, G. F. (2001). Former chronic methylenedioxy methamphetamine (MDMA or ecstasy) users report mild depressive symptoms. *Journal of Psychopharmacology, 15*(3), 181–186.

12. Depression and college students. 2012 *National Institute of Mental Health.* Retrieved from http://www.nimh.nih.gov/health/publications/depression-and-college-students/index.shtml.

13. Eisenberg, D., Golberstein, E., & Hunt, J. (2009, May). Mental health and academic success in college. B. E. *Journal of Economic Analysis & Policy.* Retrieved from http://www-personal.umich.edu/~daneis/papers/hmpapers/Eisenberg%20et%20al%20(2009).pdf.

14. National Institute of Mental Health. (2009, February 14). College depression: What do these students have in common? *Mental Health Matters.* Retrieved from http://www.mental-health-matters.com/index.php?option=com_content&view=article&id=632.

15. Ibid.

16. Ibid.

17. Farrell, E. F. (2005, December 16). Need therapy? Check your in box. *The Chronicle of Higher Education, 52*(17), A35.

18. Celebrity meltdown. (1999, November/December). *Psychology Today*. Retrieved from http://www.psychologytoday.com /articles/pto-19991101-000035.html.

19. Celebrity meltdown. (1999, November/December). *Psychology Today*. Retrieved from http://www.psychologytoday.com /articles/pto-19991101-000035.html. Liecht, L., & Colina, S. (2011, August 31). 43 inspiring celebs who lived with depression. *Huffington Post*. Retrieved from http://www.huffingtonpost .com/2011/08/31/celebs-with-depression_n_942771. html#s344898&title=Angelina_Jolie_.

20. Anxiety disorders: What you need to know. (2013). *Mental Health America*. Retrieved from http://www.nmha.org/go/go /information/get-info/anxiety-disorders/anxiety-disorders.

21. Sieben, L. (2011, March 14). Nearly a third of college Students have had mental-health counseling, study finds. *The Chronicleof Higher Education*. Retrieved from http://chronicle .com/article/Nearly-a-Third-of-College/126726/.

22. Marano, H. E. (2004). Up against the ivy wall in 2004. *Psychology Today*. Retrieved from http://www.psychologytoday.com /articles/200405/against-the-ivy-wall-in-2004.

23. Benton, S. A., Robertson, J. M., Tseng, W., Newton, F. B., & Benton, S. L. (2003). Changes in counseling center client problems across 13 years. *Professional Psychology: Research and Practice, 34*(1), 66–72.

24. Astin, A. W., Astin, H. S., & Lindholm, J. A. (2010). *Cultivating the spirit: How college can enhance students' inner lives.* San Francisco: Jossey-Bass.

25. Astin, A. W., Astin, H. S., Lindholm, J. A., & Bryant, A. N. (2005). *The spiritual life of college students: A national study of college students' search for meaning and purpose.* Los Angeles: Higher Education Research Institute, UCLA.

26. Astin et al., *The spiritual life of college students*; Bartlett, T. (2005, April 22). Most freshmen say religion guides them. *The Chronicle of Higher Education, 51*(33), A1. Retrieved from http:// chronicle.com/article/Most-Freshmen-Say-Religion/9956.

27. Saenz, V., & Wolf, D. (2006, February 16). Your first college year survey: Highlights from the 2005 YFCY. *National Resource Center Resources*. Retrieved from http://www.sc.edu /fye/resources/assessment/essays/Saenz-2.16.06.html.

28. Marsh, N. (2011, February). How to make work-life balance work. *TedTalks*. Retrieved from http://www.ted.com/talks /nigel_marsh_how_to_make_work_life_balance_work.html.

29. Ibid.

30. Bregman, P. (2010, July 30). Don't regret working too hard. *Harvard Business Review Blog*. Retrieved from http://blogs.hbr .org/bregman/2010/07/dont-regret-working-too-hard.html.

31. Nelms, L. W., Hutchins, E., Hutchins, D., & Pursley, R. J. (2007). Spirituality and the health of college students. *Journal of Religion and Health, 46*(2), 249–265.

32. Segerstrom, S. C., & Miller, G. E. (2004). Psychological stress and the human immune system: A meta-analytic study of 30 years of inquiry. *Psychological Bulletin, 130*(4), 601–630. (2004, July 4). Stress affects immunity in ways related to stress type and duration, as shown by nearly 300 studies. *APA Press Release*. Retrieved from http://www.apa.org/news/press /releases/2004/07/stress-immune.aspx.

33. Adelson, R. (2005, January 1). Hard-hitting hormones: The stress-depression link. *Monitor on Psychology, 36*(1). Retrieved from http://www.apa.org/monitor/jan05/hormones .html.

34. Ross, S. E., Niebling, B. C., & Heckert, T. M. (1999). Sources of stress among college students. *College Student Journal, 33*(2), 312–317.

35. Largo-Wight, E., Peterson, P. M., & Chen, W. W. (2005). Perceived problem solving, stress, and health among college students. *American Journal of Health Behavior, 29*(4), 360–370.

36. Hudd, S. S., Dumlao, J., Erdmann-Sager, D., Murray, D., Phan, E., Soukas, N., & Yokozuka, N. (2000). Stress at college: Effects on health habits, health status and self-esteem. *College Student Journal, 34*(2), 217–227.

37. Miller, W. C., Staples, B. & Bravender, T. (2008). Risk factors associated with overweight and obesity in college students. *Journal of American College Health, 57*(1), 109–114; Gruber, K. J. (2008). Social support for exercise and dietary habits among college students. Adolescence, *43*(171), 557–575.

38. Strout, E. (2007, September 21). The obesity epidemic-comes to campuses. *Chronicle of Higher Education, 54*(4), A1. Retrieved from http://chronicle.com/article/The-Obesity -Epidemic-Comes-to/21074.

39. Racette, S. B., Deusinger, S. S., Strube, M. J., Highstein, G. R., & Duesinger, R. H. (2005). Weight changes, exercise, and dietary patterns during freshman and sophomore years of college. *Journal of American College Health, 53*(6), 245–251.

40. *CDC FastStats*. Obesitiy and overweight. Retrieved from http://www.cdc.gov/nchs/fastats/overwt.htm.

41. Dietary guidelines for Americans (2005). Retrtieved from http://www.health.gov/dietaryguidelines/dga2005/docu ment/pdf/dga2005.pdf.

42. U.S. Department of Agriculture. (2010). Dietary guidelines for Americans. Retrieved from http://www.cnpp.usda.gov /DGAs2010-PolicyDocument.htm.

43. U.S. Department of Agriculture. (2011). ChooseMyPlate.gov.

44. USDA Dietary Guidelines for Americans 2005. Retrieved from http://www.health.gov/dietaryguidelines/dga2005/recommenda- tions.htm.

45. USDA Food safety and inspection service. *Food facts sheet: How temperatures affect food.* Retrieved from http://www .fsis.usda.gov/wps/portal/fsis/topics/food-safety-education /get-answers/food-safety-fact-sheets/safe-food-handling /how-temperatures-affect-food.

46. Eating disorders boom as kids enter college. *USAToday*. Retrieved from http://www.usatoday.com/story/news/nation /2012/12/27/college-kids-eating-disorders/1794057/.

47. Tracy, N. (2009). Eating disorders in college women, overview. *Healthy place.com*. Retrieved from http://www.healthyplace .com/eating-disorders/articles/eating-disorders-in-college -women-overview/.

48. U.S. Job satisfaction at lowest level in two decades. (2010, January 5). *The Conference Board*. Retrieved from http:// www.prnewswire.com/news-releases/us-job-satisfaction -at-lowest-level-in-two-decades-80699752.html.

49. Seligman, M. E. P. (2002). *Authentic happiness.* New York: Free Press.

50. Achor, S. (2010). *The happiness advantage: The seven principles of positive psychology that fuel success and performance at work.* New York: Crown Business.

51. Ibid.

52. Killingsworth, M. (2012). Matt Killingsworth: Want to be happier? Stay in the moment. *TedTalks*. Retrieved from http://www.ted.com/talks/matt_killingsworth_want_to_be _happier_stay_in_the_moment.html.

53. Prouty, A. M., Protinsky, H. O., & Canady, D. (2002). College women: Eating behaviors and help-seeking preferences. *Adolescence, 37*(146), 353–363.

54. Lowery, S. E., Kurpius, S. E. R., Befort, C., Blanks, E. H., Sollenberger, S., Nicpon, M. F., & Huser, L. (2005). Body image, self-esteem, and health-related behaviors among male and female first year college students. *Journal of College Student Development, 46*(6), 612–623.

55. Shuster, W. G. (2001). Less stress? Yes! *Jewelers' Circular Keystone, 172*(2), 98.

56. Huggins, C. E. (2005, January 17). Best fitness routine may depend on personality. *American Medical Network*. Retrieved from http://www.health.am/ab/more/best_fitness _routine _may_depend_on_personality/.

57. Bray, S. R., & Born, H. A. (2004). Transition to university and vigorous physical activity: Implications for health and psychological well-being. *Journal of American College Health, 52*(4), 181–188.

58. Seo, D., Torabi, M, R., Jiang, N., Fernandez-Rojas, X., & Park, B. (2009). Correlates of college students' physical activity: Crosscultural differences. *Asia-Pacific Journal of Public Health*. Retrieved from http://aph.sagepub.com/content/21/4/421.

59. Jozefowicz, C. (2004, June). Sweating makes you smart. *Psychology Today*, 56–58.

60. Brown, F. C., & Buboltz, W. C., Jr. (2002). Applying sleep research to university students: Recommendations for developing a student sleep education program. *Journal of College Student Development, 43*(3), 411–416.

61. Jensen, D. R. (2003). Understanding sleep disorders in a college student population. *Journal of College Counseling, 6*(1), 25, 34.

62. (2009, February 11). The science of sleep. *60 Minutes* (CBS news transcript). Retrieved from http://www.cbsnews.com/stories/2008/03/14/60minutes/main3939721.shtml.

63. Brown, F. C., & Buboltz, W. C., Jr. (2002). Applying sleep research to university students: Recommendations for developing a student sleep education program. *Journal of College Student Development, 43*(3), 411–416.

64. Greer, M. (2004, July/August). Strengthen your brain by resting it. *Monitor on Psychology, 35*(7). Retrieved from http://www.apa.org/monitor/julaug04/strengthen.aspx.

65. Pilcher, J. J., & Walters, A. S. (1997). How sleep deprivation affects psychological variables related to college students' cognitive performance. *Journal of American College Health, 46*, 121–126.

66. Kelly, W. E., Kelly, K. E. & Clanton, R. C. (2001). The relationship between sleep length and grade-point average among college students. *College Student Journal, 35*(1), 84–86.

67. Kelly, W. E. (2003). Worry content associated with decreased sleep-length among college students: Sleep deprivation leads to increased worrying. *College Student Journal, 37*, 93–95.

68. Kerkstra, P. (2006, February 5). Online poker 101: A lesson in losing. *The Philadelphia Inquirer*, A01.

69. Farrell, E. (2005, September 2). Logging on, tuning out. *The Chronicle of Higher Education, 52*(2), A46.

70. Kelly, W. E. (2004). Sleep-length and life satisfaction in a college student sample. *College Student Journal, 38*(3), 428–430; Teli, P. (2002, September 24, updated 2010, March 7). College students' sleep habits harmful to health, study finds. *The Daily Orange*. Retrieved from http://www.dailyorange.com/2002/09/college-students-sleep-habits-harmful-to-health-study-finds/; (2013, October 26). Facts and stats. DrowsyDriving.org. *National Sleep Foundation*. Retrieved from http://drowsydriving.org/about/facts-and-stats/.

71. Killgore, W. D. S., Kahn-Greene, E. T., Lipizzi, E. L., Newman, R. A., Kamimori, G. H., & Balkin, T. J. (2008). Sleep deprivation reduces perceived emotional intelligence and constructive thinking skills. *Sleep Medicine, 9*, 517–526.

72. (2013, October 26). Facts and stats. DrowsyDriving.org. *National Sleep Foundation*. Retrieved from http://drowsydriving.org/about/facts-and-stats/.

73. Kelly, W. E. (2004). Sleep-length and life satisfaction in a college student sample. *College Student Journal, 38*(3), 428–430.

74. Brown, F. C., & Buboltz, W. C., Jr. (2002). Applying sleep research to university students: Recommendations for developing a student sleep education program. *Journal of College Student Development, 43*(3), 411–416.

75. Teli, P. (2002, September 24, updated 2010, March 7). College students' sleep habits harmful to health, study finds. *The Daily Orange*. Retrieved from http://www.dailyorange.com/2002/09/college-students-sleep-habits-harmful-to-health-study-finds/.

76. Coren, S. (1996). *Sleep thieves: An eye-opening exploration into the science and mysteries of sleep*. New York: Free Press.

77. Geranios, N. K. (2012, December 2). Marijuana legalized in Washington, Colorado, but still banned on college campuses. Oregon Live. Retrieved from http://www.oregonlive.com/pacific-northwest-news/index.ssf/2012/12/marijuana_legalized_in_washing.html

78. Mohler-Kuo, M., Lee, J. E., & Wechsler, H. (2003). Trends in marijuana and other illicit drug use among college students: Results from 4 Harvard School of Public Health College Alcohol Study surveys: 1993–2001. *Journal of American College Health, 52*(1), 17–24; Hales, *An invitation to health*, p. 269.

79. Bon, S. R., Hittner, J. B., & Lawandales, J. P. (2001). Normative perceptions in relation to substance use and HIV-risky sexual behaviors of college students. *Journal of Psychology, 135*(2), 165.; Hales, *An invitation to health*, p. 269.

80. Hales, *An invitation to health*, p. 299.

81. College Alcohol Study. (2005). *Harvard School of Public Health*. Retrieved from http://www.hsph.harvard.edu/cas/.

82. Killough, A. C. (2009, June 15). Study finds drinking by college students on the rise. *The Chronicle of Higher Education*. Retrieved from http://chronicle.com/article/Study-Finds-Drinkingby/47745.

83. Malinauskas, B. M., Aeby, V. G., Overton, R. F., Carpenter-Aeby, T., & Barber-Heidal, K. (2007). A survey of energy drink consumption patterns among college students. *Nutrition Journal*. Retrieved from http://www.nutritionj.com/content/6/1/35.

84. Bogle, K. A. (2008, March 21). "Hooking up": What educators need to know. *The Chronicle of Higher Education*. Retrieved from http://chronicle.com/article/Hooking-Up-What-Educators/26465.

85. Nelson, T. F., Naimi, T. S., Brewer, R. D., & Wechsler H. (2005). The state sets the rate: The relationship of college binge drinking to state binge drinking rates and selected state alcohol control policies. *American Journal of Public Health, 95*(3), 441–446. Eigan, L. (1991). Alcohol Practices, Policies and Potentials of American Colleges and Universities, U.S. Department of Health and Human Services.

86. Ariniello, L. (2002, October). Young brains on alcohol. *Society for Neuroscience*. Retrieved from http://www.sfn.org/Press-Room/News-Release-Archives/2003/SCIENTISTS-MAP-MATURATION.

87. Townshend, J. M., & Duka, T. (2005). Binge drinking, cognitive performance and mood in a population of young social drinkers. *Alcoholism: Clinical & Experimental Research, 29*(3), 317–325; (2005). Binge Drinking Impairs Mood, Cognitive Performance. *ACER News Release*. About.com: Alcoholism. Binge Drinking Impairs Mood, Cognitive Performance. Retrieved from http://alcoholism.about.com/od/dementia/a/blacer050315.htm.

88. Lederman, G. (2004, March 25). Heavy drinking among college students can be predicted. *Pacific Institute for Research and Evaluation*. Retrieved from http://resources.prev.org/HeavyDrinking AmongCollegeStudentsMediaRelease.pdf.

89. Hingson, R. W., Zha, W., & Weitzman, E. R. (2009). Magnitude of and trends in alcohol-related mortality and morbidity among U.S. college students ages 18–24, 1998–2005. *Journal of Studies on Alcohol and Drugs*.

90. Jennison, K. M. (2004). The short-term effects and unintended long-term consequences of binge drinking in college: A 10-year follow-up study. *The American Journal of Drug and Alcohol Abuse, 30*(3), 659–684.

91. Strano, D. A., Cuomo, M. J., & Venable, R. H. (2004). Predictors of undergraduate student binge drinking. *Journal of College Counseling, 7*, 50–63.

92. Sheffield, F. D., Darkes, J., Del Boca, F. K., & Goldman, M. S. (2005). Binge drinking and alcohol-related problems among community college students: Implications for prevention policy. *Journal of American College Health, 54*(3), 137–141.

93. Marczinski, C. A., Bryant, R., Fillmore, M. T. (2005). The relationship between cognitive preoccupation with alcohol and alcohol use in male and female college students. *Addiction Research and Theory, 13*(4), 383–394.

94. Nelson, T. F., Naimi, T. S., Brewer, R. D., & Wechsler H. (2005). The state sets the rate: The relationship of college binge drinking to state binge drinking rates and selected state alcohol control policies. *American Journal of Public Health*,

95(3), 441–446. Eigan, L. (1991). Alcohol Practices, Policies and Potentials of American Colleges and Universities, U.S. Department of Health and Human Services.

95. Jaslow, R. (2013, April 25). Binge drinking in college may lead to heart problems later in life. *CBS News*. Retrieved from http://www.cbsnews.com/8301-204_162-57581413/binge -drinking-in-college-may-lead-to-heart-problems-later-in-life/.

96. Woodyard, C. D., Hallam, J. S., & Bentley, J. P. (2013). Drinking norms: Predictors of misperceptions among college students. *American Journal of Health Behavior*, 27(1), 14-24.

97. Facts about alcohol poisoning. (2005). *College Drinking: Changing the Culture*. Retrieved from http://www .collegedrinkingprevention.gov/OtherAlcoholInformation /factsAboutAlcoholPoisoning.aspx.

98. (2011). Get facts and statistics. *SmartSex.org*. Retrieved from http://www.smartersex.org/resources/behind.asp.

99. Patterson, R. (2008, March 30). Students of virginity. *The New York Times*. Retrieved from http://www.nytimes .com/2008/03/30/magazine/30Chastity-t.html. Yabroff, J. (2008). Campus sexperts. *Newsweek*. Retrieved from http:// www.highbeam.com/doc/1G1-175042711.html.

100. CDC. (2013, February). *CDC*. CDC fact sheet: Incidence, prevalence, and cost of sexually transmitted infections in the United States. Retrieved from http://www.cdc.gov/std/stats /sti-estimates-fact-sheet-feb-2013.pdf.

101. French, S. E., & Holland, K. J. (2013). Condom negotiation strategies as a mediator of the relationship between self-efficacy and condom use. *Journal of Sex Research*, 50(1), 48–59.

102. Hales, *An invitation to health,* p. 174.

103. Ibid, p. 163.

104. Laumann, E., Gagnon, J. H., Michael, R. T., & Michaels, S. (1994). *The social organization of sexuality: Sexual practices in the United States.* Chicago: University of Chicago Press.

105. Stammers, T. G. (2003, August). Abstinence under fire. *Post-graduate Medical Journal, 79,* 365–366.

Chapter 12

1. Farrell, E. F. (2006, December 12). Freshmen put high value on how well college prepares them for a profession, survey finds. *The Chronicle of Higher Education;* Farrell, E. F. (2007, January 5). Report says freshmen put career prep first. *The Chronicle of Higher Education, 53*(18), A32. Retrieved from http://chronicle.com/article/Report-Says-Freshmen-Put-Ca /19260/.

2. Irvine, M. (2007, January 22). Polls say wealth important to youth. *NewsOK*. Retrieved from http://newsok.com/polls -saywealth-important-to-youth/article/3002446.DTL; Schwartz, B. (2004, January 23). The tyranny of choice. *The Chronicle of Higher Education, 50*(20), B6. The top jobs for 2013. *Forbes*. Retrieved from http://www.forbes.com/pictures/efkk45mkkh /top-10-jobs-for-2013/.

3. *Celebrity Net Worth*. Retrieved from http://www.celebrity networth.com/richest-athletes/nfl/peyton-manning-net -worth/; http://www.celebritynetworth.com/richest-athletes /olympians/shaun-white-net-worth/;Crow,A.(2012,March20). Peyton Manning contract details: Broncos will pay $18 million in 2012. *SB Nation*. Retrieved from http://www.sbnation .com/2012-nfl-free-agency/2012/3/20/2887461/peyton -manning-contract-denver-broncos.

4. Koeppel, D. (2004, December 5). Choosing a college major: For love or for the money? *The New York Times,* section 10, p. 1, column 4. Dunham, K. J. (2004, March 2). No ivory tower: College students focus on career. *Wall Street Journal* (Eastern Edition), pp. B1, B8.

5. Plumer, B. (2013, May 13). Only 27 percent of college grads have a job related to their major. *Wonkblog: The Washington Post*. Retrieved from http://www.washingtonpost.com/blogs /wonkblog/wp/2013/05/20/only-27-percent-of-college-grads -have-a-job-related-to-their-major/.

6. Bissonnette, Z. (2010, November 3). Your college major may not be as important as you think. *The New York Times*. Retrieved from http://thechoice.blogs.nytimes.com/2010/11 /03/major/.

7. Malgwi, C. A., Howe, M. A., & Burnaby, P. A. (2005). Influences on students' choice of college major. *Journal of Education for Business, 80*(5), 275–282.

8. Leppel, K. (2005). College persistence and student attitudes toward financial success. *College Student Journal, 39*(2), 223–241; http://wiki.answers.com/Q/What_are_the_highest _paying_jobs.

9. Saleh, A. (2001). Brain hemisphericity and academic majors: A correlation study. *College Student Journal, 35*(2), 193–200.

10. Simpson, J. C. (2003). Mom matters: Maternal influence on the choice of academic major. *Sex Roles, 48*(9/10), 447–460.

11. Rask, K. N., & Bailey, E. M. (2002). Are faculty role models? Evidence from major choice in an undergraduate institution. *The Journal of Economic Education, 33*(2), 99–124.

12. Levine, M. (2005). *Ready or not, here life comes.* New York: Simon & Schuster, p. 4; Levine, M. (2005, February 18). College graduates aren't ready for the real world. *The Chronicle of Higher Education, 51*(24), B11.

13. *Dictionary of occupational titles.* (1991). Washington, DC: Bureau of Labor Statistics. Or see *O*Net Online* (Occupational Information Network) at http://online.onetcenter.org/find/.

14. Based on Schwartz, The tyranny of choice.

15. See J. K. Rowling Biography at http://www.biography.com /people/jk-rowling-40998.

16. Levine, *Ready or not, here life comes.*

17. Based in part on Gordon, V. N., & Sears, S. J. (2004). *Selecting a college major: Exploration and decision making, 5th edition.* Upper Saddle River, NJ: Pearson Education.

18. Based on Hansen, R. S., & Hansen, K. *Using a SWOT analysis in your career planning. Quintessential Careers.* Retrieved from http://www.quintcareers.com/SWOT_Analysis.html.

19. Association of American Colleges and Universities. (2011). *The LEAP vision for learning: Outcomes, practices, impact, and employers' views.* Washington, DC: Association of American Colleges and Universities.

20. Partenheimer, D. (2004, January 11). Abilities required for success in school don't differ greatly from those required in the real world. *APA Online*. Retrieved from http://www.apa.org /news/press/releases/2004/01/success.aspx.

21. Rowh, M. (2003, February–March). Choosing a major. *Career World, 31*(5), 21–23.

22. Ezarik, M. M. (2007, April–May). A major decision. *Career World, 35*(6), 20–22.

23. Rask & Bailey, Are faculty role models?

24. Goldhaber, G. M. (1986). *Organizational communication* (4th ed.). Dubuque, IA: Wm. C. Brown, p. 236. In Staley, R. S., II, & Staley, C. C. (1992). *Communicating in business and the professions: The inside word.* Belmont, CA: Wadsworth.

25. Peters, T. (1997, August 31). The brand called you. *FastCompany*. Retrieved from http://www.fastcompany.com/28905 /brand-called-you.

26. Pan, J. (2012, August 28). Students, here's how to kick-start your personal brand online. *Mashable*. Retrieved from http:// mashable.com/2012/08/28/personal-branding-for-students.

27. Weed, J. (2012, November 26). Business cards give way to cell-phone apps for networking. *The New York Times*. Retrieved from http://www.nytimes.com/2012/11/27/business/business -cards-give-way-to-cellphone-apps-for-networking.html.

28. Jay, M. (2013, February). Why 30 is not the new 20. *TedTalk*. Retrieved from http://www.ted.com/talks/meg_jay_why_30 _is_not_the_new_20.html.

29. Schawbel, D. (2010). *Me 2.0: 4 steps to building your future.* New York: Kaplan Publishing.

30. Pan, J. (2012, August 28). Students, here's how to kick-start your personal brand online. *Mashable*. Retrieved from http:// mashable.com/2012/08/28/personal-branding-for-students.

31. Gallo, A. (2011, March 18). Where Will You Be in Five Years? *HBR Blog.* Retrieved from http://blogs.hbr.org/2011/03/where-will-you-be-in-five-year/.

32. Brooks, K. (2009). *You Majored in What?* New York: Viking.

33. Kanter, R. M. (2011, March). Managing yourself: Zoom in, zoom out. *HBR Blog.* Retrieved from http://hbr.org/2011/03/managing-yourself-zoom-in-zoom-out/ar/1.

34. Gallo, A. (2011, March 18). Where Will You Be in Five Years? *HBR Blog.* Retrieved from http://blogs.hbr.org/2011/03/where-will-you-be-in-five-year/.

35. Buhl, L. (2013, May 24). How to survive the interview from hell. *AOL jobs.* Retrieved from http://jobs.aol.com/articles/2013/05/24/survive-the-interview-from-hell/.

36. Bradt, G. (2013, January 2). Acing the only three true job interview questions. *Forbes.* Retrieved from http://www.forbes.com/sites/georgebradt/2013/01/02/acing-the-only-three-true-job-interview-questions/.

37. Friedman, T. (2013, May 28). How to get a job. *The New York Times.* Retrieved from http://www.nytimes.com/2013/05/29/opinion/friedman-how-to-get-a-job.html?_r=0.

38. Based on J.K. DiTiberio & A.L. Hammer (1993). Introduction to Type in College. Palo Alto, CA: Consulting Psychologists Press.

39. DiTiberio, J. K., & Hammer, A. L. (1993). *Introduction to type in college.* Palo Alto, CA: Consulting Psychologists Press; Hammer, A. L. (1993). *Introduction to type and careers.* Palo Alto, CA: Consulting Psychologists Press.

40. Myers, I. B., & McCaulley, M. H. (1985). *Manual: A guide to the development and use of the Myers-Briggs type indicator.* Palo Alto, CA: Consulting Psychologists Press. In Golden, V. J., & Provost, J. A. (1987). *"The MBTI and career development;" Application of the Myers-Briggs type indicator in higher education.* Palo Alto, CA: Consulting Psychologists Press.

41. Coplin, B. (2003). *10 things employers want you to learn in college.* Berkeley, CA: Ten Speed Press.

PREFACE

1. Hamilton, J. (2008, October 9). Multitasking teens may be muddling their brains. NPR: Your Health. Retrieved from http://www.npr.org/templates/story/story.php?storyId=95524385; Tierney, J. (2009, May 5). Ear plugs to lasers: The science of concentration. The New York Times. Retrieved from http://www.nytimes.com/2009/05/05/science/05tier.html?scp=1&sq=%22ear%20plugs%20to%20lasers:%20the%20science%20of%20concentration%22&st=cse; Tugend, A. (2008, October 25). Multitasking can make you lose … um … focus. The New York Times. Retrieved from http://www.nytimes.com/2008/10/25/business/yourmoney/25shortcuts.html?scp=1&sq=%22multitasking%20can%20make%20you%20lose%22&st=cse; Walls, C. (2006, March 19). genM: The multitasking generation. Time. Retrieved from http://www.time.com/time/magazine/article/0,9171,1174696,00.html.

2. Khawand, P. (2009). *The Accomplishing More with Less Workbook.* On the Go Technologies, LLC.

Index

Note: Page numbers followed by a "b" indicate boxes; by an "e" indicate exercises; by a "f" indicate figures.

Rapid eye movement (REM) sleep, 384
Rapid-fire lecturer, defined, 226
Rapt: Attention and the Focused Life
(Gallagher), 44
Rath, Tom, 340
Reading rate, 254e–255e
Reading skills, 252–253, 256
Reading style, 258
Reading/read, 253–255e, 257–258
Read/write learning strategy/modality, 83,
85. *See also* VARK
critical thinking and, 156
defined, 235
example for, 83f
focus and, 398
importance of, 252–254
introduction, 82–83
learning strategies, 94, 99
memory, 294f, 295f
multiple intelligences and, 77, 99
notes and, 252
outlines, using, 214
paraphrasing and, 178
reading, 252–254, 257–258, 264, 281
relationships, 324
skills, 252–253, 256
tests, 286, 306, 309, 311
time management, 104
wellness and, 362
Readers, good, 256–257, 264, 280b
Ready or Not, Here Life Comes (Levine), 403
Reagan, Ronald, 151
Reasoning, 147–156
adequacy, 150
argument analysis, 148–150
assumptions, 38, 150–151
case study, 1534e–155e
claims, 151–152
faulty, 152–153, 156
focus and, 157f
introduction, 147–148
relevancy, 149–150
Rebalancing, 130–131
Receptive skills, defined, 152
Recite, defined, 263
Recording, 290–293
defined, 290
memory and, 257, 289–292
reading and, 77, 231
Red Cross, 20b
Reed, Carson, 2–4
Reeves, Keanu, 347
Reflect, 263
Rehash, 263
Rehearsal
memory and, 289, 294f
notes and, 260
presentations and, 278
Reinartz, Werner, 171
Relate/relating, 312, 328
Relationships. *See also* Diversity; Groups
bad, effects of, 341
building, 340
on campus, 17e–18e
college success and, 324–326
communicating in, 111, 340–341
conflict in, 341–345
critical thinking and, 145e
EI and, 326–329
families, 54b
listening and, 340
love and, 56, 104, 340, 370
mental health and, 341

negativity and, 340
positive actions and, 340
personality type, 345
romantic, 13, 56, 117, 191, 145e,
193, 338, 340
sleep and, 384
Relaxed alertness
calmness and, 219
defined, 69
quieting the mind, 223
Relearning, defined, 245
REM sleep. *See* Rapid eye movement
(REM) sleep
Remen, Rachel Naomi, 226
Repetition, learning and, 67, 294f
Reply-to-All key, 195
Reproductive thinking, defined, 168
Research
on academic performance, 45
active experiencing, 291
on body image, 382
on brain, 45, 67, 68–71, 329, 333b
on challenges, 92
on college success, 42, 52
on communication, 54b, 345
on decision making, 161
defined, 177, 184
on depression, 340–341, 369
on discrimination, 348, 349
on diversity, 349
on drinking, 387
on drugs, 368–369
on EI, 327, 329–330, 385
on exercise, 382, 383
on flow, 172
on friends, 340–341, 349
on grades, 276b
on group, stages of, 339
on happiness, 381
on human attention span, 03
on illness, 340–341
on influential people, 319
information literacy, 200f
on intelligence, 53, 55
on learning, 37, 67, 93
on liberal arts, 152b
on love, 370, 402
on majors/careers, 440–405
on MBTI, 88, 161
on memory, 70, 291, 292, 297, 291, 292, 297
on mental health, 341, 368, 368
on minority students, 348
mistakes, 37, 198b
on multitasking, 33–34, 44
on note-taking, 235
on nutrition, 70, 378
on optimism, 328
on people skills, 333b
on personality, 161
preliminary research, 404–405
on procrastination, 126
on psychological types, 345
on reading, 258, 263
on relationships, 319, 341
on self esteem, 382
on sleep, 94, 110, 382, 384–385
on "social loafing", 338
on social networking, 190
on speaking anxiety, 276b
on SQ6R, 263
on stress, 69, 377
on studying, 94
on suicide, 365, 370

on teamwork, 338
on technology stimulation, 33, 333b
on test-taking, 299, 302
on "the system," 36
on work-life balance, 130, 373
when writing, 270
Research universities, 6
Research skills, 196–199
Researchers, on essay questions, 313
Resilience, 2–4, 22–26
EI and, 328
environment, observation of, 26
as a process, 25
scale of, 23e
self-contribution to, 26
stages of, 25f
suggestions for, 24–26
Resourceful, in creative style, 170
Resources
academic, 20b
audiovisual, 199
campus, 20b
careers/majors, 20b
counseling, 331, 370, 371
finances, 20b
health, 20b
library as, 197–199
miscellaneous, 20b
online, 20b
support services, 17e, 20b
technological, 20b
Responding, 222, 325e–326e
Responsibility
assertions and, 156
attitude and, 43
for checking accuracy of statements,
189, 202
for communication, 228, 337–339
financial, 133, 136b
groups and, 334, 338
healthy lifestyle and, 366
for learning, 428
listening and, 220
as personal quality, 49, 373, 409
outcomes, 46
sex and, 364e, 388, 389, 391
social, 409
success and, 392
Résumé, 413e, 420b
Retaining, 292–293
defined, 292–293
memory and, 257, 290, 292–293
reading and, 257, 258
Rethink, 142–143, 263
Retrieving, 292–293
defined, 293
memory and, 292–293
tests and, 301
Review/reviewing
described, 245
learning and, 181
notes and, 231
reading/studying and, 263
tests and, 297, 305, 306
Review-the-text lecturer, defined, 228
Revision, 271–272. *See also*
Rewriting
Rewriting, 271–272
Rewards, 318
Right-brained, 165
Riney, Earl, 326
Rise of the Creative Class, The (Florida),
166–167